CONTENTS

Chapter 1

"IT'S GOING TO CHANGE YOUR LIFE"

Chapter 2

NURSERY NECESSITIES: CRIBS, DRESSERS & MORE

Chapter 3

Baby Bedding & Decor

Chapter 4

The Reality Layette: Little Clothes for Little Prices

BABY
Bargains ®

Secrets to saving **20% to 50%** on baby furniture, equipment, maternity wear and much, much more!

Money-Back Guarantee

Denise & Alan Fields
Authors of the best-seller, **Bridal Bargains**

Copyright Page and Sustainability Credits

The reviews in this book are made from scratch
The ink used to print this book contains no GMO's
The paper used in this book is locally sourced and gluten-free
The cover/interior design by Epicenter Creative is hormone-free
The index in this book was wild caught by New West Indexing
The back cover photograph by Moses Street utilizes all-natural light
Computers used to produce this book were powered by fair trade electrons

To order this book, go to BabyBargains.com or call 1-800-888-0385. Baby Bargains is published by Windsor Peak Press, 436 Pine Street, Boulder, CO 80302. Questions or comments? E-mail the authors at authors@babybargains.com. Call us at (303) 442-8792.
Learn more about this book online at BabyBargains.com

Distributed to the book trade by Ingram Publisher Services, 866-400-5351.

Library Cataloging in Publication Data

Fields, Denise
Fields, Alan
   Baby Bargains: Secrets to saving 20% to 50% on baby furniture, equipment, clothes, toys, maternity wear and much, much more/ Denise & Alan Fields
    640 pages.
    Includes index.
    ISBN 978-1-889392-49-3
    1. Child Care—Handbooks, manuals, etc. 2. Infants' supplies—Purchasing—United States, Canada, Directories. 3. Children's paraphernalia—Purchasing—Handbooks, manuals. 4. Product Safety—Handbooks, manuals. 5. Consumer education.
    649'.122'0296—dc20. 2015.

Version 11.0

Chapter 5

MATERNITY/NURSING CLOTHES

Chapter 6

FEEDING BABY: BREASTFEEDING, BOTTLES, HIGH CHAIRS

Chapter 7

AROUND THE HOUSE: MONITORS, DIAPER PAILS, SAFETY & MORE

Chapter 8

CAR SEATS

Chapter 9

STROLLERS, DIAPER BAGS AND OTHER TO GO GEAR

Chapter 10

CARRIERS

Chapter 11

CONCLUSION: WHAT DOES IT ALL MEAN?

ICONS

 Getting Started

 Money-Saving Secrets

 Sources

 Best Buys

 Best Online Sources

 The Name Game

 What Are You Buying?

 Do it By Mail

 Safe & Sound

 Email from the Real World

Smart Shopper

 More Money Buys You . . .

 Wastes of Money

Bottom Line

CHAPTER 1

"It's Going to Change Your Life!"

Inside this chapter

That had to be the silliest comment we heard while we were pregnant with our first baby. Believe it or not, we even heard this refrain more often than "Are you having a boy or a girl?" and "I'm sorry. Your insurance doesn't cover that." For the friends and relatives of first-time parents out there, we'd like to point out that this is a pretty silly thing to say. Of course, we knew that a baby was going to change our lives. What we didn't realize was how much a baby was going to change our pocketbook.

Oh sure, we knew that we'd have to buy triple our weight in diapers. What we didn't expect was the endless pitches for cribs, gear, toys, clothing and other items parents are required to purchase by FEDERAL BABY LAW.

We quickly learned that having a baby is like popping on the Juvenile Amusement Park Ride from Consumer Hell. Once that egg is fertilized, you're whisked off to the Pirates of the Crib ride. Then it's on to marvel at the little elves in StrollerLand, imploring you to buy brands with names you can't pronounce. Finally, you take a trip to Magic Car Seat Mountain, where the confusion is so real, it's scary.

Consider us your tour guides—the Yogi Bear to your Boo Boo Bear, the Fred to your Ethel, the . . . well, you get the idea. Before we enter BabyLand, let's take a look at the Four Truths That No One Tells You About Buying Stuff For Baby.

The Four Truths That No One Tells You About Buying Stuff for Baby

1 **BABIES DON'T CARE IF THEY'RE WEARING DESIGNER CLOTHES.** Babies just want to be comfortable. They can't even distinguish between the liberals and conservatives on "Meet the Press," so how would they ever be able to tell the difference between Baby Gucci crib bedding and another less famous brand that's just as comfortable, but 70% less expensive? Our focus is on making your baby happy—at a price that won't break the bank.

2 MOST BABY GEAR ISN'T TESTED FOR SAFETY. One of the biggest myths about baby gear is that every product you see on the shelf at a baby superstore is safety tested before it hits the market. Sadly, that isn't true.

Here are the scary facts: 74,900 children under age five were injured (requiring emergency room visits) by nursery products in 2013 (the latest year figures are available). During a recent three-year period, those same baby products caused 112 deaths per year. (Source: 2014 Consumer Product Safety Commission report based on 2013 data).

Yes, there are safety regulations for a couple of baby gear categories (cribs and car seats). But most other categories (strollers, high chairs, etc) only have *voluntary* safety rules and standards. You read that right—anyone can sell a stroller, for example, that doesn't meet safety guidelines. (Maybe federal regulators will catch it before it injures children—or maybe not).

So it is up to you as a parent to understand the basic safety guidelines for baby gear. Each chapter of this book has a section called "Safe & Sound" to arm you with in-depth advice on keeping your baby out of trouble. We'll tell you which products we think are dangerous and how to safely use other potentially hazardous products.

3 MURPHY'S LAW OF BABY TOYS SAYS YOUR BABY'S HAPPINESS WITH A TOY IS INVERSELY RELATED TO THE TOY'S PRICE. Buy a $200 shiny new wagon with anti-lock brakes, and odds are baby just wants to play with the box. In recognition of this reality, we've included "wastes of money" in each chapter that will steer you away from frivolous items.

4 IT'S GOING TO COST MORE THAN YOU THINK. Whatever amount of money you budget for your baby, get ready to spend more. Here's a breakdown of the average costs of bringing a baby into the world today:

The Average Cost of Having a Baby

(based on industry estimates for a child from birth to age one)

Crib, mattress, dresser, rocker	$1570
Bedding / Decor	$350
Baby Clothes	$615
Disposable Diapers	$865
Maternity / Nursing Clothes	$1300
Nursery items, high chair, toys	$515
Baby Food / Formula	$1015
Stroller, Car Seats, Carrier	$730
Miscellaneous	$490

TOTAL   **$7,450**

The above figures are based on a survey of 1000 readers, buying name brand products at regular retail prices.

Bedding/Decor includes not only bedding items but also lamps, wallpaper, and so on for your baby's nursery. Baby Food/Formula assumes mom breastfeeds for the first six months and then feeds baby jarred baby food ($385) and formula ($630) until age one. If you plan to bottle-feed instead of breastfeed, add another $630 on to that figure. (Of course, the goal is to breastfeed your baby as long as possible—one year is a good target.)

Sure, you do get a tax write-off for that bundle of joy, but that only amounts to about $975 this year (if you are in the 25% tax bracket). Plus, there is a child care tax credit for up to $3000 depending on your income. But those tax goodies won't nearly offset the actual cost of raising a child. And as you probably realize, our cost chart is missing some expensive "extras" . . . like medical bills, childcare, saving for college, etc. Here's an overview of those extras.

Scary Number: The Cost of Raising Baby to 18

$245,340. That's what the federal government says it costs to raise a child born in 2015 to age 18. Those costs include food, transportation, housing, clothes and child care.

But let's talk about child care. Critics say the federal government grossly underestimates this cost (the feds say parents spend $2,200 to $5,500 on child care each year for the first two years).

So what does child care really cost? According to the National Association of Child Care Resource and Referral Agencies, the average annual bill for center care ranges from $3,852 in Mississippi to $18,773 in Massachusetts (2014 statistics).

College is another expense the government leaves out of their figures. The College Board estimates that four years at a public college averages $75,772 (tuition, fees, room and board). At a private college, that same figure is $169,676. Given current rates of return, you have to put away $5,181 a year every year for 18 years to afford that public school.

The take-home message: raising a baby ain't cheap. It's important to start saving your pennies now, so you can start saving for those important items (college, etc.) down the road.

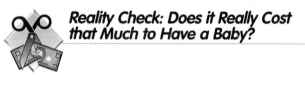

Reality Check: Does it Really Cost that Much to Have a Baby?

Now that we've thoroughly scared you enough to inquire whether the stork accepts returns, we should point out that children do NOT have to cost that much. Even if we focus just on the first year, you don't have to spend $7450 on baby gear. And that's what this book is all about: how to save money and still buy the best. Follow all the tips in this book, and we estimate the first year will cost you $4323. Yes, that's a savings of over $3100!

Now, at this point, you might be saying "That's impossible! I suppose you'll recommend shopping garage sales and dollar stores." On the contrary, we'll show you how to get *quality* name brands and safe products at discount prices. Most importantly, you will learn how not to WASTE your money on dubious gear. And much more. Yes, we've got the maximum number of bargains allowed by federal law.

A word on bargain shopping: when interviewing hundreds of parents for this book, we realized bargain seekers fall into two frugal camps. There's the "do-it-yourself" crowd and the "quality at a discount" group. As the name implies, "do-it-yourselfers" are resourceful folks who like to take second-hand products and refurbish them. Others use creative tricks to make homemade versions of baby care items like baby wipes and diaper rash cream.

While that's all well and good, we fall more into the second camp of bargain hunters, the "quality at a discount" group. We love discovering a name brand stroller for 75% off on Craigslist. Or the discount version of an expensive designer furniture brand, sold at a 20% discount. We also realize savvy parents save money by not *wasting* it on inferior goods or useless items.

While we hope that *Baby Bargains* pleases both groups of bargain hunters, the main focus of this book is not on do-it-yourself projects. Our emphasis is on identifying best buys for the dollar and not wasting your money, as well as on the best discount online sources.

What? No One Paid You to Recommend Their Product?

Yes, it's true. We don't get paid by companies to recommend or review products.

We also do not accept samples or other freebies from companies we review—if we are doing a first-hand inspection of a product, we purchase it on our own at regular retail prices. When we visit factories or other company facilities, we pay for our all our travel expenses. We don't accept gifts from companies we review.

Why? We believe that when you take a freebie, there is an obvious quid pro quo—a baby gear company isn't going to give you a $500 stroller and not expect anything less than a nice review in return. To remain objective, we think you can't be on the take.

Here's how we make a living: we sell the book you are reading. We also sell online subscriptions to our web site, as well as ebooks.

To keep our online subscription fees as low as possible, we do have affiliate links on our web site. When you read our review of a car seat and you click through on a link to purchase it, we may make a small commission from the site selling the product. If you hate the car seat and return it, we don't make any commission.

We also use software to affiliate links posted by users of our message boards, which are free. There are ads on our message boards (visible only to unregistered users) and other parts of our web site. These revenue sources are used to pay for bandwidth and server maintenance.

Of course, given the sheer volume of baby stuff, there's no way we can personally test everything. To solve that dilemma, we rely on reader feedback to help us figure out which are the best products to recommend. We receive over 200 emails a day from parents; this helps us spot overall trends on which brands/products parents love. And which ones they want to destroy with a rocket launcher.

Of course, one bad review from one parent doesn't mean we won't recommend a product—we combine multiple review sources to come up with an overall picture as to which brands are best.

The prices you see in our book were accurate as of press time. We aim to print actual selling prices (versus suggested retail prices) in our book—we do this by surveying stores and web sites. While the publisher makes every effort to ensure their accuracy, errors and omissions may exist. That's why we update this book with every new printing—make sure you are using the most recent version (go to BabyBargains.com and click on Book and then Which Version?).

Our door is always open—we want to hear your opinions. Email us at authors@BabyBargains.com or call us at (303) 442-8792 to ask a question, report a mistake, or just give us your thoughts.

So, Who Are You Guys Anyway?

Why do a book on saving money on baby products? Don't new parents throw caution to the wind when buying for their baby, spending whatever it takes to ensure their baby's safety and comfort?

Ha! When our first child was born, we quickly realized how darn expensive this guy was. Sure, as a new parent, you know you've got to buy a car seat, crib, clothes and diapers . . . but have you walked into one of those baby "superstores" lately? It's a blizzard of baby stuff piled to the ceiling, with a bewildering array of "must have" gear, gadgets and gizmos, all claiming to be the best thing for parents since sliced bread.

Becoming a parent in this day and age is both a blessing and curse. The good news: parents today have many more choices for baby products than past generations. The *bad* news: parents today have many more choices for baby products than past generations.

Our mission: make sense of this stuff, with an eye on cutting costs. As consumer advocates, we've been down this road before.

The 7 Commandments of Baby Bargains

Yes, we've come down from the mountain to share with you our SEVEN commandments of *Baby Bargains*—the keys to saving every parent should know. Let's review:

1 SAFETY IS JOB ONE. As a parent, your baby's safety is paramount. We never compromise safety for a bargain—that's why we don't recommend hand-me-down cribs or used car seats, no matter how cheap they are. Good news: you can subscribe to our free blog to get an email or text message when a baby product is recalled. Go to BabyBargains.com/blog and enter your email address in the box at the right.

2 FOCUS ON THE BASICS. Big box baby stores are so overwhelming, with a blizzard of baby products. Key on the basics: setting up a safe place for baby to sleep (the nursery) and safe transport (car seats). Many items like high chairs, toys, and so on are not needed immediately.

3 WEED OUT THE FLUFF. Our advice: take an experienced mom with you when you register. A mom with one or two kids can help you separate out needed items from the rest.

We researched bargains and uncovered scams in the wedding business when we wrote *Bridal Bargains*. Then we penned an exposé on new homebuilders in *Your New House*.

Yet, we found the baby business to be perplexing in different ways—instead of outright fraud or scams, we've instead discovered some highly questionable products that don't live up to their hype—and others that are outright dangerous. We were surprised to learn that most juvenile items face little (or no) government scrutiny, leaving parents to sort out true usefulness and safety from sales hype.

So, we've gone on a quest to find the best baby products, at prices that won't send you to the poor house. Sure, we've sampled many of these items first hand. But this book is much more than our experiences—we interviewed over 17,000 new parents to learn their experiences with products. Our message boards have over 47,000 members, buzzing with all sorts of product feedback and advice. We also attend juvenile product trade shows to quiz manufacturers and retailers on what's hot and what's not. The insights from retailers are especially helpful, since these folks are on

4 **TWO WORDS: FREE MONEY.** As a parent, you NEVER pass up free money! From tax deductions to tax credits, being a parent means freebies. And don't overlook your employer: take advantage of benefits like dependent care accounts—using PRE-TAX dollars to pay for child care will save you HUNDREDS if not THOUSANDS of dollars.

5 **MORE FREEBIES.** Many companies throw swag at new parents, hoping they will become future customers. We keep an updated freebie list on our web site—get free diapers, bottles, and more. Go to BabyBargains.com/freebies for the latest update!

6 **SHOP AT STORES THAT DO NOT HAVE "BABY" IN THEIR NAME.** Costco for diapers? Pet web sites for safety gates? IKEA for high chairs? Yes! Yes! Yes! You can save 30% or more by not buying items at baby stores.

7 **ONLINE SHOPPING SAVVY.** Let's face it: as a new mom and dad, you probably won't have much time to hit the mall. The web is a savior—but how do you master the deals? One smart tip: ALWAYS use coupon codes for discounts or FREE shipping. We keep a list (updated daily!) of the best coupon codes on our Bargain Alert Forum on our free message boards (BabyBargains.com).

What you need, when

Yes, buying for baby can seem overwhelming, but there is a silver lining: you don't need ALL this stuff immediately when baby is born. Let's look at what items you need quickly and what you can wait on. This chart indicates usage of certain items for the first 12 months of baby's life:

	MONTHS OF USE				
ITEM	BIRTH	3	6	9	12+
Nursery Necessities					
Cradle/bassinet					
Crib/Mattress					
Dresser					
Glider Rocker					
Bedding: Cradle					
Bedding: Crib					
Clothing					
Caps/Hats					
Blanket Sleepers					
Layette Gowns					
Booties					
All other layette					
Around the House					
Baby Monitor					
Baby Food (solid)					
High Chairs					
Places to Go					
Infant Car Seat					
Convertible Car Seat*					
Full-size Stroller/Stroller Frame					
Umbrella Stroller					
Front Carrier					
Backpack Carrier					
Safety items					

You can use a convertible car seat starting immediately with that first ride home from the hospital. However, it is our recommendation that you use an infant car seat for the first six months or so, then, when baby grows out of it, buy the convertible car seat.

the front lines, seeing which items unhappy parents return.

Our focus is on safety and durability: which items stand up to real world conditions and which don't. Interestingly, we found many products for baby are sold strictly on price . . . and sometimes a great "bargain" broke, fell apart or shrunk after a few uses. Hence, you'll note some of our top recommendations aren't always the lowest in price. To be sensitive to those on really tight budgets, we try to identify "good, better and best" bets in different price ranges.

We get questions: Top 6 Questions & Answers

From the home office here in Boulder, CO, here are the top five questions we get asked here at *Baby Bargains*:

1 HOW DO I KNOW IF I HAVE THE CURRENT EDITION? We strive to keep *Baby Bargains* as up-to-date as possible. As such, we update it periodically with new editions. But if you just borrowed this book from a friend, how do you know how old it is? First, look at the copyright page. There at the bottom you will see a version number (such as 11.0). The first number (the 11 in this case) means you have the 11th edition. The second number indicates the printing—every time we reprint the book, we make minor corrections, additions and changes. Version 11.0 is the initial printing of the 11th edition, version 11.1 is the first reprint of the 11th edition and so on.

So, how can you tell if your book is current or woefully out-of-date? Go to our web page at BabyBargains.com and click on Book and then "Which version?"—this shows the most current version. (One clue: look at the book's cover. We note the edition number on each cover. And we change the color of the cover with each edition.) We update this book every two years (roughly). About 30% to 40% of the content will change with each edition. Bottom line: if you pick up a copy of this book that is one or two editions old, you will notice a significant number of changes.

2 I AM LOOKING FOR A SPECIFIC PRODUCT BUT I DON'T KNOW WHERE TO START! HELP! Yep, this book is 600+ pages long and we realize it can be a bit intimidating. But you have a friend in the index—flip to the back of the book to look up just about anything. You can look up items by category, brand name and more. If that doesn't work, try the table of contents. We sort the book into major topic areas (strollers, car seats, etc).

FYI: some companies have sub-brands or private label offerings—we list these aliases alphabetically and refer you to the main company review (for example, Fisher Price cribs are made by Bivona; we discuss these cribs in Bivona's review.)

3 **WHY DO YOU CHARGE A SEPARATE FEE FOR YOUR WEB SITE?** There are two parts to our web site at BabyBargains.com: free and paid (subscriber's only).

The free side includes our blog, which tracks the latest news on baby gear, safety recalls and more. Our message boards are also free. We also post "bonus material" online for free—these are reviews of smaller companies that didn't fit in our book.

The paid or subscriber side of our web site ("Reviews") includes all the reviews you see in this book, plus a few online exclusives (example: baby food processors).

We charge a separate subscription fee because some folks prefer online access to our review. Bandwidth and web developers are expensive, so in order to maintain a quality digital experience, we charge a small subscription fee.

While the reviews online basically duplicate what we have in book form, we are able to update the web site reviews with any changes that happen after we go to press (pricing, recalls, new products, etc).

FYI: We sell a bundle of both the print book and web site access at a discounted price online. If you purchased the book in a bookstore and discover you'd also like a web site subscription, email us a copy of your receipt (authors@babybargains.com) with the magic words (We love Baby Bargains!) and we'll send you a discount code.

4 **CAN I ASK A QUESTION?** Sure, our door is always open—email us at authors@babybargains.com. We value your feedback, so feel free to tell us how to make our book or web site better.

5 **WHY DO YOU SOMETIMES RECOMMEND A MORE EXPENSIVE PRODUCT THAN A CHEAPER OPTION?** Yes, this is a book about bargains, but sometimes we will pick a slightly more expensive item in a category if we believe it is superior in quality or safety. In some cases, it makes sense to invest in better-quality products that will last through more than one child. And don't forget about the hassle of replacing a cheap product that breaks in six months.

To be sure, however, we recognize that many folks are on tight budgets. To help, we offer "Good, Better, Best" product suggestions that are typically sorted by price (good is most affordable, best is usually more expensive). Don't torture yourself if you can't afford the "best" in every category; a "good" product will be just as, well, good.

Another note: remember that our brand reviews cover many options in a category, not just the cheapest. Don't be dismayed if we give an expensive brand an "A" rating—our ratings are often based on quality, construction, innovation and more. Yes, we will try to identify the best values in a category as well. But we realize that some folks want to spend more on certain items (car seats, for example)—hence

Social & Save

Flash sale and social bargain sites are an important new tool in the bargain hunter's toolbox. In case you're new to this world, let's go over how to use social media to rack up baby bargains.

◆ **Deal of the day sites.** The best known of these sites is Groupon.com, but there are many others. In case you're a Groupon newbie, here's how it works. Groupon posts daily deals, including baby stuff with deals tailored to your city. When it comes to baby stuff, we've seen 50% off coupons to local baby stores, discounts from local baby proofers and more. Here's how it works: deals change by the day, you buy the certificate the day it appears on Groupon, typically within six hours or before it sells out. Then you take the certificate to the store, restaurant or other location and use it like a prepaid gift card.

◆ **Go deeper.** Of course, there is more than just Groupon! We have a list of deal-of-the-day sites on our web site at BabyBargains.com/deals. We also recommend checking out DailyDeals.Oohey.com, which aggregates deals from Groupon and several other sites. And many regular retail sites have jumped into the deal of the day game—Garnet Hill, Company Store, LL Bean are just a few examples.

◆ **Don't forget:** regular web sites offer deals of the day. Examples include Target, Amazon and more. These are typically limited time specials on a small selection of items. Many of these sites post their deals on their social media feeds (Facebook, Twitter).

◆ **Cash Back/Rewards sites.** If you are a heavy online shopper, consider signing up with an online cash back or rewards site. Ebates.com is probably the most well known—you earn cash back when you shop any one of 1200 web sites. Ebates also sends out coupons and promo codes for major sites. Upromise.com is a similar site that helps you pay for a child's college tuition. A great site that compares rebates from various sites is eReward.com.

we try to identify the best of the best, not just the cheapest.

6 **WHAT OTHER PARENTING BOOKS DO YOU PUBLISH?** Yes, we do have three other best-selling books: *Expecting 411*, *Baby 411* and *Toddler 411*. Co-authored by an award-winning pediatrician, these books answer your questions about pregnancy, your baby's sleep, nutrition and more. See the back of this book for details.

What's New in This Edition?

Welcome to the 11th edition—this year marks our 22nd year of covering the baby biz. Yes, we started writing this book way back in 1993. Before Google. Before Facebook. When dinosaurs roamed the Earth.

This new edition includes dozens of brand reviews for cribs, car seats and strollers. New this year: more eco-friendly baby products. We focus on green cribs and nursery furniture, with an expanded look at eco-friendly crib mattresses.

We've beefed up our car seat reviews with the government's ease of use ratings. And the booster seat reviews now include whether the seat is recommended by the Insurance Institute for Highway Safety.

Look for expanded reviews of carriers in this book, with a model-by-model look at the top brands. We've increased our coverage of video baby monitors with new streaming cams.

Of course, we've kept the features you love about *Baby Bargains*, including those nifty comparison charts that sum up our picks and our ever-popular baby registry at-a-glance (Appendix B). New this year is an online version of our registry picks—go to BabyBargains.com and click on the Registry button.

Don't forget to check out our other extensive online offerings—click on the Bargain forum on our message boards (shortcut: BabyBargains.com/coupons) to get news on the latest discount codes and more. Our "Bargain Alert" message board has dozens of posts by readers each day, sharing deals, steals and more.

Ebooks

Prefer to read this book as an ebook? We've got your covered with ebook versions of this book available for your Kindle, iPad/iPhone, Nook and other e-readers.

Let's Go Shopping!

Now that all the formal introductions are done, let's move on to the good stuff. As your tour guides to BabyLand, we'd like to remind you of one key rule: the Baby Biz is just that—business.

The juvenile products industry is a $10.3 BILLION DOLLAR business. While all those baby stores may want to help you, they are first and foremost in business to make a profit. As a consumer, you should arm yourself with the knowledge necessary to make smart decisions. So let's get rolling!

CHAPTER 2

Nursery Necessities:
Cribs, Dressers & More

Inside this chapter

How can you save 20% to 50% off cribs, dressers, and other furniture for your baby's room? In this chapter, you'll learn these secrets, plus discover smart shopper tips that help clarify all those confusing crib options and features. Then, you'll learn which juvenile furniture has safety problems and which cribs to avoid. Next, we'll rate and review over 40 top brands of cribs, focusing on quality and value. Finally, you'll learn which crib mattress is best, how to get a deal on a dresser, and several more items to consider for your baby's room.

Getting Started:
When Do You Need This Stuff?

So, you want to buy a crib for Junior? And, what the heck, why not some other furniture, like a dresser to store all those baby gifts and a changing table for, well, you know. Just pop down to the store, pick out the colors, and set a delivery date, right?

Not so fast, o' new parental one. Once you get to that baby store, you'll discover that most don't have all those nice cribs and furniture *in stock*. No, that would be too easy, wouldn't it? You will quickly learn that you have to *special order* much of that booty.

To be fair, we should note that in-stock items vary from store to store. Some (especially the larger chain stores) may stock a fair number of cribs. Yet Murphy's Law says the last in-stock crib you want was just sold five minutes ago. And while stores may stock a good number of cribs, dressers are another story—these bulky items almost always must be special-ordered.

So, let's cut to chase: when should you order nursery furniture? The answer depends on WHERE you plan to buy furniture. *If you choose an independent baby store, order at your 20th week of pregnancy.* Yes, it really takes 10-14 weeks on average to have specialty-store nursery furniture ordered and delivered (we figured you want it there a few weeks before baby arrives!).

Major caveat: some brands take as long as 16 weeks to order . . . ask your local retailer for advice, as lead times for brands can shift.

What about chain stores like Babies R Us? You need less time than specialty stores, but it isn't lighting quick either. Babies R Us says IF the furniture is in stock at their warehouse, it takes seven to 21 business days to be delivered to a store. If the furniture is NOT in stock, you'll have to wait four to six weeks. Bottom line: *if you choose a chain store, order at your 25th week of pregnancy.* That way you have left plenty of time, even if the furniture is on a six-week delay.

Why does it take so long to get nursery furniture? Most furniture today is made in Asia (primarily China). Manufacturers wait until they receive enough orders of a certain collection before they go into production. Then the furniture is loaded into a shipping container and sent on a four-to-six week ocean journey to the U.S. Assuming all goes well (no hurricanes, port strikes, etc.), the furniture is delivered to a manufacturer's distribution center. From there, it is trucked to the retailer.

Yes, you might get lucky and find your nursery furniture in stock at a manufacturer or retailer's warehouse. But don't bet on it.

We should note that some parents wait until after a baby is born to take delivery of nursery furniture. Why? Certain religious and ethnic customs say it is bad luck to have any baby gear in the house before baby is born. These families will order baby furniture, but not have it delivered until baby is born—needless to say, if you go this route, you have to find a retailer willing to store your furniture until that time.

First-time parent question: so, how long will baby use a crib? Answer: it depends. Most babies will use a crib for two or three years. Yes, some babies are out of the crib by 18 months, while others may be pushing four years. One key factor: when does baby learn they can climb out of the crib? Once that happens, the crib days are numbered, as you can understand. Of course, there may be other factors that push baby out of a crib—if you are planning to have a second child and want the crib for the new baby, it may be time to transition to a "big boy/girl" bed. We discuss more about the transition out of a crib in our other book, *Toddler 411.* See the back of this book for more info.

Cribs: Sources to Find

This year, more than one million households plan to buy infant/nursery furniture, according to a survey by *Kids Today*. That translates into $1.8 billion in sales of infant furniture—yes, this is big business. In their quest for the right nursery, parents have four basic sources for finding a crib, each with its own advantages and drawbacks:

1 INDEPENDENT BABY SPECIALTY STORES. Indie baby specialty stores are pretty self-explanatory—shops that specialize in the retailing of baby furniture, strollers, and accessories. Independents come in all sizes: some are small boutiques; others are as large as a chain superstore. A good number of indie retailers have joined together in "buying groups" to get volume discounts on items from suppliers—these groups include Brixy (brixy.com), Baby News (BabyNewsStores.com), and USA Baby (USAbaby.com).

Like other independent stores, many baby specialty shops have been hard hit by the expansion of national chains like Babies R Us. There are only a handful of specialty stores left in the U.S. Yet, those that have survived do so by emphasizing service and products you can't find at the chains. Of course, quality of service can vary widely from store to store . . . but just having a breathing human in a store is a nice plus.

The problems with specialty stores? Readers complain the stores only carry expensive brands. One parent told us the only baby specialty store in her town doesn't carry any cribs under $600. We understand the dilemma faced by mom and pop retailers—in order to provide all that service, they have to make a certain profit margin on furniture and other products. And that margin is easier to get on high-end goods. That's all well and good, but failing to carry products in entry-level price points only drives parents to the chains.

Another gripe with some indie stores: some shops can be downright hostile if they think you are price-shopping. A reader said she found this out when comparing high-end nursery furniture in her town. "When I asked to price cribs and dressers at two baby stores, I met with resistance and hostility. At one store, I was asked if I was a 'spy' for their competition! The store managers at both baby stores I visited said they didn't want people to comparison shop them on price, yet both advertise they will 'meet or beat' the competition's prices."

The bottom line: despite the hassles, if you have a locally owned baby store in your town, give them a shot. Don't assume chains always have lower prices and better selection. See the box nearby for our picks of the top indie baby stores in the U.S.

The Best Baby Stores in America

Who are the best independent baby stores in America? In researching this book, we have visited hundreds of baby stores from coast to coast during the past 15 years. Along the way, we've met some of the smartest retailers in the U.S.—folks we often turn to to find out what's REALLY happening in the baby gear biz. Which cribs, strollers and car seats are selling and winning raves from parents . . . and what are the bombs.

Readers often tell us they want to support indie stores—but which ones are most reputable? If you are tired of the chains, we offer our list of stores to check out.

A few notes: just in case you are wondering, NO retailers paid us to be on this list. We don't take advertising, commissions or fees to recommend stores in our book or blog. The retailers we think are best earned it the old fashioned way—by focusing on their customers.

We compiled this list from reader feedback and store visits; we also asked baby gear manufacturers to name their top retailers. This list focuses on baby stores in major metro areas (with a few exceptions). Most of these stores sell baby furniture/products in a wide range of prices; these aren't expensive boutiques, but mainstream retailers.

So . . . drum roll . . . here are the Best Baby Stores in America (in alphabetical order):

Baby Furniture Plus (North and South Carolina)
Baby Super Mart (Broomall, PA)
Baby's & Kid's 1st (Houston, TX)
Behr's (Metro NY)
Berg's Baby & Teen (Cleveland, OH)
Cribs to College Bedrooms (Naperville, IL)
Galt Toys + Galt Baby (Chicago)
Georgia Baby and Kids (Atlanta)
Great Beginnings (Washington DC: Maryland, Virginia)
Ideal Baby & Kids (Miami); also known as La Ideal.
Juvenile Shop (Sherman Oaks, CA)
Kids Stuff Superstores (South Dakota, Nebraska)
Lazar's (Chicago)
Magic Beans (Boston metro, Connecticut)
Planet Kids (New York City)
Treasures Room (St Louis)

2 THE CHAINS. There are two types of chains that sell baby products: specialty chains like Babies R Us and Buy Buy Baby and discounters like Walmart, Target, and Kmart that have small baby departments. We'll discuss each in-depth later in this chapter. The selection at chains can vary widely—some carry more premium brands, but most concentrate on mass-market names to appeal to price-conscious shoppers. Service? Fuggedaboutit—often, you'll be lucky to find someone to help you check out, much less answer questions.

In recent years, we've seen a third type of chain enter the baby market: specialty chains such as Pottery Barn Kids (PBK) and Restoration Hardware. The former has stores that sell some baby furniture; the latter (Restoration Hardware) has an online-only baby boutique.

3 ONLINE. Long before the web, companies tried to sell furniture via mail order, albeit with mixed results. Perhaps the best example is JCPenney (jcpenney.com), whose mail-order catalog (and now web site) specializes in affordable cribs and dressers. Despite the challenge of shipping bulky items like dressers, web sites and specialty retailers are still piling into the online nursery niche. We'll discuss the pros and cons of this approach later in the chapter.

Some web sites try a hybrid approach: online and retail. The RightStart.com has nine stores including a Denver flagship that has nursery furniture on the floor. You can see it in the store and then have it drop-shipped to your home.

Even if you decide to order your entire nursery online, there are several roadblocks. Shipping charges can be exorbitant—and that assumes you can get items shipped at all (most sites don't ship furniture to Hawaii, Alaska, Canada or military addresses). Along with high shipping fees, you then have the issue of damage, delays and worse. Some companies do a better job of packing items than others—we note this in the reviews later in this chapter.

To address these issues, companies have turned to ready-to-assemble (RTA) furniture for bulky items like dressers (cribs always are shipped disassembled). RTA furniture has come a long way in recent years, with improvements in quality and ease of assembly.

4 REGULAR FURNITURE STORES. You don't have to go to a "baby store" to buy juvenile furniture. Many regular furniture stores sell name-brand cribs, dressers and other nursery items. Since these stores have frequent sales, you may be able to get a better price than at a juvenile specialty store. On the other hand, the salespeople may not be as knowledgeable about brand and safety issues.

What Are You Buying?

Ok, let's break this down. Outfitting a nursery usually means buying three basic furniture items: a crib, dresser (which doubles as a place to change baby's diaper) and rocker. Here's a quick discussion of each.

◆ **Crib.** Crib prices start at $150 for an inexpensive crib at a discounter like Walmart. The mid-range for cribs is probably best typified by what you see at chains stores such as Babies R Us and Baby Depot—most of their cribs are in the $300 to $600 range (the stores seem to be a bit more pricey while their online sites offer more lower price options). Specialty stores tend to carry cribs that run $500 to $1000. And what about the top end? We'd be remiss not to mention the modern-design and solid wood cribs, which run $1000 to $2000.

Surprise! The vast majority of cribs don't come with mattresses; those are sold separately ($100 to $400). Bedding is also extra ($100 to $500). We'll discuss mattresses later in this chapter; bedding gets its own entire chapter (Chapter 3).

The big decision here is whether to get a plain crib or one that is convertible. As the name implies, convertible cribs morph into three or four different uses (crib, toddler bed, day bed and finally, double bed). A quick word on this—a toddler bed is a crib with the front rail replaced by a partial rail that is designed to keep a toddler from rolling off the mattress. A day bed is a crib with the front rail removed. We'll discuss the pros and cons of convertible cribs later in this chapter.

◆ **Dresser.** Most nurseries need a place to store clothes, diapers, supplies and so on. Known in the baby biz as case pieces (because they are, uh, a case), dressers range from simple, ready-to-assemble four-drawer chests to elaborate armoires (and their smaller cousins, chiffarobes).

Now, there is no federal law that says you MUST buy a dresser or armoire that exactly matches the finish of your crib. Some folks simply re-purpose a dresser from another room to baby's nursery—or pick up a dresser second-hand or at a discount from a regular furniture store. Either way (new or used) is perfectly acceptable, of course.

But . . . we realize the allure of matching nursery furniture convinces many new parents to pony up the cash. So here are some general price guidelines: a ready-to-assemble dresser from IKEA or a discount store runs $150 to $250.

Now, if you'd like to have something fancier (and already assembled), prices for dressers range from $300 to $1000 in chain stores. Step into a specialty store and you'll find plenty of fancy dressers, armoires and chiffarobes . . . for $700 to $1500 and higher.

Most dressers also double as a place to change baby—some have tops specifically designed for that purpose. These changer tops remove after baby is done with diapers (usually right before college). So most parents today do not need to buy a separate changing table.

◆ **Rocker.** A place to sit and nurse baby is an important part of any nursery's function—so the next question is . . . where to sit? Again, you can re-purpose a rocker from grandma's house or pick up one secondhand. If you have the room, a small loveseat or over-sized chair is a workable solution for nursing baby.

Brand new "glider-rockers" run the gamut from wooden chairs with thin pads to fully upholstered models. And the price range reflects this: you can spend as little as $200 for a rocker from Target or Walmart . . . as much as $2000 for a tricked out leather model from a specialty store. Most folks probably buy a basic model from chain stores like Babies R Us for about $400. Yes, ottomans are a nice extra—but cost $200 to $300 more.

Glider rockers get their own section later in this chapter.

The Grand Total. As you can see, the bare-bones budget for a nursery would be $600 (simple crib, mattress, basic dresser and rock-er). The mid-range would run about $1400 . . . and on the designer end, you could easily spend $2000 to $3000 on nursery furniture.

And these figures are BEFORE you get to any of the other décor items: bedding, lamps, paint, artwork, window treatments, etc.

More Money Buys You . . .

Here's a little secret expensive crib makers don't want you to hear: ALL new cribs (no matter what price) sold in the U.S. or Canada must meet federal safety standards. Yes, the governments of both the U.S. and Canada strictly regulate crib safety and features—that's one rea-son why most cribs have the same basic design, no matter the brand or price. So, whether you buy a $150 crib at a discount store or a $1500 wrought iron crib at a posh specialty boutique, either way you get a crib that meets federal safety requirements.

Now, that said, when you spend more money, there are some perks. The higher the price-tag of the crib (generally), the fancier the design (thicker corner posts, designer colors, etc.). That's nice, but is it really necessary? No—a basic, safe crib in a simple finish is all a baby needs.

The biggest sales pitch for cribs is convertibility: more expensive cribs are convertible. They morph into beds for older kids: toddler bed (basically, a crib with one side removed and a short rail), day bed (no rail) and (finally) full-sized bed. This uses the sides of the crib to become a headboard and footboard—some cribs even trans-

Three Golden Rules of Buying Nursery Furniture

◆ **Don't over buy**—think about your needs first. Here's a common first time parent mistake: rushing out to a local baby store and falling in love with that fancy cognac finish on a chiffarobe. Instead, think about what you really NEED. Start with the size of your baby's nursery—most secondary bedrooms in a typical suburban home are small (10′ x 12′ is common). That barely leaves room for a crib, dresser and rocker. Don't let a baby store sell you on a double dresser PLUS an armoire when you don't have room. For urban apartment dwellers, space is at a premium. Closets need to be tricked out to provide maximum storage. Expect furniture to do double duty.

◆ **Three words: set a budget.** Don't waste your time with designer furniture if you haven't done the math. As you saw from the discussion on the last few pages, a three-piece nursery set (crib, dresser, rocker) runs anywhere from $600 . . . up to $3000. Pick a budget and stick with it. Then read the brand reviews later in this chapter—you'll quickly realize which ones are in your budget and which aren't! Again, it pays to think outside the box: can you re-purpose a dresser from another room? Get a hand-me-down rocker from a friend or off Craigslist?

◆ **Decide on nursery style.** There are two theories of nursery design: either a baby's room should look, well, babyish . . . or it should be more adult-looking, able to adapt as the child grows. There is no right or wrong answer. If you subscribe to the baby-theme, then go with a simple (non-convertible) crib and dresser that you will later swapped out for a twin bed and desk/hutch. If you prefer the other path, then buy a convertible crib (which converts to a full size bed) and dresser that can do double duty. Some brands have dressers that are first a changing area for diapers . . . and then convert to a computer area complete with pull out keyboard drawer.

form into queen-size adult beds.

Convertible cribs are pitched to parents as "lifetime cribs" (your child will somehow shoehorn a full-size bed into their dorm room). Here's what the pitch leaves out: to convert the crib, you often have to buy a conversion kit (sold separately, naturally). And think about the SIZE of the average kids' bedroom these days: most can barely squeeze in a TWIN bed and dresser . . . a full or queen size bed is often impossible. We'll discuss this issue more, later in the chapter.

Some crib extras also have dubious value—take the under-crib storage drawer. Often seen on cribs that run $500 or more, this feature appeals to parents who have a storage crunch in their home (you can put blankets, extra clothes in the drawer). The problem? The drawer usually doesn't have a top. So, anything inside will be a dust magnet.

Ok, so now you know the typical prices of nursery furniture . . . and what more money really buys you. How do you decide what is best for your baby's nursery? See the previous box for our Three Golden Rules of Buying Nursery Furniture.

Safe & Sound

Here's a fact to keep you up at night: cribs are the third-biggest cause of injuries and deaths among all nursery products. In the latest year for which statistics are available, 12,400 injuries and 48 deaths were blamed on cribs and mattresses (source: CPSC Injuries and Deaths Associated with Nursery Products Among Children Younger than Age Five, 2014).

In 2011, the government strengthened crib safety standards and outlawed drop-side cribs. Now, all cribs sold in the U.S. must have fixed sides.

Even with the new safety rules, there are some basic guidelines when it comes to buying safe nursery furniture. Here's an overview:

♦ **Don't buy a used or old crib.** Let's put that into bold caps: **DON'T BUY A USED OR OLD CRIB.** And don't take a hand-me-down from a well-meaning friend or relative. Why? Because old cribs account for most of the injuries and deaths when it comes to cribs. Surprisingly, these old cribs may not be as old as you think—cribs made before 2011 don't meet current standards.

Most folks realize that cribs made in the 70's and 80's aren't safe . . . but that never seems to stop a well-meaning relative from bringing down a "family heirloom" crib from the attic. These are death traps: slats that are too far apart, cutouts in the headboard, and other hazards that could entrap your baby. Decorative trim (like turned posts) that looks great on adult beds are a major no-no for cribs—they present a strangulation hazard. (Note: cribs with TALL posts are fine; it is the shorter posts that are prohibited—see the graphic below).

Some old cribs have lead paint, a dangerous peril for a teething baby. Another hazard to hand-me-down cribs (regardless of age): missing parts and directions. It only takes one missing screw or bolt to make an otherwise safe crib into a danger. Without directions, you might incorrectly assemble the crib and create additional safety hazards. So, even if your friend wants to give/sell you a recent model crib, you could still have problems if parts or directions are missing.

It may seem somewhat ironic that a book on baby bargains would advise you to go out and spend your hard-earned money on a new crib. True, we find great bargains on Craigslist for baby gear. However, you have to draw the line at your baby's safety. Certain second-hand items are great deals—toys and clothes come to mind. However, cribs (and, as you'll read later, car seats) are no-no's, no matter how tempting the bargains.

And second hand stores have a spotty record when it comes to selling safe products. A recent report from the CPSC said that a whopping two-thirds of all U.S. thrift/second-hand stores sell baby products that have been recalled, banned or do not meet current safety standards (specifically 12% of stores stocked old cribs). Even though recently strengthened laws prevent the resale of banned products like drop-side cribs, some second-hand stores still sell these items, either knowingly or unknowingly in violation of the law.

Readers often ask us why we don't give tips for evaluating old or hand-me-down cribs for safety. The reason is simple: it's hard to tell whether an old crib is dangerous just by looking at it. Cribs

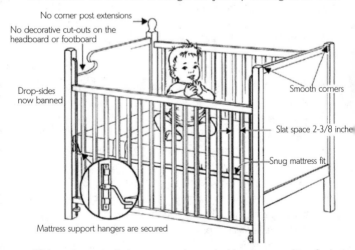

Older cribs typically have many hazards. Here's a graphic of what is dangerous. Note: all new cribs sold today are required by law to NOT have any of these features.

don't always have "freshness dates"—some manufacturers don't stamp the date of manufacture on their cribs. Was the crib made before or after the current safety standards went into effect in 2011? Often, you can't tell.

Today's safety regulations are so specific (example: strength of side slats) that you just can't judge a crib's safety with a cursory examination. Another problem: if the brand name is rubbed off, it will be hard to tell if the crib has been involved in a recall. Obtaining replacement parts is also difficult for a no-name crib.

What about floor model cribs? Is it safe to buy a crib that has been used as a floor sample in a baby store? Yes—as long as it is in good working condition, has no missing/broken parts, etc. Floor model cribs CAN take a tremendous amount of abuse from parents, who shake them to check stability and so on. As a result, the bolts that hold the crib together can loosen. Obviously, that can be fixed (just have the store tighten the bolts) . . . and as a result, we think floor model cribs are fine.

What if a relative insists you should use that "family heirloom" crib we mentioned earlier? We've spoken to dozens of parents who felt pressured into using an old crib by a well-meaning relative. There's a simple answer: don't do it. As a parent, you sometimes have to make unpopular decisions that are best for your child's safety. This is just the beginning.

◆ **Cribs with fold-down rails.** A handful of cribs have fold-down rails— the upper one-third of the railing is hinged and folds down. These are also called swing gate cribs (see picture).

One major crib maker uses these rails for some of their models: Baby's Dream. While we like the quality of Baby's Dream's furniture overall, we do not recommend any crib with a fold-down rail. Why? Older babies who can stand (which happens around a year of age) can get a foothold on the hinged rail to climb out of the crib, injuring themselves as they fall to the floor.

A reader in Seattle, WA recently emailed us with exactly that story: her 13 month old son fractured his fibula (calf bone) after falling out of his Baby's Dream drop-gate crib. "We liked how the drop gate was easy to operate and worked better for a shorter person," she said. "However, we didn't foresee that the drop gate would provide a ledge for him to prop his foot on and fall out."

We should point out that even though swing gate cribs ARE legal (they meet the new safety standard), we don't personally recommend them based on our own research.

◆ **Inspect monthly.** Many cribs that were recalled in past years had defective hardware or spindles that broke. While drop-side cribs (which had more hardware failures than static side cribs) are no longer on the market, all cribs should be inspected monthly. Make sure all bolts are tightened, no slats are loose, etc.

The 2011 crib safety standards require hardware that doesn't need to be retightened—however, wood furniture is wood furniture. Changes in humidity or temperatures in a nursery may still require hardware or bolts to be tightened from time to time.

If a part has broken on your crib, immediately stop using it. Don't attempt to repair it yourself—and never use a crib with missing, broken or loose parts.

◆ **Lead paint.** Lead paint scares of the late 2000's fed into fears of cribs and other baby gear made in China. Should you be concerned?

While there have been numerous toys and other children's products recalled for lead paint, there was only one nursery furniture recall for this reason (Munire recalled 3000 cribs and 5000 matching dressers for lead paint in 2008). Most nursery furniture companies have their paint and stains independently tested to verify they are lead-free—one (Sorelle) even posts its test results online. Yet, as the Munire recall shows, even a diligent company can have lapses.

Still, we realize some folks still don't trust China and want to avoid Chinese-made furniture. To help, we have a box (later in this chapter in the brand reviews) that lists all the nursery furniture makers who make their furniture in countries other than China.

◆ **Formaldehyde.** Most of us are familiar with this chemical from those middle school biology classes. A gas at room temperature, formaldehyde is an organic compound that was classified as a probable human carcinogen back in 1987. It is linked to increased risk of childhood asthma and allergies.

Of course, you probably don't plan to be dissecting frogs in your child's nursery, so there's no need to worry about formaldehyde, right? Wrong—formaldehyde sneaks into your house in other ways. It is found in furniture, specifically the glue in engineered wood products like particle board, chip board and some types of medium density fiberboard (MDF).

The Environmental Protection Agency regulates the amount of formaldehyde that can off-gas from furniture and other wood products. And some states (California) have even stricter limits. In fact, the state of California sued five baby furniture makers in 2008 for unsafe levels of formaldehyde.

So how can you avoid this hazard in your nursery? One alternative is to stick with solid wood furniture, but this can be pricey (that's why furniture makers use engineered wood like MDF and particle board: it's cheaper). A second recommendation is to consider furniture that is GREENGUARD certified (greenguard.org). In order to pass this certification process, furniture must meet strict chemical emission limits.

Yes, it is an environmental paradox: engineered wood products like MDF are better for the environment, since you don't have to cut down a tree to make a dresser. But the resin that holds MDF together can contain formaldehyde, which contributes to bad indoor air quality. To get around this conundrum, some eco-friendly nursery companies claim they use MDF that has low-emission glue. While this is hard to verify, you might look for this if you have a history of allergies and/or asthma in your family.

Another obvious tip: if your freshly-delivered nursery furniture has a strong chemical smell, let it air out before baby arrives. If it continues to stink, don't use it.

◆ Be aware of the hazards of putting a baby in an adult bed.

Co-sleeping is where a baby shares a bed with adults. While common in other parts of the world, co-sleeping is controversial here in the U.S.—on one side are attachment parenting advocates who insist it is safe, a big convenience for nursing moms and an important part of parent/child emotional bonds.

On the other side are safety advocates, including the Consumer Product Safety Commission and the American Academy of Pediatrics. A CPSC report blamed 122 infant deaths on co-sleeping in a previous three-year period. Of those deaths, many were caused when a child's head became entrapped between the adult bed and another object (a headboard, footboard, wall, etc). Other deaths were caused by falls or suffocation in bedding. The American Academy of Pediatrics agreed with the CPSC's concerns, issuing a recommendation against co-sleeping in 2005 and again in 2011.

We have an expanded discussion of this debate in our other book, *Baby 411*. Our basic advice: the safest place for a baby to sleep is a separate sleep space (a crib or bassinet that meets current safety standards).

◆ When assembling a crib, make sure ALL the bolts and screws are tightened.

A recent report on *Good Morning America* pointed out how dangerous it can be to put your baby in a miss-assembled crib—a child died in a Child Craft crib when he became trapped in a side rail that wasn't properly attached to the crib. How did that happen? The parent didn't tighten the screws that held the side rail to the crib. Cribs (including the Child Craft one here in question) are safe when assembled correctly; just be sure to tighten those bolts! Also: watch out for stripped screws that attach a mattress support to a headboard.

◆ **Recalls: where to find information.** The U.S. Consumer Product Safety Commission has a toll-free hotline at (800) 638-2772 and web site (cpsc.gov) for the latest recall information on cribs and other juvenile items. Both are easy to use—you can also report any potential hazard you've discovered or an injury to your child caused by a product. FYI: The CPSC takes care of all juvenile product recalls, except for car seats—that's the purview of the National Highway Traffic Safety Administration (nhtsa.gov).

Here's a great feature on the CPSC's newest site, SaferProducts.gov: you can now search for reports of injuries or problems for any product or brand. Filed by consumers, these reports sometimes include company responses.

A great "all-in-one" site for recalls is Recalls.gov. Also: subscribe to our blog—we will send you an email or text message when a product is recalled. Go to BabyBargains.com/blog and enter your email at the box at the right and hit subscribe. It's free!

◆ **Safety is more than a crib.** Be sure to have a smoke and carbon monoxide detector for your baby's nursery. And if you haven't had your home tested for radon yet, this would be a good time. (We discuss radon and other environmental hazards in depth our book, *Toddler 411*.)

Smart Shopper Tips

Smart Shopper Tip #1
The Art and Science of Selecting the Right Crib.
"How do you evaluate a crib? They all look the same to me. What really makes one different from another?"

Selecting a good crib is more than just picking out the style and finish. You should look under the hood, so to speak. Here are our nine key points to look for when shopping for a crib:

◆ **Brand reputation.** Later in this chapter, we will rate and review the biggest crib brands. Our advice: stick with a brand that gets a B or better rating. We formulate these ratings from parent feedback as well as our analysis of a brand's track record—we've been researching and writing about cribs for 20+ years! We look at recall history, customer service, delivery reliability and overall quality to assign a rating. And we're not afraid to tell you when we think a company has dropped the ball.

◆ *Mattress support.* Look underneath that mattress and see what is holding it up. The best cribs use a metal spring platform or a grid of wooden slats. Other cribs use cheap vinyl straps or a piece of particle board. We think the last two are inferior—vinyl straps aren't as secure as metal springs or wood slats; and concerns have been raised over formaldehyde emissions with particle board (see earlier discussion).

◆ *Static side rails.* All cribs sold in the U.S. and Canada are now stationary or static side cribs. In years past, cribs with drop sides (where one side lowers to give assess to the baby) were linked to numerous safety recalls. Although you won't see drop-side cribs sold in stores, there are still many listed for sale on Craigslist and in second-hand stores—avoid them.

One exception to the no-drop side rule: one crib maker, Baby's Dream, still offers some cribs with a fold-down rail (also called drop gates). Instead of lowering, the rail has a hinge that allows the top portion to fold down. The CPSC deems these rails to be safe; we aren't big fans of fold-down rails for reasons we outlined earlier in this chapter.

◆ *Hardware/bolts: hidden or exposed?* Some cribs have visible bolts that attach the crib rails to the headboard; others are hidden. Is there a difference in safety or durability? No, it's just aesthetics. The more money you spend, the more likely the hardware/bolts will be hidden.

◆ *How stable is the crib?* Because all cribs sold today have stationary sides, this is less of an issue than in years past. Stationary cribs by virtue of have no moving parts, tend to be more stable than the drop-side cribs of years past. And yes, more expensive cribs are typically heavier with thicker posts and slats than low-priced options—and that makes them more stable.

◆ *How do you move the crib?* Few cribs sold today have wheels. When you move a crib, it is a two-person job. And some cribs weigh in excess of 100 pounds. Never drag a crib across the carpet, as you can damage it. One idea: if your crib has legs or bun feet, use Magic Sliders (magicsliders.com, $7) to make it easier to move a crib to clean or vacuum behind it.

◆ *How easy is it to assemble?* Ask to see those instructions—

most stores should have a copy lying around. Make sure they are not indecipherable. Yes, some stores offer set-up and delivery, but with chain superstores, you are typically on your own. Sadly, some crib makers don't put a high priority on easy-to-understand assembly instructions—check first before you buy! The good news: some crib makers now have instructions you can download from their web sites.

◆ **Which wood is best?** Most cribs are made of hardwoods: birch, beech, mahogany, etc. In recent years, crib makers have also made some models in pine. The problem? Pine is a softwood that isn't as durable as hardwood—it tends to nick, scratch and damage.

FYI: there are many types of pine—some are harder (and more durable) than others. Unfortunately, furniture makers don't tell you they are using red pine (the hardest) versus Eastern White pine (the softest).

To be clear, pine isn't a safety hazard . . . it just isn't as durable. Sometimes this is a price trade-off—later in this chapter, we'll recommend a couple of affordable crib models, two of which are made of pine. For cribs under $200, most of your choices will be pine.

So, which wood is best? If the budget allows, we recommend you go with a hardwood crib—it doesn't matter whether it is birch, beech, mahogany or even ramin (also called rubberwood). The latter is an Asian hardwood that is often seen in low-price cribs.

Another recent trend: modern furniture made of medium-density fiberboard (MDF) with a glossy lacquer finish. Made of wood fibers and resin, MDF has a smooth, grain-free surface, which enables manufacturers to add that high-gloss finish.

We aren't fans of composite wood—MDF simply isn't as durable as hardwood. Yes, we realize fans of modern furniture are more sold on the aesthetic . . . MDF looks cool. But as we discussed earlier, MDF and other engineered woods have been blamed for outgassing of formaldehyde and other chemical emissions that lead to bad indoor air quality.

Another quick point: don't confuse *finish* with wood. Some stores and web sites tout "cherry" cribs when they are actually referring to the finish, not the actual wood. It may be a "cherry" stain, but the wood is probably not.

Smart Shopper Tip #2
Cyber-Nursery: Ordering furniture online

"We don't have any good baby stores nearby, so I want to order furniture online. How do you buy items sight unseen and make sure they arrive in one piece?"

It's a challenge, to be sure. Ever since the dawn of ecommerce, companies have tried selling nursery furniture online . . . often with mixed results. One of the biggest challenges is shipping damage.

You can probably guess the reason: bulk. Cribs and dressers are heavy and bulky—this makes them expensive to ship and suscepti-ble to damage. Once you have a damaged furniture item, the fun begins—dealing with customer service, getting replacement items sent out, etc.

There is good news on this front: over the past few years, companies have done a better job packing furniture so it isn't damaged. Improvements in the quality of ready-to-assemble furniture like dressers have also made buying furniture online a more positive experience.

Our advice: it is still easier to order from a local store and have the items delivered/set-up. If the store doesn't have items in stock, see if they have a "site to store" shipping option—you order online, but the item is delivered to a local store where you pick it up. This helps eliminate shipping damage.

However, if you decide to order online, go with a site that has a clear return policy and a good reputation for customer service (Amazon, for example).

Smart Shopper Tip #3
When space is tight

"We have a very small room for our nursery and saving space is an imperative. What are our options for nursery furniture? Can a mini crib substitute for a full-size one?"

Urban apartment dwellers often face a challenge—how do you squeeze a nursery into a tiny space? Here's our advice.

First, let's look at the crib. There are two types of cribs on the market: full-size and mini. Full-size cribs are 52" long and 28" wide. Mini cribs have the same width, but are only 38-40" long. So are mini cribs the solution for small nurseries?

No, unfortunately. Mini cribs are at best as replacements for bassinets or for occasional overnights at grandma's house. After a year of age, however, many babies will outgrow a mini crib. That necessitates buying a full-size crib anyway, as it is unsafe to put an one year old in a toddler or youth bed. (As we mentioned earlier, most kids stay in a crib until age two or three.)

Obviously, how long one can use a mini crib can vary by child. Some larger boys can outgrow a mini crib before one year of age. Smaller girls, on the other hand, may be able to fit in a mini crib until age two or beyond.

A few crib makers offer hybrid models that are smaller than a full-size crib but larger than a mini—Bloom's Alma Papa is 49" long, or three inches shorter than a standard size crib. The downside to this option: you have to get a special mattress to fit it.

Another solution is the Stokke Sleepi crib—it starts out as a bassinet or mini crib that is 26.5″ wide by 32″ in length. It then morphs into a crib that is 29″ wide and 50″ long. Unfortunately, this solution is also expensive ($1000), plus a special mattress that is $200.

Perhaps the best solution is to economize when it comes to a dresser—that is, not have one at all in the nursery. Instead, consider a crib with under-crib storage drawers. While we aren't a fan of these (since they are usually uncovered and items in the drawers can get dusty), it might be worth the trade-off when space is tight. If you have space for a dresser, some brands (like Westwood) have smaller "urban-sized" versions of their full size dressers. Ditto for the glider-rockers—manufacturers like Dutailier have smaller-size gliders in their line to fit tiny nurseries.

Other ideas for a small nursery: go vertical. Mount inexpensive cabinetry above the crib to store clothes and essentials. Make sure accessories do double duty—a bookshelf could do double duty as a place for a lamp. Forget the separate diaper changing table—use the top of the dresser or the crib to change diapers. Take the doors off closets to gain extra space.

Wastes of Money

1 LOW QUALITY "BABY" FURNITURE THAT WON'T LAST. Baby furniture stores (both chains and independents) are sometimes guilty of selling very poor quality furniture. Take a dresser, for example. Many dressers made by juvenile furniture companies have stapled drawers, veneer construction (instead of solid wood), cheap drawer glides and worse. Now, that wouldn't be so bad if such dressers were low in price. But often you see these dressers going for $500 and up in baby stores—basically, you are paying a premium to merely match the color of your crib. While we don't see a problem buying low-end "disposable" furniture at a good price (IKEA is a prime example), paying a fortune for a poorly made dresser is crazy. In this chapter, we will point out brand names that provide more quality for the dollar. Look for solid wood construction, dovetail drawers, and smooth drawer glides if you want that dresser to last.

2 UNDER-CRIB DRAWERS. It sounds like a great way to squeeze out a bit more storage in a nursery—the drawer that slides out from under a crib. Getting a crib with such a feature usually costs an extra $100 or $150. The problem? Most of these drawers do NOT have tops . . . therefore anything kept in there will get dusty

cribs

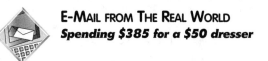

E-Mail from The Real World
Spending $385 for a $50 dresser

A reader in Ohio shared her frustration with a dresser bought online that had significant shipping damage:

"I ordered a three drawer combo dresser from a well-known baby gear web site. It had all of the things suggested in your book and was $385. The manufacturer is Angel Line. The item arrived with split wood on the corner, a knob missing, a missing wall strap and one of the drawers didn't shut completely and was crooked. I called the site and they said I had to contact the manufacturer directly to get the problem resolved. It took four calls and the best I could get was another knob and drawer sent to me with corners that did not fit together. So, I essentially paid $400 for something that looks like a dresser that's $50 at a garage sale."

in a hurry. So that nixes storing extra blankets or clothes. We say skip the extra expense of an under-crib drawer.

3 The Toddler Bed. Some crib makers tout cribs that convert to toddler beds. This is accomplished by removing the side rail and adding a toddler rail. Smaller than a twin bed, a toddler bed uses the crib mattress and is pitched as a transition between the crib and a big boy/girl bed. But, guess what? Most kids can go straight from a crib to a regular twin bed with no problem whatsoever. The toddler bed is a waste of money, in our opinion.

4 Cradle. Most pediatricians recommend "rooming in" with your newborn to help with breastfeeding. But where will the baby sleep? Cradles and bassinets are one option, but can be pricey. Cradles (basically a mini crib that rocks) run up to $400, while separate bassinets (a basket on a stand) can cost $200. A more affordable solution: just set up the crib in your room. After you establish that breastfeeding rhythm, the baby and crib can move to the nursery. If you don't have room in your master bedroom to set up the crib, consider a playpen with bassinet feature like the Graco Pack N Play (starting at $100). We'll discuss the best buys on bassinets at the end of this chapter; playpens like the Pack N Play are reviewed in Chapter 7, Around the House.

5 Cribs with "Special Features." Some stores carry unique styles of cribs and that might be tempting for parents looking to make a statement for their nursery. An example: round or elliptical cribs. The only problem: special cribs like this may require additional expenses, such as custom-designed mattresses or bedding. And since few companies make bedding for these cribs, your choices are limited. The best advice: make sure you price out the total investment (crib, mattress, bedding) before falling in love with an unusual style.

6 CHANGING TABLES. Separate changing tables are a big waste of money. Don't spend $100 to $200 on a piece of furniture you won't use again after your baby gives up diapers. A better bet: buy a dresser that can do double duty as a changing table. Many dressers you'll see in baby stores are designed with this extra feature—just make sure the height is comfortable for both you and your spouse. Other parents we interviewed did away with the changing area altogether—they used a crib, couch or countertop to do diaper changes.

Top 8 Things Baby Stores Won't Tell You About Buying Nursery Furniture

◆ *Our store may disappear before your nursery furniture arrives.* It's a sad fact: baby stores come and go. Most retailers that close do so reputably—they don't take special orders for merchandise they can't fill. A handful are not so honest . . . they take deposits up until the day the landlord padlocks their doors. Our advice: always charge your purchase to a credit card. If the store disappears, you can dispute the charge with your credit card company and (most likely) get your money back. Another red flag: stores that ask for payment up front on a special order. The typical deal is half down with the balance due upon delivery. Stores that are desperate for cash might demand the entire purchase price upfront. Be suspicious. Another piece of advice: keep a close eye on what's going on with your furniture maker. How? Read our blog or surf our message boards at BabyBargains.com. Over the years, we've seen it all—labor strikes, earthquakes, fires, port shutdowns and more. You name it, it can happen to the factory that makes your furniture. When we get a whiff of a problem, we blog about it. That way you can switch to another brand if you've haven't placed an order yet . . . or formulate a plan B if your furniture is caught by a delivery delay.

◆ *Never assume something in a sealed box is undamaged.* Always OPEN boxes and inspect items before taking furniture out of a store. Yes, that is a hassle, but we've had numerous complains about boxed furniture that someone has driven 50 miles home, only to discover a major gash or other damage. Or the wrong color is in the right box. Or a major piece is missing. A word to the wise: inspect it BEFORE going home.

◆ **If it is in stock, TAKE IT.** Let's say you see a crib that is in stock, but the matching dresser is on back order. Do you get the crib now and wait on the dresser? Or special order both? Our advice: if an item is sitting there in a store, it is ALWAYS better to take the in-stock item now.

◆ **Your special order merchandise will be backordered until 2017, despite our promise to get it to you before your baby is born.** Almost all furniture today is imported . . . and not from close-by countries like Canada or Mexico. Nope, odds are your furniture will be made in some far flung locale in Asia. A myriad of problems (backorders, labor unrest, port shutdowns, etc.) can delay orders. Our advice: ORDER EARLY. When a store gives you a 10-14 week delivery estimate, remember that is an *estimate*. It can easily morph to 16, 20 or 24 weeks. Build in a cushion just in case.

◆ **Just because the crib maker has an Italian name doesn't mean your furniture is made in, say, Italy.** Prior to the 1990's, you had domestic makers of cribs (Child Craft, Simmons) and the imports, most of which were from Italy. Those days are long gone—today almost all nursery furniture is imported from Asia (specifically, China).

Here's where it gets confusing: sometimes the very same brand will import furniture from different countries. Sorelle, for example, started out as an Italian importer. Today, Sorelle imports most of its cribs and furniture from China . . . but some of its cribs are made in Eastern Europe. Bivona's Fisher Price cribs are made in China; the upper-end Ti Amo and Dolce Babi cribs are imported from Vietnam.

Bottom line: key on the brand's reputation for quality and customer service, not so much the country the crib is made in. Yes, we realize some folks are nervous about Chinese-made products. To address those concerns, we have a box later in this chapter that points out brands not made in China. However, we don't think a crib or dresser made in China is inherently dangerous—again, it is the company's reputation for quality and customer service that is key, not the country of origin.

◆ **That special mattress we insist you buy isn't necessary.** Some baby stores are trying a new tactic to sell their pricey in-house brand of crib mattress: scaring the pants off new parents. We've heard all the stories—only OUR mattress fits OUR crib, a less expensive foam mattress is DANGEROUS for your baby and so on. Please! Government standards require both cribs and mattresses to be within standard measurements. Yes, fancy boutiques might make their mattress a bit larger to give a tighter fit . . . but that doesn't mean a regular mattress won't work just as well (and is just as safe). FYI: we have an indepth blog post on the ins and outs of fitting a mattress to your crib at at http://bit.ly/cribmattressfit. In the post, we tackle a reader question about getting a mattres to fit her IKEA crib.

◆ *Just because we say this item is discontinued does NOT mean you can't find it anywhere else.* This is especially true for chain stores—just because Babies R Us says the crib you've fallen in love with is now discontinued does NOT mean you can't find it from another store. That's because chains discontinue items all the time . . . and not just because the manufacturer is discontinuing it. Chains replace slow moving merchandise or just make way for something new. Meanwhile, the very same furniture (or for that matter, any baby gear) is sold down the street at another store.

◆ *The finish on that expensive special-order dresser may match your crib . . . or not.* Here's something baby stores don't advertise: the finishes on that expensive nursery furniture you special ordered may not match. Why? Many furniture companies use different wood species for different pieces—say birch for a crib, but pine for a dresser. The problem: each takes stain differently. As a result, a birch crib in cherry may not match a pine dresser in the same cherry stain. While the difference may be small, it bugs some folks more than others. The take home message: if matching stain is important to you, confirm all the pieces of your furniture are made of the same wood—and try to see a sample of the stain on a real piece of furniture to confirm colors (don't rely on online photos).

 Money Saving Secrets

1 CHECK OUT REGULAR FURNITURE STORES FOR ROCKERS, DRESSERS, ETC. Think about it—most juvenile furniture looks very similar to regular adult furniture. Rockers, dressers, and bookcases are, well, just rockers, dressers, and bookcases. And don't you wonder if companies slap the word "baby" on an item just to raise the price 20%? To test this theory, we visited a local discount furniture store. The prices were incredibly low. A basic four-drawer pine dresser was $250. Even maple or oak four-drawer dressers were just $450. The same quality dresser at a baby store by a "juvenile furniture" manufacturer would set you back at least $600, if not twice that. We even saw cribs by such mainstream names as Bassett at decent prices in regular furniture stores. What's the disadvantage to shopping there? Well, if you have to buy the crib and dresser at different places, the colors might not match exactly. But, considering the savings, it might be worth it.

2 GET SOCIAL. Social media is more than just status updates and tweets—sign up for "deal of the day sites" like Groupon or Zulily.com. As the name implies, deal of the day sites have one great deal (up to 70% off) available for a limited time. For Groupon, that might be a 50% discount on a local maternity store. Zulily, founded by the folks who started Blue Nile, offers cribs, designer kids clothes and baby gear at deep discounts. Of course, part of the fun with these sites is sharing the deals with your friends on Facebook.

3 THINK TWICE ABOUT MOD. Modern furniture is the rage in high-end boutiques, but what do you get for that ultra-mod look? Many "modern" cribs and furniture are made of MDF, particle board and laminates . . . and for this you're supposed to shell out $1000 for a crib and $1600 for a dresser? Can someone explain to us why modern furniture costs TWICE as much as "regular" cribs and dressers? Sure that mod furniture has a few extra coats of lacquer and looks all shiny. But we still don't get it—especially since nearly all nursery furniture (yes, even the mod stuff) is imported from Asia. Our advice: If you decide to go mod, stick with the more affordable options like IKEA . . . even Walmart now sells a modern furniture collection at reasonable prices.

4 COMPARE ONLINE PRICES. Do you wonder if that local baby store has jacked up the price of nursery furniture? We know some of you live in towns or communities with little or no local competition for nursery items. One solution: hit the web. Now, we realize we listed all sorts of caveats for online orders earlier in the book (high shipping fees, problems with damage, etc.)—but let's face it. In some parts of the country, this is really your best option. As always, don't ASSUME local stores will be higher in price than the web. Do your homework first. And always ask local retailers if they will price match what you see online. Many quietly do!

A caveat to online shopping: if you live in Alaska or Hawaii (or are overseas military with an APO address), you may be out of luck. While Walmart and Target will ship some items to Alaska and Hawaii, other sites refuse.

5 ONE WORD: IKEA. Sure, it's basic and no frills . . . but it's hard to beat the price! IKEA's ultra affordable cribs and dressers make even Walmart look expensive. Example: the HENSVIK crib for $99 and matching wardrobe for $99. Yes, you will have to assemble it yourself. And no, it won't last through three kids. But hey—it's hard to beat the price. (See the brand reviews later for more on IKEA, including some key things to know before you buy).

6 GO NAKED. Naked furniture, that is. An increasing number of stores sell unfinished (or naked) furniture at great prices. Such places even sell the finishing supplies and give you directions (make sure to use a non-toxic finish). The prices are hard to beat. At a local unfinished furniture store, we found a three-drawer pine dresser (23" wide) for $150, while a four-drawer dresser (38" wide) was $225. Compare that to baby store prices, which can top $500 to $700 for a similar size dresser. A reader in California e-mailed us with a great example of this trend in the Bay Area: Hoot Judkins in Redwood City (hootjudkins.com). Example: an unfinished double dresser in solid pine is $570—most finished versions of this dresser in a baby store would run 35% more. While unfinished cribs are somewhat rare, unfinished furniture stores often offer affordable alternatives for dressers, bookcases, and more.

7 SKIP THE SLEIGH CRIB. Lots of folks fall in love with the look of a sleigh-style crib, which looks like (you guessed it) a sleigh. The only problem? Most sleigh cribs have solid foot and headboards. All that extra wood means higher prices, as much as TWICE that of non-sleigh styles. If you have your heart set on a sleigh style, look for one with slats on the headboard instead of solid wood.

8 CONSIDER AN AFFORDABLE CONVERTIBLE CRIB. Before you jump on the bandwagon and consider a convertible crib, there is a key question to ask: do you have room in the nursery for the crib to convert to a full-size bed? If the answer is yes, then consider an affordable convertible. At chains stores like Babies R Us convertible cribs run $400 to $600. At specialty stores, brands like Westwood offer convertibles in the $400 to $600 range. Don't forget to factor in the price of the kit to convert the crib to a twin or full-size bed— this is another $60 to $200. At press time, Costco was selling a convertible crib by CaféKids (including the conversion kit) for $400. One tip: make sure the design has a true headboard and shorter footboard (many low-end convertible cribs cheat on this point by having the same size head and foot boards). This looks much better when converted to a double bed.

9 TRY CRAIGSLIST. As you probably know, Craigslist's popular online classified site has versions for dozens of cities, with a special "for sale" section for baby/kids stuff. Use Craigslist to find a local family that is unloading unneeded nursery furniture, gear and other items (but do NOT buy a used crib, as we've discussed earlier).

10 **DON'T WAIT ON THE CONVERSION KIT OR NIGHTSTAND.** Many parents like the concept of a convertible crib that can grow with your child from crib to twin or full-size bed. But to make that transition, you often need to buy a separate conversion kit (bedrails and other hardware). We recommend buying the conversion kit (and other matching items like a nightstand) when you first order your nursery furniture, instead of waiting until your child needs the crib converted. Why? Styles and colors can be discontinued at the drop of a hat; some manufacturers disappear altogether. If you wait and the conversion kit is no longer available, you've just spent a fortune on a convertible crib that can't be converted!

Baby Superstore Reviews: The Good, Bad & Ugly

There's good news and bad news when it comes to shopping for baby. Good news: there are an amazing number of stores to shop for baby gear. Bad news: there are an amazing number of

How to snag the best deals on Craigslist

Sure there are great deals on Craigslist, but how do you use this online wonder to save the most? Here are a few tips:

◆ **Be patient.** When you first go on Craigslist, you will be amazed at the prices and think you have to snap up deals quickly. But take some time to see what really are the best prices. A reader says she thought she got a good deal when she hastily bought a Baby Bjorn carrier off Craigslist for 50% retail—until she noticed the going rate is more like 75% off.

◆ **Use Craigslist list to find garage sales.** On Friday night or Saturday morning, just do a quick search in the garage sale listings for "baby."

◆ **Deals are even better than they look.** That's because there is no shipping or sales tax. Examples from our readers: a Dutailier rocker and ottoman for $260 (retail $600+), Boppy pillow for $5 (retail $35), cradle swing for $60 (retail: $140).

stores to shop for baby gear.

And as a first-time parent, you probably have never been in these stores (except for that time you bought a gift for a pregnant co-worker). Walking into a baby superstore for the first time can give even the most levelheaded mom or dad-to-be a case of the willies. It is a blizzard of pacifiers, strollers, cribs and more in a mind-numbing assortment of colors, features and options. So, as a public service, here's our overview of the major players in the baby store biz.

Babies R Us 888-BABYRUS; babiesrus.com. The 800-pound gorilla of baby stores, Babies R Us has 450+ stores nationwide and is the country's leading baby gear retailer. Love 'em or hate 'em, you'll probably find yourself in a BRU at some point—in some towns, BRU is the only baby store around.

FYI: Babies R Us comes in several flavors: there are the 248 stand-alone stores. Then there are 204 side-by-side stories (where a Toys R Us and Babies R Us are side-by-side). Finally, the chain has a flagship store in New York City's Union Square that is a Babies R Us on steroids.

For the uninitiated, Babies R Us is your typical chain store—big on selection, decent prices . . . but service? That's not the point. Sure, our readers occasionally report they found a knowledgeable sales clerk. But other times, you are lucky to find a person to check you out, much less give advice on a car seat.

To its credit, Babies R Us is trying to fix this by adding registry concierges—specially trained associates whose mission in life is to guide parents-to-be through the registry process. So far, the chain has rolled out this program at three dozen locations.

In recent years, BRU has added more private label and exclusive merchandise to combat online discounting. In some cases, BRU has manufacturers make a special line that is only sold in the chain (example: Eco-Chic Baby nursery furniture is made by Baby Appleseed). You'll also see car seats branded as "Babies R Us by Safety 1st."

The Truly Scrumptious by Heidi Klum brand is another BRU creation that you'll see in cribs, bedding, strollers (some made by Dorel/Cosco) and other products. We've also seen "Babies R Us" private label products, such as the BRU Baby Sight Video Monitor, which is made by Summer (even though Summer's name doesn't appear on the product).

These private label efforts are clearly muscling out other name brands from BRU's shelves. And if you are looking for luxury brands like UPPAbaby or Bugaboo strollers, this isn't your store.

BRU wins kudos for their web site, which has been upgraded to include a gift-finding tool, store inventory levels and wish lists. The web site features additional brands not sold in BRU's stores.

Babies R Us' ace in the hole is their gift registry, which now has a quick start option and other online tools. While no gift registry is perfect (and BRU's registry has seen its fair share of complaints on our message boards), we have noted that readers lately seem happier with BRU's registry after the company divorced itself from a disastrous partnership with Amazon.

FYI: Watch for high dollar coupon books that Babies R Us distributes in January—ask your local store for details.

So, how to grade Babies R Us? For selection, make it an A-, service gets a C, pricing a B+ and the registry, an A. Overall, let's call it a B. **Rating: B**

Baby Depot *800-444-COAT; burlingtoncoatfactory.com.* Baby Depot is a store-within-a-store concept. Tucked inside the cavernous Burlington Coat Factory, Baby Depot is a nook stuffed with nursery furniture, strollers and a smattering of other gear.

Even though there are as many Baby Depots as Babies R Us stores (370+ at last count), Baby Depot has always played second fiddle to BRU. Part of the problem has been marketing strategy: Baby Depot could use one. Burlington/Baby Depot operates in a wide range of locations, some in shiny new suburban power centers and others in dingy warehouses.

The selection of brands at Baby Depot is decent, but merchandising isn't exactly Baby Depot's strong suit. The aisles of the stores are often disorganized and cluttered.

The service at Baby Depot makes Babies R Us look like Nordstroms. We get frequent emails from Baby Depot furniture customers, complaining about late orders, botched orders and worse.

On the plus side, Baby Depot has changed their draconian return policy—now you can return items within 30 days and get cash back (as long as you have a receipt and the tags are still attached).

So, here's our advice: if you see something here that is in stock and the price is right, go for it. But forget about special ordering anything such as furniture. **Rating: C-**

Buy Buy Baby *BuyBuyBaby.com.* Owned by the Bed, Bath & Beyond chain, Buy Buy Baby is our top pick in this category. Yes, they only have 90+ locations, but the chain is expanding and may be worth a trip if one is nearby. FYI: In some markets, like Denver, CO, Buy Buy Baby operates combination stores with its parent, Bed Bath & Beyond. Basically, two stores with one entrance.

Service is the strong point here—folks at Buy Buy Baby know their stuff. Now, we realize that this might not be a fair fight—can Babies R Us with its zillion stores ever compete on service with a much smaller rival? It will be interesting to see if Buy Buy Baby can maintain that advantage as it expands into new stores.

Given the urban slant to its locations, the brands and selection skew toward the expensive. Yes, there are Graco travel systems here . . . but also Bugaboo's $1000 models. Ditto for the furniture, with Child Craft sharing floor space with more pricey options from Baby Appleseed.

The stores are merchandised much like Bed Bath and Beyond—that is crowded, with stacks of merchandise rising to the ceiling. While Babies R Us is a bit easier to navigate, Buy Buy Baby has more selection in several categories.

Buy Buy Baby's web site has improved in the past year, but still pales in comparison to competitors like Babies R Us and Amazon when it comes to parent reviews and other helpful features (like parent questions and answers about products).

Despite their web site, we still give Buy Buy Baby our top rating among chain stores—if you happen to be near one, this store is a keeper. *Rating: A*

The Discounters: Target, Walmart, Kmart

Any discussion of national stores that sell baby items wouldn't be complete without a mention of the discounters: Target, Walmart, Kmart and their ilk. In recent years, the discounters have realized one sure-fire way to drive store traffic—discount baby supplies! As a result, you'll often see formula, diapers and other baby essentials at rock-bottom prices. And there are even better deals on "in-house" brands. The goal is to have you drop by to pick up some diapers . . . and then walk out with a big-screen TV.

Of all the discounters, we think Target is best (with one big caveat—their ruthless return policy, see below for a discussion). Target's baby department is a notch above Walmart and Kmart when it comes to brand names and selection. Yes, sometimes Walmart has lower prices—but usually that's on lower-quality brands. Target, by contrast, carries Perego high chairs and a wider selection of products like baby monitors. The best bet: Super Targets, which have expanded baby products sections.

One important trend: discounters have bulked up their web sites with brands, products and models that are NOT carried in their stores. Sometimes you'll even find an upscale brand online at discount prices. We'll discuss the discounter web sites specifically below.

Of course, there are some downsides to the discounters. If you're looking for premium brand names, forget it. Most discounters only stock the so-called mass-market brands: Graco strollers, Cosco car seats, Gerber sheets, etc. And the baby departments always seem to be in chaos when we visit, with items strewn about hither and yon. Kmart is probably the worst when it comes to organization, Walmart the best. We like Target's selection (especially of feeding items and baby monitors), but their prices are somewhat higher than Walmart. What about service? Forget it—no matter which store you're in, you're on your own.

While we do recommend Target, we should warn readers about their return policy. Once among the most generous, Target now requires a receipt for just about any return. A raft of new rules and restrictions greet customers (sample: exchanges now must be made for items within the same department). This has understandably ticked off a fair number of our readers, especially those who have unfortunately chosen to register at Target for their baby gifts. Among the biggest roadblocks: Target won't let you exchange duplicate baby gifts if you don't have a gift receipt (and there are numerous other rules/restrictions as well). Of course, your friends may forget to ask for a gift receipt or throw it away. And watch out: gift receipts have expiration dates; be sure to return any item before that date. Target also limits the number of returns you can do in one year.

After receiving a fair amount of consumer complaints about this, Target now allows returns of registry gifts without a gift receipt IF the item is listed on your registry. The fine print: you will get the lowest sales price in the last 90 days, not necessarily what your guest paid for it. That's a special gotcha for new parents—many baby products and clothes go on sale frequently, rendering your gift almost worthless on an exchange. This and other concerns with Target have spawned many complaints about their registry and even blogs dedicated to dissing the chain.

Our advice: think twice about registering at Target. While we get complaints about all baby registries, be sure to read the fine print for ANY baby registry before signing up. Ask about returns and exchange policies, including specifically what happens if you have to return/exchange a duplicate item without a gift receipt. And check for limits on the number of returns you can do within a certain time period. Finally, ask about HOW the store integrates your registry with the web site—if someone buys an item online instead of at a store, will this be reflected on your registry? Check our blog and message boards for the latest buzz on baby registries.

Each of the major discounters sells baby products online. Here's an overview of each site:

◆ **WalMart.com** Hit the baby tab and you'll find yourself in Walmart's extensive online baby gear department. We like how the chain has expanded online offerings in recent years—there's much more on the web site than in the stores (particularly strollers). Walmart has steadily improved the site over the last year or so—now you can search by brand, read product reviews and get a product delivered to a nearby store at no charge. And, of course, the prices are excellent.

◆ **Kmart.com** Kmart's online outpost is a winner—we liked the graphics and easy navigation. You can search by brand, price and more. We also liked the Deals Center for the latest specials. The only bummer: unlike Target, Kmart's online selection brand-wise is much the same as the store—heavy on low-end brands like Baby Trend. And the site is confusing in some areas—in car seats, Kmart mixes infant, convertible and booster seats. That's not very helpful.

◆ **Target.com** is our pick as the best discounter web site—their online offerings go way beyond what's in the stores. We also like the user reviews, as well as the ability to sort any category by brand, price or best-sellers. Perhaps the biggest drawback with Target.com (as with other sites) is the sometimes skimpy product descriptions. You can often find more about a product by reading the user reviews than Target's own descriptions.

◆ **Diapers.com** New kid on the block, Diapers.com started off selling diapers online (naturally) and evolved into a baby gear behemoth in recent years. That caught the attention of Amazon, which scooped up the site in 2010. Diapers.com has extensive sections of nursery furniture and décor (along with other baby gear). The product reviews from pulled from Amazon's site.. For bargain hunters, zero in on the Sale tab for the latest discounts and clearance items.

Specialty Chains That Sell Baby Furniture

Inspired by the success of Pottery Barn Kids, several chains have ventured into the nursery business. An example: Room & Board (RoomandBoard.com), a 14 store chain (plus an outlet) with locations in major cities. Their well-designed web site has a nursery section with a handful of cribs ($700 to $1000), dressers and accessories. Quality is good, say our readers who've ordered from them.

And that's just the beginning: Land of Nod, a subsidiary of Crate & Barrel, has an extensive website (landofnod.com) with nursery offerings as well as five stores in Chicago, Seattle and Costa Mesa, CA. FYI: The Land of Nod is owned by Crate & Barrel—you can use gift cards from one chain at the other.

Restoration Hardware has a special web site for their nursery and children's furniture: RH Baby & Child (rhbabyandchild.com). A style and trend setter, RH Baby & Child is hardly a bargain (most cribs sell for $1000), but you can often find similar looks at other chain stores for lower prices. At a minimum, the web site is a great place to get ideas—check out the room gallery section for design inspiration.

What's driving this is a boom in babies born to older moms and dads. Tired of the cutesy baby stuff in chain stores, many parents are looking for something more sophisticated and hip. Of course, it remains to be seen what this means for bargain shoppers. On one hand, more competition is always good—having a wide diversity of places to buy nursery furniture and accessories is always a plus. On the downside, most of these chains are chasing that "upscale" customer with outrageously priced cribs and bedding. "As much as parents love the furniture at Pottery Barn Kids, some wince at the prices," said the *Wall Street Journal* in a recent article on this trend. And we agree—while we love the PBK look, our goal in life is to try to find that same look . . . at half the price!

Outlets

There are dozens of outlets that sell kids' clothing, but when it comes to furniture the pickings are slim. In fact, we found just a handful of nursery furniture outlets out there. Here's a round up:

Pottery Barn Kids has a half dozen outlets for their kids catalog, scattered around the country (go to potterybarnkids.com and click on store locator). Readers report some good deals there, including a changing table for $100 (regularly $200) and a rocker for $200 (down from $700). The outlet also carries the PBK bedding line at good discounts. A reader in Georgia said the PBK outlet there features 75% off deals on furniture and you can get a coupon book at the food court for an additional 10% discount. "The best time to shop is during the week—they run more specials then," she said. "And bring a truck—they don't deliver." One final tip: call AHEAD before you go. The selection of nursery furniture can vary widely from outlet to outlet . . . some may have no stock during certain months.

Live in the Northeast? Check out **Baby Boudoir Outlet,** an offshoot of a baby store in New Bedford, MA (babyboudoiroutlet. com, 800-272-2293, 508-998-2166). The store is an authorized dealer for Pali, Baby's Dream, Bonavita, and Romina. The Baby Boudoir Outlet has 1000 cribs in stock at any one time at prices from $250 to $450. The store also carries glider rockers, bedding and other baby products at 30% to 70% off retail. FYI: There is both a Baby Boudoir store and a warehouse outlet—you want to visit the outlet for the best deals. The outlet is around the corner from the main store.

Readers have been mixed on their opinions of the Baby Boudoir outlet. One described it as a "bare bones warehouse in a bad neighborhood." However, another reader described the outlet as "in an urban area, but safe"; she found the warehouse itself "clean and well-organized."

Check out the web site Outlet Bound (outletbound.com) for other outlets that carry kid furniture.

The Name Game: Reviews of Selected Manufacturers

Here's a look at crib brands sold in the U.S. and Canada. Our focus is on the most common nursery furniture brands you see in chains stores, independents and other furniture outlets. If you've discovered a brand that we didn't review, feel free to share your discovery by calling or emailing us (see our contact info at the end of the book).

How did we evaluate the brands? First, we inspected samples of cribs at stores and industry trade shows. With the help of veteran juvenile furniture retailers, we checked construction, release mechanisms, mattress supports, and overall fit and finish. Yes, we did compare styling among the brands but this was only a minor factor in our ratings (we figure you can decide what looks best for your nursery).

Readers of previous editions have asked us how we assign ratings to these manufacturers—what makes one an "A" vs. "B"? The bottom line is quality *and* value. Sure, anyone can make a high-quality crib for $800. The trick is getting that price down to $400 or less while maintaining high-quality standards. Hence, we give more bonus points to brands that give more value for the dollar.

What about the crib makers who got the lowest ratings? Are their cribs unsafe? No, of course not. ALL new cribs sold in the U.S. and Canada must meet minimum federal safety standards. As we mentioned earlier in this chapter, a $150 crib sold at Walmart is just as safe as a $1500 designer brand sold at a posh boutique. The only difference is styling, features and durability—more expensive cribs have thick wood posts, fancy finishes and durability to last through two or more kids. The best companies have the best customer service, taking care of both their retailers and consumers.

Brands that got our lowest rating have poor quality control and abysmal customer service. Serious safety recalls also impacts a brand's rating.

FYI: Many crib makers have sub brands, private label offerings for chain stores and other aliases. See the chart on the next page for a rundown of these names and where to look for the review.

The Ratings

A EXCELLENT—*our top pick!*
B GOOD— *above average quality, prices, and creativity.*
C FAIR—*could stand some improvement.*
D POOR—*yuck! could stand some major improvement.*

CRIB BRAND ALIASES

BRAND/ALIAS	SEE MANUFACTURER
ADELE	SIMMONS
BABY CACHE	MUNIRE
BABY MOD	MILLION DOLLAR BABY
BABY RELAX	DOREL
BABYLETTO	MILLION DOLLAR BABY
BEDFORD BABY	WESTWOOD DESIGN
BELLEFONTE KIDS	WOODCRAFT INDUSTRIES
BERTINI	DOREL
BETHANY JAMES SECURE REACH	DOREL
BROYHILL	STORK CRAFT
DAVINCI	MILLION DOLLAR BABY
DOLCE BABI	BIVONA & CO.
ECHELON	MUNIRE
ECO-CHIC BABY	BABY APPLESEED
EDDIE BAUER	DOREL
FISHER-PRICE	BIVONA & CO.
FRANKLIN & BEN	MILLION DOLLAR BABY
GRACO	STORK CRAFT
HGTV HOME BABY	BASSETT
IMAGIO BABY	WESTWOOD DESIGN
KARLA DUBOIS	BABY APPLESEED
LUSSO	SORELLE
MIRA STUDIOS	KOLCRAFT
NEST	NATART
NURSERY SMART	BABY APPLESEED
NURSERYWORKS	MILLION DOLLAR BABY
RESTORATION HARDWARE	BASSETT
ROCKLAND	JC PENNEY
ROOM & BOARD	EL GRECO
SB2	SORELLE
SERENA & LILY	MILLION DOLLAR BABY
SERTA	DELTA
SILVA	ROMINA
STATUS	STORK CRAFT
STELLA BABY	WESTWOOD DESIGN
SUITE BEBE	MUNIRE
THOMASVILLE	STORK CRAFT
TIAMO	BIVONA & CO.
TRULY SCRUMPTIOUS HEIDI KLUM	DOREL
TULIP	NATART
VINTAGE ESTATE	DOREL
WENDY BELLISSIMO	LEGACY CLASSIC KIDS
ZUTANO	STORK CRAFT

Adele The Adele furniture collection is made by Simmons in Thailand as an exclusive for Babies R Us.

AFG Furniture. *This crib brand is reviewed in the bonus section on our web site, BabyBargains.com/cribs*

Angel Line *This crib brand is reviewed in the bonus section on our web site, BabyBargains.com/cribs*

Babee Tenda See box on page 52-53.

Baby Gift Registries: Disappointing

We have a plea for tomorrow's computer science college graduates: fix the gift registries at chain stores—please!

Sure, computers can pilot a spaceship to Pluto or solve the most complex microbiology problem . . . but for some reason, such computer smarts elude the baby gift registry programmers at chain stores.

No matter how sweet the promises are about computerized registries ("Look Ma! I'm changing an item on the registry at 2 am!") the reality falls WAY short of utopia. Judging from our reader mail and message boards, folks are steamed when they must deal with registry snafus . . . and who can blame them.

While the process of registering at any chain is relatively straightforward (you can scan items in the store or pick them off a web site), USING the registry is where things start to fall apart. You name it, we've heard it: duplicate gifts, out of stock items (with no notice to the parent), endless backorders and other goofs.

Here are the frustrations:

◆ *Online versus offline.* Many stores carry items online that aren't in stores. And in some cases, items can only be found in stores, not online. So if you register online at a major retailer, your friends who visit the retailer's stores may find a large chunk of your registry can't be purchased in the store. Another frustration: at Babies R Us, online-only items can't be returned to BRU stores—they can only be returned via the mail. And then the gift-giver receives the credit, not you.

◆ *Returns.* Stores have Byzantine return policies that can frustrate the seemingly simple task of returning a duplicate gift (which shouldn't happen with registries, right?). Many stores require a gift receipt for returns—but whoops! Your gift-giver for-

---

Baby Appleseed/Karla Dubois/Nursery Smart/Eco-Chic Baby
nurserysmart.com, babyappleseed.com, karladubois. com, ecochicba-by.com Baby Appleseed is actually three separate brands: Baby Appleseed (upper-end pricing, sold in Buy Buy Baby, among other stores), Karla Dubois (modern cribs), Eco-Chic Baby (exclusive to Babies R Us) and Nursery Smart (more affordable, sold mostly online).

The company's mojo is to combine eco-friendliness and elegant design. The eco-pitch: when you buy one of their cribs, the company will plant ten trees in your baby's name, thanks to a partnership with the non-profit American Forests.

The furniture is also GREENGUARD Gold certified to be low

got to include that. No problem, just print out a copy of your registry from the web site? Whoops! The store deleted your registry 14 days after your baby was born. And so on.

◆ *Discontinued items.* You try to be smart and register early for that baby shower—but now several items are discontinued. Does the registry email you with notice? Are you kidding? Registries expect you to monitor your registry and replace items as needed. And product may disappear from an online registry, but still be available in stores.

Some of the problems with a gift registry only become apparent AFTER you've received a gift. Example: Pottery Barn's policy on gift certificates. If you want to use a gift certificate for an online or telephone purchase at Pottery Barn Kids, you must MAIL the certificate in and cool your heels for a two to three week processing period. How convenient.

Babies R Us runs the country's biggest gift registry—and comes in for a regular barbequing from our readers. To its credit, BRU has fixed many of the glitches that were apparent in recent years . . . but we still hear from readers who have problems with returns, discontinued items and more. FYI: Babies R Us changed their return policy for gift registry purchases in the past year—now you have 90 days from your due date (not when the items where purchased) to return items.

Another idea: BabyList (web: babyli.st) lets you add items from any store on one registry—it's free.

Bottom line: take a second and read the gift registry feedback from recent parents on our web site. Always READ the return policies of any gift registry BEFORE you sign up—is there a time limit for returns? Must you have a gift receipt? Are you limited to X number of returns or exchanges? Know ALL the fine print before you plunge in!

emission.

The best-selling Baby Appleseed collection is the Davenport, a curvy crib with thick rails and back board. All that chunkiness will cost you: the Davenport crib is $700, while a double dresser runs $680, armoire $750, hutch $450 and five-drawer chest $580. Rails to convert the Davenport into a full-size bed run another $120.

Finishes in Baby Appleseed are rather limited: the Davenport comes in just three (espresso, cherry and white). Other collections have just two. If you are looking for colors other than white and brown, this probably isn't your brand.

If the Davenport is too much, Baby Appleseed also sells the Stratford (a Buy Buy Baby exclusive). Here a crib runs $300 and five-drawer dresser $390.

While most of Baby Appleseed's styles are traditional, the company has recently released a collection that is more art deco (Carlisle).

Baby Appleseed's cribs are made of poplar wood; the dressers are poplar with birch veneers. While the wood is from the U.S., the cribs are produced in Vietnam. Five finishes are available, with a dark grey (slate) that recently joined the line.

On a recent visit to Buy Buy Baby, we asked the clerk in the crib department to give us her top recommendation—she pointed to the Baby Appleseed Davenport and praised its durable finish, which prevents scratches and nicks. It's clear Buy Buy Baby is this brand's biggest account, although a handful of other independent stores carry Baby Appleseed as well.

Baby Appleseed has struggled in the past with lengthy order times (sometimes up to 20 weeks), but the company says the longest wait now is 6-8 weeks for secondary colors (with four weeks average on popular finishes). Plan accordingly.

Karla Dubois is sub-line of Baby Appleseed that is also sold in Buy Buy Baby and the Right Start. As of this writing, the brand has one collection—a modern crib dubbed the Oslo ($400) with two under-crib drawers. A toddler rail runs $100 and matching two-drawer dresser is $400. Karla Dubois is basically the same as Baby Appleseed—GREENGUARD certified, crib is made from poplar wood, etc.

Nursery Smart is the company's less expensive, less fancy brand. At the time of this writing, Nursery Smart only had one collection (the Darby), but we also see a handful of mini-cribs sold online under the Nursery Smart moniker for under $200. To keep prices low, most Nursery Smart dressers are ready to assemble (Baby Appleseed dressers are fully assembled).

The newest addition to the Baby Appleseed family is Eco-Chic Baby. Exclusive to Babies R Us, Eco-Chic Baby cribs retail for $650-$700. Two collections (Clover and Dorchester) debuted in late 2014

Not made in China

From lead paint in toys to tainted baby formula, China has had its share of, uh, quality control issues. And some of our readers have asked us, not surprisingly, how to furnish a nursery with products NOT made in China. While that sounds simple, it isn't: 90% or more of baby furniture sold in the U.S. is made in China—so avoiding Chinese-made items takes some effort.

But there is good news: there ARE a handful of companies that make their furniture somewhere other than China. And yes, there are still firms that make furniture in the U.S.: ducduc, Capretti, El Greco, and Newport Cottages. Oak Designs (oakdesigns.com) makes dressers and twin beds domestically. Lolly & Me's "Eco-Friendly" collections are made in the U.S.

Other furniture makers import goods from countries other than China: Romina makes furniture in Romania; Westwood, Bratt Décor and Bivona's Dolce Babi and Tiamo have factories in Vietnam. Oeuf imports its furniture from Latvia. Natart is made in Canada and Denmark. Baby's Dream is imported from Chile.

A few caveats to this advice: first, production often shifts, so before you order, reconfirm with the manufacturer or retailer where the furniture is being made. Second, manufacturers that split production between China and other countries often don't publicize which furniture is made where. You have to ask which furniture is made where.

in two colors (slate and hickory), with more collections arriving in 2015. Like Baby Appleseed, Eco-Chic Baby touts a GREENGUARD Gold certification, where products are third-party tested to be low in chemical emissions.

This company's parent reviews have been bi-polar—readers generally like and recommend Baby Appleseed, while folks have been more mixed on Nursery Smart (their ready-to-assemble dressers are difficult to put together). And the finish on the lower end Nursery Smart furniture came in for past criticism: it scratched too easily. To address this criticism, Nursery Smart recently switched from New Zealand pine to North Carolina poplar, which is the same wood used in the Baby Appleseed and Eco-Chic Baby.

Bottom line: this is an excellent brand that would be worth the investment, if you have the budget. Yes, Baby Appleseed had growing pains, but the furniture today is excellent quality. As a result, we'll raise our rating on the brand. ***Rating: A***

Baby Cache *BabyCache.com This furniture is made exclusively for Babies R Us by Munire.*

Baby Mod *See Million Dollar Baby.*

Baby Relax *This furniture is made exclusively for Walmart by Dorel*

Baby's Dream *BabysDream.com* Georgia-based Baby's Dream's claim to fame is convertible cribs. The company was among the first to launch the trend in 1990—yes, Baby's Dream was convertible before convertible was cool.

A family-owned business, Baby's Dream splits its production between China and Chile, although the company does some final assembly at its factory in Georgia.

The furniture is sold only in specialty stores—no chain stores carry the brand. And it is rarely sold online (only BabySupermart.com sells it as of this writing). This devotion to specialty stores has a downside: Baby's Dream is hard to find in some areas. Example: states with few independent baby retailers like Washington State, Montana and Colorado have nary a single dealer for this brand.

To address the lack of dealers in some areas, Baby's Dream sells furniture direct from its own web site. You can also order online and have the furniture delivered to a Baby's Dream dealer near you.

One unusual feature for Baby's Dream: it is one of the few brands that still have cribs with drop-sides. Baby's Dream's fold down rail is one of the few (only?) designs that survived the purge of drop-side cribs for safety reasons back in 2010.

Prices for Baby's Dream are in the mid to upper ranges of the market—cribs run $500 to $700 and dressers are similar in price. That makes them more expensive than what you'd find in Babies R Us . . . but in specialty stores that carry cribs that top $1000, Baby's

Who Is Jenny Lind?

You can't shop for cribs and not hear the name "Jenny Lind." Here's an important point to remember: Jenny Lind isn't a brand name; it refers to a particular *style* of crib. But how did it get this name? Jenny Lind was a popular Swedish soprano in the 19th century. During her triumphal U.S. tour, it was said that Lind slept in a "spool bed." Hence, cribs that featured turned spindles (which look like stacked spools of thread) became known as Jenny Lind cribs. All this begs the question—what if today we still named juvenile furniture after famous singers? Would we have Lady Gaga cribs and Beyonce dressers? Nah.

Dream might be their opening price point.

Most of Baby's Dream furniture is traditionally styled, although the company has occasionally dabbled in modern designs. A typical example is the Renaissance crib.

So how is the quality, given the high prices? Well, that is a mixed picture. Baby's Dream dressers feature a "soft close" and full extension drawer glides. The overall fit and finish of the furniture is good.

But, there are two caveats: long-term wood problems and delivery snafus.

All of Baby's Dream furniture is made of pine—radiata pine from Chile. (The dressers are made of veneers over the pine). Compared to birch and beech used in other high-end furniture, pine is much softer. As a result it is prone to scratches. We also have seen scattered reports of the wood on Baby's Dream dressers splitting and cracking, especially in areas with large swings in humidity (think the East Coast). That is simply unacceptable for a $700 dresser.

Then there is the issue of delivery snafus.

If items are in stock, delivery only takes six to eight weeks. But that is the rub: items that are not in stock can go on forever backordered—retailers complain that while most items are in stock, there inevitably will be one item in an order that is back ordered for *six months* or more, frustrating retailer and consumer alike. Yes, you read that right: you may have to wait 20-24 weeks for some Baby's Dream furniture.

Another gripe: if your crib has a defective part, there may be a long wait for replacement parts. That's because Baby's Dream doesn't stock replacement rails or headboards—you have to wait until the next boat arrives from Chile (which could be weeks or months of waiting). While this is a problem that plagues many imported furniture lines, Baby's Dream could do a better job at quality control and not ship out defective furniture to begin with.

Finally, let's talk about how Baby's Dream the company is managed. Dysfunctional, in our opinion, would be the word we'd use to describe it. There is always some calamity befalling the company. After a consumer complained about late delivery of a crib on a consumer forum, the company blamed the delay on "production issues along with fewer employees due to the Holiday season." Yes, that surprise holiday season that always bedevils nursery furniture production. Really.

From Yelp to the Better Business Bureau (which rates Baby's Dream an "F"), there is a pattern here: orders run much later than the 6-8 week promised delivery, phone messages and emails to customer service go unreturned and so on. Yes, production delays can happen with any nursery furniture line . . . but Baby's Dream compounds the problem with poor customer service and other snafus that damage its brand.

We asked Baby's Dream to comment on these complaints and they noted that most of the complaints were from 2011 and 2012—in 2013, Baby's Dream hired additional customer service staff and a result, consumer contact issues have declined, says the company.

As for stock issues, Baby's Dream told us "over the last two years we have put enormous effort, energy and resources into inventory to reduce" shipping issues. The company claims they have "in stock status on almost every item in our product mix."

To address the splitting issues with dresser tops and fronts, Baby's

Babee Tenda's "safety" seminar: Anatomy of a Hard Sell

We got an interesting invitation in the mail during our second pregnancy—a company called "Babee Tenda" invited us to a free "Getting Ready For Baby" safety seminar at a local hotel. The seminar was described as "brief, light and enjoyable while handing out information on preventing baby injuries." Our curiosity piqued, we joined a couple dozen other expectant parents on a Saturday afternoon to learn their expert safety tips.

What followed was a good lesson for all parents—beware of companies that want to exploit parents' fears of their children being injured in order to sell their expensive safety "solutions." Sure enough, there was safety information dispensed at the seminar. The speaker started his talk with horrific tales of how many children are injured and killed each year. The culprit? Cheap juvenile equipment products like high chairs and cribs, he claimed. It was quite a performance—the speaker entranced the crowd with endless statistics on kids getting hurt and then demonstrated hazards with sample products from major manufacturers.

The seminar then segued into a thinly veiled pitch for their products: the Babee Tenda high chair/feeding table and crib. The speaker (really a salesperson) spent what seemed like an eternity trying to establish the company's credibility, claiming Babee Tenda has been in business for 60 years and only sells its products to hospitals and other institutions. We can see why—these products are far too ugly and expensive to sell in retail stores.

How expensive? The crib sells for $600+ and the feeding table for about $500.

We found Babee Tenda's sales pitch to be disgusting. They used misleading statistics and outright lies to scare parents into thinking they were putting their children in imminent danger if they used store-bought high chairs or cribs. Many of the statistics and "props" used to demonstrate hazards were as much as 20 years old and

Dream has "changed our (dressers) to a mix of solid wood and the highest grade of MDF with the greatest possible density. Our tops and side panels are now being produced in MDF to prevent unnecessary splitting."

While we appreciated Baby's Dream detailed response to our concerns, we still are downgrading their rating this year to reflect the above issues. If you decide to purchase this brand, make sure the pieces you want are actually in stock at Baby's Dream warehouse. ***Rating: C***

long since removed from the market! Even more reprehensible were claims that certain popular juvenile products were about to be recalled. Specifically, Babee Tenda's salesperson claimed the Evenflo Exersaucer was "unsafe and will be off the market in six months," an accusation that clearly wasn't true.

The fact that Babee Tenda had to use such bogus assertions raised our suspicions about whether they were telling the truth about their own products. Sadly, the high-pressure sales tactics did win over some parents at the seminar we attended—some forked over nearly $800 for Babee Tenda's items. Since then, we've heard from other parents who've attended Babee Tenda's "safety seminars," purchased the products and then suffered a case of "buyer's remorse." Did they spend too much, they ask?

Yes, in our opinion. While we see nothing wrong per se with Babee Tenda's "feeding table" (besides the fact it's god-awful ugly), you should note it costs nearly four times as much as our top recommended high chair, the very well made Fisher Price Healthy Care. There's nothing wrong with the crib either—and yes, Babee Tenda, throws in a mattress and two sheets. But you can find all this for much less than the $600 or so Babee Tenda asks.

A twist to the Babee Tenda pitch: invitations sent by a Babee Tenda distributor in Virginia in 2004 carried a line that their seminar is sponsored "in conjunction with the Consumer Product Safety Commission and the National Highway Traffic Safety Administration." Whoa, sounds official! Except it isn't true—neither the CPSC nor NHTSA have anything to do with Babee Tenda's seminars . . . in fact, the federal government successfully sued Babee Tenda to stop the practice. In 2007, a federal judge ruled Babee Tenda committed mail fraud, calling their sales tactics "deceitful and reprehensible."

So, we say watch out for Babee Tenda (and other similar companies like Babyhood, who pitches their "Baby Sitter" in hotel safety seminars). We found their "safety seminar" to be bogus, their high-pressure sales tactics reprehensible and their products grossly overpriced.

babyletto *babyletto.com* Babyletto is Million Dollar Baby's modern, eco-friendly sub brand. Launched in 2010, babyletto features several low-profile cribs that are available in solid or two-tone finishes.

A good example is the Hudson ($380), which is one of the line's best-sellers. You can get this crib in two solid colors (espresso, white) as well as two-tone finishes (grey frame with white spindles, espresso with white, etc).

The furniture here has a mid-century vibe; it is made in Taiwan of New Zealand pine. Cribs include the toddler rail, which is often an extra purchase with other brands.

Overall, cribs run $329 to $600, with ready-to-assemble dressers clocking in at $360 to $430.

Part of babyletto's pitch is the eco-friendly angle—the brand touts its sustainable pine wood, MDF that is compliant with California's strict indoor air pollution standards and so on. Yes, babyletto even brags its factories have with solar panels and electric vehicle charging stations. What's missing? Certifications that back up their eco-friendly talk—note, babyletto is NOT GREENGUARD certified to be low emission.

So how's the quality? We give babyletto a thumb's up—yes, these cribs are made of pine, which can easily scratch and damage from everyday use. But overall, readers say they are happy with their babyletto cribs. Fans love the fact you can get that modern, mid century look for under $400 (many other modern cribs can top $1000). The low profile of the crib makes it a favorite of shorter moms and dads.

Critics of babyletto say the assembly process for the cribs is tedious, so make sure you leave plenty of time. And while the cribs generate mostly positive feedback, consumer reviews on the dressers are more mixed. Common complaints include dressers arriving with damage (broken pieces) as well as overall quality issues (corners and edges that began to chip once the dresser is assembled). Folks knocked the assembly instructions (poorly written) and overall quality (drawers coming off the track or falling apart after a year of use).

Finally, we should note that even though babyletto calls their cribs "convertible," the cribs only convert to toddler and day beds—not into full-size beds for older kids.

Bottom line: this is good brand if you want a modern crib on a budget. But skip the dressers. ***Rating (cribs only): B+***

Bassettbaby *bassettbaby.com* Adult furniture maker Bassett traces its roots back to 1902 when the company marketed its dressers for $4.75 and beds for $1.50. Now with 100 retail locations around the country, the company has offerings in several furniture segments . . . including nursery furniture.

Bassett has shifted its strategy in nursery furniture over time. For

JPMA
CERTIFIED

Certifications: Do they really matter?

As you shop for cribs and other products for your baby, you'll no doubt run into "JPMA-Certified" products sporting a special seal. But who is the JPMA and what does its certification mean?

The Juvenile Products Manufacturers Association (JPMA) is a group of over 300 companies that make juvenile products, both in the United States and Canada. Over twenty-five years ago, the group started a volunteer testing program to head off government regulation of baby products. The JPMA enlisted the support of the Consumer Products Safety Commission and the American Society of Testing and Materials (ASTM) to develop standards for products in several categories, including cribs, high chairs and more.

Manufacturers must have their product tested in an independent testing lab and, if it passes, they can use the JPMA seal. The JPMA touts its seal as "added assurance the product was built with safety in mind."

So is a product like a crib safer if it has the JPMA seal? No, not in our opinion. In fact, the biggest crib recall in history (one million Simplicity cribs in 2007 after three deaths) involved cribs that were JPMA certified. How did that happen?

Well, the JPMA certification is a MINIMUM set of standards that mostly address adequate warning labels. While detailed warning labels for products are helpful, it doesn't stop defective design or faulty instructions (the problem in the Simplicity recall).

The Simplicity recall tarnished the JPMA's certification program—as a result, the organization undertook an extensive renovation of the certification program in recent years. The JPMA claims the more rigorous program better reflects current laws, regulations and mandates. Whether this works to prevent the next Simplicity recall disaster remains to be seen.

The take-home message: the JPMA seal is no guarantee of safety.

What about other certification programs? GREENGUARD (greenguard.org) certifies nursery furniture and mattress makers who comply with its strict standard on chemical emissions. Since this is done by an independent third party, we think GREENGUARD certification has merit—as of this writing, furniture by Baby Appleseed, Eco-Chic Baby, Natart/Tulip, RH Baby & Child, and Romina are GREENGUARD certified. Mattresses by Colgate, Contours (Kolcraft), Naturepedic, Sealy, Simmons are certified.

a while, they sold entry-price cribs under the First Choice brand on Walmart and Amazon. But those have largely disappeared in recent years, as the company focused on serving the Buy Buy Baby chain (under the moniker Bassettbaby Premier) as well as making private label offerings for Babies R Us and Restoration Hardware.

Most Bassett cribs are in the $550 and $600 range, with similarly priced dressers ($650-$750) that feature dove tail drawer contractions. While Buy Buy Baby has quite a few Bassett cribs on the floor, the brand is curiously absent from its web site. (You can see the collections online, but only buy them in store).

We'd peg Bassett's styling as traditional with a touch of bling. The Addison collection, for example, features a crib with flower appliqué carving and dressers with acrylic floral shaped knobs. Bassett's Restoration Hardware furniture is more fashion forward. (See Restoration Hardware's review later in this section for a discussion of Bassett's cribs made for that chain).

In Buy Buy Baby, Bassett also sells cribs under the HGTV Home Baby brand. Two collections feature fancier finishes with names like Dark Chocolate Cherry; the Hayden collection even features a crib that can convert into two twin beds with headboards (rails are extra). Cribs run $700 and dressers $750-$800.

All Bassett furniture is imported from China. How's the quality? We like Bassett's cribs, which we think are a good value. Yes, Bassett had two recalls in 2008 for its Wendy B cribs (one for defective bolts; another for spindles that were too far apart), but overall, Basset has a good quality record.

While we like Bassett's cribs, the case pieces are another story. Bassett's dressers didn't impress us with their overall fit and finish.

Bottom line: Bassett's cribs are a good value, but skip the dressers. **Rating (cribs only): B+**

Bedford Baby This furniture is made exclusively for JC Penney by Westwood Design.

Bellefonte Kids Bellefontekids.com Bellefonte Kids is the new nursery furniture division of Woodcraft Industries, a furniture and kitchen cabinet maker based in State College, PA. After the lead paint scare and crib recalls of the late 2000's, companies like Woodcraft saw an opportunity to market made in America furniture to parents skittish of Chinese-imported furniture.

The nursery line is comprised of two collections. Each is available in six finishes and there is a two-tone option as well. All cribs convert into full-size beds and the collections include double dressers, hutches, matching mirrors and more.

The key selling point here, besides the Made-in-America label, is solid wood construction. The styling, on other hand, is very basic and traditional. Cribs retail for $950 and a double dresser is $900 to $1000.

At those prices, Bellefonte will compete against Romina in the solid furniture niche—and Romina's prices are about 20% higher than Bellefonte. However, Romina's styling will probably win more fans than Bellefonte Kids' plain Jane looks.

This line was brand new as of this writing, so no parent feedback yet. The quality of the samples we recently viewed was good. We liked the self-closing drawer glides and dust proofing on the dressers. All the pieces are made from "Pennsylvania hardwood" and the drawers feature English dovetail joints. ***Rating: Not Yet.***

Bellini *bellini.com* Bellini pitches itself as the antidote to giant baby superstores. Instead of a cavernous building stacked to the ceiling with baby gear and clueless salespeople, Bellini boutiques are about 3,000 square feet and carry their own in-house line of furniture and accessories. The goal is personal service and a narrow focus on better merchandise. Example: some stores stock nursery accessories made by local artists.

This franchised chain had its heyday in the 80's and 90's—during those decades, its business model was selling imported Italian nursery furniture with $700 price tags. Of course, that was long before Buy Buy Baby and Pottery Barn Kids, not to mention the slew of luxury baby gear web sites.

In the last decade, like many independent retailers, Bellini found itself struggling to compete against chains selling better quality goods and the online world of baby gear discounters. After closing some locations, the chain now has 18 stores most of which are in the Eastern U.S.

As with other crib sellers, Bellini abandoned its Italian import strategy and now imports its furniture from China. Cribs run $680 to $1275, with an average price of $900. Dressers range from $605 for a simple three drawer to $1100 for a five-drawer. A double dresser runs about $1200-$1300.

Delivery takes about ten to 12 weeks on average, although some orders can be filled in just two to three weeks.

New to the line, Bellini has partnered with Newport Cottages (reviewed separately) to produce exclusives for the chain—their first effort is the Stella, a made-in-the-USA crib the chain describes as "clean, transitional" in style. Bellini has also beefed up their web site in the past year; now you can see each of the available finishes for their furniture. And yes, there are even prices online.

Quality of the furniture is good (the company has never had a safety recall) . . . but the real question here is: does Bellini's customer service justify the price premium? After all, you can buy similar furniture at a Buy Buy Baby or online for 20% to 30% less. And if you are concerned about Chinese-made furniture, Bellini won't be on your list.

Reviews of Bellini from our readers and posted on sites like Yelp are decidedly mixed (most of the complaints centered around late arriving orders and generally poor customer service). Some locations gets good marks, while other locations are lacking. We noted that most Bellini's scored a measly two stars on Yelp on average, with reviews titled "WORST CUSTOMER SERVICE EVER" outweighing the smattering of positive reports. While we take Yelp reviews with a grain of salt, you start to notice a pattern when the same complaints emerge time and again.

Some of this can be chalked up to being a franchised chain, since each store is independently owned. But if Bellini wants to compete against high-end specialty stores and chains like Buy Buy Baby and Pottery Barn Kids, it can't be inconsistent. You can't charge folks $1000 for a crib and then treat them poorly when it comes time for delivery. Many parents complained about a lack of communication from the chain when it came to delayed or backordered items.

The take home message: what you are paying for here is Bellini's design services—that coordinated look for a nursery (furniture, bedding, decor). If that is important to you and you have the bank account to tap (plus a high tolerance for middling customer service), then Bellini might be worth the time to check out. ***Rating: B***

Berg bergfurniture.com Berg got its start in 1984 and is best known for its youth and teen furniture, including bunk beds. The company sold nursery furniture from the late 90's through 2010, when it exited the crib business. At the time, Berg struggled to compete against the many upper-end brands selling in the $650 to $800 range.

Fast forward to 2015 and Berg is back. After the closing of several high-end competitors, Berg decided it was time to dip its toe back into cribs and other nursery furniture. Berg's new cribs are made of solid wood and are convertible to full-size beds. Cribs will be assembled in the company's New Jersey factory (although the actual components are imported). Pricing was set as of press time, but we assume they will be in the range of what they cost before.

Berg's dressers feature smooth glides and quality detailing.

Because this line was just shipping as of press time, we don't have parent feedback on the new Berg. However, previous feedback on Berg from the 2000's was mostly positive with one caveat—Berg in the past used pine wood in some groupings, which is susceptible to nicks and scratches. As we get more info on the new Berg collections, we'll update this review. ***Rating: Not Yet.***

Bertini See Dorel.

Bethany James The furniture is made exclusively for Walmart by Dorel. See Dorel.

Organic baby furniture

What makes nursery furniture green? As with many products marketed as organic or natural, there isn't a consensus as to what that means—and that's true with baby furniture as well.

Furniture, by its very nature, isn't the most green product on earth. A toxic brew of chemicals is used to manufacture and finish most items. Example: most furniture isn't made of solid wood but veneers (a thin strip of wood over particle board). Glue is often used to adhere the veneer onto particle board for dresser tops and sides. Some glues contain formaldehyde—as we discussed earlier, some baby furniture makers have been sued by the state of California for unsafe levels of this chemical.

For many folks, green means sustainable. So green baby furniture should be made from sustainable wood. But which wood is more eco-friendly? Some say bamboo is the most green (Natart's Tulip line of furniture is made from bamboo, but is very pricey). Others say rubber wood (ramin) is green since the tree it comes from (Para rubber tree) is usually cut down anyway after it is used to produce latex.

Given all the confusion, here is our advice for green nursery furniture shoppers:

◆ **Look for solid wood furniture that is certified.** There are a handful of non-profit environmental organizations that certify wood as sustainable: the Forest Stewardship Council (FSC) is among the best known. FSC-certified crib makers include Giggle (Harper crib)and Oeuf (both are reviewed in this chapter).

◆ **Consider a water-based paint or stain.** Romina offers a "Bees wax" finish that is about as organic as it gets. Pacific Rim also has a similar option: 100% pure tung oil with a beeswax sealant. Stokke's Sleepi crib features a formaldehyde-free varnish.

◆ **Avoid dressers made entirely of MDF or particle board.** The more solid wood, the better.

◆ **Consider an organic mattress.** We review mattresses later in this chapter.

Bivona & Co. bivonaco.com Industry veteran Larry Bivona is best known for starting LaJobi (Bonavita) in the early '90's before selling it to Kids Brands in 2008. After parting ways with the now defunct Kids Brands in 2011, Bivona launched his own eponymous company in 2013.

Bivona & Co offers cribs under different brands in a variety of price points: Fisher Price (opening price point), TiAmo (mid-price sold in Babies R Us, Target and Wayfair as well as some indies) and Dolce Babi (specialty stores, most expensive offerings). Here is a look at each:

Opening-price cribs under a Fisher-Price license are in the $150 to $300 range. These cribs are available online on Amazon, Target and Walmart and in discount retailers. One unique feature to some of these cribs: you can raise/lower the height of the crib by adjusting the crib feet (called Just the Right Height). There are nine styles and four finishes in this collection; most cribs convert into a full size bed headboard. Four ready-to-assemble dressers round out the collection.

In the past year, Bivona has expanded the Fisher Price line with more finish options and even a two-tone "modern" crib (Soho) for $300.

TiAmo is the mid-priced line ($300 to $500) with smaller scale furniture designed to fit into urban apartments. "Transitional to contemporary" is the style here with all cribs converting into toddler and then full-size beds. New in the past year is a collection (the Catania) that is exclusive to independent baby stores under the BRIXY umbrella.

Dolce Babi is the Bivona brand aimed at specialty stores: cribs run $600 to $800 and dressers $650 to $1000. As you can guess from the pricing, Dolce Babi features fancier styling and finishes than Bivona's other offerings. Dolce Babi dressers also have dove-tailed drawers with ball-bearing glides and some of the cribs convert to platform beds (which is unique). Unlike the ready-to-assemble furniture in Fisher Price and some pieces of TiAmo, the Dolce Babi dressers come fully assembled.

An example of Dolce Babi is the Naples collection with its dentil moulding and fluting, with dressers that have full-extension glides and dust covers on the drawer bottoms. The collection comes in six finishes, including a hand-rubbed grey satin. Crib: $680. Double dresser: $700-$800.

The Fisher Price cribs are made in China of New Zealand pine. The TiAmo and Dolce Babi cribs are made in Vietnam; they feature American poplar wood.

So how's the quality? Let's break it down by brand.

Fisher Price cribs generally earn kudos from readers, while a few folks report that items arrived dusty or with small nicks. Overall, good quality for the dollar.

TiAmo is the new kid on the block and so far, so good. We like the overall fit and finish of the line—and for $300-$500, these cribs are decent values if you want the style upgrade. The Moderna crib is a nice pick if you want that clean, mid-century look without spending a fortune.

As for Dolce Babi, this is probably Bivona's only stumble. While we like the overall design and finish, the features are lacking for this price point. Example: when you spend $1000 on a dresser, you'd expect self-closing (or soft-close) drawer glides . . . not the ball-bearing glides on Dolce Babi dressers.

Dolce Babi cribs are made of poplar wood—this is harder than pine, but not has hard as beech or birch. The risk: scratches and other damage from every day use. Poplar is acceptable in TiAmo's $300-$500 cribs. When you reach the $600-$900 price level, we expect harder wood than poplar. Hence, Dolce Babi earns a lower rating than the other two Bivona brands. Fisher Price. **Rating: A** TiAmo. Rating: **Rating: A**. Dolce Babi. **Rating: B**

Bloom *BloomBaby.com* Known for its modern high chairs and accessories, Bloom's flagship design in the crib category is a mini-crib called the Alma. With two mattress heights, the Alma folds for storage and is designed for babies under one year of age.

In spite of its $340 price tag, the Alma earns generally good reviews from parents. Dissenters say the mini-crib is too small for even six month olds—some folks were unhappy they couldn't use it for much longer than a bassinet. Of course, Bloom doesn't pitch the Alma as a full-size crib replacement—it is a MINI crib designed for use up to one year of age. Overall, we can see this as a bassinet alternative for urban parents who are starved for space. For others, a playpen with a bassinet feature (that you'd leave set up in your bedroom) would be a more practical alternative than the Alma.

In the past few years, Bloom has expanded the Alma line to include two larger versions: the Alma Papa and the Alma Max. Like the mini, the Papa is still not a full-size crib (49″ long versus 52″ for a typical full-size crib). The Papa fold ups and features casters for mobility. Price: $700. A conversion rail ($140) turns the Papa into a toddler bed. One major caveat to the Papa: since it is three inches shorter (in width and length) than a standard size crib, you'll have to use the special mattress to fit the Papa.

The Alma Max, however, is a standard size crib for $845 with similar features as all the Alma cribs (folding feature, etc), although the Max lacks wheel casters for some reason.

Next, Bloom offers another full size crib called the Luxo, a modern design that can be assembled without tools. Price: $1000 for a crib, with a matching dresser for another $1000.

Finally, Bloom recently released a full size crib called the Retro. Design-wise, this is a pretty cool looking crib. They describe it as a mid-century aesthetic with curved and rounded design elements. Available in Oak, Coconut White, and a combination of the two colors, this crib retails for $1200.

Bottom line: Bloom's Alma mini crib appeals to a small niche: space-starved, urban parents. But the mini crib will only buy you about a year's worth of time before you'll need a full-size crib. The minimalist, modern design is the star here, but the limited utility and high price limit Bloom's appeal. ***Rating: B-***

Bonavita See *LaJobi*.

Bratt Décor brattdecor.com   At least you have to give this company bonus points for creativity—Bratt Decor made their name with over-the-top offerings like the "Casablanca Plume" crib that was topped with (and we're not making this up) ostrich feathers. That (and the $1050 price tag) enabled Bratt Décor to earn a distinguished place on our list of the most ridiculous baby products in a previous edition of this book.

In the past year, Bratt has expanded their line to include a series of wood cribs in various "vintage" and whimsical looks. The Chelsea Sleigh crib comes in several finishes, including "antique silver." Price: $1300. Overall, prices for Bratt Décor's cribs range from $600 to $1500.

Bratt Décor's wood cribs are made in Vietnam; the metal models are imported from China. A pretty cool option: Bratt Decor has an oval iron crib that coverts from a round cradle to full-size crib to a toddler bed ($899).

What parents seem to like here is the gilded style and princess themes; Bratt Décor is one of the few crib makers out there today that makes wrought iron cribs. They also have matching accessories such as nightstands, mirrors, bookcases and other decorative options. FYI: Bratt Décor sells direct via their web site, in case you can't find a local dealer who carries the line.

How's the quality? Readers say it is very good—one reader said after two years, her Bratt Décor crib "has held up beautifully."

On the down side, this company can be incredibly slow at shipping—one source told us Bratt Décor orders require a wait of 25+ weeks on some items. Yes, that is half a YEAR. The company also discontinues product frequently—at one point in a recent year, they dropped half their line. And the company generally seems disorganized, with reports of unreturned phone calls, etc.

Hence, it is a mixed review for Bratt Décor: kudos for the clever design and overall quality. But concerns over shipping delays and discontinued products temper our rating.

FYI: Bratt Decor holds occasional warehouse outlet sales at their Baltimore, MD company store with savings up to 70%. Check their Facebook page for details. ***Rating: C+***

Broyhill See *Stork Craft.*

C&T International *CandTInternational.net* See *Sorelle.*

CaféKid *CaféKid.com* Better known for its older kid furniture (bunk beds, etc), CafeKid also sells a crib and dresser at Costco, both online and in the warehouses. The Morgan ($400 in store, $650 online—includes shipping and handling) is your standard convertible crib and features rather conservative styling.

We saw a CafeKid crib in a Costco warehouse and were impressed—made in Thailand, it features a wood slat mattress platform and converts to a full-size bed. The price includes the conversion rails to a full-size bed . . . and that's a great deal.

As for the dresser, it featured dovetail drawers, corner blocks and laminate drawer boxes. The metal glides, however, were cheap. Still, not a bad value at $400, but not as good of a deal as the crib.

Reader feedback on these items has been positive. One reader who posted to our message boards said the quality is excellent and the crib is easy to assemble. Others echoed that sentiment.

Of course, the problem with any deal at Costco is availability. Cribs are often available at Cosco in January and February although we've

Rug Burn:
How to save on nursery rug prices

Yes, it's always exciting to get that new Pottery Barn Kids catalog in the mail here at the home office in Boulder, CO. Among our favorites are those oh-so-cute rugs Pottery Barn finds to match their collections. But the prices? Whoa! $300 for a puny 5′ by 8′ rug! $600 for an 8′ by 10′ design! Time to take out a second mortgage on the house. We figured there had to be a much less expensive alternative out there to the PBK options. To the rescue, we found Fun Rugs by General Industries (funrugs.com; 800-4FUNRUGS). This giant kids' rug maker has literally hundreds of options to choose from in a variety of sizes. Fun Rugs makes matching rugs for such well-known bedding lines as California Kids and Olive Kids. A caveat: their web site lets you see their entire collection, but you can't order direct from Fun Rugs. Instead, go to one of their dealers like American Blind & Wallpaper (American Blinds.com) and, RugsUSA (RugsUSA.com). Those web sites sell Fun Rugs at prices that are significantly below similar rugs at PBK. In fact, we found most of those web sites sell rugs for 40% less than PBK or posh specialty stores.

occasionally seen them at other times of the year. Once you see them at the store, the items will probably only be at the warehouse for a limited time. Finally, sometimes you can order the crib online from Costco.com, but the prices are higher ($600-$650 for a CafeKid crib). on the plus side, that price incudes shipping and handling.

So it is a split opinion on CafeKid—if you can find it in a Costco warehouse, go for it. But the online deals are less of a bargain. **_Rating: B+ (store only)_**

Capretti Design _CaprettiDesign.com_   If money is no object, Capretti Design has got some nursery furniture for you.

This company got its start in 2007 by Mitchell Schwartz, a veteran of the old Ragazzi brand when it was made in Canada. Capretti has gone through several strategies, first importing cribs from Asia and then switching to made-in-the-USA production.

That's why Capretti's prices are so high—these cribs are now made by Amish craftsmen. Capretti features solid maple wood construction (no MDF), dust proofing and high-end drawer glides from Blum (Blumotion) that are under-mounted and self-closing.

So how expensive is Capretti? How about cribs for $1500 to $2500? Or a double dresser for $1600 to $2000?

If you are still with us, you might ask, is Capretti worth it? From a design stand-point, these are nice cribs and dressers, but hardly unique (the Milano is probably Capretti's most unique offering, with its curved base). Ten finishes are available for most collections—nice, but again not terribly special.

What you are buying here is the solid maple construction, Finishworks "scratch resistant" finish and made in the USA by Amish construction.

Perhaps the best feature of Capretti is the ability to customize the furniture (colors, sizes, dimensions) . . . and when you are paying $1500+ for a double dresser, that makes sense. Want a two-tone finish? That is a 10% surcharge. An organic finish is 20% more.

The top-of-the line Capretti collection (Mid-Century) even comes on a walnut option (finished with tung oil) for $2500 for a crib, $3000 for a double dresser.

At this price level, Capretti is pretty much on its own—the closest competitor is Romina, who makes excellent solid wood furniture that costs about 25% less than Capretti. Example: Romina's Nerva crib runs $1145, while the similar Capretti Umbria crib is $1500. Double dressers from Romina run $1425-$1545, while Capretti's charges $1600 to $2000.

Of course, Romina makes its furniture in Romania, not in the USA by the Amish. Whether folks see that as enough of a reason to part with the extra cash is hard to say.

There is good news on the price front: Capretti recently debuted a new, less expensive collection dubbed New England Shaker. The furniture runs 5% to 20% less than Capretti's other furniture—a crib runs $1100, a double dresser $1200.

Also new: Capretti will now give the folks the option of trading down to a less fancy drawer glide and omiting the dust proofing on its drawers. This will shave about $25 per drawer off Capretti's regular prices. Hence, a 7-drawer double dresser with this option would be $150 less.

Quality-wise, Capretti is impressive. Yes, you are paying through the nose for the Amish construction, but this furniture is excellent. We also like the eight week turnaround, which is quicker than most upper-end brands.

One last caveat to Capretti: the company only has a handful of dealers (27 at last count). In some states (Texas), there is just a single dealer (in Houston). In others (California), there are just two stores that carry the line. Georgia? Arizona? Zip. So seeing this brand in person may be a challenge.

Bottom line: if you want to avoid imported furniture, don't want to wait 12-16 weeks or would like a custom look to your nursery furniture and have the bankroll, Capretti should be on your short list. **Rating: B+**

Caramia *This crib brand is reviewed in the bonus section on our web site, BabyBargains.com/cribs*

Child Craft *child-craft.com* Here's a sad case study of American business and failure to adapt to changing times.

Child Craft, the Indiana-based crib maker that traces its roots back to 1911, was once among the top brands of nursery furniture. In recent years, however, the company has had a slow, painful slide into obscurity. Some of this has been bad luck (a 2004 flood knocked the company offline for several months) . . . while most of the blame can be laid at the feet of the company's managment, which never fully adapted to the flood of Asian-produced nursery furniture, both on the high and low end of the market.

Adding to the brand's woes, the company has gone through several changes in ownership. The latest: commercial crib maker Foundations acquired the assets of Child Craft in 2009.

Foundations relaunch of the Child Craft brand focused on entry-price cribs sold mostly online. Example: the low-profile London Euro crib is $200 and available on sites like Amazon and Target. A limited number of ready-to-assemble dresser styles run $160 to $290.

While we like Child Craft for its value, there is one major caveat—we see many reports from readers of shipping damage, including parts rolling around loose in boxes. Cracked headboards, wood scratches and dents indicate Child Craft needs to beef up its packaging. We'd suggest buying this crib from a store (Buy Buy Baby sells the London Euro) and inspecting the contents of the box for damage before paying.

Less enthusiastic are the reviews of Child Craft's dressers, which are made by ready-to-assemble king Sauder. We heard more than one parent complain about freight damage to the dressers; assembly is difficult and time consuming. Given the majority of negative reviews on the dressers, we say steer clear.

Style-wise, Child Craft introduced a couple two-tone and grey crib styles in the past year that are, dare we say, hip? This is a change from recent seasons, when the line seemed content to churn out very safe and traditional styles. A new mid-century modern crib joined the line in recent months.

So it is a mixed review for Child Craft: a thumbs up for the affordable cribs (especially the London). But thumbs down for the shipping damage and dressers. **Rating: C+**

Corsican Kids corsican.com Looking for a wrought iron crib? California-based Corsican Kids specializes in iron cribs that have a vintage feel, with detailed headboard and footboard decoration. Before you fall in love with the look, however, be sure to turn over the price tag. Most Corsican Kids iron cribs sell for a whopping $1600 to $6000!

Yes, you can choose from a variety of cool finishes like aged pewter and antique bronze. So if you just won the lottery and have to have a crib no one else on the block has, here's your brand. **Rating: C+**

Cosco See *Dorel*.

DaVinci See *Million Dollar Baby*.

Delta DeltaEnterprise.com Imported from China and Indonesia, Delta (also known as Delta Luv and Babies Love by Delta) is perhaps best known for their low-price cribs sold in big box stores.

Unfortunately, the company became known for something else in 2008: one of the biggest crib recalls in history. Nearly 1.6 million Delta cribs were recalled by the CPSC for defective hardware—two babies suffocated to death in their Delta cribs after the cribs' side rails detached. The 2008 recall came on the heels of two smaller recalls in 2004 (high levels of lead paint) and 2005 (defective slats).

Obviously, this was a big black eye for Delta, which responded by redoubling their safety testing. The company built an extensive testing laboratory in their New Jersey warehouse, which an article in the New York Times described:

"Eight hours a day, five days a week, cribs are beaten and battered by machines, subjected to the kind of malevolence a demonic toddler could only dream of doling out."

Of course, Delta had little choice in setting up this lab—tougher new safety standards for cribs went into effect in 2011 and that forced low-price king Delta to face an unsettling reality: it's low-end cribs wouldn't be allowed to be sold without improving their quality and durability.

So far, Delta has been recall free since the meltdown of the last decade. Prices range from $130 to $500, although most Delta cribs sold in chains like Babies R Us range from $200 to $300. Among Delta's big selling point: the cribs don't require any tools to assemble, making them a favorite of grandparents everywhere.

A good example of this line is the Canton 4-in-1 convertible crib. At $200, this crib includes a toddler rail to convert into a toddler bed—which is nice, since this can be an extra purchase. But, like many of these 4-in-1 cribs, the conversion rails to convert top full-size bed are an extra $100 purchase. And while this crib is a good value, one trade-off is the exposed bolts and screw holes. This doesn't impact the crib's safety, just aesthetics.

We are less enamored with Delta's dressers, which are affordable ($221 for a double dresser). The problems are myriad: the dresses are made of low quality pine which scratches easily. As one parent posted, "if you looked at the Delta dresser funny, it would scratch." The pre-assembled drawer fronts "were literally held in place by no more than 3/16ths of a screw tip." said another reviewer.

More than one parent tells us the dressers, often sold as a package of "Lifetime" furniture, barely last a year before falling apart.

The take-home message: the cribs are fine, but skip the dressers. And customer service at Delta is lacking—the company has to do a better job returning customer emails and phone calls.

FYI: Delta also owns the Simmons brand, reviewed separately.
Rating: B-

Dolce Babi See Bivona & Co.

Dorel djgusa.com Canadian conglomerate Dorel is best known for their Eddie Bauer car seats and Safety 1st gadgets—but the company is also a big player in the nursery furniture biz. Just don't look for Dorel nursery furniture under the name Dorel.

Dorel's furniture subsidiary Dorel Asia employs a blizzard of aliases in the furniture market: Truly Scrumptious (Babies R Us), Bella D'Este

(Babies R Us), Bertini (Babies R Us), Vintage Estate (Sears), Heritage Collection (K-Mart), Bethany James/Secure Reach, Baby Relax (Walmart), Eddie Bauer (Target) and so on. (Okay, Amazon is selling Dorel Asia cribs under their own name, but that is the exception).

Why more aliases than a Jason Bourne movie? Perhaps it has to do with the numerous recalls that Dorel endured during the 1990's under their main Cosco label. In fact, Dorel/Cosco was fined nearly $2 million for failure to report product defects to the government in the early 2000's.

So, if you were the marketing whiz at Dorel, what would you do? Start calling your furniture anything but Dorel or Cosco.

Unfortunately, the company's safety woes didn't end with the name change. A Babies R Us alias (Jardine) suffered one of the biggest crib recalls in history in 2008 when 320,000 cribs were yanked from Babies R Us for defective slats. Readers flooded our blog with complaints about how the recall was handled (Jardine and Babies R Us set up a Byzantine process to replace the defective cribs, with multiple steps and long waits). Like the name of a bad hurricane, Jardine is now retired in the pantheon of Dorel furniture brands.

Yes, these cribs are cheap (a Dorel Baby Relax is $140 at Walmart), but here are the trade-offs. Parents tell us the quality is slapdash—the crib arrives with wood that is chipped and damaged. Paint and stain appears to have been applied randomly by small marsupials. The soft pine of these cribs easily scratches. If you really want to buy one of these crib despite these warnings, we'd suggest buying at a retail store and inspecting it carefully before walking out the door.

You'd think the more expensive Dorel cribs would have better quality than the Walmart offerings . . . but no. "Poor craftsmanship," started another online review for a $450 Truly Scrumptious crib at Babies R Us. "There are multiple nail holes and gashes on the crib that were not finished appropriately. The company said this is to create a 'distressed' look, but frankly looks cheap." We guess when Dorel Asia does a distressed crib, they don't do it half way.

Given Dorel's longstanding troubles with safety in this segment, we don't recommend their nursery furniture, no matter what name they use. ***Rating: F***

Dream on Me DreamOnMe.com The portable/folding crib market has been rife with problems in recent years, with major players like Evenflo and Delta recalling their models for safety reasons. Yet small player Dream on Me has a winner with their "2 in 1 Portable mini crib." Sold online for about $110-$200, this crib is a good bet for Grandma's house—it converts from a crib to a playpen and changing table.

cribs

Bait and Switch with Floor Samples

Readers of our first book, *Bridal Bargains*, may remember all the amazing scams and rip-offs when it came to buying a wedding gown. As you read this book, you'll notice many of the shenanigans that happen in the wedding biz are thankfully absent in the world of baby products.

Of course, that doesn't mean there aren't ANY scams or rip-offs to be concerned about. One problem that does crop up from time to time is the old "bait and switch scheme," this time as it applies to floor samples of baby furniture. A reader in New York sent us this story about a bait and switch they encountered at a local store:

"We ordered our baby furniture in August for November delivery. When it all arrived, the crib was damaged and both the side rails were missing paint. We were suspicious they were trying to pass off floor samples on us—when we opened the drawer on a dresser, we found a price tag from the store. The armoire's top was damaged and loose and the entire piece was dirty. There was even a sticky substance on the door front where a price tag once was placed. Another sign: both the changing table and ottoman were not in their original boxes when they were delivered."

The store's manager was adamant that the items were new, not floor samples. Then the consumer noticed the specific pieces they ordered were no longer on the sales floor. After some more haggling, the store agreed to re-order the furniture from their supplier.

Why would a store do this? In a tough economy, a store's inventory may balloon as sales stall. The temptation among some baby storeowners may be to try to pass off used floor samples as new goods. Of course, you'd expect them to be smarter about this than the above story—the least they could have done was clean/repair items and make sure the price tags were removed! But some merchants' dishonesty is only matched by their stupidity.

Obviously, when you buy brand new, special-order furniture that is exactly what you deserve to get. While this is not an everyday occurrence in the baby biz, you should take steps to protect yourself. First, pay for any deposits on furniture with a credit card—if the merchant fails to deliver what they promise, you can dispute the charge. Second, carefully inspect any order when it arrives. Items should arrive in their original boxes and be free of dirt/damage or other telltale signs of wear. If you suspect a special-order item is really a used sample, don't accept delivery and immediately contact the store.

Dream on Me also makes full-size cribs for $175 to $270.

Overall, quality is good. Negatives include vague directions that make first-time assembly difficult, say some parents. Dream on Me's iffy customer service (unreturned emails, phone calls) is another drag on this brand.

Dream on Me's newest crib is touted as an "electronic" crib—the Wonder crib has a motor that moves the mattress up or down, to enable easier access to baby. A newer version (Wonder Crib II) is available now and both versions are Dream On Me's answer to the ban on drop-side cribs. They run a whopping $700 to $1000 (although we saw one discounted online to $490 or so). The Wonder Crib is also pitched as a combo crib and changing table— the crib mattress can rise high enough to become a changing table. In the real world, however, the crib mattress doesn't adjust high enough to make it useable as a changing table, says one consumer who bought the Wonder crib.

Customer service at Dream on Me is wanting—readers tell us of cribs that arrive with missing parts or broken rails. Calls to a customer service line are either not returned or the company promises to ship out replacement parts . . . but never does. That might be acceptable for a $150 crib, but Dream on Me can't get away with this if they want to sell $700 Wonder cribs. Our advice: if you want to buy a crib from Dream on Me, make sure the web site has a good return policy just in case.

Bottom line: Dream on Me's folding cribs are a good alternative for grandma's house. But the expensive Wonder crib is a stretch for this brand. ***Rating: B-***

ducduc *ducducnyc.com* New York-based ducduc was among the first entrants into the modern nursery category with an eco twist: all furniture is made in the U.S. (their plant is in Connecticut), contains no MDF or particleboard and features finishes that are air pollutant-free.

Of course, all this eco-fabulousness is going to cost you: a ducduc crib runs $1300 to $2000; matching dressers are $795 to $2900. No wonder this company's distribution is limited to pricey boutiques on the coasts (new this year, you can buy ducduc direct from their web site).

ducduc divides its furniture into two groups: modern and classic. We couldn't tell the difference between the two, but the classic furniture is more likely to feature a traditional color palette. On the modern side, the Parker crib runs $1425—you can customize the end panel color, end frame and rails/interior panels to your hearts content (18 different finishes). Shipping is another $225 if you are on the East Coast; or $300 to the Western U.S.

New this year, ducduc has added more designs with upholstered end panels plus a canopy option on their Cabana crib and a $6000 "crib system" which includes three pieces: a "bonding bench" (whatever that is), crib and dresser. If you just don't know what to do with a spare $6000, here's an option.

Quality is good, but we have blogged about one customer's disappointment with the ducduc's "white glove delivery." Given that experience, perhaps one would be better off buying this brand from a boutique instead of direct from the manufacturer. **Rating: B**

Dutailier *dutailier.com* Canadian rocker-glider maker Dutailier is best known for their chairs, but the company also dabbles in nursery furniture.

For several years, Dutailier turned out traditional nursery furniture made in China. After China's lead paint scare in the late 2000's, Dutailier decided to make some big changes: first, production was moved back to Canada. And then the line got a major design make-over: modern was in, traditional was out.

Dutailier's eight furniture collections feature a mix of zebra wood and colored accents, all named for fruits. The exception to the fruit/color matching nomenclature is the Apricot, which features a dark espresso finish. (Perhaps they meant to call it Apricot Pit?).

Prices are in the $1000 to $1500 range for most cribs and dressers. For most collections, you can choose from 32 finish choices and Dutailier offers many accessories (computer desks, night stands, etc). Yes, you can even purchase these cribs on Amazon.

How's the quality? All in all, we like Dutailier. We toured the company's plant outside of Montreal in 2012 and were impressed with their attention to detail.

Examples: the drawer casings are made of solid wood and drawers use French dovetail assembly. Dutailier has recently added dust proofing to the bottom of its drawers. One disappointment: there are no corner blocks on the dresser drawers.

A couple of caveats: waits can be long for some items (up to 18 weeks, reported one reader who ordered a Dutailier crib). And bolts and other hardware are sometimes visible on the cribs—not something we'd expect at this price point.

Bottom line: if modern is your thing and you have the budget, we'd recommend Dutailier. **Rating: B+**

DwellStudio *DwellStudio.com* Fashionable home designer DwellStudio made a splash with their licensed bedding line in Target a few years ago. Now, the company is debuting a nursery furniture collection—but don't look for it in discount stores.

The first effort is the Mid Century crib, available in three finishes (French White, Natural and Espresso). It is sold on Amazon and for $600 to $800.

The basic crib features an unusual "x-base structure" and tapered cone-shaped legs. The effect is a minimalist, 1950's aesthetic (Dwell dubs it "vintage classic")—but we wonder if it will be darn difficult to vacuum under the thing. Made in Canada, the crib has exposed bolts—which is disappointing at this price level.

To compliment the crib, Dwell sells a matching three-drawer dresser for $800, which has ball-bearing drawer glides, dove-tail joints and a "soft-close" drawer mechanism. The dresser is also made in Canada and features both solid birch and birch veneer, as well as something Dwell dubs "recovered wood." So for those keeping score at home, a Dwell crib and dresser will run $1400 to $1600. And, oh, the toddler rail for the crib is another $190. And, no the crib doesn't convert to a full-size bed.

DwellStudio's nursery furniture joins a crowded modern nursery furniture market, where a sagging economy has seen competitors such as Oeuf roll out less expensive versions of their $1000+ cribs. On the other hand, Dwell has a well-known brand name and good reputation . . . so perhaps it will find success at a price point that is hard to sell in today's economy.

One negative note: we've seen several reports from readers of shipping damage and poor packaging. Making matters worse, customers said they were disappointed with Dwell's customer service in fixing glitches. If you're going to sell folks nearly $1000 nursery furniture, you've got to do better than that. ***Rating: B-***

Echelon See Munire.

Eddie Bauer See Dorel.

Eden EdenBaby.com This LA-based crib importer sells a small collection of traditional and convertible cribs to a handful of independent stores nationwide. Eden offers five collections with matching dressers, armoires, hutches and combo dressers. The styling is very plain vanilla, with prices running $365 to $575 (convertible cribs are on the higher end of that scale). A three-drawer dresser is about $400. This brand is imported from China and is sold online by Sears and Amazon, among other sites.

In the past year, Eden has expanded their modern and contemporary-styled offerings. Example: the Madison crib is $550 and a matching dresser is the same price.

As for Eden's quality, we are not impressed (some dressers featured stapled drawers that lacked a smooth glide). Given the competition on the market, Eden needs to step up the quality in order to better compete.

That said, the reviews on the modern crib have been positive—

folks are understandably happy at finding a decent modern crib for less than $1000! However, we'd probably suggest folks look at Baby Mod (Million Dollar Baby), for a similar look from a brand that has a better quality track record. ***Rating: C+***

El Greco *ElGrecoFurniture.com*   Here's a rare bird in the nursery furniture business: a company that still makes furniture in the U.S.

Based in Jamestown, New York, El Greco has been making furniture since 1975 but largely flies under the radar of the industry. Why? Because most of El Greco's cribs and dressers are sold as private label offerings by Land of Nod and Room & Board (El Greco's web site lists which cribs they make for each chain on their web site). Yes, the brand is also sold in a handful of furniture stores, but most are regular furniture stores, not baby retailers.

Quality is excellent—cribs are made of poplar and maple, although some of the dressers are made of MDF. Dressers have corner blocks, dovetail joints, metal glides and solid wood drawer faces.

FYI: Readers in upstate NY have told us they have been able to buy furniture direct from El Greco's Jamestown factory store—one snagged a crib for $200 under the regular retail price. Most cribs and dressers sold in the outlet store are factory seconds, with small finishing defects. El Greco helpfully posts an inventory of what's currently at the outlet on their Facebook page. Note: the factory store appears to be open only for special periodic sales. Check their Facebook page for the latest schedule.

As for El Greco's regular prices, be prepared to spend a pretty penny for a U.S.-made crib: prices range from $750 to $1100. A three drawer double dresser is $700 to $1000 depending on finish. While those prices are about twice as much as a Chinese-made crib sold in Babies R Us, El Greco's prices are in line with other made-in-the-USA furniture companies.

Given their overall quality and safety, El Greco earns our highest rating—for parents who want to avoid Chinese-made furniture and can afford the price tags, this is an excellent choice. ***Rating: A-***

Fisher-Price See *Bivona & Co.*

Franklin & Ben *FranklinandBen.com* In 2012, Million Dollar Baby rolled out an entire new brand: Franklin & Ben. Described as "new traditionalist," this furniture takes its cues from Federalist styling and features American poplar accents and birch veneers over MDF. The result is sort of an updated vintage feel, complete with antique walnut and weathered grey finishes.

Cribs run $360 to $750; and a four-drawer dresser is $850. Double dressers are $800. Conversion rails for cribs are $200.

Franklin & Ben is mostly sold in specialty stores. That's a departure for Million Dollar Baby, a company that got its start selling low-price Jenny Lind cribs to discount stores and then its DaVinci brand via ecommerce during the web's early days.

We say "mostly" sold in specialty stores because a couple of Franklin & Ben's cribs are sold online on Amazon as well as other sites.

The web site for Franklin & Ben is impressive, with detailed info on the brand and how it beats industry safety standards. We also liked the explanation of the company's materials, stains and paints. We wish more manufacturers were this transparent. And there are even prices for the cribs and accessories posted online! What a concept.

The company has been slowly adding to their line over the past year which continue the early Americana meets distressed vintage look. New for 2015, a metal crib ($600) dubbed the Winston.

So how's the quality? Good, say readers who've been among the early purchasers of this furniture. At this price range, Franklin & Ben competes with mid-priced brands such as Pali. And they stack up well.

One black eye for the brand: a 2014 recall of 1000 cribs for fronts that separated from the side panels, creating a hazardous gap. While there were no injuries associated with this defect, it does raise questions about whether Million Dollar Baby is expanding too quickly with its new brands and not keeping an eye on quality control.

And let's talk about the wood used in this line—poplar is harder than pine (seen in cheaper baby furniture), but is still soft when compared to birch and beach. Hence, we have concerns that over time, this furniture could scratch and damage. It is possible that is would be less visible given the distressed finishes used in the line, however.

As a result of the recall, we are dropping this brand's rating a half grade. We still like Franklin & Ben for its innovative designs and decent pricing. Quality is good, with the caveat that poplar wood is soft and prone to scratching. We'll be watching to see if the safety recall was just a one-time hiccup. ***Rating: B+***

Giggle *giggle.com* Specialty chain Giggle sells cribs from Oeuf, DwellStudio, Bloom and Stokke, but the company also imports a few exclusive models. An example is the "Better Basics" Harper crib for $600. This crib is actually made by Latvian manufacturer Troll Nursery (troll.lv), which has been in business since 1994 and mostly sells cribs in Europe and Russia. The Harper crib features birch rails and plywood end panels and uses low VOC paint. A matching three-drawer dresser is $800 while a changing table is $350 and a conversion kit (to a toddler bed) is $125.

The Harper is available in two finishes: natural and walnut. Giggle claims the glue used in the plywood end panels is nontoxic, but the crib is not GREENGUARD certified, so it is hard to verify any emission claims. Reader feedback on Giggle's Harper crib has been positive—quality and durability is good. ***Rating: A-***

Graco See *Stork Craft*

Haven These cribs are made by Westwood for the Brixy group of independent juvenile retailers. See *Westwood's* review for details.

HGTV Home Baby See *Bassettbaby*. Sold exclusively at Buy Buy Baby.

IKEA *ikea.com* IKEA is an incredibly affordable option for cribs and other nursery furniture items. For example, their simple Sniglar is just $70. IKEA has five other crib options: Gulliver ($100-$130), Hensvik ($99), Gonatt ($189), Stuva ($199) and Sundvik ($119). Yes, all these cribs meet U.S. safety standards—they are so inexpensive because they are very simply styled.

IKEA carries much more than just cribs: you can buy dressers ($80 to $300), twin beds ($100), lamps, bedding and more.

So what's the catch? Well, most items require assembly that can drive just about any sane person off a cliff—although we should point out, that assembling an IKEA crib is just as easy as assembling any brand of crib. The assembly challenge usually comes in with IKEA dressers or other storage units.

The quality of IKEA's dressers and other furniture items can best be described as no-frills (example: their crib mattress didn't impress us—too soft, in our opinion). Obviously, IKEA furniture isn't intended to be heirloom quality that will last until your kid goes to college. But this is a great stop gap if you need something affordable (even if you plan to replace it down the line).

New to the IKEA line is the company's first crib with additional storage, the Stuva ($200). As readers of our book may note, we aren't big fans of cribs with under crib storage drawers. Why? That's because most of the time, these drawers are uncovered . . . that makes them (and the items stored there) dust magnets. But good news: the Stuva has drawers with covered tops. This eliminates the dust concern. FYI: The Stuva comes in six colors: green, pink, natural, black, blue or white drawers (the crib is white).

Reader feedback on IKEA nursery furniture has been positive. If you can survive the assembly process (especially for the dressers), then this is a good choice. ***Rating: A-***

Imagio Baby See *Westwood Design*.

JCPenney *jcpenney.com* JCPenney is a big player in the online crib business—their site has 40+ crib styles to choose from, along with a raft of other nursery furniture and accessories.

Penney's takes a different approach to the nursery furniture biz than other chains: it uses aliases of big crib makers to make the furniture look exclusive to the company. Hence, most furniture sold here is made by major manufacturers under assumed names. Example: Bedford Baby is really Westwood, ABC/DaVinci is Million Dollar Baby. Only the Rockland and Savanna furniture are Penney's private label. These are made by Yu Wei, a Taiwan-based furniture company, exclusively for JCPenney.

New in the past year, Penney has added cribs from Ragazzi and Munire in the $500-$700 range.

We review all the above brand names separately in this section. As for Rockland and Savannah, most readers tell us they are happy with the quality. Prices for cribs range from $300 to $790 (most are under $500); most of the dressers are $300 to $600.

In the past year, we've noticed Penney's has added several nursery packages (crib plus one or two dressers) to their web site, with prices in the $700 to $1500 range. FYI: These don't necessarily equate to savings, as the package price is the same as the pieces bought individually.

On the upside, Penney's has a good reputation for safety. Yes, the company has had recalls for some defective side rails and drop-side cribs in the past two years, but overall Penney's has had a good safety track record. (Drop-side cribs are no longer sold on the market for safety reasons, so all previous models had to be recalled).

Penney's customer service has been up and down in recent years. Although complaints are generally down compared to five years ago, we still see stories like this posted to our message board: a reader ordered a nursery set and it arrived three weeks early. So far so good, right? Yes, but when the reader opened the box with the dresser, she found it damaged (dropped on the corner and the top had buckled). Interestingly, the box was flawless, so someone had dropped the dresser before it had been packed.

So the customer takes the dresser back to Penney's, which promised to ship a replacement. The replacement arrives a week later . . . but is the wrong color. When the customer calls back Penney's to get this fixed, she finds the entire set has now been discontinued. Bottom line: our reader has to return the entire nursery set and start again.

The moral of this story is that, yes, freight damage can happen with any furniture order. But Penney's compounds the error by shipping the wrong color as a replacement—there's no excuse for that.

Bottom line: we only recommend Penney's if you live in a place with few other retail baby store alternatives. ***Rating: C+***

Jenny Lind *This is a generic crib style, not a brand name. We explain what a Jenny Lind crib is in a box earlier in this section.*

Karla Dubois *See Baby Appleseed.*

Kidz Décoeur *kidzdecoeur.com* College Woodwork makes this eco-friendly, made-in-Canada furniture line sold in specialty stores. Started by a Seventh-day Adventist school in a suburb of Toronto, College Woodwork began as a wood working class in 1921. The goal was to provide students of the bible school experience at furniture making. Still owned by the school (now called Kingsway College), College Woodwork employs students who make bedroom furniture, both adult and nursery. The adult line is sold under the College Woodwork brand, while nursery furniture is marketed as Kidz Décoeur.

Kidz Décoeur features quality finishing touches—dovetail drawer construction, full-extension slides, solid birch construction, etc. Design wise, Kidz Décoeur ranges from traditional to modern. Examples: the Greenwich collection features two-tone finishes, while the Augusta features curved legs on both the crib and dresser. The top-selling crib is the Carson, which features a traditional four-square design.

Sixteen finishes are available, including Toasted Cranberry (you probably didn't realize one could toast a cranberry, but we digress). New in the past year is a "storm grey" finish that is available in standard or "weathered" looks. Also new: the Madison collection, which aims for a more feminine look.

Prices range from $800-$1300 for cribs; dressers are $700-$1300.

How's the quality? We were generally impressed with the line—the one-inch thick tops on dressers as well as self-closing drawers are good signs. It was odd at this price point to not see corner blocks on the drawers, however.

Overall, we would recommend this brand. At these prices, Kidz Décoeur competes with Romina (who probably has them beat when it comes to solid wood construction) and Natart (a fellow Canadian company that offers more high style). But Kidz Décoeur does deserve a look if you are in that price range. ***Rating: B***

LA Baby *LABabyCo.com* Importer LA Baby's main business is commercial-grade, portable cribs sold to hotels and day care centers. In addition, LA Baby has a line of full-size convertible cribs made in China in the under $200 price range. For example, they offer their Window Crib with plexiglass end panels for $176. The company also has a line of organic crib mattresses.

Recently, LA Baby discontinued many of their upper-end cribs, which sold for up to $400. What remains are their bare bones models. They all have a bit of an industrial feel to them.

We aren't impressed with LA Baby's quality. Drawers on the dressers are stapled, not dovetailed. The full-size cribs are okay, but there are better choices at this price level. ***Rating: C***

LaJobi LaJobi's parent Kid Brands declared bankruptcy in 2014, ceasing production of wood furniture under the LaJobi and Bonavita brands.

Land of Nod landofnod.com An off shoot of the Crate and Barrel chain, the Land of Nod (LON) offers a half dozen cribs and a selection of matching accessories (including bedding, bassinets, and other gear.) It ain't cheap: cribs range from $600 to $1200. Dressers are priced from $400 to $1000. Design-wise, most are very simple, modern styles with one sleigh option.

The company has shifted its furniture strategy over the years. For a while, they sold Million Dollar Baby cribs with custom finishes. Today, the catalog offers cribs from El Greco, a U.S.-based manufacturer we reviewed earlier. LON also recently added a grouping of private-label cribs made in China and Vietnam. The El Greco cribs include the Low-Rise, Sleigh, Straight-up and Anderson; the Chinese-made cribs are the Elemental and Carousel; and the Vietnamese are Keepsake cribs.

As for Land of Nod's customer service and quality, readers give the company high marks. But one reader was upset that her furniture order arrived damaged—twice. Land of Nod was accommodating in shipping out replacement pieces, but getting it right in the first place would be nice for a brand that sells such pricey items.

All in all, we like Land of Nod—the El Greco-made cribs are safe and sturdy (the private-label cribs are new, so no reader feedback on those as yet). And while the prices aren't a bargain, many readers say the custom finishes and other coordinating accessories make it worth the investment. Style and quality-wise, these cribs aren't much different than what you see on Target.com for a $200 Graco crib. The difference is the made-in-the-U.S. label (at least for the El Greco models). If that's important to you and you're willing to pay the premium, the Land of Nod is a good alternative. **Rating: A**

Legacy Classic Kids No, this brand isn't related to Child Craft, which used the Legacy brand on some of its nursery furniture for decades. Legacy Classic Kids (also known as LC Kids) is a North Carolina-based importer of bunk beds and teen furniture that launched in 1999 and then branched into nursery in 2008.

Made in Vietnam, cribs run $500 to $900, while dressers (Chinese) are $500 to $600. A set sold on Amazon.com that includes an armor and dresser runs $1366. Legacy Classic Kids dressers feature plywood drawers with corner blocks and dove-tail drawer joints. Some designs feature wood-on-wood drawer glides, while newer models feature metal glides with a ball bearing mechanism.

We liked the fact that the cribs feature metal spring mattress supports, but most models also come with under-crib storage drawers. As we've discussed, these drawers are less practical then they seem—since they lack tops, they are dust collectors.

New in the past year, Legacy Classic Kids teamed with designer Wendy Bellissimo on her line of nursery furniture, reviewed separately. FYI: Legacy Classic Kids' distribution is a bit limited so feedback is minimal. Bottom line: this brand offers neither innovative styling, nor amazing value. **Rating: B-**

Little Miss Liberty *This crib brand is reviewed in the bonus section on our web site, BabyBargains.com/cribs*

Lolly & Me *lollyandme.com* Minneapolis-based crib maker Lolly & Me is a relative newcomer to the nursery biz with a made-in-the-USA focus. Founded in 2012 and sold semi-exclusively online on Target and Kohl's, Lolly & Me's cribs run $310 to $580. Combo dresser/changers run $270 to $550. The company offers nursery packages (crib plus dresser) for $600. (A handful of designs are also sold on Amazon).

Co-owner and designer Julie Kinsley has 15 years experience designing cribs for companies like Ragazzi, Graco and College Woodwork. She also has designed exclusives for Target, although not in the nursery furniture area. Lolly & Me was born after the company pitched its designs as a affordable nursery furniture with eco-friendly touches.

To that end, Lolly & Me has two collections (McKinley and Sawyer) designated as "eco-friendly." These collections are made in the U.S. at a small, family-owned factory in Utica, MI. (The rest of the Lolly & Me's furniture is made in Vietnam).

FYI: Three of Lolly & Me's seven finishes are what the company refers to as "Earth Smart"—Chocolate, Whitewash Driftwood and Natural are water-based, low VOC and made in the U.S.

Lolly & Me's web site is a bit vague when it comes to how their furniture is eco-friendly. The company says the furniture is "100% Earth Smart", but is somewhat nebulous on what that means (example: the site claims its finishes are non-toxic . . . but so are every other crib maker's).

Lolly & Me claims that its collections are GREENGUARD certified—but GREENGUARD doesn't list Lolly & Me among their certified companies. (We still see GREENGUARD certification as part of the furniture description on Amazon as of this writing).

We asked Lolly & Me's Kinsley about this discrepancy and she said that while the company has designed its cribs to meet GREENGUARD's strict requirements, it hasn't paid GREENGUARD's certification fee yet and therefore isn't listed on their web site.

While we understand why a start-up furniture company would be cash-strapped to start (GREENGUARD certification costs $30,000—the testing isn't cheap), this excuse doesn't cut it for us. You don't list a certification until your products are, well, certified. GREENGUARD certification assures parents furniture meets strict low chemical emission standards. It is deceptive for Lolly & Me to list this on their web site (and on resellers) and not actually hold the designation. (Since we first wrote about this issue, Lolly & Me has quietly dropped the GREENGUARD claim from their web site and Target product listings; but there still is a GREENGUARD question on the company's online FAQ. And as we went to press, we spotted a listing on Amazon for a Lolly & Me crib that still touted GREENGUARD certification).

And the product puffery didn't end with GREENGUARD—Lolly & Me claimed its furniture was also JPMA safety-certified. That also isn't true. Lolly & Me is a member of the JPMA and claims its products meet JPMA's safety standards, but the company is NOT listed as JPMA certified as of this writing. Certification and membership are two different things. Again, that is deceptive.

When we pointed out this issue to Lolly & Me, owner Julie Kinsley told us they were planning to get their products certified by both the JPMA and GREENGUARD . . . in 2013. Well, as we write this, it is 2015 and the company is *still* not certified. And they are still claiming incorrect certifications as part of their product descriptions on Target and Amazon.

How is the quality of Lolly & Me furniture? In general, good. Yes, Lolly & Me has had some quality issues as it ramped up for production, admitting they have struggled to fill demand. As a result, some cribs shipped out with incorrectly drilled holes for bolts and other quality glitches. We still see the occasional report of misdrilled screw holes in online reviews, but in general, the feedback on this furniture is positive. (One issue that comes up time and again: the "white" finish Lolly & Me claims for its cribs is actually off-white or cream. That has frustrated some buyers).

Bottom line: Lolly & Me makes good furniture that is a decent value. But the bogus claims of GREENGUARD and JPMA certification give us pause—after we confronted the company's owners with these issues and they promised us they'd correct the situation, they didn't as of this writing. That's a major red flag. As a result, we can't recommend this brand. ***Rating: F***

Lusso LussoNursery.com See *Sorelle*.

Million Dollar Baby Classic milliondollarbaby.com Million Dollar Baby (MDB) is one of the industry's best survival stories. Among the first to jump on the import bandwagon (the company launched in 1989), MDB has thrived by selling its wares in a large variety of stores under a series of aliases. It also didn't hurt that the company was the first to see the potential of the Internet to sell furniture.

Even though this company got its start selling low-price Jenny Lind cribs to discount stores, you'll now find it everywhere from specialty stores to Walmart. The company's cribs are sold under the aliases ABC in JCPenney and Baby Mod at Walmart.

The company divides its line into six brands: DaVinci, Million Dollar Baby Classic (MDBC), babyletto, Nurseryworks, Franklin & Ben and ubabub. We review Franklin & Ben and babyletto separately. Here's an overview of the rest of the brand.

DaVinci is the entry-level price point, sold online. A good example is the DaVinci Kalani, a 4-in-1 convertible crib sold on Amazon. The Kalani's affordable price tag ($219) and ability to convert to a full-size bed make the crib a good pick for those on a budget.

MDBC is somewhat more expensive than DaVinci and sold in retail stores. Style-wise, MDBC and DaVinci are similar. The difference: DaVinci's dressers are ready-to-assemble (and hence easier to ship), while MDBC's are pre-assembled.

Cribs in the DaVinci lines are $200 to $280; dressers are $250 to $500. Million Dollar Baby Classic cribs are $400 to $750, with

True Colors: Swatches and Samples

What's the difference between oak and pecan? When you order baby furniture, those terms don't refer to a species of wood, but the color of the stain. And many parents have been frustrated when their expensive nursery furniture arrives and it looks nothing like the "cherry" furniture they expected. Here's our advice: when ordering furniture, be sure to see ACTUAL wood samples stained with the hue you want. Don't rely on a web site picture or even a printed catalog. And remember that different types of wood take stain, well, differently. If you order your furniture in a pecan finish and the crib is made of beech wood while the dresser is pine, they may NOT match. That's because beech and pine would look slightly different even when stained with the exact same finish.

Ordering online makes this more of a challenge. Most sites don't offer wood samples—you have to rely on an online picture (and how that is displayed on your monitor). Bottom line: you'll have to be flexible when it comes to what the final stain looks like. But if you have your heart set on a particular hue for your nursery furniture, it might be best to order off-line . . . and see a stained wood sample first.

dressers for $450-$830–in the past year, the MDBC brand has become more upscale with new cribs in the $600-$700 range.

All Million Dollar Baby furniture is made in Taiwan by Bexco (Million Dollar Baby's parent).

We'd describe MDBC and DaVinci as traditionally styled; the company puts its modern offerings in the babyletto sub brand–although MDB sells a series of modern cribs called Baby Mod at Walmart with less fancy detailing for $250.

Million Dollar Baby's two most expensive brands are Nurseryworks and ubabub. We'd describe these offerings as nursery porn. Take Nurseryworks' Gradient crib, made of solid maple with a "3D skin that generates the slats which form an asymmetrical organic surface that explores continuos movement with no visual end."

Right.

Australian import ubabub similarly targets the trust funder new parent market with its $2300 Pod model with clear acrylic sides. Too much? The Nifty Clear is an affordable $1550. Affordable in the "my tech start-up was just was bought by Google" way.

So, how's the quality overall for Million Dollar Baby? The cribs are good; the dressers, not so much. Our biggest beef with MDBC/DaVinci: their heavy use of pine, a soft wood that is can easily scratch and damage from everyday use. How easily? Of the 745 reviews posted of the DaVinci Kalani crib on Amazon, 194 (26%) mention/complain about how easily the crib scratches.

You could argue that scratches and dents aren't safety issues–and for $200, you probably aren't expecting an heirloom quality piece of furniture you will hand down from generation to generation. Yet, we think MDB could improve the finish process to prevent some of the damage.

Low-end pine is common for $200 cribs . . . but even the more pricey furniture in the MDBC line (like the Arcadia double dresser for $750) is made of pine and MDF. At this price level, you can get better quality from the other brands we recommend.

How is MDB's customer service? We've heard mixed reports. Retailers seem happy with MDB's customer service and deliveries. Consumers are less enthusiastic, telling us about unreturned emails, poor assembly instructions and overall lackluster customer service. One particular issue is items arriving damaged, either from shipping or from MDB's lack of quality control. Be sure to order from a retailer with no hassle returns.

Bottom line: we recommend DaVinci and MDBC's cribs, at least the ones under $400 with one major caveat–the soft pine wood can and will easily scratch and damage. Skip the dressers. **Rating (cribs only): B**

Mira Studios *Kolcraft.com* Kolcraft joined the nursery furniture market in 2014 with Mira Studios, a pricey line of cribs and dressers. Better known for its affordable strollers and crib mattresses, Kolcraft lured away the former head and designer of Westwood Design to give the line a jump start. As such, there is a similarity between Westwood and Mira, both in style and overall approach to the market.

Mira's currently has two crib styles, which are traditional in design. The Bridgehampton is a panel crib that features a multi-layer finish. The Continental is a Shaker style crib. Price: $700. Dressers to match range from $770 to $800 and include double dressers and five-drawer chests.

Mira Studios' furniture is made in Vietnam and China and features just two finish choices. The quality of the dressers was OK—most have ball bearing glides and a soft close. At $800, these dressers compete with the likes of Pali and other better brands. And compared to Pali, the quality just isn't here for the $800 price point.

Oddly, Kolcraft also offers ready-to-assemble dressers under its own name (a three-drawer model is $240). This seems out of sync with Mira's more premium price offerings.

Mira Studios was brand new as we went to press, so no parent feedback yet. While our initial impression of Mira's quality was disappointing, we'll await more reader feedback before we assign a rating. ***Rating: Not Yet.***

Munire *Munire declared bankruptcy in 2014 and was sold to a new owner, Heritage Baby Products. Heritage aims to relaunch the brand in 2015. While we previously recommended Munire , we will await the relaunch to assign a rating to this brand.* ***Rating: Not Yet.***

Natart *natartfurniture.com* Quebec-based Natart is one of the few survivors of the shake-out of Canadian nursery furniture makers, most of which succumbed to competition from Asian imports.

While Natart did briefly flirt with making its cribs and dressers in China in the late 2000's, the company now produces all its furniture in the small hamlet of Princeville, Quebec.

Natart's mojo is high style furniture—designs you won't see elsewhere in the market. Touches like silver paint finishes and sculptured dressers help Natart stand out from the crowd.

Prices for Natart cribs average about $1000, with models that feature upholstered back panels running $1300. FYI: we don't recommend cribs with upholstering inside the crib, for the same reason we don't recommend crib bumpers—these are a safety concern, in our opinion..

Yes, that is expensive, but the quality is there. Dressers features

self-closing glides, center stabilizer bars and other quality touches. New for 2015, Natart has rolled out several "rustic" collections
that feature visible wood grain (the Ithaca, Rustico).

Price and style-wise, Natart is on par with Restoration Hardware—
except Natart is made in Canada, while RH imports form Asia.

We recently toured Natart's Quebec factory and were
impressed—Natart's emphasis is on eco-friendly furniture, married
with an Italian design influence (founders Tony and Michel De Bonis
moved Natart from Rome to Quebec in 1995).

Natart features three division: Natart, Tulip Leander and Nest.

While all of Natart's furniture are GREENGUARD certified to be
low emission, Natart's Tulip sub-line takes the eco-angle one step
further: all its cribs and dressers feature "all engineered recycled
wood (MDF) and bamboo components." Tulip cribs run $1100,
which include the conversion kits to confer to a double bed. A
three-drawer dresser is about $1000.

Newest to the Natart family is the Leander line, which is made in
Denmark and features an oval crib that converts to a twin bed (like
the Stokke Sleepi). Price: $1300, which includes the conversion rails.

Nest is a collection of less expensive furniture, with cribs at $600-
$800. While Nest furniture is simpler in design she compared to
Natart, the line still features some of the touches you see in the
upper-end brand (example: the rustic look of the Provence collection; self-closing drawers for dressers, etc).

In a nutshell, Natart is an excellent choice if you want to avoid
Chinese-made furniture and are willing to pay extra for the eco-
focus. ***Rating: A***

Nest See *Natart.*

Newport Cottages *NewportCottages.com* When it comes to over-
the-top nursery furniture, Newport Cottages turns the knob to 11.

With their trademark look of two-toned nursery furniture and
neon-bright finishes (30 in all), Newport Cottages is a mix of
both vintage and contemporary aesthetics. The company got its
start in 1996, when designer Cristina Alvarez was disappointed in
the plain offerings on the nursery furniture market.

But all this style will cost you: a colorful crib is $975 to $1700. A
dresser will set you back $1600—or more. Newport also sells various
accessories and accent pieces, including toy chests, dresser mirrors
and more.

Yep, that is darn pricey . . . but at least the furniture is manufactured in the U.S. (which makes Newport Cottages one of the few
remaining domestic makers of nursery furniture).

Newport Cottages furniture is mostly sold in pricey boutiques, but we noticed their simple Devon crib is now on Amazon for $975, with eight finishes from Bahama Blue to Coral pink. The simple Hampton breadboard crib is also sold online.

Quality is a mixed bag—the samples we previewed looked fine (Newport Cottages doesn't use MDF or particle board), but this company has struggled with consistency when it comes to quality and shipping. And at that these prices, we'd expect perfection. Bottom line: what you are paying for here are unique finishes/colors, not top-of-the-line furniture quality. **Rating: C**

Nursery Smart *See Baby Appleseed.*

Nurseryworks *Nurseryworks.net See Million Dollar Baby.*

Oeuf *Oeufnyc.com* Oeuf (literally, egg in French and pronounced like the "uff" in stuff) traces its roots to 2003, when French-American designers Sophie Demenge and Michael Ryan launched the company (and a family) in Brooklyn, New York. Their goal: pair eco-consciousness with modernist design elements. The result: the Oeuf Classic crib, which takes its cues from minimalist Euro styling.

The Oeuf crib's fixed side rails, headboard and footboard remove, converting the whole unit to a toddler bed. Like many modern cribs, the Oeuf Classic has a wood base (in this case, birch) and MDF panels covered in a white lacquer finish. Price: $970. A matching double dresser is $1350. Oeuf also sells a variety of other baby items, including mattresses, clothes and toys.

In recent years, Oeuf debuted a slightly less expensive grouping called the Sparrow. The crib is $760 and a three drawer dresser is $920. Sparrow features natural birch wood accents in three colors—there is no MDF in this crib (although the matching dresser is made of MDF with Baltic birch plywood drawer fronts).

The Rhea crib is like a mash up of the Classic crib's base and the Sparrow's side rails. The design is frameless, however which helps make it a bit less expensive than those other two cribs. It sells for $670 and a six drawer dresser goes for $1350.

Finally, there is the Elephant crib ($675), a grey design which can be assembled in ten minutes without tools. Oeuf notes the Elephant is influenced by Spanish designer Carlos Tiscar, and is made with what Oeuf calls "eco-MDF."

So where does Oeuf fit in the modern furniture universe? Price-wise, Oeuf is on the more affordable end of the modern crib biz—especially the Elephant and Sparrow. With modern crib prices often topping $1000, it's nice to have an option that doesn't break the bank. On the other hand, Baby Mod (Million Dollar Baby) sells a similar crib without all the eco-goodness for under $300.

What's disappointing with Oeuf is the quality of the dressers—we noticed the drawers lack corner blocks and had low-end metal glides. When you are paying $1300+ for a six drawer dresser, you are in the same price range as Romina and other better brands. Compared to the competition on dresser quality, Oeuf pales, in our opinion.

FYI: Oeuf was forced to recall its Sparrow crib in July, 2014, when consumers reported the slats and spindles detached. They offered a repair kit and no children were injured by the crib, but this does give the company a bit of a black eye. As a result, we've decided to lower their rating slightly.

We understand the point here of all the eco-goodness, made-in-Europe pedigree and minimalist design aesthetic. And to its credit, Oeuf has good customer service, according to retailers we've interviewed. Whether the brand is worth the price tag compared to competitors that use more solid wood and better dresser construction is an open question. ***Rating: B***

Pacific Rim Woodworking *This crib brand is reviewed in the bonus section on our web site, BabyBargains.com/cribs*

Pali *pali-design.com* Italian furniture maker Pali traces its roots to 1919, when the Pali family started out making chairs in Northern Italy. The company switched its focus to juvenile furniture in 1962 and then rode a wave of popularity in the 90's, when its Italian-made cribs and dressers won fans for their craftsmanship and stylish looks.

Pali has had its ups and downs in the past decade, but lately they've been mounting a comeback. To compete on price, the company switched production to Vietnam (made with wood from Europe) and lowered their prices—cribs now start in the $500's, down from $700 in years past. A double dresser in the mod-looking Trieste collection is $900; other dressers are in the $600 to $800 range.

In recent years, Pali began selling furniture sets (crib plus dresser) for $1000 to $1400. Also new: cribs can either be ordered with a high or flat headboard. And, in the category of Everything Old is New Again, Pali has re-introduced furniture made in Italy. These cribs run $700 and five-drawer dressers about the same. At the time of this writing, there are five collections made in Italy; the other two dozen collections are made in Vietnam.

New for 2015 is the Cristallo collection which features a crib with upholstered headboard for $750 (we aren't fans of upholstered headboards for safety reasons—there shouldn't be any soft cushions inside a crib). Also new is the Cortina, which features two tone (white/grey) crib and dresser.

How's the quality? Better—Pali has improved quality in recent years. Yes, Pali uses birch veneers in some collections instead of solid wood like Romina. Of course, you'll pay much more for a Romina dresser than Pali. FYI: Pali is now using three woods in its collections: poplar, New Zealand pine and rubber wood.

Critics of Pali knock the brand's customer service, especially when folks order online. In recent years, Pali has been selling cribs like the Imperia on Amazon—reports of shipping damage, order delays and unreturned customer service calls for missing parts are concerning. If you can, it may be best to buy this brand from a store instead of online.

We should note these customer service issues are scattered—while we see complaints on Amazon, customer reviews on WayFair and Babies R Us (as well as our own readers) are more positive on Pali.

Bottom line: Pali is a good, mid-price brand that offers a dash of European design flair and decent quality. ***Rating: A***

Pottery Barn Kids *potterybarnkids.com* It's rare when one retailer can change an entire industry. Pottery Barn Kids (PBK) scored that coup during the 2000's when their contemporary nursery décor (accented by vintage motifs and a bright color palette) literally changed the rules. Out went cutesy baby-ish décor; in came a more modern yet still whimsical look, thanks to PBK.

Pottery Barn Kids sells a mixture of name brand and private label furniture from their site. Prices range from a simple $500 crib to more ornate designs, like the Larkin crib at $800. Occasional sales knock cribs prices as low as $400.

Matching dressers range from $400 to $1200 and run the gamut from simple three-drawer options to extra-wide double dressers. Of course, PBK has all manner of accessories: nightstands, armoires, bookcases, and more.

Watch out for shipping—PBK shipping on expensive items is 10% of the total from $200 to $2999 and 5% on purchases over $3000. That charge can make the final price a bit higher than what you see online. Example: a $700 crib actually costs $770 with shipping.

While most parents are happy with PBK's customer service and delivery, we've had more than one parent tell us about quality woes with PBK furniture: peeling paint on a bookcase, splintering wood on a dresser, etc. While the cribs are fine, it's the other furniture items that draw complaints. To PBK's credit, the web site or store usually takes care of the problem and replaces the defective item. But as one reader, who told us PBK's home delivery service miss-assembled her crib, described it, "it's always a canned apology with a pipe dream solution—we'll send someone out, but they never show up."

Quality-wise, you are paying a premium for the PBK look (many items have custom finishes only available at PBK). But take a look under the hood: that $600 crib is cute, but why pay this much for a crib with exposed bolts? You could spend a $100 less on a similar Baby Cache crib from Babies R Us and get a more finished look. And competitors have long since caught up with PBK on style and design, so we're not sure the price premium is justified anymore.

Bottom line: use PBK for décor items like bedding or lamps and order the furniture elsewhere. **Rating (furniture): C**

Ragazzi *Ragazzi was the upper-end brand launched by Stork Craft in 2008. As of press time, Ragazzi's web site has been shuttered and the furniture is being closed out on sites like JCPenney. It appears the brand is on hiatus at this moment. A spokesperson for Ragazzi told us "the product lineup is currently under review for 2015." Given the uncertainty regarding this brand, we do not recommend it.*

Relics *This crib brand is reviewed in the bonus section on our web site, BabyBargains.com/cribs*

Restoration Hardware RHBabyandChild.com Restoration Hardware has joined other chains like Pottery Barn in rolling out a luxe kids line, complete with furniture, linens, lighting, apparel, gifts and more.

Sold online only, Restoration Hardware's neo-classical nursery furniture is arranged in over 50 collections, each with crib, dresser, and (sometimes) a bookcase and armoire. Finish options are limited: two choices in most cases, although new distressed options have been added along with upholstered end panels on some designs for those of you doing a Louis XVI theme for your nursery.

Most of Restoration Hardware cribs are made by Bassettbaby, reviewed separately. Obviously, these are upgraded models compared with what Bassett sells to other chain stores—hidden hardware, distressed finishes, etc. Dressers include English dovetail joints, cedar-lined drawers and tip guards.

So, what's not to like? Well, the prices are in the stratosphere: $700 to $1300 for a crib. And that doesn't include "unlimited delivery" fees ($149-$349, depending on your distance to a RH store; Hawaii & Alaska are $500) and hotel mini-bar prices for accessories (a $600 bookcase, anyone?).

And here's the kicker: cribs only convert to toddler beds, not twin or full size beds as most convertible cribs. Hard to imagine, but Restoration Hardware has managed to make even the most expensive nursery brands sold in specialty stores look like a bargain. At least if you are spending $1000 for a crib in such stores, most likely you are getting a convertible model that turns into a full-size bed. We suppose the point here is you are supposed to go back to Restoration Hardware and spend another $1000 on a big kid bed.

Reader feedback has been mixed on RH—one reader complained that much of her nursery furniture order was on backorder . . . for months! And the quality? "Many of the things I ordered (the mobile in particular) were sub par in terms of quality or arrived broken, however highly priced."

So it is a mixed review for RH: we liked the coordinated collections and the upgraded Bassett furniture . . . but at these prices, we are hard pressed to give RH anything higher than an average rating. The value just isn't there—you can spend *half* the price of these cribs and dressers and get *better* quality and durability. **Rating: C**

Rockland *See JCPenney.*

Romina *RominaKidsFurniture.com* Romina got its start as a supplier to a Canadian nursery furniture maker; the company went solo in 2008 and has built a successful high-end brand focused on solid wood furniture.

Romina's success here could be attributed to two factors: first, good timing. Romina launched in the midst of the Chinese recall crisis—with furniture made in Romania, the company was one of the few non-China options out there in the late 2000's.

Second, Romina doesn't cut corners when it comes to quality—the line features 100% solid beech wood construction. No MDF, no rubberwood, no veneers over particle board, etc. Romina dressers feature dove-tail joints, corner blocks and self-closing drawer glides that are smooth "like butter," as one retailer described them.

Of course, this isn't cheap—and if you want Romina, you're going to pay for it. Cribs run $850 to $1300; a double dresser is $1200 to $1400. Yes, that's $400 to $500 more than other upper-end brands charges for a similar dresser—you'll have to decide if avoiding an Asian import is worth that premium.

Romina's other major emphasis is their eco-friendly "Bees Wax" finish, which as the name implies, is all-natural. Romina touts it as the ultimate organic finish. If you prefer a darker stain or painted look, Romina also offers eight other finishes, including a navy, white and brown metallic. Adding to their eco-focus, all Romina cribs are now GREENGUARD certified to be low in chemical emissions.

Realizing those prices are a bit rich for the average nursery shopper, Romina in 2014 debuted a new, lower-priced line dubbed Silva. These cribs retail for $700 or less with a double dresser coming in at $900. We know, $700 is hardly "low price" for a crib—but as crib prices even in chain stores creep toward $500, Silva is in the ball park. The difference between Silva and Romina? Silva dressers have veneers with one-inch solid wood borders (Romina is solid wood). Silva dressers still feature self-closing drawer glides, although the styling is simpler and less ornate than Romina.

Romina has upgraded Silva in the past year—they are now using beech wood components for the dressers and poplar plywood faces. The drawers in the Silva dressers have increased in size in the past year and now three finishes are available. Silva is also GREEN-

8 tips to lower the risk of SIDS

Sudden Infant Death Syndrome (SIDS) is the sudden death of an infant under one of year of age due to unexplained causes. Sadly, SIDS is still the number one killer of infants under age one—over 2000 babies die each year.

So, what causes SIDS? Scientists don't know, despite studying the problem for two decades. We do know that SIDS is a threat during the first year of life, with a peak occurrence between one and six months. SIDS also affects more boys than girls; and the SIDS rate in African American babies is twice that of Caucasians. Despite the mystery surrounding SIDS, researchers have discovered several factors that dramatically lower the risk of SIDS. Here is what you can do:

Put your baby to sleep on her back. Infants should be placed on their back (not side or tummy) each time they go to sleep. Since the campaign to get parents to put baby to sleep on their backs began in 1992, the SIDS rate has fallen by 50%. That's the good news. The bad news: while parents are heeding this message, other care givers (that is, grandma or day care centers) are less vigilant. Be sure to tell all your baby's caregivers that baby is to sleep on his back, never his tummy.

Encourage tummy time. When awake, baby should spend some time on their tummy. This helps prevent flat heads caused by lying on their backs (positional plagiocephaly). Vary your child's head position while sleeping (such as, turning his head to the right during one nap and then the left during the next nap). Minimize time spent in car seats (unless baby is in a car, of course!), swings, bouncer seats or carriers—any place baby is kept in a semi-upright position. A good goal: no more than an hour or two a day. To learn more about plagiocephaly, go online to plagiocephaly.org

Forget gadgets. Special mattresses, sleep positioners, breathing monitors—none have been able to reduce the risk of SIDS, says the American Academy of Pediatrics. Just put baby to sleep on her back.

Use a pacifier. Consider giving baby a pacifier, which has been shown in studies to reduce the rate of SIDS. Why? Scientists don't know exactly, but some speculate pacifiers help keep the airway open.

GUARD certified.

Design-wise, Romina furniture is traditionally styled, although the company recently debuted a couple of modern collections with two-tone finishes (the New York, for example). We liked all the available accessories: each collection features nightstands, armoires, bookcases and the like. Our fave Romina style: an over-the-top crib (Cleopatra) that looks like a handlebar mustache, complete with a footboard that can be carved with your baby's name.

Okay, we should acknowledge that pacifiers are controversial—key concerns include breastfeeding interference, tooth development and ear infections. But if you introduce the pacifier after breast-feeding is well-established (around one month), there are few problems. Stop using the pacifier after one year (when the SIDS risk declines) to prevent any dental problems. While pacifiers do increase the risk of ear infections, ear infections are rare in babies when the risk of SIDS is highest (under six months old). Bottom line: Use pacifiers at the time of sleep starting at one month of life for breastfed babies. If the pacifier falls out once the baby is asleep, don't re-insert it. Stop using pacifiers once the risk of SIDS is over (about a year of life).

Don't smoke or overheat the baby's room. Smoking during pregnancy or after the baby is born has been shown to increase the risk of SIDS. Keep baby's room at a comfortable temperature, but don't overheat (do not exceed 70 degrees in the winter; 78 in the summer). Use a wearable blanket or swaddle baby with a blanket.

Bed sharing: bad. Room sharing: good. Why does bed sharing increase the risk of SIDS? Scientists say the risk of suffocation in adult linens (pillows, etc) or entrapment between bed frame and mattress, or by family members is a major contributor to SIDS. That said, *room sharing* (having baby in the same room as the parents, either in a bassinet or crib) is shown to reduce the rate of SIDS. Again, researchers don't know exactly why, but it's possible parents are more attuned to their baby's breathing when baby is nearby.

No soft bedding. Baby's crib or bassinet should have a firm mattress and no soft bedding (quilts, pillows, stuffed animals, bumpers, etc). We will discuss soft bedding more in depth in the next chapter. Also: consider using a swaddling blanket, footed sleeper or SleepSack instead of a blanket. More on these items in Chapter 3.

Make sure all other caregivers follow these instructions. Again, you might be vigilant about back-sleeping . . . but if another caregiver doesn't follow the rules, your baby could be at risk. Make sure your day care provider, grandma or other caregiver is on board.

All in all, this is one of the best nursery furniture lines on the market . . . there are many expensive nursery furniture brands on the market that aren't worth the asking price when it comes to quality. Romina is the real deal. ***Rating: A***

Room & Board *This chain sells cribs made by El Greco.*

Room Magic *This crib brand is reviewed in the bonus section on our web site, BabyBargains.com/cribs*

Sauder *This crib brand is reviewed in the bonus section on our web site, BabyBargains.com/cribs*

SB2 See *Sorelle.*

Secure Reach by Bethany James See *Dorel.*

Serena & Lily *serenaandlily.com* This web site's cribs are actually made by different manufacturers.

The Hudson crib is made by Million Dollar Baby's babyletto division. The Liberty Crib is made by Franklin and Ben, which is reviewed under Million Dollar Baby.

The Soho crib is made by Bratt Décor.

Silva See *Romina.*

Simmons *simmonskids.com* Here's an interesting rags to riches and back again tale of an American company. Simmons Juvenile was once one of the country's biggest nursery furniture makers, selling cribs and dressers to many generations of parents.

Started in 1917 by Thomas Alva Edison to provide wooden cabinets for one of his recent inventions (the phonograph), Simmons morphed into a furniture company that also made mattresses. The company spun off its juvenile division in the 1980's (just to confuse you, there is still a separate Simmons company that makes mattresses).

Then the company began its slow decline. Simmons made a couple major mistakes, chief among them never adapting to the changing nursery furniture market, which soon became flooded with low-price imports from Asia. Simmons stuck to making its cribs and dressers in plants in Wisconsin and Canada.

By 2004, Simmons' deteriorating fortunes prompted the management to sell their crib mattress biz and then shutter the Wisconsin plant. Simmons sold the rights to their name to Delta, which then relaunched Simmons as a separate, upscale division aimed at specialty stores.

However, the re-launch of Simmons has been bumpy for Delta. Their first collection (imported from China and Vietnam) was a bust—$800 cribs and $700 dressers were met with little enthusiasm from shoppers.

Delta/Simmons went back to the drawing board and decided to change strategies: instead of competing in the upper end of the market, they'd aim for the entry-level price point among specialty stores. Hence, Simmon's recent collections feature cribs that are priced in the $300's and are sold in stores like Babies R Us and Target online. There's even a $200 Simmons crib on Amazon.

Simmons other offerings run $400 to $600 for cribs, $500 to $600 for dressers. At the top end, Simmons' Jessica McClintock line of cribs features three collections running $600 to $1000 for a crib, $700 to $1000 for a dresser.

How's the quality? Simmons is all over the board: the upper-end dressers features self-closing drawers and other quality touches. But the lower end Simmons features drawer glides more at home on a Delta dresser at Walmart than a specialty store. A parent who purchased a $550 five-drawer dresser from Babies R Us said she was returning it after she found the dresser to be "very cheaply made and constructed."

While most parent reviews of Simmons cribs are positive, there were quite a few complaints about shipping damage. If you can purchase this item from a store and inspect the contents of the box before leaving, that may make more sense than ordering online.

Simmons customer service also lags: more than one reader said they emailed Simmons with questions and received no response. Bottom line: if Simmons is trying to compete against other upper-end crib brands, they've got to do better than this.

So it is a mixed review for Simmons: kudos for the new lower prices . . . but the scattershot quality drags down their overall marks. It seems Simmons is still a brand in search of an identity. ***Rating: C+***

Sorelle *sorellefurniture.com, lussonursery.com, sb2furniture.com*
Sorelle is one of the baby gear industry's survival stories. In business since 1977, the company has constantly changed and morphed over time.

Sorelle first imported Italian cribs. It switched gears in the 2000's to importing furniture from Vietnam and China (today most items are imported from Vietnam and China). Sorelle has succeeded by pursuing a value niche: its furniture is generally regarded as giving consumers more bang for the buck.

Sorelle has also survived by selling its furniture in a variety of channels: specialty stores (under the Sorelle and Lusso brands), chain stores (under Golden Baby and C&T) and online.

In recent years, Sorelle has divided its brand into three parts: high-end (Lusso), mid-price (Sorelle) and entry-level (SB2).

Lusso is sold just in specialty, brick-and-mortar stores—prices range from $500 to $700 for cribs, which includes the toddler conversion rail. Quality touches here include dovetail drawer construction and poplar wood.

Sorelle is the brand you'll see in chain stores—it is similar to Lusso in quality, but scaled down a bit. Cribs run in the $400's. In the past year, Sorelle has added more crib and dresser combination units to the line up.

SB2 is Sorelle's entry-price point brand sold online. Cribs run $150 to $300; dressers are ready-to-assemble. Under the SB2 brand, Sorelle offers entire five-piece nursery sets for $400 to $500—crib, four-drawer dresser, hamper, changing table, and toddler conversion rail.

Style-wise, Sorelle is middle-of-the-road traditional furniture; yes there are one or two modern groupings with two-tone finishes, but that is the exception to the rule.

In the last couple of years, this brand looks like they've been treading water, style-wise. The lack of innovation and me-too designs are disappointing.

So, how's the quality? If you take a look at the reviews of Sorelle posted to our message boards, you'll note the opinions are all over the board. For every parent who tells us they are pleased with the quality and finish of their Sorelle furniture, another will write to blast a series of problems—quality woes, "nonexistent and rude" customer service, poor assembly instructions, missing parts and more.

It's the lack of customer service that bothers us most here: the attitude at Sorelle seems to be "you're getting a good price on this furniture, so don't complain if we don't return your call for parts." Sorry, but that doesn't cut it.

In general, the cribs get better marks than the dressers, based on our reader feedback. Complaints about the dressers include stains that don't match cribs, uneven finishes, freight damage and more.

Bottom line: great prices but a mixed quality picture and weak customer service drag down Sorelle's rating. **Rating: C+**

Spot On Square spotonsquare.com California-based Spot on Square launched its modern nursery furniture in 2007. The company offers five crib styles, all with an eco-angle: low VOC paints and formaldehyde-free glue.

Like most modern furniture companies, Spot on Square uses MDF (which it pitches as a recycled material) along with birch, bamboo and walnut. Prices are moderate, at least for modern: the Eicho crib is $690, while a matching dresser/changer is $790. The Hiya crib comes in three color variations, ranging in price from $750 (all white MDF) to $900 for a version with walnut stained end panels. The most expensive crib in the collection is the high-end Roh crib, made of walnut for $1700.

Overall, we were a bit disappointed in the lack of accessories: at most, cribs have a single matching dresser in one configuration. And Spot on Square's cribs do not convert to full size beds. Also, it might be hard seeing this furniture in person, as distribution is limited to a handful of small boutiques (although you can buy pieces direct through their company web site).

How's the quality? Most online reviews of this brand are lukewarm at best. Quality control seems to be an issue—one Amazon reviewer point out that her fully assembled dresser arrived with one door that was a completely different color than the other. How does a company miss that in shipping? Others knocked the furniture for "poor workmanship," "drawers that keep falling out and apart," and more. That's disappointing when you are selling furniture at these prices, to say the least. Bottom line: the modern vibe and eco-goodness of this line are nice, but the quality and lack of accessories is disappointing. ***Rating: C***

Status *statusfurniture.com* See Stork Craft.

Stella Baby See Westwood Design.

Stokke Sleepi *stokkeusa.com* Norwegian juvenile gear maker Stokke pitches its ultra-expensive crib as a "system" that grows with your child: the Sleepi morphs from a bassinet to a crib, then a toddler bed and finally two chairs . . . all for a mere $1000. You can buy just the crib for $656 (without the toddler bed conversion kit).

A separate changing table (the Care) converts to a play table and desk for $500. As with all these funky European products, you'll have to buy specially made bedding with limited choices ($30 to $35 from Aden & Anais or $40 from Stokke). Yes, you read that right: $40 for a single sheet.

Fans of the Sleepi love its clever oval shape (fits through narrow doorways) and overall ease of use. The Sleepi is perhaps best suited to urban apartment dwellers with little space for a standard-size crib.

Detractors cite the limited choices of bedding, as mentioned above. Quality issues (as noted in online reviews) also dog the Sleepi—parts that don't fit right, wheel casters that don't lock, misaligned screw holes, etc.

For $1000, we'd expect better quality control than this. Hence, we've lowered Stokke's rating this time around to reflect this disappointment. ***Rating: B-***

Stork Craft *storkcraft.com* Stork Craft is an entry-level price brand that's sold in chain stores from Walmart to Babies R Us.

Stork Craft's cribs start at $99 at Walmart, although most cribs are in the $150 to $200 range. At the top end, a $350 crib model features sleigh styling and the ability to convert to a full-size bed.

All Stork Craft furniture is imported from China. While Stork Craft sells most of its furniture under its own name, it also uses a series of aliases especially for more pricey options. Example: Zutano, Thomasville and Broyhill. These cribs can top $500.

Stork Craft also makes a wide array of matching accessories, including dressers, rocker gliders and other items—the dressers are an affordable $180 to $300. All of the furniture is ready-to-assemble; readers report assembly ranges from difficult to frustrating, thanks to minimal directions and a lack of labeling for screws and parts. A significant amount of patience is necessary, say most readers.

New in the past year, Stork Craft began selling fully assembled dressers for $500.

So, let's talk quality. Parents generally give Stork Craft low marks, based on reviews posted to our web site. Fans like the affordable pricing and the fact you can order most of this furniture online. But detractors say items often arrive damaged, with missing parts and worse. One parent who paid $450 for a Stork Craft crib said she was extremely disappointed in the poor finish which looked very cheap—and the under-crib drawer's bottom constantly fell off its track when moved. Another parent who bought a $300 Stork Craft dresser said it arrived severely damaged and "looks as if it were purchased at a garage sale." Customer service also came in for criticism, with delays in fixing defective merchandise and parts among the top gripes.

Finally, Stork Craft has downgraded the quality of its cribs in recent years, in our opinion. Example: gone are the spring mattress supports. Now Stork Craft uses a MDF board to support the mattress, which is not our preferred choice.

In this price rage, Stork Craft competes against Million Dollar Baby and Fisher Price (made by Bivona). We'd recommend either of those brands over Stork Craft.

Bottom line: if you have your heart set on this brand, stick with the low-price items (the $100 cribs at Walmart are a good bet). Skip the dressers, glider rockers and anything expensive (the $250+ cribs). And be sure to set your expectations accordingly.

FYI: As we were going to press, Stork Craft had taken over the Graco crib license after the previous maker (LaJobi) went out of business. These cribs were too new as of this writing to rate or review. ***Rating: C-***

Suite BeBe See *Munire*.

Summer The big headline with Summer's cribs is their Simple Adjust feature—this let's you adjust the mattress height without any tools. (Nearly all other cribs require you to practically dissemble the crib before changing the mattress height.)

Granted, you don't adjust the mattress height every day . . . the mattress stays in the highest position until baby starts to stand. That's when you lower the mattress.

Summer offers seven crib styles, four of which feature Simple Adjust. An example: the Bryant crib for $190 at Target. Made in China, this crib can convert into a full size bed—but the resulting look is a bit funky since the headboard and footboard are about the same height.

One innovative Summer crib is the 3-in-1 Symphony convertible crib with bassinet. As the name implies, this $350 crib comes with a bassinet insert and changing area that fits onto the top of the crib rail. It's hard to believe no one has thought of that before! We were impressed with the overall utility of this set up, especially for folks who are starved for space. The one caveat: since the bassinet and changing area are at the top of the crib, this might be hard to reach for shorter parents.

Most parent reviews on Summer cribs are positive. Fans like the easy assembly—about an hour, said one parent. On the downside, folks are much less effusive about the matching ready-to-assemble dressers. Yes, they are affordable at $240-$400, but cheap wood, unlined drawers and shipping damage outweigh the bargain price. Bottom line: cribs are good; skip the dressers. **Rating (cribs only): B**

Thomasville See *Stork Craft*

TiAmo See *Bivona & Co.*

Today's Baby This crib brand is reviewed in the bonus section on our web site, BabyBargains.com/cribs

Truly Scrumptious by Heidi Klum This furniture is made by Dorel and sold exclusively at Babies R Us. See Dorel review for details.

Tulip See *Natart*.

Vintage Estate This furniture is made by Dorel.

Wendy Bellissimo See *Legacy Classic Kids*

Westwood Design _westwoodbaby.com_ Westwood Design was launched in 2005 by several veteran nursery furniture executives who partnered with an adult furniture company for distribution expertise. The company has found success in a crowded market by offering a good quality product with extra features at affordable prices.

Westwood is sold in a variety of outlets, from specialty stores to chains like Buy Buy Baby and online on Amazon. You'll find the brand under the aliases Bedford Baby at JCPenney and Hart at Baby Depot. At the chains, a Westwood crib runs $450 to $550; dressers are similar in price.

In specialty stores, Westwood tends to be a bit fancier in style and higher in price. Example: a new modern two-tone grouping features a $600 crib; dressers are in the $500 to $700 range.

If that is too rich, Westwood has a new entry-level price brand that debuted in the past year: Imagio Baby. Cribs run $200-$250. Imagio Baby is sold at Walmart, Amazon, and Buy Buy Baby.

In other news, Westwood recently added several scaled-down furniture pieces (the company calls them "euro-sized") for folks trying to fit furniture in a small nursery.

In recent years, Westwood has expanded their offerings in specialty stores. These are sold under the Stella Baby brand, which has its own web site (stellababyandchild.com). Stella has collections with prices that range from $400 to $600 for convertible cribs. Basically, the same furniture as Westwood but with fancier finishes and detailing.

Also in specialty stores, Westwood has devoted an exclusive collection for the Brixy independent baby retailer group. Dubbed "Brixy Haven," the collection has two cribs and four dressers in two finishes. Cribs run $600-$700 and dressers are $600-$800.

FYI: Westwood cribs now ship with "always there hardware"— pre-installed hardware that doesn't detach from the crib. That makes it safer when you disassemble and reassemble a crib. Another unique feature: Westwood dressers feature "no tools assembly" (under both the Westwood and Imagio Baby brands), which enable quick assembly without any hardware or tools.

All Westwood furniture is made in Vietnam.

Quality-wise, Westwood is a good value. Most of the cribs are made from solid hardwood (poplar and rubberwood are most common—one collection, the Cypress Point, is made of pine). The exception to the hard wood construction: cribs with panel headboards are made of MDF with cherry veneers. The dressers are made of solid wood frames (poplar again) with veneered MDF on the sides and top.

You'll see some adult furniture touches here and there (hutches with built-in lights; dressers with height-adjustable feet), which is unusual in the nursery market. We like how transparent Westwood is; they even post detailed pictures of their dresser drawer boxes to highlight English dovetail drawer joints and ball bearing drawer glides.

The downsides? Well, the company only offers a limited number of finishes. And Westwood probably uses more veneers and MDF than its competitors in this price range. That said, parent feedback on Westwood has been very positive—readers love the sturdy construction, ease of assembly on the cribs and overall finished look. Another plus: customer service at Westwood is excellent. **Rating: A**

Young America by Stanley *This company shut down their crib and juvenile furniture production in April 2014.*

Zutano See *Stork Craft.*

See the chart on pages 100 to 101 for a summary of the major crib brands.

Brand Recommendations: Our Picks

Good. Our top pick for the best budget crib goes to Bivona's Fisher Price. As an example, we like the **Fisher Price Newbury** ($150-$180) or the **Charlotte** ($160-$180). Another option: *IKEA's Sniglar* crib is $70. Funky name, good value. The same goes for *IKEA's Gulliver* crib ($100 in white; $130 in natural).

Better. Step up to the $300 to $500 range and you'll find more convertible models that turn from a crib to full-size bed. Our favorites here include *DaVinci* and *Westwood.* As an example, we like the *DaVinci Kalani*, $220, or the *Westwood Stratton*, $529. If you don't want a convertible model, *Imagio Baby's* (Westwood) *Midtown Cottage* crib is $250 at Amazon and BuyBuyBaby.com.

Best. Who's got the very best quality when it comes to cribs and dressers? In the $500 to $800 range, we like *Pali*, *Natart* and *Baby Appleseed* (including their sub-brand, *Eco-Chic Baby*). Each makes excellent cribs and very good dressers. The *Pali Imperia* crib ($400) is a good buy in this category.

Is someone buying your nursery furniture as a gift? Do you want to avoid Chinese-made nursery furniture? If so, we suggest *Romina* or *El Greco*. Romina/Silva offers sold-wood cribs ($700 to $1300) and dressers imported from Romania. El Greco makes its cribs and dressers in the U.S.; they are sold online at sites like Land of Nod. Prices: $650 to $1600 for a crib.

Continued on page 102

CRIB RATINGS

NAME	RATING	COST	WHERE MADE?
BABY APPLESEED	A	$$ TO $$$	VIETNAM
BABYS DREAM	C	$$ TO $$$	CHILE/CHINA
BABYLETTO	B+	$$ TO $$$	CHINA
BASSETTBABY	B+	$$$	CHINA
BELLINI	B	$$$	CHINA
BIVONA & CO	A/A/B	$ TO $$$	VIETNAM
BLOOM	B-	$$ TO $$$	CHINA
BRATT DECOR	C+	$$$	VIETNAM/CHINA
CAFEKID	B+	$$ TO $$$	THAILAND
CAPRETTI	B+	$$$	USA
CHILD CRAFT	C+	$	ASIA
CORSICAN KIDS	C+	$$$	USA
DELTA	B-	$ TO $$	ASIA
DOREL	F	$ TO $$	CHINA
DREAM ON ME	B-	$	CHINA
DUCDUC	B	$$$	USA
DUTAILIER	B+	$$ TO $$$	CANADA
DWELL STUDIO	B-	$$$	CANADA
EDEN	C+	$$ TO $$$	CHINA
EL GRECO	A-	$$$	USA
FRANKLIN & BEN	B+	$$ TO $$$	ASIA
IKEA	A-	$	ASIA
JCPENNEY	C+	$$ TO $$$	ASIA
KIDZ DECOEUR	B	$$$	CANADA
LA BABY	C	$	CHINA
LAND OF NOD	A	$$$	USA
LOLLY & ME	F	$$ TO $$$	USA/VIETNAM
MILLION $ BABY/DA VINCI	B	$ TO $$$	ASIA
MUNIRE	-	$$$	INDONESIA
NATART	A	$$$	CANADA
NEWPORT COTTAGE	C	$$$	USA
OEUF	B	$$$	LATVIA
PALI	A	$$$	VIETNAM/ITALY
POTTERY BARN KIDS	C	$$$	ASIA
RESTORATION HARDWARE	C	$$$	ASIA
ROMINA	A	$$$	ROMANIA
SIMMONS	C+	$$ TO $$$	CHINA/VIETNAM
SORELLE	C+	$ TO $$$	CHINA/VIETNAM
SPOT ON SQUARE	C	$$$	USA/EUROPE
STOKKE/SLEEPI	B-	$$$	SLOVENIA
STORK CRAFT	C-	$ TO $$	CHINA
SUMMER	B	$ to $$	CHINA
WESTWOOD	A	$$ to $$$	VIETNAM

Key:
RATING: Our opinion of the manufacturer's quality and value.
COST: $=under $250, $$=$250-500, $$$=over $500.
GREENGUARD: Are these cribs GREENGUARD certified? See p 55.

EENGUARD?	COMMENTS
◆	Eco-friendly, traditionally styled. New line at BRU for $650.
	Still have some folding rails; long waits for backorders.
	Mid-century vibe, made from pine.
	Cribs good; case pieces bad. Sold in Restoration Hardware.
	Sold only in namesake pricey boutiques.
	3 brands: Fisher Price, Ti Amo mid-price; Dolce Babi pricey.
	Alma mini crib good bassinet alternative for urbanites.
	Vintage looks, bright colors. Long lead times.
	Sold in Costco; includes conversion rails. Good value.
	Very pricey, made by Amish. Cribs start at $1500!
	Affordable, but freight damage issues. Skip dressers.
	Very pricey wrought-iron cribs; vintage feel.
	Entry price level, many cribs can be assembled without tools.
	Affordable, but quality issues. Soft pine wood.
	Affordable mini crib maker, also sells pricey Wonder crib.
	Retro, modernist furniture. Expensive.
	Quality has improved; expensive, 32 finishes.
	Pricey, mid century looks. Exposed hardware disappoints.
	Mid-price line with a couple of modern crib designs.
	Excellent quality, sold at Land of Nod, Room & Board.
	Early American, distressed vintage looks.
	Do-it-yourself assembly; low prices; very simple styling.
	Sells furniture under several private label brands.
	Eco-focus. Pricey. 16 finshes.
	Simple bare bones models; average quality.
	Stylish but pricey; good service, Made by El Greco.
	Sold in Target; eco-friendly with some items made in U.S.
	Da Vinci brand sold online; focus on traditional styling.
	Brand in transition after bankruptcy filing.
◆	Innovative storage; whimsical touches but very pricey.
	Two-tone, distressed finishes; quality/service inconsistent.
	Eco-style meets modernism; lowest price of modern group.
	Good quality; traditional design.
	Design leader but overpriced; high shipping charges.
	Upgraded line made by Bassett; very pricey.
◆	Pricey, but very well-made furniture. Solid wood.
	Owned by Delta; average quality, plain styling.
	Decent prices; mixed customer service reputation.
	Miminalist design, limited accessories. Pricey.
	Pricey crib "system" best for those with little space.
	Opening price point cribs sold in chains, Amazon.
	Clever 3-in-1 crib with bassinet feature. Affordable.
	Traditional looks; good quality. Affordable line is Imagio.

cribs

Short. If you are under 5'5", you may find reaching into a standard-size stationary crib challenging. Since drop-side cribs were phased out in 2011, shorter parents may find it difficult putting baby in a stationary crib

when the mattress in its lowest position. For those parents, a lower profile crib may be just the ticket. A good bet: *babyletto's Modo 3-in-1* crib ($330) is made from New Zealand pine.

Green. *Romina* wins the crown in the green nursery race—their uber-natural "Bees Wax" finish is offered on any of their five furniture collections. Romina also earns green points for their 100% solid beech wood and formaldehyde-free construction (no particle board or MDF). Another plus: all furniture is made in Romania.

Also worth a look: *Natart's Tulip*, made in Canada from recycled wood (MDF) and bamboo.

Grandma's house. If you need a secondary crib for Grandma's house, consider a portable mini crib from Dream on Me for $120, which folds for easy storage or transport. Delta cribs are also a good bet for Grandma's house—they can be quickly assembled.

Bassinets, Cradles & Mini Cribs

A newborn infant can immediately sleep in a full size crib, but some parents like the convenience of bassinets, mini cribs or cradles to use for the first few weeks/months. Why? These smaller beds can be kept in the parents' bedroom, making for convenient midnight feedings.

What's the difference between a bassinet and a cradle? Although most stores use the terms interchangeably, we think of **bassinets** as small baskets that are typically put onto a stationery stand (pictured at top right). **Cradles**, on the other hand, are usually made of wood and rock back and forth (center right).

A third option in this category is **"Moses baskets,"** basically woven baskets (lower right) with handles that you can use to carry a newborn from room to room. (Moses-Baskets.com has a good selection). Moses baskets can only be used for a few weeks, while you can typically use a bassinet or cradle for a couple of months.

Mini cribs are yet another alternative: most are similar in size to a bassinet (40″ long by 28″ wide). By comparison, a full-size crib is about 52″ long and 28″ wide. We recommend a specific mini crib in the previous section (see Grandma's house). FYI: mini cribs, like bassinets, are NOT a substitute for a full-size crib, which is the safest place for a baby to sleep after the first few weeks or months. Mini cribs are fine for newborns or at grandma's house for the occasional overnight visit.

Key mini crib makers include Bloom, Dream on Me, Nursery Smart and Stokke. See reviews earlier in this chapter.

Co-sleepers are similar to bassinets, but attach to the parent's bed. We used to recommend this type of product in a previous edition. However, the American Academy of Pediatrics recently came out against co-sleepers (or any device attached to a parent's bed). Pediatricians cited the risk of a parent unknowingly rolling over and injuring a newborn in a co-sleeper. As a result, we don't recommend these products.

Bassinets go for $100 to $200 and include bedding (sheets, liners, skirts, etc). Cradles run $120 to $400, but only need a mattress and sheet. Moses baskets run $50 to $200 and include all the bedding.

So, which should you buy? We say none of the above. As we mentioned at the beginning of this section, a newborn will do just fine in a full-size crib. If you need the convenience of a bassinet, we'd suggest skipping the ones you see in chain stores. Why? Most are very poorly made (stapled together cardboard, etc) and won't last for more than one child. The bedding is also low-quality. One reader said the sheets with her chain store-bought bassinet "were falling apart at the seams even before it went into the wash" for the first time. And the function of these products is somewhat questionable. For example, the functionality of a Moses basket, while pretty to look at, can be easily duplicated by an infant car seat carrier, which most folks buy any way.

Instead, we suggest you borrow a bassinet or cradle from a friend. . . or buy a **portable playpen** with a bassinet feature. We'll review specific models of playpens in Chapter 7, but basic choices like the Graco Pack 'N Play start at $60. The bassinet feature in most playpens (basically, an insert that creates a small bed area at the top of the playpen) can be used up to 15 pounds, which is about all most folks would need. Then, you simply remove the bassinet attachment and voila! You have a standard size playpen. Since many parents get a playpen anyway, going for a model that has a bassinet attachment doesn't add much to the cost and eliminates the separate $80 to $200 expense of a bassinet. Another way to save: consider a stroller with a bassinet option. Yes, you can typically add this as an accessory to full-size strollers for $100 to $200—and some companies even sell a bassinet stand for use in your bedroom.

If you would still like a traditional bassinet, we like the *Halo Bassinest Swivel Premiere Sleeper* ($250), which includes vibration, lullabies and a nightlight.

Mattresses

Now that you've just spent several hundred dollars on a crib, you're done, right? Wrong. Despite their hefty price tags, most cribs don't come with mattresses. So, here's our guide to buying the best quality mattress for the lowest price.

Safe & Sound

The key issue in mattress safety is Sudden Infant Death Syndrome (SIDS), the leading cause of death among infants under one year of age, claiming over 2000 lives per year. We have a detailed discussion of SIDS in our book, *Baby 411* (see back of this book for info), but here is the take-home message when it comes to SIDS and mattresses: buy a FIRM mattress that correctly fits your crib, bassinet or cradle. See the box earlier in this chapter for more tips on preventing SIDS.

Smart Shopper Tips

Smart Shopper Tip #1
Foam or Coil?

"It seems the choice for a crib mattress comes down to foam or coil? Which is better? Does it matter?"

Yes, it does matter. After researching this issue, we've come down on the foam side of the debate. Why? Foam mattresses are lighter than those with coils, making it easier to change the sheets in the middle of the night when Junior reenacts the Great Flood in his crib. Foam mattresses typically weigh less than eight pounds, while coil mattresses can top 20 or 30 pounds! Another plus: foam mattresses are less expensive, usually $100 to $200. Coil mattresses can get pricey, with prices that range from $150 to $350.

Sounds easy, right? Just buy a foam mattress? Well, as always, life can be complicated—many baby stores (and even chains like Babies R Us) only sell coil mattresses, claiming that coil is superior to foam.

We've consulted with pediatricians and industry experts on this issue and have come to the conclusion that the best course is to choose a *firm* mattress for baby—it doesn't matter whether it's a firm coil mattress or a firm foam one. What about the claim that foam mattresses need to be replaced constantly? In the 20 years we've been researching this topic, we've never heard from even one parent whose foam mattress had to be replaced!

What's going on here? Many baby stores try to make up for the thin profit margins they make on furniture by pitching parents to buy an ultra-expensive mattress. The latest rage are so-called "2 in 1" mattresses that combine foam *and* coil (foam on one side; coil on the other). These can run $300 or more! While these mattresses are nice, they are totally unnecessary. A $100 foam mattress will do just as well.

Bottom line: foam mattresses are the best deal, but can be hard to find (they are sold online). As a result, we'll recommend mattresses in both the coil and foam categories just in case the baby stores near you only stock coil.

Smart Shopper Tip #2
Coil Overkill and Cheap Foam Mattresses

"How do you tell a cheap-quality coil mattress from a better one? How about foam mattresses—what makes one better than the next?"

Evaluating different crib mattresses isn't easy. Even the cheap ones claim they are "firm" and comparing apples to apples is difficult. When it comes to coil mattresses, the number of coils seems like a good way to compare them, but even that can be deceiving. For example, is a 150-coil mattress better than an 80-coil mattress?

Well, yes and no. While an 80-coil mattress probably won't be as firm as one with 150 coils, it's important to remember that a large number of coils do not necessarily mean the mattress is superior. Factors such as the wire gauge, number of turns per coil and the temper of the wire contribute to the firmness, durability and strength of the mattress. Unfortunately, most mattresses only note the coil count (and no other details). Hence, the best bet would be to buy a good brand that has a solid quality reputation (we'll recommend specific choices after this section).

What about foam mattresses? The cheapest foam mattresses are made of low-density foam (about .9 pounds per cubic foot). The better foam mattresses are high-density with 1.5 pounds per cubic foot. Easy for us to say, right? Once again, foam mattresses don't list density on their packaging, leaving consumers to wonder whether they're getting high or low density. As with coil mattresses, you have to rely on a reputable brand name to get a good foam mattress (see the next section for more details).

Smart Shopper Tip #3
New crib mattress = dangerous fumes?

"I read on the 'net that some crib mattresses give off dangerous fumes that can cause SIDS."

This internet myth has its roots in New Zealand. In the mid 90's, a New Zealand chemist launched a web site that claimed Sudden Infant Death Syndrome was caused by toxic gasses given off by crib mattresses. His solution: wrap the mattress in a gas-impenetrable cover, which naturally, was sold on his web site.

This theory has been discredited by SIDS researchers and scientists, who have studied SIDS causes for years and have found no link between mattress chemicals and infant deaths. Yet, there is still much online buzz about this theory, amid general concern over exposure of infants to household chemicals.

It is true that conventional crib mattresses (whether foam or coil) are made from scary-sounding chemicals. Most mattresses have these chemicals to meet fire retardant standards, which are mandated by both federal and state rules. *Bottom line: to date, there is no research that links sleeping on traditional crib mattresses to any disease or illness.*

That said, we can understand why new parents want to limit their newborns exposure to environmental hazards—you can't control all chemical exposure, but one place you do have some say is your child's nursery. In recent years, an entire industry of organic crib mattresses have sprung up to meet this concern.

Here's the take-home message: we think conventional crib mattresses (foam or coil) are safe. If you decide you want to go the organic route, however, we will provide some recommendations in that category later in this section.

Here are a few more shopping tips/myths about crib mattresses:

◆ **What's the best way to test the firmness of a crib mattress?** Test the center of the mattress (not the sides or corners)—place the palm of one hand flat on one side of the mattress and then put your other hand on the opposite side. The greater the pressure needed to press your hands together, the more firm the mattress.

◆ **Are all crib mattresses the same size?** No, they can vary a small amount—both in length/width and thickness. Most coil mattresses are 4″ to 6″ in depth. What's the best thickness? It doesn't matter, but 5″ should be fine. FYI: 5″ mattresses are often less expensive then 6″ mattresses. And some crib sheets won't fit the six-inch thick mattresses. It is unsafe to use a sheet that doesn't snugly fit OVER the corner of a mattress and tuck beneath it.

Remember the safest crib mattress is the one that snugly fits your crib—you shouldn't be able to fit more than two fingers between the headboard/side rails and the mattress. A tip: the mattress should be CENTERED on the crib mattress platform, not jammed up to one side or the other!

FYI: For the curious, full-size cribs sold in the U.S. and Canada must be between 27 5/8″ and 28 5/8″ wide (and 51 3/4″ to 53″ in length). Hence most crib *mattresses* are about 27 1/4″ to 28 5/8″ in width.

◆ *All foam mattresses look alike—what separates the better ones from the cheaper options?* Test for firmness (see above). The more firm, the better. Another clue: weight. A slightly heavier foam mattress usually means they used a better-quality foam to make the product. Finally, look at the cover: three layers of laminated/reinforced vinyl are better than a single or double layer. What about quilted covers? They are a waste of money, in our opinion.

Smart Shopper Tip #4
Mattresses & bacteria
"I saw a study that linked crib mattresses with a lack of water-proofing to SIDS. What should I do to protect my baby?"

In a study published in 2008 in the Journal of Applied Microbiology, scientists from the United Kingdom discovered foam crib mattresses that lacked waterproofing near an infant's head could cause bacteria growth. Some researchers believe this can be linked to Sudden Infant Death Syndrome.

Of course, most mattresses sold in U.S. have water-resistant covers (typically a layer of vinyl). However, a new crop of "organic" mattresses without such waterproofing have come on the market, appealing to parents who don't want any petrochemical-based products in their baby's nursery.

Here's our recommendations:

◆ *Get a mattress with a vinyl cover that is triple-laminated* (this provides better waterproofing).

◆ *Don't use a hand-me-down mattress*, since it might not have been water-protected.

◆ *Consider changing out the mattress with each child* (new baby, new mattress) since no matter how hard you try, some leakage might happen.

◆ *Use a waterproof pad* over the mattress. A good bet is the *Carter's "Keep Me Dry"* fitted quilted crib pad ($16). If you prefer to go the organic route, the **Naturepedic Waterproof Fitted Crib Pad** ($70) is made of 100% organic cotton with a thin polyurethane waterproof barrier in the center. The pad features "DrySleep" technology, which allows for liquid to pass through the fabric while "still allowing the material to 'breathe.'" Naturepedic is one of our top recommended mattress brands—we generally like this company for their quality and durability. This material passes the GREENGUARD tests for emissions standard. It is machine washable.

The big difference between these two pads (besides the price differential, which is substantial) is the type of waterproofing—the more affordable Carter's option uses vinyl. Naturepedic uses what it calls "food-grade" polyurethane—that is, the same polyurethane approved for food contact. We think either is fine and safe.

FYI: The Naturepedic pad comes in two versions: waterproof and non-waterproof. Be sure to get the waterproof one! That way you don't have to clean the top of the mattress when an accident happens.

The Name Game: Reviews of Selected Manufacturers

Colgate *colgatekids.com* Colgate has long been one of our favorite brands for affordable foam crib mattresses. The company offers three types of mattress: foam, innerspring and natural/organic. All of Colgate's foam mattresses (regular or organic) are GREENGUARD certified to be low in chemical emissions.

Perhaps the best selling Colgate mattress is their simple Classica 1 ($143) foam mattress with a triple layer nylon reinforced cover. Colgate also sells an "eco" version of this mattress (cleverly called the Eco Classica, $190) that replaces most of the petro-chemical foam with plant-based foam. Of course, Colgate sells more than just two models—there are several versions of the Classica mattress, some of which have dual firmness zones, memory foam and other upgrades. That's nice, but unnecessary.

In recent years, Colgate expanded their collection of eco-mattresses. The EcoFoam Supreme is made of a unique foam. Instead of soy foam, like many of their competitors, this foam is derived from non-food plants which grow in rocky soil. It has square corners and a damask cover that is coated on the underside to be waterproof. The Postura mattress has a dual firmness option with one inch thick memory foam and a medical grade water proof cover of PVC3. It has square corners plus inverted seams. Prices are reasonable: $130 for the EcoFoam Supreme and the Postura is $260.

Another eco mattress option is the Nuzzle Snuze, which debuted in the past year. This mattress' mojo? AirWeave, made of recyclable and recycled materials, creates a firm mattress that also allows for airflow through the mattress. Complete with a organic cotton waterproof cover, the Nuzzle Snuze is Colgate's most expensive mattress at $370-$400.

Jumping on the memory foam train, Colgate also has the Visco Classica. This $222 mattress has dual firmness with memory foam made with cooling gel on one side and the Classica 1 foam on the other. It also has inverted seams and a polyester waterproof cover.

Also new: Colgate has launched a new division of premium mattresses: EverTrue (evertruemattress.com). This group of five mattresses runs $175-$350 and features GREENGUARD certification and something Colgate calls SecureCore Technology, which is supposed to enhance air circulation in the mattress. These mattresses were too new as of this writing to gauge any parent feedback.

Overall, we're impressed with Colgate's wide range of offerings. Quality is very good—all mattresses are made in the USA. ***Rating: A-***

Greenbuds Baby GreenBudsBaby.com Looking for an eco crib mattress that costs less than your crib? Greenbuds recently entered the now crowded eco crib mattress market with two offerings: the Primrose and Magnolia crib mattresses.

The Primrose has a three inch core of coconut coir and another inch of natural latex. The cover is made of organic quilted cotton, which is removable and washable. Price: $340. There is also a deluxe version of the Primrose that runs $400 and features an upgraded cover made from blended organic wool and cotton(again, this is removable and washable).

The Magnolia is billed as a 2-in-1 crib mattress with a thicker (four inch) core made of coconut coir and an inch of natural latex. There is a firm side for infants and a softer side for toddlers. Like the Primrose, the Magnolia comes in both regular and deluxe versions (cotton vs. wool blend covers). Price: $390 to $410.

The company also sells water proof mattress pads made of organic cotton and a food-grade polyethylene waterproof membrane. Price: $35 to $54.

Greenbuds seems to be trying to find the middle ground pricewise in the eco-market. It is a bit less than Naturalmat's coconut coir mattress (which clocks in at $450+) but more than Naturepedic's eco mattresses (which don't have coconut coir cores, however).

Feedback on Greenbuds has been positive, so we'll give them a recommended rating. ***Rating: B+***

Kolcraft/Sealy kolcraft.com Baby gear maker Kolcraft is also a big player in crib mattresses and one key reason is price: these are some of the most affordable mattresses on the market. An example is their Kolcraft Pure Sleep Therapeutic coil mattress with 150 coils for $50-$70 online—a good deal if you want to go for coil.

Kolcraft also has had a hit with their soybean foam mattresses, which replace some of the typical petrochemical foam found in other crib mattresses with a soybean foam. Made under Kolcraft's sister brand Sealy, these mattresses are affordable and good quality. Example: the Sealy Soybean Foam-Core mattress for $133 is a good deal.

The major new addition to the Kolcraft mattress line in the past year are foam mattresses that feature CoolTex gel—these mattresses feature a gel that is cool to the touch. This feature addresses a concern that some memory foam mattresses trap heat. Kolcraft makes two versions of this mattress: the Sealy Signature Cool Beginnings 2-stage mattress for $200; the similar Sealy Select 2-Cool 2-State at Buy Buy Baby is $200. These mattresses are GREENGUARD certified.

Recently, Kolcraft added a new brand for eco mattresses called Stearns & Foster, which is a kids' version of the luxury adult mattress line. They're offering two options: the Baby Dynasty Sunset 2-Stage crib mattress (foam core on one side, micro-coil on the other), and the Baby Dynasty Sunrise 2-Stage crib mattress (coil with cotton filling on one side, soybean cool gel memory foam on the other). Both use high density soy foam and include stain resistant covers for $360. As of this writing, they are being sold only on Stearns & Foster's web site.

Bottom line: we like Kolcraft's crib mattresses and would recommend the brand. While the cool gel and memory foam mattresses are nice, they are overkill—the simple soybean foam or coil mattress for under $150 is what we'd recommend. ***Rating: A***

LA Baby *lababyco.com* This company is probably better known for its mini-crib, but they also sell a line of mattresses that include foam, inner spring and natural. An example is the Organic Cotton 2-in-1 Orthopedic mattress for $85, which the company claims is made from certified organic cotton. This mattress gets generally good reviews from parents, but a few complained about its lack of firmness and fumes when first removed from packaging.

In the past year, LA Baby has expanded their Naturals line of eco-friendly mattresses, made in Southern California. The latest offering is their "Pediatrician's Choice Mattress with Medical Grade Cover" for $83 on Walmart.com.

While we think these mattress are ok, other brands like Colgate and Naturepedic offer better overall quality and durability. LA Baby mattresses lack GREENGUARD certification for low emissions and their claims of organic materials aren't certified by any third party standards group. ***Rating: C***

Lullaby Earth *lullabyearth.com* Lullaby Earth is a new division of Naturepedic (reviewed separately) that is aiming for affordable eco crib mattresses priced under $200. Yes, you read that right—an eco crib mattress priced as a conventional mattress.

Lullaby Earth's Super Lightweight crib mattress is made of polyethylene foam (a non-toxic, food-grade foam that requires no fire retardant chemicals) and weighs just 7 lbs. (Most other foam mattresses on the market are made of polyurethane). It features seamless edges and GREENGUARD-certification. Price: $170. A two-stage version of this mattress is $200.

Lullaby Earth's newest mattress is the Breeze, which takes their two-stage crib mattress and adds a waterproof, breathable and removable cover for $280. The cover is an "advanced 3D honeycomb structure (that) creates a cushion of air under. . . baby for airflow and breathability," according to the company. So what does all this mean? It replaces the need for a waterproof mattress pad. Our concern: the implication is that babies can safely sleep on their stomachs on this cover. Even though Lullaby Earth doesn't make this claim, it could be easily misunderstood by parents. So, let us repeat our mantra: *infants under one year of age should only be put to sleep on their backs!*

While the Breeze is a nice mattress, the simpler and less expensive Super Lightweight is our pick here. Feedback on Lullaby Earth's mattresses has been very positive—the quality and durability is good. We highly recommend these mattresses. ***Rating: A***

Moonlight Slumber moonlightslumber.com Moonlight Slumber was one of the first entrants into the "premium" crib mattress market when they debuted a few years ago. Their mojo: "medical grade" and natural crib mattresses. Moonlight Slumber defines medical grade as PVC/vinyl free, non-toxic, antimicrobial and hypoallergenic.

Of course, to claim something is medical grade is fuzzy, as there is no formal definition. But Moonlight Slumber points to their welded seams and a "medical grade" stretch knit fabric cover as key features.

The company's Starlight Sparkle mattress ($250) comes in various sizes (crib, bassinet, cradle, etc). Readers tell us they love the dual-zone firmness, with a less-firm side for toddlers. They also have a Starlight Supreme all foam mattress with dual firmness for $270.

FYI: Moonlight Slumber makes a standard and supreme version of its mattress—the latter ($270) has a layer of memory foam. And the company makes a more affordable version of their foam mattress (the Little Dreamer, $150 for one firmness to $185 for dual firmness), which is five inches thick (the Starlight is 6").

New in the past year, Moonlight Slumber debuted a mattress priced between the Little Dreamer and the Starlight Support—the Starlight Shimmer ($220) is a 6" mattress that features "BabyCool" foam on the toddler side, which is an upgrade from the plain foam in the Little Dreamer.

Quality is good and most reviews from parents on Moonlight Slumber are quite positive.

One minor quibble: in the past year, Moonlight Slumber has been touting a Green Safety Shield certification for its products, saying this means its products meet indoor air quality standards, product performance and material contents standards. So who invented the Green Safety Shield? Answer: Moonlight Slumber. Moonlight Slumber claims the test the mattresses to a standard higher than GREENGUARD, but there is no third party documentation of that. It would be more impressive if Moonlight Slumber achieved third-party certifications like GREENGUARD's testing for indoor air quality.

In the end, however, this is a minor issue. Overall, we recommend Moonlight Slumber and think their quality is excellent. *Rating: A*

Natura *naturaworld.com* Natura started in 1994 with natural adult bedding and branched into baby mattresses (Baby Natura) in the past few years. The company's mattress offerings come in "classic" and organic varieties.

While both are made of a latex core, the organic mattress adds in a two-inch layer of natural coconut coir (the toddler side is the softer coconut coir; the newborn is the firmer latex). The Classic crib mattress ($375) includes a cotton cover, while the Organic crib mattress ($555 retail; $322 on Amazon) has a 100% organic cotton cover that is lined with wool.

You'll note that both of these mattresses are not waterproof—and that's the biggest downside to Natura. These mattresses just aren't practical in the world of diaper leaks. And the prices? Too high, when natural alternatives are available for 30% less from competing brands. Quality is good, but the value is not here. *Rating: B*

Naturalmat *naturalmatusa.com* UK-based Naturalmat offers three organic mattresses made of coir (the husk of a coconut), latex or mohair. The Coco Mat is $360, the Latex Mat is $440 and the Mohair Mat is $563.

Unfortunately, none of these mattresses are water-proof; for that, you need a $70 Naturalmat mattress protector (we've seen it online for $45 for an organic version and $37 for the regular version).

As for quality, readers generally praise Naturalmat, especially for the coconut mattress (Coco Mat). The few complaints we see center on the latex mattress, which some parents deem too soft. We see similar complaints about the Mohair Mat version (their most expensive). One mom told us that the cover shrank on her latex mattress after washing according to the manufacturer instructions.

Of course, the biggest issue here is the sky high retail price—and the additional cost for a mattress protector. Even when discounted on Amazon, the Coco Mat is over $300. On the other hand, if you want to splurge, at least you know this is a high quality product. Of Naturalmat's three models, the Coco Mat seems to receive the best overall reviews. *Rating: B+*

Naturepedic *naturepedic.com* Naturepedic's No Compromise Classic coil mattress ($260) features feature 150 coils, organic cotton fabric and filling and a food-grade polyethylene cover that is waterproof. The company also makes this mattress in a seamless version (like Moonlight Slumber's design) and a 252-coil version, each $300.

The No Compromise Organic Cotton Lightweight Classic mattress swaps out the coils for closed-cell air pockets made from food-grade polyethylene. As a result, this mattress is half the weight of a traditional coil mattress. This seamless mattress is $260 and is Naturepedic's best-selling model; a dual-firmness model is $290 and an "organic cotton ultra" with deluxe fabric is $330.

The Ultra series was added recently and comes with a stronger, more durable cover and more support for $360 to $380.

In specialty stores only, Naturepedic sells the Classic Seamless 2-stage 180 coil mattress for $300.

Quality is excellent—Naturepedic is GREENGUARD certified. We also liked the company's detailed web site, with extensive FAQ's, articles and a blog about shopping for a natural mattress. ***Rating: A***

Nook *nooksleep.com* And now for a crib mattress that costs as much as your crib: the $400 Nook Pebble Pure mattress features an organic coconut core layered with one inch of natural latex foam. The mattress' cover is made of eucalyptus fiber, zinc and organic cotton and is machine washable/dryable. It weighs a considerable 25 lbs.

The company claims the pebbled cover design "creates valleys for airflow on the mattress surface." The obvious implication is that other crib mattresses without said valleys are somehow inferior or dangerous—that claims seems baseless to us.

Made in the U.S., Nook also sells a lighter weight version of the mattress (Pebble Lite, 16 lbs.), which features a non-toxic eco-foam core and dual support for $265. The cover is the same as the Pebble Pure. While these mattresses are certainly unique (they come in six bright colors for the Pure, three pastels for the Lite), neither has a water-proof cover (they claim the mattress is "water resistant").

Feedback on this mattress is generally positive, but there is one major drawback. Since the cover isn't waterproof, you have to buy multiple extra covers (at $100 each) to make sure the mattress is usable when one cover is in the wash. Wrestling the cover off and on in the middle of the night isn't easy either, in our opinion. We'd just get a waterproof mattress cover or two, but that might negate the airflow advantage the company touts.

Nook's major competitor in this space is Naturalmat, whose Coco Mat mattress costs about as much as the Pebble Pure. Both mattresses would need a waterproof pad (or you'll be buying another cover for the Pebble). But . . . the Pebble's cover is difficult to remove, as we mentioned above. So the advantage there goes to Naturalmat.

So it is mixed review for the Nook—readers like the eco-goodness of the coconut fiber mattress, but the price and practical limitations of this mattress curb the Pebble's appeal. Between the two, parents seem to prefer the Pure over the Lite. ***Rating: B-***

Serta by Delta Serta crib mattresses are in transition as of this writing. The brand was made by LaJobi, which declared bankruptcy in 2014. Delta (the crib maker) has subsequently announced they will start selling Serta crib mattresses in 2015. We'll await the relaunch before rating this brand.

Simmons *simmonskids.com* Part of the Delta crib company, these mattresses are sold under several names: Beautyrest, Beautysleep and Slumber Time, but the bulk seem to be Beautyrest models. Most of the models are coil mattresses.

The most popular mattress from Simmons is the Beautyrest Beginnings Sleepy Whispers Ultra Deluxe 2 in 1 Crib and Toddler Mattress. Whew! Let's just call it Sleepy Whispers for brevity's sake. This coil mattress has 231 pocketed coil springs, extra corner support, 100% cotton fire protection (no chemicals used to make it fire resistant), and it's GREENGUARD certified. This mattress retails for $175, although online it sells for as little as $145.

If you're looking for something a little less expensive, the Beautyrest Studio Grand Dreams Infant & Toddler foam mattress sells at Walmart for $100. It comes with an eco-friendly organic blend cover that has a medical grade waterproof backing. It is GREENGUARD certified as well. We're impressed with a mattress at this price level that has this certification.

Two other foam mattresses are available from Simmons under the BeautySleep name: the Happy Nights and Sleep Whispers. They are both GREENGUARD certified again with cotton fire protection but the Sleep Whispers has a hypo-allergenic waterproof vinyl cover. Price: $98 for the Happy Nights and $124 for the Sleep Whispers.

Overall feedback on this brand is mixed—the low-end mattresses (under $100) are often knocked for poor quality, but the more expensive units (like the Sleepy Whispers Ultra Deluxe above) get better marks. Complaints included seams that ripped and mattresses that arrived dirty or damaged. Bottom line: there are better bets out there than Simmons. ***Rating: C+***

Sopora Sopora is owned by Munire, which declared bankruptcy in September 2014. The company has been sold to a new owner, Heritage Baby Products, which plans to relaunch the brand in 2015. We'll await the relaunch before we assign a rating.

Brand Recommendations: Our Picks

Good. The *Sealy Soybean Foam-Core* crib mattress is a good deal at $133. Yes, the foam is made from soybeans. At just 8.3 pounds, this lightweight but firm mattress makes changing sheets easy.

Lullaby Earth's Super Lightweight mattress is made of polyethylene foam (a non-toxic, food-grade foam that requires no fire retardant chemicals) and weighs just 6.5 lbs. Most other foam mattresses on the market are made of polyurethane. It features seamless edges and GREENGUARD-certification. Price: $170.

Better. *Moonlight Slumber's Little Dreamer* foam crib mattress is $170-$190 and features stitched seams and a PVC-free, "hospital-grade" vinyl cover. Bonus: it has two firmness zones (one for baby, another for toddler).

Best. *Naturepedic's Organic Cotton Lightweight* mattress, which swaps out coils for closed-cell air pockets made from food-grade polyethylene. As a result, this mattress is half the weight of a traditional coil mattress. It runs $260; a dual-firmness model is $300. If you want a coil mattress, Naturepedic's Organic Cotton Classic 150 coil mattress is a good bet at $260. In a nutshell, Naturepedic balances the best of both worlds: organic cotton filling, a firm foam or coil innerspring AND a waterproof cover. All of Naturepedic's mattresses contain no PVC's, polyurethane foam or chemical fire retardants.

Green. *Naturepedic* would be our top pick here—see above for model info. A runner-up best pick in the green category goes to **Naturalmat's Coco Mat** ($400), made from coconut fiber. The only bummer: the cover isn't waterproof (you have to add a $70 mattress protector to get that feature).

Dressers & Changing Tables

Now that you've got a place for the baby to sleep, where are you going to put baby's clothes? The juvenile trade refers to dressers, armoires, and the like as "case pieces" since they are essentially furniture made out of a large case (pretty inventive, huh?).

Of course, a dresser is more than just a place to store clothes and supplies. Let's not forget that all-too-important activity that will occupy so many of your hours after the baby is born: changing diapers. The other day we calculated that by our baby's first birthday, we had changed over 2300 diapers! Wow! To first-time parents, that may seem like an unreal number, but we're not exaggerating. On average, that is about SEVEN diaper changes a day during the first year . . . but for a newborn, expect up to 15 diaper changes a day. So, where are you going to change all those diapers? Most parents use the dresser top, but we'll also discuss changing tables in this section.

What are You Buying

1 **DRESSERS.** As you shop for baby furniture, you'll note a wide variety of dressers—three drawer, four drawer, armoires, combination dresser/changing tables, and more. No matter which type you choose, we do have three general tips for getting the most for your money.

First, focus on the drawer glides. Test this in the store—drawers with an easy glide typically have tracks on BOTH sides of the drawer. Cheaper dressers have drawers that simply sit on a track at the bottom center of the drawer. As a result, they don't roll out as smoothly and are prone to coming off the track.

Look at the drawer glide itself. Cheaper dressers have simple metal glides. Better dressers use more elaborate mechanisms including ball-bearings or self-closing glides (you push the drawer nearly closed and it automatically/slowly closes the rest of the way). A few dresser makers use wood-on-wood glides, more commonly seen in adult furniture.

Our second piece of advice: look at the drawer sides—the best furniture makers use "dove-tailed" drawer joints. There are two types of dove-tail drawers: English and French (see pictures at right). Both are acceptable. What's not good? Drawers and drawer fronts are merely stapled together.

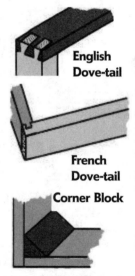

English Dove-tail

French Dove-tail

Corner Block

A third quality indicator: drawers with corner blocks (pictured). Pull the drawer out and turn it over to look at the corners—if there is a small block that braces the corner, that's good. Cheaper dressers omit this feature, which adds to the stability of the drawer. Also check the sides of the drawers: are they solid wood? Or particle board?

Finally, when it comes to drawers, consider how far they extend: fully extending drawers are ideal. Cheapers dressers use partially extended drawers.

Step back a moment and look at the entire dresser—do the drawers fit? Are the hinges for an armoire adjustable (like what you'd see in good kitchen cabinets)? Is the back of the dresser a flimsy piece of chipboard that is stapled? Most folks don't look at the back of a dresser—but how a manufacturer treats this piece (using screws to attach the back, for example) is a mark of quality.

Let's talk about wood for a second. Unlike cribs (most of which are made of solid wood), dressers are usually a compromise—solid wood on the parts you see (drawer fronts, front panels) and wood substitutes for the parts you don't see (basically, everything else).

Most dresser makers use fiberboard (sometimes referred to as MDF, medium density fiberboard) and particleboard as well as veneers (thin strips of wood glued over particleboard).

The key shopping tip: how much solid wood is there in the dresser? The better quality the dresser, the more solid wood. While one furniture maker (Romina) uses all solid wood, that is the exception. The better quality furniture makers use solid wood drawer boxes, drawer fronts, tops and sometimes even sides. Or if veneers are used, they are over less expensive solid hardwood instead of MDF (Pali uses birch veneers over rubber wood, for example).

In recent years, we've seen more MDF used in baby furniture. Why? It's cheap, easy to sculpt and smooth (there is no wood grain or knots). Many modern furniture designers are using MDF as a design statement. While we don't see anything wrong with that, we do object to the sky-high prices for this—paying $1500 for a dresser made of MDF is like spending four-figures for a fake-leather jacket.

What are the concerns with MDF and other wood substitutes? In general, fake wood isn't as durable as solid wood, which means more possible warping or splitting in very humid or dry climates. Why? MDF is made by compressing/gluing together wood waste fibers. That compression/gluing can be affected by the moisture content in the air—and hence your expensive MDF dresser can warp.

Another concern with MDF: formaldehyde. This chemical can be found in high concentrations in MDF and particle board, thanks to that glue that binds the fibers together. The more MDF or particle board, the more possible formaldehyde, which can lead to unhealthy indoor air. In high concentrations, formaldehyde can cause a burning sensation and nausea . . . as well as a possible link to cancer

The take-home message: when evaluating a dresser, look beyond the pretty finish. Evaluate drawer construction, glides, corner blocks and the amount of solid wood.

2 CHANGING AREA. Basically, you have two options here. You can buy a separate changing table or use your dresser as a changing area. As mentioned earlier, we think a separate changing table is a waste of money (as well as a waste of space).

So most folks look for dressers to do double duty: not only a place to store clothes, but also change diapers. Basically, you need a changing area of the right height to do this—evaluate your and your spouse's heights to see what you'd need.

FYI: We aren't big fans of those combination cribs, where a changing table or dresser is attached to the crib. The reason is safety: attached dressers give older babies a place to climb out of the crib and potentially fall from a higher distance.

In fact, a 2011 study from the Nationwide Children's Hospital found 9,600 babies and toddlers are injured a year in cribs, most from falls. While the study didn't have specific statistics on falls from cribs with attached dressers, we think these items are an obvious hazard.

Where do you keep the diaper changing supplies? Well, you can use a drawer in the dresser Or, a rolling storage cart is another solution (cost: about $25 in many catalogs and stores such as Container Store; containerstore.com).

Safe & Sound

Safety doesn't stop at the crib—consider these tips:

◆ *Anchor dressers to the wall.* Why? When baby starts exploring her nursery, she can tip over dressers, bookcases or shelves—no matter how heavy they are. Some furniture brands include anchor straps; in other cases, you'll need to visit a local hardware store. One solution: the Anti-Tip Kit ($10) from HangmanProducts.com.

◆ *Baby proof the diaper station.* If your diaper changing area has open shelves, you may have to baby proof the bottom shelves. As your baby begins to climb, you must remove any dangerous medicines or supplies from easily accessible shelves.

◆ *Air out all that new nursery paint, furniture and decor.* A University of Maryland study suggests new parents should air out freshly painted or wallpapered rooms before baby arrives. New furniture and mattresses also "out-gas" fumes for a brief time, so consider ventilating the nursery when they arrive as well. How much ventilation? The study suggested four to eight weeks of open window ventilation. Another idea: look for environmentally friendly paints that have lower out-gas emissions (VOC's). If you install new carpet in the house, leave during the installation and open the windows (and turn on fans) for two days.

Our Picks: Brand Recommendations

Our picks for dressers mirror what we picked for cribs. For contact information on these brands, refer to the reviews earlier in this chapter. Here's a round up:

Good. Just as in cribs, *IKEA's* affordable dressers (about $100 to $230) are our top pick if money (or space) is tight. Yes, assembly can be challenging. And these dressers probably won't last until your kid goes to college. But $230 for a double dresser? You can't beat that price.

Better. The dressers from brands like *Baby Appleseed* (and their sister brand *Eco-Chic Baby*) as well as *Pali* are good bets. Eco-Chic at Babies R Us runs $550 for a five drawer dresser or $700 for a double dresser. These dressers feature dove-tail drawers, metal ball-bearing glides and GREENGUARD certification. Pali's double dressers are in the $700 to $900 range with similar quality.

Best. If you've got the bankroll, the very best quality in dressers can be found in *Natart* and *Romina*. A double dresser from Natart typically tops $1000 and features top notch construction. Romina is even better, with all solid-wood construction and the very best drawer glides—but a double dresser from this brand can top $1200.

Changing Table Pads

Changing table pads turn a dresser into a diaper changing station. A couple of shopping tips: look for a pad with elevated sides. This will help keep your baby on the mattress pad. A word of caution: elevated sides don't guarantee your baby won't still roll off the mattress pad, so never walk away when changing your baby.

Our picks: *Simmons' Two Sided Contour Dressing Table Pad with Non-Skid Bottom* ($40). Also good: *Summer Infant's Contoured Changing Pad* ($16 to $25). Both pads are available at Amazon.com, Target, Babies R Us and Walmart. If you prefer an organic or natural option, consider *Naturepedic's Organic Cotton Contoured Changing Table Pad* ($100).

Glider Rockers

More than a mere rocking chair, glider rockers feature a ball-bearing system so they glide with little or no effort. They've earned a place in the nursery to help with those long hours of breastfeeding. Many are then repurposed later into a living room.

Here are some shopping tips when looking at rocker gliders:

◆ *Go for padded armrests.* You'll be cradling a newborn and spending many hours here. The more padding in the chair, the better.

◆ *Consider a chair with a locking mechanism.* Some brands

(notably Shermag) have an auto-locking feature; when you stand up, the chair can no longer rock. Very helpful if you have a curious toddler who might end up with pinched fingers.

◆ *Extra width is always smart.* Some of the cheapest glider rockers are quite narrow, which might not seem bad if you are a small person. But remember you will most likely be using a nursing pillow with your newborn . . . and having the extra width to accommodate this pillow is most helpful!

The Name Game: Reviews of Selected Manufacturers

Best Chair besthf.com This Indiana-based rocking chair maker entered the baby biz in 2002, although they trace their roots to the 1960's. We were very impressed with their quality and offerings. Basically, Best specializes in upholstered chairs with over 700 fabric choices. They also make traditional glider rockers and furniture for other rooms in the house.

Best claims their gliders have the longest glide in the industry. They also offer an optional 10-position glide lock that makes it easier to get in and out of the chair. The traditional wood designs have a closed base for safety.

Delivery is four weeks and prices are decent for an all-upholstered look: most are $400 to $700. A matching ottoman is $160 to $300. Best is sold only in specialty stores and on JCPenney.com (one model, the Jacob, in seven colors).

Best Chair's most recently began offering a "bonded" leather fabric option dubbed PerformaBlend. Bonded leather is made of leather scraps and costs less than a full leather chair (about $600 compared to $700 or more for leather).

Feedback from readers has been mostly positive on Best—a few complaints centered on Best models sold on JCPenney.com that had backs that were too short for some taller parents. Most folks had no problem, however and generally loved Best's overall quality and durability. For taller parents, it might be good to try out this chair in person before purchasing. *Rating: A*

Brooks brooksfurnitureonline.com. Tennessee-based Brooks sells glider-rockers that are old school—traditional chairs feature basic fabrics and exposed wood. Prices run $388 to $700 for the glider rockers, while the ottomans are $180-$250. One plus: all 75 Brooks fabrics are available on any style chair (over 15 styles and ten finishes). Brooks chairs feature solid base panels (Dutailier has an open base), which the company touts as safer. While we liked Brooks' quality, one baby storeowner told us he found the company very disorganized with poor customer service. ***Rating: B***

Dutailier *dutailier.com.* Quebec-based Dutailier is to glider-rockers what Google is to online search. Thanks to superior quality and quick delivery, Dutailier probably sells one out of every two glider rockers purchased in the U.S. and Canada each year.

Dutailier has an incredible selection of over 90 models, seven finishes, and 80 different fabrics. The result: over 37,000 possible combinations. All wood is solid maple or oak and features non-toxic finishes. You have to try real hard to avoid seeing Dutailier—the company has 3500 retail dealers, from small specialty stores to major retail chains. In the past year, Dutailier's Montreal designer has added a cool modern style chair ($800 and up) to match its Papaya crib, dresser and nightstand (see cribs for more info).

Prices for Dutailier start at about $500 (chair & ottoman) for their "Ultramotion" line sold at discount stores like Target.com. The Ultramotion gliders are entry-level: you get basic fabric cushions and exposed wood accents. Other models are exclusive to Babies R Us and Amazon, priced around $420 to $530. Some fancier fabrics can run as much as $700 for the chair only. The good news about Dutailier at chain stores: models are often discontinued and then discounted—BRU often sells these chairs and floor models for prices in the $200's.

You can spend much more than that—Dutailier's specialty store line lets you customize a glider-rocker to your heart's content . . . add a swivel base, plush cushions or leather fabric and you can spend $600. Or $1000. The latest rage: all upholstered glider rockers run $1000 to $1700 and come in leather or fabric.

If you like the upholstered look but don't have that much coin, Dutailier offers an option: chairs with fully upholstered arms (but open bases) for $600 to $650 with ottoman in six fabrics and five finishes. Basically, much the same look, half the price.

Realizing all these choices can be a bit daunting, Dutailier moved in the past to simply its offerings: now, all fabrics can be used on any chair. Dutailier's web site now divides its wood gliders into two categories: modern and traditional.

Dutailier offers an "auto lock" feature on some chairs—it's always locked when no one is sitting in it and then automatically unlocks when you sit down. Also new: a "nursery chair" for $430 with drop-down nursing pillows.

If we had to criticize Dutailier on something, it would have to be their cushions. Most are not machine washable (the covers can't be zipped off and put into the washing machine). As a result, you'll have to take them to a dry cleaner and pay big bucks to get them looking like new. A few of our readers have solved this problem by sewing slipcovers for their glider-rockers (most fabric stores carry pattern books for such items). Of course, if the cushions are shot, you can always order different ones when you move the glider-rocker into the family room—but that can be expensive, as replacement cushions are $150 to $300.

It can take ten to 12 weeks to order a custom Dutailier rocker (more for leather options), but the company does offer a "Quick Ship" program—a selection of around 15 to 20 chair styles in two or three different fabric choices that are in stock for shipment in two weeks. We have received occasional complaints about how long it takes to order a Dutailier—one reader special-ordered a Dutailier from Babies R Us, only to find out some weeks later that the fabric was discontinued (Dutailier "forgot" to tell Babies R Us, who, to their credit, tried to fix the problem immediately). Other readers complain about fabric backorders, which cause more delays in delivery. Our advice: make sure the store double checks the order with Dutailier.

Quality here is excellent. We toured Dutailier's Quebec plant recently and were impressed with the high tech wizardry used in production—laser-guided water jets slice huge sheets of top-quality leather, computer-controlled ovens make sure stains are baked on chairs for an even finish and so on. At each step, quality is hand checked by an army of workers to insure consistency of fit and finish.

So, who's got the best deals on Dutailier? At the moment, we'd have to give the crown to Target. At both their Super Target locations and online (target.com), you can get a Dutailier for about $390. Yes, Target only carries one or two styles, so your choices are limited.

An optional accessory for glider rockers is the ottoman that glides too. These start at $150 at discounters like Target, but most cost about $170 to $300. FYI: We've noticed more web sites selling glider and ottoman packages today with prices starting around $450.

One tip on rocking ottomans: we suggest skipping this and ordering an inexpensive "nursing" footstool (about $30). Why? Some moms claim the ottoman's height puts additional strain on their backs while breast-feeding. While the nursing footstool doesn't rock, it's lower height puts less strain on your back. (That said, we should note that some ottoman fans point out that once their mom/baby get the hang of nursing, that gliding ottoman is a nice luxury).

One safety note: don't leave an older child sitting in a glider-rocker. Many can be tipped over by a toddler when they climb out of it. (Safety tip: some glider rockers have a lever that locks it in position when not in use). *Rating:* ***A***

Little Castle littlecastleinc.com. Expensive, but good quality is how we'd describe Little Castle's glider rockers. Little Castle specializes in all-upholstered, swivel gliders. An example is their popular Cottage model, a soft, over-stuffed chair for $710. Other styles start at $450 on

Target.com. Custom styles can easily top $1000, although the opening price for Little Castle in most specialty stores is $650.

As you'd expect for that price level, you get a wide choice of fabrics (all of which are online at Little Castle's web site) and other perks like a hidden release button to recline the chair.

FYI: Little Castle gliders are made in Oxnard, California. Each chair is custom made; delivery is about ten weeks.

New in the past year, Little Castle released a leatherette chair ($700 to $800 in white, brown or black) that can be customized with cushions using fabric from their entire line or your own fabric. These extra cushions run $130 for a set.

To differentiate from the gliders it sells to chains like Walmart, Little Castle is launching a collection of chairs under the "Castle Home Furnishings" brand that will be sold in independent stores only. Prices will be similar to Little Castle's main line. FYI: Little Castle is sold under the alias Enchanted on Walmart.com.

Readers generally like this company, but we heard from more than one that had quality issues with their expensive Little Castle gliders. One had a spring that popped out of the bottom of the chair; another said her Cottage Chase glider developed a hole in the arm after just eight months of use. Worse, Little Castle told these reader there was nothing they could to do help her since the fabric was discontinued (even though the chair comes with a one year warranty). In the case of the spring, Little Castle refused to repair the chair since it was outside of their one year warranty. Maybe we're crazy, but when you spend a $1000 on a custom Little Castle chair, we think the company should stand behind the product for more than 12 months.

Bottom line: most folks are happy with their Little Castle gliders, but if you have a problem, you are probably on your own for the repair bill. *Rating: B*

Monte *montedesign.net* Toronto-based Monte's gliders epitomize the modern nursery look—simple lines, tailored fabrics, etc. Monte has four basic styles, but you can customize each chair to your heart's content.

All this doesn't come cheap: most chairs run $1000-$1200; swap the fabric for leather and you can add another $200.

Example: the Grazia rocker in a grey fabric is $1200. A lumbar pillow (pictured with many rockers) is $85 extra. New in the past year, Monte has added limited edition chairs made of Italian wool and walnut bases ($1300).

So is it worth it? Well, the samples we recently inspected were impressive: solid walnut bases, high quality fabrics, quality foam for the seats, etc. Yes, all that is nice, but other glider makers (Dutailier, for example) do a similar look and quality for about 25% less. Hence, we get the feeling here you are paying a premium for . . .

exactly what, we're not sure.

Feedback from parents has been positive, with fans citing the high-quality fabrics and tailoring.

Delivery is about 5-7 weeks. While we do see a couple of Monte gliders on Amazon, the brand is mostly sold specialty stores and chains like Giggle and Land of Nod. FYI: Monte gliders are made in Canada.

Bottom line: beautiful chairs, but at premium prices. ***Rating: B***

Newco *newcointernational.com* Sold online at Walmart and Amazon, Newco makes upholstered gliders at discount prices. Walmart currently has a $377 Newco glider that features chenille fabric and matching ottoman for $144. Amazon also carries this brand—one of the best selling styles (the Bella) is $624-720.

Feedback on Newco has been mixed. While a good number of reviews are positive and say the chair is a great value, more than a few parents complained of quality issues (freight damage, bases that broke after three months of use, etc). One reader told us she was a bit surprised at how short the back of the chair was (and she wasn't particularly tall). Another said her Newco glider broke after less than a year. We also saw quite a few complaints about gliders that became noisy/squeaky after only a short time of use.

As a result of these durability and quality questions, we have lowered Newco's rating this year. ***Rating: C+***

Nursery Classics by Klaussner *klaussner.com* Klaussner Home Furnishings is a large North Carolina manufacturer of adult upholstered furniture. They recently decided to market their upholstered rockers to the nursery biz (dubbed Nursery Classics by Klaussner).

Priced competitively at between $500 and $700, these upholstered rockers are manufactured in the U.S. The company offers 125 frame styles including glider rockers, regular rockers and recliners. Shipping takes three to four weeks. Wayfair sells these gliders online—the Finney is $616.

Initial reviews of this line are positive, but a few detractors complain of quality issues (squeaks, etc) and the overall small size of these chairs (you might want to try them out in the store before ordering).

So we'll give Klaussner a qualified recommendation for now, as we await more feedback. ***Rating: B***

Shermag/Chanderic *shermag.com* Canada-based Shermag's strategy is to under-price Dutailier. Their gliders (which include an ottoman) are sold online for as little as $235. Shermag's focus is the entry glider market, similar to Dutailier's Ultramotion rockers.

Most models are in the $250-$400 range with combo packages (rocker plus ottoman) about $500. A few leather and upholstered options are in the $500-$600 range.

So what's the catch with Shermag's affordable line? First, these styles are a bit smaller in size than other glider-rockers—they fit most moms fine, but those six-foot dads may be uncomfortable. The color choices are also limited (just one or two, in most cases). And you should try to sit in these first to make sure you like the cushions (no, they aren't as super comfy as more expensive options but most parents think they're just fine).

Shermag's pricier options are found at stores like Babies R Us, where $350 (including ottoman) is the average price point. For that extra money, you'll get a bigger chair, more fabric and frame color options.

How's the quality of Shermag gliders? Not great, according to a review of the feedback we've received from parents in the past year. We've noticed a deterioration in the reviews Shermag has received, both from our readers and other online postings. Concerns range from freight damage to squeaking—and long-term durability is another weak spot here. More than one parent told us their Shermag glider broke after less than two months of use.

Shermag's cheapest options often come with very cheap fabric and thin cushions, making this bargain not worth the hassle. And even Shermag's more expensive gliders are dogged by quality issues. Bottom line: there are better choices out there. **Rating: C-**

Stork Craft Like their cribs and dressers, Stork Craft's glider rockers are priced for the entry-level part of the market: Amazon and Walmart sell glider and ottoman packages for as little as $125—no, that's not a typo.

An example of these deals is the Hoop Glider and Ottoman Set, $125-164 depending on the frame color and fabric.

What's the catch? Well, quality for one. More than one parent told us they loved their Stork Craft glider . . . for about four months. Then the squeaking started. Other complaints center on the cheap cushions. Or that their Stork Craft glider simply fell apart after regular use. After two months.

Customer support is non-existent. Bottom line: a bargain glider is no bargain if the chair drives you nuts with squeaking . . . or breaks after a few months. Spend a bit more for one of our better rated glider companies (example: Dutailier) and you'll be happier in the end. **Rating: C**

Tulip/Natart Nursery furniture maker Natart entered the glider rocker market in 2014 with upholstered chairs that feature memory foam seating, adjustable armrests and a nifty accessory: an optional tray for your iPad.

Made in Quebec, the chairs run $1250; the extra tablet shelf is $150. Among the three models available, most have a choice of five wood finishes and multiple upholstery colors (leather and fab-

NURSERY NECESSITIES

ric) in a muted color palette.

While expensive, we like the quality touches—solid wood frames, bonded leather that are hand-washable, and the aforementioned memory foam seats with lumbar support and more.

Parent feedback on these new gliders has been sparse, but given Natart's reputation for quality, we will recommend them. ***Rating: A***

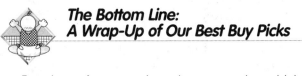

The Bottom Line: A Wrap-Up of Our Best Buy Picks

For cribs, you've got two basic choices: a simple model that is, well, just a crib or a convertible model that eventually morphs into a twin or full size bed.

For a basic crib, the Fisher Price Newbury or Charlotte cribs are good choices under $200. Another good bet: IKEA's affordable cribs which are under $150.

When it comes to convertible cribs, look at DaVinci (Million Dollar Baby Classic) or Westwood. These models run $300 to $500. Yep, it costs more money up-front but you get a crib that converts to a full-size bed.

The best mattress? We like ***Sealy Soybean Foam-Core*** crib mattress for $133. For organic mattresses, ***Naturepedic's Organic Cotton Lightweight*** mattress is our top pick at for $260.

For glider rockers, Dutailier earns our top mark. A simple glider rocker runs $350, but fancy all-upholstered styles can push $1000.

So, here's a sample budget for an affordable nursery

Fisher Price Newbury crib	$150
Sealy Soybean Form mattress	$133
Eco-Chic Baby five-drawer dresser	$550
Dutailier Ultramotion glider-rocker	$400
Miscellaneous	$200
TOTAL	**$1433**

By contrast, if you bought a designer modern crib ($1500) and paired it with a high-end dresser (plus mattress, glider rocker, etc.), you'd be out $3500 by this point. So by following our budget, you will have a safe yet affordable nursery . . . and saved $2067.

Of course, you don't have any sheets for your baby's crib yet. Nor any clothes for Junior to wear. So, next we'll explore those topics and save more of your money.

CHAPTER 3

Baby Bedding & Decor

Inside this chapter

Where can you find brand new, designer-label bedding for as much as 50% off the retail price? We've got the answer in this chapter, plus you'll find eight smart shopper tips to help get the most for your money. We'll share the best web sites for baby linens and learn the ten important tips that will keep your baby safe and sound. Finally, we've got a chart of the top bedding manufacturers and a must-read list of seven top money-wasters.

Getting Started: When Do You Need This Stuff?

Begin shopping for your baby's linen pattern in the sixth month of your pregnancy, if not earlier. Why? If you're purchasing these items from a baby specialty store, they usually must be special-ordered–allow at least four to eight weeks for delivery. If you leave a few weeks for shopping, you can order the bedding in your seventh month to be assured it arrives before the baby does.

If you're buying bedding from a store or web site that has the desired pattern in stock, you can wait until your eighth month. It still takes time to comparison shop, and some stores may only have certain pieces you need in stock, while other accessories (like wall hangings, etc.) may need to be special ordered.

No matter where you buy your baby's bedding, make sure you take the time to wash it (perhaps more than once) to make sure it doesn't shrink, pill or fall apart. You'll want to return it as soon as possible if there is a problem with the quality.

Sources

There are five basic sources for baby bedding:

1 BABY SPECIALTY STORES. These stores tend to have a limited selection of bedding in stock. Typically, you're expected to choose the bedding by seeing what you like on sample cribs or by looking through manufacturers' catalogs. Then you have to special-order your choices and wait four to eight weeks for arrival. And that's the main disadvantage to buying linens at a specialty store: THE WAIT. On the upside, most specialty stores do carry high-quality brand names you can't find at discounters or baby superstores. But you'll pay for it—most specialty stores mark such items at full retail.

2 DISCOUNTERS. The sheer variety of discount stores that carry baby bedding is amazing—you can find it everywhere from Walmart to Target, Marshall's to TJ Maxx. As you'd expect, everything is cash and carry at these stores—most carry a decent selection of items in stock. You pick out what you like and that's it; there are no special orders. The downside? Prices are cheap, but often so is the quality. Most discounters only carry low-end brands whose synthetic fabrics and cheap construction may not withstand repeated washings. There are exceptions to this rule, which we'll share later in this chapter.

3 DEPARTMENT STORES. The selection of baby bedding at department stores is all over the board. Some chains have great baby departments and others need help. For example, JCPenney carries linen sets by nearly ten such manufacturers like Trend Lab and Waverly while Sears carries lines like Lambs & Ivy and Sweet JoJo. Prices at department stores vary as widely as selection; however, you can guarantee that department stores will hold occasional sales, making them a better deal.

4 BABY SUPERSTORES. The superstores reviewed in the last chapter (Babies R Us, Baby Depot, Buy Buy Baby etc.) combine the best of both worlds: decent prices AND quality brands. Best of all, most items are in stock. Unlike in Walmart or K-Mart stores, you're more likely to see 100% cotton bedding and better construction. Yet, the superstores aren't perfect: they are often beaten on price by online sources (reviewed later in this chapter). And superstores are more likely to sell bedding in sets (rather than a la carte), forcing you to buy frivolous items.

5 **ONLINE.** Most of our readers shop for their bedding online. And if there were a perfect baby product to be sold on-line, crib bedding is it. The web's full-color graphics let you see exactly what you'll get. And bedding is lightweight, which minimizes shipping costs. The only bummer: you can't feel the fabric or inspect the stitching. As a result, we recommend sticking to well-known brand names when ordering online. See the next section on best online sources for baby bedding and don't forget to check out online-only bedding on Walmart and Target's web sites.

Best Online Bargains

Baby Supermall

babysupermall.com. As you'd expect from a site with "mall" in its name, BabySupermall tries to be all things to moms and dads. From safety gear to furniture to toys, this site carries quite a wide selection. In the baby bedding department, they had nearly 500 different bedding options available. Manufacturers include Lambs & Ivy, Glenna Jean, Bananafish and MiGi. Prices are usually affordable, although frequent sales (up to 50% off) make this site a real bargain. You can even click on a link for a bedding set and BabySupermall will send you an email when that bedding goes on sale in the future.

Perhaps the best part of the site is its baby bedding finder. You can choose categories like gender, price range, color, brand and up to four themes. These themes include floral, bugs and butterflies, frogs and 17 other options. Another plus: free shipping if you spend over $69 and fabric samples are available for a small charge. The site claims to have the fastest delivery because they warehouse "nearly 10,000 nursery bedding sets" at their shipping facility.

Our only complaint: the site is very cluttered. It can be as overwhelming visually as your first visit to a Babies R Us store. ***Rating: A***

Baby Supermarket

babysupermarket.com. This online outlet for a Jackson, MS baby store is a good option to consider for bargain bedding. They carry about ten bedding lines, including some of our top picks (Cotton Tale, Sumersault and Lambs & Ivy) and prices are good. For example they sell a four-piece set from Trend Lab for $155 (regular price $170). Baby Supermarket also has a decent selection of separates including bedding for cradles and small cribs. The site is easy to navigate and we like the options available to search by brand, collection, color, price and gender. ***Rating: B***

Diapers.com

diapers.com. Diapers.com is really the land of discounts. Everywhere you look there are coupon codes, cash back offers, free shipping over $49, and free returns. The site is a bit busy with all the free/discount offers, but you can easily narrow your bedding search by gender, theme, brand and price. We were impressed that they offered so many mini crib sets and sheets (51 total on our visit). These can be tough to find, so here's a great resource.

Manufacturers include the usual crowd as well as some different names like Clouds & Stars zip off sheets (see box later in this chapter), DwellStudio and Babyletto. The site calls out sale prices and any out of stock items clearly, a nice plus. Overall, Diapers.com is one of our favorites for great selection and price. ***Rating: A***

Overstock

overstock.com. Overstock.com is a master at finding closeout deals in all kinds of categories. We always buy our regular bed sheets from these guys in amazing Egyptian cotton with incredibly high thread counts. So we figured they'd have some great deals on baby bedding too. And we weren't disappointed. On a recent visit we saw over 160 baby bedding sets from companies like Sweet JoJo, My Baby Sam, Cotton Tale and more. Prices are 25% to 50% off. Baby bedding is sold as sets and separates.

But remember, if you see something you want on Overstock.com, don't wait too long. They sell out quick! And some designs do not offer a la carte sheets so you're stuck with what comes in the package. Be sure you check customer reviews before you buy to verify you're really getting a deal. ***Rating: A***

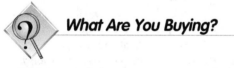

What Are You Buying?

Walk into any baby store, announce you're having a baby, and stand back: the eager salespeople will probably pitch you on all types of bedding items that you MUST buy. We call this the "Diaper Stacker Syndrome," named in honor of that useless (but expensive) linen item that allegedly provides a convenient place to store diapers. But what do you really need? Here's our list of the absolute necessities for your baby's linen layette:

◆ ***Fitted sheets***—at least three to four. This is the workhorse of your baby's linens. When it comes to crib sheets, you have three choices: woven, knit and flannel. Woven (also called percale) sheets are available in all cotton or cotton blend fabrics, while knit and flannel sheets are almost always all cotton. As to which is best, it's up to you. Some folks like flannel sheets, especially in colder climates. Others find woven or knit sheets work fine. One tip: look for sheets that have elastic all-around the edges (cheaper ones just have elastic on the corners). See the "Safe & Sound" section for more info on crib sheet safety issues.

If you plan to use a bassinet/cradle, you'll need a few of these special-size sheets as well . . . but your choices here are pretty limited. You'll usually find solid color pastels or white. Some specialty linen manufacturers do sell bassinet sheets, but they can get rather pricey. And you may find complete bassinet sets that come with all the linens for your baby. Just be sure to check the fabric content (all cotton is best) and washing instructions. By the way, one mom improvised bassinet sheets by putting the bassinet mattress inside a king size pillowcase and taping the excess fabric underneath.

◆ **Mattress Pads/Sheet Protector.** While most baby mattresses have waterproof vinyl covers, many parents use either a mattress pad or sheet protector to protect the mattress or sheet from leaky diapers. A mattress pad is the traditional way of dealing with this problem and is placed between the mattress and the crib sheet. A more recent invention, the sheet protector, goes on top of the crib sheet.

A sheet protector has a waterproof vinyl backing to protect against leaking. And here's the cool part: it Velcro's to the crib's posts, making for easy removal. If the baby's diaper leaks, simply pop off the sheet protector and throw it in the wash (instead of the fitted crib sheets). You can buy sheet protectors in most baby stores or online. See "Email from the Real World" nearby for information on sheet savers.

◆ **Blanket?** Baby stores love to pitch expensive quilts to parents and many bedding sets include them as part of the package. But remember this: *all babies need is a simple, thin cotton blanket.* Not only are thick quilts overkill for most climates, they can also be dangerous. The Consumer Product Safety Commission's report on Sudden Infant Death Syndrome (SIDS) concluded that putting babies face down on such soft bedding may contribute to as many as 30% of SIDS deaths each year in the U.S. (As a side note, there is no explanation for the other 70% of SIDS cases, although environmental factors like smoking near the baby and a too-hot room are suspected). Some baby bedding companies have responded to these concerns by rolling out decorative flannel-backed blankets (instead of quilts) in their collections.

But what if you live in a cold climate and think a cotton blanket

E-MAIL FROM THE REAL WORLD
Sheet savers make for easy changes

Baby bedding sure looks cute, but the real work is changing all those sheets. Karen Naide found a solution:

"One of our best buys was 'The Ultimate Crib Sheet.' I bought one regular crib sheet that matched the bedding set, and two Ultimate Crib Sheets. This product is waterproof (vinyl on the bottom, and soft white poly/cotton on the top) and lies on top of your regular crib sheet. It has six elastic straps that snap around the bars of your crib. When it gets dirty or the baby soils it, all you have to do is unsnap the straps, lift it off, put a clean one on, and that's it! No taking the entire crib sheet off (which usually entails wrestling with the mattress). It's really quick and easy! While the white sheet may not exactly match your pattern, it can only be seen from inside the crib, and as you have so often stated, it's not like the baby cares about what it looks like. From the outside of the crib, you can still see the crib sheet that matches your bedding. Anyway, I think it's a wonderful product, and really a must."

There are a couple of options for quick change cribs sheets. The Ultimate Crib Sheet (summerinfant.com) retails for $20 to $22 and is sold online and in stores.

Another good bet is the Quick Zip crib sheet from Clouds and Stars (cloudsandstars.com). While the Quick Zip isn't waterproof, it has a sheet base that covers the bottom of the mattress and stays in place. The top of the sheet is secured via a plastic zipper. When you need to change sheets at two in the morning, you zip off the top of the sheet and zip on a spare. No lifting of the mattress (except when you first set it up). The white or ecru sheet sets are $35 to $45 for the starter set (a zipper base plus top sheet) and additional top sheets are $17 to $30.

Between the two, we'd suggest the Quick Zip—even though it is more expensive than the Ultimate Crib Sheet, the quality is better and they are easier to use.

won't cut it? Consider crib blankets made from fleece (a lightweight 100% polyester fabric brushed to a soft finish) available in most stores and online. For example, **Pottery Barn Kids** sells a micro fleece crib blanket for $30. Of course, polar fleece blankets are also available from mainstream bedding companies like **California Kids**. Or how about a "coverlet," which is lighter than a quilt but more substantial than a blanket? Lightweight quilts (instead of the traditional thick and fluffy version) are another option for as little as $30 online.

Halo Innovations' (halosleep.com) SleepSack was the first of its kind "wearable blanket" that helps baby avoid suffocating. Available in four sizes and eight fabrics, the SleepSack is $25 to $40. A portion of the sale price goes to First Candle/SIDS Alliance. Swaddling blankets are also now the rage. Examples include the **Miracle Blanket** ($30; miracleblanket.com) and the **Summer Infant Swaddle Me** ($13). See the box nearby for more swaddling blanket picks. Note: Be sure when swaddling your infant, you leave the baby's waist and legs loosely enclosed in the blanket. Recent concerns were raised that tight swaddling could lead to hip dysplasia in some infants.

More Money Buys You . . .

Baby bedding sets vary from as little as $40 in discount stores up to nearly $1000 in specialty stores. The basic difference: fabric quality and construction. The cheapest bedding is typically made of 50/50 cotton-poly blends with low thread counts (120 threads per inch). To mask the low quality, many bedding companies splash cutesy licensed cartoon characters on their offerings. So what does more money buy you? First, better fabric. Usually, you'll find 100% cotton with 200 thread counts or more. Cheap quality crib sheets often lack elastic all the way around and some shrink dangerously when washed (see Safe and Sound next for details), while more money buys you preshrunk or oversized (to allow for shrinkage) sheets with elastic all around the edge.

Beyond the $300 price point, you're most likely paying for a designer name and frilly accessories (coordinating lamp shade, anyone?). At the upper end of the crib bedding market, you find luxury fabrics and finishes—silks, brocades, matte lasse, etc.

Safe & Sound

When it comes to baby safety, most folks think of outlet covers and coffee table bumpers—but your baby's crib bedding should be a key priority. Why? Your baby will be spending more time in the crib than any other place in the house. Here are several safety points to remember:

Swaddling & Wearable Blankets

Swaddling and wearable blankets have become increasingly popular in recent years—they keep baby warm and avoid safety concerns with quilts or regular blankets. Swaddling blankets are rectangular, light weight blankets used to fold your baby up like a burrito. Wearable blankets are pouches made of blanket fabric that your baby zips into (there arms are usually unrestricted. Here's an overview:

The original *SleepSack* (made by Halo) started the wearable blanket trend and is available in a variety of fabrics for $25 to $40. Halo has expanded their line to include swaddling blankets. The SleepSack Swaddle ($27 to $35) is a SleepSack with added flaps and Velcro closures that fold over to hold baby's arms close to their body.

Of course, there's more than just the Sleep Sack out there. Here are some of our reader favorites for swaddling blankets.

Aden & Anais (AdenandAnais.com) makes two types of swaddling blankets: muslin swaddle wraps and Easy Swaddles. The muslin swaddles are do-it-yourself swaddling blankets, while Easy Swaddles have snaps. Prices are $35 to $45 for a pack of four muslin swaddles; Easy Swaddles are $20 to $25 each. Double layer blankets, organic and bamboo collections are available. Bonus: Aden & Anais' web site includes helpful how-to videos on swaddling.

Another option: *Swaddle Designs* (swaddledesigns.com) swaddling blankets and wearable blankets are also excellent, say readers. This site offers both a wearable blanket option called the zzZipMe Sack ($27 to $45) with a cool two-way zipper for easy diaper changes plus their Ultimate Receiving blanket ($25) and Marquisette Swaddling blanket ($15). Both blankets have easy directions on a sewn-on tag.

Finally, a small company out of Connecticut makes a wearable blanket/swaddler called the *Woombie* (thewoombie. com). This option is similar to a SleepSack without the arm holes. You just zip it up and it hugs your baby's arms to his chest. Cost: $26. Winter weight, summer weight and organic fabrics are available.

One note: the International Hip Dysplasia Institute (hipdysplasia.org) points to the potential for increases in hip dysplasia problems when parents swaddle children too tightly around the hips and legs. The institute has an online pamphlet that explains hip dysplasia and the risks of improper swaddling. FYI: wearable blankets from Halo, Swaddle Designs and Woombie help parents avoid a too-tight fit when swaddling a baby.

◆ *Make sure the crib sheets snugly fit the mattress.*

Let's talk about crib sheets. As you might guess, it is the elastic on a sheet that helps it fit snugly to a mattress. But not all sheets have the same amount of elastic.

One quality sign: check to make sure the sheet's elastic extends around the ENTIRE sheet (cheaper quality crib sheets only have elastic on the ends, making a good fit more difficult to achieve).

One of our favorite brands with this feature are made by the American Baby Company (ababycompany.com). Their affordable sheets ($9 to $20) for both cribs and portable playpens come in a variety of fabrics (percale, flannel, cotton jersey, etc.).

Another issue to consider with crib sheets: shrinkage. *Never use a sheet that has shrunk so much it can no longer be completely pulled over the bottom corners of the mattress.*

Unfortunately, some sheets shrink more than others. Generally, the cheapest sheets sold in discount stores shrink the most. We will offer our recommendations of bedding brands later in this chapter. Those with our highest recommendations typically have sheets that are pre-shrunk. Others make their sheets larger to allow for shrinkage.

Our advice: for any crib sheet you buy, be sure to wash it several times *according to the directions* and see if it correctly fits your crib. If not, return it to the store.

◆ *No soft bedding in the crib.*

Yes, we've said it before and here it is again: studies on Sudden Infant Death Syndrome (SIDS, also known as crib death) have linked SIDS to infants sleeping on fluffy bedding, lambskins, or pillows. A pocket can form around the baby's face if she is placed face down in fluffy bedding, and she can slowly suffocate while breathing in her own carbon dioxide. The best advice: put your infant on her back when she sleeps. And don't put pillows, comforters or other soft bedding or toys inside a crib.

Sheets with All Around Elastic

Here is a list of manufacturers who make their crib sheets with elastic all around the sheet:

American Baby	Circo (Target)	Maddie Boo
BB Basics	Fleece Baby	Bobble Roos
Baby Basics	Garnet Hill	Restoration
Baby Gap	Hoohobbers	Hardware
Carousel	Land of Nod	Sweet Kyla

The Consumer Product Safety Commission now recommends that parents not use ANY soft bedding around, on top of, or under baby. If you want to use a blanket, tuck a very thin blanket under the mattress at one end of the crib to keep it from moving around. The blanket should then only come up to baby's chest. Safest of all: avoid using any blankets in a crib and put baby in a blanket sleeper (basically, a thick set of pajamas) and t-shirt for warmth. (More on blanket sleepers in the next chapter).

See the picture nearby for an example of the correct way to use a blanket

One mom wrote to tell us about a scary incident in her nursery. She had left a blanket hanging over the side of the crib when she put her son down for a nap. He managed to pull the blanket down and get wrapped up in it, nearly suffocating. Stories like that convince us that putting any soft bedding in or near a crib is risky.

How much bedding is too much? A new father emailed us this question: "With all the waterproof liners, fitted sheets and ultimate crib sheets we're worried that our firm mattress is now becoming soft and squishy. How many layers are safe?"

Good point. We know that some parents figure it is easier to change crib sheets at 2 am if they simply pile on several layers of sheets on the crib mattress. (This way, you simply remove the top wet layer when changing the sheets). While we admire the creative thinking, we suggest NOT doing this. One sheet over a waterproof liner is enough. Or use an Ultimate Crib Sheet over your sheet—you won't need an additional liner since the Ultimate Crib Sheet is waterproof. The take-home message: any more than TWO layers on top of a mattress is dangerous.

♦ **Beware of ribbons and long fringe.** These are possible choking hazards if they are not attached properly. Remove any questionable decoration.

♦ **We DO NOT recommend crib bumpers.** Do not use bumpers in your baby's crib, cradle or bassinet. They are a risk factor for suffocation.

Yes, in past editions of this book, we tried to discourage people from using bumpers, but did not outright reject them. Why did we change our mind? New evidence shows that bumpers can and do cause suffocation deaths in infants. An investigation by the *Chicago Tribune* detailed a link between crib bumpers and two-dozen infant deaths in the past decade. The article ("Hidden Hazard of Crib Bumpers," December 12, 2010) prompted the CPSC to open a review of the safety of crib bumpers.

An earlier study by a Washington University pediatrician, Dr. Bradley Thach "concluded that 27 babies' deaths were attributed to bumper pads from 1985 to 2005." This study, however, has been largely ignored by both the industry and the CPSC, although the American Academy of Pediatrics discourages parents from using bumpers.

In 2011, Chicago became the first city in the U.S. to outright ban the sale of bumper pads in their jurisdiction. The *Chicago Tribune* story mentioned earlier prompted the ban. The state of Maryland has also weighed in on bumpers, considering either an outright ban on their sale or the adoption of voluntary safety standards. As of press time, they were still studying the issue.

As a side note, Canada has discouraged bumper use for many years. One Canadian reader noted: "We are not supposed to use bumper pads due to the increased risk of SIDS. No one I know uses them. When the health nurse comes to visit you in the home, she checks to make sure you don't have bumper pads." It's time parents in the U.S. followed similar guidelines.

Now we know what you're thinking: "What if my baby hits his head on the hard wood slats?" or "What if she gets her arm or leg stuck between the slats?" First, these issues are rare—few kids are injured by knocking their heads against the slats and even fewer get limbs stuck. The only product we recommend for parents who truly have a problem with babies who get their limbs stuck is the Breathable Baby Crib liner ($30).

A fashion note: for parents who miss the attractive side view of a crib that has bumpers, consider sheets from Skip Hop. They are now printing a design on the sides of their crib sheets that makes them look like bumpers (an enlarged graphical item that coordinates with the bedding design). Expect to see more manufacturers adopt this style now that bumpers are becoming verboten.

◆ *Never use sleep positioners.* A recent recall of sleep positioners lead us to urge parents not to use them. These $10 to $20 blocks of foam are supposed to hold baby in place on their back when sleeping. However, the Consumer Product Safety Commission (CPSC.org) issued a "warning to parents and caregivers to stop using sleep positioners." They have received reports of 12 infants who suffocated when positioners were used. In past editions, we discouraged sleep positioners because they were a waste of money, but now we know they are also a serious hazard. Simply put your baby to sleep on his back—no pillows, no rolled up towels.

◆ **Never use an electric blanket/heating pad.** Babies can dangerously overheat, plus any moisture, such as urine, can cause electric shock.

◆ **Avoid blankets that use nylon thread.** Nylon thread melts in the dryer and then breaks. These loose threads can wrap around your baby's neck, fingers or toes or break off and become a choking hazard. Cotton or cotton/poly thread is best.

◆ **Watch out for chenille.** Its popularity has waned in recent years, but we still see some chenille accents on baby bedding and in luxe items like blankets. The problem? With some chenille, you can actually pull out fibers from the fabric backing with little effort. And that might be a choking hazard for baby.

◆ **Travel.** Now that you've created a safe nursery at home, what about when you travel? Parents who frequently travel are often frustrated by hotels, which not only have unsafe cribs (see previous chapter) but also questionable sheets. At one hotel, we were given queen size bed sheets to use in a crib! A solution: one reader recommended bringing a crib sheet from home. That way you know your baby will be safe and sound. (When you reserve a crib at a hotel, find out if it is a portable crib or a standard crib so you know what size sheet to bring.)

◆ **All linens should have a tag** indicating the manufacturer's name and address. That's the only way you would know if the linens were recalled. You can also contact the manufacturer if you have a problem or question. While this is the law, some stores may sell discounted or imported linens that do not have tags. Our advice: DON'T buy them.

Smart Shopper Tips

Smart Shopper Tip
Pillow Talk: Looking for Mr. Good Bedding

"Cartoons or more cartoons—that seems to be the basic choice in crib bedding at our local baby store. Since it all looks alike, is the pattern the only difference?"

There's more to it than that. And buying baby bedding isn't the same as purchasing linens for your own bed—you'll be washing these pieces much more frequently, so they must be made to withstand the extra abuse. Since baby bedding is more than just another set of sheets, here are several quality points to look for:

1 **RUFFLES SHOULD BE FOLDED OVER FOR DOUBLE THICKNESS—INSTEAD OF A SINGLE THICKNESS RUFFLE WITH HEMMED EDGE.** Double ruffles hold up better in the wash.

2 **COLORED DESIGNS ON THE BEDDING SHOULD BE PRINTED OR WOVEN INTO THE FABRIC, NOT STAMPED** (like you'd see on a screen-printed t-shirt). Stamped designs on sheets can fade with only a few washings. The problem: the pieces you wash less frequently (like dust ruffles and bumpers) will fade at different rates, spoiling the coordinated look you paid big money for. In case you're wondering how to determine whether the design is printed rather than stamped, printed fabrics have color that goes through the fabric to the other side. Stamped patterns are merely applied onto the top of the fabric.

3 **MAKE SURE THE PIECES ARE SEWN WITH COTTON/POLY THREAD, NOT NYLON.** While nylon threads can be a safety problem (see earlier discussion), they also are a quality issue. When nylon threads break in a dryer, the filling can bunch up.

4 **CHECK FOR TIGHT, SMOOTH STITCHING ON APPLIQUÉS.** If you can see the edge of the fabric through the appliqué thread, the work is too skimpy. Poor quality appliqués will probably unravel after only a few washings. We've seen some appliqués that were actually fraying in the store—check before you buy.

5 **HIGH THREAD-COUNT SHEETS.** Unlike adult linens, many packages of baby bedding do not list the thread count. But, if you can count the individual threads when you hold a sheet up to the light, you know the thread count is too low. High thread-count sheets (200 threads per inch or more) are preferred since they are softer and smoother against baby's skin, last longer and wear better. Unfortunately, most affordable baby bedding has low thread counts (80 to 120 thread counts are common)—traditionally, it's the design (not the quality) that sells baby bedding. But there is good news on this front: most mid- to upper-priced brands are at least 200 count.

6 **THE DUST RUFFLE PLATFORM SHOULD BE OF GOOD QUALITY FABRIC**—or else it will tear. Longer, full ruffles are more preferable to shorter ones. As a side note, the dust ruffle is sometimes referred to as a crib skirt.

7 **REMEMBER THAT CRIB SHEETS COME IN DIFFERENT SIZES—** bassinet/cradle, portable crib, and full-size crib. Always use the correct size sheet.

BABY BEDDING

Wastes of Money/Worthless Items

"I have a very limited budget for bedding, and I want to avoid spending money on stuff that I won't need. What are some items I should stay away from?"

It may be tempting to buy every matching bedding accessory. And you'll get a lot of sales pressure at some stores to go for the entire "coordinated" look. Yet many baby-bedding items are a complete waste of money—here's our list of the worst offenders:

1 **DIAPER STACKER**. This is basically a bag (in coordinating fabric, of course) used to store diapers—you hang it on the side of a changing table. Apparently, bedding makers must think stacking diapers on the shelf of your changing table or storing them in a drawer is a major etiquette breach. Take my word for it: babies are not worried if their diapers are out in plain sight. Save the $20 to $50 that bedding makers charge for diaper stackers and stack your own. By the way, we've even seen $100 diaper stackers—these typically coordinate with equally expensive bedding sets. Another note: many of the new super cheap 8, 9 and 12-piece+ bedding sets (see #3 below) may include a diaper stacker. Of course, it's up to you whether to use it or not.

2 **PILLOWS.** Some bedding sets still include pillows or pillowcases. Are the bedding designers nuts, or what? Haven't they heard that it's dangerous to put your baby to sleep on a pillow? What a terrible safety hazard, not to mention a waste of your money. We don't even think a decorative pillow is a good idea—what if another caretaker puts your baby to sleep in her crib and forgets to remove the decorative pillow? Forget the pillow and save $30 to $50.

3 **SETS OF LINENS.** Sets may include useless or under-used items like those listed above as well as dust ruffles, bumpers and window valances. Another problem: sets are often a mixed bag when it comes to quality. Some items are good, while others are lacking. Here's an example from Overstock.com: a 13-piece set on sale for $98 included a quilt, two valances, skirt, crib sheet, bumper, diaper stacker, toy bag, two pillows and three wall hangings. No surprise, this set was made of a poly/cotton blend fabric. A better bet: many baby stores or even chains now sell bedding items a la carte. That way you can pick and choose just the items you need—at a substantial savings over the all-inclusive sets.

4 **CANOPIES.** Parents-to-be of girls are often pressured to buy frilly accessories like canopies. The pitch is a feminine look for her nursery. Don't buy into it. The whole set-up for a canopy is going to be more expensive (you'll need a special crib, etc.)—it'll set you back $60 to $175 for the linens alone. And enclosing your baby's crib in a canopy won't do much for her visual stimulation or health (canopies are dust collectors).

5 **ALL-WHITE LINENS**. If you think of babies as pristine and unspoiled, you've never had to change a poopy diaper or clean spit-up from the front of an outfit. We're amazed that anyone would consider all-white bedding, since keeping it clean will probably be a full-time job. Stick with colors, preferably bright ones. If you buy all-white linens and then have to go back to buy colored ones, you'll be out another $100 to $200. (Yes, some folks argue that white linens are easier to bleach clean, but extensive bleaching over time can yellow fabric.)

Money Saving Secrets

1 **IF YOU'RE ON A TIGHT BUDGET, GO FOR A GOOD BLANKET AND A NICE SET OF HIGH THREAD-COUNT SHEETS.** What does that cost? A good cotton or fleece blanket runs $30, while a decent quality fitted sheet is another $20 to $40. Forget all the fancy items like embroidered comforters, duvet covers, window valances, diaper stackers and dust ruffles. After all, your baby won't care if she doesn't have perfectly coordinated accessories.

2 **DON'T BUY A QUILT.** Sure, they look pretty, but do you really need one? Go for a nice cotton blanket, instead—and save the $50 to $200. Better yet, hint to your friends that you'd like receiving blankets as shower gifts.

3 **SKIP EXPENSIVE WALL HANGINGS—DO DECOR ON THE CHEAP.** One of the best products we've discovered for this is *Elephants on the Wall* (elephantsonthewall.com). This company sells patterns that you just tape to the wall trace and then paint so you can create paint-by-number masterpieces in your baby's room. Paint a six-by-eight foot mural or just add some decorative borders. Cost: $30 to $100 depending on size and complexity (plus the cost of paints).

A new idea: wall decals. These creative graphic "stickers" can be positioned and repositioned, removed and replaced. Choose from animals, flowers, abstract designs and more. *Blik Re-Stik* (whatisblik.com) sells designs that start at $30 while *WallPops!* (wallpops.com) has decals starting at $15. While these are reusable, take care when removing them as they may fray along the edges. *Wallies* (wallies.com) are similar to decals except that they are pre-pasted shapes. You wet the backing and stick them wherever you like. FYI: Some Wallies aren't reusable—you have to strip them off

License	**Who makes what brand of bedding**

A perennial trend in crib bedding is licensed characters—just about every cartoon character imaginable has been licensed to one of the big bedding makers for use in juvenile bedding. But how can tell you tell who makes what? Here is a list of popular licensed characters and their bedding makers:

License	**Is Made By**
Baby Looney Tunes	Crown Crafts
Care Bears	Baby Boom
Carter's Infant	Crown Crafts
Classic Pooh	Crown Crafts
Disney Baby	Pem America
Disney Baby	Crown Crafts
Dr. Seuss	Trend Lab
Dora the Explorer	Baby Boom
Eddie Bauer	Crown Crafts
Fisher-Price	Crown Crafts
Hello Kitty & Friends	Crown Crafts
Jonathan Adler	Crown Crafts
Kathy Ireland	Thank You Baby
Lalaloopsy	Crown Craft
Laura Ashley	Pem America
NauticaKids	Crown Crafts
Nojo	Crown Crafts
Paddington Bear	Trend Lab
Precious Moments	Baby Boom
Sesame Street	Crown Crafts
Snoopy	Lambs & Ivy
Taggies	Crown Crafts
Thomas and Friends	Baby Boom
Too Good by Jenny	Pem America
Wamsutta	Spring
Waverly Baby	Trend Lab

like wallpaper. A pack of Cute Fairies (21 pieces) runs $15. They now offer bigger, mural size Wallies starting at $40.

Of course, crafts stores are another great source for do-it-yourself inspiration. Michaels Arts & Crafts (michaels.com) sells stencils and supplies for nursery decor.

4 **MAKE YOUR OWN SHEETS, DUST RUFFLES AND OTHER LINEN ITEMS.** Think that's too complicated? A mom in Georgia called in this great tip on curtain valances—she bought an extra dust ruffle, sewed a curtain valance from the material and saved $70. All you need to do is remove the ruffle from the fabric platform and sew a pocket along one edge. I managed to do this simple procedure on my sewing machine without killing myself, so it's quite possible you could do it too. A good place for inspiration is your local fabric store—most carry pattern books like Butterick, Simplicity and McCalls, all of which have baby bedding patterns that are under $10. There are other pattern books you can purchase that specialize in baby quilts—some of these books also have patterns for other linen items like valances, crib skirts or wall hangings. Even if you buy good quality fabric at $10 per yard, your total savings will be 75% or more compared to "pre-made" items.

5 **SHOP AT OUTLETS.** Scattered across the country, we found a few outlets that discount linens. Among the better ones: Garnet Hill and Carousel (also known as babybedding.com)—we recommend them as a Best Bet later in the chapter. Another reader praised the Pottery Barn Outlet. They have nine locations at the time of this writing. The discounts start at 50% on bedding and furniture from their web sites and retail stores. Other outlets: Carter's, Baby Gap, and Nautica.

6 **DON'T PICK AN OBSCURE BEDDING THEME.** Sure, that "Exploding Kiwi Fruit" bedding is cute, but where will you find any matching accessories to decorate your baby's room? Chances are they'll only be available "exclusively" from the bedding's manufacturer—at exclusively high prices. A better bet is to choose a more common theme with lots of accessories (wall decor, lamps, rugs, etc.). The more plentiful the options, the lower the prices. Winnie the Pooh is a good example, although you'll find quite a few accessories for other common themes like Noah's Ark, teddy bears, rocking horses, etc.

7 **GO FOR SOLID COLOR SHEETS AND USE THEMED ACCESSORIES.** Just because you want to have a Disney-themed nursery doesn't mean you have to buy Disney *bedding*. A great money-saving strategy: use low-cost solid color sheets, blankets and other linen items in the crib. Get these in colors that match/compliment theme accessories like a lamp, clock, poster, wallpaper, rugs, etc. (Hint: register for these items, which make nice shower gifts). You still have the Disney look, but without the hefty tag for Disney bedding. Many of the online sites we reviewed earlier in this chapter are excellent sources for affordable, solid-color bedding. Another bonus: solid color sheets/linens from these web sites we recommend are often much higher quality (yet at a lower price) than theme bedding.

8 SURF THE WEB. Earlier in this chapter, we discussed the best web sites for baby bedding deals. The savings can be as much as 50% off retail prices. Even simple items like crib sheets can be affordably mail ordered.

Tips on green bedding

Like many organic products today, there is no standard for "organic" or natural baby bedding. This leaves it up to bedding manufacturers to determine for themselves what's organic. So, let's review some terms you'll see.

Many organic crib bedding makers claim their items are made from organic cotton. Organic cotton simply means cotton that's been grown with a *minimum* amount of toxic pesticides or fertilizers. That doesn't mean it is completely free of all pesticides and fertilizers.

Next let's talk sheet dyes. Conventional cribs sheets are dyed with synthetic chemicals—so how are organic bedding companies addressing this issue? Can an organic sheet be colored anything other than the natural shade of cotton (that is, an off-white)?

Turns out, the answer is yes. Organic cotton can be grown in a few colors. Yes, that's right, just like you can buy naturally orange or purple cauliflower, cotton can be cultivated in colors. Three colors are available: pink, light brown and green. Another solution: vegetable dyes. Look for manufacturers that sell baby bedding made with low-impact vegetable dyed cotton.

Of course, all this comes for a price: organic crib bedding is often 20% to 35% more expensive than conventional bedding.

Our favorite brands that offer organic crib bedding includes Aden +Anais, American Baby and Carousel. FYI: not all of these brands' bedding is organic; only certain designs.

The Name Game:
Our Picks for the Best Brands

Perhaps the biggest challenge with baby bedding is there are so many choices! To help you whittle down the list a bit, we present our Best Bets, Good But Not Great and Skip It list of bedding brands on the following page. (Individual reviews of each bedding manufacturer listed below can be found on the subscription side of our web site at BabyBargains.com).

The Best Bets are the brands that have the best quality and durability. Typically, they feature sheets that are 100% cotton. While some of these brands can be pricey, most offer good value for the dollar.

Good But Not Great picks are just that—not our first choices for quality, but a close runner-up. In some cases, these are lines that have good quality but poor overall value. Example: Annette Tatum makes great quality bedding, but the price for a single sheet is a whopping $66. Whoa!

The Skip-It brands are the poorest quality: they shrink in the wash or fall apart. They may be made of poly/cotton blends, which tend to be less comfortable. Poor stitching on appliqués as well as stamped designs lead to bedding that wears out fast so even if it's very affordable, it's a waste of money.

Some of these brands sell direct; others just through retailers.

SAFETY NOTE: We do NOT recommend parents use bumpers in their babies' cribs. See the Safe and Sound section earlier for an in depth explanation. Note that many brands below sell bedding sets that include bumpers.

Affordable Artwork

Framed artwork for baby's room has to be very expensive, right? Nope, not if you buy a framed print from *Creative Images* (www.crimages.com). This Florida-based company sells prints, growth charts, wall hangings and more at very affordable prices—just $30 to $100. Each print is mounted on wood and laminated (no glass frame) so baby can enjoy it at eye-level (just sponge it off if it gets dirty). Best of all, there are hundreds of images in any theme to choose from: Pooh, bunnies, Noah's Ark, plus other collections of animals, sports and pastels. Check out their web site for samples.

Best Bets

AMERICAN BABY COMPANY	ABABYCOMPANY.COM
BOBBLE ROOS (BLANKETS)	BOBBLEROOS.COM
CADEN LANE	CADENLANE.COM
CALIFORNIA KIDS	CALKIDS.COM
CAROUSEL	BABYBEDDING.COM
COTTON TALE	COTTONTALEDESIGNS.COM
GLENNA JEAN	GLENNAJEAN.COM
HOOHOBBERS	HOOHOBBERS.COM
KIMBERLY GRANT	KIMBERLYGRANT.COM
LAMBS & IVY	LAMBSIVY.COM
LAND OF NOD	LANDOFNOD.COM
LIVING TEXTILES	LIVINGTEXTILES.COM
PINE CREEK BEDDING/OVER THE MOON	PINECREEKBEDDING.COM
SERENA & LILY	SERENAANDLILY.COM
SUMERSAULT	SUMERSAULT.COM
ULTIMATE CRIB SHEET	SUMMERINFANT.COM
SWEET KYLA	SWEETKYLA.COM

Good But Not Great

ANNETTE TATUM	ANNETTETATUM.COM
BB BASICS ONLINE	BUYBUYBABY.COM
BANANAFISH	BANANAFISH.COM
NOJO	NOJO.COM
DWELLSTUDIO	DWELLSTUDIO.COM
GRAHAMKRACKER	GRAHAMKRACKER.COM
JOJO DESIGNS	SWEETJOJODESIGNS.COM
KOALA BABY	BABIESRUS.COM
MADDIE BOO	MADDIEBOOBEDDING.COM
MY BABY SAM	MYBABYSAM.COM
POTTERY BARN KIDS	POTTERYBARNKIDS.COM
RESTORATION HARDWARE	RHBABYANDCHILD.COM
SLEEPING PARTNERS/TADPOLES	SLEEPINGPARTNERS.COM
SUMMER INFANT	SUMMERINFANT.COM
TADPOLE BASICS	TARGET.COM
TREND LAB BABY	TREND-LAB.COM
WHISTLE & WINK	WHISTLEANDWINK.COM

Skip It: CROWN CRAFTS (DISNEY BABY, NAUTICA KIDS, HELLO KITTY, SESAME STREET, TAGGIES, CARTER'S, LALOOPSY, JONATHAN ADLER); GERBER; CIRCO (TARGET); TOO GOOD BY JENNY

Brand Recommendations : Our Picks

Bedding Basics (sheets)

Good. *My Baby Sam* makes good crib bedding—sheets run $24 each and three and four-piece sets sell for $100 to $200. Parents tell us the quality is acceptable and the sheets fit their mattresses well. *Pottery Barn Kids* chamois sheets ($30 for one) are a great option for cold climates. Readers love their softness.

Better. *Land of Nod* makes stylish bedding, but you don't have to buy an entire set—they sell 100% cotton fitted sheets separately. Priced at $24 each, the sheets have all around elastic and wash well.

Best. Crib sheets from the *American Baby Company* are an affordable $13 to $20, yet are excellent in quality (all cotton, all around elastic, 9" deep pockets). Another top pick is *Carousel* (babybedding.com)—at $40 per sheet, they are a bit more pricey, but quality is also excellent. And there are many patterns and choices to customize your nursery's look.

Organic. *Aden & Anais, American Baby* and *Carousel*. FYI: only certain patterns from these brands are organic. Shop carefully.

Coordinated Sets

Our favorites here include *Skip Hop, Cottontale, Sumersault, Sweet Kyla* and *California Kids*. Got an aunt who just cashed out of her high-flying tech start-up? If she is paying, bedding from *Maddie Boo* sets the standard for top-of-the-line luxury in crib bedding.

Sheets for play yards, bassinets

Our pick here is *American Baby Company's fitted play yard sheet*, which fits the Graco Pack N Play bassinet/play yard mattress (as well as many other brands). At $10, it is a good deal and is made of organic cotton. If the organic thing doesn't matter to you, the same company makes a non-organic fitted play yard sheet from 100% cotton jersey knit for $9.

Blankets and wearable blankets

Bobble Roos are our top pick for plain blankets. These 100% cotton flannel blankets are great to have around the house or throw in the diaper bag. At $11 to $25, they are a pretty great deal too.

Looking for a wearable blanket? We like the *Halo SleepSack* and the *zzZipMe Sack* from *Swaddle Designs*. Also excellent: *Aden & Anais* (AdenandAnais.com)'s muslin cotton wraps (for do-it-yourselfers; $43 for a pack of four) or their Easy Swaddle ($25).

BEDDING RATINGS

NAME	RATING	COST	ORGANIC?
ADEN & ANAIS	A-	$$	◆
ANNETTE TATUM	B	$$$	
BANANA FISH	B	$ TO $$	
BB BASICS ONLINE	B-	$	
CADEN LANE	B+	$$$	
CALIFORNIA KIDS	A	$$	
CAROUSEL	A	$$	
COTTON TALE	A-	$$	◆
CROWN CRAFTS	C+	$ TO $$	◆
DWELL	B+	$$	◆
GERBER	D	$	
GLENNA JEAN	B+	$$	
HOOHOBBERS	B+	$$$	
KOALA BABY	C+	$	
LAMBS & IVY	B+	$	
LAND OF NOD	B	$$	◆
LIVING TEXTILES/LOLLI LIVING	A-	$$	
MADDIE BOO	A	$$$	
MY BABY SAM	B+	$$	
PINE CREEK	A-	$$$	
POTTERY BARN	C+	$$	◆
RESTORATION HARDWARE	B-	$$ TO $$$	◆
SERENA & LILY	B+	$$	◆
SKIP HOP	A	$$	
SLEEPING PARTNERS	B	$	◆
SUMERSAULT	A	$	◆
SUMMER	A	$	◆
SWEET JOJO DESIGNS	B	$ TO $$	
SWEET KYLA	A	$$	◆
TARGET (CIRCO)	C	$	
TL CARE	A-	$	◆
TREND LAB	B-	$ TO $$	
WHISTLE & WINK	B+	$$$	

KEY

COST: Cost of a sheet. $=under $20; $$=$20 to $50; $$$=over $50

ORGANIC: Does the bedding maker offer any organic options? Yes/No. Note: this does not mean that ALL of the maker's offerings are organic.

A quick look at some top crib bedding brands

bedding

Fiber Content	Notes
100% cotton	Famous for swaddling blankets. Sheets are excellent.
100% cotton	Pricey, shabby chic vibe.
100% cotton	MiGi line starts at $90 per set. Adult-like fashions.
100% cotton	Buy Buy Baby's private label; quality is mixed.
100% cotton	Modern vintage collections; 230 thread ct sheets.
100% cotton	Bright, whimsical patterns; most made in California.
100% cotton	Nursery designer tool online for custom looks
100% cotton	Whimsical prints, soft pastels. Made in USA.
Mix	Baby-ish designs; sold in major chain stores.
100% cotton	Stylized prints to match mid-century cribs.
Poly/Cotton	Cute patterns, but poor quality.
100% cotton	Low price line Sweet Potato features modern looks.
100% cotton	Made in U.S.; bright designs. Many accessories.
100% cotton	Sold in BRU, recent quality improvements.
Poly/cotton	Snoopy, Hello Kitty licensed designs.
100% cotton	Nice selection of accessories such as lamps.
100% cotton	Affordable 5-pc sets, designed in Australia.
100% cotton	Sophisticated looks, accented by silk and linen.
100% cotton	Affordable, readers love quality and soft fabrics.
100% cotton	Custom-made or off-the-shelf designs, pricey.
100% cotton	Peter Rabbit and other themed bedding.
100% cotton	600 thread count sheets; muted neutral looks.
100% cotton	Crisp, clean look with color accents.
100% cotton	Clever no-bumper sheet designs. Wash well.
100% cotton	Sold as Tadpole Basics in Target.
100% cotton	Traditional nursery looks; sold in chain stores/online.
100% cotton	Maker of Ultimate Crib Sheet; separates line.
100% cotton	9-piece beddings sets offer value; sold online.
100% cotton	Quality is good; sets can be ordered w/o bumpers
100% cotton	Low price, low thread counts. Shrinkage issues.
100% cotton	Affordable basics line sold in Buy Buy Baby
Mix	Sheet are good quality, textured fabrics.
100% cotton	Vintage looks with embroidery accents.

Fiber Content: Some lines have both all-cotton and poly/cotton blends—these are noted with the word "Mix."

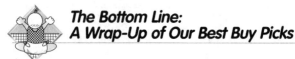

The Bottom Line:
A Wrap-Up of Our Best Buy Picks

All your baby really needs is a set of sheets and a cotton blanket. Web sites like BabyBedding.com and Land of Nod sell affordable, high-quality basics like sheets ($21 to $30) and blankets ($16 to $60). Instead of spending $300 to $500 on bedding sets with uneeded items like bumpers and diaper stackers, use creative solutions (like wall decals) to decorate the nursery affordably and leave the crib simple.

And if you fall in love with a licensed cartoon character like Pooh, don't shell out big bucks on a fancy character-themed bedding set. Instead, we recommend buying solid color sheets and accessorizing with affordable Pooh items like lamps, posters, rugs, etc.

Who's got the best deals on bedding? Web sites like Amazon (for sheets), BabySuperMall.com, Diapers.com and Overstock.com have the best bargains. If you're lucky to be near a manufacturer's outlet, search these stores for discontinued patterns.

Let's take a look at the savings. Here is a sample bedding budget:

American Baby Co. sheets (three)	$42
Wearable blanket (instead of a blanket)	$30
Miscellaneous (lamp, other decor)	$150

TOTAL **$222**

By contrast, if you go for a designer brand and buy all those silly extras like diaper stackers, you could be out as much as $800 on bedding alone—add in wall paper, accessories like wall hangings, matching lamps and you'll be out $1200 or more. So, the total savings from following the tips in this chapter could be nearly $1000.

Now that your baby's room is outfitted, what about the baby? Flip to the next chapter to get the lowdown on those little clothes.

CHAPTER 4

REALITY LAYETTE

The Reality Layette:
Little Clothes for Little Prices

Inside this chapter

What the heck is a "Onesie"? How many clothes does your baby need? How come such little clothes have such big price tags? These and other mysteries are unraveled in this chapter as we take you on a guided tour of Baby Clothes Land. We'll reveal our secret sources for finding name brand clothes at half off retail prices. Which brands are best? Check out our picks and our nine tips from smart shoppers on getting the best deals. Next, read about the many outlets for children's apparel that have been popping up all over the country. At the end of this chapter, we'll even show you how to save big bucks on diapers.

Getting Started:
When Do You Need This Stuff?

◆ **Baby Clothing.** You'll need basic baby clothing like t-shirts and sleepers as soon as you're ready to leave the hospital. Depending on the weather, you may need a heavy fleece sleeper at that time as well.

You'll probably want to start stocking up on baby clothing around the seventh month of your pregnancy—if you deliver early, you will need some basics. However, you may want to wait to do major shopping until after any baby showers to see what clothing your friends and family give as gifts.

Be sure to keep a running list of your acquisitions so you won't buy too much of one item. Thanks to gifts and our own buying, we had about two thousand teeny, side-snap shirts by the time our baby was born. In the end, our son didn't wear the shirts much (he grew out of the newborn sizes quickly and wasn't really wild about them anyway), and we ended up wasting money.

◆ **Diapers.** How many diapers do you need for starters? Are you sitting down? If you're going with disposables, we recommend 600 diapers for the first six weeks (about 14 diapers a day). Yes, that's six packages of 100 diapers each (purchase them in your eighth month of pregnancy, just in case Junior arrives early). You may think this is a lot, but believe us, we bought that much and we still had to do another diaper run by the time our son was a month old. Newborns go through many more diapers than older infants because they feed more frequently. Also, if you're a first time parent, you'll find yourself taking off diapers that turn out to be dry. Or worse, you may change a diaper three times in a row because baby wasn't really finished.

Now that you know how many diapers you need for the first six weeks, what sizes should you buy? We recommend 100 newborn-size diapers and 500 "size one" diapers. This assumes an average-size baby (about seven lbs. at birth). But remember to keep the receipts—if your baby is larger, you might have to exchange the newborns for size one's (and some of the one's for two's). Note for parents-to-be of multiples: your babies tend to be smaller at birth, so buy all newborn diapers to start. And double or triple our recommended quantity!

If you plan to use a diaper service to supply cloth diapers, sign up in your eighth month. Some diaper services will give you an initial batch of diapers (so you're ready when baby arrives) and then await your call to start up regular service. If you plan to wash your own cloth diapers, buy two to five dozen diapers about two months before your due date. You'll also probably want to buy diaper covers (six to ten) at that time. We'll discuss cloth diapers in depth later in this chapter.

Even if you plan to use disposable diapers, you should pick up one package of high-quality, flat-fold cloth diapers. Why? You'll need them as spit-up rags, spot cleaners and other assorted uses you'd never imagined before becoming a parent.

 **Sources**

There are nine basic sources for baby clothing and diapers:

1 BABY SPECIALTY STORES. Specialty stores typically carry 100% cotton, high-quality clothes, but you won't usually find them affordably priced. While you may find attractive dressy clothes, play clothes are typically a better deal elsewhere. Because the stores themselves are frequently small, selection is limited. On the upside, you can still find old-fashioned service at specialty stores—and that's helpful when buying items like shoes. In that case, the extra help with sizing may be worth the higher price.

As for diapers, you can forget about it—most specialty baby stores long ago ceded the diaper market to discounters and grocery stores (who sell disposables), as well as mail-order/online companies (who dominate the cloth diaper and supply business). Occasionally, we see specialty stores carry an offbeat product like specialized eco-friendly disposable diapers. And some may have diaper covers, but the selection is typically limited.

2 **DEPARTMENT STORES.** Clothing is a department store's bread and butter, so it's not surprising to see many of these stores excel at merchandising baby clothes. Everyone from Sears to Nordstrom sells baby clothes and frequent sales often make the selection more affordable.

3 **SPECIALTY CHAINS.** Our readers love Old Navy (see money-saving tips section) and Gap Kids. Both sell 100% cotton, high-quality clothes that are stylish and durable. Not to mention their price adjustment policies—if you buy an item at Gap/Old Navy and it goes on sale within seven days, you get the new price. Old Navy's selection of baby clothes is somewhat limited compared to Gap Kids. Other chains to check out include Gymboree, and Children's Place. All are reviewed later in this chapter.

4 **DISCOUNTERS.** Walmart, Target and K-Mart have moved aggressively into baby clothes in the last decade. Instead of cheap, polyester outfits that were once common at these stores, most discounters now emphasize 100% cotton clothing in fashionable styles. Target has vastly expanded their baby clothes with their in-store brand, Cherokee. Not only have they expanded, but the quality is terrific in most cases. Many of our readers shop Target for all cotton play clothes and day care clothes. Durability is good.

Diapers are another discounter strong suit—you'll find both name brand and generic disposables at most stores; some even carry a selection of cloth diaper supplies like diaper covers (although they are the cheaper brands; see the diaper section later in this book for more details). Discounters seem to be locked into an endless price battle with warehouse clubs on baby items, so you can usually find deals.

5 **BABY SUPERSTORES.** Babies R Us, Baby Depot and Buy Buy Baby carry a decent selection of name-brand clothing at low prices.

Most of the selection focuses on basics, however. You'll see more Carter's and Little Me than the fancy brands common at department stores. Over the years, Babies R Us has tried to upgrade their clothing options with a bit of embroidery here or an embellishment there.

Diapers are a mixed bag at superstores. Babies R Us carries them, but Baby Depot doesn't. When you find them, though, the prices are comparable to discounters. We've seen diapers priced 20% to 30% lower at Babies R Us than grocery stores.

6 WAREHOUSE CLUBS. Members-only warehouse clubs like Sam's, Costco and BJ's sell diapers at rock-bottom prices. The selection is often hit-or-miss—sometimes you'll see brand names like Huggies and Pampers; other times it is an in-house brand. While you won't find the range of sizes that you'd see in grocery stores, the prices will be hard to beat. The downside? You have to buy them in "bulk," huge cases of multiple diaper packs that might require a fork-lift to get home.

Check out the clubs' infant and toddler clothing as well. We'll talk later about some of the bargains we've found.

7 WEB SITES. There are a zillion web sites that offer clothing for infants. The choices can be quite overwhelming, and the prices can range from reasonable to ridiculous (don't worry, we'll give you the best bets). It's undeniably a great way to shop when you have a newborn and just don't want to drag your baby out to the mall. Another strength of the web: cloth diapers and related supplies. Chains and specialty stores have abandoned these items, so online suppliers have picked up the slack. Check out Best Online Sources

CPSC Issues Thrift Shop Warning

In a recent report from the Consumer Product Safety Commission (CPSC), the agency reported that in a survey of thrift shops nationwide, "an estimated 69 percent of the stores were selling at least one type of hazardous consumer product. Many of these were children's products." One of the most dangerous items for children are clothes with drawstrings. The CPSC reports 27 deaths and 70 non-fatal accidents involving drawstring between 1985 and 2008. If you buy clothing at a consignment or thrift store or from a garage sale, be sure to avoid clothes with draw-strings. Keep your smart phone handy at resale shops when you're looking gear—that way you can immediately determine if an item was recalled by going to cpsc.gov and searching the site.

later for more information on great web sites.

8 **CONSIGNMENT OR THRIFT STORES.** You might think of these stores as dingy shops with musty smells—purveyors of old, used clothes that aren't in great shape. Think again—many consignment stores today are bright and attractive, with name brand clothes at a fraction of the retail price. Yes, the clothes have been worn before, but most stores only stock high-quality brands that are in excellent condition. And stores that specialize in children's

Second Hand Shopping Tips & Advice

Experienced moms know: it's a great idea to buy used. Especially when you're talking about infant clothing. After all, infants don't do much damage to their clothes. They aren't playing in puddles, sucking down OtterPops or finger painting yet. So you can bet the wear and tear on used infant clothing is minimal.

Most towns and cities have a variety of resale shops, but not all of them concentrate on baby clothes. The good news: there is now a national chain plus some great online resellers frugal moms can target.

That national chain, Once Upon a Child (onceuponachild. com), is a favorite among our readers. Sheila Bayer of Connecticut wrote: "We have seven locations of Once Upon a Child and I love them! The clothes and toys are of great quality and very affordable." With locations in all but a few states (even Alaska has two locations!), most people should be able to find a store. The company claims their inventory is as much as 70% off retail. If you read the company policy on what items they'll resell, you'll be impressed with their stringent requirements. This weeds out the less desirable items. And finally, if you want to resell items, you can bring them into the stores where they pay cash (30-50% of estimated retail price) for the items they like. No waiting for your money!

While we're talking about baby clothing here, many resale shops carry gear as well. One caution about these second hand stores—if you buy an item like a stroller or high chair at a resale shop, you may not be able to get replacement parts. One mom told us she got a great deal on a stroller that was missing a front bar . . . that is, it was a great deal until she discovered the model was discontinued and she couldn't get a replacement bar from the manufacturer.

REALITY
LAYETTE

apparel are popping up everywhere, from coast to coast. Later in this chapter, we'll tell you how to find a consignment store near you. Look for the box on second-hand shopping tips nearby.

9 GARAGE/YARD SALES. Check out the box nearby for tips on how to shop garage sales like the pros.

Garage & Yard Sales
Nine Tips to Get The Best Bargains

It's an American bargain institution—the garage sale. Sure you can save money on baby clothes online or get a deal at a department store sale. But there's no comparing to the steals you can get at your neighbor's garage sale.

We love getting email from readers who've found great deals at garage sales. How about 25¢ onesies, a snowsuit for $1, barely used high chairs for $5? But getting the most out of garage sales requires some pre-planning. Here are the insider tips from our readers:

1 CHECK CRAIGSLIST FIRST. Many folks advertise their garage sales a few days before the event—zero in on the ads/posts that mention kids/baby items to keep from wasting time on sales that won't be fruitful.

2 FIRE UP THE GPS. Make sure you've mastered the Google Maps app on your phone or your car's GPS to pinpoint obscure streets and cul de sacs.

3 START EARLY. The professional bargain hunters get going at the crack of dawn. If you wait until mid-day, all the good stuff will be gone. An even better bet: if you know the family, ask if you can drop by the day before the sale. That way you have a first shot before the competition arrives. One trick: if it's a neighbor, offer to help set-up for the sale. That's a great way to get those "early bird" deals.

4 DO THE "BOX DIVE." Many garage sale hosts will just dump kids clothes into a big box, all jumbled together in different sizes, styles, etc. Figuring out how to get the best picks while three other moms are digging through the same box is a challenge. The best advice: familiarize yourself with the better name brands in this chapter and pluck out the best bets as fast as possible. Then evaluate the clothes away from the melee.

Baby Clothing

So you thought all the big-ticket items were taken care of when you bought the crib and other furniture? Ha! It's time to prepare for your baby's "layette," a French word that translated literally means "spending large sums of cash on baby clothes and other such items, as required by Federal Baby Law." But, of course, there

5 **CONCENTRATE ON "FAMILY AREAS."** A mom here in Colorado told us she found garage sales in Boulder (a college town) were mostly students getting rid of stereos, clothes and other junk. A better bet was nearby Louisville, a suburban bedroom community with lots of growing families.

6 **HAGGLE.** Prices on big-ticket items (that is, anything over $5) are usually negotiable. Another great tip we read in the newsletter *Cheapskate Monthly*: to test out products, carry a few "C" and "D" batteries with you to garage sales. Why? Some swings, bouncers and other gear use such batteries. Pop in your test batteries to make sure items are in good working order!

7 **SMALL BILLS.** Take small bills with you to sales—lots of $1's and a few $5's. Why? When negotiating over price, slowly counting out small bills makes the seller feel like they are getting more money. A wad of 20 $1's for a high chair feels like a more substantial offer than a $20 bill.

8 **DON'T BUY A USED CRIB OR CAR SEAT.** Old cribs may not meet current safety standards. It's also difficult to get replacement parts for obscure brands. Car seats are also a second-hand no-no—you can't be sure it wasn't in an accident, weakening its safety and effectiveness. And watch out for clothing with drawstrings, loose buttons or other safety hazards.

9 **BE CREATIVE.** See a great stroller but the fabric is dirty? And non-removable so you can't throw it in the washing machine? Take a cue from one dad we interviewed. He takes dirty second-hand strollers or high chairs to a car wash and blasts them with a high-pressure hose! Voila! Clean and useable items are the result. For a small investment, you can rehabilitate a dingy stroller into a showpiece.

are some creative (dare we say, sneaky?) ways of keeping your layette bills down.

At this point, you may be wondering just what does your baby need? Sure you've seen those cute ruffled dresses and sailor suits in department stores—but what does your baby *really* wear everyday?

Meet the layette, a collection of clothes and accessories that your baby will use daily. While your baby's birthday suit was free, outfitting him in something more "traditional" will cost some bucks. In fact, a recent study estimated that parents spend $13,000 on clothes for a child by the time he or she hits 18 years of age—and that sounds like a conservative estimate to us. Baby clothes translate into a $20 *billion* business for children's clothing retailers. Follow our tips, and we estimate that you'll save 20% or more on your baby's wardrobe.

Best Online Sources

Bargain Childrens Clothing

bargainchildrensclothing.com. This site carries lots of "workhorse" brands like Hanes, and OshKosh, as well as character items from Sesame Street, Thomas the Train Engine and Dora the Explorer. The site also carries higher-quality brands such Wes and Willy, Izod or Flapdoodles, at discounts of up to 85%. For example, we found a long sleeve girls coverall by New Potatoes regularly priced at $38 for only $24.90, a 31% savings. The site is a bit of a mishmash making it difficult to find the good stuff, but take your time and you'll see some really great money saving bargains. ***Rating: A-***

Chez Ami

patsyaiken.com or chezami.com. Once upon a time, independent baby stores carried a much wider selection of adorable outfits for babies. And the brand they all carried was Patsy Aiken. You can't get it from a store anymore, but thankfully Patsy still make their clothes under the name Chez Ami. And the clothes are still as wonderful as we remember. These U.S.-made clothes are all cotton with amazing embroidery and appliqué. You'll find beautiful, bright colors with fun accents. They've cut out a lot of the super dressy designs and seem to be concentrating on fun casual clothes. Prices average around $30 to $50 for the typical dress or overall. Not cheap but the quality is terrific and they put them on sale occasionally. This is a great site for grandmas looking for a cute shower gift.

Besides selling directly online, Chez Ami is also available through distributorships modeled on the old Tupperware parties. You get a group of your friends together and have a Chez Ami clothing party. Check out the web site for more details. ***Rating: A***

Forget Me Not Kids

foregetmenotkids.com. Selection at Forget Me Not Kids is amazing. You'll see brand names like Plum Pudding, Le Top, Hartstrings and Baby Lulu. We also saw shoes, baby blankets, hair bows, dress-up clothes and accessories, even diaper bags, slings and carriers for parents. While regular prices can be quite stiff, selection is great and they were offering seven pages of sale items when we visited. ***Rating: B***

Hanna Andersson

hannaandersson.com Hanna Andersson claim to fame is "Swedish quality" 100% cotton clothes. And our readers agree—they rank HA a top favorite. Unfortunately, Swedish quality is going to set you back some big American bucks. For example, a cute hooded romper was a whopping $39. At that price, it's hard to imagine buying a complete wardrobe here, no matter how cute their clothes are.

These aren't clothes you'd have your baby trash at daycare—Hanna Andersson's outfits are more suitable for weekend wear or going to Grandma's house. One note of caution: while the quality is very high, some items have difficult diaper access (or none at all). Another negative: Hanna Andersson uses "European sizing," which can be confusing. Thankfully, they are now including the age range for each size. On the plus side, we liked their web site especially the sale section—makes them a bit more reasonable. ***Rating: B-***

LL Bean

llbean.com Rugged basics are what LL Bean is known for, and that's reflected in their baby collection. Lots of fleece, flannel and fashion are what you'll find on their site. We love the bold floral prints for girls and the lumberjack plaids for boys. While the collection isn't huge, the quality is terrific. No shrink cottons top our list of decent buys at $20 for long sleeve t-shirts. Sales prices are about 15-25% off and they sell lots of cold weather items plus some gear like BOB strollers. ***Rating: B***

MiniBoden

bodenusa.com Designed in London, MiniBoden is a children's off-shoot of Boden, a terrific women's and men's clothing line. Chock full of fun patterns and great colors, we were thrilled when they added a kids line. Ok, it's not cheap ($26 t-shirt anyone?), but Boden offers many year-round sales and the children's line is sold at Nordstrom.com, where sales are common as well. Our readers think these Brits have great fashion sense and style—they aren't making the same old t-shirts and jeans. Quality is excellent as well. ***Rating: B+***

REALITY
LAYETTE

The Preemie Store

preemiestore.com Preemiestore.com is a wonderful oasis for parents of preemies. Sizes start as small as one to three lbs.! If you need clothes for the NICU like IV shirts, open sided shirts, NICU wraps and more, this is the place. But that's not all. Basic gowns and onesies as well as designer baby clothes for preemies are available at super low prices on this site. New items are called out as are christening gowns and even preemie pacifiers! The site is run by the mom of a former preemie and she really knows what parents need. We highly recommend this site for parents of preemies. ***Rating: A***

Wooden Soldier

woodensoldier.com If you really need a formal outfit for your child for a wedding or special occasion, Wooden Soldier has the most expansive selection of children's formalwear we've ever seen. Unfortunately, the prices are quite expensive—a girls' smocked corduroy dress is $78; a boy's corduroy coverall with embroidery plus shirt is $74 to $79. And those are for infant and toddler sized clothes (6 to 24 months)!

On the plus side, the quality is certainly impressive. And you won't find a bigger selection of dressy clothes around. They even offer some matching adult outfits. Wooden Soldier also continues to expand their casual offerings, which now include overalls, jumpsuits and cotton sweaters. If you've got the cash and the occasion for these clothes, they're pretty cool. But for most people, these items, even the casual clothes, are way out of range. ***Rating: B-***

Zulily

zulily.com This deal of the day site focuses on upper-end brands—sales open at 6pm Pacific and run 72 hours, although some sales are just a day. The baby and maternity section is a mix of baby/kids clothing, gear (strollers, carriers) as well as maternity and nursing clothes. The deals are impressive, but always comparison shop to make sure you are getting the best price. Example: we saw a Combi infant car seat here for $120, down from a purported list of $200. But Amazon was selling the same seat for $133. Add in $10 shipping and that Zulily "deal" was less than it looked! ***Rating: A***

What Are You Buying?

Figuring out what your baby should wear is hardly intuitive to first-time parents. We had no earthly idea what types of (and how many) clothes a newborn needed, so we did what we normally do—we went to the bookstore to do research. We found three-dozen books on "childcare and parenting"—with three-dozen different lists of items that you *must* have for your baby and without which you're a very bad parent. Speaking of guilt, we also heard from relatives, who had their own opinions as to what was best for baby.

All of this begs the question: what do you *really* need? And how much? We learned that the answer to that last, age-old question was the age-old answer, "It depends." That's right, nobody really knows. In fact, we surveyed several department stores, interviewed dozens of parents, and consulted several "experts," only to find no consensus whatsoever. So, in order to better serve humanity, we have developed THE OFFICIAL FIELDS' LIST OF ALMOST EVERY ITEM YOU NEED FOR YOUR BABY IF YOU LIVE ON PLANET EARTH. We hope this clears up the confusion. (For those living on another planet, please consult our *Baby Bargains* edition for Mars and beyond).

Feel free to now ignore those lists of "suggested layette items" provided by retail stores. Many of the "suggestions" are self-serving, to say the least.

Of course, even when you decide what and how much to buy for your baby, you still need to know what *sizes* to buy. Fortunately, we have this covered, too. First, recognize that most baby clothes come in a range of sizes rather than one specific size ("newborn to 3 months" or "3-6 months"). For first time parents buying for a newborn, *we recommend you buy "3-6 month" sizes (instead of newborn sizes)*. Why? Because the average newborn will grow out of "newborn" sizes way too fast. The exception to this rule: preemies and multiples, who tend to be on the small side. (See previous section for a great preemie website).

No matter how big or small your newborn, a smart piece of advice: keep all receipts and tags so you can exchange clothes for larger sizes—you may find you're into six-month sizes by the time your baby hits one month old! (Along the same lines, don't wash all those new baby clothes immediately. Wash just a few items for the initial few weeks. Keep all the other items in their original packaging to make returns easier).

Ever wonder how fast your baby will grow? *Babies double their birth weight by five months . . . and triple it by one year!* On average, babies grow ten inches in their first year of life. (Just an FYI: your child will average four inches of growth in her second year, then three inches a year from ages 3 to 5 and two inches a year until puberty.) Given those stats, you can understand why we don't recommend stocking up on "newborn" size clothes.

Also: remember, you can always buy more later if you need them. In fact, this is a good way to make use of those close friends and relatives who stop by and offer to "help" right after you've suffered through 36 hours of hard labor—send them to the store!

We should point out that this layette list is just to get you started. This supply should last for the first month or two of your baby's life. Also along these lines, we received a question from a mom-to-be who wondered, given these quantities, how often do we assume you'll do laundry. The answer is in the nearby box.

The "Baby Bargains" Layette

Let's talk quality when it comes to baby clothes.

First, you want clothing that doesn't shrink. Look at the washing instructions. "Cold water wash/low dryer setting" is your clue that this item has NOT been pre-shrunk. Also, do the instructions tell you to wash with "like colors?" This may be a clue that the color will run. Next check the detailing. Are the seams sewn straight? Are they reinforced, particularly on the diaper area?

Go online and check message boards for posts on different brands. On our boards (Babybargains.com), parents comment frequently on whether a brand shrinks, has plenty of diaper room, falls apart after a few washings, etc. Spend a little time online to get some intel on the best brands—and which ones to avoid.

Now, let's get to the list:

◆ **T-Shirts.** Oh sure, a t-shirt is a t-shirt, right? Not when it comes to baby t-shirts. These t-shirts could have side snaps, snaps at the

---

E-MAIL FROM THE REAL WORLD
How Much Laundry Will I Do?

Anna B. of Brooklyn, NY had a good question about baby's layette and laundry:

"You have a list of clothes a new baby needs, but you don't say how often I would need to do laundry if I go with the list. I work full time and would like to have enough for a week. Is the list too short for me?"

Our answer: there is no answer. Factors such as whether you use cloth or disposable diapers (cloth can leak more; hence more laundry) and how much your baby spits up will greatly determine the laundry load. Another factor: breast versus bottle-feeding. Bottle-fed babies have fewer poops (and hence, less laundry from possible leaks). An "average" laundry cycle with our layette list would be every two to three days, assuming breast feeding, disposable diapers and an average amount of spit-up.

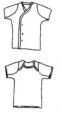

crotch (also known as infant bodysuits, Onesies, creepers) or over-the-head openings. If you have a child who is allergic to metal snaps (they leave a red ring on the skin), you might want to consider over-the-head t-shirts. (FYI: While some folks refer to Onesies as a generic item, the term Onesie is a registered trademark brand by Gerber.)

By the way, is a t-shirt an outfit or an undergarment? Answer: it's both. In the summer, you'll find Onesies with printed patterns that are intended as outfits. In the winter, most stores just sell white or pastel onesies, intended as undergarments.

HOW MANY? T-shirts usually come in packs of three. Our recommendation is to buy two packages of three (or a total of six shirts) of the side-snap variety. We also suggest buying two packs of over-the-head t-shirts. This way, if your baby does have an allergy to the snaps, you have a backup. Later you'll find the snap-at-the-crotch t-shirts to be most convenient since they don't ride up under clothes.

◆ **Gowns.** These are one-piece gowns with elastic at the bottom. They are used as sleeping garments in most cases. (We'll discuss more pros/cons of gowns later in this chapter.)

HOW MANY? This is a toss-up. If you want to experiment, go for one or two of these items. If they work well, you can always go back and get more later.

◆ **Sleepers.** This is the real workhorse of your infant's wardrobe, since babies usually sleep most of the day in the first months. Also known as stretchies, sleepers are most commonly used as pajamas for infants. They have feet, are often made of flame-retardant polyester, and snap up the front. As a side note, we've seen an increase in the numbers of cotton sleepers in recent years. Another related item: cotton long johns for baby. These are similar to sleepers, but don't have feet (and hence, may necessitate the use of socks in winter months).

One parent emailed us asking if she was supposed to dress her baby in pants, shirts, etc. or if it was OK to keep her daughter in sleepers all day long. She noted the baby was quite comfortable and happy. Of course, you can use sleepers exclusively for the first few months. We certainly did. As we've said all along, a comfortable baby is a happy parent!

HOW MANY? Because of their heavy use, we recommend parents buy at least four to eight sleepers.

◆ **Blanket Sleepers/wearable blankets.** These are heavy-weight, footed one-piece garments made of polyester. Used often in winter, blanket sleepers usually have a zipper down the front. In recent years, we've also seen quite a few fleece blanket sleepers, their key advantage being a softer fabric and a resistance to pilling.

Another option is a wearable blanket or swaddling blanket. See the previous chapter for a box on "Swaddling and Wearable Blankets." We have a few recommendations for parents who want to try one of these items. You may want to put a t-shirt on baby and then wrap her up in a swaddling blanket or wearable blanket.

HOW MANY? If you live in a cold climate or your baby is born in the winter, you may want to purchase two to four of these items. As an alternative to buying blanket sleepers, you could put a t-shirt on underneath a sleeper or stretchie for extra warmth.

◆ **Coveralls.** One-piece play outfits, coveralls (also known as rompers) are usually cotton or cotton/poly blends. Small sizes (under 6 months) may have feet, while larger sizes don't.

HOW MANY? Since these are really play clothes and small infants don't do a lot of playing, we recommend you only buy two to four coveralls for babies less than four months of age. However, if your child will be going into daycare at an early age, you may need to start with four to six coveralls.

◆ **Booties/socks.** These are necessary for outfits that don't have feet (like gowns and coveralls). As your child gets older (at about six months), look for the kind of socks that have rubber skids on the bottom (they keep baby from slipping when learning to walk).

HOW MANY? Three to four pairs are all you'll need at first, since baby will probably be dressed in footed sleepers most of the time.

◆ **Sweaters.** HOW MANY? Most parents will find one sweater is plenty (they're nice for holiday picture sessions). Avoid all-white sweaters for obvious reasons!

◆ **Hats.** Believe it or not, you'll still want a light cap for your baby in the early months of life, even if you live in a hot climate. Babies lose a large amount of heat from their heads, so protecting them with a cap or bonnet is a good idea. And don't expect to go out for a walk in the park without the baby's sun hat either.

HOW MANY? A couple of hats would be a good idea—sun hats in summer, warmer caps for winter. We like the safari-style hats best (they have flaps to protect the ears and neck).

◆ **Snowsuit/bunting.** Similar to the type of fabric used for blanket sleepers, buntings also have hoods and covers for the hands. Most buntings are like a sack and don't have leg openings, while snowsuits do. Both versions usually have zippered fronts.

FYI: Snowsuits and buntings should NOT be worn by infants when they ride in a car seat. Why? Thick fabric on these items can compress in an accident, compromising the infant's safety in the seat. So how can you keep your baby warm in an infant car seat? There are car seat covers that fit over the top of the car seat to keep baby warm. Cozy Cover (Cozy-Cover.com, $20), makes a variety of styles and fabrics to protect your child from the cold or the sun.

Clothing: What you need, when

If you're new to this baby thing, you may be wondering how to pair the right clothing with your baby's developmental stage (if you're back for another round, think of this as a refresher). Here's a little primer on ages and stages.

◆ *0-3 months:* Newborns aren't even lifting their heads and they aren't able to do much besides eat, sleep and poop. Stick with sleepers, wearable blankets, and nightgowns for these guys. They don't need overalls or shirts and pants. Look for items sized by weight if possible since 0-3 month sizes can be all over the board.

◆ *3-6 months:* By the end of this stage your little one will be rolling over, sitting up and sleeping somewhat less. Still need those sleepers, but you're probably going to expand the wardrobe to include a few more play clothes. Two new items you will need now: bibs and socks. Depending on your baby's growth, you may find that you're buying nine and 12-month sizes.

◆ *6-12 months:* Finally, your baby is crawling, standing, maybe even cruising. At the end of a year she's likely tried those first tentative steps! Play clothes are a layette mainstay during these months. You'll also need good, no-skid socks that stay on (or very flexible shoes). You may find you're buying into the 18-month sizes.

clothes

How many? Only buy one of these if you live in a climate where you need it. Even with a Colorado winter, we got away with layering clothes on our baby, then wrapping him in a blanket for the walk out to a warmed-up car. If you live in a city without a car, you might need two or three snowsuits for those stroller rides to the market.

◆ **Kimonos.** Just like the adult version. Some are zippered sacks with a hood and terry-cloth lining. You use them after a bath.
How many? Are you kidding? What a joke! These items are one of our "wastes of money." We recommend you pass on the kimonos and instead invest in good quality towels.

 ◆ **Saque Sets.** Two-piece outfits with a shirt and diaper cover.
How many? Forget buying these as well.

 ◆ **Bibs.** These come in two versions, believe it or not. The little, tiny bibs are for the baby that occasionally drools. The larger versions are used when you begin feeding her solid foods (at about six months). Don't expect to be able to use the drool bibs later for feedings, unless you plan to change her carrot-stained outfit frequently.
How many? Skip the drool bibs (we'll discuss why later in this chapter under Wastes of Money). The exception: if your baby really can't keep dry because he's drooling the equivalent of a bathtub full every day, consider buying a few of these. When baby starts eating solid foods, you'll need at least three or four large bibs. One option: plastic bibs for feeding so you can just sponge them off after a meal.

 ◆ **Washcloths and Hooded Towels.** OK, so these aren't actually clothes, but baby washcloths and hooded towels are a necessity. Why? Because they are small and easier to use . . . plus they're softer than adult towels and washcloths.
How many? At first, you'll probably need only three sets of towels and washcloths (you get one of each per set). But as baby gets older and dirtier, invest in a few more washcloths to spot clean during the day.

 ◆ **Receiving Blankets.** You'll need these small, cotton blankets for all kinds of uses: to swaddle the baby, as a play quilt, or even for an extra layer of warmth on a cold day.
How many? We believe you can never have too many of these blankets, but since you'll probably get a few as gifts, you'll only

need to buy two or three yourself. A total of seven to eight is probably optimal.

What about the future? While our layette list only addresses clothes to buy for a newborn, you will want to plan for your child's future wardrobe as well. For today's baby, clothes come in two categories: play clothes (to be used in daycare situations) and dress-up clothes. Later in this chapter, we'll discuss more money-saving tips and list several recommended brands of play and dress-up clothes.

 ## More Money Buys You . . .

Even the biggest discounters now offer good quality clothing. But with more money you tend to get heavier weight cottons, nicer fasteners, better quality embellishments and more generous sizing. At some point, however, considering how fast your little one is growing, it's a waste to spend top dollar on baby clothes!

 ## Safe & Sound

Should your baby's sleepwear (that is, the items he'll wear almost non-stop for the first several months of life) be flame retardant? What the heck does "flame retardant" mean anyway?

According to the Consumer Product Safety Commission (CPSC), items made of flame retardant fabric will not burn under a direct flame. Huh? Doesn't "flame retardant" mean it won't burn at all? No—that's a common myth among parents who think such clothes are a Superman-style second skin that will protect baby against any and all fire hazards.

Prior to 1996, the CPSC mandated that an item labeled as sleepwear be made of "flame retardant fabric." More often than not, that meant polyester because the alternative (untreated cotton fabric) DOES burn under direct flame. While there were a few companies that made cotton sleepwear chemically treated to be fire retardant, the prices of such items were so high that the de facto standard for children's sleepwear for many years was polyester.

Then the government changed its mind. The CPSC noticed that many parents were rebelling against the rules and putting their babies in all-cotton items at bedtime. After an investigation, the CPSC revised the rules to more closely fit reality.

First, pajamas for babies nine months and under were totally exempt from the flame-retardant rules. Why? Since these babies

One Size Does Not Fit All

A six month-size t-shirt is a six-month-size t-shirt, right? Wrong. For some reason, baby clothing companies have yet to synchronize their watches when it comes to sizes. Hence, a clothing item that says "six-month size" from one manufacturer can be just the same dimensions as a "twelve-month size" from another. All this begs the question: how can you avoid wide-spread confusion? First, open packages to check out actual dimensions. Take your baby along and hold items up to her to gauge whether they'd fit. Second, note whether items are pre-shrunk—you'll probably have to ask (if not, allow for shrinkage). Third, don't key on length from head to foot. Instead, focus on the length from neck to crotch—a common problem is items that seem roomy but are too tight in the crotch. Finally, forget age ranges and pay more attention to labels that specify an infant's size in weight and height, which are much more accurate. To show how widely sizing can vary, check out the following chart. We compared "six-month" t-shirts from six major clothing makers (sold at Babies R Us and Amazon.com) plus two popular web sites, Hanna Andersson, and Baby Gap. Here's what these six-month t-shirts really translated to in terms of a baby's weight and height:

What a six month t-shirt really means

MAKER	WEIGHT	HEIGHT
BABY GAP	17-22 LBS.	27-29"
CARTER'S/OSHKOSH	12.5-16.5 LBS.	24-26.5"
GYMBOREE	17-22 LBS.	25-29"
HANNA ANDERSSON	14-21 LBS.	26-30"
GERBER	16-20 LBS.	26-28"
LITTLE ME	12-16 LBS.	24-27"
LUVABLE FRIENDS	16.5-20.5 LBS.	26.5-28.5"
SPASILK	12-18 LBS.	24-26.5"

Here's another secret from the baby clothing trade: the more expensive the brand, the more roomy the clothes. Conversely, cheap items usually have the skimpiest sizing. What about the old wives' tale that you should just double your baby's age to find the right size (that is, buying twelve-month clothes for a six-month old?). That's bogus—as you can see, sizing is so all over the board that this rule just doesn't work.

aren't mobile, the odds they'll come in contact with a fire hazard that would catch their clothes on fire is slim. What if the whole house catches fire? Well, the smoke is much more dangerous than the flames—hence, a good smoke detector in the nursery and every other major room of your house is a much better investment than fire-retardant clothes.

What about sleepwear for older babies? Well, the government admits that "close-fitting" all-cotton items don't pose a risk either. Only flowing nightgowns or pajamas that are loose fitting must meet the flame retardant rules today.

If you still want to go with "flame retardant" baby items, there are a couple of options beyond plain polyester. Look for fleece PJ's—Old Navy cells fleece sleepers for $16.50. There use to be a few treated cotton pajama options on the market, but now that the rules have changed to allow close fitting, untreated cotton pajamas, we don't see the treated ones anymore.

Finally, one last myth to dispel on this topic: does washing flame-retardant clothing reduce its ability to retard flames? Nope—fabrics like polyester are *naturally* flame retardant (that is, there is no magic chemical they've been doused with that can wash out in the laundry).

There is one exception to the laundry rule: if you do choose to buy flame-retardant clothing, be sure to avoid washing such clothing in soap flakes. Soap flakes actually add a flammable chemical residue to clothes. And so do dryer sheets and liquid fabric softeners. For more advice on washing baby clothes, see the discussion in the next section.

What about other safety hazards with children's clothing? Here are a few more to consider:

◆ *Check for loose threads.* These could become a choking hazard, or the threads could wrap around fingers or toes, cutting off circulation.

◆ *Be careful about appliqués.* "Heat-welded" plastic appliqués on clothes can come off and cause choking. Poorly sewn appliqués can also be a hazard as the thread can unravel. Look for appliqués that have thick layers of thread attaching them to the clothing.

◆ *Avoid outfits with easy-to-detach, decorative buttons or bows—these may also be a choking hazard.* If you have any doubts, cut the decorations off.

◆ *Watch out for drawstrings.* In recent years, most manufacturers have voluntarily eliminated such drawstrings. But if you get hand-me-downs or buy second-hand clothes, be sure to remove any strings. We're amazed at the continued use of drawstrings by some manufacturers of new children's clothing. We get frequent alerts from the Consumer Product Safety Commission (CPSC) about recalls of new items with drawstrings.

◆ **Lead in jewelry.** Cheap jewelry from China has consistently turned up on the CPSC's recall list. These items are sold in mall stores and from vending machines. Best bet: never purchase jewelry for infants and toddlers. Items like necklaces are likely to end up in their mouths and can be a potential lead and choking hazard. If you choose to pierce your child's ears, stick with high-quality hypoallergenic metals like gold.

Laundry Conundrum: What's Best for Baby's Clothes?

Ever since Dr. Spock's best-selling tome on taking care of baby came out in 1946, most parenting authors have advised washing baby's clothes and linens in mild soap or detergents. The implication is that baby's skin is delicate and could be irritated by harsh chemicals.

So should baby's clothes be washed only in expensive detergents like Dreft? The answer is a definite no. But we do recommend you choose a dye-free, fragrance-free detergent like **All Free & Clear**, which, by the way, is HALF the cost of Dreft.

More advice: do not use fabric softeners on any sleepwear. Most sleepwear is polyester, which is a flame retardant material. However, fabric softeners will leave a residue on polyester and that residue is flammable.

What if your child develops eczema or a reaction to your detergent? Consider cleaning your baby's clothes with a natural pure soap product. One such brand: **Cal-Ben's Seafoam Liquid** laundry soap (CalBenPureSoap.com). Unfortunately, this soap does NOT clean as well as detergent, especially in the laundry, so be prepared. And it's expensive: $28 for one gallon of liquid laundry detergent, about 20% more expensive than Dreft.

Soap flakes are another laundry option. Ivory Snow and Dreft no longer make soap flakes so you have to buy them online. One brand, **Dri-Pak,** is available at Soap-Flakes.com. Soap flakes can also leave a residue on flame retardant clothing—don't use it for sleepwear.

Pure soap products are hard to find and expensive, although some natural food stores carry these brands as well. What about "natural" detergents found in health food stores? Read the labels carefully before you buy since some items contain detergents and others may have allergenic fruit or vegetable ingredients.

Smart Shopper Tips

Smart Shopper Tip
Tips and Tricks to Get the Best Quality

"I've received several outfits from friends for my daughter, but I'm not sure she'll like all the scratchy lace and the poly/cotton blends. What should she wear, and what can I buy that will last through dozens of washings?"

Generally, we recommend dressing your child for comfort. At the same time, you need clothes that can withstand frequent washings. With this in mind, here are our suggestions for baby clothing:

1 SEE WHAT YOUR BABY LIKES BEFORE INVESTING IN MANY GARMENTS. Don't spend $90 on fancy sweaters, only to find baby prefers cotton Onesies.

2 WE GENERALLY RECOMMEND 100% COTTON CLOTHING. Babies are most comfortable in clothing that breathes.

3 IF YOUR CHILD DEVELOPS A RED, ITCHY RASH, IT COULD BE AN ALLERGY. Culprits could include metal snaps on a t-shirt, zippers or even the ink on tagless labels. One idea: consider alternatives such as shirts that have ties or that pull over the head. Stick with clothes that have plastic snaps and zippers.

4 IN GENERAL, BETTER-MADE CLOTHES WILL HAVE THEIR SNAPS ON A REINFORCED FABRIC BAND. Snaps attached directly to the body of the fabric may tear the garment or rip off.

5 IF YOU'RE BUYING 100% COTTON CLOTHES, MAKE SURE THEY'RE PRE-SHRUNK. Some stores, like Gymboree (see review later in this chapter), pre-wash their clothes to prevent shrinkage. With other brands, it's hard to tell. Our advice: read the label. If it says, "wash in cold water" or " tumble dry low," assume the garment will shrink (and hence buy a larger size). On the other hand, care instructions that advise "wash in warm water and tumble dry" usually indicate that the garment is already preshrunk.

6 GO FOR OUTFITS WITH SNAPS AND ZIPPERS ON BOTH LEGS, NOT JUST ONE. Dual-leg snaps or zippers make it much easier to change a diaper. Always check a garment for diaper accessibility—some brands actually have no snaps or zippers, meaning you would have to completely undress your baby for a diaper change!

Another pet peeve: garments that have snaps up the back also make diaper changes a big hassle.

7 BE AWARE THAT EACH COMPANY HAS ITS OWN WARPED IDEA ABOUT HOW TO SIZE BABY CLOTHES. See the box "One Size Does Not Fit All" earlier in this chapter for more details.

8 BEWARE OF APPLIQUES. Some appliqué work can be quite scratchy on the inside of the outfit (it rubs against baby's skin). Feel the inside of the outfit before you buy to make sure it's soft. Some manufacturers will use additional fabric between the appliqué and baby's skin.

9 KEEP THE TAGS AND RECEIPTS. A reader emailed us her strategy for dealing with baby clothes that shrink: until she has a chance to wash the item, she keeps all packaging, tags and receipts. If it shrinks, she returns it immediately.

Wastes of Money

Waste of Money #1
Clothing that Leads to Diaper Changing Gymnastics
"My aunt sent me an adorable outfit for my little girl. The only problem: it snaps up the back making diaper changes a real pain. In fact, I don't dress her in it often because it's so inconvenient. Shouldn't clothing like this be outlawed?"

It's pretty obvious that some designers of baby clothing have never had children of their own. What else could explain outfits that snap up the back, have super tiny head, leg and arm openings, and snaps in inconvenient places (or worse, no snaps at all)? One mother we spoke with was furious about outfits that have snaps only down one leg, requiring her baby to be a contortionist to get into and out of the outfit.

Our advice: stay away from outfits that don't have easy access to the diaper. Look instead for snaps or zippers down the front of the outfit or on the crotch. If your baby doesn't like having things pulled over his head, look for shirts with wide, stretchie necklines.

Waste of Money #2
The Fuzz Factor
"My friend's daughter has several outfits that aren't very old but are already pilling and fuzzing. They look awful and my friend is thinking of throwing them out. What causes this?"

Your friend has managed to have a close encounter with that miracle fabric known as polyester. Synthetics such as polyester will often pill or fuzz after washing, making your baby look a little rag-tag. Of course, this is less of a concern with sleepwear—the flame retardancy of polyester fabric outweighs the garment's appearance.

However, when you're talking about a play outfit, we recommend sticking to all-cotton clothes. They wash better, usually last longer, and generally look nicer—not to mention they feel better to your baby. Cotton allergies are rare, unlike sensitivities to the chemicals used to make synthetic fabrics. You will pay more for all-cotton clothing, but in this case, the extra expense is worth it. Remember, just because you find the cheapest price on a polyester outfit doesn't mean you're getting a bargain. The best deal is not wasting money on outfits that you have to throw away after two washings.

If you get polyester outfits as gifts, here's a laundry tip: wash the items inside out. That helps lessen pilling/fuzzing. And some polyester items are better than others—polar fleece sweatshirts and pajamas are still made of polyester, but are softer and more durable.

Waste of Money #3
Do I Really Need These?

"My mother bought me a zillion gowns before my baby was born, and I haven't used a single one. What the heck are they for?"

"The list of layette items recommended by my local department store includes something called a saque set. I've never seen one, and no one seems to know what it is. Do I really need one?"

"A bath robe with matching towel and washcloth seems like a neat baby gift for my pregnant friend. But another friend told me it probably wouldn't get used. What do you think?"

All of these items come under the heading "Do I Really Need These?" Heck, we didn't even know what some of these were when we were shopping for our baby's layette. For example, what in the world is a saque set? Well, it turns out it's just a two-piece outfit with a shirt and diaper cover. Although they sound rather benign, saque sets are a waste of money. Whenever you pick up a baby under the arms, it's a sure bet her clothes will ride up. In order to avoid having to constantly pull down the baby's shirt, most parents find they use one-piece garments much more often than two-piece ones.

As for gowns, the jury is still out on whether these items are useful. We thought they were a waste of money, but a parent we interviewed did mention that she used the gowns when her baby had colic (that persistent crying condition; see our other book *Baby 411* for a discussion). She believed that the extra room in the gown made her baby more comfortable. Still others praise gowns for their easy access to diapers, making changes easy, especially in the middle of the night. Finally, parents in hot climates say gowns keep their infants more comfortable. So, you can see there's a wide range of opinions on this item.

There is no question in our minds about the usefulness of a baby bathrobe, however. Don't buy it. For a baby who will only wear it for a few minutes after a bath, it seems like the quintessential waste of your money (we saw monogrammed options for a whopping $90!). Instead, invest in some good quality towels and washcloths and forget those cute (but useless) kimonos.

Waste of Money #4
Covering Up Those Little Piggies

"I was looking at baby shoes the other day and I saw a $60 pair of Nike Jordan Retro sneakers! This is highway robbery! I can't believe babies' shoes are so expensive. Are they worth it?"

Developmentally, babies don't need shoes until after they become quite proficient at walking. In fact, it's better for their muscle development to go barefoot or wear socks. While those expensive Merrells might look cute, they're really a waste of time and money. Of course, at some point, your baby will need some shoes. See the box nearby for our tips on how to buy babies' first shoes.

Waste of Money #5
To Drool or Not to Drool

"I received a few bibs from my mother-in-law as gifts. I know my baby won't need them until she's at least four to six months old when I start feeding her solids. Plus, they seem so small!"

What you actually received was a supply of *drool* bibs. Drool bibs are tiny bibs intended for small infants who drool all over everything. Or infants who spit-up frequently. Our opinion: they're pretty useless—they're too small to catch much drool or spit-up.

When you do buy bibs, stay away from the ones that tie. Bibs that snap or have Velcro are much easier to get on and off. Another good bet: bibs that go on over the head (and have no snaps or Velcro). Why? Older babies can't pull them off by themselves.

Stay away from the super-size vinyl bibs that cover the arms, since babies who wear them can get too hot and sweaty. However, we do recommend you buy a few regular-style vinyl bibs for travel. You can wash them off much more easily than the standard terry-cloth bibs. As for sources of bibs, many of the catalogs we review in this book carry such items.

Money Saving Secrets

1 **REMEMBER THESE TWO STORES: OLD NAVY AND THE CHILDREN'S PLACE.** Old Navy (oldnavy.com) is the hip, discount offshoot of the Gap (gap.com) with 1000+ stores in the U.S. and Canada. Readers rave about the buys they find at Old Navy (sample: "adorable" 100% cotton Onesies for just $25 per 3-pack; gripper socks, three pair for $6), although most admit the selection is lim-

Baby Needs a New Pair of Shoes

As your baby gets older, you may find she's kicking off her socks every five minutes. And at some point she's going to start standing, crawling and even walking. While we suggest waiting to buy shoes until walking is firmly established, there will come a day when you will need to buy that first set of shoes. Here are some suggestions:

First, look for shoes that have the most flexible soles. You'll also want fabrics that breath and stretch, like canvas and leather—stay away from vinyl shoes. The best brands we found were recommended by readers. Reader Teri D. wrote us about Canada's **Robeez** (robeez.com, now a division of Stride Rite). "They are the most AWESOME shoes—I highly recommend them," she said in an email. And Teri wasn't the only one who loves them. Our email has been blitzed by fans. Robeez are made of leather, have soft, skid-resistant soles and are machine washable. They start at $24 for a basic pair. Another reader recommended New Zealand-made **Bobux** shoes ($29, bobuxusa.com). These cute leather soft soles "do the trick by staying on extremely well," according to a reader. Finally, we also like **PediPeds** (pedipeds.com). The soft-soled shoes are hand stitched and made of leather. They are sized from 0 to five years and start at $35.

What about shoes for one or two year olds? We've found great deals at Target, where a wide selection of sizes and offerings was impressive. Another good source: Gap Kids/Baby Gap. Their affordable line of sneakers are very good quality. Parents have also told us they've had success with Babies R Us' in-house brand; others like Stride Rite shoes, which are often on sale at department stores. Many of the sites we list in the Best Online Sources earlier in this chapter sell shoes as well.

ited. The options change rapidly and Old Navy's sales and clearance racks are "bargain heaven," say our spies. An insider tip to Old Navy and Gap Kids: the stores change out their merchandise every six weeks, moving the "old" stuff to the clearance racks rather quickly. Ask your local Old Navy or Gap Kids which day they do their mark-downs (typically it is Tuesday night, effective Wednesday).

Here's another tip for folks who shop Old Navy or the Gap regularly: check to see if your recent purchases have been marked down. You may be able to get a refund if items you've bought are marked down even more. One reader emailed us her great deal: "Last month I found a hooded sweatshirt for baby on clearance. It was originally $15 marked down to $10.50. The next week, I went back and the same sweatshirt had been marked down from $10.50 to $1.99. So they refunded me $8.60!" Both Old Navy and the Gap allow you a price adjustment within 14 days of purchase. You don't have to bring the clothes back, just your receipt.

A Gap employee emailed us the inside scoop on their markdowns. She told us that prices ending in $.97 are the lowest price you'll see on the markdown rack. After 14 days at the $.97 price, the stores have the authority to cut the price in half to "kill" the item. Finally, if you have a Gap credit card, you can get an additional 10% off everything on the first Tuesday of every month. And our source says don't forget to take the register surveys—they'll save you 10% as well.

The Children's Place (childrensplace.com) has over 1000 stores in the U.S. and Canada. They're about as ubiquitous as Old Navy, and the prices are just as good. They offer their clothing in sizes newborn to 4T. One reader wrote: "I found that this chain has really great looking and durable clothes for extremely reasonable prices." She did note that sizes run a bit small, so buy up a size. An example of their offerings: we saw a striped girl's cardigan for a mere $19.95. If you order online, the site offers free shipping plus you can make returns at their stores.

2 WAIT UNTIL AFTER SHOWERS AND PARTIES TO PURCHASE CLOTHES. Clothing is a popular gift item—you may not need to buy much yourself.

3 STICK WITH BASICS—T-SHIRTS, SLEEPERS, CAPS, SOCKS AND BLANKETS. For the first month or more, that's all you need since you won't be taking Junior to the opera.

4 SALES! The baby area in most department stores is definitely SALE LAND. At one chain we researched, the baby section has at least some items that are on sale every week! Big baby sales occur throughout the year, but especially in January. You can often snag bargains at up to 50% off the retail price. Another tip: consider buying for the future during end-of-season sales. If you're pregnant during the fall, for example, shop the end-of-summer sales for next summer's baby clothes. Hint: our research shows the sale prices at department stores are often better deals than the "discounted" prices you see at outlets.

5 CHOOSE QUALITY OVER LOW PRICE FOR PLAYCLOTHES AND BASICS. Sure that polyester outfit is 20% cheaper than the cotton alternative. HOWEVER, beware of the revenge of the washing machine! You don't realize how many times you'll be doing laundry—that play outfit may get washed every couple of days. Cheap polyester clothes pill or fuzz up after just a few washings—making you more likely to chuck them. Quality clothes have longer lives, making them less expensive over time.

6 FOR SLEEPWEAR, TRY THE AFFORDABLE BRANDS. Let's get real here: babies pee and poop in their sleepers. Hence, fancy designer brands are a money-waster. A friend of ours who lives in Texas uses affordable all-cotton Onesies as sleepwear in the hot summer months. For the winter here in Colorado, we use thermal underwear, which we've found for as little as $15 in Target.

7 CAN'T RETURN IT? Did you get gifts of clothing you don't want but can't return? Consign it at a local thrift store. We took a basketful of clothes that we couldn't use or didn't like and placed them on consignment. We turned these duplicates into $40 cash.

8 SPEAKING OF CONSIGNMENT STORES, HERE IS A WONDERFUL WAY TO SAVE MONEY: Buy barely used, consigned clothing for your baby. We found outfits ranging from $5 to $7 from high quality designers like Alexis. How can you find a consignment or thrift shop in your area specializing in high-quality children's clothes? Besides a quick Google or Yelp search, check out web sites like the National Association of Resale & Thrift Shops (narts.com, click on the shopping guide icon). Here are two tips for getting the best bargains at second-hand stores: First, shop the resale stores in the richest part of town. Why? They are most likely to stock the best brands with steep discounts off retail prices. Such stores also have clothes with the least wear (we guess rich kids have so many clothes they don't have time to wear them all out)! Second: ask the consignment store which day is best to shop. Some stores accept new consignments on certain days; others tell us that days like Tuesday and Wednesday offer the best selection of newly consigned items.

9 **CHECK OUT DISCOUNTERS.** In the past, discount stores like Target and Walmart typically carried cheap baby clothes that were mostly polyester. Well, there's good news for bargain shoppers: in recent years, these chains have upgraded their offerings, adding more all-cotton clothes and even some brand names.

For basic items like t-shirts and play clothes that will be trashed at day care, these stores are good bets. Walmart sure impressed one of our readers: "I spent $25 for a baby bathing suit in a specialty store, and for a little over twice that (about $60) I bought my daughter's entire summer wardrobe at Walmart—shorts, t-shirts, leggings, Capri pants, overalls and matching socks. Some of the pieces were as low as $2.88." And don't forget other discounters like Marshalls, TJ Maxx and Ross. Bargain tip: ask the manager when they get in new shipments—that's when selection is best.

By the way, Carter's makes Child of Mine brand clothing sold at Walmart and Just One You at Target.

10 **WAREHOUSE CLUBS.** Warehouse clubs like Sam's, BJ's and Costco carry baby clothes at prices far below retail. On a recent visit to Costco we saw Carter's fleece sleepers for only $7.29. All-cotton play clothes were a mere $13 while all-cotton pajamas (2T-10) were $12. Even baby Halloween costumes and kids outerwear (raincoats, fleece jackets) are terrific seasonal deals.

11 **DON'T FORGET ABOUT CHARITY SALES.** Readers tell us they've found great deals on baby clothes and equipment at church-sponsored charity sales. Essentially, these sales are like large garage/yard sales where multiple families donate kids' items as a fund-raiser for a church or other charity.

Outlets

Here's a round up of our favorite outlet stores for baby and kids clothes. Remember: outlet locations open and close frequently—check their web sites or OutletBound.com for up-to-date information on locations.

CARTER'S
Locations: Over 150 outlets.

It shows you how widespread the outlet craze is when you realize that Carter's has over 150 outlets in the U.S. That's right, 150. If you don't have one near you, you probably live in Bolivia.

We visited a Carter's outlet and found a huge selection of infant clothes, bedding, and accessories. Prices were generally marked

50% off retail although sharp-eyed readers noted that department store sale prices are often just as good.

The best deals, however, are at the outlet's yearly clearance sale in January when they knock an additional 25% to 30% off their already discounted prices. A store manager at the Carter's outlet we visited said that they also have two other sales: back-to-school and a "pajama sale." In the past, we noted that all the goods in their outlet stores were first quality. However, they have added a couple "seconds" racks (called "Oops" racks) in most of their stores with flawed merchandise. Our readers report that most seconds have only minor problems and the savings are worth it.

GAP

Locations: Over 150 outlets.

Gap sells such great play clothes, you probably find yourself buying them at full retail sometimes. But now you don't have to. With so many outlet stores, you can buy your baby those cute little mini skinny jeans, Fair Isle sweaters and itty bitty swim trunks at drastically reduced prices. And check out the $1.99 rack. Readers tell us these are amazing deals. Some parents complain that the outlet stores are a bit trashed, but pants for $4 and shirts for a dollar make it worth the mess.

HANNA ANDERSSON

Outlets Stores: Lake Oswego, OR; Michigan City, IN; Kittery, ME; Woodinville, WA; Williamsburg; VA, Wrentham, MA; Clinton, CT

If you like Hanna Anderson's catalog, you'll love their outlet stores, which feature overstocks, returned items and factory seconds. For more information on Hanna Anderson, see Best Online Sources earlier in this chapter.

HARTSTRINGS

Locations: 34 outlets

Hartstrings' 34 outlet stores specialize in first-quality apparel for infants, boys, and girls and even have some mother/child outfits. Infant sizes range from three months to 24 months; savings up to 50%.

OSHKOSH

Locations: 137 outlets.

OshKosh, the maker of all those cute little overalls worn by just about every kid, sells their clothes direct at over 140 outlet stores.

With prices that are 30% to 70% off retail, buying these play clothes staples is even easier on the pocketbook. They split the store up by gender, as well as by size. Infant and toddler clothes are usually in the back of the store.

The outlet also carries OshKosh shoes, socks, hats, and even stuffed bears dressed in overalls and engineer hats. Some clothes are irregulars, so inspect the garments carefully before you buy.

The Name Game: Our Picks for the Best Brands

Walk into any department store and you'll see a blizzard of brand names for baby clothes. Which ones stand up to frequent washings? Which ones have snaps that stay snapped? Which are a good value for the dollar? We asked our readers to divide their favorite clothing brands/stores into three categories: best bets, good but not great and skip it.

The Best Bets tend to be clothes that were not only stylish but also held up in the wash. The fabric was usually softer and pilled less. Customer service also comes into play with the best brands. Hanna Andersson is a great example of a company that bends over backwards for their customers. Gymboree, on the other hand, seems to be less satisfactory for many parents, souring them on the brand. Keep in mind, some brands are pricey, so look for sales and second hand deals. Or just point Grandma to these sites!

Good but not Great clothes were pretty good, just not as soft or as stylish as Best Bets. The Skip-It brands were most likely the poorest quality: they shrunk in the wash, pilled up or fell apart. Inconsistent sizing was also a problem with brands like Babies R Us' Koala Kids.

Some of these brands sell direct; others just through retailers.

Best Bets

BABY GAP	(800) GAP-STYLE	BABYGAP.COM
BABY LULU		BABYLULU.COM
CARTER'S	(770) 961-8722	CARTERS.COM
CHEZ AMI		CHEZAMI.COM
COZY TOES		COZYTOESDESIGNSTUDIO.COM
FIRST IMPRESSIONS		MACYS.COM
FLAP HAPPY	(800) 234-3527	FLAPHAPPY.COM
FUNTASIA! TOO	(214) 634-7770	FUNTASIATOO.COM
H & M		HM.COM
HANNA ANDERSSON		HANNAANDERSSON.COM

HARTSTRINGS/KITESTRINGS	(212) 868-0950	HARTSTRINGS.COM
JANIE AND JACK		JANIEANDJACK.COM
KISSY KISSY		KISSYKISSYONLINE.COM
LITTLE ME	(800) 533-5497	LITTLEME.COM
LL BEAN		LLBEAN.COM
MINIBODEN		MINIBODEN.COM
MULBERRIBUSH (TUMBLEWEED TOO)		MULBERRIBUSH.COM
OLD NAVY		OLDNAVY.COM
OSHKOSH B'GOSH	(800) 692-4674	OSHKOSHBGOSH.COM
PUMPKIN PATCH		PUMPKINPATCHUSA.COM
SARAH'S PRINTS	(888) 477-4687	SARASPRINTS.COM
TEA COLLECTION		TEACOLLECTION.COM
WES & WILLY		WESANDWILLY.COM
ZUTANO		ZUTANO.COM

Good But Not Great

CHILDREN'S PLACE	CHILDRENSPLACE.COM
GOOD LAD OF PHILADELPHIA	GOODLAD.COM
GYMBOREE	GYMBOREE.COM
LE TOP	LETOP-USA.COM
TARGET (LITTLE ME, CARTER'S JUST ONE YOU, HALO, CIRCO)	TARGET.COM
WALMART (FADED GLORY, CARTER'S CHILD OF MINE)	WALMART.COM

Skip It: GERBER, HANES, KOALA KIDS (BABIES R US), DISNEY, CARTER'S JUST ONE YEAR AT TARGET, GEORGE BY WALMART

Our Picks: Brand Recommendations

What clothing brands are best? Well, there is no one correct answer. An outfit that's perfect for day care (that is, to be trashed in Junior's first painting experiment) is different from an outfit for a weekend outing with friends. And dress-up occasions may require an entirely different set of clothing criteria. Hence, we've divided our clothing brand recommendations into three areas: good (day care), better (weekend wear) and best (special occasions). While some brands make items in two or even three categories, here's how we see it:

Good. For everyday comfort (and day-care situations), basic brands like Carter's, Little Me, and OshKosh are your best bets. We also like the basics (when on sale) at Baby Gap (Gap Kids) for day-care wardrobes. For great price to value, take a look at Old Navy and Target.

Better. What if you have a miniature golf outing planned with friends? Or a visit to Grandma's house? The brands of better-made casual wear we like best include Baby Gap, Flapdoodles, and Gymboree. Also recommended: Jake and Me, MulberriBush, and Wes and Willy. For online sites, we like the clothes in Hanna Andersson and MiniBoden as good brands, especially on sale.

Best. Holidays and other special occasions call for special outfits. We like Chez Ami, and the dressier items at Baby Gap. Of course, department stores are great sources for these outfits, as are consignment shops. As for catalogs, check out Wooden Soldier.

Diapers

The great diaper debate still rages on: should you use cloth or disposable? On one side are environmentalists, who argue cloth is better for the planet. On the other hand, those disposable diapers are darn convenient.

Considering the average baby will go through 2300 diaper changes in the first year of life, this isn't a moot issue—you'll be dealing with diapers until your baby is three or four years old (the average girl potty trains at 35 months; boys at 39 months). Yes, you read that last sentence right . . . you will be diapering for the next 35 to 39 MONTHS.

Now, in this section, we've decided NOT to rehash all the environmental arguments pro or con for cloth versus disposable. Fire up your web browser and you'll find plenty of diaper debate on parenting sites like BabyCenter.com or ParentsPlace.com. Instead, we'll focus here on the FINANCIAL and PRACTICAL impacts of your decision.

Let's look at each option:

Cloth. Prior to the 1960's, this was the only diaper option available to parents. Fans of cloth diapering claim that babies experienced less diaper rash and toilet trained faster. From a practical point of view, cloth diapers have improved in design over the years, offering more absorbency and fewer leaks. They aren't perfect, but the advent of diaper covers (no more plastic pants) has helped as well.

Another practical point: laundry. You've got to decide if you will use a cloth diaper service or launder at home. Obviously, the latter requires more effort on your part. We'll have laundry tips for cloth diapers later in this chapter. Meanwhile, we'll discuss the financial costs of cloth in general at the end of this section.

Final practical point about cloth: most day care centers don't allow them. This may be a sanitation requirement governed by state day care regulators and not a negotiating point. Check with local day care centers or your state board.

Disposables. Disposable diapers were first introduced in 1961 and now hold an overwhelming lead over cloth—about 95% of all households that have kids in diapers use disposables. Today's diapers have super-absorbent gels that lower the number of needed diaper changes, especially at night (which helps baby sleep through the night sooner). Even many parents who swear cloth diapers are best often use disposables at night. The downside? All that super-absorbency means babies are in no rush to potty train—they simply don't feel as wet or uncomfortable as babies in cloth diapers.

The jury on diaper rash is still out—disposable diaper users generally don't experience any more diaper rash than cloth diaper users.

Besides the eco-arguments about disposables, there is one other disadvantage—higher trash costs. In many communities, the more trash you put out, the higher the bill.

The financial bottom line: Surprisingly, there is no clear winner when you factor financial costs into the diaper equation.

Cloth diapers may seem cheap at first, but consider the hidden costs. Besides the diapers themselves ($100 for the basic varieties; $200 to $300 for the fancy ones), you also have to buy diaper covers. Like everything you buy with baby, there is a wide cost variation. The cheap stuff (like Dappi covers) will set you back $6 to $7 each. And you've got to buy several in different sizes as your child grows, so the total investment could be nearly $100. If you're lucky, you can find diaper covers second-hand for $2 to $4. Of course, some parents find low-cost covers leak and quickly wear out. As a result, they turn to the more expensive covers—a single Mother-Ease (see later for more info on this brand) is $13.25. Invest in a half dozen of those covers (in various sizes, of course) and you've spent another $300 to $500 (if you buy them new).

What about laundry? Well, washing your own cloth diapers at home may be the most economical way to go, but often folks don't have the time or energy. Instead, some parents use a cloth diaper service. In a recent cost survey of such services across the U.S., we found that the average is about $780 a year. While each service does supply you with diapers (relieving you of that expense), you're still on the hook for the diaper covers. Some services also don't provide enough diapers each month. You'll make an average of eight changes a day (more when a baby is newborn, less as they grow older), so be sure you're getting about 60 diapers a week from your service.

Proponents of cloth diapers argue that if you plan to have more than one child, you can reuse those covers, spreading out the cost. You may also not need as many sizes depending on the brands you use and the way your child grows.

So, what's the bottom line cost for cloth diapers? We estimate the total financial damage for cloth diapers (using a cloth diaper service and buying diaper covers) for just the first year is $900 to $1250 (less if you buy used items).

By contrast, let's take a look at disposables. If you buy disposable diapers from the most expensive source in town (typically, a grocery store), you'd spend about $700 to $800 for the first year. Yet, we've found the best deals are buying in bulk from the discount sources we'll discuss shortly. By shopping at these sources, we figure you'd spend $450 to $550 per year (the lowest figure is for private label diapers, the highest is for brand names).

The bottom line: the cheapest way to go is cloth diapers laundered at home. The next best bet is disposables. Finally, cloth diapers from a diaper service are the most expensive.

Best Online Sources: Diapers

Families that use disposable diapers really have it easy. After all, there are only three main manufacturers and a few in-store brands to choose from. Yes, each manufacturer may have a few sub lines with different features, but a disposable is still basically a disposable.

Life's not that easy for cloth diaper aficionados—the choices seem endless. After researching this topic for fifteen years, we realize cloth diaper parents are like snowflakes—no two are exactly alike. Some like pockets, some love prefolds. Others think wool is great while still others like microfiber. And some use one product during the day and another at night. A few of our readers have confessed to being cloth diaper obsessed: they've collected a wide variety of different brands and types. So if you don't find all the answers here, we recommend you check out cloth diapering message boards, both on our site and others.

Here are a few web sites our readers have recommended for both cloth and disposable diapers (in that order).

Amazon.com

Amazon.com
Yep, the 800 lb. gorilla of online retail is all in when it comes to diaper discounts. You'll find Pampers, Huggies and Luvs as well as minor brands like Sassy, Andy Pandy and Curity. They also offer chlorine free Earth's Best, Seventh Generations and Honest Company. Prices are typically pretty impressive: 13¢ per diaper for

Luvs, 19¢ for Huggies, and 20¢ for Pampers (size 1 or Newborn). And recently they added an in-house brand called Amazon Elements for members of their Prime or Amazon Mom programs. We review the Elements diapers later in the "Our Picks" section. One tip: if storage space is tight in your home, check out Amazon's Prime Pantry—for a $6 flat delivery fee, this service restocks your panty with everyday sizes of essentials like diapers. ***Rating: A***

ClothDiaper.com

clothdiaper.com. Home of the OsoCozy line of cloth diapers, ClothDiaper.com offers just about everything parents need for cloth diapering: covers, inserts, swim diapers, training pants and more. Package deals are available as well. When we first reviewed these guys, we were impressed by their All-in-One diapers. The system has soft cotton inside against baby's skin (gauze in the bleached version, birdseye weave in the unbleached), a polyurethane water-proof liner, adjustable Velcro-style closures and elastic leg openings. The cost: $17 each with quantity discounts available. The advantage of the all-in-one is pretty obvious, but if you'd rather buy prefolds or flat diapers, they are also available on this site as are organic fabric options. Package options are available on both fitted and pre-folds are up to 35% off. Cloth Diaper.com does sell Rumparooz and Bottombumpers diapers as well as Bummi, Imse Vimse, Thirsties and

---

Break glass for emergency diaper

In our never-ending quest to discover cool baby products and share them with our readers, we scour trade shows each year, meeting with hundreds of entrepreneurs who are convinced they've invented the next Diaper Genie. While the hype doesn't often match reality, we occasionally unearth a something really amazing.

Exhibit one: Diaper Buds.

Diaper Buds are vacuum-sealed, disposable diapers that you can fit in your jeans
pocket. The idea? Diaper Buds are an emergency diaper—when you're fresh out of diapers and something bad happens. And

since they are vacuum-packed, they take up little space. Diaper Buds are individually wrapped and when opened expand into a full size diaper. They come in sizes 2 to 5 and sell for 74¢ per diaper in a variety of package sizes. You can purchase a sample from their web site (DiaperBuds.com) for just $1 for two.

Gerber diaper covers. Finally, we love this sites "all the diapers your baby will need" options. Let's say you want to buy all the fitted diapers your baby will need up to 18 lbs and you don't want to wash too often. That package sells for $390. ***Rating: B***

Diapers.com

diapers.com. So you think Walmart and Amazon are aggressive discounters? You ain't seen nothin' till you've shopped at Diapers.com. Deals abound here: on a recent visit they were offering $10 of your first case of diapers plus $5 off future cases for three months. Or sign up for AutoShip and get your diapers shipped to you on a regular schedule plus get 10% off the diapers.

Once you add in regular deals, AutoShip discounts, coupons and other savings, Diapers.com is on par price-wise with discounters like Walmart and Target.

So why are diapers such a deal here? Because Diapers.com sells diapers as a loss leader, hoping that when you come to their site for diapers, you'll stay to buy a few of their over 25,000 additional products. But the real mojo of the site is their free two-day delivery if you buy at least $49 worth of stuff.

Thanks to those prices and super-fast shipping, Diapers.com has quickly become one of the top sites selling baby gear. ***Rating: A***

Green Mountain Diapers

greenmountaindiapers.com. Looking for some help figuring out the cloth diapering options out there? Check out Green Mountain Diapers. This site may not look as sophisticated as others, but the info and photos make it a useful resource. Most helpful: photos of real babies wearing the products they sell, which helps new cloth diaper parents get a better idea of what each product is like. Green Mountain Diapers sells a wide variety of products, including preemie cloth diapers. Wool and cotton is the specialty here, with flat-rate shipping. ***Rating: A***

Mother-Ease

mother-ease.com. Mother-Ease has been around for over 20 years, manufacturing its own line of cloth diapers. The company offers all-in-one diapers, one size diapers (in two levels of absorbency), and two types of diaper covers. Prices start at $13 for the original One Size diaper and range up to $15.75 depending on the type of fabric (choose from unbleached cotton, bleached cotton, bamboo/cotton and organic cotton). Sandy's diapers come in two sizes for a more custom fit and are priced from $12.75 to $16. All in One diapers run $17 to $19 each. Parents are pretty happy with Mother-Ease overall. ***Rating: B+***

Nicki's Diapers

nickisdiapers.com. Nicki's Diapers is a popular site mentioned often on our message boards here at *Baby Bargains*. And with good reason. They carry a wide range of cloth diapering supplies including their Best Bottom diapers. Best Bottoms are a water-proof, adjustable shell with a snap-in insert inside. Inserts are available in three different sizes and different materials (microfiber or hemp/organic cotton) as well. Shells sell for $17 while inserts range from $3.50 to $8.50 each. Nicki's recommends buying eight to ten shells and 18 to 24 inserts per size. But that's not all. Nicki's sells a huge number of brands including FuzziBunz, GroVia, Happy Heiny's, Bumkins, bumGenius and many more. Readers praise their customer service and give this web site a cloth diapering thumbs up. ***Rating: A***

Zoolikins.com

zoolikins.com. A reader recommended Zoolikins for their amazing inventory of cloth diapering products as well as their great articles. They carry products from Swaddlebees, Sweet Pea, Bummis, Kissaluvs, FuzziBunz, bumGenius, and our favorite: Knickernapies. Prices are regular retail, but if you live in Phoenix, you can pick up amazing bargains at their retail location, including used diapers for as little as $1. Zoolikins has a sale section online. ***Rating: B***

Our Picks: Brand Recommendations

Disposables. The evolution of disposable diapers is rather amazing. They started out in the 1960's as bulky and ineffective at stopping leaks. In the last 60 years, disposables morphed into ultra-thin, super-absorbent miracle workers that command 95% of the market.

And writing about disposable diaper brands is like trying to nail Jell-O to a wall—every five minutes, the diaper makers come out with new features and new gimmicks as they jostle for a piece of the nearly $27 billion worldwide diaper market. In the 16 years since the first edition of this book came out, the constant innovation in this category is amazing. We used to talk about three types of diapers: basic (thick, tape tabs), ultrathin (with the gel and tape tabs) and supreme (fabric-like outer layer, Velcro tabs). But in recent years, almost all diapers have added Velcro tabs, nicer outer layers and the ubiquitous super absorbent gels. So what separates the good from the bad diapers? *The key is good fit, no leaks and comfort for baby.*

No matter what brand you try, remember that sizing of diapers is all over the board. The "size two" diaper in one brand may be cut totally different from the "medium" of another, even though the weight guidelines on the package are similar. Finding a diaper that fits is critical to you and your baby's happiness.

Now, let's answer some common questions about disposables:

Q. What makes one brand different from another?

A. Surprisingly, the absorbency of diapers varies little from brand to brand. A *Consumer Reports* test of 14 families with infants and toddlers is a case in point. They tested seven types of disposable diapers. Five of them tested "very good" or "excellent" for leak protection. No matter what brand you choose, you'll probably have a diaper that fits well and doesn't leak. Yes, the premium/supreme diapers scored highest in CR's tests, but the difference between them and the cheaper options was minimal (except for the price, of course).

Q. What about store brands like Babies R Us and others? Is there much difference?

A. Although store diapers used to be less impressive than name brands, as we noted above, they've caught up in terms of cloth like covers, Velcro fasteners and ultra absorbency. And they cost as much as 30% less too.

Q. Do certain brands work better for boys or girls?

A. We used to hear anecdotal evidence from our readers that Huggies were better for boys and Pampers better for girls. In recent years, however, parents tell us there doesn't seem to be a gender difference at all.

Q. How many diapers of each size is a good starting point?

A. Most babies go through 12 to 14 diapers *per day* for the first few months. That translates into about 500 to 600 diapers for the first six weeks. As you read at the beginning of the chapter we recommend buying 100 "newborn" size diapers and 400 to 500 "size one" diapers before baby is born. Caveat: some families have large babies, so keep the receipts just in case you have to exchange some of those newborns for size 1.

So how many do you need of the larger sizes? It's a good idea to start with a case of each size as you transition to larger diapers. There are typically 100 diapers or more in a case. As you near a transition to a larger size, scale back the amount of smaller size diapers you buy so you don't have any half opened packs lying around.

Finally, remember that as your baby grows, she will require fewer diaper changes. Once you add solid foods to her feeding schedule you may only be doing eight to ten changes a day (we know—eight to ten a day still seems like a ton of changes; but it will feel much less than baby's first few weeks). Plus you'll be much more experienced about when a diaper really is wet.

REALITY LAYETTE

Q. Can disposable diapers cause rashes on my baby?

A. Good question. One look through our message boards at BabyBargains.com and you'll see more than a few threads asking this very question. The answer? We don't know. Anecdotally, parents have seen a rise in rashiness when manufacturers change the makeup of the diaper. But no studies have been done to compare brands either to each other or to new iterations of a brand. However, if you switch brands or a manufacturer changes the way they make their diapers, watch your baby's skin carefully. You may need to switch to another brand, ASAP. So keep the receipt!

Check out our comments on different diaper brands. They are arranged alphabetically. By the way, most of their web sites offer coupons of some sort—check them out and sign up for the deals.

◆ *Amazon Elements diapers.* Amazon.com recently jumped into the private-label, premium disposable diaper business. Their new line of Elements Diaper and Wipes is an attempt to complete with Costco's Kirkland diapers as well as other store brand diapers at Walmart and Target. These diapers are only available for purchase if you have are a Prime or Amazon Mom membership ($99 per year). The diapers are thin like other premium diapers with a fitted design. And while these diapers aren't organic, Amazon aims to be transparent about the diaper origins—using an app, you can scan a bar code to find out who made the diapers, where they were manufactured, manufacturing components and so on. As we were going to press, Amazon pulled these diapers from sale after initial feedback from parents was mixed—the company says they will tweak the design and relaunch the diapers shortly. So the jury is out on these diapers.

◆ *Babies R Us diapers.* Fans of BRU's diapers like their overall quality—the liner is hypoallergenic and contains vitamin E, aloe and zinc. They also have a waterproof cover and stretchy waistband. And the price is decent: size 1's are 12¢ each. Lately, BRU has been selling their house brand diapers for $10 a pack in every size. So they're definitely very cheap. But the verdict on these diapers isn't unanimous. Critics say leaks are a problem—and the stretchable grip tabs don't stretch enough.

◆ *Huggies (huggies.com).* Huggies has been a strong brand for years. They now offer five diaper options: Pure & Natural, Little Snugglers, Little Movers (regular and slip on), Snug & Dry, Snug & Dry Plus, Little Swimmers and Overnight. One of the best features of the line is the pocketed waistbands designed to avoid

diapers

blowouts. This feature is available on the Pure & Natural and Little Snugglers/Movers lines.

Huggies Pure & Natural have an organic cotton exterior and are hypoallergenic with aloe and vitamin E. The liner is also made of recycled material and they use less ink on the graphics on these diapers. Obviously, this is an attempt to convince parents that these diapers are more eco-friendly. You'll pay for it—on Walmart.com we priced size 1 Pure & Natural at 24¢ per diaper while the size 1 Little Snugglers was 22¢ per diaper.

Little Snugglers (formally Huggies Supreme) feature a cloth-like outer cover, wetness indicator and pocketed waistband. Huggies Snug & Dry are their less expensive option with Absorb Away (layers to "lock in wetness") and the SnugFit elastic waistband. The Snug & Dry Diapers are about 20% cheaper than Little Snugglers.

Overnights are made to be even more absorbent so babies can actually sleep through the night (and parents too!). And they still have their "Little Swimmers" swim diapers—great for the pool or beach.

As for wipes, Huggies offers six varieties from Triple Clean to Natural Care to Soft Skin. Feedback from parents was a thumbs up on the wipes, no matter the type.

Reader feedback on Huggies is positive. Parents note that the pocket waistband (they call it the "poop pocket") really does help avoid up-the-back blowouts.

◆ **Luvs (luvsdiapers.com).** Made by Procter & Gamble (who also makes Pampers), Luvs are marketed as a lower-price brand. They are often less expensive than even store brand diapers.

Thankfully, Luvs doesn't try to be all things to all people with multiple diaper options. They just have one diaper with basic features. Luvs stresses their Ultra Leakguard guarantee that claims Luvs will have fewer leaks than your current brand—or your money back.

So, do they work? Readers were mixed in their appraisal of Luvs. Some said they leaked, but others praised the low price and thought they worked fine. Walmart.com's price for size 1 Luvs was an amazing 13¢ per diaper. Compared to Huggies Little Snugglers at 22¢ per diaper, we'd say try Luvs first!

◆ **Pampers (pampers.com).** Pampers continues to offer an extensive line of diapers including Swaddlers Sensitive, Swaddlers, Cruisers and Baby Dry (and Extra) diapers. In our last edition, we noted that Pampers' Dry Max technology had been a bit controversial. Pampers was stung by parent criticism that claimed their babies got a rash from the super absorbing technology, a claim Pampers denies. In fact, Pampers has aggressively countered the bad press with a money-back guarantee and online FAQ's addressing the controversy. An inquiry from the Consumer Product Safety Commission found no evidence the diapers caused rashes. But regardless, they no longer emphasize Dry Max.

Baby Dry diapers are Pampers' lower-priced line. They offer pretty basic features like contoured fit and absorbent core.

Swaddlers Sensitive are Pampers' hypoallergenic option with an absorbent liner like the Baby Dry diapers.

Walmart.com sells the Baby Dry diapers for 18¢ per diaper and Swaddlers (size 1) for 25¢ per diaper; Swaddlers Sensitive (size 1) sell for 26¢ each. Overall, reader feedback on the Pampers line has been positive.

◆ *Parent's Choice by Walmart.* Walmart's private label brand, Parent's Choice, has features similar to name-brand diapers: a cloth-like cover, absorbent core, elastic leg openings and flexible fit waistband. But the price is what's impressive. On their web site,

Who's got the cheapest diapers?

What's the best place to buy disposable diapers? We did a price comparison among several major sources, listed here from least to most expensive:

Store or Web Site	Diaper Type	Count	Price	Per Diaper
TARGET.COM**	HUGGIES #1	276	$47.19	17¢
SAM'S CLUB	HUGGIES #1	276	$46.98	17¢
WALMART.COM**	HUGGIES #1	276	$47.17	17¢
BABIESRUS.COM**	HUGGIES #1	232	$42.99	18¢
COSTCO	HUGGIES #1	156	$29.99	19¢
AMAZON.COM**	HUGGIES #1	234	$46.90	21¢
DIAPERS.COM***	HUGGIES #1	234	$40.79	22¢
GROCERY STORE*	HUGGIES #2	76	$19.99	26¢

Per Diaper: The cost per diaper.

* Checked at Kroger (King Soopers).

** Free shipping; minimum order amount may be required.

*** Diapers.com offers periodic coupons and cash back offers.

Note: Prices check 2015.

we found a 112 pack of size 1 diapers for only $13.97. The per diaper price: 12¢, among the lowest prices out there. So what do readers think of Parent's Choice? Fans note that Walmart has re-engineered their diapers, changing the tabs and sizing to compare more with Pampers' diapers. This is a great brand to consider taking to daycare if you have to provide the diapers.

◆ *Up & Up by Target.* Target's in store brand, Up & Up sells for 16¢ per diaper for a pack of size 1's. These diapers feature leak guards, and the usual contoured shape. They are hypoallergenic, chlorine free and latex free. Parents apparently liked an earlier version of the diapers better—recent reviews complain they now leak and are smaller and thinner. They also scored near the bottom in the Houston test. As a result, we wouldn't recommend this brand.

Eco-friendly Disposables. Are there diapers that combine the convenience of disposables with the ecological benefits of cloth diapers? Yes—here's an overview of so-called eco-friendly disposables:

Seventh Generation (seventhgeneration.com) sells chlorine-free disposable diapers with a thin design. The diapers have a cloth like outer layer, reusable tabs, and are latex and fragrance free. Made of wood pulp, a polyolefin backing and a polyolefin outer cover, Seventh Generation also includes an absorbent polymer gel. They are careful to explain that the gel they use is non-toxic, non-carcinogenic and non-irritating. In fact, you can view material safety data sheets on all the diaper's components on their web site. A reader also recommends the company's wipes saying they are "free of chemicals and full of good stuff for my baby's skin." You can find these diapers online at Amazon or in stores such as Whole Foods and Vitamin Cottage. On Amazon.com, 224 stage 1 Seventh Generation diapers was $49.99 (a pricey 24¢ per diaper). Coupons are available on Seventh Generation's web site.

Another eco-friendly disposable is **Nature Babycare** diapers by Naty (naty.com). These diapers are chlorine free and use no plastics (corn-based materials). They were designed by a Swedish mom and are compostable. At 43¢ per diaper for the small size, they seem out of the range of most people. You'll find them on web sites like Target.com.

Earth's Best, known for its baby food line, has entered the eco friendly diaper arena with their Chlorine Free Disposable Diapers (clever name). These diapers use corn and wheat products as absorbing agents and they use fewer petro-chemicals in the manufacturing process. They are also latex-free. But what if your child has a corn or wheat allergy? We wonder if that would be a problem. And at 29¢ per diaper for size ones, they're still an expensive option.

Here's a popular new diaper that isn't quite a disposable, nor a cloth diaper–**gDiapers** are flushable cloth diapers. Yep, you read it right. Flushable. To be precise, part of a gDiaper is flushable.

A gDiapers newborn starter kit comes with 12 reusable "tiny gPants" (like cloth diaper covers), six small gPants and 80 biodegradable diaper refills for $120 on Amazon.com. Once you are ready to dispose of the diaper refills, you have a choice: flush them, compost the wet ones or throw them in the garbage. GDiapers notes you never compost a poopy diaper, only flush it. But what about throwing them out? Isn't that the same as disposables? Not necessarily since there is no plastic in gDiapers, so they degrade fast (supposedly 50 to 150 days) . . . if you don't put them in a plastic trash bag, of course.

GDiapers' web site has several videos showing their product at work. And we've heard from several moms who love this idea. It is a nice compromise in the cloth versus disposable debate. One caveat: you'll find gDiapers aren't as absorbent as disposables, simply because they use only wood pulp (fluffed for extra absorbency) rather than that super absorbent gel in most diapers. Price is probably the biggest stumbling block with gDiapers. Additional washable "little g" pants range from $14 to $18. Refills start at 35¢ each for 40 of the small size. Ouch! That's more than twice the price of disposables when bought at discount stores! You can also buy reusable snap-in liners, $20 for six.

Ultimately, while these products are promising options for parents looking for a natural alternative to mainstream disposables, the price of all these options severely limits their popularity. And there is still an issue of where these diapers will go. Until recycling centers with composting options become more widely available, there's a question as to whether these diapers won't still end up buried under tons of earth and trash waiting to decompose.

Cloth Diapers. As we noted earlier, if you ask 100 parents for their recommendations on cloth diapers you're likely to get 100 different opinions–it seems everyone has their special system or favorite brand! So what's an aspiring CD'er (cloth diaperer) to do? First let's take you through the basics with Karen F., our CD guru from our message boards:

A cloth diaper has three basic functions. Working from the inside out:

1. Wick it away. This layer is intended to keep baby from sitting in her pee. This layer lets moisture through in one direction but not back towards the skin. In cloth diapers, this layer is fleece or suede-cloth, but only certain kinds of fleece will do this. Some people just cut rectangles of fleece and lay them inside the diaper. Some diapers are lined with fleece, sewn in place while others are pocket diapers with the fleece next to the skin. And there are some people who skip this layer and change the diaper as soon as baby pees.

2. Soak it up. Typically, the absorbent layer in cloth diapers is made of cotton or hemp and is sewn in layers. There are also some diapers with a micro fiber towel for the absorbent layer. Some people add an extra layer called a "doubler" which is just layers of cloth sewn together. This allows parents to increase absorption when needed (overnight, for example). Options include paper, cotton, microfiber or even silk.

3. Keep the rest of the world dry. Remember those awful plastic/rubber pants of yesteryear? Uncomfortable for baby and noisy too! Today's options are much more comfortable to wear

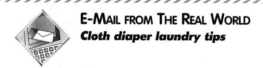

E-MAIL FROM THE REAL WORLD
Cloth diaper laundry tips

Once you make the decision to use cloth diapers, you'll want to research the "art" of cleaning them. Too many harsh chemicals can damage and fade cloth diapers and covers, not enough will leave diapers looking less than pristine. So what's a parent to do? Here's some advice from readers who've experienced lots of diaper cleaning. Rowan Cerrelli writes:

"I do not like to use chlorine bleach to wash out diapers since they are expensive and the chlorine ruins them. There are some products out there that use natural enzymes to predigest 'stuff' out of the diapers, therefore eliminating the need for bleach. Companies that have these products include Seventh Generation and Ecover. They are also available in natural food grocery stores."

Catherine Advocate-Ross recommends:
"I use BioKleen laundry powder on the diapers. Works great and you need very little."

BioKleen's web site biokleenhome.com explains their products and directs consumers to stores or web sites that carry them. They have an extensive line including liquid as well as powder detergent and stain and odor eliminator. The main ingredient in the line is grapefruit seed and pulp extract.

Kelly Small, from Wallingford, CT emailed us to say:
"I highly recommend OxyClean— it is great on the poop stains!!!"

and touch. Cloth diaper covers can be polyurethane laminate (PUL) over cotton or polyester, nylon, wool or fleece. Wool is naturally water repellent when it has natural lanolin in it. (Otherwise sheep would bulk up like a sponge in a rainstorm!). The type of fleece that is used as diaper covers is water repellent."

Okay, now that you know the mechanics of cloth diapering, what should you use for your little guy or gal? First, here's the lingo you'll need to master:

1 PREFOLDS (CPF for Chinese prefolds or DSQ for diaper-service quality). These are what most parents think of when they envision cloth diapers. They are heavyweight 100% cotton cloths that have been prefolded (so that there is extra padding in the middle) and sewn down. This process leads to a diaper with six to eight layers in the middle and two to four layers on the sides. They can

---

Finally, Rebecca Parish has some practical advice on cloth diapers:
"We (my friends and I) have run across a shortcut that I had not heard about before we attempted cloth diapering. Mainly, we have found it entirely unnecessary to rinse diapers out at all before laundering them. We own a four-day supply of pre-fold diapers and wraps. When our baby poops, we take an extra diaper wipe with us to the toilet, and use it to scrape what easily comes off into the toilet. Then we throw the dirty diaper into our diaper pail, right along with all the other dirty diapers. There's no liquid in the pail for soaking— they just sit in there dry. About every three or four days we throw the entire contents of the diaper pail into the laundry machine, add regular detergent (we use Cheer) and two capfuls of bleach (about 4 teaspoons), and run the machine. The diapers and wraps all come out clean. Just two extra loads of laundry a week (which is nothing compared to the extra loads of clothes we now wash), and no dipping our hands into toilet water. I generally use about five diaper wipes every time I change a messy diaper as it is, so using one extra one for scraping poop into the toilet seems like no big deal.

I think washer technology has improved significantly enough in recent years to allow for this much easier diaper cleaning. We own a fairly new front-loader washer. I don't think the brand name is important; we have a friend who owns a different brand of front-loader, and gets equally good results. However, one of our friends with an older top-loader uses our same system but ends up with stains; she doesn't care but I would."

Bottom line: new technologies (detergents, additives and washers) have led to great improvements in the cleaning of cloth diapers.

then be pinned onto your baby (not our favorite idea) or folded into a diaper cover. Avoid flat fold diapers—these are really just burp pads and great dust cloths!

2 **FITTED DIAPER:** Sometimes called pre-fitteds, these are prefolded diapers that have elastic sewn in for the leg openings. They don't have snaps or Velcro so they have to be secured with pins or in a cover. You'll get a more snug fit around the leg openings with these.

3 **DOUBLER (ALSO CALLED LINER).** Available in paper, cotton, microfiber or even silk, doublers are used when you need extra absorbency. They are inserted between the diaper and baby's bottom. These would be a great option at night or on a long car trip.

4 **DIAPER COVER/WRAP.** This item is placed over the diaper to stop leaks. One style of diaper cover is called a wrap—think of it as baby origami. You'll wrap your baby up and secure the Velcro tabs to the front strip. Some covers snap in place and there are other pants that can be pulled on (elastic waist).

5 **ALL-IN-ONE.** Just what you'd think, an all-in-one (AIO) is a diaper and cover sewn together. There are pluses and minuses to this design. Yes, the convenience of grabbing one item and snapping or Velcro-ing it on your baby is great, but if your baby makes a mess, you have to wash the whole thing. With a traditional diaper/cover combination, you won't have to wash the cover every time unless baby gets poop on it. So you'll end up buying more all-in-ones to keep yourself from doing laundry constantly.

6 **POCKET DIAPER.** Made famous by Fuzzi Bunz, the pocket diaper is an all-in-one with a pocket sewn into the lining. You can then customize the diaper for more absorbency by adding an insert or a prefolded diaper.

7 **SNAPPI FASTENERS.** Made in South Africa, these cutting-edge diaper fasteners replace the traditional (and potentially painful) diaper pin. Check out their website at snappibaby.com for a look at how they work.

Whew! That's a lot to remember. So anyway, what's the bottom line? What should you buy? Great question. Here's what our cloth diaper guru recommends if you're just starting out and have a newborn: Buy two to three dozen prefold diapers and four to six diaper covers. You may also want to get a few pocket diapers or all-in-ones and a couple Snappis.

Now you probably want to know which brands to buy. So we polled our readers to find out their favorites. Right off the bat, they told us "it depends." Depends on your baby's body type, whether you're looking for nighttime leak protection and many other factors. A couple of the brands readers *could* agree on were Fuzzi Bunz (fuzzibunz.com) and Snap-EZ Fleece Pocket diapers (snap-ez.com). Here is a list of the other brands readers recommend:

◆ *Fitted Diapers:*
Happy Heiney (happyheiny.com)
Kissaluvs (kissaluvs.com)
Nicki's (nikisdiapers.com)

◆ *Diaper Covers:*
Aristocrat (wool) (aristocratsbabyproducts.com)
FLIP (flipdiapers.com)
gDiapers (gdiapers.com)
Coverall Snap Wraps (blueberrydiapers.com)

◆ *All-In–Ones:*
Bum Genius (bumgenius.com)
Daisy Doodles (daisy-doodles.com)
DryBees (drybees.com)
Gro Via (gro-via.com)
Side Snap Simplex (blueberrydiapers.com)

◆ *Pockets:*
bumGenius (bumgenius.com)
Fuzzi Bunz (fuzzibunz.com)
Happy Heiny's (happyheinys.com)
Nicki's (nickisdiapers.com)
Thirsties (thirstiesbaby.com)

◆ *Inserts/Doubler:*
Babykicks Hemparoo Joey Bunz (babykicks.com)
bumGenius Stay Dry Doubler (bumgenius.com)
FLIP (flipdiapers.com)
FuzziBunz Hemp Inserts (fuzzibunz.com)
gDiaper—disposable and reusable (gdiaper.com)
Gro Via Stay Dry Booster (gro-via.com)
Happy Heiney's Stuffins (happyheineys.com)

Need more information? A good book on using cloth diapers is *Diaper Changes* by Theresa Rodriquez (M. Evans and Co., publisher; $15, Amazon.com). A new book, *Changing Diapers: the Hip Mom's Guide to Modern Cloth Diapering* by Kelly Wels (Green Team Enterprises, publisher, $18, Amazon.com) is another book with positive reviews from parents. Also, check out our online message boards on our web site at babybargains.com. They have extensive commentary from cloth diaper parents with tips and recommendations.

Wipes. Like diapers, you have a basic choice with wipes: name brand or generic. Our advice: stick to the name brands. We polled our readers and their top pick was: ***Huggies Natural Care***. The reviews were more mixed with Pampers wipes: some parents thought they were too wet and too expensive.

We found most cheap generic wipes to be inferior. With less water and thinner construction, store brand wipes we sampled were losers. There are a couple exceptions to Sensitive baby wipes. One mom emailed: "Kirkland are not as rigid as Huggies or Pampers, have a lighter scent and are stronger than any other wipe we tried." And it's hard to beat the price: 2¢ per wipe. As for Walgreens' brand, a mom emailed saying they "are as good as Huggies in thickness and durability." And they cost about 3¢ a wipe. Another mom really loves BJ's Berkely & Jensen brand of wipes. She thought they were softer than Costco's Kirkland wipes and more like Huggies for less than 2¢ a wipe.

Money Saving Secrets

Here are some tips for saving on disposable diapers (cloth diaper bargain advice is at the end of this section):

1 **THINK PRICE PER DIAPER.** Stores sell diapers in all sorts of package sizes—always compare diaper prices per diaper, not per box.

2 **BUY IN BULK.** Don't buy those little packs of 20 diapers—look for the 80 or 100 count packs instead. You'll find the price per diaper goes down when you buy larger packs. That's why grocery stores are usually the most expensive place to buy diapers—they sell diapers in smaller packages, with the highest per diaper price. Online discounters often sell packs of more than 200 at even bigger discounts.

3 **GO FOR WAREHOUSE CLUBS.** Sam's (samsclub.com), BJ's (bjs.com) and Costco (costco.com) wholesale clubs sell diapers at incredibly low prices. For example, Costco sells a 228-count package of Huggies stage 2 for just $38.99 or about 17¢ per diaper. We also found great deals on wipes at the wholesale clubs. The downside to these warehouse clubs? You buy a membership to shop at clubs, which runs about $50 a year. And clubs don't stock the usual sizes of diapers—Costco carries "size 1-2" Kirkland diapers, instead of just size 1 or 2. Readers are frustrated with this combined sizing, according to our message boards.

4 BUY STORE BRANDS. As mentioned earlier, many parents find store brand diapers to be equal to the name brands. And the prices can't be beat–many are 20% to 30% cheaper. Chains like Target, Walmart and Toys R Us/Babies R Us carry in-house diaper brands, as do many grocery stores. See the reviews earlier on these store brands. Warehouse clubs also carry in store brands: Costco's Kirkland, BJ's Little Bundles and Sam's Club's Member's Mark.

5 FORGET BRAND LOYALTY. Buy whatever diaper is on sale this week at your favorite store. Ok, some diapers are losers (Target's Up & Up are an example), but if Huggies are on sale this week, go for the Huggies. When Pampers go on sale next week, buy those. Since the name brands and most private label diapers are equivalent in quality, it doesn't pay to be brand loyal.

6 CONSIDER TOYS R US. You may not have a wholesale club nearby, but you're bound to be close to a Toys R Us (or their sister division, Babies R Us). And we found them to be a great source for affordable name-brand diapers. The best bet: buy in bulk. You can often buy diapers (both name brand and generic) by the case at Toys R Us, saving you about 20% or more over grocery store prices. Bonus: TRU and BRU often offer in-store coupons for diapers–combine these with manufacturer's coupons for double savings.

7 ONLINE DEALS MAY BEAT IN-STORE PRICES. Hard to believe, but sometimes buying diapers online and having them shipped to your house is cheaper than buying at a store. Why? Online sites often sell bigger packages of diapers than stores–and the bigger the package, the lower the cost per diaper. Walmart.com is one example according to our readers. They've seen lower prices (as much as 17% lower) online compared to the stores. With many sites offering free or low-cost shipping, online dealers may be better than shopping in store.

8 WHEN BABY IS NEARING A TRANSITION POINT, DON'T STOCK UP. Quick growing babies may move into another size faster than you think, leaving you with an excess supply of too-small diapers.

9 DON'T BUY DIAPERS IN GROCERY STORES. We compared prices at grocery stores and usually found them to be sky-high. Most were selling diapers in packages that worked out to over 25¢ per diaper. We should note there are exceptions to this rule, however: some grocery chains (especially in the South) use diapers as a "loss-leader." They'll sell diapers at attractive prices in order to entice shoppers into the store. Also, store brands can be more attractively priced, even at grocery stores. Use coupons (see below) to save even more.

10 **USE COUPONS.** You'll be amazed at how many coupons you receive in the mail, usually for 75¢ off diapers and 50¢ off wipes. One tip: to keep those "introductory" packages of coupons coming, continue signing up to be on the mailing lists of the maternity chain stores (apparently, these chains sell your name to diaper manufacturers, formula companies, etc.) or online at diaper manufacturers' web sites.

11 **IF YOU HAVE TO BUY YOUR DIAPERS FROM A GROCERY STORE OR PHARMACY, SIGN UP FOR A LOYALTY CARD**. Yes, we just said don't buy diapers at the grocery store. But we know—sometimes the grocery store is the most convenient choice for a 2 am diaper run. Our advice: sign up for the store's loyalty card, which often offers discounts on items like diapers and wipes. Combine this with in-store sales and manufacturer's coupons and you might find the price per diaper approaching what you'd pay at a discount store.

12 **ASK FOR GIFT CERTIFICATES.** When friends ask you what you'd like as a shower gift, you can drop hints for gift certificates/cards from stores that sell a wide variety of baby items—including diapers and wipes. That way you can get what you really need, instead of cute accessories of marginal value. You'd be surprised at how many stores offer gift certificate programs.

13 **FOR CLOTH DIAPER USERS, GO FOR "INTRODUCTORY PACKAGES."** Many suppliers have special introductory deals (Mother-Ease offers their One-Size diaper, a liner and cover for 30% off including shipping). Before you invest hundreds of dollars in one brand, give it a test drive first.

14 **BUY USED CLOTH DIAPERS.** Many of the best brands of cloth diapers last and last and last. So you may see them on eBay or cloth-diaper message boards. Buy them—you can get some brands for as little as a buck or two. As long as you know the quality and age of the diapers you're buying, this tip can really be a money saver.

15 **REUSE THEM.** Okay, we know this may be obvious, but hang onto your cloth diapers and use them for your next child.

Every child is different, so even if you buy a brand and it doesn't fit your baby well, it may work on your next child. And of course, you can always sell them on eBay or Craigslist when you're all finished.

16 **MANUFACTURERS' SECONDS.** Diaper site Kissaluvs.com emailed us this tip: every six to eight weeks, the site offers diaper seconds at a huge discount. The diapers are still perfectly fine, they just have minor flaws that don't affect their quality like a slightly too large waistline, a button a millimeter out of place or stitching in the wrong color. If you have a favorite cloth diaper brand, consider checking directly with the manufacturer to see if they offer any seconds deals as well.

The Bottom Line:
A Wrap-Up of Our Best Buy Picks

In summary, we recommend you buy the following layette items for your baby:

QUANTITY	ITEM	COST
6	T-shirts/onesies (over the head)	$16-$20
6	T-shirts (side snap)	$14
4-6	Sleepers/Sleep Sack	$64-$120
2-4	Coveralls	$50-$100
3-4	Booties/socks	$5-$15
1	Sweater	$16.50
3	Hats (safari and caps)	$13
1	Snowsuit/bunting	$30-$40
4	Large bibs (for feeding)	$26
3 sets	Wash cloths and towels	$36
7-8	Receiving blankets	$30
TOTAL		**$301 to $450**

These prices are from discounters, outlet stores, or sale prices at department stores. What would all these clothes cost at full retail? $550 to $650, at least. The bottom line: follow our tips and you'll save $200 to $300 on your baby's layette alone. (Of course, you may receive some of these items as gifts, so your actual outlay may be less.)

Which brands are best? See "Our Picks: Brand Recommendations" earlier in this chapter. In general, we found that 100% cotton clothes are best. Yes, you'll pay a little more for cotton, but it lasts longer and looks better than clothes made of polyester blends (the exception: fleece outerwear and sleepwear). Other wastes of money for infants include kimonos, saque sets, and shoes.

What about diapers? We found little financial difference between cloth and disposable, especially when you use a cloth diaper service. Cloth does have several hidden costs, however—diaper covers can add hundreds of dollars to the expense of this option although the cost can be spread out among additional children.

For disposables, we found that brand choice was more of a personal preference—all the majors did a good job at stopping leaks. The best way to save money on disposable diapers is to skip the grocery store and buy in bulk (100+ diaper packages) from a warehouse club. Diapers from discount sources run about $400. The same diapers from grocery stores could be $750 or more. Another great money-saver: generic, store-brand diapers from Babies R Us, Walmart, Target and the like. These diapers performed just as well as the name brands at a 20% to 30% discount.

Whew! Now that you have an advanced degree in baby clothing and diaper deals, let's talk about maternity clothes, up next!

CHAPTER 5

Maternity & Nursing

Inside this chapter

Love 'em or leave every mother-to-be needs maternity clothes at some point in her pregnancy. Still, you don't have to break the bank to get comfortable, and, yes, fashionable maternity items. In this chapter, we tell you which sources sell all-cotton, casual clothes at unbelievably low prices. Then, we'll review the biggest maternity chains and reveal our list of top wastes of money. Finally, you'll learn which nursing clothes moms prefer most.

Maternity & Nursing Clothes

Getting Started: When Do You Need This Stuff?

It may seem obvious that you'll need to buy maternity clothes when you get pregnant, but the truth is you don't actually need all of them immediately. The first thing you'll notice is the need for a new bra. At least, that was my first clue that my body was changing. Breast changes occur as early as the first month and you may find yourself going through several different bra sizes along the way.

Next, it's time for the bump. Yes, the baby is making its presence known by making you feel a bit bigger around the middle. Skirts and pants feel tight as early as your third month. Maternity clothes at this point may seem like overkill, but some women do begin to "show" enough that they find it necessary to head out to the maternity shop.

If you have decided to breastfeed, you'll need to consider what type of nursing bras you'll want. Buy two or three in your eighth

MATERNITY
NURSING

month so you'll be prepared. You may find it necessary to buy more nursing bras after the baby is born, but this will get you started. As for other nursing clothes, you may or may not find these worth the money. Don't go out and buy a whole new wardrobe right off the bat. Some women find nursing shirts and tops to be helpful while others manage quite well with regular clothes. More on this topic later in this chapter.

Sources

1 MATERNITY WEAR CHAINS. Pea in the Pod, Destination Maternity and Motherhood are probably the best known maternity stores—all owned by the same company. More on these chains later in the chapter.

2 MOM AND POP MATERNITY SHOPS. These small, independent stores sell a wide variety of maternity clothes, from affordable weekend wear to high-priced career wear. Some baby specialty stores carry maternity clothes as well. The chief advantage to the smaller stores is personalized service—we usually found salespeople who were knowledgeable about the different brands. In addition, these stores may offer other services. For example, some rent formal wear for special occasions, saving you big bucks. Of course, you may pay for the extra service with higher prices. While you're shopping at the independents look for better quality lines from manufacturers like Ingrid & Isabel (ingridandisabel.com), Juicy Couture Maternity and Olian (olianmaternity.com).

3 CONSIGNMENT STORES. Many consignment or thrift stores that specialize in children's clothing may also have a rack of maternity clothes. In visits to several such stores, we found some incredible bargains (at least 50% off retail) on maternity clothes that were in good to excellent condition. Of course, the selection varies widely, but we strongly advise you to check out any second-hand stores for deals.

4 DISCOUNTERS. When we talk about discounters, we're referring to chains like Target, Walmart and K-Mart. Now, let's be honest here—these discounters probably aren't the first place you'd think of to outfit your maternity wardrobe. Yet, each has a surprisingly nice selection of maternity clothes, especially casual wear. Later, we'll tell you about the incredible prices on these all-cotton clothes.

5 DEPARTMENT STORES. As you might guess, most department stores carry some maternity fashions. The big disadvantage:

the selection is usually rather small. Selection is much greater, however, on store websites. And department stores like Penney's and Sears often have end-of-the-season sales with decent maternity bargains. Look for maternity sections at Kohl's, JCPenney, Sears, Macy's, Nordstrom, Neiman Marcus and Saks Fifth Avenue.

6 WEBSITES. Shopping online has a hidden benefit for maternity clothes—many sites offer more generous return policies than retail stores. While maternity chains limit returns to a short period and only for store credit, online sites from the very same chains give you cash back and a longer return window. Another bonus to online shopping: it's easier to find sale items. And sites show what the clothes look like on real people, instead of a hanger.

7 NON-MATERNITY STORES. Maternity stores don't have a monopoly on pregnancy clothes—and you can save big bucks by shopping at stores that don't have the word "maternity" in their name. Some of our favorites: Old Navy, the Gap, Ann Taylor Loft. Their maternity clothes are both stylish and affordable.

8 YOUR HUSBAND'S CLOSET. Where's a good place for comfy weekend wear? Look no further than the other side of your closet, where your husband's clothes can often double as maternity wear.

9 OUTLETS. Yes, there are several outlets that sell maternity clothes and the prices can be a steal. Many of the chain maternity stores we discuss later in this chapter have outlets.

10 YOUR FRIENDS. It's a time-honored tradition—handing down "old" maternity clothes to the newly pregnant. Of course, maternity styles don't change that much from year to year and since outfits aren't worn for a long time, they are usually in great shape. Just be sure to pass on the favor when you are through with your pregnancy.

Best Online Bargains and Sources

Ann Taylor LOFT
loft.com Ann Taylor's fashion esthetic seems to be more focused on designs for work than weekend lounging. We like their trousers, top-of-the-knee length skirts and corduroys. They work well with cute cardigans, comfy jersey tops and tailored shirts. Our favorite designs are the dresses: a couple sweater dresses and jer-

sey knit dresses in great shapes and colors were affordably priced between $80 and $105. The site's fit guide is helpful with pictures of their three belly-panel options. **Rating: A**

Due Maternity

duematernity.com Due Maternity is a combo web site: they sell their in house brand as well as a plethora of designer maternity brands like Nuka, Maternal America, Olian and Egg. They have one of the nicest collections of formal wear for pregnant moms, with a wider variety of styles than we've seen on most sites. Prices are up there, but most run less than $200—not bad for formal wear. We like the section of undergarments too: belly bands, slips and camis and more. They even carry leggings. Nursing clothes are available from Japanese Weekend, Bravado, Majamas and Boob (we're not making that up). Styles are attractive, selection is great but prices are regular retail— check out sale items for better deals. **Rating: B+**

Expressiva

expressiva.com Wow! That's all we could say when we took a look at Expressiva's designs. You really never would know these are nursing clothes. And they don't make you look like a sack of potatoes. Tops, dresses, casual clothes, bras, swimsuits and sleepwear are available here. Sizes range from extra small to 3X and the site includes hints about sizing for specific outfits. We love the special collection for plus sizes. Eight styles of nursing openings are available and the site shows you exactly how each type works (click on the "why nursing wear" link). Prices are reasonable for the quality. **Rating: A**

Gap

gap.com You probably already shop the Gap for basics like jeans or t-shirts, but you can also find maternity here. There are some stores with maternity sections, but the best selection is online. You'll find classics like cardigans and jeans as well as stretch shirts, swimsuits and more. We also like their Starter Styles (lots of basics like classic shirts, tanks and pants) and their Style at Work section. If you've never been pregnant before, this is a great resource. Sizes range from 00 to 16-18 plus inseams go up to 34". Check frequently for sale items—they seem to offer more sales than most maternity retailers. Readers have been impressed with the quality of Gap maternity, according to our email. Note: the Gap only accepts mailed in returns of maternity clothes bought online—you can't take them back to the store. You also have to pay the return shipping. A few readers report they were able to return online maternity purchases to Gap maternity stores, but not regular Gap outlets. **Rating: A**

Isabella Oliver

isabellaoliver.com This stylish site offers the usual categories like work and casual, but also includes fourth trimester clothes and resort wear. While the designs are very hip, they are expensive. Sale items however, are a great deal. And we like the attitude on this site. The designers have a blog—they offer good fashion advice and interesting "style notes." ***Rating: B+***

JCPenney

jcpenney.com JCPenney may not be the source you turn to for everything in your maternity wardrobe, but you might want to take a look at some of their basics. T-shirts, jeans, bras, maternity belts and pajamas are priced reasonably. We found a lot of sale items as well: jeans marked down from $36 to $18 and more. Yes, the fashion could use a little updating, but the basics are a good value. ***Rating: B-***

Mine For Nine

MineForNine.com If the thought of buying thousands of dollars worth of pregnancy clothes to wear for a mere four or five months makes your head spin, consider renting. Mine for Nine is a new web site that offers designer maternity clothes for rent at up to 75% off the retail price. Dresses, suits, pants, skirts and more from designers like Ripe Maternity, Olian and Maternite can be rented for amazing prices. Example: a beautiful silk floor length gown that sells for $293 can be rented for just $73 for one month. For weddings, New Years and other special events, this is a great deal.

How does it work? You can rent by the month or longer if you want work or casual clothes . . . and more than one item can be rented at a time. Evening clothes can be rented for as little as 14 days. Amazingly, there are no late fees if you keep the clothes longer (you pay for the extra days on a pro-rated basis). Clothes are either new or "like new" which means they have been professionally dry-cleaned and inspected. The site has plenty of information on how to get the right fit, plus any order over $75 qualifies for free shipping. To ship your items back, use the return shipping label that comes in the box. You can even buy the clothes if something really impresses you. ***Rating: A***

Old Navy

oldnavy.com Like their parent company the Gap, Old Navy also sells maternity. Yes, the quality is less impressive here, but the prices are a steal. The category selection is similar to Gap—they carry jeans and pants, dresses and skirts, even pajamas and nursing clothes. A short-sleeve nursing top in cotton jersey goes for a mere $25. At this price, you can try one without investing a huge amount. We like their categories like "shop by semester." ***Rating: B***

One Hot Mama

onehotmama.com Nursing clothes are where One Hot Mama got their start, but they have expanded into maternity clothes as well. Their niche: hip styles from manufacturers like Snugabell and Annee Matthew. Fun fabrics and colors are highlighted in the selection on this site. Prices are regular retail and sizing ranges from 2 to 18. ***Rating: B***

What Are You Buying?

What will you need when you get pregnant? There is no short-age of advice on this topic, especially from the folks trying to sell you stuff. But here's what real moms advise you to buy (divided into two topic areas, maternity clothes and then nursing clothes):

Maternity Clothes

◆ ***Maternity Bras.*** Maternity bras are designed to grow with you as your pregnancy progresses; these bras also offer extra sup-port (you'll need it). Maternity bras are available just about every-where, from specialty maternity shops to department stores, online sites and discount chains. More on this topic later in this chapter; look for our recommendations for maternity underwear.

HOW MANY? Two in each size as your bust line expands. I found that I went through three different sizes during my pregnancy, and buying two in each size allowed me to wear one while the other was washed.

◆ ***Sleep Bras.*** Why a sleep bra, you ask? Well, some women find it more comfortable to have a little extra support at night as their breasts change. Toward the end of pregnancy, some women also start to leak breast milk (to be technical, this is actually colostrum). Sleep bras hold breast pads in place to soak up any leaks. And once the baby arrives, a sleeping bra (about $10-$20) also keeps you from leaking when you inadvertently roll onto your stomach—yes, there will come a day when you can do that again. Some women just need light support, while others find a full-fea-tured bra a necessity.

HOW MANY? Start with two sleep bras—one to wear while one is in the wash.

◆ **Underpants.** Most women today are wearing bikini underpants as standard gear. And, readers note, you can continue to wear those same styles when you're pregnant. So, save yourself some money and forget those "granny pants" maternity underpants. If you're already wearing bikini styles, stick with them. But now is a good time to consider upgrading your underpants wardrobe in case you've let your skivvies wear out a bit. After all, you'll be going to lots of check ups and eventually the hospital—your mom would be embarrassed if your unmentionables were full of holes!

HOW MANY? If you need new underpants or plan to buy maternity underpants anyway, we recommend at least eight pairs.

◆ **Maternity belts.** Pregnancy support belts can be critical for some moms. For example, Pam A., one of our readers sent the following email when she was 7 1/2 months along:

"Last week I got the worst pain/cramp that I have ever had in my life. It kept coming and going while I was walking, but it was so bad that I doubled over in pain when it hit. I went to my doctor and she said that the baby was pushing on a ligament that goes between the abdomen and the leg. She recommended that I get a "Prenatal Cradle" (PerinatalCares.com). I'll tell you what—it is the most wonderful purchase I have ever made in my life. It was about $58 (Amazon has them for as little as $36), but it works wonders. It does not totally eliminate the pain, but it gives enough support that it drastically reduces the pain and even gives me time to change positions so that it does not get worse. I have even found that wearing it at night helps to alleviate the pain at night rolling over in bed."

In our pregnancy book, *Expecting 411*, obstetrician Michele Hakakha explains the need for maternity belts for some women:

"(During pregnancy) the curvature of your spine changes and so does your center of gravity. The bigger your belly gets, the more you will feel the aching. This usually happens earlier and earlier with each subsequent pregnancy. (Maternity belts) really help lift the belly up and relieve the pressure and discomfort. But you have to wear them correctly to get relief. You need to try on many different styles and decide what fits best before you purchase."

HOW MANY? Kind of obvious, but one or two should be enough.

◆ **Career Clothing.** Our best advice about career clothing for the pregnant mom is to stick with basics. Buy yourself a coordinating outfit with a skirt, jacket, and pair of pants and then accessorize.

Now, we know what you're saying. You'd love to follow this advice, but you don't want to wear the same old thing several

Plus-size Maternity Clothing

What's the number one frustration with maternity wear? Finding the right size, particularly if you're looking for plus-size maternity clothes, say our readers. Some maternity clothing manufacturers think only women with supermodel bodies get pregnant. But what to do if you want to look attractive and your dress size starts at 16 or above? Our readers have recommended the following sites:

JCPenney	jcpenney.com
Motherhood	maternitymall.com
Expressiva	expressiva.com
Old Navy	oldnavy.com
Plus Maternity	plusmaternity.com
Simply Be	simplybe.com
Target	target.com

times a week—even if it is beautifully accessorized. I don't blame you. So, go for a couple dresses and sweaters too. The good news is you don't have to pay full price. And chances are you know someone who is finished with her pregnancy and will lend you some clothes.

Thanks to casual office wear trends, pregnant woman can spend hundreds of dollars LESS than they might have had to ten or 20 years ago. Today, you can pair a pencil skirt with a sweater set for most office situations.

◆ *Casual Clothes.* Your best bet here is to stick with simple basics, like jeans and chinos. You don't necessarily have to buy these from maternity stores. In fact, later in this chapter, we'll talk about less-expensive alternatives. If you're pregnant in the summer, dresses can be a cooler alternative to pants and shorts.

◆ *Dress or Formal Clothes.* Forget them unless you have a full social calendar or have many social engagements associated with your job. Sometimes, you can find a local store that rents maternity formalwear for the one or two occasions when you might need it. Check out Mine for Nine mentioned earlier to rent dressy clothes. And look at sale items on some of our recommended web sites. You may be able to find a nice outfit at a great price, especially right after holidays.

◆ **Spanx.** Spanx has become famous for their "slimming intimates" and their Mama Spanx support hose expand that philosophy to maternity. Made especially for pregnant bellies, these hose will smooth you out, front and back (the part you seldom see and forget about sometimes!). Available for $28, they are worth the money. And if you're not interested in hose but still want some reshaping, Power Mama ($32) is a thigh length shaper made to accommodate your pregnant belly, support your back and smooth out the bulges—and it will eliminate panty lines.

Nursing Clothes

◆ **Nursing Bras.** The one piece of advice every nursing mom gives is: buy a well-made, high quality, nursing bra *that fits you.* Easier said than done you say? Maybe. But we can offer some tips we gleaned from a reader poll we took.

Nursing bras have special flaps that fold down to give baby easy access to the breast. Access is usually with a hook or snaps either in the middle or on top of the bra near the straps. So first, our readers insist new moms should look for the easiest access they can find with a nursing bra. You'll need to be able to open your nursing bra quickly and with only one hand in most cases.

Next, avoid under wire bras at all cost. They can cause plugged ducts, a very painful condition. If you sport a large cup size, you'll need a bra that is ultra supportive. Also, in most cases, nursing moms require a sleep bra too—some for support, some just to hold nursing pads.

Mothers living near a locally owned maternity shop or specialized lingerie store recommended going in and having a nursing bra fitted to you. One reader reported that "I was wearing a bra at least three cup sizes too small. The consultant fitted me properly and I couldn't believe how comfortable I was!" In fact this should probably be our first tip: make sure your bra is comfortable! Straps shouldn't dig into your shoulders or chest, cups shouldn't look as if they are "overflowing" (we're talking to you, Kardashian sisters!) If you don't have the luxury of a shop full of specialists, HerRoom.com, a lingerie specialty site, has great online tips and videos about fitting any type bra (click the link for "bra fit guide"). Bravado (bravadodesigns.com), a pregnancy and nursing bra specialist also offers extensive sizing tips for different bras models.

If you plan to nurse, you should probably buy at least two bras during your eighth. Why then? Theoretically, your breast size won't change much once your baby is born and your milk comes in. I'd suggest buying one with a little larger cup size (than your eighth month size) so you can compensate for the engorgement phase. You can always buy more later and, if your size changes once the baby is born, you won't have invested too much in the wrong size.

HOW MANY? Buy one to two bras in your eighth month. After the baby is born, you may want to buy a couple more.

◆ **Nursing Pads.** There are two options with nursing pads: disposable and reusable. Common sense tells you that reusable breast pads make the most economical sense, particularly if you plan to have more children. Still, if you aren't a big leaker, don't plan to breast feed for long or just need something quick and easy when you're on the go, disposables are handy.

When we polled our readers, we were surprised to learn that the majority preferred disposables. Those by Lansinoh (lansinoh.com; $7 for 60 at drugstore.com) were by far the favorite followed by Johnson and Johnson ($5.94 per 60), Gerber/NUK (60 for $5.48), Curity (288 for $42), Evenflo ($7 for 60) and Medela ($7.50 for 60). What's the secret to these disposables? The same type of super absorbent polymer that makes your baby's diapers so absorbent. That makes them super thin too so you aren't embarrassed by telltale "bulls-eyes" in your bra. Moms also love the individually wrapped pads because they can just grab a couple and throw them in the diaper bag on the way out of the house. Interestingly, moms were divided on whether they like contoured or flat pads or those with adhesive strips or without.

While there wasn't one discount source mentioned for disposable breast pads, moms tell us when they see their favorite brands on sale at Walmart, Target or Babies R Us, they snapped up multiple boxes.

For the minority who preferred reusable, washable pads, Medela ($5 to $7 for two pairs), Avent ($7 for three pairs) and Gerber ($16.50 for three pair) made the top of the list. Some moms recommend Bravado's (bravadodesigns.com) Cool Max pads ($11 for three pair) for superior absorption. A few parents have raved about Danish Wool pads (danishwool.com). These soft, felted pads contain natural lanolin, a godsend for moms with sore, cracked nipples. They aren't cheap ($23.50 to $36 per pair) but we thought them worth the mention. Another pad recommended by a reader is LilyPadz by Lilypadz.com. She told us they are made from silicone and are streamlined and reusable. They can be worn with or without a bra and cost about $23 per pair.

If you have nipple soreness (you have our sympathies!), Jeri from Stoneham, MA recommended a product called Soothies made by Lansinoh. These reusable gel pads can be slipped into your bra to cool and soothe painful nipples. You can find them online or in drugstores for $10 to $12.

HOW MANY? With disposable pads, buy the smaller package—don't buy the Costco-sized box. You may not need that many or may not like the brand. As for reusable pads, we recommend starting with three pair. That gives you one to wear, one to wash and an extra just in case.

◆ **Nursing Clothes.** You may not think so (especially at 8 1/2 months), but there will come a day when you won't need to wear those maternity clothes. But what if you want to nurse in public after baby is born? Some women swear by nursing clothes as the best way to be discreet, but others do just fine with loose knit tops and button front shirts as well as discrete blanket placement. Bottom line: one obvious way to save money with nursing clothes is not to buy any. If you want to experiment, buy one or two nursing tops and see how they work for you. By the way, parents of twins found it difficult if not impossible to use a nursing top when nursing both babies at the same time.

Reader Tracy G. suggested that working moms who are nursing or expressing milk might want to check into getting a nursing camisole or tank top. "I wear them under a regular shirt and don't feel so exposed when I pump at work or nurse in public." Her favorite: a Walmart brand camisole. She thought it was softer than Motherhood Maternity options.

Another tip: a reader, Sandra F., came up with an ingenious way to use her breast pumps hands free. While Sandra's sister bought a special hands free bra, Sandra bought a zip-up-the-front sports bra and cut holes in it. She emailed us to say it worked better at holding the pumps phalanges to her breasts than her sister's, which was a tube top style that kept slipping. And Sandra saved some big bucks: her sports bra was a $6 sale item while her sister bought a $40 special pumping bra.

◆ **Nursing Pajamas.** Looking for something comfortable to sleep in that allows you to nurse easily? Nursing PJ's are one answer, although only a few moms we interviewed use them. Most hated nursing gowns and found it much simpler to sleep in pajamas with tops they could pull up or unbutton quickly

If you are interested in a specific nursing pajama, check out *Majamas* (majamas.com). One of our product testers tried out their nightgown with her newborn and thought it was great, worthy of a recommendation. It allowed her to sleep without wearing a nursing bra since it had pockets for holding breast pads and had easy nursing access. They have several pajama pant and gown designs and have expanded the line to include maternity clothes, bras and more.

More Money Buys You . . .

Like any clothing, the more you spend, the better quality fabric and construction you get. Of course, do you really need a cashmere maternity sweater you'll wear for only a few months? Besides fabric, you'll note more designer names as prices go up. For example, TopShop and Juicy Couture are making maternity clothes now.

Smart Shopper Tips

Smart Shopper Tip #1
Battling your wacky thermostat
"It's early in my pregnancy, and I'm finding that the lycra-blend blouses that I wear to work have become very uncomfortable. I'm starting to shop for maternity clothes—what should I look for that will be more comfortable?"

It's a fact of life for us pregnant folks—your body's thermostat has gone berserk. Thanks to those pregnancy hormones, it may be hard to regulate your body's temperature. And those lycra-blend clothes may not be so comfortable anymore.

Our advice: stick with natural fabrics as much as possible, especially cotton, silk, light wools and some high tech fabrics. You need fabrics that breathe. Unfortunately, a lot of lower-priced maternity clothing is made of polyester/cotton blend fabrics.

Smart Shopper Tip #2
Seasons change
"Help! My baby is due in October, but I still need maternity clothes for the hot summer months! How can I buy my maternity wardrobe without investing a fortune?"

Unless you live in a place with endless summer, most women have to buy maternity clothes that will span both warm and cold seasons. The best bets are items that work in BOTH winter or summer—for example, lightweight long-sleeve shirts can be rolled up in the summer. Cropped pants can work in both spring and fall. Another tip: layer clothes to ward off cold. Of course, there's another obvious way to save: borrow items from friends. If you just need a few items to bridge the seasons (a coat, heavy sweater, etc), try to borrow before buying.

Smart Shopper Tip #3
Petites aren't always petite

"I'm only 5 feet 2 inches tall and obviously wear petite sizes. I ordered a pair of pants in a petite size from an online discounter, but they weren't really shorter in the leg. In fact, I'd have to have the pants reconstructed to get the right fit. What gives?"

Many maternity web sites advertise that they carry a wide range of sizes but in truth you may find the choices very limited. And in some cases, "petite" is really just sizes 2 to 4. Translation: these pants aren't really shorter in the leg. How can you tell without ordering and then having to return items? Your best bet is to try on items before you buy. That's not always easy, of course, especially when ordering online. In that case, check the size charts on each site to be sure they offer *real* petites. And if a manufacturer (like the Gap, for example) makes petites that fit you in their regular clothing, chances are their maternity line will be comparable.

Here are our readers recommendations for petite maternity: Kohl's, JCPenney, Old Navy, Gap, Japanese Weekend, Juicy Couture and Rebel jeans.

Smart Shopper Tip #4
Tall isn't easy either

"At nearly six feet, I can't find any maternity pants that don't look dorky. Help!"

Just as with petites, we see lots of sites promising a wide range of sizes . . . only to find they have one style that comes in a 31" inseam. And you need a 34." I feel your pain. At 5'9" myself, I recall finding almost nothing in the right length for me. There are more choices today for tall women, but you may find yourself forced to wear more skirts and dresses than pants during your pregnancy.

Here's a partial list of sites that carry tall maternity: Mommy Long Legs (mommylonglegs.com), JC Penney, Isabella Oliver (isabellaoliver.com), Gap, and Old Navy, Long Tall Sally (longtallsally.com), and RG Maternity (rgmaternity.com). If you discover any new sites or stores with tall sizing, email us and we'll add them.

Our Picks: Brand Recommendations for Maternity Undergarments

Here are our readers top picks for maternity undergarments.
God bless Canada—those Maple Leaf-heads make one of the best maternity bras in the world. Toronto-based *Bravado Designs'* (bravadodesigns.com) maternity/nursing bra of the same name is

just incredible. "A godsend!" raved one reader. "It's built like a sports bra with no under wire and supports better than any other bra I've tried . . . and this is my third pregnancy!" raved another.

Bravado makes eight different styles and one nursing bra tank top. Prices start at $35 for the basic Original Nursing Bra. Other styles include the Body Silk Seamless bra ($49), the Bliss ($54), the Sublime ($49) and the Allure ($54). Sizes range from a B cup to J/K (a few go to H/I). The nursing tank top option includes a built in full bra (not a shelf bra) and goes up to a G cup for $54 to $60.

Another plus: the Bravado reps are knowledgeable and helpful with sizing questions. In the past, some of our readers criticized the Bravado for not providing enough support, but the Supreme should answer those concerns. FYI: *Medela*, recently acquired Bravado and have discontinued their line of bras in favor of the Bravado line.

Finally, many readers have recommended Leading Lady maternity and nursing bras (leadinglady.com). They are available widely in many department stores and maternity outlets. Leading Lady has quite a wide assortment of bras in a huge range of sizes.

Looking for maternity shorts/tights for working out? One of the best is *Fit Maternity* (fitmaternity.com; 800-961-9100). They offer an unbelievable assortment of workout clothes including unitards, tights, swimsuits, tennis clothes and more. On the same subject, *Due Maternity* (duematernity.com) offers several yoga and workout pants as well as swimsuits.

Our Picks: Brand Recommendations for Nursing Bras, Pads and Clothes

Nursing pads are a passionate topic for many of our readers with disposables beating out reusables as moms' favorites. They loved both *Lansinoh* and *Johnson & Johnson* disposable by an overwhelming number. *Medela*, *Advent* and *Bravado* make great reusable nursing pads.

Bravado is also quite popular as a nursing bra for all but the largest of cup sizes as are *Playtex* and *Medela*. If you need a size larger than DD, consider *Motherhood Maternity's* brand as well as *Leading Lady*. The web is the best place to find bras on deal including *Decent Exposures* (decentexposures.com) and *Birth and Baby* (birthandbaby.com).

Most moms found that specialized nursing clothes weren't a necessity, but for those who want to try them, nearly everyone recommended *Motherwear* (motherwear.com). *One Hot Mama* (onehotmama.com) and *Expressiva* (expressiva.com) are other stylish sites to consider. Look for discounts on clearance pages or eBay.

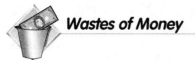

Wastes of Money

Waste of Money #1
Maternity Bra Blues

"My old bras are getting very tight. While visiting a store to get a larger size, a salesperson suggested I purchase a maternity bra for more comfort and support. Should I buy a regular bra in a larger size or plunk down the extra money for a maternity bra?

We've heard from quite a few readers who've complained that expensive maternity bras were very uncomfortable and/or fell apart after just a few washings. Our best advice: try on the bra before purchase and stick to the better brands. Compared to regular bras, the best maternity bras typically have thicker straps, more give on the sides and more hook and eye closures in back (so the bra can grow with you). Most of all, the bra should be comfortable and have no scratchy lace or detailing. Readers tell us that a good sports bra can also be a fine (and affordable) alternative.

Waste of Money #2
Overexposed Nursing Gowns/Tops

"I refuse to buy those awful nursing tops! Not only are they ugly, but those weird looking panels are like wearing a neon sign that says BREASTFEEDING MOM AHEAD!"

"I plan to nurse my baby and all my friends say I should buy nursing gowns for night feedings. Problem is, I've tried on a few and even though the slits are hidden, I still feel exposed. Not to mention they're the ugliest things I've ever seen. Can't I just wear a regular gown that buttons down the front?"

Of course you can. And considering how expensive some nursing gowns can be ($35 to $50 each), buying a regular button-up nightshirt or gown will certainly save you a few bucks. Every mother we interviewed about nursing gowns had the same complaint. There isn't a delicate way to put this: it's not easy to get a breast out of one of those teenie-weenie slits. Did the person who designed these ever breastfeed a baby? I always felt uncovered whenever I wore a nursing gown, like one gust of wind would have turned me into a centerfold for a nudist magazine. Exception: Majamas (majamas.com) are designed by people who know what it's like to breast feed.

And can we talk about nursing shirts with those "convenient button flaps for discreet breastfeeding"? Convenient, my fanny. There's so much work involved in lifting the flap up, unbuttoning it, and getting your baby positioned that you might as well forget it. My advice: stick with shirts you can pull up or unbutton down the front. These are just as discreet, easier to work with, and (best of all) you don't have to add some expensive nursing to your wardrobe.

Another tip: if possible, try on any nursing clothing BEFORE you buy. See how easy they are to use. You might be surprised how easy (or difficult) an item can be. Imagine as you are doing this that you have an infant that is screaming his head off wanting to eat NOW, not five seconds from now. You can see why buying any nursing clothes sight unseen is a risk.

Waste of Money #3
New shoes
"Help! My feet have swollen and none of my shoes fit!"

Here's a little fact of pregnancy that no one tells you: your feet are going to swell. And, sadly, after the baby is born, those tootsies

Fetal Monitors: Good or Bad Idea?

Can you buy your own Doppler ultrasound monitor to listen to your baby's heartbeat? Sure . . . but is it a good idea? To answer that question, we turned to our favorite obstetrician, Dr. Michele Hakakha. Michele is the co-author of our book on pregnancy, Expecting 411. Here's why she says pass on these gizmos:

"First of all, home Dopplers are an unnecessary expense (around $100) Secondly, using the Doppler requires the experienced hands of someone who has used one about a thousand times. And even in those experienced hands, it can be hard to find the baby's heartbeat, especially early in the pregnancy.

What ends up happening is that the pregnant couple can't detect the baby's heartbeat at home and they frantically rush into their practitioner's office. Other times, couples listen cheerfully to mom's pulse instead of baby's heartbeat!

You can do a much better job of tracking the health of your unborn baby by following your baby's movements in the womb. So, skip the panic (you'll have your share of that as new parents), save your money (you'll need it for the college fund), and leave the Fun-With-The-Doppler game up to your practitioner."

won't necessarily shrink back to your pre-pregnancy size. A word to the wise: don't buy lots of new shoes at the start of your pregnancy. But no need to despair. After your baby is born, you'll likely have a built-in excuse to go shoe shopping!

Another suggestion from reader Gretchen C. of Rochester, WA: "It is never too early to buy shoes that don't tie! I go to the gym every morning, and it was getting to be a huge ordeal just to get my shoes tied. I bought some slip on shoes at 20 weeks and I still think it's one of the smartest things I've done."

Money-Saving Secrets

1 CONSIDER BUYING "PLUS" SIZES FROM A REGULAR STORE. Thankfully, fashion continues to be heavy on casual looks . . . even for the office. This makes pregnancy a lot easier since you can buy the same styles in larger ladies' sizes to cover your belly without compromising your fashion sense or investing in expensive and

---

As a side note, the FDA says that fetal heart monitors are a medical device and, as such, require a prescription from a doctor to use at home. While some sites will not rent or sell a monitor to a parent without a prescription, others assume you have your doctor's okay.

Why do you need a prescription? After all, isn't a heart monitor just a Doppler ultrasound that checks the heartbeat? What's the big deal?

Doppler ultrasound devices use acoustical energy that is emitted continuously from the unit. It's the "continuous" part that has doctors and the FDA concerned. In your doctor's office, he or she will use a fetal heart monitor for a few minutes. But unsupervised parents at home may decide to use it every day for longer periods of time. The risk: the unit could heat up, causing damage to the fetus.

Our advice: don't bother with a fetal heart monitor.

As for the "entertainment value" of hearing your baby's heartbeat and sharing it with others we'd recommend a simple option—consider buying a good stethoscope. Then have your doctor teach you how to use it to hear your baby's heartbeat. By about 18 weeks you can usually hear a heartbeat with a stethoscope. And you can buy one for under $100.

often shoddy maternity clothes. We found the same fashions in plus-size stores for 20% to 35% less than maternity shops (and even more during sales).

One drawback to this strategy: by the end of your pregnancy, your hemlines may start to look a little "high-low"—your expanding belly will raise the hemline in front. This may be especially pronounced with dresses. Of course, that's the advantage of buying maternity clothes: the designers compensate with more fabric in front to balance the hemline. Nonetheless, we found that many moms we interviewed were able to get away with plus-size fashions for much (if not all) of their pregnancy. How much can you save? In many cases, from 25% to 50% off those high prices in maternity chains like Pea in the Pod.

2 DON'T OVER-BUY BRAS. As your pregnancy progresses, your bra size is going to change at least a couple times. Running out to buy five new bras when you hit a new cup size is probably foolish—in another month, all those bras may not fit. The best advice: buy the bare minimum (two or three).

3 TRY BRA EXTENDERS, BELLA BAND. You may be able to avoid buying lots of maternity bras by purchasing a few bra extenders. Available from fabric stores, OneHanesPlace.com and even Amazon.com among other sites, these little miracles cost as little as $2 each. You simply hook the extender onto the back of your bra and you can add up to two inches around the bust. You may still need to purchase new bras at some point, but with extenders, you can continue to use your pre-pregnancy bra for quite a while.

By the way, Candy from San Diego wrote to us about a similar product for pants called the Bella Band (bellaband.com).: "I bought the Bella Band early on in my pregnancy and love it so much that I recently bought another one. It was perfect for keeping my "normal" clothes on when I couldn't button them anymore. Then it helped me keep maternity pants on when they were still a little too big but I couldn't fit in my regular clothes anymore." Keep in mind the Bella Band is really for use in early pregnancy before you're big enough to buy true maternity pants and skirts. It will allow you to wear your regular pants during that stage where you're just not ready for maternity. Another, similar product called the Baby Be Mine Belly Band was only $18 for one while a BellaBands was $28.

4 BUT DON'T SKIMP ON QUALITY WHEN IT COMES TO MATERNITY BRAS. Take some of the money you save from other parts of this book and invest in good maternity underwear. Yes, you can find cheap bras for $20 at discount stores, but don't be penny-wise and pound-foolish. We found the cheap stuff is very uncomfortable and falls apart, forcing you to go back and buy more. Invest in better-quality bras if you plan to have more than one child—you can actually wear it again for subsequent pregnancies. No need to purchase special maternity underpants—use your own and save money.

5 CONSIDER DISCOUNTERS FOR CASUAL CLOTHES. Okay, I admit that I don't normally shop at K-Mart or Target for most of my clothes (I do like their t-shirts, workout gear and tank tops). But I was surprised to discover these chains (and even department stores like Sears) carry casual maternity clothes in 100% cotton at very affordable prices. Let's repeat that—they have 100% cotton t-shirts, shorts, pants, and more at prices you won't believe. Most of these clothes are in basic solid colors—sorry, no fancy prints. At Target, for example, I found a cotton thermal maternity shirt (long sleeves) for $20. Jeans were only $35. Even a cotton/spandex jersey dress was a mere $25. The best part: Liz Lange designs a big part of the Target line. Our readers say the quality is a bit lower than Liz's regular, specialty store version, but the style is good and the prices can't be beat. Don't forget to check Target's sale rack too. One reader found items for as little as $14 on sale.

While the discounters don't carry much in the way of career wear, you'll save so much on casual/weekend clothes that you'll be ecstatic anyway. Witness this example: at A Pea in the Pod, we found a striped cotton-knit, short-sleeved top and ponte knit pants. The price for the two pieces: a heart-stopping $245. A similar all-cotton tank top/pants outfit from Target was $50. Whip out a calculator, and you'll note the savings is an amazing 80%. Need we say more?

By the way, don't forget to check out stores like Kohl's, Marshall's, Ross and TJ MAXX. One reader told us she found maternity clothes at 60% off at TJ MAXX. Of course, as we've mentioned, readers like Old Navy and the Gap as well. Corrie, a reader from Chicago, did all her maternity shopping on line at Old Navy. She spent a total of $365 for eight pairs of pants, one pair of jeans, eleven sweaters, eight long sleeve tops, three button-down shirts, five sleeveless tops and two cardigans. This works out to less than $10 per piece!

For fans of the hip discounter H&M, there's great news: the chain has a maternity section in 20 of their stores! Granted most of them (11) are in New York, but if you live in a major metropolitan area and have an H & M, check to see if yours has a maternity section. Dubbed "Mama," our readers report these departments are selling tops for $12 to $16, camisoles for $8 and more. They carry pretty much everything except underwear. Prices are fantastic.

6 **RENT EVENING WEAR—DON'T BUY.** We found that some indie maternity stores rent eveningwear. For example, a local shop we visited had an entire rack of rental formalwear. An off-white lace dress (perfect for attending a wedding) rented for just $50. Compare that with the purchase price of $200+. Sadly, places that rent maternity wear are few and far between, but it might be worth a look-see in your local community. Another idea: try RentMaternityWear.com as an online source for rentals! Pregnant moms can rent the company's dresses for $39 to $69. Rent Maternity Wear also allows moms to rent two sizes of an item to make sure it really fits well. Shipping is a flat $8 and you can specify the exact date you want a dress. Such a deal!

7 **CHECK OUT CONSIGNMENT STORES.** You can find "gently worn" career and casual maternity clothes for 40% to 70% off the original retail! Many consignment or second-hand stores carry only designer-label clothing in good to excellent condition. If you don't want to buy used garments, consider recouping some of your investment in maternity clothes by consigning them after the baby is born. You can usually find listings for these stores in a quick Yelp or Google search. (Don't forget to look for listings of children's consignment stores as well. Some stores that carry second-hand baby gear and clothes also have a significant stock of maternity wear.) One web source to find consignment shops is narts.org.

8 **FIND AN OUTLET.** Go to OutletBound.com to find a maternity outlet near you.

9 **BE CREATIVE.** Raid your husband's closet for over-sized shirts and pants.

10 **SEW IT YOURSELF.** Pattern companies like Simplicity (simplicity.com) and McCall (mccall.com includes Butterick and Vogue as well) sell their patterns online and in fabric stores. You'll find a limited selection of designs, but if you're a sewing maven, here's a way to avoid the high prices and frustrating return policies of retail maternity stores.

11 **BEG AND BORROW.** Unless you're the first of your friends to get pregnant you know someone who's already been through this. Check around to see if you can borrow old maternity clothes from other moms. In fact, we loaned out a big box after our

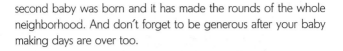
second baby was born and it has made the rounds of the whole neighborhood. And don't forget to be generous after your baby making days are over too.

12 **CHECK OUT CLEARANCE AREAS ONLINE.** Many of our most devoted discount shopping readers have scored big deals on their favorite web sites' clearance pages. Flash sale sites like Ideel (ideel.com), MyHabit (myhabit.com), Rue La La (RueLaLa.com), and Zuliliy (zulily.com) often have designer maternity for sale. Subscribe and you'll get their daily emails which include baby and children's clothes and shoes plus menswear for the guys in your life. Savings of up to 75% are common.

13 **WHEN ORDERING MATERNITY CLOTHES FROM WEB SITES, POOL YOUR ORDERS!** Most web sites offer a free shipping option on orders of $75 to $100 or more (especially after holidays and during end of season sales). Check to see what deals they're offering when you visit. Also, some chain stores will let you return items to your local store, saving you the return-shipping fee.

The Name Game: Reviews of Selected Maternity Stores

Usually this section is intended to acquaint you with the clothing name brands you'll see in local stores. But now there is only one giant chain of maternity wear in North America—Destination Maternity Corp., which operates stores under three brand names. This company is the 800 pound gorilla of maternity clothes with over 2000 locations, as well as a line of maternity clothes designed exclusively for Kohl's called Oh Baby by Motherhood. The company has leased maternity departments in Buy Buy Baby, Sears and Macy's. Destination Maternity has over a 40% share of the $1.2 billion maternity clothing market in the U.S.

FYI: keep in mind that these chains often offer a larger selection of maternity clothing online than what you see in the stores. This is, of course, frustrating since you can't try them on. On the upside, the draconian return policies of the bricks and mortar stores don't apply to online purchases. So you'll be able to return online purchases more easily.

So let's take a look at these three divisions, a new concept they've added, and their web site.

◆ ***Motherhood.*** Motherhood is the biggest sister in the chain. While most stores are located in malls and power centers, there are also Motherhood boutiques in Kohl's (called Oh! Baby by Motherhood). Motherhood carries maternity clothes in the lowest price points.

◆ ***A Pea in the Pod.*** A Pea in the Pod (APIP) is Destination Maternity's most expensive division. With dress prices ranging from $59 to $325, A Pea in the Pod's stores are positioned as designer boutiques although the quality doesn't always match the high prices.

◆ ***Destination Maternity Superstore.*** These stores combine A Pea in the Pod and Motherhood Maternity under one roof. More than just a clothing store, some of these locations also boast a spa (called Edamame) and classes in yoga, financial planning and scrapbooking.

All these stores carry merchandise designed in house, exclusively for the different divisions, plus well known brands like Spanx, C&C California, Lucky Brand and Lilly Pulitzer.

Now that you know the basics, what do real moms think of Destination Maternity's stores? First and foremost, moms dislike, no, hate their return policy. The policy is pretty basic: once you've bought an item, you have ten days to return it for store credit or exchange only (you must have the tags and receipt too).

Watch out for return policies!

Have you bought a maternity dress you don't like or that doesn't fit? Too bad—most maternity stores have draconian return policies that essentially say "tough!"

Destination Maternity stores (including their chains A Pea in the Pod and Motherhood Maternity) only allow returns to their stores if you have the receipt, the item is unworn, unopened and with all the tags. The item also must have been purchased within ten days. These returns are only for store credit or exchange—no money back. Independent maternity stores may have a similar returns policy.

Online return policies are a bit more generous from Motherhood.com: you can get cash back, given you returned the item within 30 days and have all the tags attached. Unfortunately, returning an online purchase to a Motherhood or Pea in the Pod store only gets you store credit, no cash.

No refunds. What if it falls apart in the wash on day 11? Too bad for you. By the way, if you order an item online from Mother Works web site, you'll find a more generous return policy: *Items can be returned for refund or exchange and you have 30 days to return the clothing.* You cannot return items bought online to the store or vice versa, but at least you get extra time and even the money back with an online return. Our advice, if you see it in the store, try it on. If you like it, go home and order it online.

And don't forget that Motherhood has in-store "boutiques" in Kohl's department stores as well as other department stores. In these cases, the leased stores have to comply with the same generous return policy of the department store where they lease space.

As for the individual chains, most moms agreed that the quality at Motherhood is poor. Although some readers have praised their maternity and nursing bras, in general, most agree with this reader's sum-up: "I have found the quality to be inconsistent. I've bought shirts that have unraveled within a few months. . . trashy!" The consensus seems to be that if you buy at Motherhood, you should stick to the sale rack and don't expect high quality except for their bras. However, a recent reader took issue with our review of Motherhood's quality. She told us: "Motherhood clothes are just as well made, if not better made, than Old Navy maternity."

A Pea in the Pod is just way too expensive. That's the general feeling among our readers about this store. Most moms don't think the style of clothing at this chain is anything special. Certainly not to spend $75 for a cotton t-shirt. Considering how short a time a pregnancy is it's a huge waste of money to spend over $245 on a Pea in the Pod pants outfit. And what about their "legendary" service, as Pea in the Pod likes to tout? It's a joke, say our readers. One mom summed it up best by saying: "For the price that one is paying, one expects a certain degree of customer service and satisfaction, both of which are lacking in this over-priced store. What a complete and utter disappointment!"

Consumer alert: one new mom warned us about giving personal info to a maternity chain when you make a purchase (clerks may ask you if you want to receive sales notices). The problem: you often end up on junk mailing lists. In the case of our reader, even though she specifically requested the chain not sell her information to third parties, they did so. Once on those lists, it's tough to stop the junk from arriving in your mailbox.

E-Mail from The Real World
Stay fit with pregnancy workout DVDs

Sure, there are plenty of workout DVDs targeted at the preggo crowd. But which are the best? Readers give their top picks, starting with Margaret Griffin:

"As a former certified aerobics instructor, I have been trying out the DVD workouts for pregnancy. Here are my top picks:

"**Buns of Steel: Pregnancy & Post-Pregnancy Workouts** with Madeleine Lewis ($13) gets my top rating. Madeleine Lewis has excellent cueing, so the workout is easy to follow. Your heart rate and perceived exertion are both used to monitor your exertion. There is an informative introduction. And I really like the fact that the toning segment utilizes a chair to help you keep your balance, which can be off a little during pregnancy. Most of the toning segment is done standing. This is a safe, effective workout led by a very capable instructor and I highly recommend it."

"A middle rating goes to **Denise Austin's: Fit & Firm Pregnancy** ($15). Denise has a good information segment during which she actually interviews a physician. She also provides heart rate checks during the workout. However, there are a couple of things about this workout that I don't particularly like. First, during the workout, there are times when safety information is provided regarding a particular move. This is fine and good, but instead of telling you to continue the movement and/or providing a picture-in-a-picture format, they actually change the screen to show the safety information and then cut back into the workout in progress. Surprise! You were supposed to keep doing the movement. Second, Denise Austin is a popular instructor, but I personally find that her cueing is not as sharp as I prefer and sometimes she seems to be a little offbeat with the music. My suggestion is get this DVD to use in addition to other DVDs if you are the type who gets easily bored with one workout."

Reader Laura McDowell recommended a few different workout DVDs. **Leisa Hart's FitMama: Prenatal and Postnatal Pregnancy Workout** ($20) workout DVD was a favorite. "I loved it! Leisa has great energy and her peppy attitude made me smile through the whole workout. It has about 20 minutes of salsa dancing and then modified yoga." Laura also enjoyed **Kathy Smith's Pregnancy Workout** (discontinued by manufacturer, but still available used on Amazon). It

was "a total 80's throwback; fun and energizing. She moves through the steps fast at times, but is always clear about offering ways to slow down if you need to. The hair, outfits and music are highly entertaining so the workout goes fast and feels great."

Another reader recommended **The Perfect Pregnancy Workout** DVD ($25). "It's by a former Cirque du Soleil acrobat, who leads the exercises with a French accent. It also offers beginner, intermediate and advanced options for each exercise."

Yoga is a terrific low impact exercise that does a wonderful job of stretching muscles you'll use while carrying and delivering your child. It's a terrific option for pregnant moms. And it's definitely become one of the most popular exercise options in North America. So it was only a matter of time before our readers began reviewing yoga DVDs. Here are some of their comments:

Reader Sheri Gomez recommended Yoga Zone's DVD **Postures for Pregnancy** ($15), calling it "wonderful for stretching and preventing back problems. It's beginner friendly and not too out there with the yoga thing." Her only complaint: there is no accompanying music, so she played her own DVDs along with the tape.

Reader Eufemia Campagna recommended Yoga Journal's **Prenatal Yoga** with Shiva Rea ($20). She noted that each segment of the tape is done using three women at different stages of pregnancy. "The segments are all accompanied by lovely, relaxing music and the instructor's directions are so clear that you don't even have to look at the TV to know what you need to do!" Another reader, Carolyn Oliner, also complimented this DVD: "It's not so much of a traditional yoga workout but a great series of poses and stretches that work for pregnant women and leave you feeling warm and stretched and (more gently) exercised." Finally, another reader noted that this workout is "really gentle (pretty easy for experienced yogini)."

Finally, we should note that Pilates has also been adapted for pregnancy exercise. You'll find several options on DVD including **Pilates During Pregnancy, Jennifer Gianni's Fusion Pilates for Pregnancy**, and **Prenatal Pilates** as well as many others.

If you have a Netflix subscription, you might think you can stream these videos . . . but no dice. While some title are available to rent as DVDs from Netflix, we don't see any pregnancy workout videos in the streaming service as of this writing. Ditto with Amazon Prime Instant Video. YouTube, on the other hand, has tons of pregnancy workout videos to stream! Use a Roku, Apple TV or Chromecast to stream YouTube videos to your TV..

The Bottom Line:
A Wrap-Up of Our Best Buy Picks

For career and casual maternity clothes, we thought the best deals were from the Old Navy, the Gap and H&M stores. Compared to retail maternity chains (where one outfit can run $200), you can buy your entire wardrobe from these places for a song.

If your place of work allows more casual dress, check out the prices at plus-size stores or alternatives like Old Navy. A simple pair of jeans that could cost $140 at a maternity shop are only $36 or less at Old Navy. And if you prefer the style at maternity shops, only hit them during sales, where you can find decent bargains. Another good idea: borrow from your husband's closet—many items can do double-duty as maternity clothes.

For weekend wear, we couldn't find a better deal than the 100% cotton shirts and shorts at discounters like Target, Walmart and K-Mart. Prices are as little as $10 per shirt—compare that to the $34 price tag at maternity chain stores for a simple cotton shirt.

Invited to a wedding? Rent that dress from a maternity store and save $100 or more. Don't forget to borrow all you can from friends who've already had babies. In fact, if you follow all our tips on maternity wear, bras, and underwear, you'll save $700 or more. Here's the breakdown:

1. **Career Wear: $300.**

2. **Casual Clothes: $100.**

3. **Underwear: $150 to $200.**

Total damage: $550 to $650. If you think that's too much money for clothes you'll only wear for a few months, consider the cost if you outfit yourself at full-price maternity shops. The same selection of outfits would run $1300 to $1700.

CHAPTER 6

FEEDING

Feeding Baby

Inside this chapter

How much money can you save by breastfeeding? What are the best options for pumps? Which bottles are best? We'll discuss these topics as well as ways to get discount formula, including details on which places have the best deals. And of course, we'll have tips and reviews on the next step in feeding: solid food. Finally, let's talk about high chairs—who's got the best value? Durability? Looks?

Breastfeeding

As readers of past editions of this book know, we are big proponents of breastfeeding. The medical benefits of breast milk are well documented, but obviously the decision to breast or bottle-feed is a personal call for each new mom. In the past, we spent time in this chapter encouraging breast-feeding . . . but we realize now we are preaching to the choir. Our time is better spent discussing how to save on feeding your baby, no matter which way you go. So, we'll leave the discussion of breast versus bottle to our other book *Baby 411* (as well your doctor and family). Let's talk about the monetary impact of the decision, however.

Breastfeed Your Baby and Save $900

Since this is a book on bargains, we'd be remiss in not mentioning the tremendous amount of money you can save if you breastfeed. Just think about it: no bottles, no expensive formula to prepare, no special insulated carriers to keep bottles warm/cold, etc.

So, how much money would you save? Obviously, NOT buying formula would be the biggest money-saver. Even if you were to use the less-expensive powdered formula, you would still have to spend nearly $24 per 23.4-ounce can of powdered formula. Since each can makes about 150 ounces of formula, the cost per ounce of formula is about 16¢. And, by the way, the American Academy of Pediatrics and the American Dental Association now say that parents who use powdered formula should use bottled water when they make up a bottle for baby. What kind of bottled water? Purified, demineralize, deionized, distilled or reverse osmosis filtered water. So that's going to cost you too—about a penny per ounce.

That doesn't sound too bad, does it? Unless you factor in that a baby will down 32 ounces of formula per day by 12 weeks of age. Your cost per day would be $5.12. Assuming you breastfeed for at least the first six months, you would save a grand total of $934.40 just *on formula alone*. The American Academy of Pediatrics recommends breastfeeding for 12 months (with solid foods added to the mix at six months), so in that case your savings could be as much as $1,869! That doesn't include the expense of bottles, nipples and accessories! By the way, statistically speaking, 77% of American moms breastfeed their babies at birth (as of 2013). By six months, however, the number of breastfeeding moms drops to nearly 49% (although this is an improvement up from 33% in 2007). At 12 months, the rate increased from 16% to 27% in 2013.

To be fair, there are some additional expenses that might go along with breastfeeding too. The biggest dollar item: you might decide to buy a breast pump. Costs for this item range from $30 to $50 for a good manual pump to $300+ for a professional-grade breast pump. Or you can rent a pump for $50 to $75 a month (plus a kit—one time cost of about $50 to $60). On the plus side, the new heath care law requires health insurance companies to pay for breast pumps, so your out-of-pocket expense may vary.

And of course, you'll also need some bottles—but arguably fewer than if you formula-feed.

If $934.50 doesn't sound like a lot of money, consider the savings if you had to buy formula in the concentrated liquid form instead of the cheaper powder. A 32-ounce can of Enfamil ready-to-eat liquid costs about $7.49 at a grocery store and makes up only eight 4-ounce bottles. The bottom line: you could spend over $1300 on ready-to-eat formula for your baby in the first six months alone!

Of course, we realize that some moms will decide to use formula because of a personal, medical or work situation—to help out, we have a section later in this chapter on how to save on formula, bottle systems and other necessary accessories.

Sources: Where to Find Breast Feeding Help

The basis of breastfeeding is attachment. Getting your new little one to latch onto your breast properly is not a matter of instinct. Some babies have no trouble figuring it out, while many others need your help and guidance. In fact, problems with attachment can lead to sore nipples and painful engorgement. Of course, you should be able to turn to your pediatrician, a lactation consultant and the nurses at the hospital for breastfeeding advice. However, if you find that they do not offer you the support you need, consider the following sources for breastfeeding help:

1 LA LECHE LEAGUE (llli.org). Started in 1956 by a group of moms in Chicago, La Leche League has traditionally been the most vocal supporter of breastfeeding in this country. You've got to imagine the amount of chutzpah these women had to have to buck the bottle trend and promote breastfeeding at a time when it wasn't fashionable (to say the least).

In recent years, La Leche has established branches in many communities around the world, providing support groups for nursing moms. Their web site also offers reviews and recommendations of books and videotapes on nursing, as well as other child care topics.

2 NURSING MOTHERS' COUNCIL (nursingmothers.org). Similar in mission to La Leche League, the Nursing Mothers' Council differs on one point: the group emphasizes working moms and their unique needs and problems.

3 LACTATION CONSULTANTS. Lactation consultants are usually nurses who specialize in breastfeeding education and problem solving. You can find them through your pediatrician, hospital, or the International Board of Lactation Consultants Examiners (iblce.org). Members must have: "90 contact hours of re-exam education in human lactation and breastfeeding and either be a registered/licensed/recognize health professional in their country or have completed high education in 14 subjects" before they can take the licensing exam.

At some hospitals, resident lactation consultants are available to answer questions by phone at no charge. If a problem persists, you can set up an in-person consultation for a minimal fee (about $65 to $200 per session, although your health insurance provider may pick up the tab).

Unfortunately, the availability and cost of lactation consultants seems to vary from region to region. Our advice: call area hospitals before you give birth to determine the availability of breastfeeding support. Another good source for a referral to a lactation consultant is your pediatrician.

4 HOSPITALS. Look for a hospital in your area that has breastfeeding-friendly policies. These include 24-hour rooming in (where your baby can stay with you instead of in a nursery) and breastfeeding on demand. Pro-nursing hospitals do not supplement babies with a bottle and don't push free formula samples.

5 BOOKS. Although they aren't a substitute for support from your doctor, hospital, and family, many books provide plenty of info and encouragement. Check the La Leche League web site for titles.

6 THE WEB. Our message boards (BabyBargains.com, click on Talk) include a special forum on feeding, "Kid Food." Your can discuss breastfeeding, formula feeding, bottle questions, first foods and more. With 42,000+ members and 1000 new posts a day, you can query other moms about their breast pump experiences, ask a question about food allergies and more.

7 HEALTH INSURANCE PROVIDERS. The new healthcare law mandates certain breastfeeding supplies and assistance—check with your provider for benefits.

Best Online Sources

Medela
medela.com Medela's web site offers useful info, tips and advice on breastfeeding. "Tips and Solutions" (under "Breastfeeding Info") is an excellent FAQ for nursing moms. You can even submit questions to online lactation consultants. **Rating: A**

Breast Pumps Direct
breastpumpsdirect.com Breast Pumps Direct is an online discounter of breast pumps. They carry the major brands (Medela, Avent), as well as accessories and other items. Overall, we found their prices about 5% to 10% below other discounters. The advice section includes pump reviews, comparison charts and more. **Rating: A**

◆ *Other web sites:* The major baby gear sites (Diapers.com, BabiesRUs.com, Target.com and of course, Amazon.com) have extensive offerings of breast pumps and supplies.

What Are You Buying?

Even if you exclusively breastfeed, you probably will find yourself needing to pump an occasional bottle. After all, you might want to go out to dinner without the baby. Maybe you'll have an overnight trip for your job or just need to get back to work full or part time. Your partner might even be interested in relieving you of a night feeding (okay, maybe *you're* interested in your partner taking over a night feeding). The solution? Pumping milk. Whether you want to pump occasionally or every day, you have a wide range of options. Here's an overview:

◆ **Manual Expression:** OK, technically, this isn't a breast pump in the sense we're talking about. But it is an option. There are several good breastfeeding books that describe how to express milk manually. Most women find that the amount of milk expressed, compared to the time and trouble involved, hardly makes it worth using this method. A few women (we think they are modern miracle workers) can manage to express enough for an occasional bottle; for the majority of women, however, using a breast pump is a more practical alternative. Manual expression is typically used only to relieve engorgement.

◆ **Manual Pumps:** Non-electric, hand-held pumps are operated by squeezing on a handle. While the most affordable option, manual pumps are generally also the least efficient—you simply can't duplicate your baby's sucking action by hand. Therefore, these pumps are best for moms who only need an occasional bottle or who need to relieve engorgement.

◆ **Mini-Electrics:** These breast pumps (most work either with batteries or an A/C adapter) are designed to express an occasional bottle. Unfortunately, the sucking action is so weak that it often takes twenty minutes per side to express a significant amount of milk. And doing so is not very comfortable. Why is it so slow? Most models only cycle nine to fifteen times per minute—compare that to a baby who sucks the equivalent of 50 cycles per minute!

◆ **High-End Double Pumps:** The Mercedes of breast pumps— we can't sing the praises of these work horses enough. In just ten to twenty minutes, you can pump both breasts. And high-end double pumps are much more comfortable than mini-electrics. In fact, at first I didn't think a high-end pump I rented was working well because it was so comfortable. The bottom line: there is no better option for working women who want to provide their babies with breast milk.

Today, you have two options when it comes to these pumps: rent a hospital-grade pump (which often is called a piston-electric) or buy a high-end consumer grade double-pump.

Rental Pumps. These are what the industry refers to as hospital-grade or piston electric pumps. They are built to withstand continuous use of up to eight to ten times a day for many years. Often they are much heavier than personal use pumps like the Medela Pump-In-Style. And all the interior parts are sealed to prevent contamination from one renter to the next. *In fact, the Food and Drug Administration (FDA) certifies rental pumps for multiple use.* The only item each renter must buy is a new collection kit.

WHERE TO FIND: Pediatricians, lactation consultants, doulas, midwives, hospitals, maternity stores and home medical care companies are sources to find rental pumps. You can also call La Leche League (800-LALECHE; web: lalecheleague.org) or other lactation support groups for a referral to a rental company in your area.

HOW MUCH: Prices generally average about $65 to $90 per month to rent a breast pump. Common brands of hospital-grade pumps include Hygeia and White River Concepts, although consumer brands Medela and Ameda also have hospital versions. Collection kits cost about $50 to $60 for the bottles, shields and tubes.

Professional-Grade Electric Pumps. These electric pumps are available for sale to consumers and are intended to be used no more than three or four times a day. Unlike rental pumps, they are lighter weight and easier to carry around (to work or elsewhere). Examples of these pumps include the Medela Pump-In-Style and the Ameda Purely Yours.

These pumps have an open system without sealed parts and are therefore only recommended as a single-use item. *The FDA, lactation consultants, pediatricians and manufacturers DO NOT recommend using a second-hand personal pump.* Even if you change the tubes and shields, there is a possibility of cross contamination. (The exceptions are the Bailey Nurture III and Hygeia Enjoye, which are two of the very few consumer-grade pumps certified by the FDA for multiple users).

WHERE TO FIND: Online is a primary source. Also most independent baby stores and Babies R Us carry a selection of electric breast pumps. See earlier in the chapter for some of our favorite sources.

HOW MUCH: Prices range from about $126 to $360 depending on the brand and accessories included. We will review pumps later in this chapter.

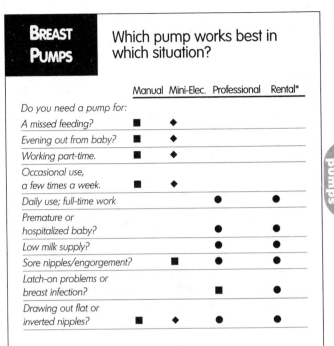

BREAST PUMPS

Which pump works best in which situation?

Do you need a pump for:	Manual	Mini-Elec.	Professional	Rental*
A missed feeding?	■	◆		
Evening out from baby?	■	◆		
Working part-time.	■	◆		
Occasional use, a few times a week.	■	◆		
Daily use; full-time work			●	●
Premature or hospitalized baby?			●	●
Low milk supply?			●	●
Sore nipples/engorgement?	■		●	●
Latch-on problems or breast infection?			■	●
Drawing out flat or inverted nipples?	■	◆	●	●

Key: ■ = Good ◆ = Better ● = Best
*Rental refers to renting a hospital-grade pump. These can usually be rented on a monthly basis.
Source: Medela.

Safe and Sound

As we mentioned in the last section, we don't recommend buying a used breast pump. Models like Medela's Pump In Style can actually collect milk in the pump mechanism. So, let's state it clearly: DO NOT PURCHASE A USED BREAST PUMP. The risk of exposing your baby to any pathogens isn't worth the savings.

Of course, it is fine to re-use your own breast pump for another child down the road. Just replace the tubing and collection bottles to make sure there are no bacteria left over from previous uses.

One more safety tip: if it hurts stop. No kidding! Pumping to express milk for your baby should not be a painful experience.

Smart Shopper Tip

Smart Shopper Tip #1
When to buy that pump.

"I don't know how long I want to breastfeed. And I'll be going back to work soon after my baby is born. When should I get a pump?"

We'd suggest waiting a bit before you invest in a breast pump or even nursing clothes. Many moms start with breast-feeding, but can't or don't want to continue it after a few weeks. For them investing in a pump would be a waste of money. If you aren't sure how long you want to breast feed, but you'd like to pump some extra bottles of milk anyway, consider renting a hospital grade pump first and trying it out before you invest a few hundred dollars. You can often rent for as little as one month, which will be much cheaper than buying a pump that can run $200 to $350.

The best milk storage options

Once you've decided to express breast milk for your child, you'll need to consider how to store it. Freezer bags are the most common method and most major pump manufactures and bottle makers sell bags. So, who's got the best storage bags? **Lansinoh** (100 pack for $17) is the hands-down winner. "They are sturdy, stand on their own and have an excellent double lock seal closure," said one mom. Others echoed that recommendation. Lansinoh also sells BPA-free storage bottles that fit most breast pumps ($12 for four).

Another good choice is **Medela**, the king of breast pumps. Their bags attach to any Medela pump and feature a zipper-top. Amazon.com sells a box of 50 for $16. Medela also sells 80 ml. breast milk containers and lids (12-pack is $13) and plastic collection bottles ($13 for four). Both options are compatible with Medela breast pumps and are BPA free.

A completely different alternative is **Mothers Milk Mate** (mothersmilkmate.com). For $29, you get a ten-bottle storage system with rack. The 5 oz. bottles are BPA free and the set

Waste of Money

Even Cows Opt for the Electric Kind

"I'm going back to work a couple of months after my baby is born. My co-worker who breastfeeds her baby thinks manual and mini-electrics pumps are a waste of money. Your thoughts?

While they may be useful to relieve engorgement, manual pumps aren't very practical for long-term pumping when you're at work. They are very slow, which makes it hard to get much milk. Mini-electric breast pumps are better but are really best only for occasional use—for example, expressing a small amount of milk to mix with cereal for a baby who's learning to eat solids. The problem with mini-electrics: some are painful and most are too slow.

Your best bet if you plan to do some serious pumping is to rent a hospital-grade pump. These monsters maintain a high rate of extraction with amazing comfort. A lactation consultant we interviewed said these pumps can empty both breasts in about ten to 15 minutes—contrast that with 20 to 30 minutes for mini-electrics and 45 minutes to an hour for manual pumps.

We note later in our reviews of pumps that the manual pump

comes with freshness dating labels.

Speaking of labels, it's pretty important to know when milk has been expressed so you don't your feed baby milk that is past its freshness date. One solution: *BabaBaby's* storage bottles, with a calendar cap you twist to date (babababy.com). Invented by mom and actress Tara Strong (best known as the voice of cartoon characters on such shows as the *Powerpuff Girls* and *Ben 10*), BabaBaby bottles are BPA-free and run $17.50 for two.

Yet another great option for freezer storage: **Milk Trays** by Sensible Lines (SensibleLines.com). It's hard to believe no one has thought of this before—Milk Trays are like old-fashioned ice cube trays but with a twist. The tray's 16 one-ounce capacity cubes are shaped like skinny cylinders, small enough to fit into any baby bottle. They come with lids to block freezer burn and are made from BPA-free, phthalate-free plastic. The trays sell for $22 for two.

Don't forget there are numerous apps for your smart phone that can help you keep track of your frozen or refrigerated expressed milk, baby feedings, diapers changes and more. Baby logs range in price from free up to $5.

that received top rating from our readers is the Avent Isis—and even though it is a vast improvement over previous options, it still is a MANUAL pump. It may not work well for moms who plan to work part or full-time and still nurse their baby. That said, one solution is to use two pumps—a mom we interviewed uses a Medela Pump In Style when she's tired (during the evening or night-time) and an Avent Isis at work (it's much quieter; doesn't need electricity, etc).

Affordable Care Act & Breast Pumps

In case you've been living off the planet since 2010 and just got back, the Affordable Care Act (ACA, Obamacare) has rolled out . . . and it includes a special benefit for new moms: a "free" breast pump.

Before you get too excited, though, there are "a few, uh, provisos. Ah, a couple of quid pro quos," as the Genie in *Aladdin* would say. The biggest catch: the ACA doesn't specify which pump you get. Not even what kind (manual, mini electric, dual electric, rental). But, you say, you'd like a top of the line Medela or Ameda personal use pump? Well, the answer is: maybe yes, maybe no.

Turns out insurance companies (and some state insurance rules) determine what pump you can get. And in most cases, you also won't be able to stop by your favorite retailer to purchase your pump. Why? Many insurance companies require customers to purchase pumps from the company's designated "durable medical equipment" company (DME). These DME's distribute a wide range of medical equipment (like oxygen bottles and nebulizers).

Yep, that means you'll have to track down one of your insurance company's DME's and then call to see what pumps they might have in stock. Parents have complained on message boards and blogs that they called their insurance providers' designated DME's and discovered they didn't even have breast pumps available. Others noted that their provider only offers a manual pump—not very helpful if you plan to pump at work!

What if you want a more powerful pump like a hospital grade option? Again, this option may or may not be covered by your insurance. Some insurers will allow you to rent a hospital grade pump but only if you have a "medical necessity." Translation: your doctor will have to fill out even more paperwork to "prescribe" a rental pump.

Bottom line in all this: you'll need to talk to your insurance provider. See our blog at BabyBargains.com for questions to ask your provider (search for Affordable Care Act and Breastpumps).

Breast Pumps (model by model reviews)

Manual Pumps

AVENT COMFORT MANUAL (SCF310/20)
Web: AventAmerica.com
Price: $40-$45.
Type: Manual.
Comments: Our readers love this pump, which Avent claims is as efficient as a mini-electric (it takes about eight to ten minutes to empty a breast). Mom feedback is very positive and at this price, it's a real winner. *Rating: A*

DR. BROWN'S MANUAL BREAST PUMP BY SIMPLISSE
Web: Simplisse.com
Price: $20.
Type: Manual.
Comments: In 2012, Dr. Brown's merged with Simplisse. The Simplesse pumps have since been renamed Dr. Brown's, including their manual pump. The company claims this pump mimics Mother Nature better than other manual pumps, which have a suck-and-release action. Fans love the soft breast cup; dissenters say it isn't as efficient as the Medela or Avent models. One online reviewer chimed in, saying "the Simplisse must be French for many ridiculous steps for assembly and disassembly and miserable to clean." *Rating: C+*

EVENFLO MANUAL
Web: Evenflo.com
Price: $18.
Type: Manual.
Comments: The Evenflo Manual features a lightweight design, "Advance MemoryFlex" fastener for better milk expression and silicone inserts for different size nipples. The unit comes with one 5 oz. collection bottle and a carry case. Reader feedback on this one has been split. Fans say it works okay for that occasional bottle. Critics, on the other hand, complain about lack of suction and pain while pumping. *Rating: C+*

LANSINOH MANUAL
Web: Lansinoh.com
Price: $30-$35.
Type: Manual.

Comments: Readers think this pump is a good runner up to Medela or Avent—Lansinoh's manual pump is easy to use and has few parts to clean. A few dissenters say it doesn't quite have the suction of the Medela, however. That was confirmed by our lactation consultant, who said her measurements showed the Lansinoh pump had about 20% less suction compared to the Avent or Medela. FYI: Lansinoh has revised the pump with new ComfortFit flanges (in two sizes) for a better seal. ***Rating: B***

MEDELA HARMONY
Web: Medela.com
Price: $30-$35.
Type: Manual.
Comments: The Harmony is a winner. Similar to the Avent Isis, it has fewer parts to wash than the Avent and is easier to assemble. Medela notes the Harmony offers a 2-phase expression technology that is supposed to stimulate let down, then slows down to mimic slower, deeper sucking action. One mom with larger breasts found this pump worked better for her than the Avent. The Harmony is also more affordable than the Avent. ***Rating: A***

Mini Electric Pumps

EVENFLO DUAL ELECTRIC
Web: Evenflo.com
Price: $36 single, $55 dual.
Type: Mini-electric.
Comments: Evenflo recently revamped its line of breast pumps. The Dual Electric breast pump is a double pump mini electric which sells for an affordable $55. The pump features an adjustable vacuum which Evenflo claims allows moms to customize the comfort level. It also has a silicone insert to "accommodate different nipple sizes" and comes with a cooler bag and two ice packs, an AC adapter and a 5 oz. bottle. This pump is also available as a single for $36.

Evenflo only recommends this pump for occasional use. In fact, they note on their web site that moms should not use it more than two times per day. So far, feedback is not very positive. Critics complain about defective units, the suction that stopped working and an overall lack of power. ***Rating: C***

First Years MiPump

Web: learningcurve.com
Price: $45-$50 single; $70-$80 double.
Type: Mini-electric.

Comments: With both a single and double mini-electric version (pictured), the First Years MiPump is affordable and quiet—but the suction is inadequate. They claim the pump offers eight levels of suction but some readers were disappointed. And more than one reader criticized the overall quality of the MiPump. Several reports of the pump breaking within a month or so of purchase make this one a loser. *Rating: C-*

Medela Swing Breast pump

Web: Medela.com
Price: $150-$170
Type: Mini electric.

Comments: This single electric pump offers Medela's 2-Phase Expression (the same system as Medela's more expensive pumps), which is supposed to copy baby's natural sucking rhythm. The pump has two different modes: first to stimulate letdown and then to simulate baby's normal sucking pattern. Moms applaud this pump's ease of use and comfort. The only negative: it's a single pump and hence is best for occasional use. In fact, some moms wished it came as a double version. Despite that, we will give it our highest rating. *Rating: A*

More mini-electrics: You'll see several other brands of mini-electric breast pumps on the market today. With the exception of the Medela Swing, most of these pumps fare poorly according to our reader feedback. For occasional use, you are better off getting a simple manual pump. Or if you need a serious pump for daily pumping, the professional-grade options (reviewed below) are the best bets.

Professional-Grade Pumps

Ameda Purely Yours

Web: Ameda.com
Price: $126 for the pump only; $160 for the Carry All version; $220 for the Backpack; $225 Ultra.
Type: Professional.

Comments: Here's a pump we've fallen out of love with. Yes, we did recommend this pump in a previous edition of our book . . . and on paper, the Purley Yours is winner. It's smaller! It's lighter! And its less expensive—the Ameda Purely Yours won a legion of fans for its Purely Yours Pump, which comes in four versions: pump only (use your own bag), Carry All (pictured) and Backpack. A new "Ultra" version throws in an extra tote bag, cooler bag and six bottles. The pump weighs about five pounds and has eight suction settings and nine speeds. The backpack includes a car adapter. The Ameda has a built-in AA battery pack, versus the Medela, which has a separate battery pack.

The Purely Yours is easy to maintain (milk can't get into the tubes, which means less cleaning than the Medela). The downside? Medela is sold in many more retail outlets than Ameda meaning you can get spare parts and supplies easier (although to its credit, Ameda has great customer service).

So what went wrong? In the past year, the reader feedback on this pump has turned sharply negative. Most complaints center around problems with suction. Moms tell us they have to constantly adjust the machine (stopping and restarting) to keep the suction at an appropriate level.

We're at a loss to explain why this pump has gone down hill—did Ameda change the specs? The motor? Or is it a quality control issue? While Ameda figures it out, we've downgraded our rating of the Purely Yours. *Rating:* **C+**

AVENT COMFORT SINGLE/TWIN ELECTRIC

Web: AventAmerica.com
Price: $131 single, $200 double.
Type: Professional.
Comments: Avent breast pumps went through a big change in the past year: moms no longer have to lean forward to use their pumps. We can hear the collective sigh of relief from our readers out there. Finally, a break for your sore backs. Avent now markets the new versions under the Comfort moniker.

Avent also improved the assembly of their single and double electric pumps making the directions easier to follow, plus they still come with their five-petal massage cushion developed to improve letdown. The pumps come with three pump settings plus an initial gentle mode to help with letdown.

The Comfort Double ($170-$200) comes with two 4 oz. bottles with nipples, breast pads, spare diaphragm, sealing disks for milk storage and travel pouch. The Comfort Single ($120-$150), however, does not include a travel bag and comes with only one bottle and nipple plus a breast pad sample pack. For an extra $50, we'd recommend the Double version: you'll empty your breasts faster with a double and get more accessories.

Our readers are generally split into two camps when it comes to pumps: Medela vs. Avent. Medela fans like the wide availability of parts and Medela's excellent customer service. Avent fans love the pump's overall quality and compatibility with Avent's very popular bottles—the pump connects directly to the bottles, for example. Avent customer service is exceptional.

A few folks criticized the suction, saying it was too weak for them to get much milk. They noted they almost never used the lower levels of suction—only the highest got enough milk for them.

Overall, most moms thought the Comfort pumps were comfortable and easy to clean. And it does the job. *Rating: A*

BAILEY MEDICAL NURTURE III
Web: BaileyMed.com
Price: $80 basic, $130 deluxe.
Type: Professional
Comments: This pump comes in two versions—basic ($130) and deluxe ($160). It's claim to fame: the Nurture III is one of the few small pump approved for multiple users by the FDA. Hence you can buy this pump and hand it down to a friend or sell it online. The Nurture III features fully adjustable suction and manual cycling, where mom can control the cycling pattern. This feature takes some practice, say our readers—and isn't a plus for sleep-deprived moms.

Fans say it does a great job at expressing milk, but others have a problem letting-down with the Nurture III. The deluxe version includes an insulated carry bag with ice pack, four extra bottles and an instructional DVD. Bottom line: this is a good pump, but hard to find in stores. It is mostly sold online. *Rating: B+*

Pumps: Have a Plan B

If you plan to return to work and will rely on pumping to feed your baby, make sure you have a Plan B in case your breast pump breaks. Yes, pumps are just machines and sometimes they break down—that means tracking down replacement parts at a store across town, or waiting for parts to arrive by mail. The best advice: have a Plan B, like a back-up manual or mini-electric pump on hand. This is especially important if you choose a brand (like Ameda) that is mostly sold online—to get replacement parts for such pumps you'll have to wait while they ship!

HYGEIA ENJOYE

Web: Hygeiababy.com
Price: $265-$340.
Type: Professional
Comments: A reader recommended this brand to us—she loved her EnJoye pump, which is comparable in suction to hospital-grade pumps. It comes in three versions: a rechargeable battery version ($299), one with an external power supply ($240) or a deluxe tote ($340, pictured).

Unique features include a "CARE button" that "records your baby's cry or other sounds for playback during pumping." This is ostensibly to help with let down. It also has independently adjustable speed and suction controls. Finally, like the Nurture III, this pump is sealed and can be used by more than one person—you can lend or sell it when you're done.

The pumps have a three year warranty. After three years, return your pump to the company and they offer to recycle or refurbish your pumps so you don't have to throw it away. One bummer: Hygeia doesn't make smaller size flanges.

Initial feedback on the Enjoye was positive, but recently moms

Nursing Pillows

Many nursing moms find a nursing pillow makes breastfeeding easier and more comfortable. Our readers have emailed us positive comments for *My Brest Friend* by Zenoff Products (zenoffproducts.com). Okay, it probably qualifies as the Most Stupid Name for a Baby Product Ever award, but it really works—it wraps around your waist and is secured with Velcro. It comes in original, deluxe, professional, travel and twins models. The original retails for about $45.

An old favorite is the *Boppy* pillow. Sold for $30 to $45 online, this perennial favorite doesn't have a waist strap, but many moms swear by it as a simple, affordable nursing pillow.

Got twins? Check out Double Blessing's *EZ-2-NURSE's* pillow (doubleblessings.com) A mom told us this was the "absolute best" for her twins, adding, "I could not successfully nurse my girls together without this pillow. It was wonderful." Cost: $70.

If you're not sold in the idea of a big, bulky nursing pillow, we did find an alternative. *Utterly Yours* (utterlyyours.com) makes a small, hand-sized pillow that you position directly under the breast. Cost: $25 (including pillow cover).

have been complaining that their pumps had suction problems and in some cases the battery or motor died. Compounding the problem is customer service (or lack thereof) from Hygeia. So we're lowering the Enjoye's rating this time out. ***Rating: C***

LANSINOH SIGNATURE PRO

Web: Lansinoh.com
Price: $105-$150.
Type: Professional.
Comments: Lansinoh's newest pump the Signature Pro is very similar to the pump it replaces, the Affinity Pro (still for sale online). The difference? Not much. The Signature Pro now allows you to pump directly into Lansinoh's baby bottles and seal and store for later use. Or you can attach a NaturalWave nipple to feed baby immediately from the collection bottle.

The Signature Pro still has the three customizable suction rhythms, LCD screen for keeping track of pumping time, and closed system so milk won't collect in the tubes or motor. These were features first introduced on the Affinity Pro. The pump is affordably priced at $150 retail and includes a carry tote, two collection bottles with nipples and caps, two nursing pads, AC adapter and a lanolin sample. This new model replaces the Affinity and Affinity Pro.

Early feedback on this pump is mixed. Some parents are disappointed in the suction power of the pump and others complain their pumps stopped working after a short while. On the other hand, fans like the light weight, easy to read LCD screen and affordable price. This might be a pump for the occasional user, not the daily user.

FYI: Be sure the item you're ordering is the Signature. We noticed on Amazon that Lansinoh pumps sometimes were listed as Signature, but were really the older Affinity pumps. ***Rating: B-***

MEDELA FREESTYLE BREAST PUMP

Web: Medela.com
Price: $306-$360.
Type: Professional
Comments: The Freestyle is Medela's latest pump and they pulled out all the stops: hands-free option, LED display, pumping session timer, memory function and more.

How does it differ from the Pump in Style (PIS)? Well, the Freestyle can be removed from its bag (unlike the PIS backpack or shoulder bag) and it features a rechargeable battery for three hours of pumping (the PIS can use AA batteries or a wall outlet). Most moms only have to charge it once a week. No, it doesn't have the PIS's "2-Phase Expression technology" but it does have the one touch let-down button. Its also missing the ability to independently control the speed and suction.

Yet it is the hands-free option that is the killer app here: fans call it "life changing," especially for moms with another toddler at home (and hence the need to multi-task). Of course, at $380, this pump better be darn impressive. And it's amazing that all this comes from a pump that basically fits in the palm of your hand (ok, if you have big hands).

So why buy the Freestyle instead of the Pump In Style? Fans of the Freestyle say it is easier to use and clean than the PIS. Even the breast shields are softer and more comfortable. The downside? The Freestyle isn't exactly quiet, although no louder than the Pump In Style. And if you don't keep the bottles at the right angle, milk can spill out. Also the Freestyle can be a bit fussy to assemble—if you don't assemble the parts just so, you can get less suction. Finally, moms complain that the battery is not as powerful as the corded Pump In Style Advance meaning you won't get as much milk or it will take longer. Those cons aside, we still think this is an good pump. The Freestyle is highly recommended.

FYI: If you receive a stripped down Medela pump from your insurance company, the company sells accessories (like carry bags) a la carte from their web site. ***Rating: A-***

MEDELA PUMP IN STYLE ADVANCED

Web: Medela.com
Price: $225-$300.
Type: Professional
Comments: It's the 800-pound gorilla of the breast pump category: the Medela Pump In Style Advance (PIS).

So what's all the fuss about? If you are serious about pumping every day, the Pump In Style allows you to carry a high quality pump with you to work. You can empty both breasts in a short amount of time with great comfort. As a nursing mom, I remember using the Original version and found it pretty comparable to a hospital-grade pump.

The PIS has evolved over the years—gone is the basic "Original" version and now we have the Advanced, which comes in three flavors: backpack, on-the-go tote bag and metro bag.

In general, the Advanced features Medela's new "2-Phase Expression" technology that mimics the way infants nurse at the breast. At first, infants apparently nurse quickly to simulate let down. Then they settle into a deeper, slower sucking action—the Pump In Style Advance simulates this pattern.

The three versions are similar: all have the same motor, just a different bag. The Metro has a removable pump motor, storage bags and two breast shield sizes.

So what's the disadvantage of the Pump In Styles? Cost is a biggie: the PIS is $50 to $100 more than the Philips Avent Double Electric Comfort, which is smaller, lighter and has several other attractive features. Medela's higher price is no doubt attributable to their "minimum advertised price" policy, which prevents Internet discounters from selling their pumps below a certain price. Hence, you'll see Medela priced about the same on most sites.

Fans of Medela love the availability of parts (sold in many retail stores) and Medela's excellent customer service. So, all in all, we will recommend the Pump in Style—it is an excellent pump. **Rating: A**

SIMPLISSE DR. BROWN'S DOUBLE ELECTRIC

Web: Simplisse.com
Price: $195-$250.
Type: Professional.

Comments: Simplesse Dr. Brown's Double Electric breast pump (yep, that is a mouthful) features "gentle compression technology to gently elicit milk expression." The pump also has flexible breast cups for better fit and adjustable pump pressure settings, as well as a purse-like tote bag that includes a cooler pack and four milk collection bottles. Moms seem a lot more impressed with the electric version than with Dr. Brown's manual pump. They tell us the pump is very comfortable and easy to use. On the other hand, we've heard a few complaints that the compression wasn't enough to get much milk. **Rating: B**

Our Picks: Brand Recommendations

◆ **Manual Pump:** The best manual pumps are the *Avent Comfort Manual* (SCF310/20; $40-$45) and *Medela Harmony* ($30). Between the two, the Medela Harmony has the edge, given its lower price and easy-to-clean design.

◆ **Mini Electric Pump:** The *Medela Swing* mini-electric is pricey ($150-$170) but very good quality. Yes, you may be tempted by other mini-electric pumps in discount stores for $40 to $50, but we have one word of advice: don't.

◆ **Professional Grade Pump:** It's been a top pick of ours for years and wins the crown again: the *Medela Pump In Style Advanced* ($225 to $300, pictured). For daily pumping, it is the gold standard. An excellent and more affordable runner up is the *Avent Double Electric Comfort* ($131 single; $200 double). If hands-free operation is important, then consider the excellent *Medela Freestyle* ($306-$360).

Before you buy a pump, we suggest RENTING a hospital-grade pump first for a week or two (or a month). After you decide you're committed to pumping and you're comfortable with how double pumps work, then consider buying one of your own. Given the hefty retail prices, it makes sense to buy only if you plan to pump for several months or have a second child.

Formula

It is a $7 billion business. But is there any nutritional difference between brands of formula? No, the federal government mandates that all formula have the same nutritional value (the same amount of protein, fat, etc). That's right—the "generic" formula sold at a dis-counter is nutritionally no different than pricey name brands. How pricey? A 23.4-ounce can of name brand powdered formula runs $24 today. Yep, 24 bucks a can. At these prices, you can see how buying formula can take a bite out of your baby budget in a hurry. Also, as we mentioned earlier, the American Academy of Pediatrics and the American Dental Association now say that parents who use powdered or concentrated formula should use bottled water when they make up a bottle for baby. What kind of bottled water? Purified, demineralize, deionized, distilled or reverse osmosis filtered water. So that's going to cost you too—add about a penny per ounce to the cost of powdered formula. Let's talk formula!

What Are You Buying?

Baby formula is just baby formula, right? Nope, it is more com-plicated than that—formula comes in several versions (powdered, liquid concentrate, ready-to-drink) as well as types (cow's milk, soy, etc). Not to mention organic, specialty formulas and more. Here's a quick overview:

◆ **Versions**. Formula comes in three different versions: powder, liq-uid concentrate and ready-to-drink. Powder is least expensive, fol-lowed by liquid concentrate—you add water to both these. Ready-

The most popular formula brands

Formula brand market share, 2013. (Sales in $ millions)

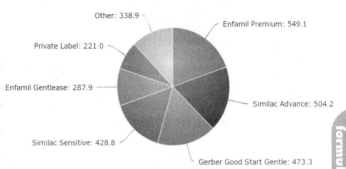

Other: 338.9

Private Label: 221.0

Enfamil Gentlease: 287.9

Similac Sensitive: 428.8

Enfamil Premium: 549.1

Similac Advance: 504.2

Gerber Good Start Gentle: 473.3

to-drink is the priciest. A recent online price survey revealed the lowest cost per ounce of powdered formula is 11¢ (we include the cost of bottled water per oz of 1¢). Compare that to liquid concentrate at 21¢ (also includes 1¢ per oz. bottled water expense), and ready to drink at 28¢ to 50¢ per ounce.

◆ *Infant stages.* Manufacturers are now making different formulas for different ages and stages of infancy. For example, Enfamil makes a formula for newborns to three month olds with additional vitamin D. Meanwhile, Enfamil's regular formula (for newborns up to 12 months) has added prebiotics to aid in the growth of good bacteria in the gut. "Enfagrow" formula is intended for older babies and toddlers (nine-24 months).

◆ *Toddler formula.* First created by Carnation ("Good Start 2" formula, now marketed under the Gerber name), then copied by other formula manufacturers, "toddler" formulas are intended to be used for older children (usually nine months old and up) instead of regular cows milk or soymilk. Typically, parents move to whole milk or soymilk when their child reaches one year of age. In order to hang on to consumers longer, formula manufacturers have developed these toddler formulas. So what's the big difference between baby formula and toddler formula? All these toddler formulas add calcium and iron as well as a variety of vitamins (E, C, D) depending on the brand.

◆ *Types.* Beside cow's milk-based formula, there is also soy-based formula. Which is best? Cow's milk formula with iron—this formula is tolerated best by the most babies and recommended first by most doctors. Of course, there are many specialty formulas for babies with special problems—we call these the "gourmet" formulas, described in more detail below. Our advice in a nutshell: buy the cheapest cow's milk based formula you can find to start with.

◆ *Organic.* These formulas are certified "antibiotic, pesticide and growth hormone free." Organic formula is almost always more expensive than regular formulas, just like organic foods typically cost more. Whole Foods and other natural grocery stores carry organic formula as well as many regular grocery chains. Other options are available online. These are the brands we've found in our research:

Baby's Only Organic (for toddlers only; naturesone.com)
Earth's Best Infant Formula (earthsbest.com)
Kroger Private Selection Organic Formula
O Organic Formula (safeway.com)
Parents Choice (parentschoiceformula.com)
Similac Advance Organic (similac.com)
Vermont Organics (pbmstore.com)

◆ *Gourmet formula.* Formula makers have been busy rolling out additional formula to accommodate a range of baby needs. For example, there is formula for babies with stomach viruses called Isomil DF, Nutramigen with Enflora LGG for colic due to milk allergy, Similac Sensitive for lactose sensitivity, Enfamil AR for babies with gastro esophageal reflux and more. We discuss these formulas in greater detail in our other book, *Baby 411.*

◆ *Packaging.* Concerns about Bisphenol-A (we've discussed this issue on our blog) have prompted formula makers to change their packaging in recent years. Newer plastic tubs and bottles are BPA-free. Other manufacturers like Nature's One have never lined their cans with BPA.

That's just a brief overview of formula—we have an in-depth discussion of formula in our *Baby 411* book. Co-written with a pediatrician, Dr. Ari Brown, the book extensively discusses breastfeeding, formula and feeding challenges for all infants. It's all in a fun-filled chapter called "Liquids." Check our web site (Baby411.com) for Dr. Brown's blog, which covers breaking news items on infant feeding.

Safe and Sound

Formula is one of the most closely regulated food items in the U.S. The Food and Drug Administration has strict guidelines about what can and cannot go into baby formula. The FDA requires expiration dates, warning labels and so on. So what are the safety hazards you might run up against? Here are a few:

1 ASK YOUR DOC FIRST. Never switch formula types or brands without discussing it with your pediatrician first. While our recommendation is to buy the cheapest cow's milk you can find, some babies have health problems that require special formula.

2 CONFUSING CANS CONFRONT SOY FORMULA USERS. Soy formula now accounts for 25% of the infant formula market. Yet, a case of mistaken identity has caused problems. Some parents mistakenly thought they were feeding their babies soy formula, when in fact they were using soymilk. The problem: soymilk is missing important nutrients and vitamins found in soy formula. As a result, babies fed soymilk were malnourished and some required hospitalization. Adding to the confusion, soymilk is often sold in cans that look very similar to soy formula. The government has asked soymilk makers to put warning labels on their products, so most should be labeled. If you use soy formula, be careful to choose the right can.

3 IRON. Another concern: low-iron formula. A myth among some parents is that the iron in standard formula causes constipation—it does not, says pediatrician Dr. Ari Brown, co-author of *Baby 411*. Yes, constipation can be a problem with ALL formulas. But babies should NEVER be on low-iron formula unless instructed by a pediatrician.

4 EXPIRED FORMULA. While formula comes in sealed cans and tubs that look like they have an infinite shelf life, they do have expiration dates. And many of our readers have written to tell us that stores don't always remove expired formula from the shelves in a timely manner. That includes grocery stores, discounters and even warehouse clubs. So read the label carefully and check your own supply of formula before you open a tub or bottle. Also, watch out for formula sold on auction sites. Be sure to ask about expiration dates.

5 DON'T BUY OFF BRAND FORMULA IN ETHNIC GROCERY STORES. While the 2008 melamine scare mainly affected families in China, a few cans did make it into the U.S. through ethnic grocery stores. Federal law bans such black market imports, but that doesn't mean they don't happen. Stick to name brand formula bought in mainstream stores.

6 DON'T FORGET THE BOTTLED WATER. Factor in the cost of bottled water, as you'll need to mix your powdered or concentrated formula with special water. What kind? Purified, demineralize, deionized, distilled or reverse osmosis filtered water. The American Academy of Pediatrics and the American Dental Association recommend this to help avoid consuming too much fluoride, which causes tooth discoloration. You can use tap water if it contains less than .3 ppm of fluoride or if you have a reverse osmosis filter. For everyone else, there will be an extra expense. Be sure to buy your water in bulk—gallon jugs are the most economical. A reasonable price per ounce will be about 1¢.

Money Saving Tips

Here are our tips on saving money when purchasing baby formula:

1 **STAY AWAY FROM PRE-MIXED FORMULA.** Liquid concentrate formula and ready-to-drink formula are 50% to 200% more expensive than powdered formula. Yes, it is more convenient but you pay big time for that. We priced name brand, ready to drink formula at a whopping 28 to 50¢ per ounce. Guess what type of formula is given out as freebies in doctors' offices and hospitals? Yes, it's often the ready-to-drink liquid formula. These companies know babies get hooked on the particular texture of the expensive stuff, making it hard (if not impossible) to switch to the powdered formula later. Sneaky, eh? What's the most popular type of formula in the U.S.? Powder. Over 60% of the formula sold in the U.S. is powdered while liquid concentrate accounts for only 27% of formula sales.

2 **CONSIDER GENERIC FORMULA.** Most grocery stores and discounters sell "private" label formula at considerable savings, at least 30% to 40% in savings. At one grocery store chain, their generic powdered formula worked out to just 7¢ per fluid ounce, a 50% savings. The largest maker of generic formula is Perrigo Nutritionals/PBM Products (known as Store Brand Formula; PBMProducts.com). This company makes generic formula under several different brand names including Bright Beginnings (BrightBeginnings.com), Member's Mark (sold at Sam's Club) and Parent's Choice (sold at Walmart). FYI: on PBM's web site you'll find a link to coupons as well. Generic formula has come a long way in recent years—now you can buy generic organic formula as well as several other special varieties. We should note that some pediatricians are concerned about recommending generic formula—doctors fret that such low-cost formula might discourage breastfeeding.

3 **BUY IT ONLINE.** Yep, you can buy formula online from eBay. You can save big but watch out—some unscrupulous sellers try to pawn off expired formula on unsuspecting buyers. Be sure to confirm the expiration date before buying formula online. And watch out for shipping charges—formula is heavy and shipping can outweigh any deal, depending on the price you pay.

4 BUY IN BULK. We found wholesale clubs had the best prices on name brand formula. For example, Costco (Costco.com) sells a 3-pack of 34 oz. cans of Similac Advance for $97.99 (12¢ per oz. of mixed formula). That is 27% less than grocery stores. And generic formula at wholesale clubs is an even bigger bargain. Costco's Kirkland brand formula was $62.99 for three 40 oz cans (7¢ per oz. of mixed formula). Don't forget to pick up bottled water to mix with formula at the wholesale club as well.

5 ASK YOUR PEDIATRICIAN FOR FREE SAMPLES. Just make sure you get the powdered formula (not the liquid concentrate or ready to pour). One reader in Arizona said she got several free cases from her doctor, who simply requested more from the formula makers.

6 SHOP AROUND. Yes, powdered formula at a grocery store can run $20 to $25 for a 25-ounce can (approximately)—but there's no federal law that says you must buy it at full retail. Readers of our book have noticed that formula prices vary widely, sometimes even at different locations of the same chain. In Chicago, a reader said she found one Toys R Us charged over a dollar less per can for the same ready-to-feed formula than another TRU across town. "They actually have a price check book at the registers with the codes for each store in the Chicagoland area," the reader said. "At our last visit, we saved $13.20 for two cases (about 30% of the cost), just by mentioning we wanted to pay the lower price."

Another reader noticed a similar price discrepancy at Walmart stores in Florida. When she priced Gerber Good Start powdered formula, she found one Walmart that marked it at $6.61 per can. Another Walmart (about 20 miles from the first location) sells the same can for $3.68! When the reader inquired about the price discrepancy, a customer service clerk admitted that each store independently sets the price for such items, based on nearby competition. That's a good lesson—many chains in more rural or poorer locations (with no nearby competition) often mark prices higher than suburban stores.

7 FORGET TODDLER FORMULA. When your child is ready for whole milk (usually at one year of age, according to most pediatricians), you can switch from formula (about 15¢ to 20¢ per ounce) to milk (about 3¢ per ounce). Yep, that is a savings of over 70%! No, you don't need toddler formula. What about the claim that toddler formulas have extra calcium, iron and vitamins? Nutritionists point out that toddlers should be getting most of their nutrition from solid foods, not formula. Toddlers should only be drinking about two cups a day of whole milk. Additional calcium can be found in foods as diverse as yogurt and broccoli; iron in red meat and spinach; vitamins in a wide variety of foods.

But what if you don't think your child is getting enough of those nutrients? Adding a vitamin and mineral supplement to your child's diet would still be less expensive than blowing your money on toddler formulas.

You may be wondering, in the day of increasing concern about obesity, why whole milk is recommended. Pediatricians tell us toddlers between 12 and 24 months of age need the fat in whole milk to foster brain development. At age two, you should switch to skim milk or 1%. For more on toddler development and nutrition, check out our *Toddler 411* book (toddler411.com).

8 CHECK OUT AMAZON. Yep, Amazon sells formula (and even diapers) in their health and personal care store. Prices for formula were about 10% to 15% cheaper than full retail and if you order more than $25 (which is pretty easy), you may qualify for free shipping. Sign up for Amazon Mom—a free membership program that gives you free two-day shipping with Amazon Prime and 30% off items like diapers and wipes. You get additional months of free two-day shipping the more you buy from Amazon's baby store.

9 JOIN A FORMULA CLUB. Several formula makers have frequent buyer clubs. Example: Enfamil's Family Beginnings offers checks for purchasing formula, a free diaper bag, and more. It's free (sign up at Enfamil.com) but be prepared to fill out lots of forms asking for information on where you live, when your baby is due and your attitudes toward breast and formula feeding. Bonus savings idea: Sam's Club accepts Enfamil's checks, which lets you stretch those freebies even farther! And you can find lots of checks for sale on eBay.com at great prices.

Bottles/Nipples

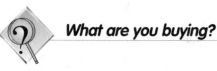

What are you buying?

What's the best bottle for baby? Actually, it's more than just the bottle. The nipple (how the milk is delivered to baby) is just as important as the container.

When it comes to nipples, there are a myriad of choices. Your first decision will be the shape of the nipple. They come in orthodontic (bulb shaped), flat-topped or original (bell shaped). See graphics at right. Experts tell us that the bell shaped nipple seems to work best for breast fed babies who are either taking an occasional bottle or permanently transitioning from breast to bottle.

Orthodontic

Most nipples are made of latex or silicone. We recommend silicone. They last longer, don't have any flavor, are heat resistant and may resist bacteria better than latex. Latex can be allergenic as well.

Finally, nipples have different flow levels. If you are starting immediately with bottlefeeding, begin with a low flow nipple so your baby doesn't become over- *Flat-topped* whelmed with formula and gag. This is also a good idea for parents who are giving an occasional bottle to a breast fed baby—it forces your baby to work harder, more like when breastfeeding. As baby grows, you may need to buy a faster flow nipple.

Flat-topped

Bell shaped

What about the bottle itself? After the government issued a report in 2008 that questioned the safety of a chemical (Bisphenol-A or BPA) used in polycarbonate bottles, manufacturers began making BPA-free bottles. So, pretty much all the new bottles on the shelves today are BPA-free. (We've posted a Q&A about BPA on our web site BabyBargains.com, click on Bonus Material). Some parents prefer glass bottles since they have always been a safe, chemical free option.

Of course, there may be older baby bottles still on the back of some store shelves—a word to the wise: make sure the package says BPA-free before buying any bottle, breast pump or sippy cup. And if a friend offers you her old baby bottles, we say politely decline. You likely wouldn't be able to tell if they had BPA or not.

Smart Shopper Tips

Smart Shopper Tip #1
Bottle confusion?

"How many bottles will I need if I formula feed? What nipple sizes do I need? Do I need a bottle sterilizer?"

Yes, the questions about bottles and feeding baby can be rather endless! To help, on our web site, we've posted a great email from a mom who's been there, done that. This email actually appeared first as a thread on our message boards, but we thought it was the most comprehensive discussion of bottle-feeding we've ever seen. Since it is eight pages long, however, we didn't have room to reprint it here. Go to Babybargains.com/Bonus to read it.

Smart Shopper Tip #2
Getting started

"I think I'm going to bottle feed for at least some of the time, but I don't want to spend a fortune on bottles. What should I buy?"

Consider getting a starter kit from one or two of our top recommended bottle makers (see Our Picks below). Starter kits usually include a selection of bottle sizes, slow flow nipples and bottle caps. They may also have accessories like a bottlebrush included. Prices range from $15 to $60 depending on brand and number of items included.

Our Picks: Brand Recommendations

Good. *First Years' Breastflow* bottles have a unique double nipple that forces baby to use both suction and compression—just like at mother's breast. Price: about $5 per 5 oz. bottle (we've seen them for as little as $7.50 for a three pack). While feedback from parents is mostly positive, some thought the double nipple design was hard to clean.

Better. *MAM* bottles may be popular for their soft silicone nipples and attractive design, but we just love the way they clean. You can unscrew the bottom of the bottle as well as the top, making it so easy to really get the bottle clean. The bottles are also microwave safe and BPA free. MAM makes an anti-colic bottle and a regular bottle ($19.50 for a 3-pack of regular MAM bottles).

Best. Tied for first place in the bottle battle are *Avent* and *Dr. Brown's*. It's a real toss up as to which is best; our readers seem to be split evenly. Avent gets a nod for its well-designed nipple, which is clinically proven to reduce colic (uncontrollable, extended crying that starts in some babies around one month of age). Ditto for Dr. Brown's Natural Flow bottle (handi-craft.com), which has a patented vent system that eliminates bubbles and nipple collapse. Avent and Dr. Brown's are pricey, however—they cost about $5 to $8 a bottle. That compares to $2 to $4 for other bottles from makers like Evenflo and Playtex.

Best Glass Bottle. *Evenflo's* glass bottles are best in class. They are very affordable, available in several sizes and quantities and the best choice for folks who don't want plastic. Prices range from $2 to $3.50 per bottle. The more expensive versions have elasticized plastic sleeve to help avoid breakage if dropped.

One quick note: in most cases, bottles and nipples aren't inter-changeable. You can't use an Avent nipple on a Gerber bottle and so on. The exception: Dr. Brown's nipples DO fit on Evenflo's glass bottles (see above), report our readers—a bit of trimming on the vent tube is required.

Bottle Warmers & Sterilizers

Do you need to sterilize bottles every time you use them? Or boil water for formula? Or use bottled water?

The answers are no, no and yes.

There's no need to sterilize baby bottles every time you use them—yes, run them through the dishwasher when you first open the package. But you can clean bottles with warm, soapy water thereafter (or use the dishwasher again).

There's also no need to boil water for formula. That's because most tap water in the U.S. is treated and is safe to drink. However, the standard recommendation today is to use bottled water to mix with formula—we have a full discussion of this in our other book, *Baby 411.*

As for the temperature of a bottle of formula, room temperature is fine—bottles neither need to be heated nor cooled.

The take-home message: bottle warmers and sterilizers are purely optional. Since we realize some readers still want to purchase these items, here are our recommendations:

Avent wins the sterilizer war with their *Express II Microwave Steam Sterilizer.* This model holds up to six Avent bottles or two Avent Breast Pumps and two bottles for $26. If you prefer a plug in sterilizer, the *3-in-1 Electric Steam Sterilizer* sterilizes six bottles in six minutes and keeps bottles sterile for up to 24 hours. Like the microwave version, it can also sterilize up to two breast pumps. Cost: about $49.

While Avent makes a good sterilizer, we would suggest getting the matching sterilizer for your bottle brand. For example, if you decide to use Born Free bottles, then the *Born Free Tru-Clean Bottle Sterilizing System* ($70-$90) is a good bet. Why? Sterilizers for one brand can sometimes damage other brand's bottles—for example, we did receive a report from a reader that Medela's Quick Clean Micro-Steam bags can melt Born Free bottles.

What about bottle warmers? *Avent* makes a good one: the *Electric Bottle and Baby Food Warmer* ($35), which warms a room temperature bottle in about four minutes. It fits baby food containers and all types of baby bottles (not just Avent).

New to the bottle warmer market is the *Kiinde Kozii Breast Milk & Bottle Warmer* ($70). This warmer accepts frozen breast

Pacifiers: Good or Bad?

Should your baby use a pacifier? Surprisingly, this is a controversial topic.

Some experts argue that early use of pacifiers may interfere with breastfeeding. But new studies show that pacifier use in children actually reduces the risk of Sudden Infant Death Syndrome (SIDS). It's unclear why pacifiers work, but studies clearly show a lowered risk of SIDS.

So, here are our recommendations for pacifier use: wait to give your child a pacifier until breastfeeding is well established (about a month of age). Discontinue pacifier use by six months of age. Why? Ninety percent of SIDS deaths occur between one month and six months of age.

So, now that you know what's good about a pacifier, which type of pacifier is best? There are two types—regular pacifiers have round nipples, while "orthodontic" pacifiers have flat nipples. Either is fine—but consult with your pediatrician if you have concerns on this topic. Our resident pediatrician, Dr. Ari Brown recommends "Soothies" (soothie-pacifiers.com) brand to her patients.

milk storage bags, liner bottles, plastic bottles, glass bottles and even food containers—any type, any brand. Kiinde's SAFEHeat technology consists of a "circulating bath of warm water" to heat a bottle. Since the water is about room temperature, Kiinde claims to prevents hot spots and allays concerns that boiling water can cause chemicals like BPA to leach out of older bottles. A timer and automatic shutoff means it won't overheat and the water reservoir does not require parents to add water each time it's used.

Feedback on the Kiinde is positive. Most folks like the warmer, despite the price tag. A few dissenters note the Kiinde requires regular maintenance (you have to clean the water scale out periodically). And we heard one or two reports of the warmer breaking after just 8 or 10 weeks. We'd like to see the company step up its customer service on these issues—more than one parent who had a problem said the company wasn't helpful in solving the issue.

Baby Food

At the tender age of four to six months, you and your baby will embark on a magical journey to a new place filled with exciting adventures and never-before-seen wonders. Yes, you've entered the SOLID FOOD ZONE.

Best Online Sources

Looking for a schedule of what foods to introduce when? Earth's Best's web site has a comprehensive chart with suggestions (earthsbest.com, click on Resource Center, then Guides and Tools, then Infant Feeding Schedule). Gerber's slick web site (gerber.com) also has lots of information. Unfortunately, you'll have to sign up on the site to get to information like recommended feeding schedules. Consider using a special Gmail address to sign up for sites like this, to prevent your main email account from being spammed.

We also liked Beechnut's site (beechnut.com), which includes suggested menus and feeding tips. Although it is designed for Canadian parents, Heinz's baby food web site, heinzbaby.com, contains extensive nutritional advice and menu planners among other information. Canadians can take advantage of rebate offers and other deals on this site (hopefully, they'll add the rest of North America to the coupon deals soon).

Safe & Sound

1 **FEED FROM A BOWL, NOT FROM THE JAR.** Why? If you feed from a jar, bacteria from baby's mouth can find its way back to the jar, spoiling the food much more quickly. Also, saliva enzymes begin to break down the food's nutrients. The best strategy: pour the amount of baby food you need into a bowl and feed from there (unless it's the last serving from the jar). And be sure to refrigerate any unused portions.

2 **DON'T STORE FOOD IN PLASTIC BAGS.** If you leave plastic bags on the baby's high chair, they can be a suffocation hazard. A better solution: store leftover food in small, Tupperware-type containers.

3 **DO A TASTE TEST.** Make sure it isn't too hot, too cold, or spoiled. We know you aren't dying to taste the Creamed Ham Surprise from Gerber, but it is a necessary task.

Another tip: a dental hygienist wrote to remind us that parents should taste baby's food with a different spoon than the one baby will be using. Why? "The bacteria from your mouth can be transferred to the baby's mouth when you use the same spoon."

4 **CHECK FOR EXPIRATION DATES.** Gerber's jarred food looks like it would last through the next Ice Age, but check that expiration date. Most unopened baby food is only good for a year or two. Use opened jars within one to two days.

5 **AVOID UNPASTEURIZED MILK, MILK PRODUCTS AND JUICES.** Babies don't have the ability to fight off serious bacterium like e. coli. Avoid these hazards by feeding your child only pasteurized dairy and juice products.

Also steer clear of feeding honey to children less than one year of age. Botulism spores can be found in honey—while not harmful to adults and older kids, these spores can be fatal to infants.

6 **WHAT ABOUT INTRODUCING HIGH ALLERGENIC FOODS?** When can you introduce nuts like peanuts and tree nuts to your baby? The advice on this has changed over the years. Until 2008, the American Academy of Pediatrics (AAP) recommended waiting on introducing peanuts and other highly allergenic foods (like shellfish) until age 3 to prevent lifelong allergies. However, the latest studies indicate there is no benefit to waiting—and even the AAP now says there is no need to wait. Our advice: consult with your pediatrician on this one, especially if you have a family history of food allergies.

Smart Shopper Tips

Smart Shopper Tip #1
Tracking Down UFFOs (Unidentifiable Flying Food Objects)
  "We fed our baby rice cereal for the first time. It was really cute, except when baby knocked the bowl to the floor . . . multiple times! Should we have bought some special stuff for this occasion?"

Well, unless you want your kitchen to be redecorated in Early Baby Food, we do have a few suggestions. First, a bowl with a bottom that suctions to the table is a great way to avoid flying saucers. Plastic spoons that have a round handle are nice, so baby can't stick the spoon handle in her eye (yes, that does happen—babies do try to feed themselves even at a young age). Spoons with rubber coatings are also recommended; they don't transfer the heat or cold of the food to the baby's mouth and are easier on the gums. One clever spoon is Munchkin's White Hot Safety Spoon (web: munchkin.com, four for $5). This spoon uses a special coating that changes color when baby's food is too hot (over 110°).

Smart Shopper Tip #2
Avoiding Mealtime Baths
  "Our baby loves to drink from a cup, except for one small prob-

lem. Most of the liquid ends up on her, instead of in her. Any tips?"

Congratulations! You have a child who is ready to join the rest of the world and give up the bottle or breast. You may have mixed feelings about this, especially when you have to wash all those additional bibs, the floor and yourself more frequently. But this is a cool milestone. Babies are developmentally able to use a cup between ten and 16 months.

So what's the solution to the inevitable mess your baby will make when learning to drink from a cup? Most parents turn to sippy cups. But we don't recommend them. Why? Sippy cups aren't exactly beloved by doctors and dentists. Turns out babies use the same sucking action to get milk from a sippy cup as they do when sucking from a baby bottle. Hence they are not learning how to drink from a cup. Plus, sippy cups direct the flow of liquid straight at the back of baby's top front teeth—this promotes tooth decay.

Is there an answer to this dilemma? When being clean and pristine aren't that important (say when eating at home in the kitchen with lots of clean up gear handy) let your baby practice with a regular plastic cup. But also try to teach her to use a straw. That way, when you're out at a restaurant, she won't be taking a bath in public.

✂ *Money-Saving Tips*

1 MAKE YOUR OWN. Let's be honest: baby foods like mashed bananas are really just . . . mashed bananas. You can easily whip up this stuff with that common kitchen helper, the food processor. Many parents skip baby food altogether and make their own. How much can you save? Mint.com estimates homemade organic baby food runs 38¢ per serving, compared with 69¢ for store bought—a 44% percent savings. There's even bigger savings for non-organic baby food—it's 30¢ per serving cheaper making it at home versus store bought. One tip: make up a big batch at one time and freeze the leftovers in ice cube trays. Check the library for cookbooks that provide tips on making baby food at home. A reader suggestion: "Top 100 Baby Purees" by Annabel Karmel ($17, Atria). This 128-page book is a best-selling guide to making your own baby food.

2 FYI: TOYS R US AND BABIES R US SELL BABY FOOD. If you think your grocery store is gouging you on the price of baby food, you might want to check out the prices at Babies R Us. We found Gerber 1st Foods in a two-pack of 3.5-ounce jars for $1.29—that works out to about 18¢ per ounce or about 15% less than grocery store prices. Toys R Us also sells four-packs of assorted dinners from Gerber's 2nd and 3rd Food collections.

3 COUPONS! COUPONS! COUPONS! Yes, we've seen quite a few cents-off and buy-one-get-one-free coupons on baby food and formula—not just in the Sunday paper but also through the mail. Our advice: don't toss that junk mail until you've made sure you're not trashing valuable baby food coupons. Another coupon trick: look for "bounce-back" coupons. Those are the coupons put in packages of baby food to encourage you to bounce back to the store and buy more.

4 SKIP ORGANIC. Organic baby food in a grocery store costs 23% more than conventional baby food. A 2012 report by the American Academy of Pediatrics states there is no nutritional difference between organic and conventional baby foods. "In the long term, there is currently no direct evidence that consuming an organic diet leads to improved health or lower risk of disease," AAP officials said in a statement.

5 SUBSTITUTE COMPARABLE ADULT FOODS. What's the difference between adult applesauce and baby applesauce? Not much, except for the fact that applesauce in a jar with a cute baby on it costs several times more than the adult version. (One caveat: make sure the regular applesauce is NOT loaded with extra sugar). Another rip-off: "next step" foods for older babies. Gerber loves to tout its special toddler meals in its "Graduates" line. What's the point? When baby is ready to eat pasta, just serve him small bites of the adult stuff. Bottom line: babies should learn to eat the same (hopefully healthy) foods you are eating, with the same spices and flavors. Toddler or graduate foods are a waste of time and money.

The Name Game: Reviews of Selected Manufacturers

Here's a round up of some of the best-known names in baby food. Unlike our brand name ratings for clothing or other baby products, food is a much trickier rating proposition. We rated the following brand names based on how healthy they are and how much they approximate real food (aroma, appearance, and, yes, taste). Our subjective opinions reflect our experience and those of our readers—always consult with your pediatrician or family doctor if you have any questions about feeding your baby. (Special thanks to Ben and Jack for their help in researching this topic.)

The Ratings

A **EXCELLENT**—*our top pick!*
B **GOOD**— *above average quality, prices, and creativity.*
C **FAIR**—*could stand some improvement.*
D **POOR**—*yuck! could stand some major improvement.*

Beech-Nut *beechnut.com* Beech-Nut was one of the first baby food companies to eliminate fillers (starches, sugar, salt) or artificial colors/flavors in its 120 flavors. While Beech-Nut is not organic, the company claims to be made of "all-natural ingredients" and are in the process of verifying that their foods do not include any GMOs. Our readers generally give Beech-Nut good marks (some like it better than Gerber). Beechnut is affordable: we've seen it on sale for as little as 13¢ per oz. New this year: toddler snack pouches. These are similar to the pouches organic baby food producers like Ella's Kitchen are using.

The only bummer about Beech-Nut baby food: it can be hard to find (not every state has stores that carry it). You can use their "where to buy" function to find a store that carries it or buy it online at Amazon.com. And check out their "Beech-Nut Rewards" for info on money saving programs. ***Rating: B+***

Bella Baby Foods *BellaBabyFoods.com* Bella Baby Food is one of a few baby food manufacturers who doesn't "can" their foods; they freeze their organic (and Kosher) ingredients. The company (named after the founders' daughter Bella) offers typical flavors like apple as well as some fun ones like mango, pumpkin and even spinach. They don't offer combinations, but encourage parents to mix and match on their own for greater flexibility. You can order directly from their site with a minimum of six packages for a flat price of $7.33 per item (includes shipping). Each package includes ten 1.5 oz. packets. That works out to 77¢ per ounce making it more affordable than other frozen food options but still twice the cost of Earth's Best. The company does have a minimum order of six units. Parents report that the taste is impressive. ***Rating: A***

Earth's Best *earthsbest.com* Earth's Best started the organic baby food trend over 25 years ago in (where else?) Vermont. Since those early beginnings Earth's Best has gone through several owners before landing in the lap of natural foods conglomerate Hain Celestial (parent of Celestial Seasonings Tea). Despite all the changes in ownership, Earth's Best has maintained its focus, with one of the

baby food

largest line of "natural" baby foods on the market—all vegetables and grains are certified organically grown (no pesticides are used), and meats are raised without antibiotics or steroids. Another advantage: Earth's Best never adds any salt, sugar or modified starches to its food. And the foods are only made from whole grains, fruits and vegetables (instead of concentrates). Yes, *Earth's Best* is more expensive (36¢ per oz.; or 15% more than conventional baby food) but as we pointed out earlier, that's works out to only about $90 more per year and ready to print coupons are easy to find on their web site.

Reader feedback on Earth's Best has been positive—fans like the extensive choice and commitment to organic principals. All in all, Earth's Best is a much-needed natural alternative to the standard fare that babies have been fed for far too many years. ***Rating: A***

Ella's Kitchen Organics EllasKitchen.com When Ella's Kitchen first entered the food and snack arena, their initial products were designed for older kids like their daughter Ella. You'll see the web site offers smoothies for older kids as well as three stages of baby foods and snacks. All their foods include just organic fruits, vegetables or grains and a bit of lemon juice to keep them from spoiling. That's it! At 43¢ per ounce (on Amazon), Ella's is pricey. And there have been allegations online of the company incorrectly labeling nutritional content—overstating iron content, for example. While the packaging has since been corrected, this gave the brand a black eye. ***Rating: C***

Gerber gerber.com Dominating the baby food business with a whopping 83% market share (that's right, three out of every four

---

E-MAIL FROM THE REAL WORLD
Making your own baby food isn't time consuming

A mom in New Mexico told us she found making her own baby food isn't as difficult as it sounds:

"My husband and I watch what we eat, so we definitely watch what our baby eats. One of the things I do is buy organic carrots, quick boil them, throw them in a blender and then freeze them in an ice cube tray. Once they are frozen, I separate the cubes into freezer baggies (they would get freezer burn if left in the ice tray). When mealtime arrives, I just throw them in the microwave. Organic carrots taste great! This whole process might sound complicated, but it only takes me about 20 minutes to do, and then another five to ten minutes to put the cubes in baggies."

baby food containers sold sport that familiar label), Gerber sure has come a long way from its humble beginnings. Back in 1907, Joseph Gerber (whose trade was canning) mashed up peas for his daughter, following the suggestion of a family doctor. Today Gerber sells over $2 billion in baby food a year.

Over the years, Gerber has tried to expand beyond jarred baby food. It launched microwavable toddler meals in 2002 and has licensed its name out for a variety of baby products, including cups, infant toys and even baby skincare items. Yet controversy has constantly dogged Gerber—in the 90's, consumer pressure forced the company to stop adding sugar and starch to its baby foods. The Federal Trade Commission has accused the company of deceptive advertising when it claimed a survey showed that four out of five pediatricians recommended the brand (the actual number was 16%).

On the upside, Gerber offers parents two key advantages: choice and availability. The line boasts an amazing 200 different flavors. And Gerber is sold in just about every grocery store on Earth at around 25¢ per oz. (26¢ on Amazon.com). We have to give Gerber credit: bowing to consumer interest in all things organic, they rolled out "Gerber Organic" to compete with Earth's Best. The new line is made with "whole grains and certified organic fruits and vegetables" and costs around 30¢ per oz. (note that Gerber's regular line still uses some fruit and vegetable concentrates). They now make the organic line in squeeze pouches similar to other brands. Finally, we noticed that Gerber is now packing its first foods in plastic rather than glass. While we like the changes Gerber has made, we still have problems with the brand: we think their "Graduates" line of "toddler" foods is a waste of money. And their juice line is overpriced compared to others on the market. Quality-wise, we will give Gerber an average rating. ***Rating: C***

HappyBaby HappyBabyFood.com How do you differentiate yourself from the competition in the baby food market. After all, even Gerber has an organic line of baby food now. If you're HappyBaby you offer food with ingredients like prebiotics and probiotics, vegan DHA, and Choline. They also use Salba, a "super grain" along with amaranth, quinoa, mangosteen and yumberry. Wow, sounds like a Whole Foods grocery store in a BPA-free pouch. By the way, if you want to know more about Salba, check the FAQ on HappyBaby's web site.

If you have an allergy prone child, you'll like the fact that HappyBaby foods are processed in a nut-free facility with no soy (only some refined soybean oil–no protein allergens), no gluten and no dairy products. If you don't like the non-recyclable pouches, HappyBaby also makes a frozen line of food. Pouches run a rather expensive 38¢ per ounce; frozen foods aren't available online. Overall, parents like HappyBaby baby foods and we'll recommend them too. **Rating: A-**

Healthy Times *healthytimes.com* Healthy Times got its start selling one of the first health-food baby products back in 1980: a teething biscuit. Since then, the company has expanded their baby food offerings to include 22 jarred baby foods, baby cereal, snacks and toiletry items. The baby food line is certified organic and contains no soy, flour or other fillers. You'll find single fruits and vegetables (stage 1), fruit and veggie blends (stage 2) and dinners (combos of several veggies, and meat and veggies). You can buy Healthy Times online on the company's web site for 30¢ per oz. jar for stage one foods. **Rating: A-**

Plum Organics *PlumOrganics.com* Plum Organics was one of the first baby foods we saw packaged in those cute little resealable pouches. Now we see similar packaging everywhere. Plums JUST fruits are made without any additives, just fruit. Second Blends include yummy sounding combinations like blueberry, pear and purple carrot (expect some heavy duty staining on your bibs with this one!). Parents seem to like the single fruit and Second Blends best; the training meals (Stage 3) were less popular. We saw Plum priced around 37¢ per ounce online and in stores. **Rating: A-**

Sprout Organic Foods *SproutOrganicFoods.com* You may have seen celebrity chef Tyler Florence on the Food Network, in ads for his many cooking products or in the cookbook section of your favorite kitchen store, but you may not realize he's the driving force behind Sprout Organic Baby Food. Started in 2008 with some friends, Sprout also claims to have invented the original baby food pouch–the fastest growing food delivery system in grocery stores today.

So what do you get for all that celebrity and innovation? For babies just starting solids, Sprout offers organically grown cereal and single fruits and veggies. We found a Sprout Starter kit of five three-ounce pouches of pears on Amazon for $8 (50¢ per ounce). Hope you didn't pass out over that!

Good news for older babies: if your family is vegetarian, they offer no-meat options at every stage. Another plus: Sprout has an online guide to starting solids. Sprout attempts to introduce more adventurous foods for older kids including quinoa and barley plus coconut milk, mango, lentils and more. The offerings actually sound like adults would like them!

Overall, our readers like Sprout. Although they are expensive compared to traditional baby food from Gerber and others, parents are impressed with the taste for the most part. We'll give them a positive rating with a slight downgrade due to the price. **Rating: A-**

Yummy Spoonfuls YummySpoonfuls.com Like almost every baby food story, Yummy Spoonfuls has a committed mom behind the creation of its organic baby food line. Founder Agatha Achindu was inspired by her love of cooking and her disgust at jarred baby foods. As she notes on her web site: "none of the (commercially jarred baby) foods was recognizable; peas were brownish green, and carrots were dull brown." Flash freezing baby food helps it keep the color and flavor of the ingredients. All the ingredients used in Yummy Spoonfuls are certified by the USDA to be grown organically. Flavors include carrots, broccoli, butternut squash, apples, green beans, pears and peas as well as variety packs.

They also make three stages of baby food: Creamy Yummy, Mushy Yummy and Chunky Yummy. Parents seem to like Yummy Spoonfuls. They note the fruits and vegetables are the right color and taste–bright orange carrots and cream colored bananas. So what's the negatives about Yummy Spoonfuls: price. At 81¢ per oz., these foods are three times as expensive as Earth's Best! Makes you want to hit the kitchen and make your own. *Rating: A-*

High Chairs

As soon as Junior starts to eat solid food, you'll need this quintessential piece of baby furniture–the high chair. Surprisingly, this seemingly innocuous product generates over 10,900 injuries each year. So, what are the safest high chairs? And how do you use them properly? We'll share these insights, as well as some money-saving tips and brand reviews in this section.

Safe and Sound

1 **STRAP ME IN.** *Most high chair injuries occur when babies are not strapped into their chairs.* Sadly, one to two deaths occur each year when babies "submarine" under the tray. To address these types of accidents, new high chairs how feature a "passive restraint" (a plastic post) under the tray to prevent this. Note: some high chair makers attach this submarine protection to the tray; others have it on the seat. We prefer the seat. Why? If it is on the tray and the tray is removed, there is a risk a child might be able to squirm out of the safety belts (which is all that would hold them in the chair). As a side note, some wooden high chairs only seem to have a crotch strap– no plastic post. Again, not much is keeping baby safely in the chair.

FYI: Even if the high chair has a passive restraint, you STILL must strap in baby with the safety harness with EACH use. This prevents them from climbing out or otherwise hurting themselves.

2 **THE SAFETY STANDARDS FOR HIGH CHAIRS ARE VOLUNTARY.** Unlike the mandatory safety rules for cribs or car seats, high chair makers only have a series of voluntary standards. This will change shortly, when the government issues mandatory safety standards for high chairs as part of the Consumer Product Safety Improvement Act. But . . . as of press time, high chair safety standards are purely voluntary.

3 **INSPECT THE SEAT PAD.** Make sure it won't tear or puncture easily.

4 **LOOK FOR STABILITY.** It's basic physics: the wider the base, the more stable the chair. Another tip: never put the high chair near a wall—babies have been injured in the past when they pushed off a wall or object, tipping over the chair. This problem is rare with the newest high chairs (as they have wide, stable bases), but you still can tip over older, hand-me-down models.

5 **CAREFULLY INSPECT THE RESTRAINING SYSTEM.** We prefer a five-point harness (straps that go over the baby's shoulders and around the waist); some high chairs only have three-point harnesses (just a waist belt).

6 **DOES THE SEAT RECLINE?** Many high chairs have a reclining seat function that makes it easier to feed a young infant. The problem? Feeding a baby solid foods in a reclining position is a choking hazard. If you want to use the reclining feature, it should be exclusively for bottle-feeding. We do think the recline feature is a plus for another reason, however: it is easier to move baby in and out of the high chair when it is reclined. And when babies start out with solid foods, they may go back and forth between the bottle and solid food during meals. Hence, the recline feature is helpful when they need to take a bottle break.

More Money Buys You

Whether you spend $30 or $500, most high chairs do one simple thing—provide you with a place to safely ensconce your baby while he eats. The more money you spend, however, the more comforts there are for both you and baby. As you go up in price, you find chairs with various height positions, reclining seats, larger trays, more padding, casters for mobility and more. From a safety point of view, some of the more expensive high chairs feature five-point restraint harnesses (instead of just a waist belt). As for usability, some high chairs are easier to clean than others, but that doesn't necessarily correspond to price. Look for removable vinyl seat covers that are machine-washable (cloth covers are harder to clean). And watch out for crevices in seats, pads and trays—these are food magnets. Models with seamless trays, seats and pads may cost more but will be easier to keep clean.

Smart Shopper Tips for High Chairs

Smart Shopper Tip #1
High Chair Basics 101

"What's the difference between a $50 high chair and one that's $400? And does it matter what color you get? I like white best."

The high chair market is basically divided into four camps:

◆ **Low-end chairs** sold in discount stores aimed at Grandma. These cost around $50 to $100 and are bare bones, without many features.

◆ **Multi-function chairs.** These range from $100 to $250 and feature seat recline, adjustable height positions, footrests and upgraded pads. The more expensive models have toys, designer fabrics and other upgrades.

◆ **Modern high chairs.** Pricey at $300 to $450, these chairs are sold mostly on aesthetics—their ultra-modern looks appeal to parents who want to make a style statement.

◆ **Wood high chairs.** Either all wood or a hybrid of wood and plastic (wood base, plastic tray), these high chairs run $150 to $200. Wood high chairs appeal to traditionalists who are turned off by the plastic-y look of most high chairs. The trade-off is a lack of features or adjustments.

As you can see, high chairs are often sold more on aesthetics than function—and that's a classic first-time parent mistake. A pretty high chair that is impossible to clean is a big headache. And while we understand that a high chair that sits in middle of your kitchen shouldn't be an eyesore, consider these practical features before falling in love with a high chair:

◆ **Tray release.** The best high chairs have a one-hand tray release that enables you to easily remove the tray with a quick motion. Of course, some are easier to use than others. Our advice: take a second in the store and remove the tray a few times from sample models. You'll note some trays are sticky; other "one-hand" tray releases really require two hands.

high chairs

◆ *Dishwasher-safe trays—NOT!* Most high chairs today come with a dishwasher-safe tray insert. This cover snaps off the main tray and pops in the dishwasher for clean-up . . . or does it? In the reviews in this section, we'll note some models whose dishwasher-safe trays are too big to fit in an actual dishwasher. A word of advice: measure the bottom rack of your dishwasher and take that dimension with you when high chair shopping.

◆ *Tray height.* Some parents complain the tray height of certain high chairs is too high—making it hard for smaller babies to use. A smart tip: take your baby with you when you go high chair shopping and actually sit them in the different options. You can evaluate the tray heights in person to make sure the chair will work for both you and baby. We'll note which chairs have the best/worst tray heights later in our reviews. Generally, a chair with a tray height of less than 8″ should work for most babies. A few models have tray heights over 8″—those can be a major problem since a child can't reach the food on the tray. Why is this important? Some day (we know it seems light years away), your baby will feed himself . . . and being able to see and reach the food is important!

◆ *Seat depth.* Most chairs have multiple tray positions and reclining seats. But what is the distance between the seat back when it is upright and the tray is in its closest position? A distance of 5″ to 7″ is acceptable. Over 7″ and you run the risk that there will be a large gap between your baby and the tray—and all their food will end up in their lap. Again, take your baby with you when shopping for a chair, as smaller babies may be harder to fit.

◆ *Cleanability.* Here's an obvious tip some first-time parents seem to miss: make sure the high chair you buy has a removable, washable seat cover OR a seat that easily sponges clean. In the latter category, chairs with VINYL trump those made of cloth—vinyl can be wiped clean, while cloth typically has to be washed. This might be one of those first-time parent traps—seats with cloth covers sure look nicer than those made of vinyl. But the extra effort to machine wash a cloth cover is a pain . . and some cloth covers can't be thrown in the dryer! That means waiting a day or more for a cover to line dry.

Watch out for seat pads that have ruffles or numerous crevices—these are food magnets and a bear to keep clean.

What color cover should you get? Answer: anything but white. Sure, that fancy white "leatherette" high chair looks all shiny and new at the baby store, but it will forever be a cleaning nightmare once you start using it. Darker colors and patterns are better.

Of course, keeping a chair clean involves more than just the pad—look at the seat and tray itself. Avoid models with numerous crevices and cracks. Seamless seats and trays are best.

FYI: Many high chair trays claim they are dishwasher safe. But some have cracks that let water collect inside the tray—this can be a mold hazard, as it is hard to get the tray to dry properly. We will note these models in our reviews later in this section.

Smart Shopper Tip #2
Tray Chic and Other Restaurant Tips

"We have a great high chair at home, but we're always appalled at the lack of safe high chairs at restaurants. Our favorite cafe has a high chair that must date back to 1952—no straps, a metal tray with sharp edges, and a hard seat with no cushion. Have restaurateurs lost their minds?

Some folks who run restaurants must search obscure foreign countries to find the world's most hazardous high chairs. The biggest problem? No straps, enabling babies to slide out of the chair, submarine-style. The solution? When the baby is young, keep her in her infant car seat; the safe harness keeps baby secure. When your baby is older (and if you eat out a lot), you may want to invest in a portable booster seat. We'll discuss and recommend hook on chairs and booster seats later in this chapter.

If you decide to use the restaurant high chair, you may want to do a quick clean with baby wipes just to make sure. Nothing grosser than a dirty restaurant high chair. In fact, there are some grocery cart covers (reviewed in the stroller section) that can also be used in restaurant high chairs.

The Name Game: Reviews of High Chair Makers

Here's a round up of the best high chairs on the market today:

The Ratings

- **A** **EXCELLENT**—*our top pick!*
- **B** **GOOD**— *above average quality, prices, and creativity.*
- **C** **FAIR**—*could stand some improvement.*
- **D** **POOR**—*yuck! could stand some major improvement.*

Baby Bjorn *babybjorn.com* Best known for its iconic carrier, Baby Bjorn has been slowly expanding into other categories in recent years. First there was the Bjorn potty, then a bouncer, and a playpen last year. And given their recent debut of kitchen ware (bowls, spoons, bibs), it's not too surprising to see Bjorn debut its first high chair, cleverly dubbed the Baby Bjorn High Chair.

The Bjorn high chair has all the Swedish minimalist design you'd expect from a Bjorn—the white/black color motif, seamless seat design and so on. It is also available in red and black. Of course, Bjorn hasn't forgotten about safety: the high chair features a "Smart Safety Lock," which is a two-stage lock that Bjorn says "ensures that children cannot open or close the safety table on their own." This is probably the Bjorn's most unique feature: the tray pivots down to enable a parent to put a child in or out of the chair. That differs from other high chairs, where the entire tray is removable—or the tray slides forward to let you move a child in or out.

So what's not to love? Well, first of all, the price: at $220, the chair is seriously overpriced. At this lofty price point, the Bjorn high chair is competing against both modern high chairs such as the Bloom Fresco and Boon Flair (both beat the Bjorn on style) and multi-function models like the Perego Tatamia, which transforms into a baby swing and recliner. The Bjorn doesn't transform into anything. And considering Bjorn's emphasis on safety, we were disappointed to see the chair lacks a five-point harness (instead it has a three-point harness).

Real world feedback on the Bjorn high chair has been positive overall. Parents like the seamless design (easy to clean) and easy assembly. The compact fold (a mere 10" wide when folded) also is a plus. But the small size of the seat had more than one parent grumbling that, despite Bjorn's claim the chair will work up to three years of age, it is too small for bigger toddlers. The chair is light weight and the footprint is small making it easy to move around the kitchen. Finally, parents praise the tray mechanism saying their clever toddlers haven't been able to figure out how to get out of the seat.

A few negatives: while the tray has a three-position adjustment (to allow more room for growing babies), there is no height adjustment for the chair. While we understand that Bjorn's intention is to have the high chair fit most kitchen tables, this seems like a major oversight. Ditto for the lack of casters to make the chair more mobile. Finally, we should note the seat doesn't recline—as a result, you won't be able to use this chair with newborns who don't have any head control. Add in the lack of a five-point harness and we are left scratching our heads at how this chair ever got out of Bjorn's R&D lab.

Bottom line: this is a pricey but good high chair if (and only if) you have a small baby. ***Rating: B+***

Baby Trend *babytrend.com* Baby Trend's high chair was one of our top picks in a previous edition of this book, but our rating of this chair continues to drift down as complaints from readers stack up. Yes, it is a credible knock-off of the Perego and Chicco chairs, yet sells for 40% less ($60 to $100 in most stores). You get all the stan-

dard features you'd expect: five-point harness, three-position reclining seat, three-position tray with one hand release, six height positions, compact fold and casters. Some models have a separate dishwasher-safe tray. And, yes, the Baby Trend high chair is generally easier to use than its competitors (it requires little assembly and the seat recline is easy to adjust, for example).

Baby Trend sells a $55 version of their high chair at Walmart (the Sit-Right) and a $70 to $100 version elsewhere. The more expensive model has a fully reclining seat and is fully assembled (the cheaper one has a partial seat recline and requires assembly). All in all, Baby Trend churns out 24 different versions of the Trend, most of which are just variations in fashion. They go by names like Feeding Center (and Deluxe Feeding Center), Accent, MyLift, Aspen LX, Tempo, Trend, Trend 2, Sit-Right and Hi-Lite. It is unclear how these chairs differ from each other—they pretty much look the same to us.

Given Baby Trend high chairs' numerous features, why all the complaints? The pad is this chair's Achilles' heel. We've received several reports that the cloth pad (which has a reversible vinyl side) fell apart or bunched up after machine washing. Even Baby Trend, in an email to us, admitted the pad "responds best to hand washing." Gee, that's nice—too bad the instructions for the chair say to machine wash the pad on the gentle cycle . . . with no mention of hand washing. Add that to the fact the pad has to be line dried and you have a deal-breaker here.

Another major complaint centers on the tray height, which is way too high for average-size babies. And finally, the crotch bar is attached to the tray making it frustrating to put it on a counter and removing any safety advantage. Of course, not all the reviews are negative: some parents have had success with this high chair. And we give Baby Trend bonus points for improving the chair over the years. But Baby Trend's customer service stumbles and the pad washing issue have convinced us that this chair isn't worthy of a recommendation. **Rating: C+**

Bloom *BloomBaby.com* Bloom's Fresco Chrome high chair is another entrant in the space-age, Jetsons-style high chair category. It's egg-shaped, seamless seat and circular base echo the Boon Flair with one big exception: the Bloom Fresco can recline, making it suitable for infants. The Fresco comes with micro-suede seat upholstery (in 14 colors) and pneumatic-assist height adjustment. But the price? $445 to $550 is way too high, in our opinion.

Feedback on the Bloom Fresco has been mixed. For every fan who loves the chair's Jetsons' look and function, others say it just isn't worth the money (the chair is very heavy, making it hard to move; assembly is a challenge; the color fades after a year or two, etc). Quality is a major complaint area: one reader said the chair's lift feature worked well for a week . . . and then broke. The Bloom Fresco is also so hard to clean, some parents have just given up and junked the chair.

Bloom has a second high chair model: the Nano, which is tagged as an "iconic minimalist" model with a flat fold and "micro leather" seat in six colors. Price: $150—that's about three times the price of other simple high chairs that don't recline, lack wheels and fold up flat. In the past year, Bloom modified the Nano so it has a smaller footprint.

Feedback on the Nano is similar to the Fresco: for every parent who likes the Nano, we found another who knocked its difficulty to clean and fold. As a result of the mixed feedback on this brand, we've decided not to recommend Bloom's high chairs. Prices are too high and the quality is too low. Yes, these chairs are cool to look at, but that's about it. ***Rating: D***

Boon *booninc.com* Boon's Flair high chair debuted in 2007, part of the modernist wave sweeping the baby products biz at the time.

At least this chair features something unique: a pneumatic lift, which gives the chair "effortless height adjustment." Basically, a button on the base will automatically lower the chair.

We do like the seamless seat, which is easier to clean than other high chairs (where food finds its way into every last crack and crevice). The pad and harness remove for cleaning and a dishwasher-safe tray within a tray is easy to use. The Flair retails for $200 to $250. (We can't help but wonder if the folks at Boon were watching the move Office Space when they named this chair).

There haven't been many changes to the Flair in the past year, except for a few new colors—currently the chair comes in white with an orange pad or grey with a green pad.

One negative for the Flair: the seat doesn't recline, making this chair inappropriate for smaller infants who are bottle-feeding. A reclining seat is a standard feature on almost all high chairs, so we wonder why Boon left this out.

Reader feedback on the Flair is mostly positive: fans love how easy it is to clean and the small footprint. Their only complaint: the straps should tighten a bit more for smaller babies. And the lack of a chest buckle means the harness can slide off the shoulders of some kids. While most folks say the Boon Flair is easy to clean, a few dissenters say there are parts of the chair that can be trouble-some—the underside of the tray and the harness buckle (which can't be removed) are two magnets for grime.

Overall, however, most folks love this chair, whose sleek look is the big draw. ***Rating: A***

Chicco chiccousa.com Chicco's Polly high chair is the successor to the Mamma, a high chair we only gave a C in a previous edition of this book. So is the Polly an improvement? Yes, but only slightly.

Retailing for $130 to $150, the Polly features an adjustable footrest, compact fold, three-position seat recline, seven height positions and removable dishwasher-safe tray. You also get two pads—one can be on the chair while the other is being cleaned. An SE model of the Polly is identical to the regular version, just different fabric patterns. FYI: The Polly has either cloth or vinyl seat pads, usually noted online. We'd avoid the cloth pads and stick with the newer, vinyl seat versions (much easier to clean).

Fans of the Chicco Polly like the tray, which can be removed with one-hand and hung off pegs on the back of the frame. The compact fold is nice, but the chair doesn't stand well by itself. Readers who like the Polly love the stylish look—it comes in one of five snazzy color combinations.

As for negatives, the Polly's pad is not machine-washable, which is a bummer. You can only spot clean it. Cleanability is a major negative to the Polly: the chair and tray have numerous seams, cracks and crevices that are food magnets. Also: the submarine protection is attached to the tray and not the seat, as we prefer for safety reasons. To top it off, the harness can be difficult to adjust.

There is also an upgraded version of the Polly available, dubbed the Polly Magic. It is similar to the regular Polly, but adds an upgraded leatherette pad, toys and a storage basket. The frame is slightly different and includes a "CradleRecline" seat and infant pad. Where's the magic? That's the price, which magically rises to $160. Parent feedback on the Polly Magic has been divided, with quite a few critics knocking the clean-ability. As of this writing, the Magic is no longer shown on Chicco's web site although it is still for sale online.

So it's a mixed review for the Chicco Polly: fans like the stylish design and easy fold—and when the chair is discounted like it is on Walmart for $116, it is a good deal. But the negative reviews outweigh the positives in our research, so the Chicco Polly only earns an average rating. There are better options out there than this. **Rating: C+**

Combi combi-intl.com Best known for its strollers, Combi has been trying to crack the high chair category for a while now but its efforts have met with little success.

Giving the category another try, Combi recently rolled out a new high chair, cleverly called the Combi High Chair. This $126 chair has all the usual features you'd expect: five-position height adjustment, three-position seat recline, removable dishwasher tray insert, etc. Unlike other chairs on the market, the fabric pad covers the entire chair, which theoretically should make it easier to keep clean. One negative: the tray has to be removed to fold the chair.

Parent feedback on the Combi High Chair is sparse still. Parents who bought it are generally happy with the seat, although one complained it was rather narrow. If you're looking for a simple, no frills high chair, this might be a good option. **Rating: B**

Cosco *djgusa.com* Like most things Cosco makes, their high chairs define the entry-level price point in this market. The Cosco Flat Fold high chair is a bare bones model for $34 at Walmart. This would do the trick for grandma's house—this simple chair has a three-position seat recline, three point harness
and, as the name implies, a flat fold for storage. Nothing too fancy to look at, but how many bells and whistles does Grandma need?

Cosco also makes a Flat Fold Deluxe ($44) and a Slim Fold ($34) option. The Deluxe adds a five point harness and comes in Disney patterns with a thicker seat pad while the Slim Fold keeps the three point harness and theoretically folds even flatter than the Flat Fold.

New this year, the Simple Fold High Chair, a $40 to $50 high chair that folds compactly to a standing position. This seat will eventually replace the Flat Fold line. Because this is a new high chair, we don't have feedback on it as of press time

While these high chairs are fine for occasional use at Grandma's house, we aren't keen on these offerings as a primary high chair. Why? A lack of safety features (example: three-point harnesses instead of a five-point) make these chairs better for occasional use. And the pad doesn't remove from the chair, making it harder to clean after repeated use.

Oddly, Cosco's high chair seats don't sit upright, so baby is always reclined—hence this may not be a good choice until your baby can sit up unassisted. We saw more than one complaint about the seat angle. Again, all these negatives would be moot if you only used it occasionally at Grandma's house; but not as a primary high chair. **Rating: C+**

Eddie Bauer *djgusa.com* Eddie Bauer offers a mash-up here: a hybrid wood chair with plastic tray. Yep, in the category of "everything old is new again," the Eddie Bauer Classic 3-in-1 high chair ($75-$125) combines the look of wood with the convenience of plastic.

So, what are the trade-offs? Well, you can forget about many of the features you'll find in plastic chairs—Eddie Bauer's chair lacks wheels, height adjustments, seat recline and more.

Reader feedback on this chair has turned sharply negative since it first debuted. Originally, the Eddie Bauer wood high chair had a full pad that covered the entire seat; subsequently, the pad design changed to a smaller size, showing more wood. We speculated in the last edition this would make it harder to clean (more food would get on the wood) and we were right—the negative reviews shot up after the design change.

"It's pretty out of the box, but impossible to keep that way," said one reader, who summed up the frustrations of many parents. Food sticks to the dark wood finish, the slats on the side of the seat, just about anywhere—and it is impossible to clean. The finish also comes off, say others, indicating Cosco cut some corners here. Most worrisome are recent quality complaints that include screws that fall out; miss-aligned screw holes, and other woes.

FYI: Babies R Us has an exclusive version of this chair, sold under the name Safety 1st Decor Wood high chair. It is basically the same as the Eddie Bauer model, but with a less fancy base. Price: $120.

New this year, Eddie Bauer returns to plastic traditional high chairs with a model called the Multi Stage ($130). This chair has six height adjustments, three-position recline, one hand tray release, infant insert, wheels and five point harness. There are two trays: an insert tray is dishwasher safe while the snack tray remains attached to the seat as part of the anti-submarine safety bar. The high chair also folds and the pad can be wiped clean. This high chair is still new to the market, so we don't have any parent feedback on it yet.

Bottom line: the Eddie Bauer wood high chair is not recommended. We will withhold our rating on the Multi Stage until we get more feedback. **Rating: F**

Evenflo *evenflo.com* Evenflo has always been an also-ran in the high chair market, thanks to quality woes and designs that lack pizzazz.

The Evenflo Convertible high chair is an effort by the company to innovate in this category. As the name suggests, this simple chair converts from high chair to table and chair for about $40. No bells and whistles here: just a removeable tray and five point harness. FYI: Evenflo makes a similar chair called the MiniMeal ($34). The MiniMeal has a lower seat back and only partial padding compared to the Convertible.

In the entry price point level, Evenflo offers the Compact Fold ($50) high chair. As you might guess from the name, it's main feature is the compact fold. This chair gets good reviews from parents, but there is one major flaw: the chair pad can't be removed for cleaning. Hence, you can only spot clean the pad with a sponge. While most folks seem happy enough with this chair even with that

high chairs

limitation, we'd only recommend the Compact Fold for occasional use at Grandma's house because of the cleaning issues. It comes with a three position tray (some parents say it's hard to adjust), dishwasher safe tray insert and rear wheels.

There's always some funky part of Evenflo's high chairs that mars an otherwise good design. Take the tray on the Compact Fold—it requires two hands to remove. And then when you go to put the tray down on a flat surface, it ends up spilling any remaining food. Why? There is ridge under the tray that keeps it from being level.

Overall, Evenflo has had a bumpy track record in the high chair category in the past decade. The low point came in 2008 when the company recalled nearly 100,000 high chairs because "plastic caps and metal screws can loosen and fall out, posing both a fall and choking hazards to children," reported the CPSC.

That said, the company's more recent offerings have earned better parent reviews as quality has improved. So we will tick up Evenflo's rating this time around. Evenflo's high chairs aren't among our top picks in this category, but the company is closing the gap. ***Rating: B***

Fisher-Price *fisher-price.com* Folks, we have a winner! Fisher-Price has hit a home run with its well-designed line-up of high chairs, including the best-sellers, Healthy Care and Space Saver.

In fact, Fisher Price now has six high chair models: the Healthy Care, Space Saver, Zen Collection, EZ Clean, Home & Away and Grow with Me. Here's an overview:

The Healthy Care high chair features a three-position seat recline, five-point restraint, one-hand tray removal, dishwasher-safe tray liner, and various height adjustments. FYI: The Healthy Care comes in three versions: a basic model (Healthy Care) that starts at $100 and then fancier versions (dubbed Adorable Animals or Precious Planet Sky Blue) for $110 to $150. Basically, these are the same high chair, but the more expensive versions include a fancier pad and more toys.

Parents universally praise the Healthy Care for its ease of use and cleanability (yep, those harness straps and toys can be thrown into the dishwasher). The major negative to this chair is the fashion—that cutesy color scheme turns some folks off. We know, you are putting it in the middle of your kitchen, so the fashion can be an issue.

Other negatives? Some complain the chair tends to collect food in crevices of the seat pad. And the Healthy Care requires quite a bit of assembly. The Healthy Care hasn't changed much in recent years either. Despite that, this is a best bet in the high chair market and we give the Healthy Care our highest rating.

The second best-selling Fisher Price high chair is the Space Saver ($40 to $50), the first high chair that sits on a dining chair (sort of a souped-up booster). This model features a full-size tray and three-position recline—plus it converts to a tod-dler booster. If you are short of space (think New

York City apartment), this is a great choice. Detractors point out that once you strap this thing to a chair, you can't push the chair under the table—hence defeating the space saving concept. We see that point, but still think this is a great solution for urban condos with little space to store a bulky high chair. Reader feedback on the Space Saver is very positive—we recommend it.

Fisher Price's first wood hybrid chair, the Zen, is an attempt to address the complaints that the fashion for the Healthy Care is too baby-ish. This $120 to $150 high chair features a plastic seat with three-position recline, a tray with dishwasher-safe insert and three-position height adjustment. The Zen is actually a combination of plastic, wood and metal—the chair is plastic (with a vinyl cover), the legs are metal and the footrest and support bars are wood.

The Zen is quite a departure for Fisher Price—this company is not exactly known for its design aesthetic. Most folks have to hide their Fisher Price chairs when guests come over; this one you can leave out and it will fit in most contemporary kitchens.

Reader feedback on the Zen is mixed, especially considering the glowing reviews for the Healthy Care or Space Saver. Critics of the Zen say the lack of a compact fold is a negative, as is the dishwasher safe tray, which is too easy for baby to remove. Although the main tray is dishwasher safe, water can get into it and that can create a mold problem if not properly drained. Bottom line: save the $50 and get a regular Healthy Care instead. FYI: Even though the Zen has an official retail of $150, we see it discounted online on many sites.

The EZ Clean is a $100 high chair that has as its main focus, if you hadn't guessed by the name, cleanability: it features a seamless pad (no crevices for food to stick), coated straps and a seamless dish-washer-safe tray. Of course, you also get the standard high chair features like four position seat recline, one-hand tray release and more. Reader feedback on this model has been quite positive (folks love the seamless pad), but a few dissenters knock the lack of wheels on the back of the chair (there are only wheels upfront). This makes it difficult to move around the kitchen. A few parents with bigger toddlers also found the seat too snug. Overall, however, we would recommend the EZ Clean. We've seen it online for $70.

The Home & Away 3-in-1 high chair ($110 to $120) converts from a high chair to a booster for use at restaurants as an alternative

high chairs

to grimy high chairs. Our only complaint: they claim it folds but it still looks big and bulky when folded, so it may not be convenient to take to restaurants. The Home & Away is probably the least popular chair in the Fisher Price line-up; feedback on it has been sparse.

Rounding out the high chair line-up is the Grow With Me, an entry-price point model for $50 to $60. This bare-bones chair features two height adjustments and machine washable pad . . . but it lacks wheels and doesn't recline, so it isn't suitable for newborns who can't sit up on their own. This chair is aimed at Grandma, but she'd probably do better with the Cosco Flat Fold, which is half the price.

Bottom line: Fisher Price is one of our top picks for high chairs. We like the Healthy Care, Space Saver and EZ Clean the best; skip the Zen. **Rating: A**

Graco *gracobaby.com* Graco is the second-biggest selling brand in the high chair category, behind Fisher Price. The company has had a hit with their flagship Blossom high chair, as well as their compact-folding Contempo.

Unfortunately, safety recalls have hit the brand in recent years, tarnishing Graco's reputation. In 2012, Graco recalled all its wood high chairs (80,000 chairs) for defective seats that detached from the base (injuring nine children). That followed on the heels of a huge 2010 recall (1.2 million units) that targeted construction defects (screws that held the chair's front legs loosened, causing the chair to tip over unexpectedly). This hazard injured 24 babies.

Graco offers eight high chair models, divided into three categories: all-in-one models in a group called Grow With Me (Ready2Dine, Blossom, pictured, Duo Diner), "classic" high chairs (Meal Time, Contempo, Slim Spaces, TableFit, Swivi) and travel models (Toddler Booster).

Graco's flagship "all-in-one" high chair is the Blossom, which strikes a much more modern pose than most Graco models. It has all the standard features you expect from today's chairs (three-position recline, six position height adjustment, dishwasher safe tray insert) plus a few surprises: an adjustable footrest and a parent tray under the chair.

The Blossom's key feature: the seat detaches and converts to an infant booster with a seat back insert that adjusts in size. But wait, there is also a separate toddler booster (it straps onto a regular chair). Once the seat is detached, the base becomes a "youth chair." Price: $145 to $190. Feedback for this chair has been positive, with fans citing its cleanability and ease of use. One negative: the t-bar is attached to the tray, not the seat (as we prefer for safety reasons). And the Blossom lacks a fold feature, which means you can't store it away. Despite those negatives, most reader feedback on the Blossom is positive.

Graco's Duo Diner is similar to the Blossom—it also converts to a booster seat for use with older children. But it is 20% cheaper ($110 to $140) and can be folded for storage. Readers are generally happy with the Duo Diner, with a caveat that the dishwasher-safe tray is too big to fit in some dishwashers (you may want to confirm yours will fit before purchasing).

If you need a compact fold, consider The Graco Contempo ($86 to $140). Feedback on this model has been quite positive, with folks loving the ultra compact fold and extra seat pad. You also get six-position height adjustment, three-position recline and a dishwasher-safe tray insert. Very similar to the Contempo is the newer Slim Spaces ($110), which has a compact fold to just 8.5". The Slim Spaces high chair comes pre-assembled, has six height adjustments, three position recline plus extra padding and body support for smaller infants.

On the more affordable price spectrum (the "classic" high chair category), the Graco Meal Time high chair ($70 to $80) features a one-hand, three-position recline, dishwasher-safe tray, four height adjustments, casters and one-hand tray release. Readers like the Meal Time, but the praise isn't as positive compared to the Contempo. Fans like the vinyl seat cover and smaller seat dimensions, but critics say this chair is rather bulky and the tray insert and even the tray itself can easily be removed by baby (which of course, is not good!).

Finally, we have the Graco SimpleSwitch, which converts from a high chair to a booster seat. At $60 to $70, the SimpleSwitch features a three position recline, five position height adjustment and washable pad. Reader feedback on the SimpleSwitch has been positive. One negative to the SimpleSwitch: the safety T-bar is attached to the tray instead of the seat, as we'd prefer to prevent babies from sliding out of the chair when the tray is removed.

The Graco TableFit is sized so it can slide right up to a dining room table. Eight height adjustments enable it to fit various tables, plus you also get a snack tray that fits over the larger tray and three position recline with infant support. One unique touch: the TableFit will have a no rethread harness (you can adjust the height of the harness without rethreading it), which is seen on some car seats but this is a first for high chairs. We also like the machine washable pad. Price: $90-$110.

Feedback on the TableFit has generally been positive, but a few vocal critics knock the tray design, which requires multiple hands to remove, hold your baby, etc. To fold the chair, you have to remove the tray . . . which then has no storage place. While most folks are happy with the TableFit, the concerns over the tray would lead us to pass on recommending this model.

New for 2015 is the Graco Swivi—a high chair where the seat rotates 360 degrees so baby can face in any one of four directions. The Swivi has a standing fold, dishwasher safe tray insert, seat recline, adjustable footrest and machine washable seat pad. Price: $200. This was model was too new as of this writing for any parent feedback.

So to sum up, Graco high chairs generally earn positive reviews from readers, especially the Blossom and Contempo. However, the company's safety record in this category tempers our enthusiasm. *Rating: A*

IKEA *ikea.com* IKEA has two minimalistic high chairs offerings. The Antilop ($15; pictured) is a plastic chair with metal legs . . . but doesn't include a tray (that's $5 extra) and doesn't fold up. A support pillow with cover is available for an extra $6. The Blames ($60) is a wood high chair with plastic tray.

These chairs are clearly designed for older kids, but the lack of a five-point harness (the "safety belt" doesn't quite cut it) or other adjustments make these a hard sell. That said, readers have generally given good reviews to the Antilop—one mom said it was incredibly easy to clean and just the ticket for her twins. *Rating: C+*

Inglesina *inglesina.com* Italian baby gear manufacturer Inglesina is probably best known for its strollers, but the company has recently expanded its high chair offerings. The flagship is the pricey Zuma, which attempts to be both high style and practical. The rounded seat echoes modern seats by Bloom and Boon, but the more traditional base echoes a bit of Pali.

The Zuma has eight height positions, three-position seat recline and a hefty price tag: $300 (although we've seen it online for less). The Zuma has a dishwasher safe snack tray, washable (but air dry only) double seat pad and five point harness. On an earlier version of the high chair the tray was too far away from baby leading to spill issues. We're happy to note that has been fixed by Inglesina. But perhaps the biggest plus: it folds down compactly so parents can shove it under the table when not in use.

Reader feedback on the Zuma is positive. They love the easy fold and seat height adjustment as well as the one hand tray. Some negatives: food sticks to the Velcro that attaches the seat pad and the instructions are difficult to follow, especially regarding the tray. The chair does come pre-assembled, so at least parents don't have to put it together. Finally, the front wheels on the Zuma are fixed, making it hard to maneuver.

New in the past year, Inglesina added the Gusto ($150) to their line-up. The seat has a compact fold, three position recline, four height adjustments and double tray (snack tray is dishwasher safe).

Unfortunately, the bar to keep a child from sliding out of the chair is attached to the tray, not the chair. That isn't our preference for safety reasons. The Gusto is still new, so we don't have much feedback yet from parents. The price is an improvement over the Zuma with a lot of the same features.

Inglesina's simplest high chair is the Club ($150). This chair doesn't really do anything but look pretty. The Club is probably best for toddlers who aren't ready for a booster seat yet. The feedback on the Club is more positive than the Zuma, although critics claim it takes up too much floor space and the seat is too shallow. The safety harness on the Cub is oddly anchored to the bottom of the chair, not the back, which is a safety concern in our opinion. Inglesina no longer lists this high chair on their web site, although we continue to see it sold online.

Bottom line: Inglesina's high chair offerings look pretty, but their drawbacks outweigh the positives. **Rating: C+**

Joovy joovy.com Joovy is best known for its strollers, but its Nook high chair ($102) is worth a look. It features a swing-open tray, plush seat cushion (fabric or leatherette), dishwasher-safe insert and compact fold. We liked the five-point harness and most reader feedback on the chair has been positive. Critics note the large gap between the tray and seat means too much food ends up in baby's lap. The sleek look has its fans, but note there are no wheels. This chair is relatively easy to clean and that super-compact fold makes this one a winner. We liked the price too, which is below that of similar simple high chair offerings from Inglesina and Bloom.

Joovy also has a convertible chair (baby to toddler) called the HiLo, with a unique flippable seat. The plastic seat sits in a solid beach frame with dishwasher safe tray, five-point harness and wheels. Price? An astonishing $350. At that price, we haven't had much feedback although the few folks who've purchased it seem to like it. **Rating: A-**

Mamas and Papas mamasandpapas.com British manufacturer Mamas and Papas is like the Graco of the UK. Now the company has landed on this side of the Atlantic, with a collection of strollers, bouncers and two high chair models.

Mamas & Papas most popular high chair is the Juice ($150, pictured), which has a 2-in-1 pitch: the high chair's legs pop off and it becomes a little chair for toddlers. The seat pad is molded foam and the design is sleek and modern. Parents note it is fairly easy to clean although the tray is pretty far away, meaning spills in baby's lap.

A second offering, the Pixi ($120) features an impressive compact fold, an extra removable tray and storage for the tray. It's low height means you can pull this high chair up to the table. Again the Pixi's tray is too far away, so expect lots of food in baby's lap. This seat might be best for Grandma's house although at $120, you can find a cheaper basic alternative.

Feedback on the Juice is mostly quite positive although slim babies have a hard time keeping the harness straps on, while parents complain a bit about the cleanability of both chairs. The Pixi has lots of nooks and crannies for food to get stuck and the pad on the Juice allows food to get stuck underneath the seat.

Overall, parents seem to like these seats. Our biggest beef is the trays are too far away. Until Mamas & Papas fixes this serious flaw, we'll downgrade their rating a bit. **Rating: B**

Nuna *nuna.eu* Dutch-based Nuna has launched a full scale U.S. invasion in the past year, leading the way with their strollers that marry Euro minimalism with modern aesthetics. That design element continues with Nuna's first high chair effort, the Zaaz ($250).

The "grow with me" Zaaz strikes a modern pose with its chunky, anodized aluminum legs. It converts into a chair for older kids when the tray and footrest are removed. Nuna touts the Zaaz's "crumb free" design that includes a smooth, crevice-free, air-filled foam seat for easier cleaning.

Nuna did their homework for the Zaaz: the tray is dishwasher safe, the seat is height adjustable, etc. What's missing? Well, there is no seat recline, so this might not be the best choice for infants who can't sit up unassisted. And the tray doesn't adjust, so there is a large space between baby and the tray—which means most of the food will end up in baby's lap.

Parent feedback has been positive overall. The ease of adjustment and clean ability are big winners for parents. The only negative is the lack of a recline. The Zaaz's distribution is limited to specialty stores and sites like Giggle and Nordstrom and it is $250. But theoretically you can use it until your child goes away to college. **Rating: A-**

OXO Tot *oxotot.com* Kitchen gadget maker OXO's first high chair, the Sprout, strikes an über modern pose, with its wooden legs and plastic seat. We liked the overall design, with two height positions, adjustable footrest and more. But at $250, we'd expect to see a dishwasher-safe insert tray (it lacks this), compact fold (the Sprout doesn't fold)  and reclining seat (again, missing). It comes in two base colors, a light birch and dark walnut. The birch comes with either an orange or taupe pad; the dark walnut has green, pink or taupe pads.

The Sprout garners mostly positive reviews, with folks liking the chair's small footprint and easy assembly. Unfortunately, the pads are surface clean only and more than one parent noted that water can easily get trapped in the tray when cleaning. This then rusts out the springs that are part of the tray's attachment mechanism. Other folks said this chair (especially the straps and Velcro) is hard to keep clean and stains easily. Several others complained about the durability of the seat pad. The OXO Tot seems to fall into that classic trap with high chairs: it looks pretty, but in real life, the usage experience falls short . . . that might be somewhat forgivable at $100, but not at $250.

OXO Tot also offers a lower-price chair, the $150 Seedling High Chair. This all-plastic chair features five height adjustments, a safety bar attached to the chair, dishwasher safe tray, one-hand adjustments, reclining seat (three positions) and even machine washable cushions. Parents seem to like the chair's light weight and maneuverability. Other pluses: easy clean ability and one hand tray release.

So it looks like OXO has learned some lessons from the Sprout's shortcomings . . . but as an all plastic chair, the Seedling looks like something Graco would sell for $100 (or 30% less than OXO Tot's pricing). Hence, it remains to be seen whether this will be a success. The Seedling was brand new as of this writing, so no parent feedback yet. FYI: OXO Tot recently debuted its first booster seat: the Nest Booster Seat is $55. ***Rating: B-***

Peg Perego *perego.com* The Peg Perego Prima Pappa high chair had been a best selling high chair for years, but its day has come and gone. Sure, it looks stylish and features a four-position reclining seat, seven height adjustments, a dishwasher-safe dinner tray, five-point restraint and compact fold. And the fabrics! Tre chic!

But let's look at the chair's key flaw: the tray. It sits a whopping 8.5" above the seat, making it too tall except perhaps for LeBron's kids. Another problem: the tray sits 7" from the back of the seat, creating a gap the size of the Grand Canyon between your baby and her food. (There is some good news on this front: in the past year, Peg added a newborn cushion to one model of the Prima Pappa to address this issue).

Then let's talk about this chair's cleanability—it's notorious for collecting food in every little nook and cranny. And the dishwasher-safe tray insert is too big to fit in most dishwashers. All this for $200+! Wow, what a deal.

Perego makes three versions of the Prima Pappa: Best, Diner and Zero 3. The Best ($250, pictured) features an upgraded, tailored seat cushion. The Diner ($200) has a seat pad made of microfiber.

The Zero 3 is the newest version of the Prima Pappa. This chair features a reclining seat (four positions), vinyl pad, simple wheels, easy fold, adjustable footrest, and the ability to store the tray on the back. Price: $200.

Perhaps the best thing about the Pappa high chair is how it looks—the fabrics are gorgeous. And this chair is made in Italy (and your only option if you want to avoid Chinese-made high chairs, which is basically everything else on the market). But when you actually use the chair, the design flaws (it lacks a compact fold, the tray is sticky and tough to remove with one hand, lack of cleanability, etc.) quickly outweigh how pretty it looks. As one mom summed it up in an online review: "this chair should only be sold together with a 2000 psi power washer!"

Besides Pappa, Perego has two other high chair offerings: The Tatamia and the Siesta.

The pricey Tatamia ($330) is billed as a "multi-purpose baby seat" since it also functions as a swing and bouncer. Given the high price, reader feedback on this model has been thin, but in general, the few who have it, like it. In contrast to the Prima Pappa, the Tatamia is easy to clean. And fans like the multi-function swing/bouncer plus the compact fold. On the other hand, critics say this chair has a steep learning curve—the directions to convert functions are complicated, etc. Other negatives: the Tatamia's large base takes up a lot of space and the swing motion can trap a baby's arm, creating a safety hazard.

The newest Perego high chair is the Siesta. Billed as a "multi-function, ultra-compact" model, the Siesta has nine height positions and a full recline. We liked the hi-tech "eco-leather" covering, which should be easy to clean. The Siesta also includes a dishwasher safe tray, wheels that have a unique "stop and go" break system and a storage net on the back. When folded it measures just 11.8". That is a bit wider than the 9" depth of the Graco Contempo when folded, but overall, impressive.

At $300, the Siesta is no bargain, but reader feedback has been mostly positive. Fans love the overall design and ease of use, but critics say the overly complicated wheels aren't user-friendly. Since the front wheels are fixed, the Siesta only pushes in a straight line. That sort of defeats the point of having wheels in the first place.

Other parents complained about the Siesta's tray (it is hard to release with one hand; it can get stuck); some say the chair is hard to adjust. Bottom line: while the Siesta has its fans, the drawbacks are too much for this pricey model.

To sum up, Peg's Italian tailored high chairs are pretty to look at—but high prices and design flaws prevent us from recommending them. If you have the space and a rich uncle, the Tatamia is probably the best of the bunch here. **Rating: C+**

Phil & Teds *philandteds.com* Stroller maker Phil & Teds offers two high chair options, the HighPod, which features a modern look and five height adjustments as well as a three position infant recline and the stripped down Poppy.

Good news about the HighPod: it's selling now for only $200 (although that's hardly cheap) down from $300 when it originally came out. Fans like the seamless chair/pad (no crevices for food to hide) and deep seat recline for infants although critics note the seat is small and bigger babies will outgrow it quickly.

But there are more negatives including a very small tray that takes two hands to remove. Plus, it is too easy for babies to remove the dishwasher safe insert, in our opinion. Add in the fact that the safety bar is attached to the tray and not the seat (for safety reasons, we like it the other way around) and the lack of wheels, and you've got a mixed review for the Highpod. This high chair feels like a version 1.0 product . . . it needs some work. Reader feedback on the HighPod is pretty positive now that the price has dropped significantly. The biggest complaints are about the tray (too small, hard to remove, clips break).

Phil & Teds Poppy is a more scaled down high chair design for $120. The lightweight chair (8 lbs.) doesn't recline or feature much in the way of adjustments but does have a relatively large tray (unlike the HighPod). It's biggest trick: after your child outgrows the high chair, the Poppy converts to a kids chair by removing the legs, similar to the Juice from Mamas & Papas. The Poppy comes in four rather bright patterns and features an "Aerocore" foam seat which is both dishwasher safe and comfortable.

Reviews of the Poppy are mixed. Readers like the tray size, but complain it's hard to remove. The harness also appears to be difficult to adjust and the shoulder straps don't stay on the child. On the other hand, the Poppy is very easy to keep clean with it's seamless seat pad. It's also very light weight.

Finally, more than one reader mentioned the leg design on the Poppy (the legs stick straight out from the chair in every direction) means you might end up tripping over it if you have limited room in your kitchen.

Bottom line: the HighPod is a much better bet at $200, and the Poppy is an interesting chair, but Phil & Teds needs to go back to the design room and fix tray issues on both chairs and the harness on the Poppy. ***Rating: B-***

Safety 1st *Safety1st.com* While parent Cosco sells bare-bones high chairs to the discount chains, Safety 1st focuses on a slightly more upscale market. Example: Safety 1st's AdapTable High Chair

high chairs

($87, pictured) has all the standard features you expect in a high chair (machine-washable cushion, three position recline, six height adjustments, one-hand tray release with dishwasher safe insert) plus an ultra-compact, standing fold. The Disney version is called the Serve n' Store; basically it is the same as the AdapTable.

The AdapTable is probably the best rated Safety 1st model, given parent feedback.

The Safety 1st Nourish high chair is an upgraded version of the AdapTable with fancier fabric and an extra infant cushion to better fit smaller newborns. Price: $120.

Safety 1st's newest high chair is the Decor, a Babies R Us exclusive for $120. This is a wood chair with plastic tray. Safety 1st parent Dorel has had a mixed track record in this category, with several Eddie Bauer wood high chairs earning less than stellar parent reviews. Parents were disappointed with the skimpy padding, flimsy straps and tray that doesn't stay in place. We don't recommend this high chair.

Overall, the quality of Safety 1st's high chairs is only average—the AdapTable is the best of the litter.

If you want a bare bones chair for Grandma, you're better off with one of Cosco's offerings for $30 less. If you want a full feature high chair, you're better off with Fisher Price or Graco, which are priced about the same as Safety 1st, yet offer enhanced features and better quality. **Rating: C+**

Stokke *stokke.com* The Stokke Tripp Trapp is the revised version of the Kinderzeat, which we recommended in a previous edition. This $250 chair has a seat and footrest that adjusts to multiple positions— the result is you can use it from six months (once baby can sit up) to age eight or beyond. By the way, we've seen this chair online for as little as $170 for discontinued finishes.

The downsides? Well, the plastic baby rail ($60 to $70), tray ($50 to $90) and seat cushion ($35 to $48) are extras—making this a very pricey investment. (Some stores are offering a two piece set of the infant rail and chair for $300–not a huge savings.) Our view: the Tripp Trapp is probably best for older toddlers who have outgrown a regular high chair (as an alternative to a booster seat). The quality of the Stokke Tripp Trapp is excellent.

Stokke expanded their high chair offerings by buying Minui, a Danish company known for its HandySitt booster chair. The HandySitt's pitch: it is a wooden portable child seat that attaches to a regular chair. Cost: $120. Compare that to a kitchen booster like the Inglesina Fast Table chair for $60.

And the reviews aren't that great. Some parents complain that the portable seat slips off chairs (say in a restaurant, for example) and toddlers can easily tip over in it. It also doesn't work on every chair.

So it is a split opinion for Stokke. The Tripp Trapp: **Rating: A-**. The HandySitt: **Rating: D** (portable seat).

Summer summerinfant.com Better known for their baby monitors, Summer has two high chairs: the Classic Comfort Wood high chair and the Bentwood high chair.

Like the Eddie Bauer wood high chairs and the OXO Tot Sprout, the Bentwood ($170; pictured) and Classic Comfort ($130) are a hybrids with wood bases and plastic trays.

The Classic Comfort has one unique feature: the seat has a three position recline unlike most wood high chairs. It also includes a permanent snack tray and full size removable dishwasher safe insert. Parents' biggest complaint is with the seat pad: it's thin and slips around a lot.

The Bentwood's key differences from similar chairs include being height adjustable with a wooden seat. It also folds. An infant insert is included with the Bentwood and the seat has four height adjustments. One reader told us the snack tray on the Bentwood is fixed (like the Classic Comfort), meaning you have to wrestle a toddler over it each time you use the chair. The chair cushion is also quite thin.

Bottom line: Summer is only a bit player in the high chair market and it shows. While models like the Bentwood show promise, Summer needs to establish more of a track record here for quality and durability before we can recommend them. **Rating: D+**

Svan of Sweden scichild.com Svan's Signet high chair is a multi-function high chair imported from Europe, much like the Tripp Trapp (discussed earlier). The all-wood Svan Signet (a plastic dishwasher-safe tray cover is included) morphs from a high chair to a chair for toddlers and then older kids.

Svan now offers two versions of the Signet: the Essential ($150 to $200) and the Complete ($240). The Complete includes a wooden tray, removable plastic tray cover and infant safety guard for use starting at 6 months. The Essential version is really just an adjustable chair for an older child with no infant safety guard or tray. You can buy a kit to convert an Essential ($200) into a Complete for $80.

Cushions are $40. Both versions now have a five-point harness.

Svan offers a more moderately priced wooden chair ($150to $180) called the Baby-to-Booster Bentwood High Chair (shorter name here please?). It mimics the Oxo Tot Sprout both in esthetics and price. It also has a foot rest that adjusts like the Tripp Trapp (but not as large). It does fold, making it convenient to store, has a one hand tray release and fits a standard table height. The post to prevent submarining is attached to the tray (we prefer it to be attached to the seat) and it doesn't have wheels. The feedback is minimal but parents seem to like it.

So is the Svan Signet worth the high price tag? Fans tell us they love how sturdy the chair is, yet it's still light enough to move around the kitchen. The aesthetics and small footprint are the key selling points. On the other hand, this is a wood high chair, so there is no seat recline or other perks you find in plastic chairs. Adjusting the chair's height requires an Allen wrench, which is a pain—and several parents complained about the Svan's numerous nooks/crannies to clean. Overall, however, most of the reviews for the Swan are positive—this is a good chair if you can get past the drawbacks and price.

FYI: Svan also makes a wooden booster seat called the Lyft. It attaches to a regular dining room chair but does not include a tray. Price: $80 to $90. **Rating: B**

Valco valcobaby.com Stroller maker Valco's simple $80 to $130 Astro is a basic high chair that folds flat (and comes with a travel bag). Reader feedback on the Astro has been quite positive— the real star here is its compact fold and light weight (about 15 lbs.), which makes it a good bet for travel.

On the downside, the tray is now dishwasher safe but requires two hands to remove. We also don't like how far it sits away from the child, although the deep lip is nice. Bottom line: this is probably a better bet for older babies and for parents with a small kitchen that need a high chair with a compact fold. **Rating: B**

◆ **Other Brands.** If you like those wood high chairs at restaurants, you can buy a similar model online: the Lipper wood high chair is $50 on Amazon.com.

Our Picks: Brand Recommendations

Here is our round up of the best high chair bets.

Good. Is space tight in your kitchen? *The Fisher-Price Space Saver* ($40-$50) lives up to its name—it straps to a regular chair and provides most of the features of a full-feature high chair, yet costs half as much. Another good option: the *Graco Contempo* ($86 to $140), which has the most compact fold of any high chair on the market and positive feedback. Also good in the compact fold, simple high chair category: *Joovy's Nook* ($102), which has a swing-out tray and a sleek, modern look.

Better. The *Fisher-Price Healthy Care* is a full feature high chair that hits all the bases—safety, ease of use, and cleanability. We like the snap-off dishwasher-safe tray, good design and easy-to-clean vinyl pad. At $100 to $150, it is a good buy. FYI: This high chair goes under several names, including Ocean Wonders, Rainforest and Precious Planet Blue Sky. The more expensive versions include an upgraded pad and toys. If you find the Fisher Price patterns too cutesy, the *Boon Flair* ($200-$250) strikes a much more contemporary pose, albeit at a higher price.

Best. *Graco's Blossom* takes the crown this year with a modern design and a slew of helpful features. Among the Blossom's best tricks: it converts to a toddler booster chair that straps to a regular kitchen chair for older kiddos. Reader feedback on this chair has been very positive. Yes, the Blossom is pricey at $145-$190, but worth it. One bummer: the Blossom doesn't fold away for storage. And the restraint bar for the chair is attached to the tray, not the chair, as we prefer. Despite these drawbacks, we recommend the Blossom for its utility and value.

Grandma's house. For grandma's house, a simple *Cosco Flat Fold* ($34) should do the trick. No, it doesn't have the bells and whistles of $100+ chairs, but Grandma doesn't need all that.

HIGH CHAIRS

High chairs, compared

NAME	RATING	PRICE	TRAY HEIGHT	TRAY DEPTH
BABY BJORN	B+	$220	5.5"	5.5"
BABY TREND	C+	$60-$100	8.5	8
BLOOM FRESCO	D	$445-$550	10	8
BOON FLAIR	A	$200-$250	5.5	7
CHICCO POLLY	C+	$130-$150	7.5	7
COSCO FLAT FOLD	C+	$34	*	*
EDDIE BAUER CLASSIC	F	$75-$125	8	5
EVENFLO CONVERTIBLE	B	$40	*	*
FISHER PRICE HEALTHY CARE	A	$110-$150	7.5	6
FISHER PRICE SPACE SAVER	A	$40-$50	7.5	5
GRACO BLOSSOM	A	$145-$190	6	6
GRACO CONTEMPO	A	$86-$140	7.5	6
IKEA ANTILOP	C+	$15	*	*
IKEA BLAMES	C+	$60	*	*
INGLESINA CLUB	C+	$150	5.5	8
INGLESINA ZUMA	C+	$300	7.5	7.25
JOVVY NOOK	A-	$102	*	*
MAMAS & PAPAS JUICE	B	$150	7	9.5
NUNA ZAZZ	A-	$250	*	*
OXO TOT SPROUT	B-	$250	7	7
OXO TOT SEEDLING	B-	$150	6	7
PEREGO PRIMA PAPPA BEST	C+	$250	8.5	7
PHIL & TEDS HIGHPOD	B-	$200	*	*
SAFETY 1ST ADAPTABLE	C+	$87	*	*
STOKKE TRIPP TRAPP	A-	$250	*	*
SUMMER BENTWOOD	D+	$170	7	6.5
VALCO ASTRO	B	$80-$130	8	9

KEY

TRAY HEIGHT: Distance from the seat to the top of the tray. Any measurement under 8" is acceptable. Above 8" is too tall.

DEPTH (tray to seat): Distance from the back of the seat to the tray. 5" to 7" is acceptable.

SUB?: Most high chairs have a special guard to prevent a child from submarining under the tray. Some models attach this to the chair; others to the tray. A better bet: those that attach to the seat. See discussion earlier in this chapter.

Sub?	Pad	Comment
Seat	None	No 5-pt. harness, easy clean, small seat
Seat	Cloth	Pad should be hand-washed, line dried.
Seat	Cloth	Seamless seat, auto height, seat reclines
Seat	Vinyl	Seamless seat; automatic height adjust.
Tray	Vinyl	Hard to clean, difficult to adjust harness
Seat	Vinyl	Lowest price, good for grandma's house.
Tray	Both	Wood with plastic tray; hard to clean.
Seat	Vinyl	Converts to table and chair
Seat	Vinyl	One of our top picks; 3 versions.
Seat	Vinyl	Attaches to chair; great for small spaces.
Tray	Vinyl	Converts to toddler booster.
Seat	Vinyl	Among narrowest fold on market.
Seat	None	Tray is $5 extra; better for older toddlers.
None	None	No harness; better for older toddlers.
Seat	Vinyl	Best for toddlers not ready for booster.
Seat	Cloth	Seamless seat, mod look, very pricey.
Seat	Vinyl	Easy fold, like a beach chair.
Seat	Vinyl	Legs pop off to convert to a chair.
Seat	Foam	"Crumb free" design for easy cleaning.
Tray	Vinyl	Doesn't fold; wood hybrid.
Seat	Vinyl	New, Plastic/Metal, Dishwasher safe tray.
Seat	Vinyl	3 versions; many colors, hard to clean.
Tray	Vinyl	Seamless pad, but small tray.
Tray	Cloth	Ultra compact, standing fold.
Seat	Cloth	Baby rail is $70 extra; no tray.
Tray	Vinyl	Hybrid wood/plastic, fixed snack tray.
Seat	Vinyl	Folds flat, comes with carry bag.

Pad: Is the seat made of cloth or vinyl? We prefer vinyl for easier clean up. Cloth seats must be laundered and some can't be thrown in the drier (requiring a long wait for it to line dry). Of course, this feature isn't black and white—some vinyl seats have cloth edging/piping.

* Not applicable or not available. Some of these models were new as of press time, so we didn't have these specs yet.

high chairs

Hook-on Chairs and Boosters

Your toddler has outgrown his high chair, but doesn't quite fit into the adult chairs at the kitchen table. What to do? Consider a booster. There are three types of kitchen booster seats on the market today:

1 HOOK-ON CHAIRS. As the name implies, these seats hook on to a table, instead of attaching to a chair. Pros: Lightweight; yet most can hold toddlers up to 35 to 40 lbs. Very portable—many parents use these chairs as a sanitary alternative when they dine out since many restaurants seemed to have last cleaned their high chairs during the Carter administration. Cons: May not work with certain tables, like those with pedestal bases. Fear of tipping an unstable table leads some restaurants to prohibit these chairs. Hook-on chairs do not recline, a feature you see on regular boosters.

2 BOOSTER SEATS WITH TRAYS. These boosters strap to a chair and usually have a tray. Pros: Most fold flat for travel. Some have multiple seat levels. Can use with or without a tray. Cons: Child may not be sitting up at table height. Some brands have too-small trays and difficult to adjust straps make for a loose fit.

3 PLAIN BOOSTERS (NO TRAY). These chairs are just boosters—nothing fancy, no trays. Pros: Better bet for older toddlers (age four or five) who want to eat at the table. Cons: No restraint system or belt, so this isn't a choice for younger toddlers.

Our Picks: Brand Recommendations

◆ *Hook-on chair. Top pick:* Chicco's two entrants in this category are excellent. The *Caddy* ($40) has a compact fold, three point harness and "quick grip" table  clamps. The seat pad is removable and machine washable. FYI: Chicco makes a version of this hook-on chair with a seat that rotates, dubbed the *360 Hook On* ($75). Either one is a good bet.

We also like the *Inglesina Fast Table Chair* ($59), which has a quick fold-flat for travel. The cover is removable and handwashable. A bit more pricey than the Chicco Caddy, but the parent feedback is excellent.

◆ ***Kitchen booster seat with tray.***
Top pick: *Fisher Price Healthy Care Booster Seat* (fisher-price.com). Fisher Price has a winner here: we liked the snap-off feeding tray that can go into the dishwasher,

easy fold and shoulder strap for road trips plus three different height settings. When your child gets older, the tray removes so the seat becomes a basic booster. The only caveat: the back does not recline, so your baby must be able to sit up on his own to use it safely. (No biggie for most toddlers, but we know some folks consider these boosters as high-chair replacements—not a good idea unless your child can sit upright). Price: $24, making this a good value.

boosters

Runner Up: *Summer Infant Deluxe Comfort Booster* (summerinfant.com). This affordable ($20) booster is similar to our top pick, but adds one nice bonus: it features a compact fold for easy transport. No snack tray, but

the full-size tray is dishwasher-safe. Be aware: this seat has a 33-pound limit—as a result this one won't work for larger toddlers. (FYI: The Fisher Price Healthy Care booster is good up to 45 lbs.).

◆ ***Kitchen booster seat without tray.***
The *Soft Gear My Booster* is our pick for kids who've outgrown their highchairs, but still need a boost in a regular chair. Designed for kids three and up, the foam seat includes a rubberized, slip-resistant grip. Price: $35.

Another good bet in this category is the *OXO Tot Perch* booster seat ($30). It quickly collapses and has a carry handle for travel. Reader feedback on this one has been quite positive.

A brief warning: The *Bumbo Seat* ($36) is a popular seat designed for younger infants to sit upright. The problem? Babies have fallen out of the seat and been injured, especially when the Bumbo is used on elevated surfaces (which

is contrary to the manufacturer's instructions that it only be used on a floor). There have also been reports of injuries to children when the Bumbo has been on the floor. As a result, the seat has been the subject of several safety recalls. We suggest passing on the Bumbo.

The Bottom Line:
A Wrap-Up of Our Best Buy Picks

What's the most affordable way to feed baby? Breastfeeding, by a mile. We estimate you can save $900 in just the first six months alone by choosing to breast-feed instead of bottle-feed.

Of course, that's easy for us to say—breastfeeding takes some practice, for both you and baby. One product that can help: a breast pump, to relieve engorgement or provide a long-term solution to baby's feeding if you go back to work. Which pumps are best? For manual pumps, we like the Avent Comfort Manual ($40-$45) and the Medela's Harmony ($30-$35) for that occasional bottle. If you plan to pump so you can go back to work, a professional-grade pump works best. Tip: rent one first before you buy. If you like it and decide you are serious about pumping, we liked the Medela Pump In Style ($225-$300).

If you decide to bottle feed or need to wean your baby off breast milk, the most affordable formulas are the generic brands sold in discount stores under various private-label names. You'll save up to 40% by choosing generic over name brands, but your baby gets the exact same nutrition.

Who makes the best bottles? Our readers say Avent and Dr. Brown's are tops, but others find cheaper options like Playtex work just was well at half the price.

Let's talk baby food—besides the ubiquitous Gerber, there are several other brands that are good alternatives. One of the best is Earth's Best, although it is more pricey than affordable brands like Beechnut. How can you save? Make your own baby food for pennies or buy jarred baby food in bulk at discount stores. And skip the toddler meals, which are a waste of money.

Finally, consider that quintessential piece of baby gear—the high chair. We felt the best bets were those that were easiest to clean (go for a vinyl, not cloth pad) and had snap-off dishwasher-safe trays. Our top pick here is the Graco Blossom ($145-$190).

Now that you've got the food and kitchen covered, what about the rest of your house? We'll explore all the other baby gear you might need for your home next.

CHAPTER 7

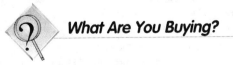

AROUND THE HOUSE

Around the House: Monitors, Diaper Pails, Safety

Inside this chapter

What's the best bathtub for baby? Which baby monitor can save you $40 a year in batteries? What's the best—and least stinky—diaper pail? In this chapter, we explore everything for baby that's around the house. From bouncer seats to safety gates, we'll give you tricks and tips to saving money. You'll learn about play yards and swings. Finally, let's talk safety—we'll give you advice on affordable baby proofing.

Getting Started: When Do You Need This Stuff?

The good news is you don't need all this stuff right away. While you'll probably purchase a monitor before the baby is born, other items like bouncer seats and even bath-time products aren't necessary immediately (you'll give the baby sponge baths for the first few weeks, until the belly button area heals). Of course, you still might want to register for these items before baby is born. In each section of this chapter, we'll be more specific about when you need certain items.

What Are You Buying?

Let's take a tour around the house to see what items you might consider for baby. Of course, these ideas are merely suggestions—none of these items are "mandatory." We've divided them into two categories: bath-time and the baby's room.

AROUND THE HOUSE

Bath

1 **TOYS/BOOKS.** What fun is taking a bath without toys? Many stores sell inexpensive plastic tub toys, but you can use other items like stacking cups in the tub as well. And don't forget about tub safety items, which can also double as toys. For example, Safety 1st (safety1st.com) makes a **TempGuard Rubber Ducky**, a yellow duck with attached thermometer (to make sure the water isn't too hot) for $7. **Tubbly Bubbly** by Kel-Gar (kelgar.com) is a $12 elephant or hippo spout cover that protects against scalding, bumps and bruises. But it doesn't fit on some spouts that have a shower diverter.

2 **TOILETRIES.** Basic baby shampoo like the famous brand made by Johnson & Johnson works just fine, and you'll probably need some lotion as well. The best tip: first try lotion that is unscented in case your baby has any allergies. Also, never use talcum powder on your baby—it's a health hazard. If you need to use an absorbent powder, good old cornstarch will do the trick.

What about those natural baby products that are all the rage, like Mustela or Calidou? We got a gift basket of an expensive boutique's natural baby potions and didn't see what the big deal was. Worse yet, the $20-a-bottle shampoo dried out our baby's scalp so much he had scratching fits. We suppose the biggest advantage of these products is that they don't contain extraneous chemicals or petroleum by-products. Also, most don't have perfumes, but then, many lower-price products now come in unscented versions as well. The bottom line: it's your comfort level. If you want to try them out without making a big investment, register for them as a shower gift.

If you have a history of allergies or skin problems in your family, consider washing baby's skin and hair with Dove, Vanicream or Cetaphil bar soap. These do not contain detergents that you find in

Moms' clubs great way to share, save

Moms' clubs today are a great way to meet other moms, learn about new products and save money. In Dallas, Metro Moms (metroplexbaby.com) holds monthly events that include dinner and numerous product giveaways. Some events feature a guest speaker (usually a parenting expert), guided museum tours, book signings and other seasonal events. In Chicago, the BumpClubandBeyond.com is aimed at both moms and moms-to-be with girls' night out, lunch and dinner seminars, shopping events and more. Many of these new moms' clubs spread the word via social media (Facebook, Twitter, Foursquare).

even the most basic baby shampoo. And remember, just because a product is "organic" or "all-natural" doesn't mean it's non-allergenic. In fact, ingredients like shea butter (made from a tree nut), calendula and chamomile all have potential for reactions including rashes, breathing problems (anaphylaxis) and eye irritation. See our other book, *Baby 411* for more on alternative ingredients and their potential side effects.

3 **BABY BATHTUB.** While not a necessity, a baby bathtub is a nice convenience (especially if you are bathing baby solo). See later in this chapter for more info on bathtubs.

Safe & Sound

◆ **BATH SEATS SHOULD NOT BE USED.** It looks innocuous—the baby bath seat—but it can be a disaster waiting to happen. These seats suction to the bottom of a tub, holding baby in place while she takes a bath. The problem? Parents get a false sense of security from such items and often leave the bathroom to answer the phone, etc. We've seen several tragic reports of babies who've drowned when they fell out of the seats (or the seats became un-suctioned from the tub). The best advice: AVOID these seats and NEVER leave baby alone in the tub, even for just a few seconds.

◆ **TURN DOWN YOUR WATER HEATER.** Ideally, your water heater should be set at no more than 120° F. At 140° F it poses a safety hazard. You can also consider installing anti-scalding devices on your showers and faucets. One such device is called *ScaldShield* and sells at hardware stores for about $50.

◆ **NO SKID RUGS IN THE BATHROOM.** Invest in rugs that have rubberized, no-skid bottoms. You don't want to slip carrying your baby, and you don't want your newly walking toddler to bang his head on the toilet or tub.

◆ **LOCK IT UP.** Install cabinet and toilet locks. This is just as important as safeguarding baby from dangers in the kitchen. And now is a great time to retrain your husband to put the lid down on the toilet seat. Locks don't work unless you actually use them.

Baby Bathtubs

Sometimes, it is the simplest products that are the best. Take baby bathtubs—if you look at the offerings in this category, you'll note some baby bathtubs convert to step stools and then, small compact cars. Okay, just kidding on the car, but these products are a good example of brand manager overkill—companies think the way to success with baby bath tubs is to make them work from birth to college.

So, it shouldn't be a surprise that our top picks for baby bathtub are, well, just bathtubs. Here's an overview

Best (full size tub). The *EuroBath by Primo* ($25; primobaby.com; pictured right) is a sturdy tub for babies, age birth to two. It weighs less than two pounds and is easy to use—just add baby, water and poof! Clean baby. The EuroBath is well designed, although it is big—almost three feet from end to end. It may be a tight fit if you have a small bathroom.

Another good choice is the ***First Year's Infant to Toddler Tub with Sling*** ($17 to $20). This simple tub includes a sling and foam pads to better fit a newborn.

Best (folding tub). The *Puj Tub* ($45) is a soft, foldable tub designed to fit in a sink. Made of foam, it unfolds when not in use and can hang on the back of a door—perfect if you live in a tiny urban apartment. The only caveat: it doesn't work with  all sinks or faucets (an oval sink with a 6.5" depth is best). And it is designed for infants to six month-olds, so this won't work for older babies and toddlers.

Boon has an excellent tub for the space deprived (and fashion forward) parent. The ***Naked*** baby bathtub is collapsible with a hook to hang it in the shower and can be placed in a reclining position. The simple, colorful design makes it a pleasure to look at and use. Cost: $60. It comes in bright teal blue and traffic cone orange.

What about tubs with bells and whistles like built-in thermometers? A waste of money, say our readers, who complain the thermometers often don't work.

A baby bathtub is a great item to pick up second-hand or at a garage sale. Or borrow from a friend. Readers say they've snagged baby bath tubs for $2 or so at garage sales—with a little cleaning, they are just fine. What if you want to give baby a bath in a regular tub or kitchen sink? A bath pad like ***Leachco Safer Bather Infant Bath Pad*** ($20) will do the trick.

Now let's talk about that big milestone, potty training.

Potty Seats

Potty seats come in two flavors: floor models and inserts. Inserts are molded (and sometimes padded) seats made for smaller bottoms. They are installed on top of the regular toilet seat. Floor models are traditional self-contained units with a base and seat.

Some potty seats start out as floor models and then the seat can be removed and used as an insert on the regular toilet. Our advice: go for the insert only. Yes, you'll need a step stool for your little one to climb up, but it's much easier to transition to a regular toilet if your child is already using one. And think about how excited your child will be to use the same toilet as his parents (trust us, it is a big deal).

Our Picks: Brand Recommendations

Best (Seat Insert). The *Baby Bjorn Toilet Trainer* ($26 to $31) has an adjustment dial to fit most toilet seats and an angled splashguard. The contoured seat works well, say readers.

Best (Potty Chair). The *Fisher Price Precious Planet Potty* ($13) is shaped like a frog and is very simple. Does the trick at an affordable price. A closer runner-up is *Baby Bjorn's Potty Chair* at $29. Very good as well.

Ceiling Fans & White Noise

Many parents swear they'd never survive without the ceiling fan in their baby's room—the "white noise" made by a whirling fan soothed their fussy baby (and quieted sounds from the rest of the house).

Interestingly, a study in the *Archives of Pediatrics and Adolescent Medicine* published in 2008, showed that babies who sleep in a room with a ceiling fan have a much lower risk of dying of Sudden Infant Death Syndrome (SIDS). Why would a ceiling fan make a difference, you ask? Turns out that by circulating the air in your baby's room, you lower the chances that he or she will "re-breathe" exhaled carbon dioxide. This re-breathing has been suggested as one cause of SIDS. So we definitely recommend a ceiling fan, both for that low hum in the background and the recirculation of the room's air.

What about other white noise generators that play rain forest or ocean sounds? Our advice is to skip them. In a 2003 study published in the journal *Science*, researchers say using white noise can be dangerous to your child's developing hearing. Our advice now is to avoid those white noise generators, although a ceiling fan is fine.

Diaper Pails

Pop quiz! Remember our discussion of how many diapers you will change in your baby's first year? What was the amount?

Pencils down—yes, it is 2300 diapers! A staggering figure . . . only made more staggering by figuring out what do with the dirty ones once you've changed baby. Yes, we can hear first-time parents raising their hands right now and saying "Duh! They go in the trash!"

Oh, not so fast, new parental one. Stick a dirty diaper in a regular trashcan and you may quickly perfume your entire home—not to mention draw a curious pet and we won't even go there.

So, most parents use a diaper pail, that specialized trashcan designed by trained scientists to limit stink and keep out babies, pets and stray relatives. But which diaper pail? Here's our Diaper Pail 411:

Diaper pails fall into two camps: those that use refill cartridges to wrap diapers in deodorized plastic and pails that use regular kitchen trash bags.

As you'd guess, pails that use special refills are more expensive (the refills cost about $8 each and wrap about 140 or so diapers). The pail can hold 20-25 diapers at a time, which is about three days worth of diapers. Bottom line: you'll about need to buy 16 refill cartridges per year—which means $125. And that's on top of the $40 to $60 that the pails cost.

So, should you just get a diaper pail that uses regular kitchen trash bags? Yes, they are less expensive to use—but there is sometimes a major trade-off. Stink. These pails tend to stink more and hence, have to be emptied more frequently (perhaps daily or every other day) than the diaper pails that use special deodorized plastic.

Obviously, the decision on which diaper pail is right for you and your baby's nursery depends on several factors. What is the distance to the trash? If you live in a house with easy access to an outside trashcan, it might be easier to go with the lower-cost alternatives and just take out the diapers more frequently. If you live in an apartment where the nearest dumpster is down three flights of

Wipe Warmers: Not Recommended

These $20 gizmos warm wipes to a comfy 90 degrees, so baby isn't surprised by a cold wipe at 2am. While this sounds like a good idea, there have been a series of safety recalls for these devices, which have caused fires, electric shock and other problems. Besides, you can just warm the wipes up in your hands for a few seconds—voila! Warm wipe without spending $20.

stairs and a long walk across a parking lot, well, it might make sense to go with an option that requires less work.

Another factor: how sensitive are you to the smell? Some folks don't have a major problem with this, while moms who are pregnant again with a second child may need an industrial strength diaper pail to keep from losing it when walking into baby's nursery. A great tip from our readers: dump the poop. Before tossing the diaper, dump the poop into the toilet.

Whatever your decision, remember you'll live with this diaper pail for three or more YEARS (that's how long before most children potty train).

And it's a fact of life: diapers get stinkier as your baby gets older . . . so the diaper removal strategy that works for a newborn may have to be chucked for a toddler. Yes, you may be able to use a plain trashcan with liner when your newborn is breastfeeding . . . but after you start solid foods, it will be time to buy a more stink-free diaper pail.

Given those caveats, here is an overview of what's out there:

ARM & HAMMER DIAPER PAIL BY MUNCHKIN

Web: munchkin.com

Type: Refill canister.

Price: $49 with ten refill bags; additional refills $13.

Pros: Baking soda+diapers = less stink.

Cons: Supposedly only needs one hand to open lid, but really difficult one handed.

Comments: This diaper pail's secret weapon is baking soda—once you put a diaper in, a built-in dispenser sprinkles the diaper with baking soda to control odor. Yes, you still have to push in the diaper (like the Diaper Genie), but the self-sealing system is a bit easier to use and does what it supposed to do: control the stink.

Reader feedback on this has been trending positive on this pail. Parents praise the lack of odor saying it seals better than other brands. And the little shot of baking soda from the refillable cartridge can't hurt. It's also easy to replace the bag and remove the dirty diapers.

Perhaps the biggest complaint we hear from readers is what's called the "squish factor." You have to really push the diaper down to get it into the pail—not fun when it's a really full diaper. And some enterprising toddlers have easily figured out how to get the door open in the base. Finally, it does take two hands to open the lid making for tough going if you have your baby in one hand.

Bottom line: Still with all it's faults, Munchkin's Arm & Hammer diaper pail is a great option for odor control. ***Rating: A***

BABY TREND DIAPER CHAMP DELUXE

Web: babytrend.com
Type: Kitchen trash bag.
Price: $38.

Pros: Did we mention no expensive refills? The Diaper Champ uses regular ol' kitchen bags, yet the contraption works to seal out odor by using a flip handle design. Easy to use. Taller design means it holds more diapers than the Genie. They do sell their own refill bags with "multiple layer odor protection," but we say skip their bags and stick with trash bags.

Cons: Not as stink-free as the Genie or Dekor, especially when baby starts solid foods. Bigger footprint than other pails.

Comments: When you redesign a best-selling product, you're supposed to improve it, right? Yes, unless you are Baby Trend, a brand that seems to botch even the simplest task. Fans loved the original Diaper Champ, which started the concept of using regular kitchen trash bags (and hence, saved hundreds of dollars in refill cartridges). The most recent version of Diaper Champ, unfortunately, is a step backwards: yes it has a wider opening, but parents tell us it doesn't work as well (diapers get stuck, the smell can be atrocious, etc). And the diaper removal process may require an EPA HazMat Rapid Response team, given the stink level. Fans of this diaper pail seem to like it . . . until their baby starts solid foods. Then the smell can be overwhelming, forcing folks to buy a Dekor or Genie. One tip: if you go with the Champ, put a fabric softener sheet in the pail with each load (this cuts down on the smell). And be prepared to scrub it every month or two with bleach, leaving it outside to air out. Also the Champ probably isn't the best bet if you have an older toddler, who can put toys into the slot (trust us, not a pretty sight). New this year, Baby Trend is offering Odor Grabber refills that can be used in any diaper pail on the market: Diaper Genie, Diaper Dekor and more. **Bottom line:** A mixed review: good for the first few months, not so good after baby starts solid food. A bargain—but beware the stink trade-offs. **Rating: C+**

DIAPER DEKOR

Web: regallager.com
Type: Refill canister.
Price: $40 to $77. Refill packs are $6-$7 each and wrap 480 diapers.

Pros: Hands free operation—you hit the foot pedal and drop in a diaper. Comes in three sizes, largest can holds 5+ days of diapers. Converts to a regular trashcan after baby is done with diapers. Parents say it is much easier to use than the Diaper Genie.

Cons: "Biodegradable" refills are terrible at containing stink, readers report. Hinges on the "trap door" seem prone to breakage, as does the foot pedal.

Comments: The only serious competition for the Diaper Genie, the Diaper Dekor comes in three sizes: Classic ($40, holds 40 newborn diapers), Plus ($48, 60 newborn diapers) and XL ($77, 105 newborn diapers). The Classic is best for newborns; the Plus is pitched for larger families (where more than one child is in diapers) and the XL is best for multiple births or a daycare center . . . or the Octomom. As of this writing, we saw more Plus versions for sale than the XL or Classic. And the Plus is available in designer colors (the Kolor Plus) for a bit more than the white. Be careful which size inserts you buy: the Classic size won't fit in a Plus can.

The Dekor was one of our top picks for diaper pails in our last edition—but then the company re-designed the refills . . . the result was disappointing. The worst part is a change in the plastic: the new refills are now "biodegradable." And in case you missed the eco-friendly message, the plastic is now green. The problem? The new refills are horrible at blocking odor, the main reason why you'd part with the big bucks to buy one of these pails.

Some good news: the stink about the new refills was so great, Regal Lager has brought back the original refills, which work great. So we will recommend this diaper pail, as long as you use the original refills. **Rating: A (original refills only)**

DIAPER GENIE
Web: diapergenie.com
Type: Refill canister.
Price: Essentials: $20 to $30; Elite: $30 to $40 (both are a lot less online depending on the web site). Refill cartridges ($8) hold 180 diapers.

Pros: Wraps each diaper in deodorized plastic. One-hand operation. Easy to remove diapers. Some say better at stink control than Diaper Champ.

Cons: Expensive, since you have to keep buying those refills.

Comments: Diaper Genie was the original "odor free" diaper pail with plastic refills. The pail has been through a few iterations over the years—the current models are the Diaper Genie Essentials and the Elite with Odor Lock Carbon Filter. Basically when using both models, diapers go in the top past a clamp which keeps the diapers (and the smell) inside the container (called the AIR-TITE system). A plus over past Genies: Playtex actually designed a cutter that, well, cuts the plastic liner so you can easily remove the dirty diapers.

The Diaper Genie Elite features a foot pedal, is taller and is made of anti-microbial coated plastic (to control odor). New this year, the Elite has an "Odor Lock Carbon Filter." Both versions use the same

diaper pails

refills (in case you find an older versions of the Diaper Genie at a garage sale, they use different refills that are still sold in some stores).

There used to be a three-way competition in diaper pails between the Genie, the Dekor and Baby Trend's Diaper Champ. But after Baby Trend muffed the re-design of the Champ, the Dekor changed the plastic in it's refills and Munchkin released its Arm & Hammer diaper pail, it looks to be a two way race for odor control between the Arm & Hammer and the Genie. (The Dekor is in the running if you use the old liners.)

That doesn't mean the Genie doesn't have its detractors, many of whom cite the cost of refill cartridges as a major negative. Those parents think a steel trashcan with tight fitting lid (with frequent emptying) is just as effective as the Genie. That is debatable, but others object to the process of putting a diaper in the Genie, which requires pushing it below a clamp (ew, we know).

FYI: Between the two pails, the Genie Essentials gets slightly better marks than the Elite—but the feedback on both is similar. **Bottom line:** The Genie is among the best in its field—but that doesn't mean its perfect. There is probably no such thing as a stink-free diaper pail, especially when baby starts solid foods. ***Rating: A***

FIRST YEARS CLEAN AIR DIAPER DISPOSAL SYSTEM
Web: learningcurve.com
Type: Kitchen trash bag.
Price: $45. Extra carbon filters $10 for two.
Pros: Uses a fan and carbon filter to trap odors. Holds 40 diapers. Uses standard kitchen trash bags.
Cons: LOUD! Requires four D batteries; smell escapes.
Comments: First Years decided they couldn't just design a regular diaper pail. They needed a gimmick! And *voila*! They came up with the first diaper pail with a fan plus carbon filter! Readers have one universal complaint: it is too LOUD! When you put a diaper in, the pail cranks up the decibels like a 747 (okay, an exaggeration, but you get the idea). Other readers report diapers that jam and a general lack of stink control. **Bottom line:** A loser. ***Rating: F***

UBBI DIAPER PAIL
Web: ubbiworld.com
Type: Kitchen trash bag or their own liners.
Price: $80 to $110 (more if it's an unusual color).
Comments: This steel diaper pail has a sliding opening with a rubber seal to keep odors in. The reason for the slide? Ubbi told us they think this keeps the smell from wafting out like other diaper pails. And the steel doesn't absorb odors like plastic. Best of all, it uses regular trash bags! The

Ubbi has received some pretty positive reviews overall, although it does get some criticism for the sliding opening. We tried it ourselves and thought the slide was a bit sticky so you may not be able to use it one-handed. Also parents note you don't want to overfill it–the bag can snag on the lid. But it's a lot less expensive than a VIPP, comes in 11 different colors and you can really use this as a trash can after baby is out of diapers. ***Rating: A-***

VIPP DIAPER PAIL
WEB: VIPP.com
Type: Refill canister.
Price: $320 for four gallon capacity. Plastic liners: $75 for 800 liners.
Pros: Uh . . . it's from Denmark?
Cons: Yes, the world's first $300+ diaper pail!

Comments: We'll let one of our readers describe her experience with the VIPP: "So I gave in and bought the VIPP diaper pail from Giggle. I thought that despite the obscene price this would be a worthwhile investment that would fight smell, not take up too much space, and look attractive in my Manhattan apartment. I saw that it is made in Denmark, used in doctor's offices and has a steel liner. Basically no plastic to absorb smell. And despite the many debates about Dekor/Genie, it seemed that neither one is quite ideal.

"Well this story does not end well. For $320, I also wanted ease of use (special bags are included but you can use trash bags)—but even their special VIPP bag is rather difficult to get in and out. Sadly, I took my 39-week pregnant self to return the trashcan and the woman at Giggle confirmed that although it is great at keeping the smell at bay, it is difficult to change the bag. I really was shocked to find that this 80-year-old Danish company did not have this down to more of a science. While this is not an official 'diaper pail' I think this is aggravating even if using this for regular trash." **Bottom line:** You don't need to spend $320 on a trashcan. ***Rating: F***

◆ ***More pails:*** There are several other basic diaper pails on the market today, such as the $20 Safety 1st Simple Step Diaper Pail. Most are simple plastic trashcans with lids. Our suggestion: if you go this route, just get a stainless steel step-on trashcan ($40 to $100 at Bed Bath & Beyond). Why steel? They are easier to clean—and less likely to stink like plastic. And you are getting a real trashcan you can repurpose to another part of the house after baby is done with diapers.

Humidifiers

We always know when its wintertime here in Colorado—the furnace kicks in and everyone's skin dries out quicker than you can say Palm Desert. Hence, humidifiers are a way of life here. But even if you live in a moist climate, running a humidifier in your baby's room in the winter can keep throats, nasal passages and skin from drying out—and make everyone happier.

Here's the 411 on buying a humidifier. First, there are two basic types of humidifiers:

1 EVAPORATIVE HUMIDIFIERS. Water is soaked into a wick and then a fan blows the moisture out. While these are affordable, they can be rather noisy (the fan) and you have to replace the filters regularly.

2 ULTRASONIC HUMIDIFIERS. Sound waves disperse the moisture, so there's no fan—hence these humidifiers are quieter. The downside: sometime these humidifiers leave a coating of white dust on furniture.

There's also one more choice to make when it comes to humidifiers: warm or cool mist. Like the name implies, warm mist humidifiers use a heating element to warm the water. While that might sound appealing if you live in a cold climate, we do NOT recommend these humidifiers for baby's room. That's because warm mist humidifiers can overheat the room—and that is a risk factor for Sudden Infant Death Syndrome. Also: the warm mist coming out of the humidifier can cause a scalding injury if touched by a wayward toddler.

Some quick additional points:

◆ **CONSIDER ROOM SIZE.** Humidifiers are rated by gallon output and most will tell you the size room they cover—match this to the size room your baby is in. You don't need a giant humidifier for most bedrooms.

Tracking Online Coupon Codes

If you've earned your black belt in online shopping, you know discount codes are a common way for web sites to lure customers or reward customer loyalty. And while there are sites that list coupon deals across the web (FatWallet.com, eDealFinder.com), how do you find the best coupon codes just for baby stuff? Check out our message boards (BabyBargains.com, click on Message Boards). On the Bargain Alert board, we keep a pinned thread with all the latest coupon deals, all submitted by our readers (spam isn't allowed). Updated regularly, this thread has all the best deals. (And there's even a separate pinned thread for freebies.)

◆ **CLEAN IT REGULARLY.** Humidifiers have detailed cleaning instructions—follow these! If not, you risk mold or mildew build-up in the unit or shortening the life of the humidifier.

◆ **ADJUSTABLE HUMIDISTAT.** A humidistat works like a thermostat, setting the humidity at a certain level and turning on or off the humidifier until it reaches that level. This is a nice feature, but not completely necessary.

◆ **REMODELING? CONSIDER A WHOLE-HOUSE HUMIDIFIER.** If you are planning to do any HVAC work on your home, consider installing a whole-house steam humidifier. These automatically kick in when your furnace runs (or can be controlled by a thermostat). Since they are permanently installed and plumbed to a water line, you never have to refill it. You do have to change the filter and clean out the unit, but that's just once a year.

◆ **SKIP THE VAPORIZER.** A vaporizer is a humidifier that lets you disperse medication in your child's room. Generally, this is NOT recommended—that's because pediatricians rarely prescribe medication that needs to be vaporized these days.

Our Picks: Brand Recommendations

Good. The *Honeywell HCM-350* is a $70 cool mist humidifier with a two gallon tank that is dishwasher safe. It is easy to clean and fill; we also found this model to be one of the quieter evaporative humidifiers on the market. One negative: it is rather large (18" long) and bulky. The HCM-350 also lacks a humidistat—you adjust the amount of output with a fan control knob. Overall, however, an excellent humidifier.

Best. The *Sunpentown SPT SU-4010 Ultrasonic Dual Mist Humidifier* ($65) is one of the most affordable ultrasonic humidifiers on the market. It features a built-in humidistat and a replaceable ion exchange cartridge to cut down on white dust. Offers either warm or cool mist (when used in a baby's room, always use cool mist). Very quiet, four liter gallon tank. Like all ultrasonic humidifiers, however, it requires regular cleaning and maintenance ($25 filter cartridges every year).

Bouncer Seat/Activity Gyms

◆ **ACTIVITY GYM.** Among our favorites is the Gymini by Tiny Love (tinylove.com). The Gymini is a three-foot square blanket that has two criss-cross arches. You clip rattles, mirrors and other toys onto the arches, providing endless fun for baby as she lies on her back and reaches for the toys. The Gymini comes in several versions that range from $35 to $60. The *Gymini Super Deluxe Lights & Music* is a good bet at $70. A runner-up: the *Fisher Price Rainforest Melodies and Lights Deluxe Gym* is $46. Both of these activity gyms fold up for travel.

◆ **ACTIVITY SEAT/BOUNCER WITH TOY BAR.** An activity seat (also called a bouncer) provides a comfy place for baby to hang out while you eat dinner, and the toy bar adds some mild amusement. The latest twist to these products is a "Magic Fingers" vibration feature—the bouncer basically vibrates, simulating a car ride. Parents who have these bouncers tell us they'd rather have a kidney removed than give up their vibrating bouncer, as it appears the last line of defense in soothing a fussy baby, short of checking into a mental institution.

What features should you look for in a bouncer? Readers say a carrying handle is a big plus. Also: get a neutral fabric pattern, says another parent, since you'll probably be taking lots of photos of baby in this bouncer and a garish pattern may grate on your nerves.

What is the best brand for bouncers? Fisher Price (fisher-price.com) makes the most popular one in the category; most are about $25 to $75, depending on the version. A good choice: the *Fisher Price Infant to Toddler Rocker* ($40). Yes, other companies make similar products (KIDS II is a good runner-up), but the feedback we get from parents is that Fisher-Price is the best.

Readers also give kudos to the *Fisher Price Newborn Rock 'n Play Sleeper* ($48) which doubles as both a place to sleep and a rocker.

One caveat: most bouncer seats have a 25-pound weight limit. If you want something that will last longer, consider the *Baby Bjorn Balance*. Yes, it is considerably more pricey than the Fisher-Price (about $175, depending on the store) and lacks a vibrating feature . . . but you can use it up to 29 lbs.

If you are on a tight budget, a simple Fisher Price bouncer like the *Comfy Time* (aka Mocha Butterfly) is $33 in Walmart.

If you are hoping for a gift in this category, consider registering for the *4Moms' MamaRoo.* Clocking in at a hefty $200, the MamaRoo's fans love the five unique motions (including car ride, ocean wave, etc) as well as the built-in nature sounds and the relatively compact foot-

print. New for 2015, the Mamaroo is Bluetooth enabled so you control it with a smartphone app. One caveat: it only works to 25 lbs.

What about those $100+ bouncers from Oeuf or Svan? Pretty to look at but not practical, say our readers. The lack of vibration or just about any other feature you find on a $50 bouncer makes these bouncers not worth the extra investment.

◆ **TOY BARS FOR YOUR CAR SEAT.** Here's another money-saving tip: turn your infant car seat into an activity center with an attachable toy bar. Manhattan Toy makes a *Whoozit Activity Spiral* with dangling toys that wraps around carrier handles for $18. Another plus: your baby is safer in an infant car seat carrier than in other activity seats, thanks to that industrial-strength harness safety system. Safety warning: only use these toy bars when the car seat is NOT inside a vehicle (that is, at home, etc.). Toy bars are not safe in a vehicle as they can be a hazard/projectile in an accident.

One caveat: some parents and pediatricians believe that leaving an infant in a car seat for extended periods of time can contribute to breathing problems in very young infants. For older babies, excessive time in an infant seat could lead to flat head syndrome (plagiocephaly). Unfortunately, doctors don't agree on how much time in an infant seat is too much. Use your common sense and move your child out of the seat frequently.

Play Yards

The portable play yard has been so popular in recent years that many parents consider it a necessity. Compared to rickety playpens of old, today's play yards fold compactly for portability and offer such handy features as bassinets, wheels and more. Some shopping tips:

◆ ***Don't buy a second-hand play yard or use a hand-me-down.*** Many models have been the subject of recalls in recent years. Why? Those same features that make them convenient (the collapsibility to make the play yards "portable") worked too well in the past—some play yards collapsed with babies inside. Others had protruding rivets that caught some babies who wore pacifiers on a string (a BIG no-no, never have your baby wear a pacifier on a string). A slew of injuries and deaths have prompted the recall of ten million playpens over the years. Yes, you can search government recall lists (cpsc.gov) to see if that hand-me-down is recalled, but we'd skip the hassle and just buy new.

◆ *Go for the bassinet feature.* Some play yards feature bassinet inserts, which can be used for babies under three months of age (always check the weight guidelines). This is a handy feature that we recommend. Other worthwhile features: wheels for mobility, side-rail storage compartments and a canopy (if you plan to take the play yard outside or to the beach). If you want a play yard with canopy, look for those models that have "aluminized fabric" canopies–they reflect the sun's heat and UV rays to keep baby cooler.

◆ *Skip the "newborn napper."* Graco has recently added a new-born napper feature to some of its playpens. This is a separate sleep area designed to "cuddle your baby." You are supposed to use this napper before you use the bassinet feature. Our concern: the napper includes plush fabrics and a head pillow–we consider this an unsafe sleep environment. As we discussed in Chapter 2, Nursery, your baby should always be put down to sleep on his back on a flat surface with no soft bedding. Graco also makes a model (the Chadwick) that has non-removeable bumpers on the bassinet. We do not recommend this model play yard for the same reason we don't recommend you use bumpers in a crib.

◆ *Check the weight limits.* Play yards have two weight limits: one for the bassinet and one for the entire play yard (without the bassinet). Graco and most other play yard versions have an overall weight limit of 30 lbs. and height limit of 35". The exception is the Arms Reach Co-Sleeper which tops out at 50 lbs. However, there is more variation in the weight limits for the bassinet attachments. Here are the weight lim-its for the *bassinet attachments* on various play yards:

Arms Reach Co-Sleeper	30 lbs.
Graco Pack N Play	15 lbs.
Chicco Lullaby	15 lbs.
Compass Aluminum	18 lbs.
Combi Play Yard	15 lbs.

Our Picks: Brand Recommendations

Good. *Joovy's Room2 Portable Play Yard* ($104-$145) has ten square feet of area–twice the size of most standard playpens, giving baby more room to play. No, it doesn't include many other features you see in other playpens (there is no bassinet, diaper changing area, etc). However, it does

what it does well–provide a large, safe area for baby to play. Readers love the easy set-up and heavy weight canvas fabric.

Better. *Chicco's Lullaby LX Play Yard* ($190) is loaded with all the bells and whistles: bassinet, changing station, toys, storage areas, remote control electronics and more. Readers love the quality and ease of set-up for the Chicco playpen, but a few

critics knocked the hefty 30-pound weight (which we admit stretches the definition of a *portable* play yard). And the two gimmicky features (a vibrating mattress that doesn't really vibrate) and a somewhat useless mobile had more than one reader scratching their heads. Overall, however, folks are generally happy with this unit.

Best (for home). Graco is the market leader in this category—and given the value and features they offer, that's no surprise. The company offers a dozen models of playpens and each is well designed. A good example is the **Graco Pack N Play On the Go** ($70), which

lacks all the whiz-bang electronics and toys of the Chicco playpen, but then again, is that really needed? It features a bassinet, toy bar and wheels. Of course, if you want all the toys and gizmos, Graco has models with those features too—but you'll pay $100 to $200 for those versions. A couple final caveats: skip the Graco models with "newborn nappers." As we explained on the previous page, we don't recommend these for safety reasons.

Best (for travel). *Baby Bjorn's Travel Crib Light* ($200). Not cheap, but this ultra-light play yard folds up like an umbrella and fits in a smaller size carry case. Parent feedback has been

universally positive. At 11 pounds, it is half the weight of a standard Graco Pack N Play. The latest version of this playpen has see-through mesh to the floor.

Swings

You can't talk to new parents without hearing the heated debate on swings, those battery-operated surrogate parents. Some think they're a godsend, soothing a fussy baby when nothing else seems to work. Cynics refer to them as "neglect-o-matics,"

Playpen Bassinets: Naps vs. Sleeping?

As you may remember from Chapter 2, we recommend the bassinet feature of playpens as an alternative to a stand-alone bassinet for newborns.

However, some readers note that manufacturers like Graco advise the product is "intended for naps and play" and question whether a newborn should sleep full time in the bassinet.

We understand the confusion, but here's our advice: when it comes to newborns, there isn't much of a distinction between "naps" and nighttime sleep—day or night, most newborns are sleeping about four hours at a stretch (they need to feed at roughly that interval). Hence, we interpret Graco's advice to only use the Pack N Play for "naps or play" applies more to older babies—the product shouldn't take the place of a full-size crib (but is fine for occasional use at Grandma's house or a hotel room). The bottom line: we believe the bassinet feature is fine for full-time use for newborns who are under the weight limits (typically 15 pounds).

FYI: Be sure to check out some of our recommendations for play yard sheets toward the end of Chapter 3. While most parents love their play yards, the cheap-o sheets that come with most are a pain (they slip off the mattress too easily, etc).

sinister devices that can become far too addictive for a society that thinks parenting is like a microwave meal—the quicker, the better.

Whatever side you come down on, we do have a few shopping tips. First, ALWAYS try a swing before you buy. Give it a whirl in the store or borrow one from a friend. Why? Some babies love swings. Others hate 'em. Don't spend $120 on a fancy swing only to discover your little one is a swing-hater.

When we last wrote on the topic of swings, you still had a choice between wind-up swings and battery-operated models. While you may still find some wind-up models at garage sales or on eBay, most swings sold in stores are battery-operated. On Craigslist, we've seen wind-up swings for as little as $20. Of course, check with the CPSC (cpsc.gov) to make sure a used swing hasn't been recalled.

If you are in the market for a new swing, remember this rule: swings eat batteries faster than toddlers can scarf M&M's. Look for swings that use fewer batteries—some use as little as two or three (others up to four). Good news: many swings now also include an AC adapter so you can plug the swing into a wall outlet. This saves tremendously on batteries. Fisher-Price has several options with adapters.

Swings range in price from $50 to $160. The more money you spend the more bells and whistles you get—toys, music, etc.

Remember to observe safety warnings about swings, which are close to the top ten most dangerous products, as far as injuries go. You must always stay with your baby, use the safety belt, and stop using the swing once your baby reaches the weight limit (about 25 lbs. in most cases). Always remember that a swing is not a baby-sitter.

Our picks: Brand recommendations

Swings today come in three flavors: full-size, compact or travel. As you might guess, the latter category folds up for easy transport. Each work fine—if you have the space, go for a full-size model. If not, try a compact or travel version.

Who makes the best swings? Here are our picks:

Good. *Kids II's InGenuity Power Adapt Portable Swing* is an affordable swing ($90) with TrueSpeed technology to keep baby swinging even when she gets heavier.

Better. *Graco's Glider LX Gliding Swing* ($93-$135) features six gliding speeds, two vibration settings and music and sounds. Bonus: this swing takes up less space that most competitors. This model is Graco's most popular full-size swing.

Best. Fisher-Price has the cradle swing down to a science. The *Fisher Price Snugabunny Cradle 'n Swing* ($150, pictured) allows for both side-to-side and front-back motion, three seat positions and a plush seat. There are six speeds, eight musical tunes and two-position seat recline. FYI: Fisher Price makes many differ-ent versions of its cradle swing in prices that range from $100 to $160— the difference is typically fashion and toys. For example, the *Papasan Cradle Swing* ($130) is a reader favorite.

Portable. How about a swing for travel to Grandma's house? We like the *Graco Swing By Me Portable 2-in-1 Swing.* This cool swing folds up for portability, making it a good bet for $60 to $70.

Monitors

For her first nine months, your baby is tethered to you via the umbilical cord. After that, it's the baby monitor that becomes your surrogate umbilical cord—enabling you to work in the garden, wander about the house, and do many things that other, childless human beings do, while still keeping tabs on a sleeping baby. Hence, this is a pretty important piece of equipment you'll use every day—a good one will make your life easier . . . and a bad one will be a never-ending source of irritation.

Smart Shopper Tips for Monitors

Smart Shopper Tip #1
Bugging your house

"I saw a TV report where a reporter was able to drive around a neighborhood and peer in on folks' video baby monitors. Are these monitors secure?"

Let's consider what a baby monitor really is: the base unit is the transmitter and the receiver is, well, a receiver. So anyone with another baby monitor on the same frequency can often pick up your monitor—not just the sound of your baby crying, but also *any* conversations you have with your mate in the nursery.

Ditto for video monitors—most work at the same frequency. If you get another receiver and drive around the neighborhood, you'll probably be able to pick up other video signals.

The take home message: most audio and video monitors are not encrypted. Therefore the best advice is to remember that your house (or at least, your baby's room) is bugged. If you want to protect your privacy, don't have any sensitive conversations within earshot of the baby monitor. You never know who might be listening. It is wise to turn OFF the baby monitor when baby isn't in the room.

So are there any monitors that are private? Until just recently, the answer was no. But there is good news: several models feature "digital" (DECT) technology—their signals can't be intercepted, unlike older analog monitors. We'll discuss DECT later in this section and point out which models feature this technology in our product reviews.

As for baby video monitors, most are analog, not digital (and hence, not secure). However, there are a few digital models. We'll note such monitors in the reviews later in this chapter.

Side note: you can use a network webcam as a baby monitor—and several of these cameras can be password protected (so not just anyone can look in on the signal). But setting up a network webcam to view online requires some geek ninja skills!

Smart Shopper Tip #2
Battery woes

"Boy, we should have bought stock in Duracell when our baby

was born! We go through dozens of batteries each month to feed our very hungry baby monitor."

Most baby monitors have the option of running on batteries or regular current (by plugging it into a wall outlet). Our advice: use the wall outlet as often as possible. Batteries don't last long—as little as eight to ten hours with continual use. Another idea: you can buy another AC adapter for $10 or less—you can leave one AC adapter in your bedroom and have another one available in a different part of the house. (Warning: make sure you get the correct AC adapter for your monitor, in terms of voltage and polarity. Otherwise you can fry the monitor. One tip: get a universal adapter like the Velleman PSSMV1USA, $14.50 on Amazon).

Another solution: several baby monitors (reviewed later in this chapter) feature rechargeable receivers! You'll never buy a set of batteries for these units—you just plug them into an outlet to recharge.

Smart Shopper Tip #3
Interference issues
"We have a cordless phone and a baby monitor. Boy, it took us two weeks to figure out how to use both without having a nervous breakdown."

If we could take a rocket launcher and zap one person in this world, it would have to be the idiot who decided that baby monitors and cordless phones should share the same radio frequency. What were they thinking? Gee, let's take two people who are already dangerously short of sleep and mess with their phone and baby monitor.

So, here are our tips to avoid frustration:

First, the higher the frequency, the longer the range of the monitor. Basic baby monitors work on the 49 MHz frequency—these will work for a few hundred feet. Step up to a 900 MHz monitor and you can double the distance the monitor will work (some makers claim up to 1000 feet). Finally, there are baby monitors that work on the 2.4 GHz frequency, where you can pick up your baby in Brazil. Okay, not that far, but you get the idea. Of course, "range" estimates are just that—your real-life range will probably be much less than what's touted on the box.

Now here's the rub: cordless phones and Wi-Fi networks can often interfere with your baby monitor. Old cordless phones worked on the 49 MHz frequency, but modern models are more likely to be found in the 900 MHz or the 2.4 GHz (or even 5.8 GHz) bands. If you've got a baby monitor at 900 MHz and a cordless phone on the same frequency, expect trouble. Ironically, as more and more devices use the higher frequency, the old 49

MHz for baby monitors now seems to be the most trouble free when it comes to interference.

Wi-Fi networks work on the 2.4 GHz band—yep, the same frequency used by some baby monitors. The same advice as above: don't get a baby monitor on the same frequency as your Wi-Fi network. FYI: Baby VIDEO monitors work on either the 900 MHz or 2.4 GHz frequencies and can have the same interference issues as audio monitors.

New to the market are digital or DECT monitors, which work in the 1.9 GHz range. Since very few other electronics operate on this band, DECT monitors are virtually interference-free and work at even longer range than 2.4 GHz monitors. Another plus: DECT monitors can't be monitored by noisy neighbors. Bottom line: if your house is buzzing with electronics, consider a DECT monitor (we'll suggest specific models later in the reviews section).

So, to sum up, here is our advice: first, try to buy a baby monitor on a different frequency than your cordless phone or Wi-Fi network. Second, always keep the receipt. Baby monitors have one of the biggest complaint rates of all products we review. We suspect all the electronic equipment in people's homes today (cell phones, Wi-Fi routers, fax machines, large-screen TVs the size of a Sony Jumbotron), not to mention all the interference sources near your home (cell phone towers, etc.) must account for some of the problems folks have with baby monitors. Common complaints include static, lack of range, buzzing and worse—and those problems can happen with a baby monitor in any price range.

So, read our monitor recommendations later with a grain of salt. ANY monitor (even those we rate the highest) can still run into static and interference problems, based on your home's electronics.

Again, the best advice: always keep the receipt for any baby monitor you buy—you may have to take it back and exchange it for another brand if problems develop.

Smart Shopper Tip #4
The one-way dilemma

"Our baby monitor is nice, but it would be great to be able to buzz my husband so he could bring me something to drink while I'm feeding the baby. Are there any monitors out there that let you communicate two ways?"

Yep, Philips has models that do just that (see review later in this chapter). Of course, there is another alternative: you can always go buy a basic intercom for about $50. Most also have a "lock" feature that you can leave on to listen to the baby when he's sleeping. Another advantage to intercoms: you can always deploy the unit to another part of your house after you're done monitoring the baby. Of course, the only disadvantage to intercoms is that they aren't portable—most must be plugged into a wall outlet.

Here are other features to consider when shopping for monitors:

◆ *Out of range indicators.* If you plan to wander from the house and visit your garden, you may want to go for a monitor that warns you when you've strayed too far from its transmitter. Some models have a visual out of range indicator, while others beep at you. Of course, even if your monitor doesn't offer this feature, you'll probably realize when you're out of range—the background noise you hear in your home will disappear from the receiver.

◆ *Low battery indicator.* Considering how quickly monitors can eat batteries, you'd think this would be a standard feature for monitors. Nope—very few current models actually warn you when you're running out of juice. Most units will just die. If you plan to heavily use your monitor on battery power (out in the garden, for example), look for this feature.

◆ *What's the frequency?* As we discussed above, the right or wrong frequency can make a world of difference. Before selecting a monitor, think about the wireless gadgets you have in your home (particularly cordless phones). Then look carefully at packages . . . not all monitors put that info up front.

◆ *Extra receivers.* It is convenient to leave one receiver in your bedroom and then tote around another receiver in your home.

◆ *Digital technology.* New models use digital technology to prevent eavesdropping by your neighbors. Digital monitors also avoid static and interference from other electronics in your home.

◆ *Great, but not necessary.* Some monitors have a temperature display, which might help you spot a nursery that's too warm. Others have a base with nightlight or play lullabies to sooth baby. Nice, but most folks don't need this.

Smart Shopper Tip #5
The cordless phone trick
"A techie friend of mind mentioned that some of the new cordless phones can double as baby monitors. Which phone does that?"

Here's a clever way to avoid spending $50 on a baby monitor. Simply use your cordless phone to monitor the baby's room.

Uniden (uniden.com), for example, sells not one but 55 cordless phone models with a room monitor feature. A typical package includes two handsets for about $40—then you can buy extra handsets for about $20. FYI: Panasonic also has several models with this feature as well.

Basically, you put one handset in the baby's room, turn on the room monitor feature and you can listen in on a second handset. One caveat: with some models you can't both monitor a room and receive a phone call at the same time. Make sure your model can receive a call when in monitor mode.

The bottom line: if you need a new cordless phone for your house, consider buying one with a room-monitoring feature.

Smart Shopper Tip #6
Video monitor shopping advice
"We want a video baby monitor. What are the key features to consider?

Video baby monitors have become increasingly popular in recent years, thanks to improved technology and lower prices, starting at just $100. Here are some key features to look for:

◆ *Fixed . . . or not.* There are three basic types of video monitors out there: fixed, PTZ and streaming. Fixed monitors have a camera that is, well, fixed and is the most economical choice. PTZ stands for point/tilt/zoom, where a camera can move and tilt: some parents prefer PTZ monitors since they can scan a room for a wayward baby or toddler. Finally, streaming baby monitors can send a video signal over the internet, so grandparents and relatives can see the baby's nursery. Each type has its trade-offs—most streaming monitors are fixed. And most PTZ monitors can be pricey.

◆ *Zero Dark Nursery.* One of the key times you use a monitor is at night—or to see in a darkened room, while baby is sleeping. To help make visible pictures, cameras use night vision—basically a series of LED lights that bathe a nursery in infrared light. While some cameras have better night vision than others (we'll note this in reviews), realize that baby monitor night vision is rather rudimentary. The goal isn't to have a super-crisp picture to see your baby's facial expressions. You just want to see if baby is sleeping. Or playing. Or standing up crying, etc. Of course, weak night vision that doesn't let you even see if your baby is sleeping or sitting up is a problem. And night vision is often limited in distance—you can't put the camera ten feet away from the crib and expect to see clearly in the dark.

◆ **Battery life.** In a word, it sucks for most video monitors. That's because portable video screens are power hogs. Expect to plug in the monitor for over-night monitoring—that's because most monitors only last two to four hours on battery power.

◆ **Resolution.** Don't expect HDTV-quality pictures from most baby monitors. Remember, you are viewing most monitors on a small (2.4″ to 3.5″) screen. The resolution should enable you to get a clear view of your baby's crib or nursery, not to count the freckles on his cute little face (no matter how tempting). The best video monitors have a resolution of 640 x 280 pixels. HDTV, by contrast, is 1920 x 1080 pixels.

◆ **VOX.** Voice-on-exchange mode is an optional setting on many monitors that only turns on the screen when baby makes a sound above a preset level. This is helpful to conserve battery. Folks either love or hate VOX—fans love not having to hear every peep or squeak from baby. Critics say VOX mode can falsely trigger, awakening sleep-deprived parents when there isn't a problem in the nursery.

◆ **Zoom.** The Z in PTZ cameras stands for zoom. And some cameras offer this feature to let you zoom in on a particular area in the nursery. Be aware that most cameras have a digital zoom. This means the pixels in the camera are enlarged when you zoom. As a result, the picture becomes grainy. Hence, the zoom feature is less helpful than you'd think.

◆ **Stream.** The latest trend in baby monitors are those that can stream a picture online—so you can check baby while you are at work. Or a grandparent can see the nursery. This type of monitor can be tricky to set up, as it requires a secure connection to the internet. Depending on your internet router, these monitors can work fabulously . . . or not at all. We'll discuss the options in detail in the reviews.

More Money Buys You

Basic baby monitors are just that—an audio monitor and transmitter. No-frills monitors start at $20 or $25. More money buys you a sound/light display (helpful in noisy environments, since the lights indicate if your baby is crying) and rechargeable batteries (you can go through $50 a year in 9-volts with regular monitors). More expensive monitors even have transmitters that also work on batteries (so you could take it outside if you wish) or dual receivers (helpful if you want to leave the main unit inside the house and take the second one outside if you need to work in the garage, etc.). Finally, the top-end monitors either have digital technology or intercom features, where you can use the receiver to talk to your baby as you walk back to the room. The most expensive monitor on the market ($100+) add vibration alerts, a room temperature thermometer, adjustable sound sensitivity, music and a night light.

For video monitors, more money buys you bigger viewing screens (four or five inch wide screens, versus cheaper models that are as small as 1.5″). More expensive baby video monitors have point-tilt-zoom capability (PTZ) as well as the ability to stream video online to a smartphone.

Audio Baby Monitors

The Name Game: Audio Baby Monitors

Here's a look at the best audio baby monitors (video monitor reviews start on page 229).

Major caveat to these reviews: ANY baby monitor, even those that earn our highest ratings, can have problems with static, poor reception or interference (see earlier discussion). The best advice: keep your receipt and buy a monitor from a store with a good return policy. It might be trial and error to find one that works for you.

A quick safety tip for monitors: always keep the cord at least three feet away from your baby's crib. Cords from cameras/monitors are a strangulation hazard.

The Ratings

A **EXCELLENT**—*our top pick!*
B **GOOD**— *above average quality, prices, and creativity.*
C **FAIR**—*could stand some improvement.*
D **POOR**—*yuck! could stand some major improvement.*

Angelcare *angelcare-monitor.com* The Angelcare monitor launched in 1997 after engineer Maurice Pinsonnault bought the patent rights to a breathing monitor sold in the UK. In a nutshell, Angelcare has two functions: first, it is a regular audio baby monitor. Second, it measures baby's "breathing movements" through a sensor placed under the crib mattress. If baby stops moving for 20 seconds, an alarm sounds on the parent unit.

Here's our problem with this concept: Angelcare clearly plays on parents' fears of Sudden Infant Death Syndrome. However, experts such as the American Academy of Pediatrics say monitors like Angelcare don't work in preventing SIDS. And Angelcare is very careful to steer clear of such promises (its website doesn't refer to SIDS, only the "anxiety which all new parents face").

Bottom line: if your baby has a medical condition that requires a breathing monitor, you need to get a medical grade monitor from your pediatrician.

In Angelcare's defense, folks who have this monitor praise it for the "piece of mind." But you can get the same piece of mind from *any* audio monitor that costs half as much as the Angelcare ($74 for a single, $110 for a double receiver).

As a side note, we should mention that Angelcare does make an audio-only model (the AC420, $50). This model omits the breathing sensor and generally gets very good marks from parents. But it is rather pricey (by comparison, the Vtech audio monitor we recommend is 40% cheaper). And there is no dual receiver version of the Angelcare audio only monitor, limiting its appeal.

In recent years, Angelcare has expanded their line of monitors to include video monitors ($270). One model can stream video to an smartphone or tablet ($260).

Bottom line: Angelcare's movement monitoring feature is not worthwhile, in our opinion. What you have left are audio or video monitors that quite pricey compared to other brands. So we will give Angelcare a failing grade: if experts say movement monitors don't prevent SIDS, what is the point? ***Rating: F***

BabySense hisense.co.il The BabySense 5s Movement Monitor ($130) is similar to the Angelcare—using sensor pads, it detects baby's movements to prevent SIDS. If she stops breathing, the parent unit sounds an alarm. But it isn't an audio monitor so you won't hear your baby crying. Regardless, we don't recommend monitors like the BabySense; see the Angelcare review for our reasoning. ***Rating: F***

First Years thefirstyears.com First Years sells one audio monitor, the Crisp & Clear ($20 single, $30 double) at Target.

This bare-bones analog monitor (using the 49 MHz range) has sound, lights, low battery and out of range alerts.

FYI: There are older, discontinued audio monitors from First Years that are still being sold online. These models had similar features to the Crisp & Clear.

Generally, First Years monitors get very poor reviews. Quality woes dog these monitors with static, connection drops, clicking and other complaints. There are better choices in this category. ***Rating: D***

Graco *gracobaby.com* Graco has been in the monitor market for many years, but they've run into stiff competition from tech brands. Here's an overview of their current offerings:

At the opening price point for audio monitors, the Sound Select analog monitor is a bare bones 49 MHz monitor that just has audio (no lights or other features) for $15 in Walmart.

A more deluxe version of this model (Sound Select LX) features sound, lights and vibration. It runs $24 at Walmart for a single, $34 for double.

For digital monitors, Graco has three offerings: the Secure Coverage, Direct Connect and imonitor.

Secure Coverage ($39 single, $54 double) is a 900 MHz monitor with vibration, sound/lights and a low battery alarm. Direct Connect ($48 single, $90 double) is similar, but adds an intercom feature as well as a display of the baby's room temperature on the parent unit.

The imonitor Vibe ($39 single, $53 double) is a simple digital monitor with 900 MHz frequency and vibration.

So how's the quality? Graco says its "static filter technology" on its analog monitors allows you to hear only baby's cry, not background noise. Readers give a thumbs down on the static filter, saying it just doesn't work. It's hard to know whether it is the 49 MHz technology that is the failure here or the numerous interference points that most folks have in their homes.

Graco's digital monitors fared even worse in reader feedback. The imonitor, for example, is often criticized for its lack of range and short battery life. Sound clarity is good, but more than one parent complained about lack of long-term durability (the monitor won't hold a charge after a year, etc.). No surprise that the imonitor is headed for the discontinued bin.

Similar complaints about quality and lack of range dog the Direct Connect monitors—Graco clearly over-promises (a 2000 foot range?) and under-performs (readers say it is more like 30 feet line of sight).

Of all the monitors, the model with the least negative feedback is probably the Secure Coverage. While it still has a large number of detractors, fans of this like this monitor . . . when it works. Unfortunately, more than one reviewer claimed it has a short life span (as little as three weeks from purchase).

Overall, Graco falls short in this category. ***Rating: D***

Motorola *binatonetelecom.com* Electronics maker Binatone has licensed the Motorola name for a line of baby monitors that include both audio and video options. While the video monitors get generally positive reviews, the audio monitors (reviewed here) score much lower with parents.

The lowest cost Motorola model is the MBP8 ($35), which features DECT transmission for a range of 165 feet—the transmitter plugs directly into a wall outlet. There is an out of range alert, sound/lights and a nightlight on the baby's unit.

Next, the simple MBP11 ($40) has a basic sound/light display, out of range indicator, rechargeable batteries on the parent unit only and . . . that's about it.

The MBP16 ($60) adds a night light, two-way intercom, lullaby player and room temperature display (see below).

New for 2015, the MBP160 is a digital DECT monitor with a 900 foot range and sound/light display. The price wasn't set as of this writing. FYI: There are several older, discontinued models by Motorola still being sold online.

So how's the quality? Motorola monitors get mixed reviews at best. The lowest price model (MBP8) gets the best marks, but that isn't saying much. The biggest complaints center on quality—units that quit working after five days, transmission that cuts out, etc.

The reviews turn even more negative for the more expensive Motorola models—they are universally panned for a series of problems. Bottom line: while Motorola's video baby monitors are well received, the audio monitors are a bust. ***Rating: D***

Philips Avent *Consumer.Philips.com* Consumer products giant Philips Avent makes an excellent line of baby monitors.

Key to the quality: DECT transmission technology that not only maintains privacy but allows for a good connection distance.

The SCD560/10 ($80) features sound/light display, intercom feature, and temperature sensor/display, rechargeable batteries and an ECO mode that saves power consumption when the monitor isn't in use.

The SCD570/10 ($95) adds a vibration alert feature, but is other wise the same as the 560.

New to the line-up is a lower-price model, the SCD501/10 ($50). This unit is just the bare essentials—a sound/light display and that's about it (no intercom, no temperature feature, etc). FYI: The SCD501 doesn't have rechargeable batteries or a sensitivity adjustment. You'll have to plug the parent monitor into an outlet or provide your own batteries.

Reader feedback has been positive on the 560 and 570—parents like the ability to adjust the microphone sensitivity to screen out background noise in baby's room. Fans also laud the interference-free reception and long rechargeable battery life (about 24 hours on a charge).

The few complaints we get on these monitors center on the display unit's screen—it's hard to read the display in certain light conditions. The screen contrast frustrates some users.

As for the new low price 501, that model was too new as of this writing to get much parent feedback. But initial reports are positive; our only concern: the lack of rechargeable batteries will add up in expense over the long term.

Bottom line: while these audio monitors are pricey, the quality is excellent. ***Rating: A***

Safety 1st *safety1st.djgusa.com* Safety 1st offers a dozen audio baby monitors, most of which are affordably priced.

Example: a bare bones 49 MHz model with no sound and light display (Crystal Clear, $16).

The Glow & Go adds sound/lights and a temperature display (on base) and comes in both single ($25) and dual ($40) versions. The baby's unit has a glow light with a 15 minute auto shut-off.

Sound Moments is a newer 49 mhz monitor available with one ($30) or two parent units ($35). It also features a quick mute button, sound and lights, power and low battery indicators and an audio jack for headphones. The Sure Glow ($22 for single version, $25 to $44 for double) is similar to Sound Moments but has only the sound and lights and audio jack.

The above models are analog monitors; Safety 1st' sole entry in the digital monitor category is the High Def Monitor. This simple monitor features DECT technology, sound/light display, rechargeable battery, out of range and low battery indicators. This monitor sells for about $39—one of the more affordable digital monitors on the market.

So, how's the quality for Safety 1st's monitors? Bad, readers tell us. The analog models are often criticized for static and generally poor sound quality. Yes, some of the interference issues are thanks to all the modern tech folks have in their homes. But when you call a model the Crystal Clear, you'd think the sound would be, well, crystal clear? Not so much, say parents who've suffered with these monitors.

Quality issues also dog Safety 1st's digital offering. Reviews for the High Def have been mixed, with quite a few complaints of poor sound quality, static and other woes.

Bottom line: yes, these models are cheap but they aren't worth it—unless you have a high tolerance for static and other glitches. Audio monitors from competitors like Philips Avent and VTech score much better than Safety 1st's monitors. ***Rating: D***

Sony *sonystyle.com* If you want to chart the decline of the Sony brand, using this baby monitor would be an apt illustration.

The Sony BabyCall NTM-910 is a 27-channel model with rechargeable batteries for $35 single, $50 dual. Yes, you read that right—the BabyCall has 27 channels (most monitors have at most one or two).

The downside? Well, the receiver is rather bulky. And since this monitor isn't digital, it is possible to eavesdrop on the signal. And the 900 MHz frequency has less range than 2.4 GHz or DECT. But this model does have an out-of-range indicator and an optional sound-activated mode that silences the receiver until sufficient noise activates it.

So all that looks good, at least on paper? Well, this monitor was first released over ten years ago. And Sony hasn't changed it much in all those years. The best-selling models today have DECT digital technology, which not only offers privacy but also helps eliminate interference from other home electronics. By sticking with ten year old technology, Sony has made a big mistake.

Even worse, the reviews of this model in recent years suggest Sony has cut corners with this model's manufacturing. Now, we see complaints about out of range alarms that go off frequently. And that's just the beginning—the reviews are downright brutal. Why Sony keeps this model in the shelf is hard to understand.

In the past year, Sony released and then discontinued a digital monitor, the NTM-DA1 ($25). Although it is still for sale online, we wouldn't recommend it—readers were disappointed with the audio quality, range and overall sensitivity. The failure of their digital model indicates the problems with Sony's baby monitors go beyond a lack of current technology.

Bottom line: Sony's baby monitor is past its prime. Yes, we did recommend this monitor years ago, but there are better options out there now. ***Rating: D***

Summer *summerinfant.com* Summer is best known for its video monitors, but the company does have a couple of offerings in the audio only category. Both models offer digital transmission for privacy.

The Baby Wave Digital Audio monitor ($30) is a basic model with rechargeable batteries, digital transmission and sound/lights. A deluxe version of this monitor ($47) adds temperature monitoring of the nursery (with an on-screen read out on the parent unit), as well as an intercom and nightlight feature.

Reader feedback has been sharply divided between fans who like range and battery life—and critics who hate the range and battery life. The deluxe version gets better marks than the basic model, which is savaged in reviews for static and limited battery life.

We wonder if some of the issues with these models are caused by the lack of DECT technology. While the digital transmission of these models insures privacy, DECT is better at preventing static and interference.

Bottom line: Summer's audio monitors are only average performers. For every reader who says it works great for them, another reports the monitor was a bust—static, interference, durability issues, etc. ***Ratings: C-***

VTech *babymonitors.vtech.com* VTech is probably best-known for their cordless phones and interactive toys. In recents years, they entered the baby monitoring market with well received audio and video models.

The Safe & Sound Digital Audio (DM221) monitor comes in both single ($30-$40) and double ($50-$60) receiver versions and boasts 6.0 DECT technology for a secure transmission that is free from most interference. There is also an intercom feature, sound/light display, vibrating sound alert, night light and rechargeable batteries. Range is rated to 1000 feet.

Parent feedback has been very positive—it's clear VTech's successful track record in cordless phones is a major help here with the technology. The few criticisms centered on the range being less than the stated 1000 feet (that's probably a given for most monitors, sorry to say).

VTech claims 18 hour battery life for this unit, which is a stretch; most folks say it barely lasts a night. For night time monitoring, we'd suggest leaving this unit plugged in, instead of running off batteries.

While we will recommend this monitor, we should note we have received occasional reports from readers about defective VTech units. One reader said the quality of the monitor was excellent, but the battery on his unit would not hold a charge. Others report monitors that don't link properly. As with all monitors, we'd recommend purchasing this unit from a store or site that has a decent return policy just in case.

FYI: VTech has one other audio monitor on its web site, the DM111 ($20 single, $30 double). This monitor is simpler, with no LCD display but still offers DECT transmission and sound/light indicators. Parent reviews for this monitor are positive, but not quite as glowing as the DM221. Part of this is probably due to the fact the DM111 is newer and has much fewer parent reviews and comments than the DM221.

Between the two models, we think the DM221 offers the better value—the intercom and vibrating sound alert features are worth the extra expense. At $30 to $40, the DM221 is still quite affordable compared to our other top pick in this category (the Philips Avent SCD560/10, $80).

Bottom line: VTech is an excellent choice for those who want a reliable, affordable audio-only baby monitor. ***Rating: A***

Our Picks: Brand Recommendations

Here are our picks for audio baby monitors, with one BIG caveat: how well a monitor will work in your house depends on interference sources (like cordless phones, wireless internet routers), the presence of other monitors in the neighborhood, etc. Since we get so many complaints about this category, it is imperative you buy a monitor from a place with a good return policy. Keep the receipt in case you have to make an exchange.

You'll note that we just have two recommendations in this category: good and best. For privacy and static-free operation, we only recommend DECT monitors.

Good. The *Philips Avent SCD560/10* ($80) features DECT digital technology to stop interference and eavesdropping. The SCD510 also has rechargeable batteries, out-of-range indicator and intercom feature. The only bummer: it doesn't have a double receiver option. Quality is very good.

Best. VTech's affordable *Safe & Sound Digital Audio Monitor* DM221 ($30-$40 single, $50-$60 double) has 6.0 DECT technology for a secure, interference-free signal. This monitor is loaded with features (intercom, vibrating sound alert, rechargeable batteries and more). It is the best of the audio bunch.

Video Baby Monitors

The Name Game:
Video Baby Monitors

D-Link DLink.com D-Link is probably best known as a Wi-Fi router and webcam company—their first baby monitor is the Wi-Fi Baby Camera, which aims to compete against Dropcam and other similar cameras out on the market today.

Interestingly, this camera comes in three configurations: 480p resolution ($75), 480p plus SD card slot ($101) and 720p HD version with SD card slot for $150. By comparison, Dropcam is 720p resolution with no SD card slot for $200.

Like other bring your own monitor baby cams, you stream video from the D-link to your smartphone or tablet via their mydlink Baby Camera app. For the monitors with a SD card slot, you can record videos and then stream them back to your mobile device . . . or at least that is the promise.

The more expensive (720p) versions of the D-Link monitor feature a temperature sensor that turns a LED on top of the monitor from blue (too cold) to red (too hot) to green (just right). All models feature lullabies.

What's missing? Well, this monitor is fixed, so there is no point-tilt-zoom feature. (A version with PTZ runs $261).

Parent reviews of this monitor have been mixed. Set-up is an issue—more than one parent said pairing this monitor with their Wi-Fi network was a challenge. This is a common problem with Wi-Fi monitors . . . and why Dropcam's simple set-up is a category killer here. D-Link's app also comes in for a fair share of criticism—a long delay hearing sound from the camera is a common issue. (The Android version of the app draws 235 1-star reviews, with folks complaining about battery usage, sluggish performance and more).

Bottom line: this monitor promises more than it delivers. Until D-Link improves the software (apps, set-up), we suggest a Dropcam instead. ***Rating: C-***

Dropcam *DropCam.com* Dropcam is a good example of a recent trend—the invasion of streaming webcams into the baby monitor category. Only a few years ago, if you wanted a baby video monitor, you bought an expensive closed system that streamed video to a handheld parent unit. There was no streaming online or the ability to view video on a smartphone or tablet.

Now owned by Google, Dropcam revolutionized webcams with a simple to use and setup model. The Dropcam Pro is a $200 Wi-Fi security camera that lets you view your baby's nursery on a computer or smartphone (there is no parent handheld unit).

Quick and easy set-up is Dropcam's secret sauce—they promise a 60 second set-up. No special software is needed and the Dropcam works on a Mac or PC. Apps are available for iPhone and Android devices—there's even a Kindle Fire app.

FYI: in the past, there were two Dropcam models—regular and pro. The regular is now discontinued but still for sale online for $144. The pro version looks almost identical to the original Dropcam but adds a wider field of view (130° vs 107°), better zoom (8x vs 4x) and improved night vision and audio quality.

Dropcam can send you a mobile alert if it detects movement or sound in your baby's nursery. You can also record video to Dropcam's cloud web site—but this incurs a monthly fee ($99 a year for seven days of recording, $299 per year for 30 days of storage) Of course, you don't have to record the video (it's free to monitor the feed online or via a smartphone. And email/mobile alerts are also free).

Dropcam uses a special low bandwidth technology (H.264) to avoid hogging your Wi-Fi bandwidth—but a Dropcam can easily use up to 60 GB of internet bandwidth during a month's time (that's because it streams video 24/7). That could be a problem if you are on a metered internet plan (which is more common in Canada than the U.S.). FYI: you'll need an internet connection with at least 0.5 Mbps of upload bandwidth to use a Dropcam.

Parent feedback on the Dropcam is excellent—it does live up to the promise of easy set-up. Of course, there are always a few trade-offs: depending on your router speed, there can be a 3-5 second delay between the sound in your baby's nursery and what you hear on your smartphone. Hence, there might be an echo-like effect. And of course if you plan to use a Dropcam for night-time monitoring, you'll need to dedicate a device to keep the app open (a retired iPhone or iPod touch would be a good bet).

We purchased a Dropcam to demo here at the home office and are generally impressed—it is probably the easiest to set up webcam we've seen. A few thoughts: the cloud storage feature is nice but expensive (adding another $100 a year if you want to store the last seven days worth of videos). And the aforementioned few second delay irks some users, understandably. Also: a few users report that the Dropcam occasionally drop/disconnects, especially if they have a weak Wi-Fi where the cameras is located—which is a good point. If your Wi-Fi router is a long distance from the Dropcam, you may need to get a Wi-Fi repeater to boost the signal near the camera.

Those issues aside, we'd recommend Dropcam. Of course, a Dropcam isn't for everyone (Blackberry and Windows phone users—you are out of luck, no app for you). And if you have a slow internet connection (say, 1-2 Mbps), this probably isn't the best choice. But if you are looking for a simple streaming solution to viewing your baby's nursery from an iPhone or Android device (as well as computer at work), Dropcam is a worthy choice. **Rating: A**

First Years thefirstyears.com Baby gear and toy maker First Years is a relative newcomer to the video baby monitor market, launching their first offering in 2012.

The Home & Away Portable ($150 to $200)) features a 3.5" monitor, 650 foot range, night vision, rechargeable batteries and the ability to expand up to four cameras. The camera is Skype-compatible, letting you view the camera from Windows-based PC's. It also has an intercom feature and can take snapshots.

Reviews of the monitor are mixed. Parents complain that the range wasn't anywhere near 650 feet—some users complain the signal drops just a few feet away from their baby's room. Other issues: the Skype feature is cumbersome (you have to tether the parent unit to a PC via USB) and is not Mac compatible. Others complained about the battery life, which sharply deteriorates over the course of a year.

The Talk & Soothe Video Monitor ($100) is a more recent model from First Years that features a two-way intercom and lullabies, plus automatic night vision and sound sensitive lights. But the screen on the parent unit is a tiny 2.4″. Many parents seem disappointed with the Talk & Sooth citing problems with the night vision function (blurry) and malfunctioning over time. Based on the feedback, we don't recommend this monitor.

Finally, First Years makes the See & Share Monitor ($129 to $200) with a 3.5″ screen, auto night vision and Skype compatibility (PC only, not Mac). One parent noted that in order to Skype to the monitor from the parent unit this parent unit has to be connected to a PC and someone has to be in the room with baby to accept the video chat. Other that this, the monitor is too new with little feedback as yet.

Bottom line: the First Years is struggling in this category with quality and usability issues. There are better choices out there than this. **Rating: D+**

Foscam *Foscam.com* Like many other new entrants into the baby monitor category, Foscam got its start as a security camera company.

While Foscam offers cameras specifically designed as baby monitors (dubbed Fosbaby), their most popular offering is a network security camera that many parents are using to monitor a nursery.

The FI8910W is an affordable ($64) cam with an impressive list of features: remote pan/tilt, night vision (you can turn this remotely on or off), two-way audio monitoring and a sharp picture. Yes, it works off your home's Wi-Fi network. The one downside: there is no monitor to view the camera—you do that from your computer or smart phone (apps are available for iPhone, iPad, Blackberry and Android).

Readers on our message boards have been quite happy with Foscam (most of this discussion was focused on an earlier, similar model). Fair warning: like many network cams, it does take a fair amount of tech skill to set it up. The Foscam Surveillance Pro app for iPhone ($5) is an easy to use app for live streaming of any Foscam camera.

In the past year, Foscam has come out with a newer version of this camera, the FI9821W. It has s a higher resolution (720p) HD picture but otherwise looks the same as the model above. It runs $90.

Foscam's traditional baby monitors feature both a camera and monitor unit. the FBM3501 ($120) is a PTZ camera with 3.5″ LCD parent unit. It does NOT connect to the internet, however . . . so no online streaming. A similar model (the FBM3502, $140) features enhanced night vision and a few other bells and whistles (lullabies, temperature display).

FYI: Foscam baby monitors have been in the news lately, as parents discovered some Foscam cameras can be easily hacked. We have blogged on this subject, but the basic advice is: change the default password. Many hacked cameras were still using the default password.

That being said, Foscam could do a better job of securing the firmware of its network cams against hackers.

So, how is the quality? Most parent reviews of Foscam are positive, but they are tempered by the reality that you need serious tech chops to set up the Wi-Fi cams. The traditional baby monitors get above average marks, but a few critics knock the overly bright infrared LEDs on the 3501, as well as the night vision picture quality of the 3502.

The take home message: while these aren't our favorite cameras in this category, they are a good runner up. Only buy one of these network cams if you have a good understanding of your home's network router. **Rating: B**

Graco gracobaby.com Graco has struggled to get traction on this category. Their last effort (the ill-fated imonitor) suffered from range, battery life and overall complaints. It is now discontinued.

Taking another swing at the category, Graco has launched the True Focus video monitor with 1000-foot range and pan and tilt feature. It also has night vision and rechargeable batteries. Price: $160.

Parent feedback on this model is much more positive then Graco's previous efforts. Fans like the True Focus's overall value, since many other baby video monitors can top $200. Other positives include the night vision (noted as good), decent range and lack of interference.

Critics don't like the fact you can't turn off the sound (and just watch the video). And mounting this camera to a wall isn't easy (Graco intends it to be on a dresser top, apparently). While the range is good, it isn't anywhere close to the 1000 feet Graco claims and over time the battery life gets shorter making it impossible to use it cordless. Also note the zoom feature is digital (not optical) zoom—which means you lose some resolution as you zoom in. And some parents say the True Focus drops its signal frequently and its quality degrades over just a few months (range worsens, buttons stop working, etc).

Finally, we should note the Graco True Focus is not a streaming monitor (you can't view it on a TV, computer or smart phone). But not everyone needs or wants that feature . . . and the price of the True Focus reflects its stand-alone capabilities. You can't add on additional cameras to this unit—it is a solo deal.

Bottom line: Graco's monitor is okay, but not great. Long term durability and reliability issues mar this model, leading us to drop its rating this time. **Rating: C-**

iBaby ibabylabs.com iBaby is the latest streaming baby video monitor to hit the market. The company offers both fixed and point/tilt/zoom models. FYI: all of these monitors are BYOD—bring your own device as a viewer (smartphone, etc).

The M2 ($105) is a fixed camera with a magnetic base that allows you to rotate it for the best view. The camera can be operated on battery only if you want to move it to another room. iBaby has an app (Apple only) that allows four users at once to see the feed. The M2 connects via Wi-Fi or ethernet to your router.

The monitor has a two-way intercom feature and the ability to capture snapshots.

The M3 is much like the M2, but adds a point/tilt/zoom feature. Price: $121. A newer version of this camera, the M5 ($162), adds the ability to have four simultaneous viewers as well as photo capturing/social sharing. The new iBaby M6 is the company's top of the line model ($200). It features a PTZ camera, lullabies, HD picture and more.

New in the past year, the M6 ($200) is a funky looking monitor with PTZ, HD picture recording, intercom feature, cloud storage and sharing.

The coolest feature of the M6: motion alert. When the camera senses motion, it records three images of a video clip and sends a push notification to your device. (The sensitivity of motion detection can be adjusted and you can just it turn off, if you don't need it).

Feedback on iBaby's cameras is mixed. Some folks report connectivity issues and others are disappointed in the video quality (for the low priced cameras, the M2 and M3; the picture is far from HD).

Unstable connections were a common gripe, with the monitor dropping its signal from some users. Lack of volume is another complaint, as is a five second delay in transmitted images. iBaby's iPhone app also gets a huge share of unlove on the iTunes store—the lack of a native iPad app (as of this writing) is also disappointing.

One of the challenges of Wi-Fi cameras is getting them to connect to your router and then to broadcast video to the 'net. Troubleshooting connectivity issues can be a challenge unless you have serious tech chops—you know there is a challenge when iBaby's web site has an entire support section on Port Forwarding. If you don't know what that is, don't buy this camera.

That said, fans of iBaby say when it is working, it is an excellent baby monitor. Unfortunately for iBaby, there is another company that has perfected the Wi-Fi camera—Dropcam. No, it doesn't have PTZ, but Dropcam runs circles around iBaby when it comes to set up and ease of use. Bottom line: iBaby needs to polish its cameras and apps before it is ready for prime time. **Rating: D**

Infant Optics InfantOptics.com Infant Optics is a good example of how online shopping has reshaped the baby gear world. This small company (part of San Francisco-based importer Genexus) has landed its DXR-5 video baby monitor on the top of Amazon's best-seller chart for video monitors. Yes, tiny Infant Optics is out-selling baby gear heavyweights like Summer and Graco and tech giants like Samsung in this category—with little more than a web site, a single product . . . and the reach of Amazon.

The DXR-5 boasts an impressive list of features: digital and secure transmission with 800-foot range (2.4 GHz with FHSS technology to avoid interference), 2.4" display, voice-triggered (VOX) or manual operation, night vision, camera that can be wall mounted, and four hours of battery life. And the unit is expandable with up to four additional cameras.

Of course, what is more amazing about this is the price: $99. No, you don't get point/tilt/zoom—but then again, most cameras with that feature are 50% more than the DXR-5. Additional cameras are just $79.

Feedback on this monitor has been largely positive: folks like the clear audio (no static), simple set-up and VOX mode. For $99, the DXR-5 is a great value.

Of course, there are a few criticisms: quality control seems to be an issue here, with scattered reports of defective units or units that broke after a week (fortunately, the company offers a one-year warranty). Some folks found the audio to be too quiet; others said it was just fine. And some said their Infant Optics monitor interfered with their Wi-Fi router (the company has troubleshooting suggestions if this happens to you).

One suggested improvement to this monitor could be a low battery warning for the parent unit—unfortunately, it just shuts off when it runs out of juice. And it would be nice to have an option to turn the screen off and just listen to the audio at night.

Bottom line: this is an excellent video monitor for the price.

Infant Optics newest model is the DXR-8—this $185 unit has pan/tilt/zoom and interchangeable lenses (normal—comes with it; zoom and wide angle, which are sold separately).The DXR-8 also has an intercom feature and temperature sensor. The screen is larger (3.5) and you can link up to four cameras to a single display, which will then cycle through the additional cameras every 12 seconds. We're not sure we see the point of the interchangeable lenses, which would easily just get lost in our house but feedback on this model has been very positive. The biggest complaint was the beep it makes before it "goes to sleep." **Rating: A**

Levana mylevana.com Canadian-based Levana is the baby monitor division of Svat, which makes security cameras. Levana has an affordable line of video monitors (mostly sold online) that are closed systems—they include a camera and parent viewer (no Wi-Fi needed, no online streaming).

Levana offers ten models, with a mix of both fixed and point/tilt/zoom models.

The most popular Levana model is the Jena, a $80 fixed camera unit that boasts 8 hour battery life, temperature monitoring and intercom feature. The Jena has a smallish, 2.4" screen.

If that is too small, you can move up to the Ayden ($120) which has a 3.5" screen. Levana's biggest screens (4.3") are in their models with point/tilt/zoom.

For example, the Stella ($200) is a PTZ camera with "smart LED" indicator ring, which gives you a visual read-out of noise in the nursery (blue for low volume; red for wailing). The Stella also has a large 4.3" screen and intercom feature and a 36 hour battery life in "peep" mode (power-on/off, energy efficient picture). Price: $260. Feedback on the Stella has been positive, although more than one parent commented about the relatively low resolution for the parent unit (don't expect HD quality).

The Astra is a $150 model with pan/tilt/zoom, sound-sensitive LED display, 3.5" screen, 720p resolution, 2.64 GHz frequency, invisible LEDS on the camera for night vision, and eight hour battery life (48 hours on a special energy-saving mode, which activates when baby cries). You can mount the Astra on the ceiling or wall, which is a nice feature. We played with a prototype of the Astra at a trade show and thought it was well designed, much more polished than Levana's previous efforts. Example: the pan/tilt feature is silent in the Astra.

The Lila ($90) has a fixed camera with 72-hour battery, intercom and invisible night vision. Feedback on this monitor is mostly positive.

The Ovia ($160) is Levana's kitchen sink monitor; they throw in just about every possible feature: 24 hour battery life, PTZ, intercom, 4.3" screen with touch screen controls, SD photo and video recording and more.

If you need to monitor two rooms, Levana has several models with two cameras.

So how's the quality? Levana got a shaky start in this category when its monitors constantly promised more than what they delivered, whether it was battery life or receiver range. Long-term reliability was also a concern—we saw more than one report of Levana monitors that just stopped working after a few months (in some cases, a few weeks).

On the plus side, we should note that Levana's reviews are trending more positive in the last year—the newer models are garnering better marks then the older ones. Levana still needs to pay attention to quality control: we saw more than one review that claimed their Levana unit was DOA (dead on arrival). Others worked great—then died after ten months. Yes, Levana has decent customer service and they will replace these units, but the best advice would be not to ship defective units in the first place.

The models with the best parent reviews are the Ayden, Sophia and Jena—these are all fixed camera models. For PTZ cameras, the Astra and Stella are probably the pick of the litter.

Bottom line: Levana's video baby monitors are in the middle of the pack. On the plus side, we like the affordable prices and extensive features (intercom, temperature monitoring). One way Levana keeps the prices down is to have non-HD cameras. That works well on smaller screens, but some folks are disappointed with the lack of resolution.

Quality-wise, Levana ranks above competitors like First Years and Safety 1st . . . but that isn't saying much. The company needs to improve long-term reliability of its monitors to be a player. We'll tick up Levana's rating this year to reflect the more positive reviews and improved newer models. We would stick with their newest models, as the company seems to be learning from its mistakes. ***Rating: B***

Lorex *lorextechnology.com* Like Levana, Lorex is a security camera maker that has branched out into baby monitors. The company has rapidly released and discontinued models over the last couple of years.

The current flagship Lorex model is the Sweet Peep video monitor (BB2411, $98). It features a 2.4" screen on the parent unit, eight hours of battery life, intercom feature and lullabies.

The Care 'n' Share comes in two flavors: the BB3521 ($110) has a fixed camera, while the BB3525 ($130) adds point/tilt/zoom. These cameras have a snapshot feature that lets you save pics with one click of a button on the parent unit. The Care 'n' Share also has an intercom feature and lullabies. FYI: There is also a version of this monitor with a larger 4.3" screen for $200 (the BB4321T).

In the past year, Lorex rolled out its first Wi-Fi baby monitor, the Little Link (LBN511, $120). This HD 720p camera connects to your Wi-Fi network and works a bit like the Dropcam. This model is BYOD (bring your own device, smartphone or tablet) for viewing.

Like most other baby monitor makers, Lorex makes versions of its monitors with larger screens (example: Star Bright, with a 7" screen) and multiple cameras.

So how's the quality? Reviews are mixed, at best. The model with the best parent feedback is the Sweet Peep, yet critics complain it dies after a short time (three months for one parent, nine months for another). Signal drops are another annoying problem, as are Wi-Fi interference and short battery life (only one hour after a full charge?).

Troubling reports of over-heating/exploding batteries for the Care 'n' Share and the general lack of reliability (plus weak customer service) make Lorex not ready for prime time. ***Rating: D-***

Mobi *GetMobi.com* This brand is reviewed on the free side of our web site here: http://bit.ly/mobimonitorreview

Motorola *motorola.com* Electronic gadget maker Binatone licensed the Motorola name for a line of baby monitors that debuted in 2011. Their claim to fame: the ability to have multiple cameras (some models, up to four) with a viewer than can show two monitor streams at once with a picture-in-picture display.

Motorola monitors are more expensive than competitors, with many models around the $200 price point. This may be partly explained by the features Motorola packs into the monitors—many have room temperature monitoring, two-way intercom, remote activated lullabies and so on. While competitors sell $100 units, they are stripped down feature-wise, compared to these monitors.

Like most security camera companies that have moved into baby monitors, Motorola offers a variety of monitors with fixed or point/tilt/zoom cameras. The viewers range from tiny 1.8" screens up to 3.5". Most of the units are closed systems, but Motorola does have one model that works off Wi-Fi and streams online.

The most popular and flagship model in the line is the MBP36S ($240), which features a PTZ camera, 3.5" screen, room temperature monitor, built-in lullabies, and two-way intercom. You can add extra cameras ($99) to monitor multiple rooms—the display can switch between the two cameras or show both on the screen with picture-in-picture.

FYI: The 36S is an upgrade of the older 36 model—the difference is better night vision and other tweaks like the picture-in-picture feature.

So what's missing in the MBP36S compared to other brands? Well, there is no VOX mode—hence the unit is always on. Folks either love or hate VOX (where the monitor is sleeping until movement or voice triggers it to come on). Some users have also complained the night video is choppy and lacks the sharpness of other competitors, namely Samsung.

To address the picture resolution complaints, Motorola is coming out with an HD version of the 36S in 2015. Pricing and other details weren't available as of press time.

If the $240 price tag on the 36S is too much, Motorola makes a version of this camera with a smaller 2.8" screen (the MBP33S, $180). There will be a HD version of the 33S in 2015 as well.

If you don't care about the PTZ feature, Motorola has several fixed camera options including the MBP25-2, $196 with two cameras (2.4" screen) and the MBP28 ($66) with a tiny 1.8" screen.

If you are looking for a Wi-Fi camera that streams to a smartphone, the Blink1 ($111), which is similar to Dropcam since it has no parent viewer (it is compatible with smartphones, tablets, etc).

New in the past year, Motorola has rolled out the MBP41 ($160), which is similar to the MBP36 but has a redesigned camera unit that sits on a pedestal slightly above its base. This allows for flexible viewing angles when the camera is mounted on a wall, compared to the MBP36. Otherwise the MBP41 is similar to the MBP36—same point/tilt/zoom features, same resolution, etc. One plus: the MBP41 has improved night vision. FYI: The MBP41 is a Babies R Us exclusive. Also: the camera comes in a two-camera version (MBP43-2, $250) which is also exclusive to BRU.

Parent feedback on Motorola video monitors has been mostly positive, with few reports of static or interference. Much of that credit probably goes to the Motorola use 2.4 GHz FHSS technology—FHSS stands for frequency-hopping spread spectrum—which enables strong, secure reception. Both the MBP33 and MBP36 have FHSS, while the simpler MBP20 works on DECT.

Perhaps the biggest complaint about these cameras is their weak night vision—compared to other brands, the Motorola night vision pictures are not very clear. That means the camera will have to be very close to the crib to get a clear picture . . . that can be an issue since cords aren't supposed to be within arm's length of a crib for safety reasons. The newer models (33S and 36S) have improved night vision, but we still see the older models for sale online. We'd steer clear of these.

Another complaint about Motorola is choppy, low quality video. This seems especially to be a problem on the low-end models with tiny screens. We wouldn't recommend the Motorola models with puny 1.8″ screens—its hard to see anything on that size parent unit.

And want to quickly adjust the volume in the middle of the night? While you think there would be dedicated buttons to do this, you'd be wrong. Users have to navigate through menus to change the volume. Or zoom in on a baby on one side of the crib. Binatone could also beef up their customer service . . . we heard many complaints of slow response, slow replacement of defective units, etc. Our advice: purchase this monitor from a retailer that allows for easy returns.

One of the biggest frustrations with Motorola monitors is long-term reliability. Parents tell us they love their Motorola monitor—until it breaks after six months. Or three months. Or a feature (like sound) stops working in less than a year.

So it is a mixed review—these monitors are better than most, with innovative features such as the picture-in-picture viewing for multiple rooms. The pick of the litter is MBP36S. But reliability and usability issues keep the brand from receiving our highest rating. ***Rating: B-***

Philips *usa.philips.com* After debuting well received audio monitors, Philips has tip toed into the video category with a digital offering, appropriately named the Digital Video Baby Monitor. While the official retail is $220, we've seen it discounted to $140 online.

The unit features a private/secure connection (DECT signal helps avoid interference), night vision and 2.4″ viewing screen. Overall quality is good—while the picture is hardly high definition, it is good enough. The rechargeable batteries last about five to six hours. Range is decent (about 400 feet) and set-up is easy enough.

So what are the negatives? Well, the screen automatically activates when noise is detected in the baby's room—that sounds good in theory (it saves battery), but is lousy in practice. That's because the monitor doesn't transmit any audio while in this rest mode. Unfortunately, it takes a very loud noise for the monitor to trigger on and that bugged more than one reader—it would make more sense for the audio to be on 24/7 and the video screen to activate when sound reaches a certain level you could set.

After complaints that their monitor couldn't be wall mounted and had a camera base that blocked it when pointed down, Philips has fixed those flaws. Be sure you're buying the SCD603 as we've seen the older models for sale on some close-out sites. (As a reminder, make sure monitor cords are at least three feet from a crib—if not, they can become a strangulation hazard).

Those negatives aside, the majority of parents who have this monitor like it. Yes, at this price point ($220 retail), you might expect a pan/tilt/zoom function like you see on the Motorola monitors—but Phillips lacks that. And Philips doesn't have a monitor that streams to the internet. So if you can live without those features, this isn't a bad choice. ***Rating: B***

Samsung *Samsung.com* Gadget king Samsung is in every possible electronic category, so no surprise, the company offers several video baby monitors. Unfortunately, Samsung has chosen confusingly similar sounding names (RemoteVIEW, SmartVIEW, etc.) for the line.

The flagship monitor in the line is the SafeVIEW (SEW-3037W), a $179 unit with point/tilt/zoom, remotely activate nightlight, voice activated mode, and a 3.5″ screen (with 320 x 240 resolution). A similar unit dubbed BabyVIEW ($169, SEW-3036WN) has all the same features of the SafeVIEW but has a fixed camera.

Samsung's voice activated mode (VOX) has its fans and detractors. In a nutshell, VOX mode saves on battery—it turns off the screen unless sound is detected above a certain level within one minute. Fans love the VOX's ability to stretch battery life. Critics hate having the screen turn on in the middle of the night when a stray sound sets off VOX.

In the past year, Samsung came out with new versions of these flagship models with larger screens (4.3"). the BrilliantVIEW (SEW-3041W, $250) is the PTZ version, while the fixed camera SimpleVIEW (SEW-3040W) runs $176. Same basic features, just bigger screens.

Like most baby monitor makers, Samsung makes less expensive versions of its monitors with smaller screens (the EzVIEW has a 2.4" screen). These models generally rate poorer than bigger screen versions.

Finally, we should note Samsung makes one Wi-Fi monitor, the SNH-1010N ($80) that allows online streaming. This model has had brutal reviews; we would pass on it. If you want to stream your nursery to your smartphone, consider a Dropcam.

So what's the verdict on Samsung? Generally, these models are winners (especially the more expensive ones with the bigger screens). We like the overall design and user interface—they are easier to use than similarly priced models by Motorola, in our opinion. Night vision and screen resolution is good. Got multiple rooms to monitor? Most Samsung models can add up to three additional cameras; in scan mode, the screen alternates between each camera in pre-set intervals.

What's not to like? Well, there are quite a few online reports of models that stop working after a year or so. Other folks say the promised range of 900 feet is more like 90 feet. Poor battery life is another common issue—it won't last for more than a few hours, so you'll need to plug the parent unit for overnight use.

Bottom line: we will recommend Samsung, but only the models with the biggest screens (SafeVIEW or BabyVIEW for PTZ cameras). *Rating: A*

Summer *SummerInfant.com* To show you how long we've been writing about baby products, we remember Summer's first baby monitor from the late 90's. It featured a bulky camera that would stream grainy black and white pictures to a giant analog TV "parent unit." Your price: $500, in today's dollars. Ouch.

Video monitors have come a long way—and Summer has done a decent job of keeping up with the times with a video line-up of ten models.

As you'd expect, there is a mix of both fixed and PTZ models, with screen sizes that range from 1.8" up to 3.5" for the parent unit.

Summer has two flagship models: The BabyTouch Digital Video Monitor and the Peek Plus Internet Baby Monitor System.

The BabyTouch Digital Video Monitor ($149) has a touch-screen parent unit with special docking station that charges the camera. This PTZ camera has a 3.5" color display and a 400-foot range (secure digital transmission). The model also has an intercom feature and you can add multiple cameras to monitor more than one child or room (both audio and video).

Parent feedback on this monitor has generally been positive. The few negatives include lack of a belt-clip for the parent unit and battery life is about half the stated ten hours. A few folks reported interference with their Wi-Fi router.

The Connect Plus Internet Baby Monitor System ($169) is a streaming monitor that has a parent handheld unit with 2.5" screen as well. The camera works on 2.4 GHz frequency with digital transmission and a 400-foot range. A "plug and play" Internet gateway connects to your wireless router and enables remote viewing (free apps for iPhone, Android, Blackberry) via a secure web site that is password protected.

So what's not to like about the Connect Plus? Well, the camera lacks a pan/tilt/zoom function—for $169, you think Summer could have thrown that in. And while the phone apps allow for remote viewing, you can't use a smartphone for regular monitoring since the app times out after five minutes. Night vision is only okay. While Summer has done an admirable job in making this monitor easy to set up, there were still some parents who couldn't get it to work with their router.

Summer has two Babies R Us exclusive models: the Privacy Plus Series Touch and Baby Touch 2.0 ($240 either model). These models are very similar to the BabyTouch Digital Video Monitor reviewed above, but add a couple more bells and whistles. Example: the Baby Touch 2.0 has "motion-tracking" technology that follows baby's movements. We're not exactly sure of the point to this—so what if your baby scoots three inches across her crib?

Reviews on these models are lukewarm at best, with several complaints about lack of range. All things considered, it would probably be a better bet at this time to stick with the BabyTouch Digital Video Monitor until Summer works out the kinks in these BRU exclusives.

New in the past year, Summer has rolled out the first monitor that works both with a dedicated parent unit and smartphone: Baby Zoom Wi-Fi. Yes, it is the holy grail of baby monitors— a 2.5" parent monitor PLUS it streams to smartphones and tablets. The Baby Zoom has PTZ, two way intercom, the ability to add extra cameras and more. Price: $260. If you want to skip the parent unit, you can buy the camera only for $134. FYI: there is a Babies R Us version of the Wi-Fi monitor (called the Baby Touch Wi-Fi) for $300 with much the same features.

So what do parents think of the new monitors? Not good. Most of the reviews slam the Baby Zoom (and Baby Touch) for poor video quality and a generally unreliable app, which gets an abysmal 1.5 star rating on iTunes.

New for 2015, Summer is launching two monitors—the Sharp

Sight ($260) features an HD picture, which clearly is an attempt by Summer to address the picture quality complaints for their other cameras. The Sharp Sight has a 4" parent screen, PTZ camera, two-way intercom. Also new: the Baby Glow ($139) with features a camera that projects a nightlight display on a wall or ceiling. It comes with a parent unit that has a 2" screen.

So what is the final verdict on Summer? These are good, but not great monitors. Fans say these units are easy to use and the night vision is good.

Perhaps our biggest gripe with Summer is their monitors' long-term reliability. "Awesome—while it worked . . . then it died" is a common review, with parent after parent reporting units dying after several months, touch screens that stop working, out of range alerts when the monitor is close to the baby's room, etc. We realize baby monitors get intense use (on 24 hours a day), but Summer can't charge premium prices and get away with such lousy reliability. If Summer wants to charge the same amount of money that Samsung, Motorola and Dropcam charge, they must achieve similar reliability. Right now, Summer is not quite measuring up.

In the past, we recommended Summer with the caveat that the monitor may not make it past your baby's first birthday. But with so much competition in this category, there are better choices of video monitors out there that won't break after a few months. Summer's face plant with its Wi-Fi monitors doesn't help its rating either.

Bottom line: we can't recommend this brand. Summer must aggressively address quality and long-term reliability issues to right its ship in this category. ***Rating: C-***

VTech babymonitors.vtech.com Cordless phone and educational toy maker VTech joined the baby video market craze in the past year with their affordable Safe & Sound Full Color Video and Audio monitor (VM321).

This $130 model (we've seen it online for $100) features a vibrating sound alert when there is sound in baby's room, intercom feature, temperature sensor, digital zoom, night vision, and a 2.8" LCD that features a 320x240 color display. The Safe & Sound camera can be wall mounted and has 1000 foot range, which is digital and secure. You can expand the system with up to four cameras (additional cameras are $42 each), although you can't hear audio from secondary cameras (only a display alert and vibration of the parent unit notes sound detected from a secondary camera).

The voice activated sound feature (VOX) is a pro and con—this turns on the parent unit's speaker when it detects sound in the nursery (instead of continuously playing the audio). While this is a plus since it saves on battery, some found it frustrating because it can't be turned off and causes the monitor to turn off and on when the slightest sound is detected. Finally, this camera features a digital zoom option, but it has one setting (zoom in or not). FYI: VTech also makes a PTZ version of this camera, the VM333 for $150.

New this year is a more affordable model, the VM311-13 ($80). It has many of the same features as the 321, like night vision, intercom, full color video and more, but it comes with a smaller parent unit and very small video screen. Feedback is not very positive with complaints about short battery life, poor picture quality and range.

Overall, feedback on the 321 monitor has been positive, with folks generally happy with the video quality and lack of interference. Yes, there are a few glitches—the parent unit lacks a belt clip, you can't remotely trigger the lullabies that the camera plays, etc. And the VOX feature is hit or miss, as far as parent feedback goes. While this probably isn't the best choice to monitor multiple rooms, for a single camera set-up, the VTech Safe & Sound is a good bet. ***Rating: B+***

Withings *withings.com* Gadget maker Withings was among the first to market a streaming baby video monitor, the Smart Baby Monitor.

Unlike many other baby monitors, this unit is just a camera with built-in night vision—there is no monitor or receiver. Your baby's image is streamed to an iPhone or Android device over your home network. You can remotely view the image/audio over cellular networks or your work Wi-Fi. The camera unit also monitors temperature and humidity in the baby's nursery, allowing you to set up personal alarms if these exceed a certain threshold. Price is $220.

Parent feedback on Withings has been all over the board. When it works, fans like the overall quality (good video images, etc.). The monitor includes such extras as temperature and humidity—the latter is unusual for this category. There is also a music and lights feature. A clever graph tracks your baby's recent movement and noise for the last 15 minutes. There also is no limit to the number of devices you can use to monitor your Smart Monitor (but you can only have three devices simultaneously viewing the feed).

Critics point out the way the camera is situated on the base, it is hard to see most of the crib without also seeing the base. You can't view the video on a desktop computer either, which is unfortunate.

Night vision was weak in the first version of this monitor, but that has been fixed. Yet there still is no point/tilt/zoom function, which you'd expect at this price level. On the plus side, Withings has made small improvements to the monitor to address complaints. Example: now streaming is unlimited, even over 3G or 4G networks (there use to be a free 15 minute viewing limit a day over cell phone networks; then a charge after that).

Unfortunately, the company hasn't significantly upgraded this unit for while . . . and competitors like Dropcam have surpassed Withings in quality, ease of use, etc. We also see reports of app crashes, especially for Android. Withings' app for iOS7 is also very glitchy, judging from the feedback on the iTunes store. That's a major bummer, since the only way this model works is with an app.

Bottom line: Withings monitor was once a winner, but now competitors like Dropcam have surpassed it. Glitches with its apps are a crippling blow. **Rating: C**

Our Picks: Brand Recommendations

Best Bet: Fixed camera. The *Infant Optics DXR-5* is an excellent, yet affordable fixed baby monitor at just $99. FHSS technology helps avoid interference and a 2.4" display provides a crisp
picture. Simple set-up and voice-activated mode are two key features.

Runner-up: Samsung's *BabyVIEW* (SEW-3036WN) is more expensive ($169), but does have a bigger viewing screen (3.5"), as well as time display and intercom. FYI: While the BabyVIEW is a fixed camera it does have a zoom feature.

Best Bet: PTZ camera. The *Samsung SafeVIEW* (SEW-3037W, $179) is the best of the PTZ (point/tilt/zoom) cameras—it features
a voice-activated option, remote nightlight and a crisp 3.5" screen. Night vision is very good.

Runner-up: The *Motorola MBP36S* ($240) is not as easy to use as the Samsung, but a good runner-up choice. It features a PTZ camera, 3.5" screen, room temperature monitor, built-in lullabies, and two-way intercom. You can add extra cameras ($99) to monitor multiple rooms—the display can switch between the two cameras or show both on the screen with picture-in-picture.

Best Bet: Streaming camera. You'd like grandma or an aunt across the country to see your baby? Then you need a camera that can stream an image over the internet. While that sounds simple,
this category of camera can be tricky to set up. The best bet here is the **Dropcam Pro**, a simple, fixed $200 camera with about the easiest set up we've seen on a Wi-Fi cam. You can view your baby's nursery via the Dropcam web site or an iPhone or Android app. The down-side: there is no parent display unit, so you'll have to re-purpose an old iPhone or iPod Touch to be a viewer.

BABY MONITORS	A quick look at baby video monitor features

BRAND	MODEL	PRICE
DLINK	WI-FI BABY CAMERA	$75-$200
DROPCAM	DROPCAM PRO	$200
FIRST YEARS	HOME & AWAY	$150-$200
FOSCOM	F18910W	$64
GRACO	TRUE FOCUS	$160
IBABY	M3S	$162
INFANT OPTICS	DXR-5	$99
LEVANA	JENA	$80
	ASTRA	$150
	STELLA	$200
LOREX	SWEET PEEP	$98
MOTOROLA	MBP36S	$240
PHILIPS	DIGITAL VIDEO MONITOR	$140-$220
SAMSUNG	SAFEVIEW	$179
	BABYVIEW	$169
SUMMER	BABYTOUCH DIGITAL	$149
	CONNECT PLUS	$169
	BABY ZOOM WI-FI	$260
VTECH	SAFE & SOUND VM321	$110
	SAFE & SOUND VM333	$170
	SAFE & SOUND VM311	$80
WITHINGS	SMART BABY MONITOR	$220

Baby Proofing

All parents want to create a safe environment for their baby. And safety begins at the place where baby spends the most time—your home.

✔ = Yes
PTZ: Point/tilt/zoom feature.
MONITOR: Included display monitor. Models without a monitor are intended to stream to a smartphone or tablet.
STREAM: Can the monitor stream video online?

PTZ	MONITOR	STREAM	OUR RATING
		✔	C-
		✔	A
	✔		D+
✔		✔	B
ZOOM ONLY	✔		C-
✔		✔	B
	✔		A
	✔		B
✔	✔		B
✔	✔		B
	✔		D-
✔	✔		B-
	✔		B
✔	✔		A
	✔		A
✔	✔		C-
	✔	✔	C-
✔	✔	✔	C-
	✔		B+
✔	✔		B+
	✔		B+
		✔	C

monitors

Getting Started:
When Do You Need This Stuff?

Whatever you do, start early. It's never too soon to think about baby proofing your house. Many parents we interviewed admitted they waited until their baby "almost did something" (like playing with extension cords or dipping into the dog's dish) before they panicked and began childproofing.

Remember Murphy's Law of Baby Proofing: your baby will be instantly attracted to any object that can cause harm. The more harm it will cause, the more attractive it will be to him or her. A word to the wise: start baby proofing as soon as your child begins to roll over.

Safe & Sound: Smart Baby Proofing Tips

The statistics are alarming—each year, over 100 children die and millions more are injured in avoidable household accidents. Obviously, no parent wants their child to be injured by a preventable accident, yet many folks are not aware of common dangers. Others think if they load up their house with safety gadgets, their baby will be safe. Yet, there is one basic truth about child safety: *safety devices are no substitute for adult supervision.* While this section is packed with safety must-haves like gates, you still have to watch your baby at all times.

Where do you start? Get down on your hands and knees and look at the house from your baby's point of view. Be sure to go room by room throughout the entire house. On our web site, BabyBargains.com (click on bonus material), we have room-by-room advice on how to baby proof on a shoestring.

Top 10 Baby Products That Should Be Banned

We asked Dr. Ari Brown, a pediatrician in Austin, TX and co-author of our book *Baby411* for a list of baby products that should be banned. Some are dangerous, others simply foolish and unnecessary. Here is her take:

1 **BABY WALKERS: NO!** There are so many cases of serious injury associated with these death traps on wheels that some countries (including Canada) completely ban baby walkers.

2 **DON'T GET YOUR KIDS HOOKED ON BABY EINSTEIN.** TV and electronic media of any type, even "educational videos" designed for babies, are bad for developing brains. Babies need active, not passive learning, and getting them used to watching TV is a bad habit.

3 **THROW AWAY THE PACIFIER AT SIX MONTHS.** As we discussed in the feeding chapter, pacifiers are now recommended after breastfeeding is well established (about one month). But . . . remember to STOP the pacifier at six months! Your baby needs to learn to fall asleep and/or comfort herself without a crutch.

4 **AVOID EAR THERMOMETERS.** They are notoriously unreliable, and since fever in infants (over 100.3 degrees) could be serious, an inaccurate reading might give parents a false sense of security. Rectal thermometers are the most accurate.

5 **DON'T FALL FOR THE BABY TOOTHPASTE HYPE.** The best way to clean your baby's teeth is to wipe them with a wet washcloth, twice daily. The sweet taste of baby toothpaste encourages your

The Most Dangerous Baby Products

The Consumer Product Safety Commission releases yearly figures for injuries and deaths for children under five years old related to juvenile products. The latest figures from the CPSC are for 2013 and show a slight decrease in the number of injuries. The following chart details the statistics:

PRODUCT CATEGORY	INJURIES	DEATHS
INFANT CARRIES/CAR SEATS*	13,700	12
CRIBS, MATTRESSES	12,400	46
STROLLERS/CARRIAGES	12,200	1
HIGH CHAIRS	10,900	1
CHANGING TABLES	5,300	< 1
BABY GATES/BARRIERS	3,800	2
WALKERS/JUMPERS	3,300	< 1
BOUNCER SEATS	3,100	3
PLAY YARDS/ PLAYPENS	2,200	13
PORTABLE BABY SWINGS	1,700	1
BOTTLES/WARMERS/STERILIZERS	1,500	0
BASSINETS/CRADLES	1,300	22
BATH SEATS	**	5
OTHER	3,900	6
TOTAL	**74,900**	**112**

Key:
Deaths: This figure is an annual average from 2009-11, the latest figures available.
* Excludes motor vehicle incidents
** In the CPSC's latest report bath seat and bassinets/cradle injuries were not tabulated due to a low sample size.

baby to suck on the toothbrush once in his mouth and you can't maneuver it around well.

6 **BEWARE OF NATURAL BABY SKIN-CARE PRODUCTS.** Over 25% of "natural" infant skin-care items contain common allergens including peanuts.

7 **NATURAL TEETHING TABLETS.** Some of these contain *caffeine* as an ingredient! Save the espresso for kindergarten! In 2010, the Food & Drug Administration recalled Hyland's Teething tablets because they contained belladonna, a potentially toxic substance that can cause serious harm at high doses. Specifically, the FDA found Hyland's Teething tablets contained "inconsistent amounts of belladonna" and has received reports of "serious adverse events in children taking this product."

8 **FORGET SIPPY CUPS.** They promote tooth decay because the flow of liquid heads straight to the back of the top front teeth. If your baby hasn't quite mastered drinking from a cup yet, offer her a straw instead.

9 **HANGING MOBILES ARE ONLY FOR NEWBORNS.** Remove all toys and decorations hanging over your baby's crib by the time he or she is five months old. They become hazardous when babies start to pull themselves up and grab for them.

10 **ENJOY THOSE BEAUTIFUL QUILTS AS WALL HANGINGS**, not in the crib.

Safety Gates: Our Picks

Safety gates are needed in four key areas:

◆ **STAIRS.** Gates should be permanently mounted at the top and bottom of stairs.

◆ **NO BABY ZONES.** You may want to gate off the dining room or other areas baby isn't allowed.

◆ **PLAY AREAS.** Some gates can be linked together to form pla-yards—a space where baby can play, but not escape.

◆ **WINDOWS/FIREPLACES.** Unless you plan to leave your windows closed and locked, safety gates are needed when a window is opened. Fireplaces hearths are another area that needs gating.

Gates come in two flavors: hardware or pressure mounted. Hardware-mounted gates are permanently affixed to walls or door openings. Pressure-mounted gates use a spring to create pressure, holding the gate in place. In general, we recommend hardware-mounted gates at the top and bottom of stairs. Pressure-mounted gates are fine for no baby zones like the laundry room.

When it comes to hardware-mounted gates, it is always best to mount the gate's brackets into solid wood (not drywall). Use a "stud finder" (sold in hardware stores) to find wood studs in walls.

Here are specific recommendations by use:

Best stair gate. *KidCo's Safeway Gate* ($43) comes in different versions: a steel gate (G20) for straight stair openings and a model that can be mounted on angled stairways. The latter is available in both steel (G22) or wood (G32). The basic gate fits openings 24.75" to 43.5" and can be used for either stairs or windows. Reader feedback on this gate is very positive, with fans loving the ease of installation and small footprint (when open, it doesn't restrict the stairway). If you have angled banisters or walls, the

E-MAIL FROM THE REAL WORLD
A solution for those coffee tables

Reader Jennifer K. came up with this affordable solution to expensive coffee table bumpers.

"When our son started to walk we were very worried about his head crashing into the glass top tables in our living room. We checked into the safety catalogs and found those fitted bumpers for about $60 just for the coffee table. Well, I guess being the selfish person that I am, and already removing everything else dangerous from my living room, I just didn't want to give up my tables! Where do we put the lamps, and where do I fold the laundry?

"My mother-in-law had the perfect solution. FOAM PIPE WRAPPING!!! We bought it at a home improvement store for $3. You can cut it to fit any table. It is already sliced down the middle and has adhesive, (the gummy kind that rolls right off the glass if you need to replace it). The only disadvantage that we've come across is that our son has learned to pull it off. But at $3 a bag we keep extras in the closet for 'touch-ups.'

"Now the novelty has worn off, so I have NOT had to replace it as often. And I'm happy to report that we've had plenty of collisions, but not one stitch!"

Safeway G22 Angle Mount gate can be installed in any position. It sells for $55.

Best soft gate. *Evenflo's Soft and Wide Gate* ($35) is 20" tall and expands from 38" to 60" wide—perfect for funky openings you need to gate. Mesh lets baby see through the gate. However, this gate isn't designed to be set-up and removed frequently—it is better to set it up and have the adults walk over it to access the non-baby zone.

Best play yard gate. Want to create a safe place for an infant to play in the living room? The **North States Superyard XT Gate Play Yard** ($90 to $120) is an expandable panel system that is 26" high and provides a play area

of 18.5 square feet. A two-panel extension kit ($18) nearly doubles the area. Some readers use this to protect a Christmas tree from toddlers. Yes, it is all plastic, but it is durable enough to corral toddlers. A few parents say it is hard to open and close the gate (the hinges are tight), but overall, readers give this play yard solution the thumbs up.

Best fireplace hearth gate. A fireplace is an obvious place baby doesn't need to visit—but how do you protect it? *KidCo's Auto Close HearthGate* ($170) is pricey but does the trick. It is 29.95" tall and works on hearths

six feet wide by two feet deep; extensions are available for bigger openings. The HearthGate also includes a walk-through gate that closes automatically.

Best window guard. *Guardian Angel* (angelguards.com) sells affordable metal window guards that fit just about any type of window. A gate that works on windows 23" to 35" runs about $77 and is hardware mounted. A must for low windows your toddler can access or if you live in a high-rise condo building. Remember babies can climb furniture and access windows you think are safe—keep them locked or install a window guard. Runner-up: Kidco sells a Mesh Window Guard ($30) in case you don't want metal bars over your windows. Another idea: the Super Stopper from Parent Units ($19; parentunits.com) is a simple device that suctions on a window, preventing it from opening too far to let a toddler out.

Top 11 Safety Must Haves

To sum up, here's our list of top safety items to have for your home (in no particular order).

◆ *Fire extinguishers* rated "ABC," which means they are appropriate for any type of fire.

◆ *Outlet covers.*

◆ *Baby monitor*—unless your house or apartment is very small, and you don't think it will be useful.

◆ *Smoke alarms.* The best smoke alarms have two systems for detecting fires—a photoelectric sensor for early detection of smoldering fires and a dual chamber ionization sensor for early detection of flaming fires. An example of this is the First Alert "Double Sensor" ($25 to $60). We'd recommend one smoke alarm for every bedroom, plus main hallways, basement and living rooms. And don't forget to replace the batteries twice a year. Both smoke alarms and carbon monoxide detectors can be found in warehouse clubs like Sam's and Costco at low prices or in Home Depot or Lowes home improvement stores.

◆ *Carbon monoxide detectors.* These special detectors sniff out dangerous carbon monoxide (CO) gas, which can result from a malfunctioning furnace. Put one CO detector in your baby's room and another in the main hallway of your home.

◆ *Cabinet and drawer locks.* For cabinets and drawers containing harmful cleaning supplies or utensils like knives, these are an essential investment. For playtime, designate at least one unsecured cabinet or drawer as "safe" and stock it with items safe for baby.

◆ *Spout cover for tub.*

◆ *Bath thermometer or anti-scald device.*

◆ *Toilet locks*—so your baby doesn't visit the Tidy Bowl Man. One of the best we've seen in years is KidCo's toilet lock ($18), an award-winning gizmo that does the trick. Check their web site at kidcoinc.com for a store that carries it.

◆ *Baby gates.* See the section earlier for recommendations.

◆ *Furniture wall straps.* Since 2000, over 100 deaths have been caused by TV's and furniture tipping over onto kids. We recommend you anchor all your large furniture to the wall, especially shelves and dressers in baby's room. Once your child becomes a climber, she'll climb anything so be prepared.

The Bottom Line:
A Wrap-Up of Our Best Buy Picks

For baby bathtubs, we like the simple EuroBath by Primo ($25) or the Puj Tub folding tub for $45.

When it comes to potty seats, a seat insert like the Baby Bjorn Toilet Trainer ($26) when paired with a step stool is the best bet for most toddlers. For potty chairs, the Fisher Price Precious Planet Potty ($13) should do the trick.

What's the best diaper pail? We like the Diaper Dekor, Diaper Genie and Arm & Hammer by Munchkin diaper pails best, although they require costly refill packages.

Many find a simple can with regular kitchen trash bags will do the trick.

Stay away from wipe warmers, which have safety concerns.

An activity/bouncer seat with a toy bar is a good idea, with prices ranging from $30 to $75—we like the Fisher Price bouncers best. An affordable alternative: adding a $10 toy bar to an infant seat.

Play yards are a great way to keep baby safe, but also provide a place to sleep (bassinet) for newborns. The Graco Pack N Play On the Go is $70 and does the trick.

Our top pick for swings is the Fisher Price Snugabunny Cradle 'n Swing ($150). Gotta love that name.

For baby monitors, our top pick for an audio baby monitor is VTech's Safe & Sound digital audio monitor for $30 single, $50 double. For video monitors, we like the Infant Optics DXR-5 for $99 for a fixed camera and the Samsung SafeVIEW ($230) as a PTZ model.

CHAPTER 8

CAR SEATS

Car Seats: Picking the right child safety seat

Inside this chapter

What's the best car seat for your baby? What is the difference between an infant, convertible or booster seat? We'll discuss these issues and more in this chapter. You'll find complete reviews and ratings of the major car seat brands as well as informative charts that compare the best choices.

Here's a sobering figure: in the most recent year's statistics, motor vehicle crashes killed 1,168 children under age 14 and injured another 169,000. And 59 infants under age one were killed in traffic accidents in 2012.

According to government research, child safety seats reduce fatal injury by 71% for infants and by 54% for toddlers. And of course, child safety seats are required in every state in the U.S. and province in Canada. So this is one of the few products every parent must purchase. In fact you may find yourself buying multiple car seats as your baby grows older—and for secondary cars, grandma's car, a caregiver's vehicle and more.

So, which seat is the safest? Easiest to use? One thing you'll learn in this chapter is that there is not one "safest" or "best" seat. Yes, we will review and rate the various car seat brands and examine their recall/safety history. BUT, *remember the best seat for your child is the one that correctly fits your child's weight and size—and can be correctly installed in your vehicle.*

And that's the rub: roadside safety checks reveal 80% to 90% of child safety seats are NOT installed or used properly. Although the exact figure isn't known, a large number of child fatalities and injuries from crashes are caused by improper use or installation of seats.

Realizing that many of today's child safety seats are a failure due to complex installation and other hurdles, the federal government has rolled out a safety standard (called LATCH) for child seats and vows to fix loopholes in current crash testing. The results so far are mixed—we'll discuss these issues later in this chapter.

Getting Started: When Do You Need This Stuff?

You can't leave the hospital without a car seat. By law, all states require children to be restrained in a child safety seat. You'll want to get this item early (in your sixth to eighth month of pregnancy) so you can install it in your car before baby arrives.

Sources to Find Car Seats

1 DISCOUNTERS. Car seats have become a loss leader for many discount stores. Chains like Target and Walmart sell these items at small mark-ups in hopes you'll spend money elsewhere in the store. The only caveat: most discounters only carry a limited selection of seats, typically of the no-frills models.

2 BABY SPECIALTY STORES. Independent juvenile retailers carry car seats, but the selection is often limited by the size of the

E-MAIL FROM THE REAL WORLD
Car seats save lives

"When I was expecting my first child, I used your book extensively. I followed your recommendation for a car seat for my baby. I'm so glad I did because we recently were involved in a potentially deadly accident. My car's left back-side (where my ten-month-old baby was sitting), hit a lamppost. To give you an idea how serious it was, the car door was pushed in nearly a foot and a half.

"My son was riding in his Graco SnugRide infant seat, installed rear facing and attached to its base. He was actually injured by the collision when the door was damaged and the air bag deployed. We rushed him to the hospital where he was found to have superficial skull fractures and minor bruises. Good news: he recovered quickly without any permanent damage. Later, when we showed the hospital staff the photos of the vehicle, they were amazed that our son survived the accident."

store (small boutiques may just have one or two brands).

3 **THE SUPERSTORES.** Chains like Babies R Us, Buy Buy Baby and Burlington Coat Factory's Baby Depot dominate the car seat business, thanks to a wider selection of models than discounters. Prices can be a few dollars higher than the discounters, but sales often bring better deals.

4 **ONLINE.** We'll discuss our favorite sites to buy a car seat online shortly, but remember this caveat: Prices are usually discounted, but watch out for shipping—the cost of shipping bulky items like car seats can outweigh the discount in some cases. Use an online coupon (sites like RetailMeNot.com catalog current discount codes) to save and look for free shipping specials.

Best Online Sources

The web is teeming with both information and bargains on car seats. Here's the best of what's out there.

◆ **NHTSA.** The National Highway Traffic Safety Administration site (nhtsa.gov) is a treasure trove of car seat info—you can read about recalls, the latest news on changing standards and installation tips. Confused about how to use your LATCH car seat? The web site offers instructional videos for both rear and forward facing seats. You can also contact the government's Auto Safety Hotline at 800-424-9393 to ask car seat related questions. Even better: NHTSA now ranks car seats on their *ease of use* (assembly, instructions, securing a child, etc). The most recent report covers over 90 seats, from infant to booster. Note: these ratings do NOT cover how well a seat does in crash tests or compatibility with different vehicles.

◆ **The American Academy of Pediatrics** (HealthyChildrebn.org, go to Safety & Prevention then On the Go) is an excellent resource for buying tips.

◆ **The National Safe Kids Campaign** (safekids.org) has a helpful interactive "safety seat guide" that helps you determine which seat is right for the age and weight of the child.

◆ **Safety Belt Safe USA** (carseat.org) has a good site with tips on picking the best seat for your child, as well as the latest recalls and info on child safety seats.

car seats

CAR SEATS

◆ *Our web site* has a message board dedicated to car seats. Go to BabyBargains.com, click on talk. Navigate to the Oh Baby! forum and scroll down to see car seats. Or just go to http://bit.ly/babybargains2

◆ *Insurance Institute for Highway Safety* does an annual report on booster car seat fit—go to iihs.org and search booster.

◆ *Where to buy online.* Our readers' favorite sites to buy car seats at a discount include Amazon, Babies R Us and Bed Bath & Beyond (owners of Buy Buy Baby). As always, look for a coupon code for additional savings, free shipping and the like. Check out the Bargain Alert message board on our site (BabyBargains.com/coupons) for a regularly updated list of coupon deals and discounts.

More Money Buys You . . .

As you'll read later in this chapter, all child safety seats are regulated by the federal government to meet minimum safety standards. So whether you buy a $50 seat from Walmart or a $400 brand from a specialty store, your baby is safe. When you pay extra money, however, there are some perks. First, on the safety front, the more expensive seats often have shock-absorbing foam that better protects a child from side-impact collisions. The more expensive seats are also easier to use and adjust . . . and clearly that is a major safety benefit. For infant seats, when you spend more money, you get an adjustable base (which enables a better fit in vehicles), a canopy to block the sun and plush padding.

Speaking of padding, the more money you spend, the cushier the seat—some makers throw in infant head pillows, body cushions and more . . . all of which raises the price. These are not marketed as a safety benefit, but more for the baby's "comfort." The problem? Newborns and infants don't really care. They are just fine in a seat with basic padding (versus the deluxe version). Of course, if you have a super long commute or an older child (say over two years), padding and comfort becomes more of a relevant issue. But for most babies, basic padding is just fine.

Smart Shopper Tips

Smart Shopper Tip #1
So many seats, so much confusion
  "I'm so confused by all the car seat options out there. For example,

are infant car seats a waste of money? Should I go with a convertible seat? Or one of those models that is good from birth to college?

Children's car seats come in four flavors: "infant," "convertible," "booster" and "hybrid." Let's break it down:

◆ **Infant** car seats are just that—these rear facing seats are designed for infants up to 35 lbs. or so and 33" in height (weight/height limits will vary; some models only works up to 22 lbs. and 29"). On average, parents get about six to 12 months of use out of an infant seat (of course, that varies with the size/height of the child). Infant car seats have an internal harness (usually five-point) that holds the infant to the carrier, which is then snapped into a base. The base is secured to the car. Why the snap-in base? That way you can release the seat and use the carrier to tote your baby around.

◆ **Convertible** car seats can be used for both infants *and* older children (most seats go up to 40 lbs., but newer models top out at 65, 70 and even 80 lbs.)—infants ride rear facing; older kids over two years of age ride facing forward. Convertible seats have different harness options (more on this later); unlike infant seats, however, most do not have snap-in bases.

◆ **Booster** seats come in three types: hybrid/combo seats, high back and backless boosters. We'll discuss each in-depth in a special section on boosters later in this chapter. In a nutshell, here's how they work: after your child outgrows his convertible seat, the booster correctly positions the safety belt. Most states have laws that require booster seat use until 60 or 80 lbs. (or up to age eight).

◆ **Hybrid** seats. Of course, real life doesn't always fit neatly into these categories—some seats pitch their use from birth to 120 lbs.! An example is the Graco 4Ever. It can be used rear-facing from 4-40 lbs. Then forward facing with harness from 20-65 lbs. Then as a high back booster from 30-100 lbs. Then as a backless booster to 120 lbs. (There will be a quiz on this later).

So, does it make more sense to buy one car seat (that is a convertible model) and just skip the infant car seat? There is considerable debate on this subject. Some safety advocates think convertible car seats are safer, pointing to recalls of infant car seats. Others deride infant car seats for their overuse *outside* of a car (as a place for baby to nap), speculating that such babies are at risk for SIDS (Sudden Infant Death Syndrome, discussed in Chapter 2). Fuel was added to this fire in 2006, when a *British Medical Journal* study generated headlines, saying that babies in infant car seats are at risk for breathing problems.

But . . . we analyzed that study and found the researchers examined only nine babies in New Zealand to come up with that conclusion (see our *Baby 411* blog for a detailed discussion). And while babies born prematurely (less than 37 weeks in gestation) are at an increased risk for breathing problems while in a car seat, full term infants ARE NOT. Sure, you should always supervise a newborn in an infant seat (have someone ride in the back seat if possible). And limit your baby's time in an infant seat. But that doesn't mean infant seats are UNSAFE or dangerous for sleeping infants.

On the other side of the debate are advocates who say infant car seats fit newborns better—most are designed to accommodate a smaller body and baby travels in a semi-reclined position, which supports an infant's head and neck. Yes, some convertible seats recline—but the degree of recline can be affected by the angle of your vehicle's seat back.

Furthermore, most babies don't outgrow their infant car seats until six months (and some as late as 12 months, depending on the baby's weight and seat's limits)—and that can be a very long period of time if you don't have an infant car seat.

Why? First, it's helpful to understand that an infant car seat is more than just a car seat—it's also an infant carrier when detached from its base. Big deal, you might say? Well, since infants spend much of their time sleeping (and often fall asleep in the car), this *is* a big deal. By detaching the carrier from the auto base, you don't have to wake the baby when you leave the car. Buy a convertible car seat, and you'll have to unbuckle the baby and move her into another type of carrier or stroller (and most likely wake her in the process). Take it from us: let sleeping babies lie and spend the additional $150 for an infant car seat, even if you use it for just six months.

Remember: babies should be REAR FACING until they reach two years of age, regardless of weight. If your child outgrows his infant car seat before one year of age, be sure to use a convertible seat in rear facing mode for as long as possible. Most convertible seats can be used rear facing until baby is 30 to 40 lbs. (depending on the model).

Smart Shopper Tip #2
New standards, new problems?

"I hear there are problems with LATCH. What is LATCH anyway?"

Stop any ten cars on the road with child safety seats and we'll bet eight or nine are not installed or used correctly. That's what road-side checks by local law enforcement in many states have uncovered: a recent study by the National Highway Traffic Safety Administration stopped 4000 drivers in four states and found a whopping 80% made mistakes in installing or securing a child safety seat.

What's causing all the problems?

Many child safety seats have failed parents, in our opinion. Installation of a car seat is an exercise in frustration—even parents who spend hours with the instructions still made mistakes. The number one culprit: the auto seat belt—it is great at restraining adults, but not so good at child safety seats. And those seats simply won't work well if they aren't attached to a car correctly . . . that's the crux of the problem. Simply put, thanks to the quirkiness of auto safety belts (different auto makers have different systems), putting a child safety seat in a car is still like trying to fit a square peg into a round hole. Some seats wobble too much; others can't be secured tightly to the back seat.

The bottom line: some child safety seats simply DON'T FIT in some vehicles. Which cars? Which seats? There is no easy answer. Often, parents find it's trial and error to see what works.

So, that's where LATCH comes in. The federal government rolled out a mandated "uniform" attachment (called LATCH or ISOFIX), required for all vehicles and safety seats made after 2002. LATCH stands for "Lower Anchors and Tethers for Children." ISOFIX stands for International Standards Organization FIX, which is the international version of LATCH.

What is LATCH? Instead of using the auto's seat belt, car seats attach to two anchor bars in the lower seatback. The result: fewer confusing installations, no more locking clips or other apparatus needed to make sure the seat is correctly attached. (Another part of the new standard: tether straps, which are discussed later in this section.) See picture of a LATCH-installed car seat on page 362.

Here is a sum up of frequent questions we get on LATCH seats:

◆ **Which manufacturers sell LATCH seats?** Answer: all. Every infant and convertible car seat sold now includes LATCH. However, booster car seats aren't required to use LATCH (although a few do).

◆ **Will I have to junk my sister's old car seat?** Yes, safety advocates do NOT recommend using a seat that is over five years old. Why? Belts, clips and interior parts in car seats wear out over time . . . hence, seats over five years old may no longer be safe to use.

◆ *My older car does not have LATCH. What is the safest seat I can buy?* All LATCH seats are backward compatible—that is, they can be safely installed and used in older vehicles that do NOT have LATCH anchors. Remember the safest seat is the one that best fits your car *and* your child. There is no one "safest" seat. Get the best seat you can afford (we'll have recommendations later in this chapter) and use it with a tether strap. And get your car seat safety checked to make sure you have the best installation and fit.

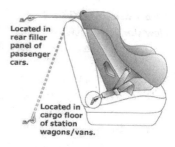

Located in rear filler panel of passenger cars.

Located in cargo floor of station wagons/vans.

◆ *I need to move my LATCH seat to a second car that doesn't have the new attachments. Will it work?* Yes, see above.

◆ *I know the safest place for a baby is in the middle of the back seat. But my car doesn't have LATCH anchors there, just in the outboard positions! Where should I put the seat?* Our advice: use the LATCH positions, even if they are only on the side. Some car seat and vehicle makers say it is okay to use a LATCH seat in the middle of the back seat if you use the LATCH anchors in the outboard positions—check with your car seat and vehicle owner's manual to see if this is permissible.

◆ *I got a LATCH seat that doesn't fit in my vehicle! I thought this was supposed to be universal.* LATCH has been sold to the public as some kind of magic pill that will instantly make all seats fit all vehicles. Hardly. Because of the wide variety of vehicles and seats (a SUV versus a compact, minivan versus pickup), it is unreasonable to expect any system would make this happen. While LATCH helps, it is not the cure-all.

◆ *I find LATCH hard to use.* You're not alone: a recent survey showed that 40% of parents aren't using LATCH. Problems with LATCH include hard-to-reach anchors that are buried in the seat back, making installation a challenge. Some LATCH clips are also easier to use than others. Car seat makers are trying to respond to these issues. Example: Evenflo's new Symphony car seat has an improved LATCH clip that is easier to install.

Smart Shopper Tip #3
Strap Me In
"What is a tether strap? Do I want one?"

Way back in 1999, the federal government mandated that all convertible child safety seats be sold with a tether strap–these prevent a car seat from moving forward in the event of a crash. How? One end of the tether strap attaches to the top of the car seat; the other is hooked to an "anchor bolt" that is permanently installed on the back of the rear seat or on the floor in your vehicle.

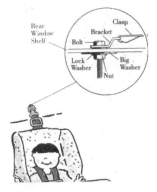

All newer vehicles already have anchor bolts, making the use of a tether strap a snap. (Hint: check your vehicle's owner's manual to find instructions on using tether straps). Older vehicles may have pre-drilled anchorage points–just ask your car dealer for the "anchor bolt installation kit" (a part number that's listed in your owner's manual in the section on installing child safety seats). You can install the bolt or have the dealer do it.

A side note: most convertible seats can only use tether straps when FORWARD FACING. A handful of seats (certain models by Combi, Peg Perego and Diono, for example) have a tether that can be used in either rear or forward facing positions. Note: tether straps are typically not used with infant seats or booster seats (but always consult your seat's directions for specific advice on this).

So, is the tether strap worth all the hassle? Yes–crash tests show car seats are SAFER when used with a tether strap. The strap keeps the car seat (and hence, your baby's head) from moving forward in a crash, lowering the chance of injury. Unfortunately, parents don't seem to be getting this message: a 2006 survey from the NHTSA revealed that only 55% of parents are using a top tether.

Are seats used *without* tethers unsafe? No, the federal government requires seats to be safe even when a tether is not in use. Of course, the tether adds that extra measure of safety and is always preferable to a tether-less installation.

Smart Shopper Tip #4
One Size Does Not Fit All

"My friend has a car seat that just doesn't fit very well into her car. Does anyone put out a rating system that says which seats are most compatible? Easiest to use? Safest?"

The National Highway Traffic Safety Administration rates car seats on their ease of use and posts the results on the web at nhtsa.gov. Note these are not crash test results. NHTSA rates seats on how a seat assembles, installs and secures a child. In the latest report, over 90 seats were rated. The government updates the report every year.

Smart Shopper Tip #5
Recalls

"I saw online that a particular car seat is being recalled. Should I be skeptical of other seats by that manufacturer?"

Here's a sobering fact of car seat shopping: most major brands of car seats have had a recall over the past five years. We've seen recalls on cheap seats sold in Walmart and $300 car seats sold in specialty stores, making recalls a reality no matter what brand you consider. So if all major brands have had recalls, how do you shop for the best seat?

First, understand that some recalls are more serious than others. Some car seats are recalled for minor problems, like incorrect warning labels. Other companies do voluntary recalls when their own testing reveals a problem. The key issue: look to see if there are any injuries associated with the defective product. Obviously, car seats that are so defective as to cause injury to babies are much more serious than minor labeling recalls.

Another issue: how does a company handle a recall? Do they fight the government, forcing regulators to order a recall? Or do they voluntarily recall the item and set up an efficient process to get replacements or retrofit kits to consumers? In the past, we have lowered our ratings for car seat manufacturers who bungled a recall effort.

When a company announces a recall, the product is typically removed from store shelves (if the recall is for the current production run). If the recall is for a product's previous production, you may still see it on store shelves (since the defect may have been corrected months before). That's why it is key to see WHEN the recalled product was manufactured. Of course, different car seats in the same manufacturer's line may be totally unaffected by a recall.

Another tip: make sure to fill out the registration card that comes with any car seat you buy . . . and send it in! In theory, this will get you expedited recall information and repair kits. Also: sign up for a recall email list on Recalls.gov.

Unfortunately, with some car seat makers, even if you fill out a registration card you may not get a recall notice.

Smart Shopper Tip #6
Watch the height limit

"My son isn't anywhere near the 26 lb. limit for his infant seat, but he's so tall I don't think it is safe anymore—he has to bend his legs when we put him in!"

Here's a little known fact about most infant seats: in addition to WEIGHT limits, all infant car seats also have HEIGHT limits. And like everything in the car seat world, each seat has different limits (check the sticker on the side of the carrier—by law, the manufacturer must list both height and weight limits). Once your baby exceeds EITHER the height or weight limit, you should move him to a convertible seat.

One note on this: while the weight limit is important, do one other test if your child is approaching the height limit—is there less than an inch of seat left above baby's head? If so, then move your baby to a convertible seat (facing the rear of the vehicle until age two).

With the bigger babies everyone seems to be having these days, this isn't a moot point. A large infant might exceed the height limit BEFORE he or she passes the weight limit. And of course, different seats have different limits.

Later in this section, we'll have a chart that lists the height and weight limits of all major infant car seats. Also, individual reviews of seats later in this chapter list weight and height limits.

Smart Shopper Tip #7
Do I have to buy THREE seats?

"My baby has outgrown his infant seat. Can I buy a combo seat that converts to a booster?"

The short answer: yes. Do we recommend it? No. Why? We think the safest place for an infant who has outgrown an infant seat is in a CONVERTIBLE seat in rear facing mode. Leave them there until they are AT LEAST two years of age—longer if they still are under the weight limit. Note: nearly all "combo" seats with five-point harnesses that convert to a belt-positioning booster are FORWARD FACING only seats.

So, what is best? When your child outgrows her convertible seat, THEN we recommend a booster seat (combo or belt-positioning). Now, we realize what you are thinking: have you lost your minds? We are recommending you buy THREE seats for your child: infant, convertible, and then a booster. Wouldn't it be cheaper to get one of those all-in-one seats or at least one that combines the convertible/booster function? We will review such seats later in this chapter.

And while those combo (harnessed) boosters are a good choice for a three or four year old child who has outgrown his convertible seat but is not mature enough to sit in a belt-positioning booster, combo seats are NOT good for babies under age two—they often don't recline and have less sleeping support than convertibles.

Smart Shopper Tip #8
European seats

"I saw a cool European car seat online—is that safe or legal to use in the U.S.?

Short answer: no.

Thanks to the web, you can order a car seat from Switzerland . . . or South Africa. Making this more tempting: the belief among some safety advocates that Europe has better car seats than the U.S. or Canada.

But let's do a reality check: European standards are DIFFERENT than the U.S. or Canada. Different does not necessarily mean better, however. European seats are designed to work in European cars, which have different safety features compared to vehicles sold in North America.

Bottom line: it is ILLEGAL (and dangerous) to use a seat from overseas here in the U.S. (Ditto for you Canadians—seats must be certified to meet Canadian standards before they can be sold or used in Canada. So if you are a Canadian reading this book, you can't buy a seat in the U.S. and use it legally in Canada.)

Smart Shopper Tip #9
Holding Your Baby Back: Safety Harness Advice
    "Which seats are easiest to adjust?"

You will adjust your baby's car seat's harness two ways: first, you will tighten or loosen it as she grows. And then you will adjust the HEIGHT of the harness as she gets taller.

The best car seats have upfront adjusters to tighten or loosen a harness. Unfortunately, some seats require you to do this from the back of the seat—that is a major pain. We'll note which seats have this feature in the review section of the book.

As for adjusting the height, the best seats have a harness that can be raised without having to re-thread the harness (which requires disassembling the seat to a certain degree). Again, we'll note this feature later in this chapter.

FYI: do not put your child in a bulky coat or snowsuit when sitting in a safety seat. In the case of an accident, the bulky coat might compress, compromising the safety of the seat. At most, only put a child in a thin coat (like a fleece) when they are riding in a child safety seat. (To keep an infant warm, you can purchase an infant car seat that comes with a boot. Or purchase one as an accessory—Graco has an infant car seat boot accessory for $8).

Here are nine more shopping tips for car seats:

◆ **How easily does it recline?** Many convertible seats have a recline feature to make sure baby is at a proper angle. Of course, how easily the seat reclines varies from model to model—and reaching that lever in a rear facing seat may be a challenge. Check it out in the store before you buy.

◆ *No-twist straps.* Better car seats have thicker straps that don't twist. The result: it is easier to get a child in and out of a seat. Cheaper seats have cheaper webbing that can be a nightmare— "twisty straps" are a key reason why parents hate their car seats. Later when we review specific car seat models, we'll note which ones have twisty straps.

◆ *Look at the chest clip.* The chest clip or harness tie holds the two belts in place. Lower-quality seats have a simple "slide-in" clip—you slip the belt under a tab. That's OK, but some older toddlers can slip out from this type of chest clip. A better bet: a chest clip that SNAPS the two belts together like a seat belt. This is more kid-proof.

◆ *Are the instructions in Greek?* Before you buy the car seat, take a minute to look at the set-up and use instructions. Make sure you can make sense of the seat's documentation. Another tip: if possible, ask the store for any installation tips and advice.

◆ *Is the pad cover machine-washable?* You'd think this would be a no-brainer, but a surprising number of seats (both convertible and infant) have covers that aren't removable or machine washable. Considering how grimy these covers can get, it's smart to look for this feature. Also check to see if you can wash the harness.

◆ *Will the seat be a sauna in the summer?* Speaking of the seat pad, check the material. Plush, velvet-like covers might seem nice in the store, but think about next August. Will your baby be sitting in a mini-sauna? Light-weight, light colored fabric pads are better than heavier weight, dark fabrics.

◆ *Does the seat need to be installed with each use?* The best car seats are "permanently" installed in your car. When you put baby in, all you do is buckle them into the seat's harness system. Yet a few models need to be installed with each use—that means you have to belt the thing into your car every time you use it. Suffice it to say, that's a major drawback.

◆ *Watch out for hot buckles.* Some inexpensive car seats have exposed metal buckles and hardware. In the hot sun, these buckles can get toasty and possibly burn a child. Yes, you can cover these buckles with a blanket when you leave the car, but that's a hassle. A better bet is to buy a seat with a buckle cover or no exposed metal.

◆ *How heavy is it?* This is a critical factor for infant car seats, but also important for convertibles. Why? First, remember you are lugging that infant seat WITH a baby that will weigh seven to ten lbs. *to start*. When your baby outgrows the infant seat, she will weigh 22 to 35 lbs. *in addition to the seat weight*! To help you shop, we list the weights for major infant car seat brands later in this chapter. What about convertible seats? If you buy one seat and plan to move it from car to car, weight may be a factor here as well.

◆ *Buying a new car?* Consider getting a built-in (also called integrated) child safety seat, which is a $225 to $600 option on vehicles like minivans. This is an option for parents who have a child who is older than one year of age and heavier than 20 lbs. The only caveat: most integrated seats lack side-impact protection and may not fit small children well. Of course, offerings vary by maker. For example, Volvo offers an integrated booster seat ($500 for two seats) that has won kudos for its innovative design.

Safe & Sound

1 **NEVER BUY A USED CAR SEAT.** If the seat has been in an accident, it may be damaged and no longer safe to use. Bottom line: used seats are a big risk unless you know their history. And the technology of car seats improves every year; a seat that is just five years old may lack important safety features compared to today's models. (And, as we discussed earlier, seats older than five years also have parts that may wear out and fail . . . a big reason not to use an old seat). Another tip: make sure the seat has not been recalled (search the National Highway Traffic Safety Administration's recall database at Recalls.gov). The bottom line: risky hand-me-downs aren't worth it. Brand new car seats (which start at $50) aren't that huge of an investment to ensure your child's safety.

2 **GET YOUR SEAT SAFETY CHECKED.** No matter how hard you try to buy and install the best seat for your child, mistakes with installation can still occur. There's nothing like the added peace of mind of having your car seat safety checked by an expert. Such checks are free and widely available. The National Highway Traffic Safety Administration's web site (nhtsa.dot.gov) has a national listing of fitting/inspection stations.

3 **DON'T TRUST THE LEVEL INDICATOR.** Yes, many infant car seats come with "level indicators" and instructions to make sure the seat is installed so the indicator is in the "green" area. When in the green, the seat is supposedly at the correct angle to protect your

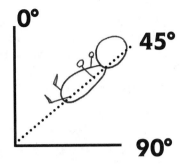

baby in case of a crash. Nice idea, but thanks to the myriad of back seat designs in dozens of cars, the seat may be incorrectly installed even if the indicator says it is fine. At car seat safety checks, many techs ignore the level indicator and instead use this test: They take a piece of paper and fold one corner to form a 45-degree angle. Then they place the side of the paper against the back of the infant car seat where the baby's back would lie. When the folded corner is level with the horizon, the seat is at the correct angle—even if the indicator says it ain't so. If you aren't sure your seat is installed to the correct angle, take it for a car seat safety check.

4 **FORGET CAR SEAT ADD-ONS.** We've seen all manner of travel "accessories" for kids in car seats, including bottle holders, activity trays and so on. The problem: all these objects are potential hazards in an accident, flying around the car and possibly striking you (the adult) or your child.

5 **HOW TALL IS TOO TALL?** You'll notice that most child safety seats utilize two types of limits: weight and height. It's the latter limit that creates some confusion among parents. Convertible seats have both a rear and forward facing height limit—this is required by federal law (for those inquiring minds, the standards are FMVSS 208, 213, 225). Most safety techs say the maximum height for a child is when their head is one inch below the top of the shell (the 1″ rule) or if your child's shoulders exceed the height of the top harness slot. The problem: some car seat makers have more strict height limits than the 1″ rule. Here's the frustrating part: kids often outgrow the seat's stated height limit *before* they reach that 1″ rule or their shoulders are taller than the top harness slot, leaving some parents to wonder if they should continue using the seat. The problem is one of interpretation: while the federal law requires every seat to have height limits, car seat makers are free to interpret this rule (and usage of the seat). Some seat makers just interpret the rules more strictly than others. Bottom line: while we understand seat makers might have their own take on federal safety standards, it is generally safe to use a seat until your child's head is 1″ below the top of the seat or their shoulders exceed the top harness slot—even if their height is slightly above the stated limit for the seat.

6 **READ THE DIRECTIONS VERY CAREFULLY.** Many car accidents end in tragedy because a car seat was installed improperly. If you have any questions about the directions, call the company or return the car seat for a model that is easier to use. Another tip: read your vehicle's owner's manual for any special installation instructions. Consult with your auto dealer if you have any additional questions.

What's the number-one problem with car seat installation? Getting a tight fit, say safety techs. Make sure the safety seat is held firmly against the back of the car seat and doesn't wobble from side to side (or front to back). One tip: put your knee in the seat and push down with your full weight while you tighten the seat belt or LATCH strap. This eliminates belt slack and ensures a snug installation.

7 **KEEP YOUR CHILD REAR FACING AS LONG AS POSSIBLE.** Safety experts agree that the longer a child is rear facing, the safer the child is in an accident. Why? Newborns and even young toddlers have undeveloped neck muscles–this can lead to an injury, especially if a child is forward facing in an accident. Good news: more and more seats have higher rear facing limits. Several infant car seats now work to 30 or 40 lbs. rear facing. And many convertibles also work up to 40 lbs. or even 50 lbs. rear facing. The take home message: keep your child rear facing as long as possible (to age two or three if you can).

8 **PUT THE CAR SEAT IN THE BACK SEAT.** Air bags and car seats don't mix–several reports of injuries and deaths have been attributed to passenger side air bags that deployed when a car seat was in the front seat. As a result, the safest place for kids is the back seat. In fact, whether the car has an air bag or not, the back is always safer–federal government statistics say putting a child in the back seat instead of the front reduces the risk of death by 27%.

And where is the safest part of the back seat? Safety experts say it's the middle–it is the furthest away from side-impact risks. The only problem with that advice is that some cars have a raised hump in the middle of the back seat that makes it difficult/impossible to safely install a car seat. Finally, consider the LATCH problem we noted above (where many vehicles have no LATCH anchors in the middle of the back seat, only the sides). Bottom line: while the middle of the back seat is the safest spot, sometimes you just can't install a seat there. The next best place is in an outboard position of the back seat with a lap/shoulder belt.

What about side curtain air bags you see in the back seats of some cars? Many new cars come equipped with side-impact air bags or curtains. These air bags are NOT as dangerous as front air bags, as they deploy with much less force in the event of a side impact crash. Therefore, putting a car seat next to a door that has a side curtain air bag is not a danger.

9 **REGISTER YOUR SEAT.** Don't forget to send the registration card back to the manufacturer so you are contacted in the event of a recall.

10 **PICKUP TRUCKS ARE OFTEN NOT SAFE FOR CAR SEATS.** "A pickup truck should not be considered a family vehicle," concluded an article by the Children's Hospital of Philadelphia on car seat safety—and we agree. Why? "Children in the rear seat of compact extended-cab pickups are nearly five times as likely to be injured as children seated in the back seat of other vehicles," according to a study by Partners for Child Passenger Safety, sponsored by the same hospital.

Of course, not all pickup trucks are alike. Some larger pickup trucks with full-size rear seats do allow car seats (check your vehicle manual for advice). Depending on the vehicle maker, pickup trucks with these seats are called SuperCrew, Double Cab, Crew Cab or Quad Cab. However, pickup trucks with jump seats should NEVER be used with car seats—these are often referred to as Extended Cab or SuperCab trucks. If your pickup truck does not have a rear seat and you must use the front seat (again, not recommended), you must disable the passenger-side air bag.

Even if your pickup truck has a full-size rear seat that allows for car seat installations, think twice about using this vehicle with car seats. Again, studies show that all passenger cars are generally safer in an accident (for kids in a car seat) compared to pickup trucks.

11 **CONSIDER SEATS WITH SIDE IMPACT PROTECTION.** About 25% of all vehicle accidents are side-impact collisions. Over the last few years, more and more seats have been adding side-impact protection. This would be especially important if your vehicle does not have rear-curtain airbags to protect rear occupants. Yes, these seats tend to cost a bit more than those without side-impact protection, but we think it is a wise investment.

Recalls

The National Highway Traffic Safety Administration (NHTSA) posts recalls online (nhtsa.dot.gov) and has a toll-free hot line to check for recalls or to report a safety problem. Call (800) 424-9393 or (202) 366-0123. Note that this is a different governmental agency than the Consumer Product Safety Commission, which regulates and recalls for other juvenile products.

Money-Saving Secrets

1 **TRACK AMAZON PRICES.** Baby gear prices on Amazon often rise or fall with little notice. Tracking web sites like CamelCamelCamel.com will send you free email alerts when prices drop. You can also look up historical price charts (a browser plug-in lets you see this even while looking at the Amazon pages). We tracked the Britax Marathon and noticed the prices varied by $100 in the past six months. And we saw Amazon drop the price on a Combi infant car seat by 31% in the past month.

2 **GET A FREE SEAT!** A reader emailed in this great tip—her health insurance carrier provides free infant car seats to parents who complete a parenting class. No specific class is required . . . you just provide proof of completion. And health insurance providers aren't the only ones with car seat deals—check with your auto insurance provider or employer as well. Some companies sell discounted car seats as a family-friendly perk, so check that too.

3 **IF YOU HAVE TWO CARS, YOU DON'T NEED TO BUY TWO INFANT SEATS.** Instead, just buy one seat and then get an extra stay-in-the-car base. Major infant seat makers sell their auto bases separately for $40 to $100. Retail stores rarely carry these bases; you'll probably have to buy an extra base online.

4 **COUPONS!** Find the latest coupons and discounts by popping over to our Bargain Alert message boards (BabyBargains. com/coupons). Right at the top, we keep a pinned thread with a list of the best online coupon codes, discounts and deals. The thread is updated regularly, so come back to visit when you need a code.

5 **EXPENSIVE MODELS AREN'T NECESSARILY BETTER.** If you spend $200 on a car seat, are you getting one that's twice as safe as a seat that's $100? Not necessarily. All car seats must meet federal minimum safety standards. In fact, we will recommend a simple Cosco Scenera Next, which costs $46 as a good bet for your second car or Grandma's vehicle.

So what do you get when you spend more? First, plusher fabric and padding. That doesn't have anything to do with safety—it's more comfort. Based on our research, extra padding isn't worth the extra money for infant car seats; however, for convertible seats or boosters, we can see the point (especially for longer trips). That's because older infants and toddlers are more likely to notice skimpy padding than newborns.

Also when you spend more you get a car seat that is easier to adjust (and that is a major plus and safety advantage). And some of the most expensive seats have added side-impact crash protection, again worthy of the extra investment.

6 **LAST YEAR'S FASHION.** Car seat makers frequently discontinue fashions (not the seat, just the fabric). Look for closeouts and save. Example: we saw a closeout pattern for a Britax seat for 40% off on Amazon.

Here are our reviews of individual car seat models. First, infant seats and then convertibles. Booster car seats are in the last section of the chapter.

Infant Car Seats (model by model reviews)

BABY TREND EZ FLEX-LOC 32

This seat is a Babies R Us exclusive; see the Baby Trend Flex-Loc review for more details.

BABY TREND FLEX-LOC

Price: Flex-Loc is $100 to $120. Extra bases $40. EZ Flex-Loc is $80-$140.

Type: Infant seat, five-point harness.

Limits: 5 to 30 lbs. and 30". EZ-Flex Loc 32 works to 32 lbs.

NHTSA ease of use rating: ★★★★☆

Pros: Top rated seat in crash test—back in 2007.

Cons: Carrier is quite heavy; hard to find in some stores—mostly sold as part of a travel system with an inferior stroller.

Comments: Baby Trend advertises this as a "top rated" infant car seat—we assume they are referring to a 2007 report from *Consumer Reports* that named the seat a "Best Buy." But that was 2007 . . . in CR's most recent report, the Flex Loc dropped to 23rd out of 25 infant car seats. And we would agree: this seat is showing its age.

Yes, it features a four-position height adjustable base and EPS foam for head protection. Some models come with a boot for extra warmth. But this seat hasn't been updated in years. It appears to exist so Baby Trend can pair it with its poorly-rated (in our opinion) strollers for cheap travel systems.

Confusingly, Baby Trend marketed two versions of this seat: Flex-Loc and EZ Flex-Loc. The only difference: the Flex-Loc has a height adjustable seat back with no rethread harness. The EZ version does not. Babies R Us has an exclusive on the EZ Flex-Loc 32 for $140.

Parent reviews for this seat are, at best, mixed. Fans like the narrow width of the base and the seat's overall value—and if you have a Baby Trend stroller, it is compatible. Unfortunately for everyone else who doesn't have a Baby Trend stroller, this infant car seat is a bust. Few stroller makers make adapters for this seat.

And more than one parent complained their infant quickly outgrew this seat, despite the stated 30 lb. limit. The weight of this seat is a major negative—tipping the scales at 9.4 lbs, it is quite heavy. More criticism: the handle release button can be hard to reach and stiff to release. And the strange triangle handle takes a bit of getting used to.

Finally, we should note that Baby Trend's customer service, or lack thereof, is also disappointing. Unanswered emails, un-returned phone calls and a general "we don't care" attitude mar Baby Trend's brand. ***Rating: D***

BABY TREND INERTIA

Price: $180 to $240.

Type: Infant seat, five-point harness.

Limits: 5-32 lbs.

NHTSA ease of use rating: ☆☆☆☆☆

Pros: Anti-rebound bar.

Cons: Rigid latch may not work in some vehicles.

Comments: The Baby Trend Inertia car seat debuted in 2013 and features a "controlled motion base" that moves the seat up and at an angle in a crash. There is also an anti-rebound bar, a first for a Baby Trend seat. The straps on this seat are easy to adjust with a knob on the back of the seat. Rounding out the features is an ergonomic handle and 32 lb. weight limit (Baby Trend's previous infant seat only went to 30 lbs).

The Inertia includes a rigid latch connector—and that could mean some trouble fitting in vehicles. Most infant seats have flexible latch straps instead of rigid for that reason. A big negative for the Inertia: you can't buy extra bases. So you'll have to move the seat and the base from car to car if you need to switch vehicles, which is a big pain.

At $180, Baby Trend is pricing this seat at almost twice as much as the company's other infant car seat (Flex Loc)—and at about the same price as the highest-rated Chicco or Britax seats.

Initially, we rated this seat an A- minus when early field reports on the seat were positive. However, now that we see more real world feedback, we are dropping the grade. Why? We've seen multiple reports that the recline feature on the seat doesn't work. We're not sure if there was a defective batch of seats or what, but that is very disappointing for such an expensive car seat. Adding insult to injury, folks had to navigate Baby Trend's notoriously lackluster customer service (40 minute waits on hold, etc.) to get replacement seats. As a result, we can't recommend the Inertia.

FYI: This seat was originally a Babies R Us exclusive. For 2015, Baby Trend tells us they are discontinuing the Inertia. The seat will get a second life, however as the Muv Kussen, which is Baby Trend's new Dutch-flavored baby gear brand. The Kussen will sell for $260 and features the Inertia base with a no rethread harness, adjustable headrest. Baby Trend calls the Kussen a second generation Inertia. We'll wait to see if this seat can improve on the Inertia's mixed track record. *Rating: C-*

BRITAX B-SAFE / 35 / 35 ELITE

Price: Original B-SAFE: $144, B-SAFE 35: $170-$210, B-SAFE 35 Elite: $200-$250.
Type: Infant seat, five-point harness.
Limits: 4-30 lbs., 32" (original B-Safe). 4-35 lbs (B-SAFE 35 and 35 Elite).
NHTSA ease of use rating: ★★★★☆
Pros: Under $200, lighter carrier. Side-impact protection, tangle-free harness.
Cons: No anti-rebound bar.
Comments: Sometimes the second time is the charm.

Britax had struggled for years in the infant car seat category, with a poor-selling offering (the Chaperone, now discontinued) and a weak line-up of strollers. So the company went back to the drawing board and improved on both fronts: the B-SAFE is a winner and Britax's latest generation of strollers (including the B-Agile) are giving the brand a lift in infant seats.

FYI: There are now three different versions of the B-SAFE—the original B-SAFE, the B-SAFE 35 and B-SAFE 35 Elite. The latter two models were released in early 2015.

The original B-SAFE works to 30 lbs. and features four harness heights and two crotch buckle positions. One of the B-SAFE's key features is a "removable comfort pillow" that better fits smaller newborns and preemies. The adjustable base has five positions and built-in lock-offs to help with belt installation. You also get premium LATCH connectors.

The B-SAFE base width is somewhat narrower than similar seats (15"), making it easier to install in smaller vehicles. For comparison, the Graco SnugRide Classic Connect base is 17.2".

The B-SAFE comes in at $144, which is a competitive price (the Chicco KeyFit, for example, is $189).

So what are the trade-offs? The B-SAFE omits the anti-rebound bar and no-thread harness you see on more expensive infant car seats. The carrier weighs 9.6 lbs., which is on the heavy side.

infant seats

The B-SAFE has what Britax calls its basic side impact protection—deep side walls that are lined with EPS foam.

Real world feedback on the B-SAFE has been generally positive. A mom's in-depth review posted on Amazon compared the B-SAFE to the similarly priced Chicco KeyFit and we agree with this assessment. She gave the Chicco higher marks for ease of install, but the Britax had better fabric (albeit only two choices) and a superior canopy. As for fit, it is probably a tie. While most parents give the B-SAFE high marks, a few detractors say the infant insert is difficult to use and the straps on the seat are too twisty.

Consumer Reports judged the B-SAFE "excellent" in crash protection, but gave the Chicco KeyFit better marks for ease of use and install (fit to vehicle). That jives with parent feedback we've heard as well.

One major consideration for this seat: stroller compatibility. If you are getting a Britax stroller, then the B-Safe would be a no-brainer. As for compatibility with other strollers, well, that's going to be hit and miss (mostly miss). Fewer strollers are compatible with Britax's infant seat, compared with Graco and Chicco.

FYI: With Britax's recent purchase of BOB strollers, Britax has rolled out a version of this car seat that matches the fabric on the BOB strollers: the BOB B-SAFE is exactly the same as the Britax B-SAFE, just different fabrics. (The BOB B-SAFE is an REI exclusive as of this writing; $200). And as you might guess, BOB's car seat adapter now works with Britax infant car seats.

The two newest models in the B-SAFE line are the B-SAFE 35 ($210) and 35 Elite ($250). As the name implies, these new seats now work to 35 lbs. Each gets improved crash protection (which Britax calls SafeCell, a system seen on its convertible seats). The 35 Elite adds additional side impact protection and a no-rethread harness (Quick-Adjust).

So we'll give the B-SAFE our recommendation—it is a step up from our "good" pick (the Graco SnugRide), but not quite as nice as our "best" pick (the Chicco KeyFit). The original B-SAFE is fine, but if you can afford the $50 upgrade, go for the B-SAFE 35 Elite with side impact protection (around $200 on Amazon as of this writing). ***Rating: A***

Chicco KeyFit 30

Price: $190, extra base $85.
Type: Infant seat, five-point harness.
Limits: 4-30 lbs., 30".
NHTSA ease of use rating: ★★★★☆
Pros: EPS foam, newborn insert, adapters available to work with other strollers.
Cons: Skimpy canopy. Large base may be tight fit for smaller vehicles. Pricey.

Comments: The Chicco KeyFit is one of our top picks for infant seats.

The KeyFit boasts a nice list of features: a seat lined with EPS foam for improved side impact protection, thick seat padding, multi-position canopy and comfort grip handle. Chicco hired a former Graco engineer who worked on the SnugRide to design the KeyFit and it shows in the details . . . the base has a "single-pull" LATCH adjustment, a leveling foot to account for uneven back seats and even a smooth underside to keep from damaging your back seat upholstery. As you'd expect from Chicco, the fashion of this seat boasts Italian flair and there is even a newborn insert for a better fit.

Our readers have been very positive about the KeyFit's ease of use, lauding the no-twist, easy-to-adjust straps, the ability to leave the handle in the up position when driving (most seats require it to be lowered), and overall ease of installation. Quibbles? The KeyFit carrier weighs 9.4 lbs., a tad heavier than other similar seats. It takes two hands to release the handle on the seat. And the sunshade is too small (even with the extended visor). A few readers also report the fabric doesn't breathe, so the seat can get hot.

Perhaps the biggest drawback to the Chicco KeyFit 30 is the large base, which may not fit in smaller vehicles. And removing the cover for cleaning can be challenging. And yes, this seat clocks in at nearly $200, so it might be a stretch for those on tighter budgets. But this seat's ease of use and overall excellent design make it worth the extra cash, in our opinion.

FYI: Chicco makes three versions of the KeyFit—one that works to 22 lbs. (called the KeyFit) and one to 30 lbs. (the KeyFit 30) and the KeyFit 30 Magic with upgraded fabrics and infant insert. Between them, we'd suggest the plain KeyFit 30 version. And also note: the same base works with either the 22 lb. or the 30 lb. carriers.

In recent years, more stroller companies have rolled out adapters for the KeyFit and that's great news. Of course, you can also use it in Chicco's strollers, which are generally well regarded.

Overall, the Chicco KeyFit 30 is an excellent seat that is highly recommended. ***Rating: A***

COMBI SHUTTLE

Price: $134. Extra base: $70.

Type: Infant seat, five-point harness.

Limits: 35 lbs., 33"

NHTSA ease of use rating: ☆☆☆☆☆

Pros: EPS foam, one-pull harness adjustment, nice padding. Works to 35 lbs.

Cons: Complex belt path and puzzle buckle. Large seat.

Comments: The Combi Shuttle works to 35 lbs. and features EPS foam for crash protection, comfort pads on the harness and one-

infant seats

pull harness adjustment. The seat has an anti-rebound bar, which keeps the seat more stable in the case of a crash. Babies R Us is selling an exclusive version, the Shuttle 33, with a weight limit of 33 lbs. It's virtually the same seat, and sells for $160. Oddly, that's a higher price than the Shuttle with a 35 lb limit sells for on Amazon ($134).

The Shuttle's base is smaller and easier to use, thanks to its new built-in lock-off design. But the belt path on the Shuttle base had us scratching our heads: it is way too complex compared to other seats. Four position height adjustment rounds out the features. All of Combi's strollers work with the Shuttle infant seat.

Reader and expert feedback on the Shuttle 35 has been mixed. *Consumer Reports* ranked it second in a recent survey of seats, giving it above average remarks for ease of use and crash protection. Our readers weren't so generous, with numerous complaints about difficulty fitting the seat into the base. The carrier is also heavy at 10.1 lbs.

Fans of the seat like that the handle can be left in the upright position when in a vehicle. But be forewarned: the Shuttle is a large seat that won't fit into some smaller vehicles (and even mid-size sedans). And the Combi infant seat is compatible with few strollers, except, of course for Combi's offerings.

Overall, readers gave the Shuttle merely average marks—other seats like the Graco SnugRide and Britax B-Safe score better in reader feedback.

Regarding safety, Combi's track record has been mixed, with several major recalls. Example: a 2008 recall for 67,000 Shuttle and Centre seats after testing revealed the seats could separate from the base in a crash. ***Rating: B-***

Cosco Comfy Carry

Price: $79; extra base $35.

Type: Infant seat, five-point harness.

Limits: 22 lbs., 29"

NHTSA ease of use rating: ★★★☆☆

Pros: Low price. Lightweight carrier.

Cons: Base isn't adjustable; no level indicator. Very basic seat.

Comments: This is Cosco's low-price infant seat. The Comfy Carry features a 22 lb. weight and 29" height limit. And that's about it: the base isn't adjustable, there isn't side impact protection and fabric/padding is basic.

As usual, Dorel makes different versions of this seat, marketed under their Cosco and Safety 1st brands. Here's an overview:

◆ The Cosco Comfy Carry: $79. As we mentioned above, it is rather bare bones: no head support insert, the harness adjusts from the rear and the base is non adjustable. Sold on Walmart.com and at other online retailers.

◆ The Cosco Light 'n Comfy. See review below.

◆ The Safety 1st Comfy Carry Elite: $63-$90. This version adds a head support insert and front harness adjuster. Available in chain stores like Sears, Toys R Us, etc.

◆ The Safety 1st Comfy Carry Elite Plus: $85. All the features of the Elite plus an adjustable base and infant insert and upgraded fabrics. Of all the versions of the seat, this is probably the best bet as we prefer the adjustable base and front harness adjuster.

Parent reviews on this seat have been mixed. Yes, this seat is affordable and is easy to install. But . . . it only works with a handful of Safety 1st or Cosco strollers—few stroller makers bother to make an adapter for this seat, given its low sales. Another complaint: some parents had to return their seats because they weren't snapping into the base properly. They were able to dislodge the seats quite easily by just wiggling it out. Twisty straps are another complain parents have.

As for *Consumer Reports*, CR says crash protection of this seat is excellent—the Elite Plus model has better ease of use (the adjustable base makes a difference here).

Bottom line: it's basic. We'd say it's "good enough" as long as it's installed correctly. ***Rating: C***

Cosco Light 'n Comfy
Price: $70-$80
Type: Infant seat, five-point
Limits: 4 to 22 lbs., 29".
NHTSA Ease of Use Rating: ★★★☆☆
Pros: Very lightweight carrier, affordable.
Cons: No side impact protection, rear harness adjustment on base model.
Comments: The Cosco Light 'N Comfy debuted in 2014 and features the lightest weight carrier on the market: 6.3 lbs. When you consider other carriers can top ten pounds, this might be a big plus for smaller moms or grandparents.

The Cosco Light 'N Comfy is clearly aimed at the entry price point ($70-$80)—it works to just 22 lbs. and lacks extra safety and ease of use features you'd see in more expensive seats (no side impact protection, etc). So this might be a good bet for occasional use by grandparents or other caregivers.

Like the similar Comfy Carry, the Light 'N Comfy comes in both a basic model and "elite" versions. The latter features upgraded details such as a front harness adjuster (the basic model will have a rear adjust) with a price point only about $10 to $20 more.

Given Cosco's track record for the similar Comfy Carry (which earned "best" crash protection ratings from *Consumer Reports*), we expect the Light and Comfy to perform similarly.

We gave the Cosco Comfy Carry a C, as its reader feedback was mixed at best. For the Light 'N Comfy, we've give this seat a B. The parent feedback is slightly better—still, it is a very basic seat with no frills. For a grandparent's occasional use, it would be fine. ***Rating: B***

CYBEX ATON 1 / 2 / Q / CLOUD Q

Price: $250-$300.

Type: Infant seat, five-point

Limits: 4 to 32 lbs., 30".

NHTSA Ease of Use Rating: Three out of five stars for Aton 1. Four out of five stars for Aton 2.

Pros: Light carrier weight, very easy to install. Short shell might fit compact cars better than others.

Cons: Funky canopy has skimpy coverage. Steep price tag. Hard to get the cover back on if you wash it.

Comments: German baby gear maker Cybex's innovative car seat, the Aton, is worth checking out despite its limited distribution.

Launched in 2011, the Aton has a striking, Euro-minimal look that boasts a secure belt-tightening system and fold-away canopy. Safety-wise, the Aton's steel base-to-car seat connectors provide a rock solid installation. You also get infant inserts (a newborn inlay for babies up to 11 lbs. and a infant insert for babies up to 22 lbs.) and a padded harness. Of course, the Aton snaps into most Cybex strollers to form a travel system. A key fact to note: you can use Maxi Cosi adapters made for other strollers with the Aton. Hence the Aton's stroller compatibility is wider than it looks.

What's not to like? Well, the seat shell is rather short—about 17" for the seatback. That compares to 20" for most other seats (like the Graco SnugRide). So some larger babies might out grow the seat before they reach 32 lbs. On the plus side, the shorter shell might work better for small, compact vehicles.

So is it worth the steep, nearly $300 price tag? Well, yes, in our opinion. We like the carrier's overall safety, ease of use and light weight (8.8 lbs). Reports from parents say the seat is very easy to install—it is very compact and a good fit for smaller vehicles. One negative: a few readers report it is difficult to reattach the Aton's padding after washing. And the large chest clip is too, well, large for smaller newborns, in our evaluation.

The Aton's canopy gets mixed reviews. Folks like how it hides away and its fabric quality. But the coverage is rather skimpy compared to other brands. And we worry the giant piece of plastic that borders the canopy might break after extended use. When the canopy is hidden away, it interferes with the carry handle.

Parent reviews for the Aton are mostly positive. *Consumer Reports* ranked the Aton 2 third out of 25 seats (the original Aton 1 scored somewhat lower). The NHTSA gives the Aton three out of five stars for ease of use.

FYI: There are actually four versions of the Aton on the market: the Aton 1, 2, Q and (new for 2015) the Cloud Q.

The Aton 1 is the original, described above. The Aton 2 ($300) adds an anti-rebound load leg that reduces forward motion in a crash. The Aton 2 also has added side impact protection—a small bar that flips up from the handle that helps cushion side impacts. That's different from most other infant seats that have side impact protection built into the carrier or headrest. Confusingly, the Aton 2 is sometimes referred to online as the Aton 2013.

In the past year, Cybex added the Aton Q (named in homage to the famed James Bond gadget maker, or at least that's how we see it). The Q includes a new, bigger canopy and top-of-the-line fabrics and padding. The Q works from 4 to 35 pounds.

The Aton Q features an enhancement to the Linear Side Impact Protection first introduced on the Aton 2. The Q now has a telescoping side impact bar for additional crash protection—yes, that is a Cybex first. The bar telescopes off the top of the carrier in whichever direction you need protection. The Aton Q also has a no rethread harness (not available on the Aton 1 or 2) and will fit any Aton base. Price: $350. The weight of Aton Q is slightly more than the Aton 2.

The new Aton Cloud Q features a seat that fully reclines—this is for use in a stroller, not while in a vehicle. While this is a nifty trick, we're not quite sure we see the point. This feels more like a gimmick than an innovation. In just about any infant seat, baby rides in a reclined position. The difference between this and completely flat

infant seats

EPP vs. EPS foam

When you take the fancy fabric cover off a car seat, you'll notice that many car seats are lined with foam for crash protection. Car seat makers use two types of foam: EPS and EPP. EPS (expanded polystyrene foam) is the hard yet lightweight foam used in bicycle helmets. EPP (expanded polypropylene foam) is similar to EPS but softer (and hence more comfortable) for older toddlers. The take-home message: either foam is fine, but more makers are using EPP foam as an upgrade.

isn't significant, in our opinion.

Besides the recline feature, the Cloud Q also has an improved version of the "telescopic linear side impact protection," which is discussed above with the Q.

So to sum up, the Aton 1 is $250; the Aton 2 is $300 and the Aton Q is $350. The Aton Cloud Q is $400.

Bottom line: the Aton is a great seat if you have a compact car and would like a lighter carrier. We would recommend the Aton 2 or the Q. ***Rating: A-***

EDDIE BAUER SUREFIT *See the Safety 1st OnBoard.*

EVENFLO EMBRACE (LX, SELECT, SELECT WITH SURESAFE)

Price: $60; extra base $45.

Type: Infant car seat, five-point harness.

Limits: 4 to 35 lbs.

NHTSA ease of use rating: ★★★★☆

Pros: Three-position adjustable base, easier to release base and handle.

Cons: Recalled in 2007 for faulty handle.

Comments: Here, in a nutshell, is why Evenflo is in last place in the car seat biz: the Embrace infant seat was supposed to be a fresh start for Evenflo, after their last major car seat (the PortAbout) was recalled for failing a crash test back in 2005. The Embrace features a new, easier release mechanism for the carrier (this was a gripe for past models). The seat also has a three-position adjustable base and an ergonomic handle that releases with one hand.

Yet, Evenflo had to recall 450,000 Embrace infant seats in 2007 after 679 reports of the handle of the carrier unexpectedly releasing, causing 160 injuries to children. (As a side note, 679 reports? 160 injuries? At what point did Evenflo think it was time to pull the plug?). Thankfully, there haven't been any more recalls of this seat since then. (We realize this recall was way back in 2007, but it still damages Evenflo's reputation to this day, in our opinion).

As for ease of use, the Embrace scored second to last in *Consumer Reports* most recent infant car seat rankings; Evenflo's Discovery 5 was in last place. The Embrace was judged better for crash protection than the Discovery 5, but otherwise ranked far behind the competition.

FYI: Evenflo sells the Embrace in three flavors: the entry-level LX is $60 and features basic fabrics. The Embrace Select is $72 and features upgraded fabrics. The top-of-the-line model is the Embrace Select with SureSafe is $90 and features premium LATCH connectors to ease installation.

Reader feedback on this seat has been mixed. Fans like the under $100 price point. But critics point out the flimsy canopy is disappointing and the buckle can be hard to open. There also are no lock-offs on the base for seat belt installation.

About the best we can say for this seat is it is a bit easier to install and use than the Evenflo Nurture/Discovery . . . but that's not saying much. Given the past safety issues with this seat and Evenflo's track record, we say pass. **Rating: D+**

EVENFLO NURTURE (DISCOVERY)
Price: $50 to $60; extra base $25.
Type: Infant car seat, five-point harness.
Limits: 5 to 22 lbs., 26″
NHTSA ease of use rating: ★★★☆☆
Pros: Lightweight carrier, affordable price.
Cons: Not easy to use.
Comments: This bare-bones seat got its start as the Discovery and is sold in discount stores like Walmart. Newer versions of this seat are dubbed the Nurture. We still see the Discovery for sale on Amazon, but that version has disappeared from most other stores.

The carrier (at 6.5 lbs.) is one of the lightest on the market. And yes, Evenflo has added EPS foam to the seat (a few years after the competition). But . . . you don't get many features with this seat—the base doesn't adjust, there is just one crotch strap position and so on. Want to adjust the straps? You'll have to do that from the back of the seat, a major pain.

And the list of negatives goes on: the handle must be in the down position when travelling in a car, an extra step that takes up extra space. Amazingly, a version of this seat first debuted in 1998, yet it is still on the market (albeit, in an updated form). Using a car seat with 90's technology is hard to imagine, considering all the advances in child passenger safety since then.

That probably explains why the Evenflo Discovery scored at the very bottom of *Consumer Reports* most recent report on infant car seats—that report weighed ease of use heavily in their rankings. And our feedback from parents is similar: yes, this seat is cheap, but in this case, you get what you pay for.

The Nurture didn't do much better in CR's safety tests, ranking 8th out of nine infant seats rated to 22 lbs.

FYI: The main difference between the Nurture and the Discovery is the handle—the Discovery featured a Z-shaped handle. The Nurture has a more traditional, plain handle.

Bottom line: yes, this seat is cheap . . . but that is about it. The lack of upgrades and old technology here is disappointing. A basic low-end Graco SnugRide would be a better bet than this seat if you are on a tight budget. **Rating: F**

GB Asana35 AP

Price: $250.

Type: Infant seat.

Limits: 35 lbs., up to 32".

NHTSA ease of use rating: Not yet.

Pros: No rethread harness, load leg for additional crash protection. Premium LATCH connectors. Carrier weighs 9.2 lbs.

Cons: Babies R Us exclusive. Little parent feedback since seat is so new. Only works with GB's own stroller, the Evoq,

Comments: GB stands for Good Baby, the little-known Chinese baby gear behemoth that owns Evenflo and Cybex. Good Baby also markets its car seats and strollers under the Urbini brand in Walmart.

The new GB Asana35 AP is the more expensive cousin to the Urbini Petal infant car seat sold in Walmart for $100. FYI: GB is exclusive to Babies R Us, while Urbini is a Walmart exclusive.

GB Asana35's load leg provides additional stability for the seat in a crash.

The GB Asana35 AP features several upgrades over the Petal,

What is the lightest infant car seat carrier?

Here at *Baby Bargains*, we have Ivy League-trained scientists who help us determine important stuff like which infant car seat weighs the least (and hence, is easiest to lug around).

Oh, we're just kidding. Actually, we the authors just went to our local baby store and stood there in the aisles lifting each infant seat and saying things like "Yep, this one is lighter!" For this edition, we actually employed a scale to get accurate readings (and you thought only the folks in lab coats at *Consumer Reports* got to play with such toys). Our official results: the lightest seat is the Cosco Light 'N Comfy (6.3 lbs.) followed by the Safety 1st onBoard Air (9.4 lbs.). The heaviest seats? That crown goes to the Orbit at 12 lbs. The Combi Shuttle and Peg Perego Primo Viaggio were close behind at 11.1 lbs.

We list the weights for infant car seat carriers in a chart later in this chapter (pages 434-435). Of course, the weight of an infant seat isn't the only factor we used to decide which was best, but it certainly is important.

which GB dubs the "FirmFit" system. The FirmFit load leg is essentially an anti-rebound bar that keeps the seat from moving forward in a crash. Load legs are more common in other countries than the U.S., so this will be the first widely available here (the Cybex Aton and Nuna Pipa both have load legs).

The second upgrade for the Asana35 AP is the FirmFit Arm—this feature is a lever inside the base that gives the Asana a tighter fit to the car back seat. Finally, the Firm Fit harness is a no re-rethread harness system that adjusts both the headrest and harness in one pull.

So is this all worth the $250 price tag for the Asana35 AP, considering the Urbini Petal is $100 and no slouch in terms of features? Well, both seats have side impact protection, adjustable bases and side impact protection. Of all the upgrades, the FirmFit harness is probably the best addition—you have to manually rethread the harness on the Urbini Petal.

Still new as of press time, GB Asana35 AP has garnered little to no parent feedback as of this writing. However, the feature list of this seat is impressive and our first impression is quite positive. It is clear that GB is borrowing upper-end features from their Cybex brand and putting them in more affordable seats (Cybex infant seats are $100 or more than this). We like the premium LATCH connectors and the carrier weight that clocks in at 9.2 lbs.—not the lightest on the market, but less other premium seats.

Of course, one major downside to the GB Asana 35 AP—it only works with GB's own strollers as of this writing. No other stroller makers have adapters for the Asana . . . and it is unclear if it works with other brands like Maxi Cosi adapters.

So the jury is still out on this one. We'll revise this review as we get more feedback. ***Rating: Not Yet.***

GRACO SNUGRIDE
Price: $70-$220; extra base $50-$75.
Type: Infant seat.
Limits: SnugRide 22: 22 lbs., 29"; SnugRide 30: 30 lbs., 30"; SnugRide 35: 35 lbs., 32"; SnugRide 40: 40 lbs., 35".

NHTSA ease of use rating: ★★★★☆

Pros: Lightweight carrier (for the base model), level indicator, canopy, easy to use. Front belt adjuster on some models. Works with many strollers.

Cons: Only one crotch position for some models. Other seats have better side-impact protection.

Comments: Here is the country's top-selling infant car seat—and it deserves the crown. The Graco SnugRide is an affordable infant seat with excellent features: good crash protection, EPS foam lining, adjustable base (in some versions) and good fit in most vehicles. Stroller compatibility is excellent: the SnugRide not only works with Graco strollers but many other stroller makers have SnugRide adapters.

Graco has had such success with the SnugRide that they've rolled out several different versions of the seat over the last few years, keeping the SnugRide name. And that's where it gets confusing: there are now six different SnugRides. With so many versions, be sure to carefully check the box or online description before buying.

Before we wade knee deep into the SnugRide specific models, we should note that current SnugRide car seats are part of the Click Connect family. Click Connect refers to the way these car seats attach to strollers—they take one step to snap in. (At one point, Graco also sold a version of these seats called Classic Connect which required two steps. The Classic Connect versions of the SnugRide are now discontinued).

Here's a quick overview of the versions:

◆ **SnugRide 22.** This seat work to 22 lbs., 29". This is the least expensive SnugRide that is sold as part of low-price travel systems. This model lacks a front harness adjuster (requiring you to adjust the harness from the back, a major pain).

◆ **SnugRide 30** works to 30 lbs., 30". Graco sells two versions of this seat. Entry-level SnugRide 30's have rear-adjust harnesses and non-adjustable bases. More expensive versions of this seat have front-adjust harnesses and adjustable bases (which we prefer). These seats sell for $110-$130.

◆ **SnugRide 35 / 35LX** works to 35 lbs., 32". Yep, there are two versions of this model—the basic 35 that runs $130-$140. And the 35 LX ($150-$190) which adds a no-rethread harness and base with seat belt lock-offs. The LX also has upgraded fabric.

◆ **SnugRide 40.** This is the newest SnugRide and, until recently, a Babies R Us exclusive ($170-$220). As the name implies, it is the first SnugRide to work to 40 lbs. This top-of-the-line model features a no-rethread harness and an adjustable base that slides back to give 8" of additional legroom—allowing babies to use the seat up to age two. That's nice . . . but the downside is the seat then takes up a lot of space in the backseat and that could make it a no go in smaller vehicles. The SnugRide 40's base is also much larger/longer than other SnugRide bases, again making fit in smaller cars a challenge.

So, which one should you get? The pick of the litter, in our opinion, is the SnugRide 35LX and SnugRide Click Connect 40. We like the no-thread harness and seat belt lock-offs for easier installations. Both models are $150-$170 on Amazon. If the budget is tight, the SnugRide 30 runs about $40 less than the 35LX. The version of this seat sold on Amazon has the front adjust harness and adjustable base.

One caveat: if you plan to use a non-Graco stroller, check compatibility before buying a SnugRide. Some strollers makers have adapters that only work with the older Classic Connect SnugRides (now discontinued).

Overall, readers give the SnugRide a thumbs up for ease of use and overall quality. The no rethread harness on the 35LX and 40 is excellent. We also like the machine washable covers.

Is the SnugRide perfect? No. Even the most expensive SnugRide's lack premium (push-on) LATCH connectors. And the low-end SnugRides that have rear-adjust harnesses and non-adjustable bases should be avoided. Those seats also have only one crotch buckle position, which some larger babies can quickly outgrow.

Are there trade-offs between the SnugRide and more expensive seats? Well, the SnugRide does lack extra side-impact protection like you see on the Peg Perego and Britax seats. And the seat lacks an anti-rebound bar, seen on the Cybex Aton. Of course, these seats also cost almost $100 more than a SnugRide, so there's your trade-off.

It would be nice if Graco beefed up the side-impact protection in the SnugRide. If this concerns you, make sure your car has rear-curtain airbags if you use a SnugRide. If not, consider a seat with additional side impact protection (Britax, Chicco or Peg Perego).

Despite those points, overall, this seat is a winner—good crash protections, excellent ease of use and features. Add in the afford-able price and we have a winner. ***Rating: A***

INGENUITY INTRUST 35 PRO
Price: $170.
Type: Infant seat, five-point harness.
Limits: 4-35 lbs., 32″
NHTSA ease of use rating: Not yet.
Pros: Headrest and harness adjust simultane-ously for proper fit; side impact protection. No rethread harness, premium LATCH connectors.
Cons: Too new for parent feedback; only works with brand's own stroller.
Comments: Ingenuity is a new name in the infant car seat busi-ness—the brand is part of Kids II, a baby gear and toy company that is best known for its Bright Starts and Baby Einstein activity gyms and toys. And not to mention the popular Taggie gear/toys, cur-rently fascinating thousands of toddlers at this moment.

Ingenuity launched the new InTrust 35 Pro infant car seat and matching stroller (InVenture) in fall 2014, after previously entering the high chair/booster, playpen and bouncer/swing categories.

The headline for the InTrust 35 Pro is the seat's "SmartAdjust" headrest—with one step, you can simultaneously tighten and adjust both the headrest and harness to the correct position. With other car seats, you have to separately adjust the headrest and harness. This is an impressive innovation.

Of course, the InTrust 35 Pro has all the other standard features you'd expect in a $170 car seat: a 35 lbs./32" harness limit, side-impact protection, no-rethread harness and premium push-on LATCH connectors.

We were impressed with the little details of the seat: a "SeatRelief" smooth base feature to avoid damage to back seats, "AirInfuse" ventilated panels/mesh, a soft grip carry handle.

All in all, a very good first effort for Ingenuity.

So what's not to like? As of this writing, the infant seat is only compatible with Ingenuity's stroller—a $200 multi-function stroller that may not be everyone's cup of tea.

This seat was too new as we went to press to gather any real world feedback from our readers. So we'll wait on a rating until then. ***Rating: Not Yet.***

Maxi Cosi Mico AP / Nxt / Max 30

Price: $140 to $200.

Limits: AP/Nxt: 22 lbs., 29". Max: 30 lbs.

NHTSA ease of use rating: ★★★★☆

Pros: Works with Quinny strollers, Air Protect foam, four harness heights, deep side wings.

Cons: Canopy doesn't stay up, pricey for what is essentially a Cosco seat.

Comments: Cosco imports these seats from their European subsidiary, adapted for the U.S. market and designed to work with its Quinny strollers.

There are two Micos now on the market: The original Mico (now rebranded as the Mico Nxt) and the Mico AP, its more plush cousin.

The AP is slightly different from the Next with a new seat pad, visor and air protect technology (hence the AP). Both seats are among the lighter infant seats on the market. The AP is 8.7 lbs. while the Next is slightly less. Maxi Cosi has improved the carrier release on the Mico's base, both for the original and AP models.

Reader feedback has been mixed: fans say it is easy to use and install, plus the EPP foam is softer than the EPS foam you see on most other seats.

Critics universally hate the canopy (which does not stay in place) and others note it's expensive for a low maximum weight seat.

In the past year, the feedback on this seat has trended in a more positive direction. Fans point out that even though the weight limit is 22 lbs., it is one of the biggest seats (the shell is longer) compared to other 22 lb. seats. And at eight pounds, the carrier is among the lighter weight options out there. The Maxi Cosi scored second in *Consumer Reports* latest tests for infant seats that have a 22 lb.

capacity; and the government gives this seat (both versions) a four star rating for ease of use.

For 2015, Maxi Cosi plans a new version of the Mico, dubbed the Mico Max 30. And as you might guess from the name, this version will now work up to (drumroll) 30 lbs. Price: $230. You'll be able to customize the Mico Max 30 with a choice of frame color, seat cushion, canopy, toys and other details—a customized Mico will take three weeks to ship. Also new: an anti-rebound bar for additional crash protection.

Bottom line: the Maxi Cosi Mico is a good seat—but at $200, the Mico is rather pricey considering our top picks (like the Chicco KeyFit or Britax B-SAFE) cost less and work to 30 lbs. (We'll have to wait and see how the Mico Max 30 performs in the real world before we can rate that version). ***Rating for AP/Nxt: B***

MAXI COSI PREZI INFANT SEAT
Price: $290.
Limits: 30 lbs., 29"
NHTSA ease of use rating: ★★★★☆
Pros: Anti-rebound bar, easy-out no-rethread harness, extra side-impact protection.

Cons: Very pricey, heavy carrier, stroller adapters may not work.
Comments: The Prezi is Maxi Cosi's latest infant car seat: it features a 30 lb. weight limit, five-position adjustable base, anti-rebound bar and no-rethread, "easy out" harness. The last feature is unique: Maxi Cosi claims this is a quicker way for parents to buckle in or out their child.

Maxi Cosi has borrowed the "Air Protect" technology from their sister-line, Safety 1st, for the Prezi's side impact protection.

So, what's not to like? Well, the Prezi carrier weighs in at a hefty 11.7 lbs. empty. Add an average-size newborn and you've got 20+ pounds to haul around—hope you've been doing your pregnancy upper arm workouts.

Another negative: stroller adapters that work for the Maxi Cosi Mico don't necessarily work for the Prezi—that's because the Prezi has a completely different base and attachment system. Since the Prezi is still relatively new, we expect stroller makers will eventually catch up with correct adapters. But, meanwhile, just because a stroller maker says they make adapters for Maxi Cosi seats, don't assume the Prezi will work.

And the $290 price tag is steep—about a third more than other top-rated car seats. We're not sure if the seat's features justify that premium.

Real world feedback has been limited so far and mixed overall. Fans like the overall sleek design and high-tech plush fabric—with special kudos to the fancy canopy. Detractors say the fabric is very hot and the carrier weight is a major negative. Several wish the neato canopy extended further over the seat. Others complained that the seat's space interior was small and cramped for larger babies.

Most disappointing: the Prezi scored only "basic" for crash protection, as judged by *Consumer Reports*. Given the anti-rebound bar and side impact protection cushions, this was a major disappointment. The magazine put the Prezi 21st overall out of 25 seats, knocking it for lower ease of use scores compared to other seats. One example we saw in parent feedback: the fixed harness straps are difficult to use with newborns.

Bottom line: at nearly $300, we expected a lot out of the Prezi. And while it has a sleek look and an impressive set of safety features (at least on paper), the real world performance of this seat—based on reader feedback and third party testing—has been a disappointment. The heavy weight of the carrier is the final nail in the coffin. ***Rating: C+***

MUV KUSSEN
Price: $260.
Type: Infant seat, five-point harness.
Limits: 4-32 lbs.
NHTSA ease of use rating: ★★★★★
(rating for previous version, Baby Trend Inertia).
Pros: Anti-rebound bar.
Cons: Previous life as the Baby Trend Inertia only earned mixed parent reviews.
Comments: MÜV is the new upper-end division of Baby Trend that plans to launch both an infant car seat and strollers in 2015.

If the MÜV Kussen (Dutch for "cushion") looks familiar, that's because it is the Baby Trend Inertia. MÜV told us this is the second generation Inertia, but it has much the same specs (4-32 lbs., rigid LATCH, no rethread harness, rebound bar, etc). The price, however, is going up: $260 at retail.

This seat wasn't out as of press time, so no parent feedback yet. Unfortunately, the parent reviews on the Inertia were mixed at best. So we'll have to wait to see if changing the name will make any difference here. ***Rating: Not Yet.***

NUNA PIPA
Price: $300, extra base $150.
Type: Infant seat, five-point harness.
Limits: 4-32 lbs., 32".
NHTSA ease of use rating: ★★★★☆
Pros: Sleek look, anti-rebound leg for additional crash protection, cool canopy, lightweight.
Cons: $300? Limited stroller compatibility. Few retail stores carry it.

Comments: Dutch baby gear maker Nuna landed in the U.S. in 2013 with a handful of products, including the Pipa infant seat. Nuna's mojo is "simple, smart, chic" design, with a green spin (fabrics are Oeko-Tex certified for sustainability, etc.).

The big headline for the Pipa infant seat is the "true lock" installation, with indicators that turn green when correctly installed. Also somewhat unique: an anti-rebound leg (called a stability leg) that is common in Europe, but somewhat rare here in the U.S. That helps with crash protection.

The Pipa's "dream drape" is a car seat cover that uses hidden magnets to stay in place and then stores away in a hidden compartment— which is a nifty trick. (One parent who's used the seat tells us they love the dream drape—but when you are carrying the Pipa with the dream drape closed and brush against the carrier, the drape can easily disengage. Hence, Nuna should make the magnets stronger).

The Pipa has rigid LATCH connectors that can rotate for the best fit, depending on the slope of your vehicle's back seat.

Overall, we were impressed with the carrier's lightweight design

The NYC Taxi Dilemma

Here's a common email we get from parents in New York and other urban areas: are there any portable car seats that can be used in taxis? Something that is lightweight, easy to install and collapses to fit inside a small purse when not in use? Well, the answer is no—there's no perfect solution. But we have a few ideas. Let's break out our advice for New Yorkers by age:

◆ **Infant (birth to six months).** The safest way for an infant to ride in a taxi is in an infant car seat. Most (but not all) can be strapped in without the stay-in-the-car base. However, always check the manual BEFORE buying any seat to confirm this feature.

◆ **Babies/toddlers (six months to four years).** Many infant car seats can be used up to 30 or 32 lbs.—use the seat as long as you can. For older babies, there aren't many good options. If you use a car service to go to or from an airport, you can usually request a car seat in advance. Otherwise, using public transport is probably the safest option.

◆ **Older kids.** A booster seat is the safest way to go—and a simple backless booster such as the Graco TurboBooster (backless version) or Bumblebum. Both are lightweight and portable.

(7.7 lbs.) and overall design.

So what's not to like? Well, the $300 price for one. Want a second stay-in-the-car base for another vehicle? That's $150. Yes, this car seat has an impressive design . . . but we aren't sure that alone justifies the price tag.

The Pipa lacks a no-rethread harness—that means you have to manually thread through the harness to change the height. Not a big deal . . . but for $300, that's disappointing.

And which strollers is the Pipa compatible with? Also disappointing—Nuna only has adapters for a handful of UPPAbaby, Bugaboo and Stokke strollers (plus one model from Mamas and Papas). So if you are planning to use this with an UPPAbaby Vista, you're in luck. Baby Jogger? Britax? Bob? Not so much. Yes, you can use the Pipa with Nuna's own PEPP stroller . . . but the adapters are a separate purchase. For the company's own stroller! (Nuna is debuting a stroller frame called the Tavo that will fit the Pipa in early 2015, but it will cost $300+).

Bottom line: the limited number of "official" Nuna adapters means you'll have to take the chance it will work with a Maxi Cosi adapter if you want a travel system with another stroller brand.

Based on initial parent feedback, we'll give the Nuna Pipa a qualified thumbs up—the seat's innovative design and features are impressive and most parents say it performs well in the real world. But the high price and limited stroller compatibility makes the Pipa at best a niche player in this category.

Finally, the Pipa may be hard to see in the real world, as it is sold only in a handful of specialty stores. ***Rating: B+***

ORBIT

Price: $980, as part of a travel system with stroller frame. $440 sold as a stand-alone seat.
Limits: 4-30 lbs., 32"
NHTSA ease of use rating: ★★★★☆

Pros: You'll have a seat none of your friends has.
Cons: Did we mention it is sold as part of a travel system that's nearly $1000?
Comments: Orbit aims to be the Apple of juvenile gear—a company whose innovative products set the bar for everyone else. Do they succeed? Let's discuss.

Orbit's flagship is the Orbit Baby Infant System, which includes an infant car seat, in-car base and stroller frame that attempts a Bugaboo-like chic vibe. The infant car seat is a bit strange looking (one parenting blog compared it to a crock pot), with an innovative soft-strap handle and rotating base. We liked Orbit's "SmartHub" base technology, that lets you "dock" the seat at any angle. The base also has a front knob that ensures a tight fit to the vehicle.

The feedback on the Orbit has been mixed. Fans love the Orbit's technology and ergonomic design. Tall parents particularly love the stroller's tall handles; others love how it is a conversation starter with other parents.

But . . . detractors point out the bulky 12 lb. carrier is beyond HEAVY, providing a serious upper body workout as baby gets bigger. The bulk of the Orbit seat makes for a tight fit in even mid-size cars.

And let's get real for a second: does anyone really need to spend nearly $1000 on an infant car seat and stroller frame? Most babies will outgrow the Orbit infant car seat at or before their first birthday. Then you have to pony up another $200 for a toddler stroller seat. So if are scoring along at home, that adds up to $1200+. (A bassinet cradle that docks to the stroller frame is another $200).

In the past year, Orbit began offering the infant car seat separately, for an eye-popping $440 retail.

As for crash testing, *Consumer Reports* ranked the Orbit only 14th out of 18 seats, giving it only a "basic" mark for crash protection. Other seats did better and had better ease of us and fit to vehicle.

In the past year, Orbit rolled a out the third generation (G3) versions of its car seat and stroller. The new travel system has more customization options and a raft of improvements to the stroller (bigger storage basket, faster fold, better steering).

Bottom line: most parent feedback on this seat is positive—fans like the design and durability. You'll get stopped in the park or the mall with folks commenting on the seat. But the extreme weight, bulk and price of this seat limit its appeal. If you don't want to get the entire Orbit travel system, there is no point to the Orbit infant seat as it isn't compatible with other strollers.

So, it's a mixed review for the Orbit. Kudos to the company for their innovative features and design. But does Orbit reach the Apple level of cutting edge tech *and* accessible pricing? No. Let's do the math. You could buy an Orbit system for $980. . . or buy a Graco SnugRide for $150 plus a stroller frame for $50 and take the $780 savings and start a college fund for your child. ***Rating: B***

PEG PEREGO PRIMO VIAGGIO 4.35

Price: $280. extra base: $100.

Limits: 4-35 lbs., 30"

NHTSA ease of use rating: ★★★☆☆

Pros: No rethread harness, new tensioning system for solid installations, anti-rebound bar, canopy with UV protection.

Cons: Price. Other stroller makers may not have adapters for this new seat yet.

Comments: Peg Perego has made slow but steady improvements to their best selling Primo Viaggio seat. The latest version (dubbed 4.35) works up to 35 lbs. (the previous version worked only to 30 lbs.) and features a series of other improvements: a no-rethread harness adjustable from the rear of the seat, anti-rebound bar, and a canopy that now boasts UV sun protection.

The 4.35 also has two inserts for smaller newborns, an adjustable base, and a tensioning system to tighten the belt or LATCH installation. Another nice new improvement: the handle can be left up or down when travelling in a vehicle. The base of the 4.35 is also compact enough to fit in smaller vehicles (it is similar to the Chicco KeyFit, based on our measurements).

The carriers weighed in at 9.1 lbs., which is almost 20% lighter than the previous version.

Reader feedback on the 4.35 has been positive—like Peg's other infant car seat, the 4.35 is easy to use and install. So what's not to love, besides the hefty $280 price tag? We're hard pressed to find a negative here. Many stroller brands have Peg adapters, so you're covered in case you want to go with another stroller maker. The anti-rebound bar is excellent.

One important caveat: as a reader pointed out below in the comments section, other stroller makers have yet to make 4.35 adapters since the seat is still relatively new. That means when you see a stroller that says it has a "Peg Perego adapter," they mean adapters for the Primo Viaggio SIP 30/30. The adapters that fit the SIP 30/30 may NOT fit the 4.35. As of this writing, we only see Britax/BOB offering an adapter that specifically says it is both SIP 30/30 and 4.35 compatible. Baby Jogger has two different adapters for Peg— one that works for just the 4.35 and one that works for either the 4.35 and SIP 30/30. Confusing, we know. **Rating: A**

PEG PEREGO PRIMO VIAGGIO SIP 30-30

Price: $250. extra base: $80-100.
Limits: 5-30 lbs., 30"
NHTSA ease of use rating: ★★★★☆
Pros: Side impact protection, auto harness adjustment, improved canopy, luxe fabrics.
Cons: Price.
Comments: Peg Perego has had much success in this category, despite the seat's high price tag. Some of that success can be chalked up to Peg's slow but steady improvements to the Primo Viaggio. In recent years, the company has added side impact protection, an automatic adjustable harness and a better canopy to the seat, which now works up to 30 lbs. and can be used with or without the base.

Of course, a big part of Peg's mojo here is their Italian fabrics and style—plus the fact this seat mates with many of Peg's fashionable strollers. The luxe Italian fabrics are sharp, but most of Peg's competitors have caught up in the looks department in recent years.

As for ease of use, most of our readers give the Viaggio good marks, although not quite as high as the Graco SnugRide. Negatives include a bulky, heavy carrier that clocks in at 11.1 lbs. That said, the majority of the reader feedback on this seat is very positive.

Obviously, the price of the Viaggio is its biggest drawback—Peg has let the retail price of this seat creep dangerously close to $300. While it is a well made, safe infant car seat, it's hard to justify the nearly 50% price premium over similar seats from Chicco and Graco.

That said, we should note that we occasionally see the Primo Viaggio SIP 30-30 discounted online under $200. And there are many bargain Primo Viaggio seats from past years sold online in the $170 to $200 range. Be aware, however, that many earlier models only work to 22 lbs. and omit the side impact protection.

As for the latest crash tests, the Primo Viaggio scores in the middle of the pack in *Consumer Reports* latest tests—above average crash ("better") protection but only fair fit to vehicle using a safety belt. The government gave this seat a four-star rating for ease of use.

FYI: In the past year, Perego rolled out a new version of the Primo Viaggio, dubbed the 4.35. The SIP 30-30 continues to live on, but the new seat's improvements make it a more attractive buy. ***Rating: A-***

PHIL & TEDS ALPHA
Price: $200.
Limits: 4-35 lbs., 32"
NHTSA ease of use rating: Not yet.
Pros: EPS foam lined seat, infant insert, works to 35 lbs.
Cons: Little feedback; no third party testing.

Comments: Stroller maker Phil & Teds quietly entered into the infant car seat category in spring 2014 with a new seat dubbed the Alpha.

Sold on online and on Phil & Ted's web site, the Alpha features a 35 lb. weight limit, removable infant insert and EPS foam lined seat. The carrier is lightweight at 8.3 lbs. Phil & Ted's sells a rain cover for the Alpha for $35 and extra bases for $80.

As for stroller compatibility, the Alpha works with Phil & Ted's strollers . . . and that's about it. As of press time, it was sold in just a handful of stores, so it is hard to see in person.

Reader feedback has been thin on this car seat and there is little third party testing available (no NHTSA ease of use rating; no testing by *Consumer Reports*). Phil & Teds has a good reputation for safety and quality, but given how new this seat is, we are unable to assign a rating as we went to press. ***Rating: Not Yet.***

RECARO PERFORMANCE COUPE
Price: $270.
Limits: 4-35 lbs., 32"
NHTSA ease of use rating: Not yet.
Pros: Memory foam lined seat, side impact protection, no rethread harness.
Cons: No anti-rebound bar or load leg. Little stroller compatibility.

Comments: Best known for their convertible and booster seats, Recaro entered the infant car seat category in 2014 with the Performance Coupe. The headline on this seat is memory foam, which lines the seat to provide a more cushy ride.

That's nice, but most infants don't really care about padding—this is more an issue for toddlers in convertible and booster seats on longer drives.

Otherwise, the Performance Ride offers what you'd expect for an upper-end seat: included infant insert, side impact protection and a no-rethread harness with five height positions. The base is adjustable with a flip foot and level indicator. We liked the fact that the fabric is easily removable, but the pad isn't machine washable.

The premium infant seat market ($250+) is crowded, so given the competition, what is the Performance Coupe missing? There is no anti-rebound bar, found in seats like the Peg Perego Primo Viaggio 4.35. Seats like the Cybex Aton Q and Nuna Pipa have load or stability legs, which are an added measure of crash protection (in a front collision, the leg distributes some of the force and prevents the seat from striking the front seat or console). So does the Performance Coupe have this? Nope.

Stroller compatibility is another missing component—the Performance Coupe works with one Recaro stroller . . . and that's about it. Most stroller brands do not have Recaro adapters.

Early reader feedback on this seat has been positive: most folks say the Performance Coupe is easy to use and install. So we'll give Recaro a B on its first effort in this category. The Performance Coupe is a decent infant seat—but given the competition at this price, it falls short of a top ranking. ***Rating: B***

SAFETY 1ST ONBOARD 35/AIR/AIR PLUS
Price: onBoard 35 is $90 to $119. onBoard 35 Air is $110 to $160. onBoard 35 Air Plus is $190. Extra base: $35-$70.
Limits: 35 lbs., 32"
NHTSA ease of use rating: ★★★☆☆
Pros: Among the least expensive seats with side impact protection.

Chocolate donuts with sprinkles?

Here's a confusing thing about car seat shopping: most car seat makers offer their models in a plethora of versions. At one point a couple of years ago, one infant seat maker had FIVE different versions of the same seat: the Classic, Plus, Elite, Supreme and the Extra Crispy. Okay, there wasn't an Extra Crispy, but you get the point. The key thing to remember: the seat was basically the very same seat in each configuration, just with minor cosmetic variations (an extra bit of padding here, a pillow there, etc). Yes, sometimes there are more significant variations like a front versus rear harness adjuster or an adjustable base. But often there isn't much difference. Think of it this way: car seat makers produce a chocolate donut and top it with different color sprinkles—the rainbow sprinkle version goes to Walmart, the green sprinkle donut goes to Target, etc. That way the companies can offer "exclusives" on certain models to large retailers, so the chains don't have the same exact offerings. But remember this: basically, it's the same donut. Bottom line: don't get caught up in all the version stuff. If the basic seat has the features you want, it doesn't really matter whether you buy the Plus or the Elite. Or the Extra Crispy.

Cons: Canopy only offers minimal coverage. No harness pads. Stroller compatibility an issue.

Comments: The flagship infant car seat for Dorel's Safety 1st is the onBoard. Like many Dorel offerings, however, the onBoard comes in multiple versions that can be confusing. So let's break it down.

The basic onBoard features a newborn insert that works well with preemies as small as four pounds. It features a carrier lined with EPP foam, four harness height positions and an adjustable base.

Step up to the onBoard Air and you get additional side impact protection in the form of Safety 1st's Air Protect cushions. The onBoard Air Plus adds additional crash protection in what Safety 1st calls its "GCell HX" padding. The more expensive onBoard Airs features a premium base with belt-lock offs, premium LATCH "push on" connectors and more adjustable positions.

For release in early 2015, Safety 1st plans a complete refresh for the onBoard car seat, with a base that will have more adjustable positions (five versus three previously). Also new: an easier to carry handle. As before, the 2015 version of the onBoard will come in three price points: onBoard 35 ($120-$130), onBoard Air ($160) and onBoard Air Plus ($180).

The Safety 1st OnBoard is sold widely in chain stores and online. Reader feedback on the Air version of this car seat has been pos-

infant seats

itive. As for crash tests, *Consumer Reports* gave the onBoard Air a "best" rating, ranking it fourth overall out of 20+ seats tested. And for ease of use, all versions of the onBoard scored three out of five stars by the NHTSA. Another plus: the onBoard is a relatively light-weight carrier at 8-8.3 lbs., depending on the version.

What's missing? Well, the seat lacks harness pads, which you find on seats in the $150 to $200 price range. The canopy also lacks the coverage and overall finish you'd expect for a car seat in this price range.

But those are small quibbles compared to the big negative here: stroller compatibility. While this seat works with Safety 1st strollers and other models in the Dorel universe (Quinny, etc.), most other brands do NOT sell adapters for the onBoard Air.

Bottom line: this is a good seat, as long as you plan to pair it with a Safety 1st or other Dorel brand stroller. Between the versions, we'd suggest the onBoard Air or onBoard Air Plus. ***Rating: B***

SUMMER PRODIGY

Price: $191; extra base $67.

Limits: 35 lbs., 32"

NHTSA ease of use rating: ★★★★★

Pros: Auto height harness adjustment, high-tech screen to advise on correction installation. Top rating for ease of use.

Cons: Version 1.0 of any car seat is usually best to skip.

Comments: Summer's first infant car seat, the Prodigy, debuted in 2011 to generally positive reviews—yet it barely made a blip on the sales radar.

On paper, the Prodigy looked good: features included a no-rethread harness that automatically tightens with one pull. There's also SmartScreen, a LCD readout tells you when you've correctly installed the belt, testing the install to ensure safety. A special vehicle belt-tightening system enables a parent to tighten the belt with one hand. A newborn head and body support pillow allows use for preemies starting at four pounds (top capacity is 32 lbs.).

The only negatives: At 9.9 lbs., the carrier (which has two crotch positions) is on the heavy side, but oddly lacks any EPS foam.

Clearly, Summer put a lot of thought and design effort behind this seat. And by attaching a $200 price tag to the Prodigy, Summer hoped to compete with top-rated seats from Britax and Chicco, not to mention category leader Graco.

However, the sales of the Prodigy clearly disappointed Summer. The company "re-launched" the Prodigy in 2012. It's not a good sign when you launch a new product—and then need to re-launch it six months later.

Part of the problem here is the difficulty in launching an infant car seat without a strong stroller line to pair it with—Summer is better known for its video monitors than travel gear. And few (no?) stroller makers offer adapters for the Prodigy. So if you buy this infant car seat and want to snap it into a stroller, you'd have to buy a stroller from Summer as well.

On that score, Summer dropped the ball—its first matching stroller for the Prodigy weighed in at nearly 30 lbs. and lacked much pizzazz. And at $330 for the travel system, Summer simply priced itself out of the market.

Reader feedback and online reviews of this seat have been thin—and considering the seat has been on the market since 2011, that's probably an indication of very low sales.

So it is a mixed review for Summer—a good first effort with the Prodigy, but the weak line-up of compatible strollers and high price make this one a tough sell. *Rating: C*

Uppa Baby Mesa

Price: $280.

Limits: 35 lbs., 32"

NHTSA ease of use rating: ★★★★★

Pros: No-rethread harness, side impact protection, adjustable headrest, hideaway canopy with stretch fabric, innovative base with self-retracting LATCH system.

Cons: Pricey, version 1.0 seat. Uppa's first effort in this category. No anti-rebound bar.

Comments: Stroller maker Uppa Baby entered the crowded infant car seat market with the Mesa in 2013.

Uppa's effort here is nothing if not ambitious—the Mesa is loaded with top end features. Examples: a no-rethread harness, side-impact protection with an adjustable headrest, a canopy made of lightweight stretch material (similar to the Maxi Cosi Prezi) and a base that has a self-retracting LATCH system. Innovations include a tension indicator (Smartsecure) on the base that shows when you've tightened the belts correctly.

They've even thought of the little things, like a base with a smooth bottom surface, so it won't mar your auto's back seat (parents are tempted to use seat protectors with other seats, which are not recommended by safety techs). And the canopy (which disappears when folded) has a 50 SPF protection rating.

Since the Mesa came out after the Vista (Uppa Baby's flagship stroller) was designed, the Mesa doesn't quite integrate smoothly with the Vista. It requires a separate two-piece adapter (which Uppa Baby includes). That disappoints many Uppa Baby fans, who had visions of using this seat seamlessly with the Vista. On the other hand, the Uppa Baby Cruz DOES work seamlessly with the Mesa.

infant seats

What's missing? Well, there is no anti-rebound bar as you see on the Maxi Cosi Prezi or Peg Perego Primo Viaggio 4.35. And at 10.5 lbs., the Mesa's carrier is HEAVY. Parents using the seat in the real world noted that the extra three pounds (compared to Graco, for example) really made a difference. And let's talk about stroller compatibility. Few other stroller brands make adapters for the Mesa. Yes, Baby Jogger has one for the City Select and Versa, but other major brands don't.

At $280, the Mesa is priced at the top of the market.

The Mesa's launch has been bumpy—at one point, complaints surfaced about water-spotting on the canopy. When exposed to the rain, water spots left marks on the canopy. We asked Uppa Baby about this problem and they blamed it on a small batch of defective canopy fabric—they said they have taken steps to correct the issue. One could argue this is a small quibble, but we can see how parents who shelled out $300 for this seat would be disappointed that the seat's canopy became stained when being exposed to a few rain drops.

Despite the initial launch hiccups, the Mesa boasts an impressive design and feature list. Whether folks will pony up nearly $300 for it is an open question, however. After all, if you want an Uppa Baby stroller, you can use just about any major brand car seat with it, thanks to Uppa's extensive adapter accessory list.

Reader feedback has been largely positive. Most folks say the Mesa works well and is easy to install and use. As a result, we'll raise the rating. ***Rating: A-***

URBINI PETAL
Price: $100.
Limits: 4-35 lbs., 32″
NHTSA ease of use rating: Not yet.
Pros: Adjustable base with built-in lock offs, side impact protection, lightweight carrier (8 lbs.), preemie insert, affordable.
Cons: Twisty harness straps. 1.0 version seat. Only works with Urbini's own strollers, as other stroller makers don't offer Urbini adapters.
Comments: Urbini is the new brand from Chinese baby gear behemoth Goodbaby, which owns Evenflo and Cybex as well as makes baby gear for a host of other brands. The company sells strollers under the GB brand.

Sold exclusively at Walmart, the Urbini Petal is impressive—we like the lightweight carrier (8 lbs.) and the adjustable base with built-in lock offs. Goodbaby both designed and manufactured car seats for such brands as Maxi Cosi and Dorel (before parting ways with Dorel in 2014)—hence, their experience shows in the Petal.

With a padded preemie insert, the Petal can work for preemies as small as four pounds.

So what's not to like? Well, like any version 1.0 seat, the Petal as a few rough edges–velcro on the harness can sometimes snag on the harness slots when you tighten the seat. And the harness itself is thin and is prone to twisting, which is a pain to deal with.

Yes, you have to rethread the harness when charging the harness height (the Petal even has two hip adjustments, as well as two crotch positions). While it would be nice to have a no-rethread harness, that is a feature one wouldn't expect on a $100 car seat.

As of this writing, Urbini is only sold at Walmart. The company sells the Petal as a stand-alone seat or as part of a travel system with the Urbini Omni ($199), Touri ($149) or Avi ($299) strollers. (See our review of Urbini strollers in the stroller section.) Unfortunately, that is your only option for strollers that work with the Petal–as of this writing, no other stroller makers make adapters that fit the Petal.

Overall, parent feedback on the Petal has been positive and we will recommend the seat. *Rating: B+*

Convertible and Forward Facing-Only Car Seats (model by model reviews)

ALPHA OMEGA THREE IN ONE *See Eddie Bauer Three In One convertible seat.*

BRITAX ADVOCATE
Price: $300 to $420.
Type: Convertible seat.
Limits: 5 to 40 lbs. rear facing, 20 to 65 lbs. forward facing. Height limit: 49" (G4) or 54" (ClickTight).
NHTSA ease of use rating:

★★★☆☆ Rear-facing
★★★★☆ Forward-facing

Rating is for G4 version.
Pros: Same as Boulevard but with added side impact protection.
Cons: Price. Big seat—may not fit into smaller vehicles.
Comments: This seat is the same as the Britax Boulevard, with one major difference: the Advocate has added side impact protection cushions that compress to protect the child during a crash. Yep, think of these as side-impact air bags for your car seat.

FYI: There are two versions of this seat–G4 and ClickTight. The latter (ClickTight) is the newest version with a seat that pops forward for easier belt installations. The ClickTight version also has a higher harness height (19.5" versus 17.4" for the G4)–this enables the seat to be used for kids up to 54" tall (six more inches than the G4).

convertible seats

The new ClickTight version of the Advocate features seven position seat recline and fourteen harness height positions. Also new: the side impact protection is integrated closer to the seat compared to the G4 seats. As a result, the Advocate is narrower than previous versions: 19.4" vs 20.5". That may not sound like much, but this slimmer profile may enable you to fit three Advocates in the back seat of a mid-size vehicle.

Britax is selling both the G4 and ClickTight versions for the time being; we'd recommend the ClickTight.

One nice feature can also be a negative: the cover is easy to remove for washing. But we noted more than a few readers said it came off way too easily when in the car.

As with all Britax convertible seats, you get SafeCell technology to minimize seat movement in a crash, integrated steel bars for strength and an energy-absorbing tether strap.

FYI: Babies R Us has an exclusive version of this seat called the Advocate Ultra Comfort Series—this is the same as the Advocate, but adds a cup holder, an exclusive fabric and added memory foam in the seat. Price: $330-$380. Is the Advocate Ultra Comfort Series worth the upgrade? Well, the memory foam is nice, especially if you are taking long trips. Otherwise, a regular Advocate is fine for most folks.

Reader feedback on the Advocate has been very positive—at least for the G4 version (the ClickTight was too new as of this writing, but we expect it to perform similarly). The G4 version scored well in *Consumer Reports'* most recent report on convertible seats. Perhaps the only knock to this seat is ease of use—the government only gives it a three-star rating when used rear-facing, with "installation features" coming in for criticism (again, the G4 version, not the ClickTight). And we heard from more than one reader who was stumped by the instruction manual, which is heavy on illustrations and light on text.

Overall, this is an excellent seat—the rating only falls short of a full A because of the high price. Topping $400, the Advocate ClickTight may simply be out of reach. The G4 version is less expensive (about $100 less), but we think the upgrades for the ClickTight make it worth the investment if you can afford it. **Rating: A-**

BRITAX BOULEVARD
Price: $270-$370.
Type: Convertible seat.
Limits: 5 to 40 lbs. rear facing, 20 to 65 lbs. forward facing, G4: 49" tall. ClickTight: 54" tall.
NHTSA ease of use rating:
★★★★☆ Rear facing
★★★★☆ Forward facing
(Rating is for previous version.)

Pros: Same as the Marathon, but seat adds a no rethread harness. Additional side impact protection with headrest.

Cons: Price. Big seat—may not fit into smaller vehicles. EPS foam only in headrest.

Comments: This seat is virtually the same as the Marathon, with one significant difference: what Britax calls "true impact protection." Basically, this is a reinforced headrest that protects your child in a side-impact collision. The Boulevard also has SafeCell HUGS pads and a top harness slot that is about two inches higher than the Marathon (hence you can use it for a longer period of time).

As with Britax's other convertible seats, the Boulevard comes in two versions: G4 and ClickTight. ClickTight, which is the newest version, features a seat that pops forward for a quick and easy install without any tugging on the belt (or dealing with LATCH issues). The ClickTight base also has seven recline positions.

Like all of Britax's current seats, the Boulevard comes with SafeCell and an integrated steel frame for crash protection.

Because ClickTight is new as of this writing, most of the feedback we have on the Boulevard is for the previous G4 version. Reader feedback has been very positive. The few complaints we've heard about the Boulevard have been addressed by the new ClickTight version (higher harness heights, more recline positions, etc).

The Boulevard gets very good crash test marks from *Consumer Reports*; the government's ease of use rating indicates the Boulevard is easier to install forward facing than rear facing.

Are there any disadvantages to the Boulevard? Well, this is a bulky (and heavy) seat. So moving it from car to car would be a major chore. The Boulevard may not fit well in smaller vehicles, especially rear-facing. Bottom line: this is an excellent seat and a worthy upgrade to the Marathon if you can afford it. ***Rating: A***

BRITAX MARATHON

Price: $200-$300.

Type: Convertible seat.

Limits: 5 to 40 lbs. rear facing, 20 to 65 lbs. forward facing, 49" tall.

NHTSA ease of use rating:

★★★★☆ Rear facing:
★★★★☆ Forward facing:

(Rating is for previous version.)

Pros: New ClickTight version makes belt install a snap. Basic side impact protection, no thread harness.

Cons: Other Britax models have more side impact protection.

Comments: The Marathon is Britax's best-selling seat and it's no wonder: this model was one of the first to work to 65 lbs. with a harness. Since its release, Britax has done a series of Marathon spin-offs that add side impact protection (Boulevard, Advocate). Despite being more old school, the Marathon is still worthy of consideration.

What's so great about the Marathon? Yes, it works to 65 lbs., but there are many seats on the market that work to that spec. Britax's secret sauce is the seat's ease of use—from installation to adjusting the harness, the Marathon is a winner. The emphasis on safety is impressive: steel bar construction, "SafeCell" technology in the base to absorb crash impacts, built-in seat belt lockoffs.

Britax has made steady improvements over the years—the most recent version is the Marathon ClickTight, with a new seat base that pops open to allow for easier installation with a safety belt. The new base also has a multi-position recline, matching a feature seen on the Chicco NextFit.

Confusingly, there are now two Marathons on the market: the G4 and ClickTight. So what's the difference? Besides the base (described above), the seats are very similar—the G4 has a slightly lower top harness height (17.4" vs. 17.7"). The overall height limit is the same (49").

Another major difference: the G4 costs about $50-$75 less than the ClickTight. But the ClickTight so markedly improves the installation process (with a safety belt) that it is probably worth the extra cash. The extra recline positions for the ClickTight are also impressive.

So, what's not to like about the Marathon? Well, first, this is a big seat. At 23.5" tall (the seat back), the Britax is a few inches taller than other convertible seats. That means it may not fit into smaller cars, especially when in rear facing mode. The Marathon is also a beast at nearly 30 lbs.—you won't be moving this seat from vehicle to vehicle without the help of a standby Sumo wrestler.

And if you are concerned about side impact collisions, the Marathon only has what Britax calls its basic side impact protection. The more expensive Britax Boulevard and Advocate add additional protection in the form of headwings and cushions. Those cushions have both fans and detractors—the safety benefit is obvious, but some kiddos don't like the wings/cushions around their heads, limiting vision and movement.

Bottom line: the Marathon does have side impact protection (deep side walls) and that might be enough protection . . . depending on your vehicle. If your car has rear side curtain air bags (more common on newer vehicles) and you can install a seat in the middle position of the back seat, then the Marathon may be all you need. If your vehicle lacks rear side curtain air bags, then the Boulevard or Advocate may be worth the safety upgrade ($100 to $200 extra).

Reader feedback on this seat has been very positive, with fans citing its ease of use and installation. All in all, we recommend the Marathon—IF you have a vehicle in which it can fit! **Rating: A**

BRITAX ROUNDABOUT

Price: $144-$190

Type: Convertible seat.

Limits: Rear-facing: 5-40 lbs. (Roundabout G4.1), 5-35 lbs. (Roundabout 50 Classic). Forward-facing: 55 lbs. (Roundabout G4.1), 50 lbs. (Roundabout 50 Classic). Height limit: 46″ (Roundabout G4.1), 49″ (Roundabout Classic).

NHTSA ease of use rating:

☆☆☆☆☆ Rear facing
☆☆☆☆☆ Forward facing. (Rating is for G4 version.)

Pros: Excellent features–EPS foam, no-twist straps, easy to adjust harness, double-strap LATCH.

Cons: Harness not as easy to adjust as Marathon.

Comments: The Roundabout was Britax's first convertible sold in the U.S. and has been a best-seller thanks to its affordable price and rock-solid installation–the lock-off clips provide snug belt installations and Britax's double-strap LATCH connectors are among the best in the business.

Today the Roundabout is the entry price point for Britax's convertible car seat offerings. Sales of this seat have been eclipsed in recent years by the Marathon, which earned our top recommendation. Yes, the Marathon costs $90 to $150 more than the Roundabout (depending on the version). But we think it is worth the upgrade–the no rethread harness, the higher 65 lbs. weight limit and other upgrades make the Marathon a superior choice.

The Roundabout still is a good seat, however. If you only have $150 to spend on a seat, you won't be disappointed.

FYI: Britax sells two versions of the Roundabout: the Roundabout (also called G4.1) and the Roundabout 50 Classic. The Roundabout 50 Classic is the basic model that works to 50 lbs. The Roundabout G4.1 works to 55 lbs. and features deeper sidewalls for side impact protection and a new, lower first harness height (8″). That addresses a complaint we had about previous Roundabouts, whose lowest harness height was too tall for the smallest infants. Other small differences: the 50 Classic lacks built-in lock-offs for the seat belt (which makes installation more tight). And the 50 Classic doesn't have Britax's newer SafeCell technology, which absorbs energy in a crash.

Both Roundabouts have an harness that is easy to use and adjust with straps that don't twist.

What's not to like about the Roundabout? Well, despite the lesser 50 or 55 lbs. weight limit the Roundabout is about the same size as the Marathon (26″ in height). That makes it a tight fit when rear-facing in smaller vehicles. On the plus side, the Roundabout weighs significantly less than the Marathon (17.6 lbs. vs 30 lbs.). The

convertible seats

Marathon also has a cover that easily removes for cleaning, a feature the Roundabout lacks.

Bottom line: the Roundabout is a good convertible seat if your car seat budget is under $200. We'd suggest the newer Roundabout G4.1 versus the older Roundabout 50 Classic. And if your budget allows, the Marathon has numerous upgrades that make the additional expense worth it. **Rating: A**

CHICCO NEXTFIT

Price: $280.

Type: Convertible seat.

Limits: 5-40 lbs. rear-facing, 22-65 lbs. forward facing. 50" or less.

NHTSA ease of use rating: ★★★★☆

Pros: Nine recline positions. Side impact protection with deep side wings. Easy to install. Premium LATCH connectors. No rethread harness. Belt lockoffs for seatbelt installs. Cover can be machine washed.

Cons: No anti-rebound feature. Early version had harness pads that were too close to a baby's neck, generating some complaints from users. Also the harness was hard to adjust. This was fixed in a revised version. Large seat may not work in smaller vehicles.

Comments: After successfully topping the infant car seat charts with their KeyFit infant seat, Chicco's NextFit launched in 2013 as the brand's first effort on the convertible car seat market.

The seat features nine (!) recline positions, dual level indicators and a harness rated for 65 lbs. forward-facing (40 lbs. rear-facing). The NextFit has a small footprint (to work well with smaller cars) as well as an infant insert cushion.

The NextFit features "Super Cinch" LATCH technology, which Chicco says will make it easier to install than competing seats. Also innovative: the seat's harness widens to accommodate larger toddlers. The no rethread harness is a major plus. And yes, the NextFit has side impact protection.

What does all this Chicco car seat goodness cost? $280, which makes this seat quite competitive with Britax's offerings. We were surprised the price for this seat is under $300, considering the KeyFit infant seat runs a bit more than most other infant seats.

Feedback on this seat has been positive, although some parents have complained about the strap adjustment–they find the straps get twisted and have to be "dug out" from underneath the child. The high harness height (17.5" for the NextFit; for comparison, the Advocate is 17") is a plus.

It's clear Chicco has done its homework with the NextFit: the seat is very easy to install, either with LATCH or vehicle belt. We like the harness adjuster and recline, which are as easy to use as any Britax seat. The attention to detail is obvious: note the storage compartment for the LATCH and tether straps; the fabric is also excellent quality and soft to the touch. Many parents say their kids prefer the Chicco NextFit to other convertibles when it comes to comfort.

As with any version 1.0 seat, there are always bugs to work out. Example: unlike the Britax Advocate, there is no velcro on the sides of the NextFit to hold the harness when the seat isn't in use. As a result, once a child is put in the seat, the parent has to fish around under the child to find the harness. Ditto for the crotch strap.

Other negatives include the seat's large bulk (yes the base is narrow, but the rest of the seat is huge) and weight (you won't want to haul this on an airplane).

And a few folks complained about the NextFit's deep side walls (which are there for side impact protection)—getting a squirmy toddler in and out of the seat can be a challenge, thanks to these walls. So even though the NextFit expands to better fit toddlers, the deep side walls somewhat defeat the innovation when it comes to ease of use.

Another minor negative: we also see reports that the rear-facing harness position is too small/tight, positioning the straps too close together—this has annoyed some babies.

Perhaps the biggest initial complaint area for the NextFit is the harness. The harness pads are universally panned by readers—too bulky/rough, they cut into a baby's neck, etc. Others complained the harness is hard to tighten. And the chest clip is way to easy to unbuckle (for enterprising toddlers).

Chicco quietly moved to address the harness issues in late 2013—now the hated harness pads are removable (if you choose), a revised crotch strap is now longer and the harness is easier to adjust.

Unfortunately, Chicco hasn't changed the model name to reflect these refinements to the NextFit. The models made after November 2013 have the tweaks. So if you decide this is the convertible seat for you, make sure you are getting a seat made after that time. (One clue: see if the harness pads are removeable. Initial NextFits did not allow for the harness pads to be removed. Revised NextFits have removable harness pads).

FYI: Chicco has launched a couple of spin-offs of the NextFit in the past year—the NextFit Zip ($280, a Target exclusive) includes a cover that zips off for easy cleaning. Also new: the NextFit CX ($300) adds a "comfort flex" harness that keeps the harness "up and out-of-the way for easy in/out." Our view: these are nice upgrades but not necessary if you decide you want this seat.

Bottom line: this is a excellent seat that we will recommend. Installation is a snap and the overall safety features are excellent. ***Rating: A***

CLEK FLLO

Price: $370-$400.

Type: Convertible seat.

Limits: 14 to 50 lbs. rear facing, 22 to 65 lbs. forward facing, 49″ tall.

NHTSA ease of use rating: Not yet.

Pros: More compact version of Clek's flagship seat. Unique crumple zone for crash protection. Anti-rebound bar.

Cons: Can't be used for infants who are not sitting up on their own yet. Pricey.

Comments: Clek's flagship seat the Foonf made a splash when it debuted with advanced crash protection, rigid LATCH connectors and an anti-rebound bar. But the seat's large bulk and weight quickly became an issue, as some parents complained it required a cavernous rear seat to work.

So Clek has rolled out the Fllo, which it bills as a more compact version of the Foonf. Here are the main differences:

◆ The rigid LATCH detachable base on the Foonf is replaced by a non-removable base that is more compact and has an integrated rear-facing recline feature.

◆ The Fllo weighs about 10 lbs. less than the Foonf.

◆ The Fllo is about four inches smaller from front to back, if you remove the anti-rebound bar. The shell is about an inch shorter.

The Fllo suffers from the same drawbacks as the Foonf—namely, the lack of seat padding that makes it about as comfortable as a gym bleacher. This is an odd oversight for a seat that is close to $400. On the plus side, the changes to the Fllo trim about $100 off the retail price of the seat compared to the Foonf.

We're a bit perplexed about the marketing of this seat as compact. Yes, it shaves an inch here and there compared to the massive Foonf. But a seat with a shell that is 31″ tall is still huge compared to market leader Britax's seats, whose shell is 28.5″ tall with the headrest fully extended on the Boulevard. (Yeah, 2.5″ may not sound like much, but it could be the difference between fitting in a vehicle and not).

We'll give this seat the same rating as the Foonf—we like the lower price and overall emphasis in safety, but the lack of seat padding and large size limit its appeal. ***Rating: A-***

CLEK FOONF

Price: $370-$500.

Type: Convertible seat.

Limits: 14 to 50 lbs. rear facing, 20 to 65 lbs. forward facing, 49″ tall.

NHTSA ease of use rating:

⭐⭐☆☆☆ Rear-facing
⭐⭐⭐☆☆ Front facing

Pros: Premium seat that can fit three across in a backseat. Rigid LATCH for front-facing mode. Unique crumple zone for crash protection. Anti-rebound bar.

Cons: $500? And it doesn't work with infants who can't sit up alone?

Comments: Clek is the Canadian company known for its popular booster seats with rigid LATCH connectors and funky names. The Foonf is their first effort in the convertible seat category.

The Foonf is ground-breaking. It features a narrow base that allows three-across seating, an aluminum "crumple zone" in the seat for energy absorption, anti-rebound bar more and more. There are also little interesting touches like magnets that hold open the harness when putting baby in or out of the seat. With all these over-the-top safety features, the Foonf is like the Volvo of car seats.

So is it worth the nearly $500 price tag? (Ok, previous year versions of the Foonf can be found online for $370, but the official retail is $500).

Well, you do get quite a few premium features, such as the IMMI flexible LATCH attachments for rear facing and rigid LATCH for forward-facing mode. Like Clek's Oobr, there is also an integrated headrest. And there is a recline feature when the seat is rear-facing. The Foonf's weight limits are 40 lbs. rear-facing and 65 forward-facing.

The biggest negative: the Foonf is not rated for infant use—a child must be at least 14 lbs. and be able to sit up alone to use the seat, which is practically unheard of for a seat that can be used rear-facing. And in case your wondering, the average age a child can sit up unassisted ranges from five to eight months.

Clek continues to tweak the Foonf with improvements. In the past year, Clek has made some minor tweaks to the Foonf: the crotch buckle is now adjustable, with a longer length for bigger kids. Clek has also refined the anti-rebound bar, so it is easier to use and install. Feedback from parents is mostly very positive, although the seat does have its critics. The negatives we've heard include stiff straps, a poorly written manual and a lack of seat padding. Another concern: the lack of recline when the seat is in its forward-facing position frustrates parents of napping toddlers. And the Foonf is very heavy—38 lbs.

The Foonf's bulk and footprint are another negative if you have a smaller vehicle. With the headrest extended the Foonf is 32.5" tall (for comparison, Britax's seats are about 26").; when installed rear-facing, it extends 33" from the back of the seat to the anti-rebound bar—one parent commented that it was so large, she had to take care to avoid hitting her child on the door jam when she removed her baby from the Foonf.

Of all the complaints, the lack of seat padding is the Foonf's biggest flaw, in our opinion. For nearly $500, you'd think Clek

convertible seats

would have lined the seat with expensive memory foam imported from Sweden ... making the Foonf the most comfortable, cushiest car seat on the market. Yet, the Foonf is as hard as a gym bleacher, as one parent put it. (For folks who have a smaller vehicle, Clek makes a more compact version of this seat called the Fllo).

Bottom line: is the Foonf really worth the hefty price tag? We will recommend it, as long as you don't plan to do any long road trips or commutes, thanks to the lack of seat padding. Fans love this seat's construction and safety features. Ease of installation is another plus. But you'll need a vehicle with a spacious back seat to make the Foonf work. *Rating: A-*

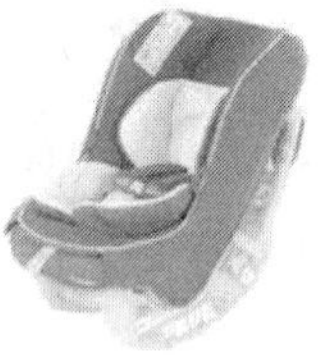

COMBI COCCORO
Price: $202-$235
Type: Convertible seat.
Limits: 3 to 33 lbs. rear facing, 20 to 40 lbs. forward facing, 40" tall.
NHTSA ease of use rating:
★★★☆☆ Rear-facing
★★★☆☆ Forward-facing

Pros: Small size = good fit for compact vehicles.
Cons: Can be hard to install rear facing.
Comments: The Coccoro is a compact car seat (it weighs just 11 lbs.), pitched for parents with small cars. Thanks to its small base size, Combi offers this seat as a solution for parents who need to fit three car seats across the backseat. The top harness slot is 15," which is impressive for a compact seat. Another plus: the Coccoro has built-in lock off clips, a nice safety feature. And the Coccoro comes in a series of bright colors.

Parent feedback on this seat has been positive, although a few have complained that it is hard to install rear facing. *Consumer Reports* echoed that view, with a "poor" rating for the Coccoro's fit to vehicle, rear facing. That dragged down CR's overall opinion of the seat, which scored LAST overall, even though crash protection was judged very good. The NHTSA gives the Coccoro an overall three-star rating for ease of use, although again installation in rear facing mode comes in for criticism.

So it is a mixed review for the Coccoro—this is a good seat if you have a smaller child (and only need a seat with a 40 lb. limit) and/or you have a smaller car. The Coccoro's biggest fans are those with the smallest vehicles, such as a VW Beetle or Honda Civic. Overall parent feedback on the Coccoro is quite positive. But be aware of the poor fit and installation issues when in rear facing mode. *Rating: B*

SEATS

CAR

(Reorganized:)

Cosco Apt 40 RF/50
Price: $46 to $70
Type: Convertible seat.
NHTSA ease of use rating:
⭐⭐☆☆☆ Rear facing
⭐⭐⭐☆☆ Forward facing

Limits: Apt 40: 5 to 40 lbs. rear facing, 22 to 40 lbs. front-facing. Apt 50: to 50 lbs. front-facing.

Pros: Budget friendly seat that works to 40 lbs. rear-facing. Five harness slots; three crotch positions. New Apt 50 has six harness slots.

Cons: Built-in cup holders make seat wider than others. Top harness slot on Apt 40 is only 13", meaning older toddlers will outgrow this seat quickly.

Comments: The Apt debuted in 2012 and is basically an updated Scenera, Cosco's popular and affordable convertible seat. The differences? The Apt has deep side walls for side impact protection and two intergraded cup holders.

Feedback on the Apt has been positive—the seat is easy to install and is one of the more affordable options on the market for rear-facing use up to 40 lbs. (Walmart sells this seat for under $50). On the other hand, critics note the low top harness slot (13") means bigger kids will outgrow this seat by height more quickly than the 40 lb. weight limit.

Another issue: the built-in cup holders make the seat wider than the Cosco Scenera—and that makes the Apt a tight fit in some back seats where space is an issue (or when trying to fit three seats across). Finally, in order to clean the cover (which features all-over elastic), you must first remove the harness, which is a pain.

FYI: there are now two Apts on the market: the Apt 40 RF and the Apt 50, which is new for 2015. The Apt 50 features another harness slot position, allowing for the higher forward-facing limit of 50 lbs. Also new: a cover that can be machine washed and dried.

Bottom line: it is a mixed review for the Apt. We know kids love cup holders, but that design features makes the Apt much wider than the similarly priced, entry-level Cosco Scenera. And that could be a deal-killer if you have a smaller back seat. ***Rating: B***

Cosco Scenera/Scenera Next
Price: $39 to $60
Type: Convertible seat.
NHTSA ease of use rating:
⭐⭐⭐☆☆ Rear facing
⭐⭐⭐☆☆ Forward facing

Limits: 5 to 35/40 lbs. rear facing, 22 to 40 lbs. front-facing.
Pros: Affordable car seat for a second car. Good for airplane travel.
Cons: No side impact protection or EPS foam. Fabric and padding is very basic. Top barness slot only 13" tall.

Comments: This simple seat is our top pick for that occasionally-used second car or Grandma's vehicle. The Scenera isn't fancy: you get a five-point harness with four height positions and three crotch slots. The padding is very simple and there isn't any EPS foam, side-impact protection or other goodies. But then again, this seat starts at just $40—perfect when you need an affordable seat that is easy to install and use.

Consumer Reports picked this seat as a best buy in their most recent rankings, giving it an "excellent" in crash protection. As for ease of use, the Scenera earned just two stars from the NHTSA, with rear facing installation holding the seat's rating down. Nonetheless, we think this is a good, basic seat for secondary use.

Most reader feedback on this seat has been positive, with most parents finding it easy to install and use. The only hitch: the Scenera has a kick-stand that has to be flipped out when forward facing. Some folks forget to do this and complain about difficulty of installation. FYI: Cosco has eliminated this feature from the new, similarly priced Apt seat, (which is somewhat wider).

Critics note the lack of padding or fancy fabric; the Scenera also lacks an infant insert, which means the smallest infants may not fit well in the seat. And the top harness slot is only 13", so it is doubtful a kid will hit the 40 lb. weight limit before outgrowing this seat by height. But that's the trade-off for getting the price so low—again, we think this seat is best for that little-used second car or Grandma's car. Fans love the light weight, which is especially nice for airplane travel.

FYI: The Cosco Scenera is a Walmart exclusive, although we occasionally see this seat pop up on other web sites.

New for 2015, Cosco has debuted a updated version of this seat called the Scenera Next, which works to 40 lbs. rear-facing and has a new narrow profile (17" wide). It is a Walmart exclusive at $46 to $50. Later in 2015. Cosco will phase out the older Scenera in favor of this new model. ***Rating: B+***

DIONO OLYMPIA
Price: $259
Type: Convertible to belt-positioning booster
Limits: 5-45 lbs. rear-facing, 20-70 lbs. front-facing, 50-100 lbs. as a booster.
NHTSA ease of use rating:
★★☆☆☆ Rear facing
★★☆☆☆ Forward facing
★☆☆☆☆ Booster mode

Comments: The new Diono Olympia is based on the Radian R100, an older Diono model reviewed later in this section. It has the same enhanced weight limits as the Diono Pacifica and Rainier, but is more basic.

The Olympia omits the infant body support pillow, cup holder and protective headrest seen on the Rainier. Hence, the Olympia might be best for older babies that don't need the infant support pillow.

Like all the revised Diono models, the Olympia has added side impact protection (compression walls at the head area, a rigid double wall structure on the sides) and upgraded fabrics (called Silk Tech) that are wipeable and wick for comfort in hotter temperatures. The added side impact protection to the Olympia doesn't expand the seat's width, which is rather impressive.

The Olympia gets good marks from readers—fans like the seat's overall ease of use and design. The narrow base lets you fit three seats across in most vehicles.

The biggest negatives include the amount of space the seat needs in rear-facing mode—if you have a smaller vehicle, it might not fit. LATCH installation can be tricky in some vehicles, especially rear-facing, thanks to the location of the LATCH attachments. (We discussed this issue in the review for the Rainer, which is a sister model to the Olympia).

The NHTSA ease of use ratings for this seat are quite low (just two out of five stars when used with a harness). That's primarily due to the seat's mediocre instruction manual, which lacks illustrations of properly restrained children among other deficiencies.

We'll give this seat a B+ . . . overall, we like the Diono Rainer better, since it provides more value (the side impact cushions at the headrest, for example). The Rainer is only $75 more than the stripped down Olympia. **Rating: B+**

DIONO PACIFICA
Price: $261 to $278
Type: Convertible to belt-positioning booster
Limits: 5-50 lbs. rear-facing, 20-90 lbs. front-facing, 50-120 lbs. as a booster.
NHTSA ease of use rating:
★★★☆☆ Rear facing
★★☆☆☆ Forward facing
★★☆☆☆ Booster mode

Comments: The Diono Pacifica is the revised version of the Radian R120, a convertible seat that converts to a belt-positioning booster. This seat is the same as the new Diono Rainier, but omits the Rainier's headrest (side impact protection headwings). The Pacifica is about $50 less than the Rainer (at retail pricing).

Like all the revised Diono models, the Pacifica has added side impact protection (compression walls at the head area, a rigid double wall structure on the sides) and upgraded fabrics (called Silk Tech) that are wipeable and wick for comfort in hotter temperatures. The added side impact protection to the Pacifica doesn't add

convertible seats

to the seat's width, a definite plus.

The Pacifica does have the infant support cushions, same as the Rainier. Reader feedback on the Pacifica has been thin (the seat debuted in May 2014 but was backordered for a while), however, what we are hearing is positive. Fans love the memory foam in the seat (great for comfort for longer trips) and the seat's overall ease of use. The Pacifica is one of the few seats on the market that can be used rear-facing to 50 lbs., which is excellent (although we suspect few kids will make it to 50 lbs. and still be rear-facing in the seat). We also like the narrow base width—you can fit three of these in the back seat of most vehicles.

On the downside, the NHTSA rates for this seat are quite low—the government didn't like the labels on this seat and that dragged down the rating to an abysmal two out of five stars for booster and forward-facing mode.

Despite that negative note, we will recommend the Pacific. It is an excellent seat. If your car has side curtain air bags in the rear seat, then the Pacifica would be a very good choice. (If you vehicle does NOT have side curtain air bags in the rear seats, then upgrading to the Rainer with its additional side impact protection would be our recommendation).

FYI: As of this writing, Amazon is selling the Rainer for just $336, while the Pacifica is still $319. Given that small price difference, we'd probably suggest the Rainer for the added side impact protection. ***Rating: A***

DIONO RADIAN RXT / R120 / R100
Price: RXT $270, R120 $250, R100 $208
Type: Convertible (RXT converts to belt-positioning booster)
Limits: to 100 or 120 lbs. Height up to 57".
NHTSA ease of use rating:
R100: Rear-facing: 3 out of 5 stars. Forward-facing: 2 out of 5 stars. Booster mode: 2 out of 5 stars.

R120: Rear-facing 2 out of 5 stars. Forward-facing: 2 out of 5 stars. Booster mode: 2 out of 5 stars.

RXT: Rear-facing 2 out of 5 stars. Forward-facing: 2 out of 5 stars. Booster mode: 1 out of 5 stars.

Pros: Folds up! Works to 100/120 lbs., depending on the model. EPS foam. RXT has added side impact protection. Narrow base lets you fit three across.

Cons: Heavy weight. Biggest kids may find crotch strap too tight. Not as ideal for kids under one year of age riding rear facing. Low ratings on ease of use.

Comments: The Radian is Diono's flagship car seat brand that boasts three key advantages: extended harness use (up to 80 lbs.), a narrow base and a seat that is car pool friendly—yes, they fold up!

The Radian accomplishes its folding trick by omitting the base you see on so many convertible seats—the seat actually sits along the back of the vehicle's seat. One plus to this: the Radian's narrow base allows for a three-across install in the back of a vehicle.

The Radian has recently been refreshed and now comes in three versions: RXT, R120 and R100. All the seats feature steel alloy frames. And you can use LATCH up to 80 lbs. (65 lbs. for the R100), much higher than other seats on the market.

The RXT is the flagship and features a new trick: the harness removes so the seat can become a belt positioning booster (up to 120 lbs). The pitch: you can use this from birth (starting at 5 lbs.) rear-facing for infants, forward-facing for toddlers with a harness that works to 80 lbs. . . . and then in belt-positioning mode to 120 lbs. The RXT also features memory foam and side impact protection (wings that are near the top of the seat).

The R120 omits the side impact protection wings, but otherwise is much like the RXT (example: you still get the memory foam, etc) and has the same weight limits.

The entry level R100 is more bare bones: no memory foam and the booster mode is only rated to 100 lbs.

Reader feedback on the Diono Radian has generally been very positive. Folks love the narrow, low profile of the seats and their overall quality. Yes, you can fit three Radians in a back seat in most vehicles, which is difficult with many other seats.

What's not to like? Well, these seats are rather tall and that can make the fit rear-facing difficult in smaller vehicles. And even though these seats fold up, they are rather heavy (20+ pounds)—so lugging them around is no picnic. And for some reason, Diono bombed on the government's ease of use ratings, earning very low scores. That's odd because most parents tell us these seats are easy to use and install (except the previously noted rear-facing install in smaller vehicles).

Bottom line: the Diono Radian line is an excellent choice, especially for those who car pool or frequently travel. ***Rating: A***

DIONO RAINIER
Price: $288
Type: Convertible to belt-positioning booster
Limits: 5-50 lbs. rear-facing, 20-90 lbs. front-facing, 50-120 lbs. as a booster.

NHTSA ease of use rating:

⭐⭐☆☆☆ Rear facing

⭐⭐☆☆☆ Forward facing

⭐☆☆☆☆ Booster mode

Comments: The Diono Rainer is a new, improved version of the Radian RXT. The Rainer is Diono's top-of-the-line model.

The Rainier has a few enhancements over the RXT, chief among these higher weight limits (90 lbs. forward facing with harness for the Rainer vs. 80 lbs. in the harness for the RXT).

Like all the revised Diono models, the Rainier has added side impact protection (compression walls at the head area, a rigid double wall structure on the sides) and upgraded fabrics (called Silk Tech) that are wipeable and wick for comfort in hotter temperatures. The added side impact protection to the Rainer doesn't add to the seat's width, a plus.

The Rainier also includes new, deluxe infant body support cushions.

Reader feedback on this seat has been very positive. Fans love the seat's overall ease of use and added comfort (the memory foam in the seat, for example). The infant insert means you can use this seat with newborns. The narrow base means you can fit three of these seats in the back seat of most vehicles, a major plus with multiple car-seat age kids. The fabric also comes in for kudos—parents in hot climates say the Rainer's fabric remains cool despite summer heat.

So what's not to like? Well, the Rainer does not have a no-rethread harness—yep, that means you'll be rethreading the harness to change the height. For a $300+ seat, that is a glaring omission.

We also see a few complaints about the position of the LATCH buckles in rear-facing mode, which makes for difficult LATCH installation and adjustment in some vehicles. We see fewer complaints about belt installation, however.

Another negative: the Rainer's epic fail at the NHTSA ease of use ratings—a measly two out of five stars for rear and forward facing modes. An abysmal one out of five stars in booster mode. Poor instructions and labels (poor routing labels, the lack of pictures of a properly restrained child are examples) contributed to the low ratings. Another negative: you must remove the harness when converting to booster mode, but there is no place to store the harness in/on the seat. That means it could be misplaced if used later for another child.

Yep, it is pricey at nearly $300, but it's been significantly discounted on Amazon below the manufacturer's price. Considering the Diono Pacifica (which is like the Rainer but omits the additional side impact protection headwings) is pretty close in price, the Rainer probably makes more sense given the small upgrade in price but big improvements in features.

Bottom line: despite the NHTSA's ease of use ratings and somewhat lacking instructions, we will recommend the Rainer. It is an excellent seat, if you can live without a no-rethread harness. ***Rating: A***

Eddie Bauer XRS 65
Price: $172
Type: Convertible seat.
NHTSA ease of use rating:
⭐⭐ Rear facing
⭐⭐⭐ Forward facing

Limits: 5 to 40 lbs. rear facing, 22 to 65 lbs. front-facing.
Pros: 40 lb. rear facing; compact seat. EPP foam. Easy to install.
Cons: No recline. Must rethread harness to adjust height.
Comments: The Eddie Bauer XRS 65 features a 40 lb. rear-facing limit, four harness slots, three crotch positions and a relatively compact size. We liked the multi-position headrest, although the clunky cup holder might make installation near a door problematic (the cup holder is removeable).

The key downside to the XRS 65: you have to rethread the harness to adjust the harness height, which of course is common on lower price convertibles. And there are no recline positions for the Easy Fit 65.

Feedback on this seat seems split evenly between folks who like it and those who don't. The overall fit and easy install plus the EPP foam are mentioned as pluses, while critics say it is hard to install rear-facing . . . and the seat lacks many amenities (the harness is a pain to rethread). We've lowered the ratings on this seat based on continued installation frustration.

This seat used to be sold as the Easy Fit 65, which was discontinued. The fabric on the XRS is an upgrade from the Easy Fit although we don't quite see why the XRS is $40 more–it's not silk or something.

One caveat: you can find this exact seat minus the infant body pillow sold as the Safety 1st Guide 65 for just $78 at Walmart. If you don't need the infant pillow, save yourself $50 and go for the very similar Safety 1st Guide 65. ***Rating: B-***

Evenflo SureRide
This seat is reviewed on the free side of our web site at BabyBargains.com. Go to http://bit.ly/evenflosureride

Evenflo Symphony
Price: $165 to $230
Type: All in one: convertible seat and booster.
Limits: 5 to 40 lbs. rear-facing, 22 to 65 lbs. forward-facing with five-point harness, 40 to 110 lbs. as a belt-positioning booster.
NHTSA ease of use rating:
⭐⭐⭐ Rear, forward facing, booster
IIHS rating for booster mode:
Base model: Good bet; e3 version: Best bet.

Comments: The Symphony is Evenflo's attempt at that car seat holy grail—the all-in-one seat that works with newborns up to kids who weigh 110 lbs., which would be your average 12 year old.

SureLATCH is the headline here: Evenflo's new LATCH connectors that tout a "super-fast, tight and safe installation." SureLATCH features built-in retractors that eliminate belt slack—this makes the Symphony one of the easier seats to install with LATCH.

Confusingly, Evenflo makes seven different versions of the Symphony, all with different suffixes (Symphony LX, Symphony DLX, etc). Then to add even more confusion, there are also Platinum and ProComfort versions of the seat—a Platinum LX and Platinum DLX, as an example.

So we'll try to make some sense of this. The lowest price versions of the Symphony are called the LX and omit the e3 side impact protection and SureLATCH—the LX runs $168-$200. Step up to the DLX version of the seat and you get the extra side impact protection (called e3) and SureLATCH—the DLX costs $190-$230.

The next level are the ProComfort Symphonys—these add "Gel Matrix" padding and no rethread harnesses on top of the DLX features. This seat is a Target exclusive for $240.

At the top end are the Platinum Symphonys—Evenflo adds Outlast fabric (which absorbs hot and cold temperatures) as well as a few other upgrades like buckle pockets to hold a harness when a child isn't in the inset. The Platinum seats run about $250.

Parent feedback on the Symphony overall has been positive. Fans like the removable padding for infants and excellent harness adjuster.

As for ease of use, the Symphony earned three out of five stars— not the best, not the worst. *Consumer Reports* gives the Symphony a "very good" rating for crash protection.

We found the Symphony's booster mode better designed than a similar model by Dorel's Safety 1st—it's easy to adjust and will provide a good fit for older kids. BUT, the Symphony is not a very tall booster . . . that means kids will probably outgrow it by height long before the stated 120 lb. limit.

Bottom line: this seat is probably one of the better attempts at an "all in one" seat. If you have your heart set on buying just one seat that works from birth to 120 pounds, skip the Safety 1st option and go with this one. ***Rating: B+***

EVENFLO TITAN
Price: $100.
Type: Convertible seat.
Limits: 5 to 40 lbs. rear facing, 20 to 65 lbs. forward facing.
NHTSA ease of use rating:
⭐⭐⭐☆☆ Rear facing
⭐⭐☆☆☆ Forward facing

Pros: Affordable seat that works to 65 lbs. Premium LATCH connectors (Walmart version).

Cons: Hard to clean cover and adjust straps. Twisty straps.

Comments: Here's another seat to consider for grandma's car—the Evenflo Titan is a bare-bones seat where the price ($100) is right. Nothing fancy here: you get a five-point harness, four shoulder positions and simple padding.

FYI: Evenflo makes several versions of the Titan. The Walmart version of this seat (called just the Titan) includes premium LATCH connectors (called SureSafe). And we should note the Titan is very similar to the Evenflo SureRide, another Evenflo affordable convertible.

Like the Cosco Scenera, the Evenflo Titan has little side-impact protection, fancy padding, but, hey, it's affordable. Most reader feedback on the Titan is positive, with folks saying the Titan provides good value with basic features. The big gripe we heard from parents on the Titan were the straps—some found the harness hard to adjust, especially when the seat is rear facing. Yes, you have to rethread the harness when you change the harness height, which is common on low-price convertible seats.

Between the Evenflo Titan and the Coscco Scenera, we think either would be a good bet for Grandma. If you are on a tight budget, the Scenera is a good deal at $40 to $50. But if you step up to the Evenflo Titan, you get a seat that works to 65 lbs. (versus 40 or 50 lbs. for the Scenera) and premium LATCH connectors (SureSafe) that will ease installation. ***Rating: B+***

EVENFLO TRIBUTE
Price: $45-$70
Type: Convertible seat.
Limits: 5 to 35 (or 40 depending on version) lbs. rear facing, 20 to 40 lbs. forward facing.
NHTSA ease of use rating:
⭐⭐☆☆☆ Rear and forward facing.
Pros: Least expensive Evenflo seat. Works to 40 lbs. rear-facing.

Cons: Competitors have better ease of use. Skimpy padding.

Comments: The Tribute is Evenflo's opening price point seat: starting at $50, the Tribute comes in several trim levels (Sport, Select and LX). The only difference between the trims is fabric: Sport is the least fancy, LX is the "deluxe" version which also adds a cup holder. Walmart sells a version of the Tribute called the Select; same basic seat, different fabric, no cup holder.

Like the Cosco Scenera (the Tribute's main competition at this price point), the Tribute is a bare bones seat: while you do get EPS foam for crash protection, there is no added side impact protection. The padding is very basic. Want to change the harness height? You'll have to rethread the harness. And the seat only works to 40 lbs. (more expensive seats work up to 50 or 65 lbs., like the Evenflo Titan).

On the plus side, the Tribute works rear-facing to 40 lbs., which will enable the average child to be rear-facing to age two (as is the recommendation). FYI: A couple older versions of the Tribute that only work to 35 lbs. rear-facing are still be sold in some stores and online.

So if you are looking at the Evenflo Tribute versus the Cosco Scenera, which one would be best for a second vehicle or Grandma's car? Well, the Cosco Scenera scored much higher on *Consumer Reports* tests than the Tribute. While both seats have similar crash protection, the Cosco Scenera has better rear-facing fit to vehicle.

As for ease of use, the Tribute scores a low two out of five stars on the NHTSA's tests; the Scenera scored higher (three out of five stars). Most parent reviews on the Tribute are positive—fans say this seat is great for airplane travel (rental cars). But the lack of padding will make it uncomfortable for long driving trips. And some parents complain it is difficult to install rear facing.

Bottom line: Between the two entry level seats (Cosco Scenera and the Evenflo Tribute), we like the Cosco Scenera better. But the Tribute is not a bad second choice for that second vehicle. ***Rating: B***

EVENFLO TRIUMPH
Price: $80 to $160.
Type: Convertible seat.
Limits: 5 to 40 lbs. rear facing, 20 to 65 lbs. forward facing.
NHTSA ease of use rating:
⭐⭐⭐☆☆ Rear and forward facing.
Pros: Special harness "remembers" last setting, EPP foam, up-front five-position recline and harness adjustment (no re-threading). Half the price of similar Britax seats.
Cons: Tension knob is hard to adjust when seat is in rear facing mode. Wide base may not fit in smaller cars. Can only use the top harness slot when forward facing, making the seat difficult to use for larger (but young) infants. Deep recline only works when rear-facing.
Comments: The Triumph used to be Evenflo's flagship car seat offering, but has since been eclipsed by the Symphony. The Triumph soldiers on as a mid price convertible offering ($110 to $160) with an impressive list of features.

As always, Evenflo makes the Triumph in a series of versions, four at last count. Hence, you'll see a basic, stripped-down Triumph in Walmart (Triumph Select) for $79 . . . and then the top-of-the-line version in Babies R Us for $160.

The Triumph's key feature are the TensionRight knobs on either side of the seat that tighten the harness from the side of the seat and the infinite slide harness adjustment system (no rethreading). All the knobs on the Evenflo seat have both fans and detractors—give it a try in the store to see if you find it easy to adjust.

Another stand-out: a no rethread harness. Yes, even on the $79 version sold at Walmart, which is probably the lowest price convertible on the market with this handy feature.

The cheapest Triumph has clip-on cup holders, basic fabric and basic LATCH connectors. Step up to the Triumph with SureSafe and you get premium LATCH connectors (SureSafe). The ProComfort Triumph LX adds "gel matrix" seat padding and integrated cup holders. The most expensive Triumph (Platinum Triumph) has "OutLast" fabrics that absorb heat and cold temps—this is a Babies R Us exclusive for $160.

So, should you buy one? Looking at parent feedback, we see quite a split opinion on this seat. Take ease of use, for example. The current Triumph scores just three out of five stars for ease of use in the NHTSA's evaluation. *Consumer Reports* echoed that view, with average ease of use ratings weighing down the seat's overall score (18th out of 24 seats ranked). That's probably due to the difficulty in adjusting the TensionRight knob when the seat is rear facing. Another negative: the wide seat width (19.5") means this seat will eat up much of your backseat, a problem if you drive a small to mid-size vehicle.

Fans say this seat is easy to install and the no-rethread harness is a big plus, especially at this price. Critics point out the Triumph has frustrating limitations. The Triumph has two recline position, but the deepest recline feature on the Triumph only works when the seat is rear-facing. And you can't switch between the semi-reclined and upright position without un-installing and re-installing the seat . . . which is crazy.

The new "Outlast" fabrics on the Platinum Triumph don't wash well, report more than one parent dismayed at the fabric that frayed. Some even said the Outlast fabric frays without washing. You'd think Evenflo would have done more testing on this special expensive fabric before touting it as a premium feature. And the integrated cup holders sound great in theory—but in the real world, they don't even hold a sippy cup. The Triumph lacks harness covers or belt lock-offs, which ease belt installations.

Bottom line: the Triumph is an affordable seat whose ace in the hold is the no-rethread ("infinite slide") harness. But various glitches mar this seat and prevent us from recommending it. ***Rating: C***

convertible seats

GRACO 4EVER

Price: $300 (at Babies R Us exclusively).

Type: Convertible seat, booster.

Limits: 4-40 lbs. rear-facing, 20-65 lbs. in harness mode forward facing and 30-100 lbs. as a belt-positioning booster. Backless booster 40-120 lbs.

NHTSA ease of use rating: Not yet.

IIHS rating for booster mode: Not yet.

Pros: All-in-one seat works from 4 lbs. through booster mode. No rethread harness. Six recline positions; ten position adjustable headrest. Side impact protection.

Cons: New seat has little third party ratings yet or crash tests. Pricey at $300. Only at Babies R Us.

Comments: The all-in-one car seat is the Fountain of Youth for car seat makers—the mythical seat that works from birth to college (ok, as a belt-positioning booster to 120 lbs., or when kids age out of booster seats and can correctly fit in a regular seat belt).

Yet like Ponce De Leon, Graco's quest for the perfect all-in-one seat has been one of frustrating missteps. Their last effort, the SmartSeat, received mixed reviews from parents, many of whom cited negatives like the seat's bulk and a harness that was hard to use.

Amid that backdrop, we now have Graco's latest effort in this category: the Graco 4Ever. This seat is similar to the new Graco Milestone, which is an exclusive to Target and Walmart. The big difference is the booster mode: the 4Ever converts to a backless booster for use up to 120 lbs. The Milestone works as a belt-positioning booster to 100 lbs. . . . but no backless mode.

There are some other small differences as well—the 4Ever has two built-in cup holders. The Milestone has a single cup holder attached to the side of the seat. The 4Ever has six recline positions and a headrest with ten positions that can be adjusted with one hand. The Milestone has only four recline positions. Of course, the 4Ever costs $70 more than the Milestone, which seems like a lot of cash for the backless booster mode (a backless booster can be bought for $20 or so in most stores).

Graco clearly has put a lot of thought into the 4Ever. Little touches like the harness that stores away in booster mode (you don't have to remove it from the seat) are very nice. Unlike the giant SmartSeat, the 4Ever is easier to fit in a vehicle in rear-facing mode. The steel reinforced frame and EPS lined seat are pluses. You also get premium "push-on" LATCH connectors, which you would expect at this price point.

What's not to love? Readers say in rear-facing mode, the seat's harness can be tricky to tighten. There is little third-party testing of the seat so far, as it debuted in summer 2014. (The NHTSA's ease of use and IIHS booster mode evaluation are pending; *Consumer Reports* hasn't weighed in with an independent crash test). Early adopters of this seat tell us it is easy to use . . . but the lack of a belt lock-off when used with a seat belt is a curious omission for a $300 seat.

As a Babies R Us exclusive, you won't be able to snag this seat on discount from Amazon.

We'll give this seat an A-. If you like the concept but find $300 hard to swallow, the Milestone at $230 would be a good alternative. ***Rating: A-***

GRACO CLASSIC RIDE 50

This seat is reviewed on the free side of our web site at BabyBargains.com/?p=20367

GRACO COMFORTSPORT

This seat is reviewed on the free side of our web site at BabyBargains.com/?p=1109

GRACO CONTENDER 65
Price: $140
Type: Convertible seat.
Limits: 5-40 lbs. rear facing; 20-65 lbs. forward facing.
NHTSA ease of use rating:
★★★★☆ Rear-facing
★★★☆☆ Forward-facing

Comments: Based on the Size4Me platform, the Contender 65 is a lower-priced version of that model. What's missing? Gone is the fancy sliding recline feature, replaced by a simple three-position bar recline. There's also a single LATCH strap instead of two in the Size4Me. Other than that, you basically get the same seat as the Size4Me (aka the Fit4Me).

Official retail for the Contender convertibles is $160. That would make them about $20 to $40 less than the Size4Me/Fit4Me seats. Our only caveat to Contender would be the single LATCH strap—we've seen complaints about installation of other Graco seats that have this set-up . . . so the jury is out on that.

The Contender is exclusive to Walmart at this time. We'll rate the seat essentially what its parent seat is rated. ***Rating: C.***

GRACO HEAD WISE
Comments: This seat is the same as the Graco My Size, but adds side impact protection in the form of Graco's "Safety Surround" headrest. The Head Wise 70 retails for $200 at Target. See the review of the Graco Size4Me for specs and a rating.

convertible seats

GRACO MILESTONE

Price: $229 (at Target and Walmart exclusively).
Type: Convertible seat, booster.
Limits: 5-40 lbs. rear-facing, 20-65 lbs. in harness mode forward facing and 30-100 lbs. as a belt-positioning booster
NHTSA ease of use rating: Not yet.

IIHS rating for booster mode: Not yet.

Pros: All in one seat works from 4 lbs. through booster mode. Affordable. No rethread harness.

Cons: New seat has little third party ratings yet or crash tests. Doesn't work as a backless booster, as sister model 4Ever does.

Comments: Graco has had limited success in the "all in one" car seat category (most notably with the Smart Seat), but the company is giving it another try with the Milestone. In fact, the Milestone has similar specs to the Smart Seat with one exception: the Milestone retails for $229, while the Smart Seat is $300.

The Milestone omits the Smart Seat's stay in the car base, which was a funky feature for a convertible seat that made the SmartSeat very heavy and wide.

Key feature of the Milestone include EPS foam lined seat, side impact protection headwings, four position recline and an adjustable headrest. The seat pad is removable and machine washable. We liked the no rethread harness, which is impressive at this price level.

The Milestone was released in mid 2014 and (as of this writing) there is little crash test or safety ratings for it—the NHTSA hasn't reviewed it for ease of use, nor has the IIHS weighed in on the seat in booster mode. Ditto for *Consumer Reports* crash tests—the Milestone didn't make it into their most recent report.

That leaves us with a smattering of reader reviews, who generally give the Milestone a thumbs up. Fans like the seat's overall comfort and value—at $229, the extended use of the seat (from convertible to high back booster) wins many fans.

So what's the difference between the Milestone and Graco's other new all-in-one seat, the 4Ever? The big difference is the booster mode: the 4Ever converts to a backless booster to 120 lbs. The Milestone has no backless mode and stops at 100 lbs. The 4Ever also has more recline positions than the Milestone, plus works better for preemies (the 4ever starts at 4 lbs.; the Milestone at 5 lbs.). The downside? The 4ever is $300 and a Babies R Us exclusive—you could argue the $70 isn't worth it since you can buy a backless booster for $20.

We'll give the Milestone our recommendation, despite the somewhat thin parent feedback and lack of third party testing. We will revise this review as we see more data. ***Rating: B+***

GRACO MY RIDE 65 / 70

Price: $118 to $180.

Type: Convertible seat.

Limits: 4 to 40 lbs., rear facing, up to 65/70 lbs. forward facing

NHTSA ease of use rating:

★★★★☆ Rear facing

★★★★☆ Forward facing. FYI: The version with Safety Surround earned three out of five stars in both positions.

Pros: Affordable seat that works to 40 lbs. rear-facing and up to 70 lbs. forward. One version (with Safety Surround) has enhanced side impact protection.

Cons: Difficult LATCH installation, strap adjustments.

Comments: This is Graco's effort at an affordable convertible seat that works to 65 pounds. Reaction from readers, however, is mostly negative. Yes, folks love the 40 lb. rear-facing limit, but the complicated LATCH installation (Graco uses a single strap that runs under the seat in rear facing mode) makes a tight fit difficult in some vehicles. The recessed cup holders are now built into the seat (in earlier versions of the My Ride, they weren't—and that generated quite a few complaints). Adjusting the straps is also quite difficult, especially when compared to Britax's seats.

Despite the mixed reader feedback, the 65 version earned four out of five stars in the government's ease of use ratings (although the 65 with Safety Surround earned only three out of five). And *Consumer Reports* picked this seat as a best buy, even though it ended up scoring ten out of 23 in their most recent report on convertible car seats. We can see their point on affordability: $120 to $150 for a seat that works to 65 or 70 lbs. is a value.

Given the split opinion, we'll side with our readers on this seat and only give it an average rating. Bottom line: while we salute Graco's effort to make an affordable 65 lb. limit seat, the trade-offs in ease of use and design drag down the My Ride's rating.

By the way, the "Safety Surround," version adds an optional/removeable head cushion for infants and built-in side impact protection for older kids. The head cushion for infants adjusts up or down to accommodate a growing child. The My Ride 65 with Safety Surround is $180 at Buy Buy Baby.

FYI: Some versions of the My Ride 65 feature special newborn insert cushions that enable the seat to fit infants as small as four pounds (parents of preemies, take note). And we should also note there is a My Ride 70 sold at Target for $160. It basically the same as the My Ride 65 but works to 70 lbs. forward-facing. ***Rating: C***

convertible seats

GRACO READY RIDE

This seat is reviewed on the free side of our web site at BabyBargains.com/?p=20371

GRACO SIZE4ME (AKA FIT4ME & MY SIZE)

Price: $150-$180

Type: Convertible seat.

Limits: 4-40 lbs. rear facing, 20 to 65 lbs. forward facing.

NHTSA ease of use rating:

★★★★☆ Rear and forward facing.

Pros: No rethread harness, adjustable headrest, seat recline, extended rear-facing use. Integrated cup holder.

Cons: Harness can be difficult to tighten; buckle hard to release. Skimpy padding in base.

Comments: This seat is Graco's mid-price offering and goes under several names: Size4Me, Fit4Me and My Size.

The seat features an adjustable headrest, no-rethread harness, three-position recline and upgraded LATCH connectors (called Right LATCH). There's also a removable head/body support for newborns.

Parent feedback on this seat has been mostly positive—fans laud the extended rear-facing weight limit, easy to clean fabric, and easy LATCH installation. The top harness height is a generous 17"—that means kids will be able to use the seat with a five-point harness to age six or even seven.

The negatives? Well, the harness can be tricky to adjust, with even Graco addressing this issue with tips on their blog. The buckle can also be hard to release. Other critics note the lack of padding in the base of the seat, which could be uncomfortable for toddlers on longer trips.

On the plus side, this seat scored four out of five stars for ease of use in NHTSA's evaluation. And *Consumer Reports* ranked it seventh (out of 23 seats tested) overall, which isn't too shabby.

Given the more recent positive parent feedback, we'll raise our rating for this seat this time out. While this seat doesn't quite compare with the Britax seats on ease of use and overall features, it is a good runner-up choice. And it runs $100 less than most Britax offerings. ***Rating B+***

GRACO SMART SEAT

This seat is reviewed on the free side of our web site at BabyBargains.com/?p=5595

MAXI COSI PRIA 70 / 85

Price: Pria 70: $200;
Pria 70 with TinyFit: $232;
Pria 70 Leather: $700;
Pria 85: $240

Type: Convertible seat.

Limits: 4 to 40 lbs. rear facing (with TinyFit insert; 9 to 40 lbs. without), 22 to 70 lbs. forward facing (up to 85 lb. forward facing for Pria 85.).

NHTSA ease of use rating:

★★☆☆☆ Rear facing
★★★★☆ Forward facing.

(Ratings for Pria 70 only.)

Pros: TinyFit infant insert good for preemies (starting at 4 lbs.). Side impact protection. Small footprint means seat will fit into smaller vehicles. Removable washable/dryable seat pad. Pria 85 one of the few (if only) seats with 85 lb. harness limit.

Cons: TinyFit makes install rear-facing somewhat challenging. Must rethread harness when changing height–only available on 70 lb. version.

Comments: Maxi Cosi is Dorel's European subsidiary that has been imported to the U.S. to help shore up Dorel's car seat offerings on the high end.

The Pria 70 aims to solve two problems: car seats that don't fit small infants well–and seats that don't fit small cars.

On the first score, the Pria 70 features "TinyFit"–basically an infant insert for newborns as small as four pounds. It even has a smaller chest clip for newborns. (FYI: There are two Pria 70 models: a basic model without the Tiny Fit insert for $250 and one with the TinyFit for $290).

Unlike other competing seats that stop at 65 lbs., the Pria 70 has higher rear-facing limit (40 lbs.) and a 70 lbs. forward facing limit. And the Pria 70 has the Air Protect feature for side impact protection (seen on Safety 1st seats). The seat also has three recline positions.

New in the past year is the Pria 85. This $240 seat starts at 14 lbs. rear-facing (unfortunately, no infant insert for this seat) and goes up to a maximum of 85 lbs. with harness, which is unique. The Pria 85 is the only seat on the market (as of this writing) with an 85 lb. harness limit.

The seat also includes a removable machine washable and dry-able seat pad. In fact, all three cloth versions of the Pria now have washable/dryable seat pads. The 70 comes with a bamboo and charcoal seat pad with anti-bacterial and wicking properties. (There is a leather version of the 70 which, as you might guess, isn't washable). The 85 includes harness holders you can use when your child is not in the seat.

So is the Pria worth it? At these prices, Dorel/Maxi Cosi is com-

convertible seats

peting against Britax and Diono . . . and as such, our expectations are high. On some scores (padding, crash protection) the Pria 70 is equal to Britax. And the TinyFit seat does Britax one better (the Pria 70 starts at four pounds; Britax at five) . . . so if you know you're going to have a small newborn (parents of twins, take note), then the Pria is an excellent choice.

More than one parent we spoke with said they preferred the fabric on the Pria over Britax—the Pria's smooth fabric might be a better choice in hot/humid climates than the current crop of Britax seats, which features fabric that can get hot. Another plus for the Pria 70: its relatively small footprint means it will fit nicely in a compact vehicle.

For the Pria 85 the ability to keep your baby in the same seat until they reach 85 lbs. is a huge advantage.

Most parent feedback on the Pria is quite positive although a few complain installation with Tiny Fit can be tricky. Tightening or loosening the harness when it is routed through the Tiny Fit insert can be a challenge. Other downsides? The cover for the headrest isn't removable, which makes it tricky to clean.

And while the TinyFit seat is innovative, it makes the installation of this seat more complex than others (especially rear-facing). That probably explains the low (two star) rating the Pria earned in rear-facing mode on the NHTSA's ease of use ranking. Finally, the Pria 70 lacks the no rethread harness feature you get on a Britax Marathon or Boulevard, which are similar in price to the Pria.

Overall, we'll give this seat a B+. While not perfect, the Pria 70 is a good option, especially if you know you will be having a newborn on the small side. ***Rating: B+***

MAXI COSI VELLO 65

Price: $230.

Limits: 9-40 lbs. rear-facing, 22-65 lbs. forward-facing.

NHTSA ease of use rating: Not yet.

Pros: First Maxi Cosi seat to be under $200. No rethread harness. Excellent fabric.

Cons: Starting weight is 9 lbs. rear-facing, so this seat isn't for small newborns. Soft cup holders may get detached, lost.

Comments: This seat debuted in February 2015 and is basically a scaled down Pria. It only work to 65 lbs. and omits the Air Protect side impact protection (instead the Vello has EPP foam). The seat has soft cup holders on the sides of the seat (the Pria has a built-in cup holder).

Like the Pria, the Vello features a no rethread harness that can be adjusted with one hand. FYI: The starting weight for this seat is 9 pounds, so this isn't the choice if you have a small newborn.

While the official retail price of the Vello 65 is $230, we'd guess the actual street price will drop under $200. That's because the Pria 70 is already $200 on Amazon. So there is no point in getting this seat if you can snag a Pria for $200! ***Rating: Not Yet.***

ORBIT G3 TODDLER CAR SEAT

This seat is reviewed on the free side of our web site at BabyBargains.com/?p=1115

PEG PEREGO PRIMO VIAGGIO SIP CONVERTIBLE

Price: $329

Type: Convertible seat

Limits: Rear facing 5-45 lbs., forward facing 22 to 65 lbs.

NHTSA ease of use rating:
★★★★☆ Rear-facing
★★★★☆ Forward-facing

Pros: Adjustable side impact protection. Made in Italy.

Cons: Pricey.

Comments: Stroller maker Peg Perego has long been a player in the infant car seat market, but this seat marks their first effort at a convertible. The Primo Viaggio SIP Convertible works to 65 lbs. with a five-point harness and features an adjustable headrest, three recline positions and a newborn insert. The winged headrest provides a measure of side impact protection and shock absorbing foam in the base adds to crash protection.

Perego offers two options for the cover: fabric for $329 and leatherette $380.

This seat first debuted in 2012 and reader feedback has been very positive. Folks say the seat is easy to install and use, plus the fabric is excellent. And of course, the seat is one of the very few not made in China (all Perego products are made in Italy). So we'll recommend this one, despite the stiff price tag. ***Rating: A***

RECARO PERFORMANCE CROSSOVER

Price: $400.

Type: Convertible seat.

Limits: Rear facing 5-40 lbs., forward facing 23-65 lbs.

NHTSA ease of use rating: Not yet.

Comments: This brand new convertible seat debuted in 2015 as we were going to press. An exclusive to Buy Buy Baby, the big headline on this $400 convertible seat is a stay in the car base. Yep, like the ones sold with infant car seats, the "EasySwap" base installs once and lets you move a seat from car to car (extra bases are $99). Another bonus to the base: when you switch the car seat from rear to forward facing after your child stays two, the base stays put (you only switch the direction of the seat). Graco tried this approach a few years ago with the SmartSeat, but that model was a commercial flop.

The Performance Crossover also features a new "Genius" harness adjustment system—basically, this is a no-rethread harness on steroids. It automatically adjusts not only the harness height, but also the headrest and shoulder position. To make getting in and out of the seat easier, Recaro also is debuting a new "AutoOpen" feature that pops the harness and headrest open/up.

Like Recaro's other convertible seats, the Performance Crossover features the brand's HERO harness technology, memory foam and a cover that comes off easily for cleaning. Yes, there are even two up holders.

The Performance Crossover was too new as of this writing for any parent feedback. We will update this review once we get more info. **Rating: Not Yet.**

Recaro ProRIDE / PerformanceRIDE
Price: $210 to $225.
Type: Convertible seat.
Limits: Rear facing 5-40 lbs., forward facing 20-65 lbs.
NHTSA ease of use rating:
★★★★☆ Rear facing
★★★★☆ Forward-facing

Pros: Adjustable headrest, EPP foam, side-impact protection wings. CoolMesh air ventilation. Memory foam in luxe version.
Cons: May not fit rear facing in smaller vehicles. Hard to find in stores.
Comments: German car seat maker Recaro is probably Britax's biggest competitor on the upper-end of the convertible car seat market. And Recaro's flagship seat, the ProRIDE, is a winner.

Among the ProRIDE's unique features: side-impact protection wings made of cushy EPP foam. Similar to the Britax Boulevard, these wings provide both crash protection and head support for napping toddlers. The seat has many seat adjustments and the plush, microfiber fabric is impressive.

The negatives? Well, like the Britax Marathon, this is a big seat—it may not fit rear facing into smaller vehicles. A few parents told us they found the ProRIDE's head pillows to be too restrictive for their older toddlers. And Recaro's thinner distribution (as of this writing, Recaro isn't in as many stores as Britax) means you may have to search for a local store that carries it to see this seat in person.

There is also a luxe version of this seat called the PerformanceRIDE.

It has all the features of the ProRIDE but adds an integrated harness and headrest (called HERO), built-in cup holders, memory foam and other upgrades. Price: $230 to $300.

In general, parent feedback on both versions of this seat is quite positive—most folks say they are easy to use, although more than one noted their large size makes for a tight fit in smaller vehicles. Compared to the similar Britax seats, readers like the head cushions (side-impact protection) somewhat better. Overall, these are excellent seats that may be hard to find in stores. ***Rating: A***

SAFETY 1ST ABLE 65
Price: $100.
Type: Convertible seat.
NHTSA ease of use rating:

⭐⭐⭐☆☆ Rear facing
⭐⭐⭐☆☆ Forward facing

Limits: 5 to 40 lbs. rear facing, 22 to 65 lbs. front-facing.

Pros: 40 lb. rear facing; compact seat. EPP foam. Easy to install. Three position seat recline.

Cons: No recline.

Comments: This seat features a 40 lb. rear-facing limit, a no rethread harness with five positions, three crotch positions and a relatively compact size. We liked the multi-position headrest, although the clunky cup holder might make installation near a door problematic (the cup holder is removeable).

The no rethread harness is a great feature for a $100 car seat—you typically have to spend $50 to $100 more for that feature alone.

Feedback on this seat has been mostly positive. Folks like the overall fit and easy install plus the EPP foam is a nice feature at this price point. Critics say it is hard to install rear-facing . . . and the seat lacks much in the way of side impact protection.

FYI: This seat is also sold as the Eddie Bauer XRS 65 at Target for $130. Same seat, just upgraded fabric. And if you used to own an old Safety 1st Uptown or Avenue and think this seat looks familiar, it is—the Able 65 has the same shell as those seats (but adds the headrest). ***Rating: A-***

SAFETY 1ST ADVANCE 70 AIR+/SE 65+
Price: $146 to $190
Limits: 5-40 lbs. rear-facing, 22-70 lbs. forward-facing.
NHTSA ease of use rating:

⭐⭐⭐⭐☆ Rear-facing
⭐⭐⭐⭐☆ Forward-facing

Pros: Side-impact protection, yet priced at only $190.

Cons: Large, bulky seat. Fabric may be hot in summer.

Comments: The Safety 1st Advance 70 Air+ is the brand's first seat to feature both the Air Protect side impact cushions and GCell HX. What is that? Well, it is patented foam with hexagonal shapes that Safety 1st says was inspired from Indy race-car protection technology—the claim is more full body protection, not just the head, in side impacts.

Unfortunately, there are no federal side impact crash tests or standards, so it is hard to evaluate this claim—or even how this seat would compare with competitor's seats that are lined with basic foam.

The Advance 70 also has a few other impressive features: a deep, four-position recline feature, plus color-coded belt bath for easier install. There is a a no-rethread harness, and a nice cup holder built in to the arm rest.

The down side to the Advance 70: it is a BIG, bulky seat. Unless you have a large SUV, this one will be a tight fit. Some parents also thought the quality of this seat was cheap. And we saw a few complaints from readers that the seat's velvety fabric, while plush, can be hot in the summer.

These complaints aside, most folks are happy with the Advance 70. Yes, it is a large seat, but as long as you have a big enough vehicle and don't see yourself moving it from car to car, this would be a good seat to consider.

FYI: The Advance 70 is a Target-exclusive. So that means you won't be able to price shop it (although we have to say the $190 retail price is affordable). Safety 1st has also come out with a version of this seat that is more widely available: the Advance 65 SE Air+. It is very similar to the Advance 70 Air+, but only works to 65 lbs. and has an one-hand headrest adjustment. Price: $150. ***Rating: A-***

SAFETY 1ST ALL IN ONE (AKA EDDIE BAUER DELUXE 3-IN-1, SAFETY 1ST ALPHA OMEGA ELITE/ELITE 65)

This seat is reviewed on the free side of our web site at BabyBargains.com/?p=1097

SAFETY 1ST CHART AIR 65

Price: $113

Limits: 5-40 lbs. rear-facing, 22-65 lbs. forward-facing.

NHTSA ease of use rating:

★★☆☆☆ Rear facing

★★★☆☆ Forward facing

Pros: Side-impact protection, yet priced under $200.

Cons: Large seat can be difficult to install rear-facing in smaller vehicles.

Comments: This member of the "Air" family from Safety 1st features a 65 lb. weight limit and a headrest that adjusts separately from the back of the seat.

The headline here is the Air Protect side impact protection cushions—this is one of the lowest price seats with this enhanced crash protection and a 65-lb. rated harness.

Feedback on this seat has been sparse but so far positive. While folks like the head cushions, more than a few parents commented on how difficult the seat is to install rear-facing in smaller vehicles, thanks to its large size. ***Rating: B***

SAFETY 1ST COMPLETE AIR 65

This seat is reviewed on the free side of our web site at BabyBargains.com/?p=1122

SAFETY 1ST ELITE 80 AIR+

This seat is reviewed on the free side of our web site at http://bit.ly/elite80air

SAFETY 1ST GUIDE 65

This seat is the same as Safety 1st's Able 65 (and Eddie Bauer XRS 65).

SAFETY 1ST ONSIDE AIR

This seat is reviewed on the free side of our web site at BabyBargains.com/?p=5637

As you can imagine, the child safety seat world changes quickly—read our blog (BabyBargains.com) for the latest news, recalls and more with car seats.

Our Picks: Brand Recommendations

Here are our top picks for infant and convertible seats. Are these seats safer than others? No—all child safety seats sold in the U.S. and Canada must meet minimum safety standards. These seats are our top picks because they combine the best features, usability (including ease of installation) and value. Remember the safest and best seat for your baby is the one that best fits your child and vehicle. Finding the right car seat can be a bit of trial and error; you may find a seat CANNOT be installed safely in your vehicle because of the quirks of the seat or your vehicle's safety belt system. All seats do NOT fit all cars. Hence it is always wise to buy a seat from a store or web site with a good return policy.

FYI: See the chart on pages 436-437 for a comparison of features for both infant and convertible/front-facing car seats.

Best Bets: Infant Car Seats

Good. The *Graco SnugRide Click Connect 40* ($170-$220) is the top-of-the-line model in the SnugRide family. It features a no-rethread harness and an adjustable base that slides back to give 8" of additional legroom—allowing babies to use the seat up to age two. That's nice . . . but the downside is the seat then takes up a lot of space in the backseat and that could make it a no go in smaller vehicles. The SnugRide 40's base is also much larger/longer than other SnugRide bases, again making fit in smaller cars a challenge. FYI: this seat used to be a Babies R Us exclusive, but now Amazon has it for $170.

If backseat space is at a premium, the *Graco SnugRide 35 LX* ($150-$190) is a good runner-up. It also has a no-rethread harness and a base with seat belt lock-offs. The base for the 35LX is smaller than the Click Connect 40.

Better. The *Chicco KeyFit 30* ($190-$260) earns our second best pick. Crash protection is excellent, with added side impact protection making a difference. The KeyFit gets high scores from our readers on ease of use (somewhat higher than the Graco seats)—installation is a snap and adjusting the harness is easy. The seat also features EPS foam and a newborn insert. What's missing? The KeyFit's harness must be manually rethreaded to adjust the harness height. The canopy coverage is also somewhat skimpy compared to other seats. On the plus side, more strollers brands have rolled out adapters for the popular KeyFit, making stroller compatibility better than before.

Best. The *Britax B-SAFE 35 Elite* ($200-$260) earns the top spot in our car seat picks for this edition. The B-SAFE 35 Elite is a new, improved version of the already excellent B-SAFE, which gets very good marks from readers for usability and fit. The 35 Elite adds a no-rethread harness, additional side impact protection and an improved base that makes installation even easier with LATCH. Stroller compatibility is good but not as extensive as the Graco SnugRide—besides Britax strollers, the B-SAFE now works with Britax's BOB brand.

Best Bets: Convertible Car Seats

Good. For a decent, no-frills car seat, we recommend the *Cosco Scenera Next*. It works to 40 lbs. rear-facing or forward-facing and has a new narrow profile (17″ wide). It is a Walmart exclusive at $46 to $50—perfect for that little-used second car or Grandma's vehicle. With the prices of some car seats pushing $300, it's nice to know you can find a good, safe seat for well under $100.

Better. The secret sauce of the *Chicco NextFit* ($280) is its ease of installation. Whether with LATCH or a safety belt, the NextFit is a breeze to install, thanks to what Chicco calls its Super Cinch feature. The NextFit features nine recline positions, a no rethread harness, side impact protection and a cover that can be machine washed. The downside? This seat is heavy and bulky—you won't be moving it from car to car or taking it on an airplane.

Best. So, what is our top recommendation for convertible car seats? The *Britax Boulevard ClickTight* ($280) takes the crown this year. This seat combines both ease of installation and use with excellent safety features. The new ClickTight base pops open to enable a super simple install with a safety belt. The Boulevard ClickTight features a no rethread harness, seven recline positions, enhanced side impact protection and an easy to remove cover for cleaning. Bonus: this seat doesn't take as much room in the back seat when installed rear-facing (except when it is fully reclined).

FYI: there are two versions of the Boulevard on the market: ClickTight and G4. G4 is the older model with much the same features, but lacks the ClickTight base.

If Grandma is buying. What if money isn't an issue when buying a seat? One obvious seat that we'd suggest is the top-of-the-line *Britax Advocate ClickTight* ($315), which is much like the Boulevard, but adds additional side-impact protection in the form of a protective shell on the sides of the seat. The downside? This additional side impact protection adds to the seat's width, possibly making it harder to fit in smaller vehicles. If your vehicle lacks rear side curtain air bags, however, the Advocate may be worth the upgrade.

Another excellent seat if Grandma is buying would be the *Peg Perego Primo Viaggio SIP* ($330). This seat boasts excellent reader feedback on ease of use and installation; the adjustable side impact protection is impressive. Premium LATCH connectors and fabrics complete the seat.

CAR SEATS

INFANT SEATS

The following is a selection of better known infant car seats and how they compare on features:

MAKER	MODEL	PRICE	WEIGHT/ HEIGHT LIMITS
BABY TREND	FLEX-LOC 32	$80-$140	32 LBS./30" *
BRITAX	B-SAFE	$144	30 LBS./32"
	B-SAFE 35 ELITE	$200-$250	35 LBS./32"
CHICCO	KEYFIT 30	$190	30 LBS./30"
COMBI	SHUTTLE	$134	35 LBS../33"
COSCO	COMFY CARRY	$79	22 LBS../29"
CYBEX	ATON 1/2/Q	$250-$300	32 LBS./30"
EVENFLO	EMBRACE	$60	35 LBS./30"
	NURTURE	$50-$60	22 LBS./26"
GB	ASANA35 AP	$250	35 LBS./32"
GRACO	SNUGRIDE 40	$170-$220	40 LBS./35"
MAXI COSI	PREZI	$290	30 LBS./29"
NUNA	PIPA	$300	32 LBS./32"
ORBIT	ORBIT	$440	30 LBS./32"
PEG PEREGO	PRIMO VIAGGIO 4.35	$280	35 LBS./30"
RECARO	PERFORMANCE COUPE	$270	35 LBS./32"
SAFETY 1ST	ONBOARD 35 AIR	$110-$160	35 LBS./32"
UPPA BABY	MESA	$280	35 LBS./32"
URBINI	PETAL	$100	35 LBS./32"

CONVERTIBLE SEATS

The following is a selection of popular convertible car seats and how they compare on features:

MAKER	MODEL	PRICE	WEIGHT LIMITS (IN LBS.) REAR	FORWARD
BRITAX	BOULEVARD CT	$370	40 LBS.	65 LBS.
	MARATHON CT	$250	40	65
	ROUNDABOUT 55	$144-$190	40	55
CHICCO	NEXTFIT	$280	40	65
COSCO	SCENERA NEXT	$46	40	40
DIONO	RADIAN RXT	$270	45	80/120
EVENFLO	SYMPHONY	$165-$230	40	65/110
GRACO	4EVER	$300	40	65/120
MAXI COSI	PRIA 85	$240	40	85
PEG PEREGO	PRIMO VIAGGIO SIP	$329	45	65
SAFETY 1ST	ABLE 65	$100	40	65

SIDE IMPACT: Does the seat have side-impact protection?
FOAM TYPE: Does the seat have a EPS or EPP foam (or none at all)? This is for crash protection; EPP foam is softer (more comfortable) than EPS.
LEVEL IND.: Does the seat have a level indicator for easier installation?
CARRIER WEIGHT: This is the weight of the carrier only (not the base).

SIDE IMPACT	LEVEL IND.	FOAM TYPE	BASE WIDTH	CARRIER WEIGHT	OUR RATING
◆	◆	EPS	16.5"	9.7 LBS.	D
◆	◆	EPS	17.5	9.8	A
◆	◆	EPS	17.75	11.5	A
◆	◆	EPS	17	9.4	A
	◆	EPS	17	11.1	B-
		NONE	17	6.6	C
◆	◆	EPS	15	8.8	A-
	◆	EPS	18	7.0	D+
		EPS	17.5	5.5	F
◆	◆	EPS	17.5	9.2	NOT YET
	◆	EPS	15	10.1	A
◆		EPP	17	11.6	C+
◆		EPS	12.5	8.6	B+
	◆	EPP	15.25	12	B
◆	◆	EPS	15.5	11.1	A
◆	◆	EPS	15.5	9.8	B
◆	◆	EPP	15	9	B
◆	◆	EPS	14.25	10.5	A-
◆	◆	EPS	17.5	9.7	B+

RATING	COMMENT
A	7 RECLINE POSITIONS; ENHANCED SIDE IMPACT PROTECTION
A	BASIC SIDE IMPACT PROTECTION; NO-RETHREAD HARNESS
A	ENTRY-LEVEL PRICE SEAT; MUST MANUALLY RETHREAD HARNESS
A	NO RETHREAD HARNESS; 9 RECLINE POSITIONS.
B+	SIMPLE SEAT, GREAT FOR AIR TRAVEL OR GRANDPARENTS.
A	SEAT FOLDS UP; SIDE IMPACT PROTECTION
B+	EASY TO INSTALL WITH LATCH; SMOOTH HARNESS ADJUSTER
A-	6 RECLINE POS; SIDE IMPACT PROTECT; NO-RETHREAD
B+	85 LB HARNESS LIMIT IS UNIQUE; MACHINE WASHABLE PAD
A	SIDE IMPACT PROTECTION, ADJUSTABLE HEADREST.
A-	EASY TO INSTALL, 3 POS SEAT RECLINE. MANUAL HARNESS.

Booster Seats

So what is a booster? Simply put, this seat boosts a child to correctly sit in an auto safety belt. Yes, some boosters have five-point harnesses (more on this later), but most boosters work with your vehicle's safety belt.

Most parents know they have to put an infant or toddler into a car seat. What some folks don't realize, however, is that child passenger safety doesn't end when baby outgrows that convertible car seat—any child from 40 to 80 lbs. and less than 4'9" (generally, kids age four to eight) should be restrained in a booster seat (or one of the new harnessed seats that work up to 80 lbs.). And in most states, booster seat use is mandated by law. Numerous states have passed laws requiring the use of booster seats. And more states are following their lead.

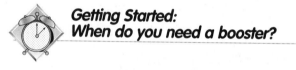

Getting Started:
When do you need a booster?

Your child needs a booster seat when he outgrows his convertible seat. This happens when he exceeds the weight limit or when he is too tall for the harness (his shoulders are taller than the top slots in the seat). For most children, this happens around ages three to five.

Booster seats use the vehicle's safety belt and hence require your child to be mature enough to stay in the seat. The seat belt is all that is holding your child in the seat—unlike the escape-proof five-point harness of a convertible seat.

What if your child has outgrown a convertible seat but isn't mature enough to stay in a booster? Then consider a hybrid seat that uses a five-point harness up to 65 lbs. or more.

Best Online Sources

◆ **The Insurance Institute for Highway Safety** (iihs.org) produces an annual report that evaluates booster car seats based on their fit to vehicle. We list these ratings for each booster later in this chapter.

◆ **The National Highway Traffic Safety Administration** (nhtsa.gov) has excellent videos showing proper booster seat installation and use. Click on Driving Safety, then Child Safety, then on Installation Tips. Also helpful: the NHTSA now rates and reviews booster seats for ease of use and other factors.

Smart Shopping Tips

Smart Shopper Tip #1
Booster Laws

"My daughter just turned four, and my state doesn't require her to use a car seat anymore. Does she really need a booster?"

A majority of states have enacted booster car seat laws, usually requiring children to use "appropriate restraints" until age six or 60 lbs. (some state laws are now up to age eight or nine and 80 lbs.). But other states still only require a car seat until a child turns four (some even just two) years old. So why should you continue to hassle with a car seat or booster after this time?

We like to remind parents that there is the law . . . and then there is the law of physics. Car seat belts are made for adults, and children (as well as some short adults) just don't fit well, and don't get good protection from those belts. Lap belts used with four- to eight-year old children routinely cause such severe injuries and paralysis that the injuries even have their own name: "lap belt syndrome." Children using lap/shoulder belts often put the shoulder belt behind their back (since it is so darn uncomfortable), giving them no more protection than a lap belt alone. Ejections are another common problem with young children in adult belts, even if they are using both the lap and shoulder belt.

Booster seats (and of course regular car seats) work very simply to eliminate this problem. Boosters properly position the lap part of the belt on a child's hip bone, not their soft internal organs. They elevate the child and include a special adjuster so that the lap shoulder belt fits right on the strong shoulder bones. Booster seats should be used until a child fits the adult belts like an adult. Try out the Five Step Test (later in this section) to see if your child is ready.

See our web page for pictures of good and bad fit for a booster (BabyBargains.com, click on Bonus).

Smart Shopper Tip #2
Different seats, lots of confusion?

"When I was shopping for a booster seat, I was confused with all the types of seats out there. Why isn't there just one type of booster?"

Good question. We've noticed that buying a booster seat can be a bit more complex than buying another car seat. For example, an infant car seat is, well, an infant car seat. But a booster can come in several versions: high back boosters, backless boosters, combination seat/boosters, and more.

In this chapter, we'll try to simplify things a bit. Any time we refer to a *belt-positioning booster*, we mean a seat that uses the lap/shoulder belt to secure the child. Most other car seats (like convertible seats) use an internal harness to hold the child, while the seat itself is attached to the car with the seat belt or the LATCH system.

What's made this so confusing is that car seat makers have blurred the lines between convertible seats and boosters in recent years by coming out with hybrid models that use a five-point harness up to 65 (or 80) lbs. and then convert to a belt-positioning booster. The Britax Frontier and Graco Nautilus are two examples.

Confusing, yes we know. But we want this section to cover all the options for older children who've outgrown their traditional convertible seat . . . so you'll see a variety of options in this section. Let's break down what's out there:

◆ **High back boosters (HBB):** Belt-positioning boosters come in two flavors: high back boosters and backless boosters. High back boosters have often been called "kid's captain's chairs," which they kind of resemble. They are designed to be simple, but provide vital safety features for children who've outgrown a harnessed seats. These boosters properly position the lap belt on a child's strong hip bones, rather than letting it ride up on the soft internal organs. And they provide correct positioning of the shoulder belt, so the child can comfortably wear it and get critical upper body support. The high back also protects the child's head from whiplash if there are no head restraints in the vehicle, and the high back may also give some side sleeping support. ALL of these boosters require a lap and shoulder belt. FYI: Some high back boosters convert into backless boosters for older kids.

◆ **Backless boosters:** These belt-positioning boosters work the same way as high back boosters—they just don't have a back. Safety-wise, these can be a bit better than a high back booster, since the child sits against the vehicle seat. They do the same job positioning the lap belt, and usually include some sort of strap to adjust the shoulder belt. But they don't provide head support if you have low seat backs, and they don't give any side or sleeping support. On the other hand, they are often popular with older kids, since they can be quite inconspicuous.

◆ *Hybrid/Combo seats:* These are probably the most confusing "booster" seats because sometimes they are a booster, and sometimes they aren't. They come with a five-point harness, which can generally be used up to 40 lbs. (some seats now to 65 and even 80 lbs.). Then the harness comes off, and the seat can be used as a belt-positioning booster, usually to 80 or 100 lbs. They get the name "combination," or "combo" for short, from the two jobs they do.

A recent report by the Insurance Institute for Highway Safety criticized many older combo seats, saying they poorly fit kids when in booster mode. We factored this report into our ratings.

Newer combo seats (namely the Britax Frontier, Graco Nautilus, among others) now work to 65 lbs. and beyond. These combo seats do a better job at fitting older kids, whether in harness or booster mode.

The take-home message: hybrid/combo boosters are great for children that have outgrown their convertible seats but aren't mature enough to sit in a belt-positioning booster (the types described earlier). The five-point harness provides that extra measure of safety and security while they are still young (typically, a child has to be three or older to be mature enough to handle the belt-positioners).

◆ *Special Needs Seats:* There are a few seats on the market now that don't really fit into any category. One is the Britax Traveler Plus, which is designed for special needs kids up to 105 lbs.

Smart Shopper Tip #3
Avoid Seat Belt Adjusters

"The shoulder belt was bugging my son's neck, so I bought a little adjuster thing. Is that as good as a booster?"

Several companies make inexpensive belt adjusters ($10 or so), which help to properly position the shoulder belt on your child. Sounds good, right? Wrong. Look closely at the pictures on the box. In order to pull the shoulder belt down, and make it more comfortable for a short passenger, virtually all of these devices also pull the lap part of the belt UP, right back onto the tummy. Marketed to kids 50 lbs. and up, these devices are also packed with statements that confuse even the most safety conscious parents, like "designed to meet FMVSS 213," a reference to a federal safety standard in crash testing. What's wrong with that picture? That federal standard doesn't even apply to items marketed for children 50 lbs. and up! Worse yet, government crash tests show that a three-year-old dummy is less protected when using one of these adjusters compared to using the regular

boosters

vehicle safety belt. When tested with a six-year-old dummy, same result. Bottom line: forget these adjusters and use a booster seat.

Smart Shopper Tip #4
Cars with only lap belts
"What if my car has only lap belts in the back seat?"

While lap belts are just fine with infant and convertible seats, they are a no-no when it comes to boosters. If your vehicle doesn't have shoulder belts, check with your vehicle's manufacturer to see if they offer a retrofit kit. If that doesn't work, consider buying a newer vehicle with lap/shoulder belts in the back seat. In the meantime, you can use a seat with a five-point harness for kids over 40 lbs. See the convertible seat reviews earlier in this chapter for details on such seats.

Smart Shopper Tip #5
LATCH system and boosters
"My car has LATCH attachments. Do booster seats work with this?"
"My car does NOT have LATCH. Do boosters require LATCH?

We discussed LATCH earlier in this chapter; in short, most booster seats do NOT work with LATCH—you secure them with the regular seat belt. There are a few exceptions: see reviews of Clek, Diono, and Graco (Affix) boosters.

If your vehicle does NOT have LATCH, no worries—the vast majority of booster seats don't require LATCH.

Smart Shopper Tip #6
Back Harness Adjuster
"I loved our combo seat—until the day I discovered its fatal flaw. When it was cold, my daughter's thick coat required me to loosen the belts on her five-point harness. I discovered this could only be done from the BACK of the seat! What a pain!"

More booster seats are adding five-point harnesses so they can be used at younger ages/weights (some seats start as little as 20 lbs.). The problem? The cheapest combo boosters do NOT have up-front belt adjustments. You must adjust the belts from the back of the seat, which is a pain especially in cold weather. A word to the wise: if you get a combo seat, make sure the belt adjustments are UP FRONT and easy to access. The question of coats/snowsuits and car seats comes up frequently—we should stress that most safety advocates suggest that a child in a safety seat wear a coat that is no thicker than a polar fleece. Big bulky coats are a hazard. Why? In the event of a crash, the coat will compress, creating a gap between the child and the restraint (and possibly ejecting the child from the seat).

Smart Shopper Tip #7
Too Tall for a Convertible

"My daughter is too tall for her convertible car seat but is only 32 lbs. Now what?"

Many children outgrow their convertibles by height before weight. Most convertibles say that they are good from 40" to 50" tall, but a better measure is to make sure the child's shoulders are no higher than the top harness slot. Another guideline: when a child's ears reach the top of the car seat shell, he's outgrown the seat.

Remember that while weight limits are set in stone, height rules are more like guidelines. Example: two children could both be 48" tall, but one still fits in her convertible car seat while the other clearly needs to be a booster. Why? Because a child could be 48" tall, but have a long torso—and if a child's ears are at the top of the car seat shell, it's time to move to a booster. Yet the other child who is 48" tall may be shorter in the torso (but have longer legs) and may still fit in the convertible.

Smart Shopper Tip #8
Who crash tests booster seats?

"Are there independent sources to find boost seat crash test ratings?"

There are three sources for booster seat ratings: *Consumer Reports,* The National Highway Traffic and Safety Administration (NHTSA) and the Insurance Institute for Highway Safety (IIHS).

Consumer Reports magazine independently crash tests and evaluates boosters for ease of use. The NHTSA assigns ease of use ratings (on a one to five star scale) for booster seats—these are based on "vehicle installation features" and how well the seat secures a child. In the review section later in this chapter, we list this as the NHTSA ease of use rating.

The Insurance Institute for Highway Safety (IIHS) evaluates how well a booster seat fits the lap and shoulder belt on a four to eight year old child. The IIHS doesn't crash test seats, just evaluates belt fit. Seats are judged best bets, good bets or not recommended. In the review section, we list the IIHS rating for each booster. FYI: In some cases, the IIHS says a booster is rated "check fit." That means these seats may work in *some* vehicles; you need to check the fit.

At *Baby Bargains*, we look at tests and information from these three sources and combine that with parent feedback to come up with our booster seat ratings.

Safe & Sound

1 **CHECK YOUR VEHICLE'S OWNERS MANUAL.** We're amazed at the detailed info on installing child safety seats you can find in your vehicle's owners manual, especially for newer vehicles. Car seats also include detailed installation instructions.

2 **ALWAYS USE THE LAP/SHOULDER BELT WITH THE BOOSTER**—this provides crucial upper body protection in the case of an accident. NEVER use just the lap belt with a belt-positioning booster.

3 **DON'T EXPECT TO USE THAT BOOSTER ON AN AIRPLANE.** FAA rules prohibit the use of booster seats on airlines. Why? Booster seats must be used with a shoulder belt to be effective—and airplanes only have lap belts. Our advice: if you travel a lot, consider a harnessed seat that works to 65+ lbs. that is certified to work on airplanes.

4 **BE CAREFUL OF HAND-ME-DOWN AND SECOND-HAND BARGAINS.** Most old booster seats don't meet current safety standards. If you do find a newer used booster, make sure you ask the original owner if it has been in a crash, and then check the seat for recalls (Safety Belt Safe has a great recall list at carseat.org). And if your seat has been in a crash, is over six years old or missing its proper labels, stick it in a black garbage bag and throw it away.

5 **ONLY USE CARDBOARD CUPS IN BOOSTER SEAT CUP HOLDERS.** You'll note that some seats now come with cup or juice box holders. These are a great convenience, but most manufacturers only recommend cardboard cups (like to-go cups) or juice boxes be used. Anything harder could become a dangerous projectile in a crash.

6 **WHEN IS A CHILD BIG ENOUGH TO USE JUST THE AUTO'S SAFETY BELT?** When a child is over 4'9" and can sit with his or her back straight against the back seat cushion (with knees bent over the seat's edge), then he or she can go with just the auto's safety belt. Still have doubts? Try this Five-Step Test from Safety Belt Safe, USA:

◆ Does the child sit all the way back against the auto seat?
◆ Does the belt cross the shoulder between neck and arm?
◆ Is the lap belt as low as possible, touching the thighs?
◆ Can the child stay seated like this for the whole trip?
◆ Do the child's knees bend comfortably at the edge of the seat?

If you answered no to any of these questions, your child needs a booster seat, and will probably be more comfortable in one too.

7 **DON'T USE A BOOSTER TOO SOON.** Most safety techs say a child should stay in a harnessed seat as long as possible—many seats can now keep a kid harnessed until 65, 70 or even 80 lbs. Some parents try to switch a too-young toddler to a booster . . . but kids that are under four are often not mature enough to correctly sit in a belt-positioning booster.

Booster Car Seats (model by model reviews)

BABY TREND HYBRID 3-IN-1
Booster type: Combo
Weight: up to 100 lbs.; 22 to 65 lbs. with harness, belt-positioning booster for 30 to 100 lbs. Backless 40-100 lbs.
Price: $90
IIHS rating: Good bet in high back mode, best bet as backless booster.
NHTSA ease of use rating: Not yet.
Pros: Side impact protection on headrest with six positions. Harnessed works to 65 lbs. Machine washable seat pad and harness covers. Insert cushion for smaller kids. Two cup holders. LATCH connectors.
Cons: 2014 recall of previous version of this seat. Twisty straps. Chest buckle can slide down. Some complain buckle is hard to use. Can't adjust the crotch strap
Comments: The headline here is the six position headrest support with side impact protection, as well as the affordable $90 price. The Baby Trend Hybrid 3-in-1 has three uses: as a harnessed booster to 65 lbs., then as a belt-positioning booster to 100 lbs. And as a backless booster, again to 100 lbs.

Fans of this seat say it is a good value, since many harnessed boosters sell for over $100. FYI: Even though this seat starts at 22 lbs., it would be best to wait until your child is at least two before using it. That's because it is best (and safest) to have your child rear-facing until age two and this seat is only forward-facing.

Critics of this seat say it can be difficult to install. That may be because the belt path is rather narrow, which makes it tough to get a tight fit. While the six position headrest is a key feature, adjusting the headrest back up can be challenge (it requires some force). And there is only one position for the crotch belt—that makes it harder to fit bigger kids.

Other criticisms of this seat focused on the straps (which are thin and can twist easily), as well as the chest buckle that some found hard to use.

That's the same issue that prompted a 2014 recall of a previous version of this seat (the Fastback). A sticky harness buckle promoted the recall of 16,000 seats.

Bottom line: we're not big fans of Baby Trend and while this seat is priced well, there are better choices out there for ease of use. **Rating: C-**

BRITAX FRONTIER CLICKTIGHT

Booster type: Combo
Weight: 20-90 lbs. with harness, 40-120 lbs. as a belt-positioning booster. For kids at least two years old and 25 lbs. and 30-58" for the harness; 45" to 62" in height for belt-positioning booster.
Price: $247

IIHS rating: Best Bet.
NHTSA ease of use rating:
★★★★☆ Booster mode
★★★★★ Harness mode

Pros: Works to 90 lbs. with five-point harness. A bit wider, deeper than the Graco Nautilus.

Cons: Large seat, expensive.

Comments: The Frontier aims for a market similar to the Graco Nautilus—it is a harnessed seat that works to a whopping 90 lbs. and then a belt-positioning booster to 120 lbs. after that. The Frontier is targeted at kids at least two years old who have outgrown their convertible seats but aren't mature enough to sit in a belt-positioning booster.

Britax has steadily improved this seat over the years. Overall weight and height limits have moved higher and there are a series of small enhancements (example: the cup holders are inset in the seat, rather than stick out from the side, etc.). The Frontier also has:

◆ *A ClickTight seatbelt installation system*. This system automatically tightens and tensions the seat belt—no more locking clips or concerns about LATCH seat limits.

◆ *SafeCell* crash protection in base. Seen in Britax's other models, this system absorbs energy in a crash.

◆ *Higher top harness adjustment*. The top harness slot is now 20.5", which is the tallest in the industry. That will keep kids from outgrowing the seat in harness mode too soon. Other small improvements to the seat include a better recline feature and now the harness hides away when you convert the seat to booster mode (before it had to be removed completely).

Are there any negatives to this seat? Well, just as before, this is a big, bulky seat. Carrying it through an airport isn't going to be fun (the Frontier is certified for use in an airplane, but only with its five-point harness—not as a booster).

The Frontier is 19.5" wide—that means fitting three across in a carpool won't be easy for most vehicles. Also: the Frontier has limited recline settings and that might be a negative for some.

In the most recent booster seat ratings from the Insurance Institute for Highway Safety (IIHS), the Frontier improved its ratings from a Check Fit to a Best Bet.

The price of the Frontier is perhaps its biggest draw-back—the similar Graco Nautilus is about HALF the price. And the Graco Nautilus has an extra use as a backless booster (the Frontier only works as a belt-positioning, high back booster). That said, the Britax Frontier is an excellent seat and is highly recommended.

FYI: If you want additional side impact protection, there is a special version of the Frontier with Side Impact Cushion Technology (SICT). This model is called the Pinnacle ClickTight, $250 to $260. **Rating: A**

BRITAX PARKWAY SG / SGL
Booster type: High back
Weight: 40 to 120 lbs., 38-63" in height, as a belt-positioning booster.
Price: SG: $104, SGL $110
IIHS rating:
Parkway SG backless: Check fit.
Parkway SG high back: Best bet.
Parkway SGL backless: Check fit.
Parkway SGL high back: Best bet.

NHTSA ease of use rating: ★★★☆☆
Pros: Side-impact protection, plush cover.
Cons: Pricey, narrow seat, skimpy armrests.
Comments: The Britax Parkway is Britax's entry-price point booster, competing against the Graco TurboBooster. The SG in the model name refers to the seat's Slide Guard (SG) feature—this keeps a child from submarining out of the seat in a crash. Like other models in this category, the Parkway converts from a high back to a backless booster for older kids (hence the separate ratings from IIHS for each mode).

There are two versions of this seat: SG and SGL. The Parkway SGL includes LATCH connectors (SGL model), which keep the seat anchored when it is unoccupied. It runs $120-$160. Otherwise, the SGL is the same as the SG.

Comparing the Parkway to the Graco TurboBooster, we'd give Britax the advantage when it comes to seat covers—the fabric Britax uses is much nicer than Graco's. That said, the Graco TurboBooster's armrests are bigger than the Parkway's, which are not adjustable. And the Parkway has a somewhat narrower seat than the TurboBooster, which might mean a tight fit for larger toddlers. As for crash protection, *Consumer Reports* rated the TurboBooster as better than the Parkway. And the TurboBooster is about $50 less expensive than the Parkway.

FYI: Britax added a few enhancements in the past year. The Parkway SGL now boasts enhanced side impact protection with deeper head wings and adds the SafeCell technology (seen in Britax's convertible seats) in the base.

Bottom line: this is a good seat, but at a price that is double the Graco TurboBooster, we'd give the Graco seat the edge in overall value. ***Rating: A-***

BRITAX PINNACLE CLICKTIGHT

Booster type: Combo
Weight: 90 lbs. with harness, up to 120 lbs. as a belt-positioning booster. For kids at least two years old, 25 lbs. and 30-58" for the harness, 45" to 62" in height for belt-positioning booster.
Price: $260
IIHS rating: Best Bet.
NHTSA ease of use rating:

★★★★☆ Booster mode
★★★★★ Harness mode

Comments: This seat is the same as the Britax Frontier, but adds Side Impact Cushion Technology (SICT). This gives additional protection if the vehicle is in a side-impact crash.

The Britax Pinnacle debuted in mid 2013 and has received mostly positive parent reviews, according to our research. Readers say it is very easy to install and overall quality is excellent.

As you might expect, one negative here is the seat's large bulk—those side impact cushions add significantly to the seat's width, which might be a concern for fit in smaller vehicles. That said, since this is basically a Frontier with a new feature, we'll recommend it with the same rating we do for the Frontier. ***Rating: A***

BRITAX PIONEER

Booster type: Combo
Weight: 25-70 lbs. with harness, 40 to 110 pounds as a belt-positioning booster. For kids 2 years old and 25 lbs. and up. Heigh limit: 30-56" for harness mode; 45-60" in booster mode.
Price: $172
IIHS rating: Best Bet.
NHTSA ease of use rating:

★★★★☆ Booster mode
★★★★★ Harness mode

Comments: This is a less expensive version of the Britax Frontier and Pinnacle. At under $200 retail, the Pioneer is about $50 less than a Frontier.

What are the trade-offs? As you can probably tell from the model name, the Pioneer only works to 70 lbs. (and has a lower height limit as well—60″ versus 65″ for the Frontier). The top seated shoulder height is 19.5″, about 2″ in less than the Frontier. The Pioneer has less fancy fabric and padding—noticeably lower quality than Britax's other seats.

The Pioneer does have SafeCell technology in its base for energy absorption in a crash, as well as True Side Impact Protection. But you miss the ClickTight belt system found on the Pinnacle and Frontier (the Pioneer does have a no-rethread harness, however).

Our take: unless you have a small child who won't be hitting the Frontier/Pinnacle's higher weight/height limits, we don't see the point of the Pioneer 70. We'd spend the extra $50 and get the Frontier. The ClickTight belt system is worth the upgrade. And we've often seen the Frontier (which has wider distribution) discounted online to just about the same price as the Pioneer 70.

Parent feedback on the Pioneer 70 has been mostly positive, but a few dissenters knock the single LATCH strap on the Pioneer (versus dual straps on the Frontier and Pinnacle). That made LATCH harder to install for some parents. The downgraded fabric and pad (again, compared to other Britax seats) was too much of a compromise for some.

Bottom line: given the trade-offs of this seat, we'd suggest a Frontier instead if you want a Britax booster. We understand that some folks simply can't afford a Frontier (at least at its official retail price). But Britax made too many quality trade-offs with this seat to earn our top rating. ***Rating: B***

BUBBLEBUM
Booster type: Backless
Weight: 40 lbs. to 100 lbs. (kids over age 4)
Price: $30
IIHS rating: Best Bet.
NHTSA ease of use rating: ★★★★★★

Pros: Small and lightweight. Deflates and rolls up into carry bag for travel. Good for three-across situation.
Cons: Unstable, wobbly to sit on. Not comfortable for a long car ride.
Comments: BubbleBum is an inflatable, backless booster seat invented by a certified car seat tech from Northern Ireland. The idea was to have an easy-to-carry booster seat option for travel, rental cars, etc. But it's also a great option if you live in a place like New York and need a portable option for taxis.

Another plus: it's cheap ($30). But does it work well? Car seat techs

boosters

report that the BubbleBum does provide good lap and shoulder belt fit (the IIHS gave it a "Best Bet" rating). The seat belt is threaded through a lap belt positioner, which keeps the belt in the proper position.

Critics note it can be confusing to use the positioner at first. Techs recommend threading the seat belt through the positioner after you have buckled your child into the seat to get a tighter fit. Also, it's a small seat and doesn't provide much thigh support. So the BumbleBum isn't going to be comfortable for long-term use. On the plus side, however, the small size of the seat makes it possible to use it in a three-across situation. Most readers are happy with the Bumblebum, although a few noted quality issues with a BumbleBum that developed a slow leak (the company provided replacements).

We like the BumbleBum for it's portability, price and safety. When used for short-term situations and travel, it's a great option. **Rating: A**

CHICCO KIDFIT

Booster type: High back and backless
Weight: 30-00 lbs. high back, 40-110 lbs., backless.
Price: $100.
IIHS rating: Not yet.
NHTSA ease of use rating: Not yet.

Pros: Adjustable headrest with side impact protection has ten positions, SuperCinch to make installation easier, foam padding in seat.
Cons: Only at Target.
Comments: The new Chicco KidFit debuted in 2015 as a new, more affordable booster from Chicco (their previous effort, the Strada, clocked in at $150). The headline here is Chicco's "DuoZone" side impact protection—a headrest with ten positions. Also new: Chicco brings its SuperCinch LATCH tightener system (seen on the NextFit convertible seat) to the KidFit, making installation and tightening of the belt easier.

The KidFit is billed as a 2-in-1 seat—it can be used as a high back booster and then can be converted to a backless model (up to 110 lbs). The seat also has two cup holders and the back has two positions to better fit vehicle back seats.

As of this writing, the KidFit is brand new and a Target exclusive at $100—that's a good price, considering the features like the extra foam padding in the seat. Since the seat is so new, there hasn't been any reader feedback as of press time. **Rating: Not Yet.**

CLEK OLLI/OZZI

Booster type: Backless booster
Weight: 40 to 120 lbs., 57" tall.
Price: $100 Olli; $60 Ozzi

IIHS rating: Check fit.
NHTSA ease of use rating: ⭐⭐⭐⭐☆
Pros: LATCH backless booster. Removable, washable seat cover.
Cons: High price. Only scored "fair" in latest crash tests by *Consumer Reports*.
Comments: Canadian car seat maker Magna's (magnaclek.com) backless booster is unique: it is one of only a few backless boosters that use LATCH for a secure fit to the car. Your child then buckles in with the auto safety belt. The main advantage of the Clek is that the LATCH connectors hold the seat in place when it is unoccupied. Nice, but is it worth $100 when most other (LATCH-less) backless boosters run $20?

Reader feedback on the Clek Olli (pictured) has been positive—readers love how easy it is to install and use. One past gripe (a lack of cup holders) has been remedied. There are still older, cup holder-less versions of the Olli on the market, so double check your order if you value this feature.

FYI: Clek makes a scaled down version of the Olli called the Ozzi: it omits the quick release strap, mesh side storage pocket, carry bag, cup holder and armrest padding. The Olli comes in several colors and is made of a micro fiber; the Ozzi comes in one color (black) and has less expensive fabric (accessory color covers run $25 to $35). FYI: The Ozzi is about $20 or so cheaper than the Olli.

Consumer Reports latest crash tests put the Olli at the bottom of the pack, rating it only "fair" for crash protection. As a result, we've dropped our rating of this seat this time out. ***Rating: B-***

CLEK OOBR
Booster type: High back and backless
Weight: 33 to 100 lbs., 57" tall.
Price: $300
IIHS rating:
Backless: Check fit.
High back: Best Bet.
NHTSA ease of use rating: ⭐⭐⭐⭐⭐

Comments: The Clek Oobr is a high back booster that has a removable back. As with the Clek Olli/Ozzi, the Oobr features LATCH for a secure fit to the car. The Oobr's other main point is that the seat reclines up to 12 degrees and has an adjustable head restraint. At prices topping $250, however, this is a tough sell for most parents. With the top-selling high back booster (the Graco TurboBooster) selling for less than $50, it is unclear whether these features make it worth the investment.

Despite the price, reader feedback on this seat has been very positive, with folks saying the overall ease of use (the NHTSA gives

boosters

it five stars) and LATCH feature outweigh the cost issue. Quality and safety-wise, this seat would earn an A if it wasn't priced so high.

Critics knock the skimpy padding of the seat, especially when compared to the similarly priced Britax Frontier (which has a five-point harness). On the plus side, the Clek Oobr scored "very good" in crash protection in *Consumer Reports* latests tests. ***Rating: B***

COMBI KOBUCK
Booster type: High back and backless booster.
Weight: 33 to 125 lbs.; 33" to 57" in height.
Price: $80
IIHS rating: Good Bet.
NHTSA ease of use rating: ★★★★☆
Pros: Side impact protection; can be used as a backless booster. Picked as a "good bet" by IIHS.
Cons: Funky cup holder; not sold in many stores so it may be hard to see in person.
Comments: Want side impact protection but turned off by the restrictive wings of other booster seats? Combi's Kobuk aims to fill this niche with a protective headrest, minus the tight-fitting wings. We liked the padding of this seat (even the armrests are padded), but the cheesy cup holder that sticks straight out of the seat and relatively high price (twice the price of a Graco TurboBooster) are negatives.

On the plus side, the entire seat is lined with EPS and "egg shock" (comfort) foam. Combi's pitch for the Kobuk includes a claim that its front air vents allow for "healthy ventilation." Well, given parent feedback, we don't think this seat is any cooler than other boosters, but it's hard to measure that claim. In the past year, Combi hasn't made many changes to this seat but it is now rated to 125 lbs. (up from 100 lbs.).

Parent feedback on this seat has been positive. The Kobuk scored as a good bet on the latest IIHS rating and four out of five stars in the government's ease of use tests.

Unfortunately, like many Combi products, this seat may be hard to find at retail. That is more of a problem for a booster seat, as it is best to sit your child in the seat before purchasing. ***Rating: B+***

COSCO AMBASSADOR / HIGHRISE
Booster type: Backless booster
Weight: 40-100 lbs. Kids must be between 43" and 57" tall.
Price: $11.20 to $17.49
IIHS rating: Check fit.
NHTSA ease of use rating: ★★★☆☆
Pros: Cheap backless booster. Cup holder.
Cons: None.

Comments: Very simple and affordable backless boosters. Both versions have padded armrests and a fold-down cup holder. Most parent feedback is positive, but quite a few parents noted the padding on the seat is rather skimpy when compared to Graco boosters.

FYI: This seat is sold as the Ambassador in Walmart and the HighRise on other sites; it is basically the same seat. ***Rating: B***

COSCO HIGH BACK

This seat is reviewed on the free side of our web site at BabyBargains.com/?p=1146

COSCO PRONTO
Booster type: High back and backless booster
Weight: 30-100 lbs. as belt positioning booster, 40-100 lbs. as backless booster.
Price: $34
IIHS rating:
Backless mode: Check fit.
High back mode: Best Bet.
NHTSA ease of use rating: ★★★★☆

Pros: Low price, machine washable pad, cup holder.
Cons: None.
Comments: This booster has a roomy seat and adjusts for taller kids. We also like the machine washable pad. And you can't beat the price. This might be a good booster for Grandma's car.

Unlike Cosco's High Back Booster, this seat earns a better rating from the government for ease of use (four out of five stars) and a Best Bet from the IIHS in high back mode. Reader feedback has also been positive—no, the fabric and padding isn't as nice as the Graco TurboBooster. And Evenflo's similar model has armrests that move up (the Pronto has fixed armrests, which makes climbing in and out of the seat a bit more challenging). But the Pronto is less expensive than those options, so there's your trade-off. ***Rating: B***

COSCO STACK IT
Booster type: Backless booster
Weight: 40-100 lbs.
Price: $25

IIHS rating: Check fit.
NHTSA ease of use rating: ★★★★☆
Pros: Cheap backless booster. Two cup holders.
Cons: None.
Comments: This simple backless booster features two cup holders and a removable/machine-washable pad. Parent feedback on this seat has been positive. We will recommend it. ***Rating: A***

Cosco Top Side / No Back

This seat is reviewed on the free side of our web site at BabyBargains.com/?p=12041

Cybex Solution X-Fix / Q-Fix / M-Fix

Booster type: High back
Weight: 33-80 lbs.
Price: X-Fit: $170; Q-Fix: $305; M-Fix (price not set).
IIHS rating:
X-Fix: Best Bet.
Q-Fix: Good Bet.
M-Fix: Not rated yet.
NHTSA ease of use rating: X-Fix ★★★★☆

Pros: Rigid LATCH, side impact protection.

Cons: Pricey, doesn't convert into a backless booster.

Comments: This LATCH-compatible booster is coming back from the grave. After being discontinued in 2012, Cybex has decided to give it a second chance.

The X-Fix's main feature is a rigid LATCH connector, much like the Clek Oober. We like the Solution X-Fix's adjustable back and side impact protection. One unique feature: the headrest reclines in three positions.

Reader feedback on this seat was positive before and the IIHS gave the last version a Best Bet rating. We assume it will perform similarly, since it isn't changing in its reincarnation. Cybex also offers a beefed up version of this seat called the Q-Fix, with extensive side impact protection. As you raise up the headrest, the Q-Fix's sides expand, giving a bigger toddler more room in the seat. Like the X-Fix, the Q-Fix has rigid LATCH.

Coming in 2015, the Q-Fix will be getting a revised headrest and a new name, the Solution Q2-Fix. The headrest keeps a sleeping child from slumping forward in the seat. This booster also features an automatic height and width adjustments, plus additional side impact protection. No price was set as of press time.

Also new in 2015: the Solution M-Fix. This seat is similar to the Q-Fix, but features an independently adjustable headrest with three positions and button-operated side impact protection that pops out of the side of the seat. How is this different than the Q-Fix? On the Q-Fix, both the headrest and torso move together; the M-Fix's headrest now moves independently. And the Q-Fix has fixed side impact cushions. Pricing for the M-Fix wasn't available as of this writing. It is due out in the first half for 2015.

Reader feedback on these seats has been sparse, probably due to Cybex's thin distribution in stores and online. However, the IIHS picked it as a Best Bet and the government scored it as four out of five stars in ease of use. So we'll recommend this one, even though it is pricey. ***Rating: B+***

DIONO CAMBRIA/SOLANA

Booster type: High back.
Weight: 50 to 120 lbs.
Price: $92
IIHS rating: For the Cambria: Not yet. For the Solana: Best Bet
NHTSA ease of use rating: Not yet.
Pros: LATCH connectors, adjustable deep headwings for side impact protection. Seat lined with EPS foam.
Cons: Fewer height adjustments than previous model. Sides aren't adjustable. No five-point harness.

Comments: As Diono's newest high back booster, the Cambria is designed to be more of an entry-price point seat than Diono's previous high back offering (the Monterey, now discontinued). The Cambria features LATCH connectors, swing-out cup holders and deep head wings for side impact protection.

The trade-offs include fewer height adjustments (six) and no adjustable seat width. But you do get a seat that works to 120 lbs. Some parents noted the padding is rather skimpy on the Cambria.

At about $100, the seat is competitive with other LATCH-compatible seats like the Graco Affix.

A backless version of the Cambria is sold as the Solana; it works from 30 to 120 lbs. and runs $32. It has the same features as the Cambria (LATCH connectors; dual swing-out cup holders, etc.).
Rating: B

DISNEY BOOSTERS

These models are made by Cosco; see Cosco Pronto review. Basically, the same seat but with Disney fashions.

EDDIEBAUER DELUXE BELT-POSITIONING BOOSTER

This seat is reviewed on the free side of our web site at BabyBargains.com/?p=1154

EVENFLO AMP HIGH BACK BOOSTER

Booster type: High back booster, converts to backless
Weight: 30 to 100 lbs.
Price: $36
IIHS rating: Amp High Back: Not Available
Amp High Backless: Best bet.

boosters

NHTSA ease of use rating: ✮✮✮✮✮

Pros: Affordable. Deeper side wings for more side impact protection. Comfort touch padding.

Cons: None.

Comments: The Amp High Back Booster is similar to the Evenflo Big Kid with a couple of differences: the Amp has a bigger headrest for more side impact protection. And the Amp has two integrated cup holders (the Big Kid's cup holders can retract into the base). Price-wise, they are about the same. Both seats convert into backless boosters for older children.

As with Evenflo's other Amp seats, the emphasis here is on bright, neon color accents. And just to confuse you, there is also a backless Amp booster (that's how the Amp line started). And for a while, Evenflo even marketed a version of the Big Kid called the Big Kid *Amp* (it's still for sale on some sites). In the past year, Evenflo has tried to separate the Big Kid and Amp boosters into separate lines.

Parent feedback on this seat has been positive. We'd still give the Graco TurboBooster a slight edge in how well kids fit in the seat, but the Amp High Back is a close second. **Rating: A-**

EVENFLO BIG KID

Booster type: High back booster
Weight: 30 to 100 lbs.
Price: $30-$60.
IIHS rating:
Big Kid LX: Check fit.
Big Kid LX No Back: Best Bet.
Big Kid Sport No Back: Best bet.
Big Kid Sport high back: Check fit.
Big Kid Advanced: Not yet.

NHTSA ease of use rating: Big Kid LX only: ✮✮✮✮✮

Pros: Low price, extras like reading lights, EPS foam.

Cons: Skimpy padding in low-end version.

Comments: Evenflo's answer to Graco's TurboBooster, the Big Kid adds a few bells and whistles that Graco doesn't have. The Big Kid is adjustable in both height and lap depth (most boosters are just height adjustable). One version of the Big Kid actually comes with reading lights. Like the TurboBooster, the Big Kid's back removes as kids grow bigger, adding a discreet boost to older kids.

On the plus side, the Big Kid is less expensive than the Graco Turbo Booster (a $40 version called the Big Kid Amp at Babies R Us is especially affordable). On the downside, the padding is a bit skimpier than the Graco, making this seat less comfy for longer trips. And the Big Kid has less side impact protection than other seats. As usual, it is the little things about Evenflo that drive you crazy: the reading lights are nice, but lack an auto shut-off feature (and hence, will consume batteries fast if left on).

Like most Evenflo products, the Big Kid comes in several different versions, including an Advanced, LX, DLX (DLX, pictured) and Sport. The more expensive versions include upgraded fabric and padding. The Sport omits the activity lights, the one-hand adjustment, energy-absorbing foam liner and pivoting armrests. (Other older versions may still be available online, but Evenflo notes these are the versions going forward.)

Reader feedback on this seat has been positive, with parents lauding the many features and adjustments. And the government awarded this seat its top rating for ease of use. However, the Insurance Institute for Highway Safety only gave this seat a "check fit" rating (a backless version of the this seat did earn a best bet).

Between the two seats, we'd give the Graco TurboBooster the edge in overall quality—it tends to fit kids better than the Evenflo Big Kid. On the other hand, you can often find this seat for a lower price than the TurboBooster. *Rating: B*

EVENFLO CHASE (LX & DLX) / MAESTRO

These older model Evenflo boosters are reviewed on the free side of our web site at BabyBargains.com/bonus.

EVENFLO NO BACK BOOSTER
aka: Big Kid Elite, AMP LX, AMP Performance
Booster type: Backless booster
Weight: 40-110 lbs. Kids must be 57" or less.
Price: $22 to $30.
IIHS rating: Best bet.

NHTSA ease of use rating: ★★★★★
Pros: Neon colors; affordable.
Cons: None.
Comments: Basic backless booster that aims to appeal to kids with bright neon colors. Parent feedback has been very positive.

The Big Kid Elite has a fancier, thicker pad than the AMP versions, but they all use the same platform. And they all go up to 110 lbs. *Rating: A*

EVENFLO PROCOMFORT AMP LX
Booster type: High back, converts to backless
Weight: 30 to 110 lbs.
Price: $70
IIHS rating: (for previous version)
Amp High Back: Check fit.
Amp High Backless: Best bet.

NHTSA ease of use rating (previous version): ⭐⭐⭐⭐⭐

Pros: Easy to use, side impact protection, ProComfort padding for a more cushy ride.

Cons: Twice as expensive as a regular Amp. Only at Target.

Comments: The ProComfort Amp LX is basically the same as the regular Amp, but adds a more cushy seat with "ProComfort" gel technology. It works as a belt-positioning booster from 30-110 lbs. and then as a backless booster to 110 lbs.

The ProComfort Amp differs from the regular Amp in two ways: it features cups built into the armrests; the regular Amp has cup holders built into the base. Also new: Evenflo's "ProComfort" padding that has "Gel Matrix Technology." Basically, this is a more comfortable seat.

As the top of the line Amp, Evenflo also throws in activity lights and a six-position adjustable headrest with side impact protection. The ProComfort Amp LX is a Target exclusive.

Parent feedback on this seat has been positive and we'll recommend it. The only caveat: at $70, it is twice the price of a plain Amp. If you plan on taking longer trips or have a long commute, the extra ProComfort padding might be worth it. Otherwise, you can save $35 and get a regular Amp. *Rating: A-*

EVENFLO RIGHTFIT

Booster type: High back booster

Weight: 30 to 110 lbs.; 38"-57" in height. At least four years of age.

Price: $90. Babies R Us exclusive.

IIHS rating: Best Bet.

NHTSA ease of use rating: Not yet.

Pros: Affordable, multiple seat and headrest adjustments. Side impact protection.

Cons: Top harness height of 19" means taller kids may outgrow the seat too soon. Pricey.

Comments: This booster is a Babies R Us exclusive and features some refinements over Evenflo's other booster seats. The headline here is adjustability: the back rest has four adjustments. When combined with three headrest adjustments, you have 12 possible positions. That's more than just about any other seat on the market.

The RightFit also has Evenflo's e3 side impact protection and improved lights (four LED lights on each side wing). Like most Evenflo boosters, the RightFit converts to a backless booster for older kiddos. Two built-in cup holders on the arms are well designed.

The negatives: the top belt height is only 19"—that is much shorter than the Britax Parkway (21.5") or Recaro's ProBooster (21"). Hence this may not be the right booster if you have a tall toddler, as they may grow out of the seat too soon. We also found this seat's $90 price tag a bit high, since you can buy a comparable Graco TurboBooster for $43.

Parent feedback on the RightFit has been mixed, with several folks criticizing the narrow shoulder belt guide (making it difficult to slide a seat belt through). Given some of these reviews, we've downgraded the rating. If you get this seat, make sure you keep the receipt so you can return it if the shoulder belt guide turns out to be an issue in your vehicle. ***Rating: B-***

EVENFLO SECUREKID / PLATINUM SECUREKID DLX

This seat is reviewed on the free side of our web site at BabyBargains.com/?p=9052

GRACO AFFIX YOUTH BOOSTER

Booster type: High back and backless booster
Weight: 30 to 100 lbs. as high back booster (backless, it is 40 to 100 lbs.).
Price: $67to $80 (high back); $34 (backless)
IIHS rating: Best Bet.
NHTSA ease of use rating: ★★★★☆
Pros: LATCH connectors keep seat in place when unoccupied. Side impact protection.

Cons: Pricey if you don't want to use LATCH.
Comments: The Graco Affix Youth Booster is similar to the Graco TurboBooster with Safety Surround with one main difference: the Affix has LATCH connectors to secure it to the vehicle. This keeps the seat secure if it is unoccupied. An upfront adjuster lets you tighten the LATCH connectors.

Like the TurboBooster, you also get an integrated cup holder. The downside to this seat: a basic Graco booster like the TurboBooster can be found for 40% less than this model.

What about the LATCH connectors? Well, we can certainly see why parents would want to secure a booster to the vehicle (if unoccupied and there is a crash, an unsecured booster seat could fly about in the vehicle). Graco also pitches the LATCH connection as easier for kids to buckle the seat in (since it can't move around). As far as safety of the seat itself, however, LATCH doesn't necessarily make the seat safer—a booster without LATCH connectors is just as safe for a toddler as one with LATCH.

FYI: A backless version of the Affix is $34. Buy Buy Baby has an exclusive version of the Affix that has "Safety Surround" side impact protection for $100.

Bottom line: the Affix is a good seat. If LATCH connection is important, then this is a worthy seat to consider. Given Graco's track record in this category, we will give it our recommendation. Parent feedback has been positive. ***Rating: A***

GRACO ARGOS 65/70/80 ELITE

Booster type: Combo booster
Price: 65: $160; 70: $160; 80 Elite: $215
Type: Combo.
Limits: 65: 20 to 65 lbs. with harness, up to 100 lbs. as a highback booster, up to 120 lbs. as a backless booster.

70: 20 to 70 lbs. with harness, up to 100 lbs. as a highback booster, up to 120 lbs. as a backless booster.

80 Elite: 20 to 80 lbs. with harness, up to 100 lbs. as a highback booster, up to 120 lbs. as a backless booster

NHTSA ease of use rating (Argos 70):

★★★★☆ Booster mode
★★★☆☆ Harness mode

IIHS rating (Argos 80 Elite): High back mode: Best bet.; Backless mode: Check fit.

Comments: The big headline here is a no-rethread harness. The Argos also features extra side-impact protection and EPS foam as well as its three-position recline.

Basically, the Argos is like the Nautilus, but works to 65, 70 or 80 lbs. with a five-point harness depending on the model (the Nautilus works to 65 lbs.). Then the Argos becomes a backless booster to 120 lbs. (the Nautilus stops as 100 lbs.). And the no-rethread harness is a big pro over the Nautilus.

So what's not to like? Well, the harness slots are the same height as the Nautilus. You'd think if they are promoting the higher weight, Graco would throw you a harness height an inch or so above the Nautilus. And the price premium is another issue: the Argos is between $150 and $215, while the Nautilus can be found online for as little as $140 on Walmart.

Feedback on the Argos is positive—fans generally laud the seat's quality and design. A recent upgrade to the seat is a better buckle system (IMMI) to address issues readers had in the past with the old buckles. While it is overshadowed by its better-selling sister model (the Nautilus), the Argos is worthy of consideration as well. **Rating: B+**

GRACO NAUTILUS 3-IN-1

Booster type: Combo
Weight: 20-65 lbs. with harness, 30 to 100 lbs. as high back booster. Backless booster from 40 to 100 lbs.
Price: $140-$190.
IIHS rating: High back mode: Best Bet.
Backless mode: Check fit.
Elite model: Check fit (both modes).

NHTSA ease of use rating: ★★★☆☆

Pros: Works to 65 lbs. with a five-point harness.

Cons: Harness must be re-threaded to adjust height. No LATCH connectors to keep seat in place when unoccupied.

Comments: Here's the best-selling combo booster seat on the market—the Graco's Nautilus is a combo booster that works with a five-point harness to 65 lbs. and then converts to high back booster (100 lbs.) and even a backless booster for older kids. The harness is a big plus if you have a toddler who has outgrown his convertible seat, but wish to keep him in the harness for a while longer (the 65 lb. limit should fit most five year olds).

The Nautilus' other features include over molded armrests (with side storage), three-position recline and decent padding. The seat is lined with EPS foam. Like most Graco seats, Graco makes a few different versions of the Nautilus, which boils down to fabric plushness.

The Nautilus's biggest competitor is the Britax Frontier, so let's look how they compare. The Britax Frontier is bigger and wider than the Nautilus—and the Britax seat works up to 90 lbs. with the five-point harness. Folks generally give the Frontier better marks for padding, although the more expensive Nautilus models offer similar padding.

In the past, we gave the Nautilus the edge over the Frontier for its ease of install; however, Britax redesigned the Frontier in 2010 and caught up to the Nautilus.

There are a couple of key differences: to adjust the harness height with the Graco Nautilus, you have to rethread the harness. The Frontier harness doesn't require rethreading, which makes it much easier to use. The Frontier has three crotch strap adjustments; the Graco only two. On the other hand, the mesh fabric on the Britax Frontier is much more prone to show wear and stains compared to the Nautilus, which doesn't have this problem.

So it now basically comes down to price: the basic Nautilus is HALF the cost of the Britax Frontier . . . and we know that's nothing to sneeze at.

As for reader feedback, the Graco Nautilus earns positive marks from readers for its overall ease of use. The IIHS ranks the Nautilus as a Best Bet when used in highback mode; the Britax Frontier earns the same rating.

FYI: There are many other versions of the Nautilus on the market. First, the Nautilus Elite adds an adjustable headrest and belt lock-offs (to ease installation in that mode). The Elite also has enhanced side impact protection (EPS foam lining the headrest). As you'd expect from the Elite name, this model includes upgraded pad and fabric. Oddly, the Elite scored lower on ease of use and the IIHS ratings than the regular model. And you'd think the Elite model would have premium push-button LATCH connectors, right? Nope, the Nautilus

boosters

Elite uses the same run of the mill LATCH connectors as on the basic model. The Nautilus Elite sells for $190 on Amazon.

Another alternative version of the Nautilus is the Nautilus Plus, available at Buy Buy Baby. It features a reversible body support pillow and seat protector. Price: $190. Between the Plus and Elite, the Elite is better in our opinion.

Two other versions include the Nautilus with Safety Surround Protection (enhanced side impact protectional, sold at Target for $180) and the Nautilus LX ($163; we're not sure what makes it different). Enough with the multitude of Nautilus versions—we get headaches trying to figure out what the real differences are between models. In some cases, the version is just a different pattern and name Graco sells to certain stores as an exclusive.

Bottom line: we like the Nautilus—it is among our top picks in this category. **Rating: A**

GRACO TURBOBOOSTER

Booster type: High back and backless booster
Weight: 30 to 100 lbs. as high back booster (backless, it is 40 to 100 lbs).
Price: $42-$75. Backless version is $22-$35.
IIHS rating:
High back mode: Best Bet.
Backless mode: Best Bet.

NHTSA ease of use rating: ★★★☆☆
(Rating for Graco TurboBooster with Safety Surround.)
Pros: Top choice in booster market—affordable and well designed.
Cons: No five-point harness; little side impact protection.
Comments: This is our top pick as a great, affordable belt-positioning booster seat (no harness). The TurboBooster features padded armrests that are height adjustable, EPS foam, hide-away cup holders and a one-hand adjustment for the headrest. The seat pad removes for cleaning; the TurboBooster converts into a backless booster for older kids.

As usual, Graco makes this seat in more than a dozen colors and styles. Hence, you'll find a basic version for $45 at Walmart and upgraded models for $75 in specialty stores. What's the difference? Just the fabric pad. More money, fancier pad.

So what are the drawbacks to the Graco TurboBooster? Well, unlike the Graco Nautilus or Britax Frontier, this seat lacks a five-point harness. Hence you must have an older toddler who is mature enough to sit in a regular seat belt. Also: the TurboBooster requires quite a bit of assembly with various screws (that's the reason this seat only earned three stars in booster mode for the

NHTSA's ease of use rating).

One flaw for the TurboBooster, the lack of side impact protection, was addressed recently: Graco is adding their "Safety Surround" side impact protection to one version of the TurboBooster (dubbed the Highback TurboBooster with Safety Surround, $80—a Target exclusive). Another flaw: this seat isn't as tall as other boosters, making it less attractive for larger kids.

Bottom line: the Graco TurboBooster is an excellent high back booster. If you can spare the extra cash, go for the version with the Safety Surround padding. ***Rating: A***

HARMONY

These booster seats are reviewed on the free side of our web site at BabyBargains.com/bonus.

KIDDY CRUISERFIX PRO
Booster type: High back.
Weight: 33 to 100 lbs. as high back booster.
Price: $160
IIHS rating: Best Bet.
NHTSA ease of use rating: ★★★★☆
Pros: Adjustable side impact protection wings, extendable leg extension. LATCH connectors.

Cons: No backless mode. Hard to find at retail.

Comments: Kiddy is a German car seat maker that is the latest European import to the U.S. Their CruiserFix Pro is a $160 belt-positioning booster that works up to 100 lbs. Among the CruiserFix Pro's unique features is its extendable seat depth (to nearly 17"), as well as being both height and width adjustable. Unlike Kiddy's other model (the World Plus), the CruiserFix Pro lacks a top tether or lap shield. But this seat does have rigid LATCH connectors that pop out of the seat.

If there is one downside to this seat, it would be Kiddy's rather thin distribution—this seat is hard to find in retail stores to see first hand. Hence, most folks have had to take the plunge and buy it online, sign unseen. Yet, so far, reader feedback has been very positive. Yes, it is pricey, but we like all the adjustments and the detailed side impact protection. One negative: the rigid LATCH may not work in some vehicles, especially if the anchor points don't line up with those on the seat.

Bottom line: we'll give the CruiserFix Pro a thumbs up. ***Rating: A***

KIDDY WORLD PLUS

This booster seats is reviewed on the free side of our web site at BabyBargains.com/?p=5667

KIDSEMBRACE FRIENDSHIP/FUN RIDES

Type: Combo booster
Weight: 22 lbs. to 65 lbs. with harness; booster 30 lbs. to 100 lbs.
Price: $100-$150
IIHS: Highback version: Best Bet. Backless version: Not Recommended.

NHTSA ease of use rating: ★★★★☆

Pros: One hand harness adjustment; 2-position crotch strap; wrap around headrest. Cartoon themes = toddler happiness.

Cons: Cup holders have no bottom. Straps can be twisty. Backless version is NOT RECOMMENDED.

Comments: As parents of a toddler know, getting their "buy in" to a new situation is crucial to everyone's happiness. Hence, we can see the point of the KIDSEmbrace themed car eats, featuring the likes of Sponge Bob, Dora the Explorer, Batman and Spiderman.

Even though they look jokey, these are actually well-designed boosters. Sold on Walmart.com for $118 and other sites for up to $150, KIDSEmbrace's boosters are well priced and may be the solution to toddlers who balk at sitting in a "baby seat." The booster has a one-hand harness adjustment, two-position crotch strap and side impact headrest. Parent feedback is relatively positive—it's easy to install and use. Best bet is how the IIHS rated these seats, which also scored decent ease of use ratings from the NHTSA.

In our last review, we criticized one big negative for these seats: a low top harness slot. Well, Kids Embrace has addressed this problem—their new models have a 17" top harness slot. The similar Graco Nautilus has an 18" top slot, so Kids Embrace is now in the ballpark.

As for the cartoon characters, we realize some folks turn up their nose at the commercialism. But if a Ninja Turtles car seat gets your kid excited about that long road trip, where's the harm? These seats are safe and generally well reviewed by parents. Are the Kids Embrace as cushy as other more expensive seats? No. Is there extensive side impact protection? No. But you do get a decent seat that your toddler will (probably) never argue about sitting in.

So we'll raise the rating on these seats this time out.

FYI: KIDSEmbrace makes a backless booster seat. The IIHS rating on this model is "Not Recommended." That means the seat does not "provide good belt fit;" therefore we also will not recommend KIDSEmbrace backless version. ***Rating: B (Highback version only)***

LITTLE TIKES

Comments: Made by Diono, these boosters are similar to the Diono Cambria/Solana. Pricing ranges from $17 (backless) to $60 (high back). See Diono review earlier in this chapter.

Maxi Cosi Rodi AP
Booster type: High back booster
Weight: 30 to 120 lbs.
Price: $130
IIHS rating:
High back mode: Best Bet.
Backless mode: Check fit.
NHTSA ease of use rating: ★★★★☆

Pros: Extra large side wings provide sleep support, adjustable headrest. Seat recline.

Cons: Requires vehicles with rear headrests.

Comments: The Rodi AP ($130) features Dorel's "Air Protect" side impact cushions, which are integrated into the height adjustable headrest. When you pull the headrest up, it also widens the body to better fit a growing child. The Rodi AP now goes up to 120 lbs.

Reader feedback on this seat has been mixed. Yes, the seat is lightweight. Yes, it adjusts and fits kids pretty well. But there isn't much padding in the seat area and the cup hold is flimsy. There are no LATCH connectors to hold the seat when unoccupied. Another major negative: like most Dorel boosters, the Rodi must be used in a back seat that has headrest support—something lacking in many cars.

That said, this seat is priced well and it earned a Best Bet (in high back mode) from the Insurance Institute for Highway Safety. So we'll tick up the Rodi AP's rating this year. **Rating: B**

Maxi Cosi RodiFix
Booster type: High back booster
Weight: 30 to 120 lbs.
Price: $250
IIHS Rating: Best Bet.
NHTSA ease of use rating: Not yet.
Comments: This seat has the same basic features as the Maxi Cosi Rodi AP, but adds LATCH connectors to keep the seat from moving when unoccupied. The only other minor difference: this model doesn't have armrests. While we like the addition of LATCH, the current price on this model is too high. **Rating: C**

Peg Perego Viaggio HBB 120
Booster type: High back and backless booster
Weight: 40 to 120 lbs. as high back booster or backless.
Price: $180
IIHS rating:
High Back: Best Bet. Backless: Check fit.

boosters

NHTSA ease of use rating: ★★★★☆

Pros: EPS foam, side impact protection head wings, use to 120 pounds, converts to backless. LATCH connectors, two recessed cup holders. Made in Italy.

Cons: $180? Similar seats can be had for $50.

Comments: Peg Perego continues to expand its car seat line–after debuting a convertible seat in 2011, the company added a belt-positioning booster in 2012. The Viaggio HBB 120 booster seat works from 40 to 120 lbs. (Confusingly, Perego refers to all its car seats as Viaggio, which is Italian for trip).

The booster features side impact head cushions and integrated cup holders. It comes in both fabric ($180) and leatherette ($215), the latter of which looked like a poor choice for parents in hot climates.

Our first impression of this seat was that it looked like an overpriced knock-off of the Graco TurboBooster. And since you can pick up that seat for just $50, we're not sure what justifies the big price premium here (okay, the Viaggio HBB will work to 120 lbs. versus the TurboBooster's 100 lbs.). The Viaggio does have LATCH attachments to keep the seat secure when unoccupied and it reclines, another feature the TurboBooster lacks. But most of the specs of this seat are similar to the TurboBooster, down to the two hide-away cup holders in the base.

We wish Perego had come out with some new technology or incredible adjustments (like Kiddy's seats that have amazing adjustments for the seat depth and head rests). Otherwise, this is just another me-too seat with Italian fashion that, unfortunately, is symbolic of Perego's malaise in recent years.

Parent feedback on this seat has been mostly positive. They love the latch system which makes it easy to install. One negative: readers note that if the seat can't be placed flush to the back of the seat because of protruding headrests, you can't use the seat with the high back. It did receive a four out of five rating from the NHTSA for ease of use. If you want to avoid Chinese-made products, this seat is made in Italy.

We think other competitors like Britax and Graco have set the bar very high in this category. And the $180 Perego booster just doesn't quite measure up, in our opinion. *Rating: B*

RECARO PERFORMANCE BOOSTER

Booster type: High back booster

Weight: 30 to 120 lbs., 37" to 61" tall.

Price: $120

IIHS rating: Best Bet.

NHTSA ease of use rating: ★★★☆☆

Pros: Side impact protection, works to 120 lbs.

Cons: No LATCH. No cup holders. Only works as a high back booster.

Comments: Side impact protection is the headline here—the Performance Booster works to 120 lbs. and has a wide seat. This model has "cool mesh" air ventilation and a recline feature to better fit the slope of a vehicle's back seat. Other features include memory foam, 11 position head rest, and built in LATCH system.

Reader feedback on this seat is mostly positive. One minor complaint: the LATCH strap system is not adjustable so you can't get a tight fit to the back seat. Recaro notes that the point is not to get a tight fit, rather to keep the seat from flying around when not in use. But parents note the loosely attached seat makes it hard for kids to jump in and out by themselves.

Also: a previous version of this seat drew complaints for being tippy in vehicles with bucket seats. In 2013, Recaro came out with a revised version of the Performance Booster that addressed these concerns. After this change, we saw a decrease in comments on this issue.

Bottom line: this is an excellent booster. **_Rating: A-_**

RECARO PERFORMANCE SPORT
Booster type: Combo
Weight: 20 to 120 lbs.; five-point harness to 65 lbs. Up to 59"
Price: $202
IIHS rating: Best Bet.
NHTSA ease of use rating:
⭐⭐⭐☆☆ Harness mode
⭐☆☆☆☆ Booster mode

Pros: Very comfortable, EPS foam, side impact protection.
Cons: Price. Hard to find in retail stores. Tools required to disassemble the seat for cleaning.
Comments: Like the Recaro Performance Booster, side impact protection is the star here with the Performance Sport. You also get a harness height adjustment that works without re-threading, EPS foam for crash protection, and extra seat padding. The Performance Sport also features LATCH connectors, which is handy to keep the seat in position when not occupied. Other features: additional memory foam in the seat and Recaro's new HERO system (headrest optimization system). And new this year, breathable mesh and enhanced cup holders.

Reader feedback on this seat has been very positive and it earned a Best Bet from the Insurance Institute for Highway Safety. On the downside, we heard a few complaints that the side wings can get protest votes from toddlers who think they are too confining, block their vision, etc. (you may want to sit your child in this seat first before buying). And the NHTSA gave this seat only one-star in booster mode for ease of use, criticizing Recaro for not labeling the belt path. The NHTSA also said conversion of this seat from

boosters

harness to booster mode is difficult and hand tools are needed to disassemble the seat for cleaning.

While we respect the NHTSA's ratings, we note the real world feedback from parents who've used the Performance Booster is much more positive. Priced at about same level as the Britax Frontier, we give the Recaro Performance Sport our top rating. ***Rating: A***

SAFETY 1ST BOOST AIR PROTECT

This booster seats is reviewed on the free side of our web site at BabyBargains.com/?p=5676

SAFETY 1ST BOOSTAPAK

Booster type: Backless
Weight: 40-80 lbs., 57"
Price: $58
IIHS rating: Best Bet.
NHTSA ease of use rating: ⭐⭐⭐⭐☆
Pros: It's a backpack! It's a booster
Cons: Pricey
Comments: Yes, this backless booster does its best Transformer imitation, starting out as a backless booster and then morphing into a backpack. The BoostAPak is great for carpoolers and air travel—and it earned a Best Bet rating from the IIHS as well as four out of five stars for ease of use.

The only negative? It is rather pricey at $58. Considering you can get a good backless booster for $20 to $30, the BoostAPak seems expensive to us. But you also get a storage compartment in the back, so we can see how some parents would find this a major plus especially for frequent travelers.

Parent feedback on this seat has been positive. We will recommend it. ***Rating: A***

SAFETY 1ST INCOGNITO

Booster type: Backless booster
Weight: 60 to 100 lbs.
Price: $20
IIHS rating: Not yet.
NHTSA ease of use rating: ⭐⭐⭐⭐☆
Pros: Lower profile; neutral colors.
Cons: Won't work for younger kids until they hit 60 lbs.
Comments: Safety 1st's new Incognito booster is intended for use by older kids, not toddlers. The age range for the Incognito is eight years old and up; and 60 lbs.+. As the name implies, the Incognito has a low profile to blend into a car's interior.

Kudos to Safety 1st for thinking outside the box here. This booster would work well for a small school age child that needs just a couple inches of boost for an improved belt fit.

Reader feedback has been positive, but a few folks complained that the seat is hard (uncomfortable for long trips) and, for some kids too narrow. Overall, however, we'd recommend this seat–a good solution for smaller school age kids. **Rating: A**

SAFETY 1ST STORE 'N GO
Booster type: High back.
Weight: 40-100 lbs., 57"
Price: $47 high back; $25 backless booster
IIHS rating: Not Yet.
NHTSA ease of use rating: ★★★★☆
Pros: Storage drawer. Two cup holders.
Cons: No side impact protection.

Comments: As you might have guessed from the name, the Store 'n Go's claim to fame is its under seat storage drawer. It also has a side pocket/cup holder. The Store 'n Go comes both as a high back ($47 and backless booster ($25). FYI: Walmart has a Disney version of this seat ($27).

The Store 'n Go looks like Safety 1st's attempt to knock off the Graco TurboBooster, which is similarly priced. Unfortunately, this seat omits Safety 1st's Air Protect side impact protection feature seen on the company's Boost Air Protect model. Considering that the Boost Air is roughly the same price as the Store 'n Go, we think the side impact protection is a better bet than a storage drawer.

The Store 'n Go gets good marks from parents. They like the soft padding, adjustable head rest, and kids like the bright colors. One complaint: the seat rattles. For parents who are sensitive to noises in the car this is a deal killer. **Rating: A-**

SAFETY 1ST SUMMIT, VANTAGE
The Safety 1st Summit and Vantage booster seats are reviewed on the free side of our web site at BabyBargains.com/bonus

Best Bets: Booster Seats

◆ **Best Bets: Harness Seats.** Our top pick is the **Graco Nautilus** and **Nautilus Elite**–this combo seat has a five-point harness that can be used up to 65 lbs. The Nautilus also converts to a belt-positioning booster and even a backless booster to 100 lbs. Starting at $140, the Nautilus is very affordable. If you can spring for the Nautilus Elite ($190), you get several upgrades: enhanced side impact protection, adjustable headrest and belt lock-offs to ease installation.

Runner-up: **Graco Argos 80 Elite** is a good choice if your kiddo

boosters

is on the upper end of the growth charts. With higher weight and height limits, the Argos 80 Elite also features a no-rethread harness, a three-position recline and extra side impact protection. Price: $210.

Runner-up: Despite costing twice as much as a Nautilus, we think the *Britax Frontier ClickTight* ($247) is also worth a look. Yes, it works up to 90 lbs. with a five-point harness—and that is impressive. We love the ClickTight base for quick installation, as well as the no rethread harness and side impact protection. Reader feedback on this seat has been very positive. The only downside to the Frontier: this is a large and bulky seat, making it less attractive for car pools.

◆ *Best Bets: Belt-Positioning Booster.* We have one clear winner here and several other strong runners-ups.

The *Graco TurboBooster* ($45 to $80) is the best belt-positioning booster on the market today. It packs a good number of features into an affordable package: height-adjustable headrest, open belt loop design, armrests, back recline, cup holders and more. Note it comes in two versions: a high-back version and backless (the latter is about $25). If you can afford the upgrade, the Graco *TurboBooster With Safety Surround ($80)* has additional side impact protection in the form of enhanced headrest and torso cushions.

Runner up: the *Britax Parkway SGL* ($110) gets excellent marks from readers for ease of use and safety—you get LATCH connectors and an impressive 120 lb. weight limit. Bonus: this seat has Slide Guard (SG)—it keeps a child from submarining out of the seat in a crash.

Runner up: *Recaro Performance Booster* ($120) works to an impressive 120 lbs. and features enhanced side impact protection and LATCH connectors. Recaro's reputation for quality shines here with extra EPS foam and other detailing. The only negative: it only works as backless booster (it doesn't convert to a backless model).

◆ *Best Bets: Backless Booster.* The best backless boosters on the market are the *Graco TurboBooster* backless ($18-$35) and the *Evenflo Amp* ($22-$30). Both are affordable and easy to use boosters for older kids who don't need a high back booster.

◆ *Best Bets: Booster for carpools/taxis:* BubbleBum ($40) is an affordable, inflatable booster that is perfect for carpools or taxis. The BumbleBum's small size makes it perfect when you need to fit three toddlers in one back seat. One caveat: this booster probably isn't the most comfortable for long commutes or road trips.

Whew! You made it through the car seat chapter. Yes, we know—it was slightly shorter than Moby-Dick. Next up: strollers: which brands are best? How can you pick the best stroller for what you need? We've got it covered, starting on the next page.

CHAPTER 9

Strollers, Diaper Bags & Other Gear To Go

Inside this chapter

What are the best strollers? Which brands are the most durable AND affordable? We'll discuss this plus other tips on how to make your baby portable— from diaper bags to bike trailers and more. And what do you put in that diaper bag anyway? We've got nine suggestions.

Getting Started: When Do You Need This Stuff?

While you don't need a stroller or diaper bag immediately after baby is born, most parents purchase them before baby arrives anyway. And some of the best deals for strollers and other to-go gear are found online, which necessitates leaving time for shipping.

Sources to Find Strollers

As with other baby products, discounters like Target and Walmart tend to specialize in just a handful of models from mass-market companies like Cosco, Kolcraft, Graco and so on (lately, they've been adding premium brands to their web sites that aren't available in stores). The baby superstores like Babies R Us and Buy Buy Baby have a wider selection and (sometimes) better brands. Meanwhile, juvenile specialty stores almost always carry the more exclusive brands.

Yet perhaps the best deals for strollers and diaper bags are found online—for some reason, this seems to be one area the web covers very well. This is because strollers are relatively easy to ship (compared to other more bulky furniture items). Of course, more competition often means lower prices, so you'll see many deals online. Another plus: the web may be the only way to find certain premium-brand strollers if you live in less-populous parts of the U.S. and Canada.

Beware of shipping costs when ordering online or from a catalog—many strollers may run 20 or 30 lbs., which can translate into hefty shipping fees. Use an online coupon (see Chapter 7 for coupon sites) to save and look for free shipping specials.

Strollers

Baby stores offer a bewildering array of strollers for parents. Do you want the model that converts from a car seat to a stroller? What about a stroller that would work for a quick trip to the mall? Or do you want a stroller for jogging? Hiking trails? The urban jungle of New York City or beaches near LA?

And what about all the different brand names? Will a basic brand found at a discount store work? Or do you pine after one of the stylish Euro-designed imports? What about strollers with anti-lock brakes and air bags? (Just kidding on that last one).

The $332 million dollar stroller industry is not dominated by one or two players, like you might see in car seats or high chairs. Instead, you'll find a couple *dozen* stroller makers offering just about anything on wheels, ranging from $30 for a bare-bones model to $1100 for a Dutch-designed über stroller. A recent hot trend: all-terrain strollers with three wheels, where the front wheel swivels.

We hope this section takes some of the mystery out of the stroller buying process. First, we'll look at the six different types of strollers on the market today. Next, we'll zero in on features and help you decide what's important and what's not. Then, it's brand ratings and our picks as the best recommendations for different lifestyles. Finally, we'll go over several safety tips, money saving hints, and more.

Whew! Take a deep breath and let's go.

? What Are You Buying?

There are six types of strollers you can buy:

◆ **Umbrella Strollers.** The name comes from the appearance of the stroller when it's folded, similar to an umbrella.

WHAT'S COOL: They're lightweight and generally

cheap—that is, low in price (about $20 to $40). We should note that a handful of premium stroller makers (UPPAbaby and Peg Perego) also offer pricey umbrella strollers that sell for $100 to $300—we discuss them in the next category. Pictured is a no-frills Kolcraft umbrella stroller.

WHAT'S NOT: They're cheap—that is, low in quality. You typically don't get any fancy features like canopies, storage baskets, reclining seats, and so on. Another problem: most umbrella strollers have hammock-style seats with little head support, so they won't work well for babies under six months of age.

◆ **Lightweight Strollers.** These strollers are our top recommendation: they're basically souped-up umbrella strollers with many convenience features.

WHAT'S COOL: Most offer easy set-up and fold-down; some even fold up similar to umbrella strollers. Many models have great features (canopies, storage baskets, high-quality wheels) at amazingly light weights (as little as 8 lbs.). Graco, UPPAbaby and Bab Jogger make the most popular lightweight strollers.

WHAT'S NOT: Can be expensive—most high-quality brands run $150 to $300. The smaller wheels on lightweight strollers make maneuvering in the mall or stores easy . . . but those same wheels don't perform well on uneven surfaces or on gravel trails. Skimpy baskets are another trade-off.

◆ **Full-size Strollers.** Full-size strollers used to be called carriages or prams. Sort of like a bed on wheels—the seat lies flat and the leg rest pulls up to form a bassinet-like feature. Clearly, this feature focuses on newborns . . . but these strollers can then be configured for older babies with a seat that sits upright.

WHAT'S COOL: Full recline is great for newborns—they spend most of their time sleeping. Most combo carriage/strollers have lots of high-end features like plush seats, quilted canopies and other accessories to keep the weather out. The best carriage strollers and prams have a dreamy ride, with amazing suspensions and big wheels.

WHAT'S NOT: Hefty weight (not easy to transport or set up) and hefty price tags. Some carriage/stroller models can top $500, although entry-level carriage strollers start at $200. These strollers once dominated the market but have lost favor as more parents opt for "travel systems" that combine an infant seat and stroller (see below).

strollers

◆ **Multi-function Strollers.** These
strollers morph from infant carriages to tod-
dler strollers, with either an infant car seat
adapter or bassinet accessory. With fully
reclining seats, these strollers can be used
from birth. Some multi-functions even have
second seat options, morphing from a sin-
gle to a double stroller. Examples include the UPPAbaby Vista and
the Britax B-Ready (pictured).

WHAT'S COOL: In a word, flexibility—parents who buy these
strollers love the ability to morph them into several different uses.

◆ **Jogging (or Sport) Strollers.** These
strollers feature three big bicycle-tire wheels
and lightweight frames—perfect for jogging or
walking on rough roads. The front wheel is
fixed to maximize glide.

WHAT'S COOL: How many other strollers can
do 15 mph on a jogging trail? Some have plush
features like padded seats and canopies—and fold up quickly for easy
storage in the trunk. This category was hip a few years ago, but is now
in decline: more popular are the all-terrain strollers (see below).

WHAT'S NOT: They can be darn expensive, topping $300.
Jogging strollers are a single-purpose item—thanks to their sheer
bulk and a lack of steering (joggers usually have fixed front wheels),
you can't use one in a mall or other location. On the plus side, the
flood of new models is helping lower prices. New, low-end jogging strollers run $100 to $150. The trade-offs to the new bargain
price models: heavier steel frames and a lack of features.

◆ **All-terrain Strollers.** The baby equivalent of
sport-utility vehicles, these strollers are pitched to
parents who want to go on hikes or other outdoor
adventures. All-terrain strollers are similar to joggers
with one big difference—the front wheel swivels.

WHAT'S COOL: Big air-filled tires and high clear-
ances work better on gravel trails/roads than standard strollers.
These strollers are great for neighborhoods with broken or rough
sidewalks. All-terrain strollers have many convenience features (baskets, canopies, etc.) as well as one key advantage over jogging
strollers: most all-terrains have swivel front wheels. That makes them
easy to maneuver, whether on a trail or at the mall. Pictured above
is the Phil & Ted's stroller.

WHAT'S NOT: All-terrain strollers are wider and heavier than other
strollers, which make them less useful in a mall or store with tight

aisles. And air-filled tires are great for trails . . . but a pain in the neck if you get a flat. If you really want to run with a stroller, all-terrains with a swivel front wheel are not the best choice (a jogger with a fixed front wheel is better). And let's not forget the cost—most all terrains are pricey, some topping $400.

◆ **Travel Systems.** It's the current rage among stroller makers—models that combine infant car seats and strollers. Century (now part of Graco) kicked off this craze way back in 1994 with its "4-in-1" model that featured four uses (infant carrier, infant  car seat, carriage and toddler stroller). Since then, just about every major stroller maker has jumped into the travel system market. Pictured here is a Graco travel system.

WHAT'S COOL: Great convenience—you can take the infant car seat out of the car and then snap it into the stroller frame. Voila! Instant baby carriage, complete with canopy and basket. Later, you can use the stroller as, well, just a stroller.

WHAT'S NOT: The strollers are often junk—especially those by mass market makers Cosco and Evenflo. Quality problems plague this category, as does something we call "feature bloat." Popular travel systems from Graco, for example, are so loaded with features that they tip the scales at nearly 30 lbs.! The result: many parents abandon their travel system strollers for lighter weight models after baby outgrows his infant seat. And considering these puppies can cost $150 to $250 (some even more), that's a big investment for such limited use.

Travel systems have become less popular in recent years as more strollers feature adapters for other brand infant car seats—letting you create your own travel system.

Safe & Sound

Next to defective car seats, the most dangerous juvenile product on the market today is the stroller. That's according to the U.S. Consumer Product Safety Commission, which estimates that over 11,000 injuries a year occur from improper use or defects. The problems? Babies can slide out of the stroller (falling to the ground) and small parts can be a choking hazard. Seat belts have broken in some models, while other babies are injured when a stroller's brakes fail on a slope. Serious mishaps with strollers have involved entanglements and entrapments (where an unrestrained baby slides down and gets caught in a leg opening) and lacerations when parents fold up the stroller and kids get their hands caught. Here are some safety tips:

strollers

1 **NEVER HANG BAGS FROM THE STROLLER HANDLE**—it's a tipping hazard.

2 **DON'T LEAVE YOUR BABY ASLEEP UNATTENDED IN A STROLLER.** Many injuries happen when infants who are lying down in a stroller roll or creep and then manage to get their head stuck in the stroller's leg openings. Be safe: take a sleeping baby out of a stroller and move them to a crib or bassinet.

3 **THE BRAKES SHOULDN'T BE TRUSTED.** The best stroller models have brakes on two wheels; cheaper ones just have one wheel that brakes. Even with the best brakes, don't leave the stroller unattended on an incline.

4 **FOLLOW THE WEIGHT LIMITS.** Many strollers have limits of 35 to 40 lbs., but a few models allow extended use.

5 **JOGGING STROLLERS ARE BEST FOR BABIES OVER ONE YEAR OF AGE.** Yes, some stroller makers tout their joggers for babies as young as six weeks (or six months) of age. But after consulting with pediatric experts, we suggest waiting until one year of age to run with baby in a stroller. Why? The neck muscles of infants under a year of age can't take the shocks of jogging or walking on rough paths (or going over curbs). Ask your pediatrician if you need more advice on when it is safe to use a jogger.

6 **FOLD AND UNFOLD YOUR STROLLER WHEN BABY IS NOT NEAR.** Simply because they are foldable, strollers have various pinch points where baby's fingers may get caught. While some stroller makers have included protective shields over those points, it's best to open and close strollers when your baby is not around—leave them buckled in their car seat or keep them a distance away while you set up or put away your stroller.

Smart Shopper Tips

Smart Shopper Tip #1
Give it a Test Drive
"My friend was thinking of buying a stroller online, sight unseen. Should you really buy a stroller without trying it first?"

It's best to try before you buy. Most stores have at least one stroller set up as a floor model. Give it a whirl, practice folding it up, and check the steering. One smart tip: put some weight in the stroller seat (borrow a friend's toddler or use a backpack full of books that weighs about 15 lbs.). The steering and maneuverability will feel different if the stroller is weighted—obviously, that's a more real world test-drive.

Once you've tried it out, shop both on and offline. Ask retailers if they will meet or beat prices quoted to you online (many quietly do so). What if you live in Kansas and the nearest dealer for a stroller you want is in, say, Texas? Then you may have no choice but to buy sight unseen—but just make sure the web site has a good return policy. Another tip: use message boards like those on our web site (BabyBargains.com) to quiz other parents about stroller models.

If you buy a stroller from a store, we strongly recommend opening the box and making sure everything is in there BEFORE you leave the store!

Smart Shopper Tip #2
What Features Really Matter?

"Let's cut through the clutter here. Do I really need a stroller that has automatic folding and a built-in thermometer? What features are really important?"

Walk into any baby store and you'll encounter a blizzard of strollers. Do you want a stroller with a full recline? Boot and retractable canopy? What the heck is a boot, anyway? Here's a look at the features in the stroller market today:

Features for baby:

◆ **Reclining seat.** Since babies less than six months of age sleep most of the time and can't hold their heads up, strollers that have reclining seats are a plus. Yet, the *extent* of a stroller's seat recline varies by model. Some have full reclines, a few recline part of the way (120 degrees) and some don't recline at all. FYI: just because a stroller has a "full recline" does NOT mean it reclines to 180 degrees. It may recline slightly less than that for safety reasons.

◆ **Front (or napper) bar.** As a safety precaution, many strollers have a front bar (also called a napper bar) that keeps baby secure (though you should always use the stroller's safety harness). Better strollers have a bar that's padded and removable. Why removable? Later, when your baby gets to toddler hood, you may need to remove the bar to make it easier for the older child to access the stroller. Some strollers have a kid snack tray, which serves much the same function as a napper bar.

◆ **Footrest.** Footrests can range from a simple strap extending between the two side bars of the stroller or as complex as a ratcheting adjustable footrest with leg support. FYI: If a stroller has a fully reclining seat, voluntary safety regulations require the stroller to have an adjustable footrest that can fold out to fully enclose the entire stroller seat—this keeps baby from sliding out.

◆ **Seat padding.** You'll find every possible padding option out there, from bare bones models with a single piece of fabric to strollers with deluxe-quilted padding made from fine fabrics hand woven by monks in Luxembourg. (Okay, just kidding—the monks actually live in Switzerland.) For seating, some strollers have card-

Guaranteed Frustration:
Baby gear warranties can leave you fuming

It's a fact of life: sometimes you buy a product that breaks only days after purchase. So, you pick up the phone and call the manufacturer and ask about their warranty. "Sure, we'll help," says the customer service rep. In no time, you have a replacement product and a happy parent.

Fast forward to real life. Most parents find warranties only guarantee frustration—especially with baby products like strollers and other travel gear. Numerous hassles confront parents who find they have a defective product, from unreturned emails to endless waits on hold waiting for a customer service rep.

Consider the process of actually registering an item. Filling out a warranty card often requires information that you can only find on the product box or carton. Some parents find this out the hard way . . . after they've hauled all the boxes off to the trash. Even worse: some baby product makers like Peg Perego actually request a copy of the sales receipt for their warranty form. Hello? What about gifts?

Then, let's say something goes wrong. Your new stroller breaks a wheel. That brand new baby monitor goes on the fritz after one week. If it is a gift or you lost the receipt, the store you bought it from may say "tough luck"—call the manufacturer. With many warranties, you have to return the defective item to the manufacturer at your expense. And then you wait a few more weeks while they decide to fix or replace the item. Typically you have to pay for return shipping—and that can be expensive for a bulky item like a stroller. And then you must do without the product for weeks while they fix it.

Dealing with the customer service departments at some baby product makers can add insult to injury. It seems like some companies can count their customer service staff on one hand—or one finger, in some cases. The result: long waits on hold. Or it takes days to get responses to emails. The U.S. offices of foreign baby product companies seem to be the worst at customer service staffing, while mass-market companies board platforms (these can be uncomfortable for long rides) and other models have fabric that isn't removable or machine washable (see below for more on this).

◆ **Wheel suspension.** Yes, a few strollers do have wheels equipped with shock absorbers or suspension springs for a smoother ride. This is a nice feature if you live in a neighborhood with uneven or rough sidewalks.

◆ **Wheels: plastic or air-filled?** In reality, how smooth a stroller

---

such as Graco and Evenflo have better customer service.

And customer service can go from good to bad in the blink of an eye. Recalls can cause a huge surge in customer service requests—and many companies fail to adequately staff their customer service departments during such events. Hence, even good companies can fall flat on their face during such episodes.

The bottom line: it's no wonder that when something goes wrong, consumers just consider trashing the product and buying a new one. And let's be realistic: paying $30 in shipping to send back a broken $50 stroller doesn't make much sense. Here's our advice:

Keep your receipts. You don't have to get fancy—a shoebox will do. That way you can prove you bought that defective product. If the item was a gift, keep the product manual and serial number. Ask for gift receipts when possible.

◆ **If something goes wrong, email/call the manufacturer.** We're always surprised by how many consumers don't contact the manufacturer FIRST when a problem arises. You might be surprised at how responsive some companies are at fixing an issue.

◆ **If the problem is a safety defect,** immediately stop using the product and file a complaint with the Consumer Product Safety Commission (cpsc.gov). Also contact the company.

◆ **Attack the problem multiple ways.** Don't just call; also send an email and perhaps a written letter. Be reasonable: allow the company one to two business days to reply to a phone call or email.

◆ **Let other parents know about your experiences.** The best way to fix lousy customer service? Shame companies into doing it better. Post your experiences to the message boards on our site (BabyBargains.com) and other parenting sites. Trust us, companies are sensitive to such criticism.

rides is more related to the type of wheels. The general rule: the more the better. Strollers with double wheels on each leg ride smoother than single wheels. If you plan to use a stroller on trails, air-filled tires are the smoothest ride . . . but require maintenance. New to the market are foam filled or "forever air" tires: these are a compromise between air-filled and plastic wheels in terms of ride

◆ **Weather protection.** Yes, you can buy a stroller that's outfitted for battle with a winter in New England, for example. The options include retractable hoods/canopies and "boots" (which protect a child's feet) to block out wind, rain or cold. Fabrics play a role here too—some strollers feature quilted hoods to keep baby warm and others claim they are water repellent. While a boot is an option some may not need, hoods/canopies are rather important, even if just to keep the sun out of baby's eyes. Some strollers only have a canopy (or "sunshade") that partially covers baby, while other models have a full hood that can completely cover the stroller. Look for canopies offer full coverage and pop-out sun shades (to block a setting sun) and have "peak-a-boo" windows that let you see baby even when closed.

What if the stroller you've fallen in love with only has a skimpy canopy? Or lacks a rain cover? Good news: after-market accessories can fill the gap (see box below).

Features for parents:

◆ **Storage baskets.** Many strollers have deep, under-seat baskets for storage of coats, purses, bags, etc. Yet, the amount of storage can vary sharply from model to model. Inexpensive umbrella strollers may have no basket at all, while other models have tiny baskets. Mass-market strollers (Graco, etc.) typically have the most storage; other stroller makers have been playing catch-up in the basket game. One tip: it's not just the *size* of the storage basket but the *access* to it that counts. Some strollers have big baskets but are practically inaccessible when the seat is reclined. A support bar blocks access to some baskets. Tip: when stroller shopping, recline the seat and see if you can access the basket.

◆ **Removable seat cushion for washing.** Let's be honest: strollers can get icky in a flash. Crushed-in cookies, spilt juice and the usual grime can make a stroller a mobile dirt-fest. Some strollers have removable seat cushions that are machine washable—other models let you remove *all* of the fabric for a washing. Watch out for those models with non-removable fabric/seat cushions—while you can clean these strollers in one of those manual car washes (with a high-pressure nozzle), it's definitely a hassle, especially in the winter.

◆ **Lockable wheels.** Some strollers have front wheels that can be locked in a forward position—this enables you to more quickly push the stroller in a straight line (nice for exercising).

◆ **Wheel size.** You'll see just about every conceivable size wheel out there on strollers today. As you might guess, the smaller wheels are good for maneuverability in the mall, but larger wheels handle rough sidewalks (or gravel paths) much better.

◆ *Handle/Steering.* This is an important area to consider—most strollers have a single bar handle, which enables one-handed steering. Other umbrella-type strollers have two handles. Two handles require two hands to push, but enable a stroller to fold up compactly, like an umbrella. It's sort of a trade-off: steer-ability versus easier fold.

Another important factor: consider the handle *height*. Some handles have adjustable heights to better accommodate taller parents. However, just because a stroller touts this feature doesn't mean it adjusts to accommodate a seven-foot tall parent (at most, you get an extra inch or two of height). Later in this chapter, we'll mention which have height adjustable handles as we review stroller brands. Finally, a few stroller makers offer "one-touch fold" handles. Hit a button on the stroller and it can be folded up with one motion.

◆ *Reversible seats.* Some mult-function strollers have seats that reverse. Initially, you can push the stroller while the baby faces you (better for small infants). Later, you can reverse the seat so an older child can look out at the world. A nice feature, but not critical.

◆ *Compact fold.* We call it the trunk factor—when a stroller is folded, will it fit in your trunk? Some strollers fold compactly and can fit in a

strollers

Handy stroller accessories

What if your stroller doesn't have a rain cover? One option is the **Elegance Universal Stroller Weather Shield**, which runs $16 on Amazon.

You're in love with a fancy stroller. . . except for that skimpy canopy. What's the solution? Try the *RayShade* ($15) by Summer. This shade extends your stroller canopy and is excellent for blocking low-angle sun (take note, Californians). It also blocks ultraviolet rays and has a hidden bottle pocket. Also consider: the *SnoozeShade* ($35; pictured) which is a breathable shade that covers the entire stroller.

narrow trunk. Other strollers are still quite bulky when folded—swallowing all of a trunk in even a mid-size car. Unfortunately, we are not aware of any online resource that lists size/footprint of strollers when folded. You are on your own to size up models when folded in a store, compared to your trunk (hint: take trunk measurements before you go stroller shopping). Not only should you consider how compactly a stroller folds, but also how it folds in general. The best strollers fold with just one or two quick motions; others require you to hit 17 levers and latches. The latest stroller fold fad: strollers that fold standing UP instead of down. Why is this better? Because strollers that fold down to the ground can get dirty/scratched in a parking lot.

◆ **Durability.** Should you go for a lower-price stroller or a premium brand? Let's be honest: the lower-priced strollers (say, under $100) have nowhere near the durability of the models that cost $200 to $400. Levers that break, reclining seats that stop reclining and other glitches can make you despise a cheap stroller mighty quick. Yet, some parents don't need a stroller that will make it through the next world war. If all you do is a couple of quick trips to the mall every week or so, then a less expensive stroller will probably be fine. However, if you plan to use the stroller for more than one child, live in an urban environment with rough sidewalks, or plan extensive outdoor adventures with baby, then invest in a better stroller. Later in this chapter, we'll go over specific models and give you brand recommendations for certain lifestyles.

◆ **Overall weight.** Yes, it's a dilemma: the more feature-laden the stroller, the more it weighs. And strollers are often priced via the Bikini Principle: the less it weighs, the more it costs. Yet it doesn't take lugging a 30-pound stroller in and out of a car trunk more than a few times to justify the expense of a lighter-weight design. Carefully consider a stroller's weight before purchase. Some parents end up with two strollers—a lightweight/umbrella-type stroller for quick trips (or air travel) and then a more feature-intensive model for extensive outdoor outings.

Smart Shopper Tip #3
The Cadillac Escalade or Ford Focus Dilemma
"This is nuts! I see cheap umbrella strollers that sell for $30 on one hand and then fancy designer brands for $900 on the other. Do I really need to spend a fortune on a stroller?"

Whether you drive a Cadillac Escalade or a Ford Focus, you'll still get to your destination. And that fact pretty much applies to strollers too—most function well enough to get you and baby from point A to point B, no matter what the price.

So, should you buy the cheapest stroller you can find? Well, no. There *is* a significant difference in quality between a cheap $30 umbrella stroller and a name brand that costs $150, $250 or more. Unless you want the endless headaches of a cheap stroller (wheels that break, parts that fall off), it's important to invest in a stroller that's durable.

The real question is: do you need a fancy stroller loaded with features or will a simple model do? To answer that, you need to consider *how* you will use the stroller. Do you live in the suburbs and just need the stroller once a week for a quick spin at the mall? Or do you live in an big city where a stroller is your primary vehicle, taking all the abuse that a big city can dish out? Climate plays another factor—in the Northeast, strollers have to be winterized to handle the cold and snow. Meanwhile, in Southern California, full canopies are helpful for shading baby's eyes from late afternoon sunshine.

Figuring out how different stroller options fit your lifestyle/climate is the key to stroller happiness. Later in this chapter, we'll recommend several specific strollers for certain lifestyles and climates.

One final note: name-brand strollers with cachet actually have resale value. You can sell that pricey stroller on eBay, at a second-hand store, or via Craigslist and recoup some of your investment. We'll note which brands have the best and worst resale values later in this chapter.

Smart Shopper Tip #4
Too tall for their own good

"I love our stroller, but my husband hates it. He's six feet tall and has to stoop over to push it. Even worse, when he walks, he hits the back of the stroller with his feet."

Strollers are made for *women* of average height. What's that? About 5'6". If you (or your spouse) are taller than that, you'll find certain stroller models will be a pain to use.

This is probably one of the biggest complaints we get from parents about strollers. Unfortunately, only a limited number of strollers have height-adjustable handles that let a six-foot tall person comfortably push a stroller without stooping over or hitting the back of the stroller with his or her feet. One smart shopping tip: if you have a tall spouse, make sure you take him or her stroller shopping with you. Checking out handle heights in person is the only way to avoid this problem.

The best stroller brands for taller parents: BOB and Peg Perego (particularly, the Pliko, which has height adjustable handles). The worst? Combi, a Japanese brand that has low-handle heights.

Smart Shopper Tip #5
The Myth of the Magic Bullet Stroller

"I'd like to buy just one stroller—a model that works with an infant

strollers

*car seat and then converts to full-featured stroller and then finally a
jogger for kids up to age four. And I want it to weigh less than ten
lbs. And sell for just under $50. What model do you suggest?"*

Boy, that sounds like our email some days! We hear from parents
all the time looking for that one model that will do it all. We call it
the Myth of the Magic Bullet Stroller—an affordable product that
morphs into seven different uses for children from birth to college.
Spoiler alert: it doesn't exist.

The reality: most parents own more than one stroller. A typical set-
up: one full-feature model (or a stroller frame) that holds an infant car
seat and then a lightweight stroller that folds compactly for the
mall/travel. Of course, we hear from parents who own four, five or
six strollers, including specialty models like joggers, double strollers
for two kids and more. First-time parents wonder if these folks have
lost their minds, investing the equivalent of the gross national product of Aruba on baby transportation. Alas, most parents realize that
as their baby grows and their needs change, so must their stroller.

Far be it for us to suggest you buy multiple strollers, but at the
same time, it is hard to recommend just one model that works for
everyone. That's why the recommendations later in this chapter are
organized by lifestyle and use.

Money-Saving Tips

1 STOP! DON'T BUY THAT GIANT STROLLER. Here's a classic
first-time parent mistake: buying an expensive, giant travel system stroller (a.k.a, the Baby Bus), thinking you need all those whiz-
bang features. But the huge bulk and weight of those strollers will
have you cursing the thing before your baby hits six months. A better bet: get a good quality, lightweight stroller that has an infant car
seat adapter, strap in your infant seat and voila! You have your own
travel system.

2 WHY NOT A BASIC UMBRELLA STROLLER? If you only plan to
use a stroller on infrequent trips to the mall, then a plain
umbrella stroller for $40 to $50 will suffice. One caveat: most plain
umbrella strollers do NOT recline—you will not be able to use it until
your baby is able to hold up his head (around six months). And they
may not have any storage.

3 CONSIDER A CARRIER FOR NEWBORNS. Yes, a simple baby carrier (sling, wrap, front carrier, etc.) can be a much more affordable alternative to expensive strollers. Check our new carrier chapter

(Chapter 10) for reviews of different types of carriers.

4 **CHECK FOR SALES.** We're always amazed by the number of sales on strollers. There's usually something on sale in most baby stores; online sellers (we're looking at you, Amazon) are always discounting one brand or another. Another reason strollers go on sale: the manufacturers are constantly coming out with new models and have to clear out the old. Which leads us to the next tip.

5 **LOOK FOR LAST YEAR'S MODELS.** Every year, manufacturers roll out new models. In some cases, they add features; other times, they just change the fabric. What do they do with last year's stock? They discontinue it—and then it's sale time. You'll see these models on sale for as much as 50% off in stores and on the web. And it's not like stroller fabric fashion varies much from year to year—is there really much difference between "toasted cranberry" and mauve? We say go for last year's fabric and save a bundle. See the Email from the Real World nearby for a mom's story on her last year model deal.

6 **SCOPE OUT FACTORY SECONDS.** Believe it or not, some stroller manufacturers sell "factory seconds" at good discounts—these "cosmetically imperfect" models might have a few blemishes, but are otherwise fine. An example: Peg Perego has twice yearly factory sales in the spring (late April or early May) and fall (November) at their Ft. Wayne, Indiana company store. Check their social media for specific upcoming dates.

7 **DON'T FALL VICTIM TO STROLLER OVERKILL.** Seriously evaluate how you'll use the stroller and don't over buy. If a Toyota Camry will do, why buy a Lexus? You don't really need an all-terrain stroller or multi-function stroller for mall trips. Flashy strollers can be status symbols for some parents—don't play the game.

8 **SELL YOUR STROLLER TO RECOUP YOUR INVESTMENT.** When you're done with the stroller, consign it at a second-hand store or sell it on Craigslist. You'd be surprised how much it can fetch. The best brands for resale are, not surprisingly, the better names we recommend in this chapter. Of course, the strollers with the best resale value are those that are in excellent condition. If you keep an expensive jogging stroller in your garage or on your deck, consider a cover.

9 **WAREHOUSE CLUB DEALS.** Yes, Sam's and Costco periodically sell strollers. At one point before going to press, Costco was

strollers

selling Schwinn jogging strollers from their web site (Costco.com) at 45% under retail. Of course, these deals come and go—and like anything you see at the warehouse clubs, you have to snap it up quickly or it will be gone.

10 **EBAY/CRAIGSLIST**. There's no law that says you have to buy a brand new stroller from a baby store. Increasingly, baby gear retailers are using eBay to discreetly clear out overstock. Better to unload online the stuff that isn't moving than risk the wrath of local customers who bought the model for full price last week. An example: a reader scored a brand new Peg Perego for HALF the stroller's retail price through an eBay auction. Other readers regularly report saving $100 to $200 through eBay. Hint: many strollers sold online are last year's model or fashion. Be sure to confirm what you are buying (is it in the original box? No damage? Which model year?) before bidding. And don't forget Craigslist either. Yes, this site has both junk and jewels. Be patient and search carefully to find worthwhile stroller buys.

Resale Value: Best & Worst Brands

Which stroller brands have the best resale value? To find the answer, we poured over 4000 Craigslist ads for every major city in the U.S. and calculated resale value for both brands and individual models. We excluded ads for brand new, still in the box strollers (some retailers use Craigslist to unload unsold inventory). We focused on strollers that were in good or excellent condition with minimal wear and tear.

E-MAIL FROM THE REAL WORLD
Last year's fashion, 50% off

A reader emailed her tip on how she saved over $100 on a stroller:

"When looking for strollers you can often get last year's version for a big discount. I purchased a previous year model online for $190. That compares to the $300 price tag for the current year model from Babies R Us. As far as my research could tell, the models are identical except for the color pattern. A quick web search can turn up a number of sources that are selling last year's strollers; colors are limited (dmartstores.com had the widest selection) but it is a great way to save over $100 for a very nice stroller."

Best Resale (Brand). The top three brands for resale are Britax (65.2%), Baby Jogger (63.9%) and Bugaboo (63.9%). Hence, the average Britax stroller sells for 65.2% of its original retail price on Craigslist. All of these three brands have popular models that command a premium on the resale market.

Best Resale (Model). Among the top models for resale are the Baby Jogger's City Select with second seat (79.5%) and the Baby Jogger City Mini at 75%. In general, we found double strollers scored at the top of the resale list—perhaps because they are somewhat rare and demand is high. Stores also stock fewer double strollers, making Craigslist a popular outlet.

Worst Resale (Brand). The stroller brands with the worst resale value are Graco (41.9%), Maclaren (41.4%), and Inglesina (33.3%). Graco is a mass-market brand whose strollers simply don't fetch much on a resale market. Maclaren has had its struggles with bankruptcy and safety recalls. Inglesina is a bit of surprise here—we're not sure what is driving this low resale, but folks appear to be willing to part with these models for very little cash.

Worst Resale (Model). Inglesina's Trip (26.3%) scored at the bottom of our survey—yes, that means that stroller sells for a measly 26% of its retail price on the second hand market. Of course, the seller's loss is a buyer's gain! The Peg Perego Pliko (30%), Combi Cosmo (30.7%) and Maclaren Quest (32.2%) also came in with very low resale values.

Individual brands' resale value are noted in the next section, listed as *Baby Bargains Resale Rank*. Note: some brands don't have a resale ranking because we couldn't find enough of their strollers for sale on the secondary market to make a judgment. Index ratings are excellent, good, fair and poor. Excellent resale brands were in the top 25% of resale values; poor brands were in the bottom 25% of resale values.

Of course, you can look at these resale rankings two ways: as a buyer of a brand new stroller, you'll get the most resale value for brands that have a good or excellent rating. If you are looking for a used stroller, brands with a poor or fair rating are selling at a steep discount from their resale price—and that might make for some great bargains!

The Name Game: Reviews of Selected Manufacturers

So, how do we rate and review strollers? First, we do hands-on inspections in stores and at trade shows. That involves giving the stroller a test spin, checking the fold and more. Next, we listen to you, the reader. The stroller message board on our web site is one of the most popular forums, brimming with over 1000 posts a month. As always, parent feedback is our secret sauce.

One note: the ratings in this section apply to the ENTIRE line of a company's strollers. No, we don't assign ratings to individual strollers, but we will comment on what we think are a company's best models. Following this section, we give several "lifestyle recommendations"—specific models of strollers to fit different parent lifestyles.

The Ratings

A **EXCELLENT**—*our top pick!*
B **GOOD**— *above average quality, prices, and creativity.*
C **FAIR**—*could stand some improvement.*
D **POOR**—*yuck! could stand some major improvement.*

4moms (Origami) *4moms.com* 4moms' Origami stroller's claim to fame is its power-folding feature—yes, the stroller actually folds by itself. Press a button on the handle and the stroller does the rest.

So this stroller is a conversation piece. But is it worth the $850 price tag? Weighing in at 32 lbs., it's too bad the folded stroller doesn't also levitate off the ground and into your trunk for that price.

The Origami comes with a few other bling-y features, including an LCD screen with a thermometer, speedometer, trip and lifetime odometers. Optional accessories include a cell phone charger ($40) which charges your phone when you push the stroller, Graco car seat adapter ($60), and "color kit" that lets you change the color of your stroller's fabric pad for $100.

Fans of the Origami love the stroller . . . at least initially. The stroller has a smooth glide and can handle even gravel surfaces. And it is hard to discount the "wow" factor with this stroller—you'll be asked to demonstrate the automatic fold feature for friends, family and complete strangers.

But the love affair with Origami typically fades after a year.

The downsides: the lack of a reclining seat makes this stroller only appropriate for babies that can sit up on their own (6 months +). That's because the seat only has a slight recline. To use the stroller with a newborn, you have to buy the aforementioned Graco infant car seat adapter (and have a Graco car seat, of course). That seems like a glaring omission for an $850+ stroller. Most of the Origami's competitors (Uppa Baby Vista, Britax B-Ready, etc.) include infant seating options . . . at a price $450 less than the Origami.

The other major flaw: the Origami's weight. Hauling this stroller in and out of a trunk qualifies you for a spot on the next U.S. Olympic weight lifting team. We realize the motor, batteries and gizmos to make the Origami fold require this added weight, but a stroller that tips the scales at 32 lbs. empty is borderline insane. Imagine lifting a folded Origami up to a SUV's cargo area and you'll quickly realize why a 32 lb. stroller is a killer.

On the plus side, once folded, the Origami takes up less space than other full-size strollers in a vehicle trunk, thanks to its relatively smallish footprint. And the Origami's motor is self-charging, so you don't have to plug in this stroller to have it recharge the motor.

From a practical point of view, the stroller's storage basket is decent sized; there are also other storage pockets on the side of the seat. But there is no snack tray or bumper bar for the child.

Most troubling are parent reviews and online reports of quality glitches—wheels that get stuck, a dead battery that prevents the stroller from opening, etc. Reviewers complain that the battery doesn't effectively recharge despite the claimed walking charging feature. So that means you have to plug it in each night, instead of leaving it in the trunk of your car. Other users complain that when an Origami breaks, there are no replacement parts or repairs outside of the warranty period . . . so a broken Origami that won't unlock or open is now an $850 paperweight.

Bottom line: the Origami in real life doesn't live up to the promise.

FYI: Scheduled for "late 2015," 4Moms will address the weight issue with the release of the Origami mini, a 16 lb. umbrella stroller which is the Mini Me of its flagship model. Same power folding feature, daytime running lights, etc. Price: $450. ***Rating: D-***

Babyhome *babyhome.es* Spanish stroller maker Babyhome recently debuted their first model in the U.S., the Emotion. This lightweight ($270 to $300, 16.9 lbs.) stroller features a curved frame, rain cover, mosquito net, fully reclining seat, and maintenance kit and is car seat adaptable (Chicco, Graco, Maxi Cosi).

The stroller's unique feature: polyurethane wheels (with ball bearing suspension) give a smooth ride. Made in China, the Emotion comes in six solid color fashions.

Parent feedback on the Emotion is mostly positive—fans love the smooth glide and light weight. Critics knock the low to the ground profile, lack of cup holder and skimpy hood coverage. We like that the Emotion includes a rain cover and mosquito net.

Optional accessories include a cup holder, front bumper bar, rotating snack tray and canopy extender. That might make the stroller more user friendly—but we'd argue if you're paying $300 +/- for a stroller, those should be standard. ***Rating: B***

Baby Jogger *babyjogger.com* Baby Jogger literally invented the jogging stroller category 30 years ago with the first stroller with bicycle tires designed for runners. Since then, the company has been through numerous ups and downs . . . including a bankruptcy back in 2003 and new ownership that refocused the brand on lightweight, easy-to-fold strollers. The new models have met with much success, despite the fact the company has drifted away from its "jogger" name.

The models. Baby Jogger has two main stroller lines: the City (which the brand dubs as "everyday strollers") and the Summit, which are all-terrain models designed for off-road adventures.

Baby Jogger's City strollers are divided into three sub-genres: lightweight models like the City Mini, multi-function strollers like the City Select/Versa and double versions of their popular sellers.

The secret sauce to the City Mini is the company's Quick-Fold technology: pull up on one strap and zip! The stroller collapses and folds. No complicated buttons or latches. No multi-step process. The Quick-Fold has super-sized Baby Jogger's sales of the City series, which boasts six models: the Mini, Mini GT, Elite, Lite, Versa and Select.

The tri-wheel City Mini (single $250, 17.1 lbs.; double $450, 26.6

Stroller Shopping Secret: Rear Wheel Width

Weight may be the most important factor to urban parents looking for a new stroller, but we suggest looking at one additional criteria: rear wheel width. Many new strollers have a wide spread between the rear wheels. The problem? Many urban parents have to negotiate tight spaces (grocery store aisles, subways, etc). A stroller with a wide wheelbase may not squeeze through small doorways and into tight elevators. Here is a look at the rear wheel widths for some popular urban strollers.

STROLLER	REAR WHEEL WIDTH
Bugaboo Bee	20.0
Stokke Xplory	22.0
Bugaboo Cameleon	23.0
Peg Perego Skate	23.75
Orbit	24.0
UPPAbaby Vista	25.0
Quinny Buzz	25.5

Our advice: go for the narrowest wheelbase you can find—23" and under is probably best (some doors are a narrow 24" wide).

lbs.) is Baby Jogger's best-selling stroller, featuring a full recline and large canopy. In a recent refresh, the City Mini got a few tweaks: a slightly larger seat, an easier to access storage basket and an auto lock feature when the stroller is folded.

If you aren't sold on the tri-wheel set-up, there is a four-wheel version of the City Mini (dubbed the City Mini 4-Wheel) for $260. It is identical to the three wheel version, just one more wheel. And if you prefer your four-wheel stroller with a compact umbrella style fold, consider the City Mini Zip ($250, 16.5 lbs.).

To appeal more to off-road users, the City Mini GT ($350, 21.5 lbs.) adds bigger, no-flat tires, as well as an adjustable handle bar with brake, a redesigned seat/canopy that provides more head-room, and an easier to access storage basket.

At the top end, the City Elite (single $400, 31.3 lbs.) features 12" air-filled wide tread tires and a parent console. While those air-filled tires make the Elite more of an all-terrain stroller, the trade-off is added weight.

FYI: One major difference between the City models is weight capacity. The City Elite works to 75 lbs. single, 100 double. The City Mini's limits are 50/100 lbs.

Baby Jogger is also a player in the multi-function stroller market with its City Select, which is sort of like the Swiss Army Knife of strollers. It can be configured 16 ways, with an optional second seat. With a telescoping handle and foam tires, the Select (28.1 lbs.) costs $500 (plus $170 for the second seat). A bassinet accessory is $93. In the past year, Baby Jogger has made only small changes to the Select, upping the amount of seat padding yet keeping the price the same.

If you can't decide between the City Mini and the Select, there is a third option: the City Versa (23.7 lbs.). This hybrid is a cross between those two models: the seat on the Versa reverses (like the Select), but the stroller doesn't expand to a double. You do get a full canopy and recline, an adjustable leg rest, all wheel suspension, hand brake and a flat fold. Price: $360.

In the past year, Baby Jogger has been adding more four-wheel strollers. Example: the Vue ($200)—it's claim to fame is a reversible seat on an umbrella stroller frame, which is impressive. The Vue also has a large canopy, adjustable leg rest, full seat recline (in either mode) and an optional bassinet. At 17.5 lbs., it is on the heavier side for an umbrella stroller. And the Vue does not have Quick Fold—instead you hit a latch on the side and fold the stroller over to the ground.

New in spring 2015, Baby Jogger debuts the Vue Lite ($179), which shaves three pounds off the regular Vue to weigh in at 14.6 lbs. You still get the reversible seat, a nearly flat seat recline and adjustable footrest. Also in spring 2015: a new double Vue ($400, 30 lbs.) which can hold two infant car seats or two bassinets (a separate accessory).

strollers

You can fold the Vue Double with the seats facing either direction

If you want to actually jog with a Baby Jogger, the company offers the F.I.T. ($300, 25.4 lbs.), with a fixed front wheel, deep seat recline and aluminum frame. FYI: The F.I.T. has been discontinued although you might still see a few for sale.

For serious all-terrain use, the Summit X3 comes in single ($430, 27.1 lbs.) and double ($450 to $650, 38.8 lbs.) versions. The Summit has 16" rear and 12" front air-filled tires, swivel front wheel that locks, suspension, and the same quick-fold technology you see on the City Series. The X3's handlebar has a front wheel lock feature, which is nice.

One final note: Baby Jogger sells a car seat adapter that works with most infant car seats, including Graco and Peg Perego.

Our view. Whew! That was a quite a few models! With the blizzard of strollers sporting the Baby Jogger name, which ones are our favorites?

We like the Baby Jogger City Mini as the pick of the litter here—from the canopy to the quick fold, this is an excellent lightweight stroller for the mall and smooth sidewalks. If you prefer a four-wheel stroller with a compact fold, the City Mini Zip is another excellent choice. For more off-road adventures or if you have rough sidewalks, the City Mini GT is pricey but worth it for the tire upgrade.

If you are in the market for a multi-function stroller that can carry two kiddos, we would recommend the City Select.

Bottom line: Baby Jogger has been on a roll in recent years—innovative features (that Quick Fold technology is the star here), excellent quality and overall good pricing has been a recipe for success. You can see the brand's popularity here in their strong resale prices, among the highest in the category. *Baby Bargains Resale Rank: Excellent.* **Rating: A**

Baby Trend babytrend.com Baby Trend's biggest selling stroller isn't really a stroller at all—it's a stroller frame. Here's an overview of the line:

The models. The Snap N Go is Baby Trend's claim to fame—basically, it's a stroller frame that lets you snap in most major-brand infant car seats. Presto! Instant travel system at a fraction of the price.

At least, that is the sales pitch. The truth is many infant car seats don't snap into the Snap N Go—the infant seat is strapped onto the frame. Hence, it should really be called the Strap N Go.

The stroller frame concept was innovative when it was introduced in the 90's—then few strollers had car seat adapters. Today, the Snap N Go is passé. Many stroller makers either come with car seat adapters or sell them as an affordable accessory. The only purpose we can see for this product now is perhaps for folks who are undecided on their stroller pick. In that case, the Snap N Go is a place holder.

The basic Snap & Go is $75; a double version that holds two car seats is $85. The Snap N Go has been so successful it has spawned knock-offs from several competitors, namely Graco.

Besides the stroller frame, Baby Trend also offers travel systems, double strollers and joggers. Baby Trend's travel systems combine their Flex-Loc Inertia car seat with basic low-end strollers. Example: the Envy travel system is $170 to $200 (car seat and stroller). That's a fairly low price, but the stroller (21 lbs.) is nothing fancy—steel frame, five-point harness and multi-position recline. You do get a decent canopy, one-hand fold and big basket.

Baby Trend is a big player in the all terrain/jogger stroller market—their flagship model is the Expedition. This steel frame jogger is loaded with features (reclining seat, five-point harness, parent tray with cup holders and ratcheting canopy) and is sold as a travel system ($200) or separately ($86-$120).

In the past year, Baby Trend has been rolling out Hello Kitty versions of their strollers for Target and Walmart. And the "Go Lite" collection features a $170 modular stroller system (called the Snap-N-Grow) that accepts most major brand infant seats and features a reversible seat, full recline, EVA foam tires with quick release wheels, and telescoping handle.

FYI: Baby Trend still sells the Sit N Stand stroller, a "pushcart" that combines a stroller with a jump seat for an older child.

Baby Trend recently rolled out a redesigned Sit N Stand double that holds two car seats and has a napper bar that rotates away when not in use. It comes in both steel (36 lbs.) and aluminum (30 lbs.) versions that run $135 to $180. The redesigned single Sit N Stand will let you attach a car seat in front or back.

Our view. After writing about baby gear for 20+ years, there are still some companies that are mysteries to us. Baby Trend is Exhibit One.

The company mainly exists to sell low-price travel systems to chain stores, with little innovation or change from year to year. Despite quality that our readers charitably describe as merely average, the company seems to merrily chug along. Basically, these are strollers that are sold on price—if it breaks, that's your problem. Over 70 complaints have been filed on Baby Trend with ConsumerAffairs.com website, most cite quality woes, missing parts and so on.

Yes, we did recommend the Snap & Go back in the late 90's and early 2000's, but we don't see the point of it today with all the current options for strollers and car seat adapters.

Bottom line: this isn't a brand we'd recommend. *Baby Bargains Resale Rank: Good.* **Rating: D**

BOB Strollers bobgear.com BOB has won accolades for their innovative joggers—you can tell these were designed by runners

strollers

for runners. (Trivia note: BOB stands for Beast of Burden trailers, the company's original name—the owners decided BOB was easier to spell . . . and would avoid a lawsuit from Mick Jagger).

BOB's strollers are billed as "sport utility" strollers and that's an apt moniker, as their rugged design (polymer wheels to prevent rust, for example) and plush ride make these strollers best sellers despite their $300+ price tags.

FYI: BOB is owned by Britax; the car seat maker acquired the brand in 2011. Among the first joint efforts between the brands is a revised car seat adapter that now works with Britax infant car seats. And Britax has debuted a BOB B-Safe version of its B-Safe infant car seat—same seat, just new fabric to match BOB's strollers.

The models. The best-selling BOB model is the Revolution, with its front swivel wheel, rear wheel suspension, multi-position canopy and seat recline, padded handlebar. While not as easy to fold as a Baby Jogger, the Revolution's two-step fold is a close runner-up.

BOB has tweaked the Revolution over the years to improve its features. The latest models feature an adjustable crotch strap, new multi-position canopy and a storage basket with easier access.

There are five versions of the Revolutions: SE, CE, Flex, Pro and Stroller Strides. Here's an overview:

Revolution strollers with larger polymer wheels are referred to as the Sport Experience (SE; single $330, double $536) while those with smaller, aluminum wheels are called the City Experience (CE; single $390). We weighed the current Revolution SE at 24.9 lbs.

The Revolution Flex ($390 single, $552 double) has polymer wheels with added adjustable handlebar. The Revolution Pro is the same as the Flex, but adds a hand brake. The Pro is an REI exclusive at $400 single, $570 double.

The BOB Stroller Stride model ($385 single, $550 double) is basically a BOB Revolution with an added handlebar console and tension tubing for resistance exercise.

If you are a serious runner, the BOB Ironman Stroller (single: $335, 21 lbs.; double: $455, 31.4 lbs.) is probably the pick of the litter, with smooth tires, stiffer shocks, suspension wheels and more. Plus the bright yellow color gives it great visibility.

Finally, there is also a four-wheel BOB called the Motion ($285, 23 lbs.). It features a height adjustable handle bar and air-filled tires, as well as a one-hand fold. The Motion strikes a Bugaboo-like pose, with smaller front wheels. A series of accessories (weather shield, travel bag, etc.) are available.

Our view: Parents give BOB excellent marks on quality and durability. Yes, these strollers are expensive, but worth it. The new adjustable handle bar of the Flex and Pro addresses a previous concern that the strollers didn't work well for taller parents.

The downsides? The storage could be better—yes, you can fit a diaper bag in the basket . . . but not much more. The seat recline on the Revolution is cumbersome, requiring you to adjust both from harness straps. That's much more complicated than Baby Jogger. Another issue: weight. At 25 lbs., the Revolution would never be confused with a lightweight stroller—but that is the trade-off with the all-terrain air-filled wheels.

While the BOB Revolution and Ironman receive much love, folks are more mixed on the new four-wheel Motion. The storage basket is hard to access and the model's overall bulk is an issue. The Motion isn't designed for all terrain use (its wheels are too small). . . and the strollers large size/bulk make it a no go for most mall trips. This model looks like a rare miss for BOB.

Overall, however, BOB has excellent quality and is among our top picks for all terrain strollers. *Baby Bargains Resale Rank: Excellent.* **Rating: A**

Britax britaxusa.com Best-known for its well-made car seats, Britax launched a stroller line in 2005. It took several years before the company was able to successfully crack the stroller category.

The models. Britax offers four stroller models: the B-Agile (both in single and double versions), B-Ready, B-Nimble and Affinity.

The B-Ready ($400, 28.1 lbs.) is Britax's flagship stroller and their

strollers

E-MAIL FROM THE REAL WORLD
The Weight Game

"I saw the same stroller listed with two different weights online. How can the same model weigh five lbs. less on one site?"

Good question—call it the weight shell game. We've noticed some retail web sites play fast and loose with the weights of strollers listed on their sites. Why? What parents' value most in a stroller is LIGHT overall weight—and online sellers know this. So, why not cheat and list a stroller's weight . . . minus a few items like a canopy, basket or other amenities? Another explanation: stroller manufacturers often tweak their models from year to year, adding new features. This can add additional ounces, but some retail web sites "forget" to update the weight. Yes, it is deceptive—but there are ways around the problem. First, this book lists the true weight for most models. Also check the *manufacturer's* web site, which usually lists the correct weight.

first stab at a modular stroller that works with an optional bassinet and second seat. It has 14 different configurations, much like the Baby Jogger Select and Uppa Baby Vista.

Out of the box, the stroller will work with Britax's infant car seats (a separate $40 adapter is needed for Graco and Chicco seats). The B-Ready features a seat that reverses to face forward or rear, full tire suspension, large storage basket and full seat recline. They've improved the stroller recently by adding a fourth recline position to the seatback as well as more durable foam filled rubber wheels.

Got two kids? A second seat ($120) transforms the B-Ready into a double stroller. In a recent refresh, Britax tweaked the B-Ready by adding four recline positions for the main seat including a more upright position, a deeper storage basket and foam filled rubber tires that never go flat.

The B-Nimble ($275; 15.5 lbs.) is the B-Ready's much lighter cousin—it is infant car seat compatible and features a removable/reversible seat liner, cup holder and rain cover. It works with the Britax infant seat out of the box.

The B-Agile is Britax's riff on the Baby Jogger City Mini. It weighs in at 16.5 lbs. and runs $215. It features a one-hand quick-fold, large canopy and a no-rethread harness. Recently, Britax added a B-Agile double stroller to its lineup. This side-by-side version ($320 to $380) accommodates kids up to 50 lbs. each and can carry one Britax infant seat. FYI: Babies R Us has an exclusive four-wheel version of the B-Agile (B-Agile 4) for $250. It weighs 20.2 lbs. and also features an upgraded canopy with a viewing window with magnetic closure.

In the past year, Britax added a fourth stroller to the mix with the Affinity ($480, 27.4 lbs.; $560 with color pack), a multi-function stroller with reversible seat. The Affinity fits all Britax car seats, as well as Chicco, Peg and Graco seats, and features a fully reclining seat, height adjustable handle and air-filled tires. The Affinity includes a rain cover, but is designed for babies six months or older (when using the seat). Oddly, the Affinity does not come with a canopy—that is an optional accessory that is part of a "color pack" for $80 or may be included for $560 total. On the plus side, you can fully customize the Affinity with six different fashions and a choice of three frame colors (white, black or silver).

Our view. After struggling in the stroller category with several product stumbles, Britax has scored success with the current model line up.

We liked the B-Ready's ability to morph into different configurations—many more than the comparable Uppa Baby Vista (which notably, runs $180 more than the B-Ready). And you can fold the B-Ready with the second (toddler) seat attached—that's something the competition can't do.

Critics, however, knock the B-Ready's overall bulk and weight (about two pounds heavier than the comparable Vista). To Britax's credit, however, they have made small tweaks to improve the B-Ready (example: new rubber wheels replaced the previous foam versions).

So we have the function and value, but what about style? That's probably Britax's weakness . . . and we aren't just talking about the B-Ready's paint-by-number fabric color choices. Britax strollers lack a certain je ne sais quoi when compared with Baby Jogger (see: Quick Fold, definition of) and Uppa Baby. And when you are trying to sell a $500 stroller like the B-Ready, you need some zing.

Shopping Cart Covers: Advice & Picks

Grocery store carts aren't exactly the cleanest form of transportation—yet once your baby outgrows her infant car seat, you will likely put baby in the little seat up front . . . and quickly realize that keeping the  carts clean doesn't seem to be a high priority for most stores. Some stores have added in a wipes dispenser near the carts, but you can't get the gook off the fabric belts—that's just gross.

Ditto for restaurant high chairs—they can be germ factories.

To the rescue comes the shopping cart/high chair cover, basically a fabric seat that provides a clean and safe space for baby while you shop or dine. Here are our top picks:

◆ *Infantino.* Infantino's Compact 2-in-1 Shopping Cart Cover is made of polyester and comes with a sippy cup strap, teether and loop. At $21, it's one of the most affordable options and parents like the cute fabrics.

◆ *Itzy Ritzy.* These shopping cart covers are more fashionable than the ones you see in stores and run $42-$68. Readers say Itzy Ritzy covers (itzyritzy.com; pictured) are easy to use and work on both regular grocery store carts and those large carts at Costco. Price includes a carrying case.

◆ *Bellingham Baby's* (bellinghambabycompany.com) shopping cart covers were recommended by readers for their reversible covers in cool fabrics. Covers include two toy loops plus pockets and are available in several fabric choices. Prices are about $50.

On a more positive note, the Britax B-Agile gets good marks on quality. The price (about $215) makes it a good deal. Parents like the smooth glide, large canopy and easy to adjust harness. We recommend the B-Agile as a credible alternative to the Baby Jogger City Mini.

Britax's other strollers (Affinity, B-Nimble) get more mixed reviews. The Affinity's dinky basket and two-handed seat recline draw jeers, as did the requirement to buy an $80 accessory pack to get a canopy—for a $500 stroller. Fans of the Affinity liked the adjustable handle and reversible seat, so your baby can face out or towards the parent.

The weakest link in the Britax stroller line-up is the B-Nimble, which is knocked by parents for its skimpy sunshade and a fold that collapses the canopy into the wheels, which inevitably gets the canopy dirty. The overall design and quality of the B-Nimble is disappointing.

Bottom line: we recommend Britax B-Ready and B-Agile. The B-Ready in particular is a credible and affordable alternative to the Uppa Baby Vista; and the B-Agile is a good bet compared to the Baby Jogger City Mini. *Baby Bargains Resale Rank: Excellent.* **Rating: A-**

Bugaboo bugaboo.com Bugaboo. It's Dutch for "priced as if from a hotel mini-bar."

The models. Here's an unlikely recipe for success in the stroller biz. Take a Dutch-designed stroller, attach an $800 price tag and voila! Instant hit, right? Well, chalk this one up to some creative design, marketing, and a dash of good timing.

Bugaboo's breakthrough success was the Frog, named as such for its small wheels in front that give it a frog-like look. The Frog (now discontinued) was a clever hybrid of an all-terrain and carriage stroller, pitched to parents for its multiple uses. The Frog was comprised of three parts: an aluminum frame and bassinet that could later be replaced by a stroller seat (included with canopy and basket). It weighed about 20 lbs., which is rather amazing. (Although discontinued, used Frogs can still be found online on Craigslist, eBay, etc.).

Oh, and we forgot the fourth ingredient of the Bugaboo—hype.

The Bugaboo folks were in the right place at the right time. How did the Bugaboo become so hot? Sure, it was fashionable, but that doesn't quite explain it. Nope, the answer is Bugaboo had one of the great product placements of all time . . . it was the featured stroller on HBO's Sex in the City. The rest is stroller history. In no time, celebs like Gwyneth Paltrow were swishing their Bugaboos across the pages of *People* magazine. The Bugaboo was the first baby stroller to cross paths with the white-hot supernova that is celebrity product placement.

Cleverly, Bugaboo also played on its Dutch design roots . . . even though (shhh! don't tell anyone!) Bugaboo's are made in Taiwan, not Amsterdam.

Bugaboo's sequel to the Frog—the aptly named Cameleon (20 lbs.) runs $969. The Cameleon adds a more springy suspension on the front wheels, plus a slightly larger seat frame and higher chassis. Unlike the Frog, the Cameleon is available in a wide range of color combinations—you can choose from six base colors and nine top colors, mix and match. Also new: a height adjustable handle.

Bugaboo recently rolled out a slightly revised Cameleon, dubbed the Cameleon3 (C3 for short). At first glance, there aren't many major visible differences between the new and old Cameleon. But Bugaboo points out the C3 has an easier fold (with one-hand!), a larger storage basket with lid, quick release front wheels, improved brake and new mosquito net accessory. The price on the C3 is the same as the last model. Oddly, Bugaboo is also touting the C3 s "refreshed design", which includes a more durable chassis. That seems to be a tacit admission that the old Cameleon lacked durability, which you think would come standard in a $969 stroller. Not expensive enough? How about a Complete version (with bassinet, rain cover and under seat bag) for $1109? Or the Special Edition with even nicer fabric for $1140?

In addition to the multi-function Cameleon3, Bugaboo has three other models: the compact Bee, the side-by-side double Donkey and all-terrain Buffalo.

The Bee 3 ($570-$620, 20.4 lbs.) is pitched to urban parents looking for a compact stroller. With its narrow width (20"; about four inches narrower than other Bugaboo's), the Bee has an over-sized canopy, reversible seat, and four-position seat recline.

A recent refresh of the Bee 3 included the ability to add an optional bassinet ($260), an extended canopy, larger storage basket and new all black frame (in addition to aluminum).

For $600, you'd think Bugaboo would throw in a canopy and seat pad . . . but then you don't know Bugaboo. The nifty new extended canopy is an extra $80. The seat pad (four colors) is another $70. So the Bee 3's actual price is $720-$770.

Bugaboo's first double stroller is the unfortunately named Donkey ($1150 to $1229). The unique feature here is a frame that can expand to accommodate a bassinet, storage basket or second baby seat. In its single or mono configuration, the stroller is 23" wide; for a duo, it expands to 29." Unfortunately, all this presto-chango goodness comes at a price, both literally and figuratively. The weight of the Donkey is a hefty 32 lbs. as a single and a whopping 40.3 lbs. as a duo (with the added second seat, $250). Yep, 40 lbs. before you add your kids!

Bugaboo's latest model, the Buffalo (26.2 lbs. $1000-$1180), is the company's first all terrain stroller featuring foam tires and a one-piece fold(!). The Buffalo features an included rain cover, reversible

strollers

seat, and is car seat compatible (adapters sold separately).

New for 2015, Bugaboo plans to sell a jogging stroller frame called the Runner that will work with any of their existing stroller seats. With 16" rear air-filled tires and a 14" front fixed wheel, the Runner chassis also has a hand brake, height adjustable handle and is compatible with any Bugaboo stroller. When it debuts in spring 2015, the Runner will be sold as a chassis only for $425 or as a complete system with seat for $755.

FYI: Bugaboo also sells a raft of accessories for its strollers such as cup holders (What? You thought that would be included?). Example: a $45 car seat adapter lets you attach most major brand infant car seats to the frame. That cup holder is $25; parasol $60; foot muff $130.

Our view. So, given all the hype around Bugaboo, you might be asking: is a Bugaboo stroller worth it?

When you walk into a baby super store, no doubt you'll see Bugaboo in a marquee position in the stroller department. The brand is positioned as the BMW of strollers . . . yes, it is more expensive than other options, but does the engineering, design and cache make it worth the price premium?

No, not in our opinion.

We will give Bugaboo credit for innovation—the brand's flagship multi-function model with reversible seat spurred a luxury stroller market boom. But Bugaboo slumped in recent years . . . and while economic headwinds no doubt cooled the desire for $1000 strollers, some of damage to Bugaboo has been self-inflicted.

The company's notorious slow and arrogant customer service is Exhibit One. When you spend this much on a stroller and something breaks, you expect white glove treatment from the company. Yet reader reports and online reviews again and again slam Bugaboo for indifferent customer service, long waits for parts and other hassles.

Quality issues have also dogged Bugaboo (plastic parts that break, inflated tires that go flat and so on) and that's on top of some of the built-in design hassles of the strollers, particularly on the Cameleon. In 2011, Bugaboo recalled Bee strollers in UK for defective wheels. Do recalls and quality issues happen with other stroller brands? Yes . . . but at this price level, we have higher expectations.

Readers gripe that the assembly and folding on the stroller takes too darn long. To fold a Bugaboo Frog or Cameleon, you must first remove the seat—that's a major pain, especially for folks who live in the suburbs and plan to fold it up frequently to fit in a trunk (and you'll need a big trunk). Hence, setting up the Bugaboo requires re-attaching the seat to the frame. Sure, this takes 30 seconds or so, which isn't forever—but about 25 seconds longer than most strollers.

The take-home message: a Bugaboo is probably best for urban dwellers or folks who don't plan to frequently disassemble and throw it in a trunk. (The Bee is an exception—it is easy to fold and set-up).

Fans of Bugaboo love the strollers' smooth steering, ride and suspension. The multi-function aspect of the Cameleon also earns kudos, although this has been matched in recent years by the Uppa Baby Vista and even Britax B-Ready. And while we think the Donkey's amazing expandable frame is a key innovation, the $1500 price tag for this stroller is just too steep.

Despite those kudos, we aren't sold on this brand. The price premium Bugaboo demands is simply too much given the above concerns. If you want a multifunction stroller, we like the UPPAbaby Vista or Britax B-Ready better (bonus: they cost 30%-50% less). The Bee is equally overpriced at $700+. Save $500 and get a Baby Jogger City Mini instead. *Baby Bargains Resale Rank: Excellent*. **Rating: B**

Bumbleride bumbleride.com In a stroller market stuffed with look-a-like models in varying shades of navy, Bumbleride's niche is both all-terrain and umbrella strollers with more than a touch of style. Started by a husband and wife team in San Diego, Bumbleride is a small stroller company with three basic models: Indie, Indie Twin and Flite.

The models. The Indie ($500, 20 lbs.) is a tri-wheel, all-terrain stroller with quick release 12" inflated tires, boot, adjustable handle, full recline and deep storage basket. Basically, the Indie is a more stylish version of the Mountain Buggy Urban Single or BOB Revolution. In the past year, the Indie got a new longer (and adjustable) footrest, a new included bumper bar and locks on the front wheel so it can be pushed in a straight line. The Indie now ships with a car seat adapter included in the box, which is great.

FYI: A twin version of the Indie runs $625 and now can hold two infant car seats. It weighs a rather hefty 32 lbs.

Bumbleride newest version of the Indie has four wheels and is called the Indie 4. Instead of the air-filled front wheel, the Indie 4 will have two small plastic wheels, similar to the Bugaboo Cameleon and bringing the weight down to 22 lbs. The goal is a stroller that "bridges the gap between urban and off-road terrain" strollers, says Bumbleride. Price: $600.

Finally, the Flite ($200, 14 lbs.) is a lightweight stroller with two handles (a la the Peg Pliko), a big canopy, two recline positions and car seat adapter bar. We liked all the included accessories such as a rain cover and travel bag.

FYI: Bumbleride has jumped on the sustainable wagon, rolling out eco-friendly fabrics across its entire line (50% of the exterior fabric is recycled PET plastic bottles; the interior fabric is made of 50% bamboo fabric).

Our view. Reviews for Bumbleride are mostly positive—the Indie probably gets the best marks from readers, who often compare it to the BOB Revolution. The Indie is three pounds lighter than the

strollers

Revolution and fans like its easy fold, height adjustable handle, car seat adapter and more. But critics point out the Indie doesn't have as smooth of a glide as the Revolution and the Indie only has a partial seat recline. The canopy on the Indie also gets low marks for its skimpy coverage and gaps near the frame.

As for the Flite, readers like the compact fold and car seat adapter—plus the overall style of the stroller is a winner. Critics, however, knock the small and hard to access basket. Also: the Flite doesn't have a height adjustable handle, so if you are short and your partner isn't, this could be an issue. The Flite's seat recline requires two hands to operate.

Over the past couple years, parent feedback has improved. Bumbleride still has great customer service, and the design and fashion are good So we'll up their grade a bit. *Baby Bargains Resale Rank: Excellent.* **Rating: B+**

Chicco chiccousa.com Chicco (pronounced KEY-ko) has a 50-year history as one of Europe's leading juvenile products makers. Along with Peg Perego, Chicco is one of Europe's biggest producer of baby gear and toys. When we first started writing about baby gear (way back in the early 90's), Chicco always played second fiddle to Peg, whose strollers outsold Chicco by a large margin. In recent years, their fortunes have switched: Chicco has seen a string of successes in America, with a popular infant car seat and several lightweight stroller models.

The models. The heart of Chicco's stroller line is their lightweight models: the Liteway, Echo and Capri (C6).

The Liteway ($140, 17 lbs.) features two handles, rear wheel suspension, padded five-point harness, cup holder and a full recline. We liked the boot that tucks away when not in use. New in the past year, Chicco added an enhanced Liteway (the Liteway Plus, $180) that works with the Chicco infant seat. After you are finished using it with the infant seat, you flip back the stroller seat and it becomes a toddler stroller that has an umbrella fold and weighs 19.2 lbs.

Similar to the basic Liteway, the Echo ($118 for single, $190 for twin) features a four position reclining seat and adjustable leg rest. The main difference between the Echo and Liteway: the Echo has double wheels up front, while the Liteway has single wheels.

The entry-level Capri (also known as the C6; $80, 11 lbs.) features a two-position seat recline, five-point harness and basic canopy.

As we move up in price, we come to Chicco's full-size strollers, anchored by the Cortina. It is sold separately ($180, 23 lbs.) or as part of a travel system ($330, paired with Chicco's excellent KeyFit infant seat). The Cortina features a more traditional design with height-adjustable handles and decent size basket. We thought it was well designed—we liked the one-hand fold and fully reclining seat. FYI: There is also an upgraded version of this stroller, the

Cortina Magic, that runs $200 and features upgraded fabric, a slightly larger canopy and boot plus a reversible seat insert.

The new Chicco Bravo ($230 stand-alone, $350 travel system, 22.7 lbs.) features a self-standing, quick fold. With a seat that pops off, the frame then can carry the Chicco infant seat. It is similar to the Baby Jogger City Mini 4 wheel and Britax B-Agile. FYI: The Bravo will eventually replace the Cortina over the coming year.

The Chicco Neuvo straddles the full-size and umbrella stroller categories—the Neuvo has umbrella-style handles and fold, but also features a multi-position reclining seat, child's tray and two-position footrest. The Neuvo is sold as a stand-alone stroller ($170) or travel system ($280).

Chicco has been expanding their stroller offerings in recent years, adding a multi-function stroller (the Urban), an all-terrain model (Activ3/Tre) and stroller frame (KeyFit Caddy).

The Urban ($400) is a Babies R Us exclusive until April 2015—a modular stroller with telescoping handle, alumium frame, standing fold, large basket, quick release EVA tires, included car seat adapter for the KeyFit and a reversible seat. This 24.1 lb. stroller also includes a clever seat that converts to a carry cot. The Urban is clearly aimed at the Uppa Baby Vista and is priced aggressively ($200 or so less).

The Activ3/Tre strollers are Chicco's take on the tri-wheel, all-terrain market dominated by the BOB Revolution. The Active3 features height adjustable handle, swivel/lockable front wheel, extendible canopy, large basket and included car seat adapter. The Active3 ($300; travel system $460) also has 12" foam filled tires and a standing fold plus adjustable suspension. The Tre ($380) is an upgraded version of the Active3, with bigger 16" air-filled wheels, hand brake and upgraded fabrics.

Rounding out the Chicco line is a stroller frame, dubbed the KeyFit Caddy ($100, 11 lbs.). As you might guess, it fits a Chicco KeyFit infant car seat (which pops in with a click) and has a big storage basket plus a height adjustable handle. The frame only fits Chicco infant seats, however.

Finally, lest we forget, Chicco makes two double strollers: the Cortina Together and Echo Twin. The Cortina Together ($300, 30 lbs.) is a front/back tandem stroller that holds two car seats and features an aluminum frame, a storage basket with trap door access, three-position handle and flat fold. Chicco also makes a double version of its Echo, the Echo Twin ($190, 30.5 lbs.). This stroller is a Target exclusive.

Our view. Chicco's strength is their lightweight strollers, which combine good quality and affordable prices. We like the Liteway best, but the entry-price Capri is great for travel and mall trips. Fans like the overall design, ease of use and (in the case of the Liteway

strollers

Plus) compatibility with the KeyFit infant seat. Critics note the Liteway isn't that light (at 20 lbs., it stretches the definition) and the Capri's skimpy canopy pales in comparison with Uppa Baby G-Luxe (but of course, that costs twice as much).

One caveat to Chicco's strollers are the handles, which in most models are not height adjustable. That frustrates taller parents.

Chicco's full-size strollers earn kudos, especially the Cortina. Fans cheer the easy steering, one-hand fold and padding (critics point out when folded, the Cortina is a bit bulky).

Bulk and weight are the main drawbacks with the Chicco Urban, which otherwise earns cheers for its multi-function feature that can morph into six different modes. A color pack lets you change the strollers look; the price at $400 is also attractive since competitors are in the $500-$700 range.

Overall, we think Chicco is a good brand and the prices are a decent value. *Baby Bargains Resale Rank: Good.* **Rating: B+**

Combi *combiusa.com* Japanese-owned Combi had its heyday in the '90's with a string of best-selling lightweight strollers, but the company has struggled in recent years. Combi has gone through several management changes and shifts in strategy, which has hurt its brand.

The models. Combi's focus is on lightweight, compact strollers. The company's flagship model, the Cosmo, is a good starting point. The Cosmo ($115, 13 lbs.) features a compact fold, full seat recline for infants, and removable napper bar plus it holds Combi's Shuttle infant car seat. The Cosmo SE ($130) at Babies R Us is the same as a regular Cosmo but with upgraded fabric.

Next is Combi's Cabria, which is basically a pimped out Cosmo. It features an extended canopy, larger basket, larger wheels, parent storage console and cup holder. This adds about a pound to the stroller (14.8 lbs.). Price: $135-$180 (travel system $320). In a recent update, the Cabria got a few tweaks: bigger wheels, a bigger basket and cup holder.

Combi has two offerings in the double stroller (side by side) category. The Combi Twin Savvy E ($170) is an entry-price double with partially reclining seats and independent canopies and the Twin Cosmo ($180), which features a full recline, infant "safety boots," self-standing fold and larger canopies.

Combi recently debuted the Catalyst, a very un-Combi like stroller that weighs in at 28.1 lbs. This $280 stroller features a reversible seat, extendable handles, and a bassinet that morphs into a seat. It is car seat compatible with Combi's Shuttle infant seat plus adapters for other brands (Graco, Chicco). While this stroller is innovative, we were scratching our heads at why Combi would attempt to compete in the multi-function stroller market with a nearly 30 lb. model.

On the other hand, Combi F2 is a super lightweight (8 lbs.) stroller with a one-hand, standing fold for $200.

New for 2015, Combi is debuting the Fold N Go stroller, available in both single ($229) and double ($329) versions. It features an extended canopy, auto locking mechanism, cup holds and (a first for Combi) accessory adapters for other brand infant car seats. The Fold & Go abandons Combi's tri-fold and instead adopts a Baby Jogger like quick fold, which is currently the rage.

Our view. Combi's woes in the stroller market can be traced to one major problem: its infant car seat. Unlike competitors Perego and Chicco, Combi has yet to figure out this market (its weak Shuttle car seat has suffered from slow sales amid recalls and other issues). As a result, Combi isn't much of a player in the travel system (car seat + stroller) market.

Yes, the new Fold & Go works with other brand infant seats, but most Combi strollers work only with Combi's shuttle infant car seat. This lack of cross compatibility hurts Combi.

Design snafus have also dogged the brand. Parents have complained for years about Combi's handles (too short) and storage baskets (too small, hard to access). You'd think Combi's designers would have better adapted these models to America after being here for 30 years. But, no.

And while parents universally like Combi for their lightweight and easy folds, there always seems to be some fatal flaw that pops up . . . front wheels that are easily damaged when the stroller is folded up, an overall lack of durability, etc.

When you spend $50 on a bare-bones umbrella stroller, you might put up with some of these issues. But at the $100+ price level, that's a tough sell, especially when competitors like Chicco and UPPAbaby offer similar strollers with taller handles and better storage . . . and without the quality problems. On the plus side, the new Combi Catalyst does earn mostly positive marks from readers, who like the built-in bassinet. But critics say it is too heavy and doesn't have a smooth push/ride, which you'd think you'd get for $300.

As for parent feedback, the most positive reviews for this line come for the Combi double strollers. The reviews for the Cosmo and Cabria are more mixed. *Baby Bargains Resale Rank: Poor.* ***Rating B-***

Cosco djgusa.com Baby products conglomerate Dorel takes a divide and conquer approach to its stroller offerings. In mass-market discounters like Walmart, Dorel sells travel systems under the brands Cosco and Safety 1st. For chains like Babies R Us, it sells more upscale versions of its strollers under the Eddie Bauer brand. Finally, at the top end, Dorel uses its European sister brands (Quinny, Maxi Cosi) to sell

strollers

strollers in specialty stores and upscale chains.

Since Quinny and Maxi Cosi are marketed as their own separate brands, we review them separately. Below is a review of Cosco, Safety 1st and Eddie Bauer.

The models. Cosco's divides its strollers into two groups: umbrella and full feature models. The low-end umbrella strollers are sold in discount stores for about $20 and are about as bare bones as you can get—no canopy, no basket, etc. These are disposable strollers best suited for travel.

The full feature strollers include the $34 Umbria, an 11 lb. stroller that has a simple two-position seat recline and basket. The similar Deluxe Comfort Ride runs $35.

Cosco's other main stroller business is travel systems, which come a Cosco infant seat with an affordable stroller. Example: Sprinter Go Lightly Travel System. This $117 travel system combines the Cosco Designer 22 car seat and a no-frills stroller with one-hand fold and three-point harness. These travel systems are sold under both the Cosco and Disney brands.

Eddie Bauer and Safety 1st offer more options and upscale features—these strollers are sold at Babies R Us, Target and online. Eddie Bauer's Portage (13.5 lbs.) stroller is a $100 umbrella stroller that can hold an infant car seat, while the Endurance Jogging Stroller is an all-terrain tri-wheel with air-filled wheels for $170 to $190.

Eddie Bauer travel systems include the full-feature Origin and QuadTrek strollers, as well as the tri-wheel TriTrek. Most of these travel systems are in the $200 to $250 range.

Safety 1st has the most stroller offerings of Dorel brands, with options ranging from $23 umbrella strollers emblazoned with Disney to $250 travel systems. The brand now even has a stroller frame, the Safety 1st Clic It! ($90, 13 lbs.). It features a large storage basket, two cup holders, a click-in feature for Dorel seats and a strap-in system for other infant car seats.

Safety 1st's marquee stroller is the AeroLite LX ($150 to $215), which is combined with the OnBoard Air infant car seat to make a travel system. This model features a curved frame, ultra compact fold, multi-position canopy and seat recline. There are multiple versions of this travel system ranging in price from $210 to $260.

Need to transport a baby and toddler? The Safety 1st Stand Onboard has a stroller seat and the ability to hold an infant car seat, plus a stand-on platform at the back to transport an older toddler. Price: $155, 24.8 lbs.

New for 2015, Cosco is debuting the Lift N Stroll, an $80 stand-alone stroller or $129 as a travel system at Walmart. The big feature here: a quick fold like Baby Jogger.

Our view. Let's be honest here—Cosco, Eddie Bauer or Safety

1st strollers are far from "best in class." Sold on price and paired with Cosco's middling infant car seats, these travel systems are aimed at folks on very tight budgets who can only spend $100 or so on a stroller and car seat. Yes, this is a book on bargains, but what we have here is a case where the cheap is cheap.

Sure, there's nothing wrong with those bargain basement $20 or $30 Cosco umbrella strollers—they are designed to be disposable. But when you cross $100, spending that much money on one of these strollers is absurd. "Disappointed" is the most common parent comment . . . and that's putting it charitably.

Folks soon discover why these strollers are sold so cheaply . . . wheels that squeak, canopies that break, low-end fabric, skimpy padding.

Take the Safety 1st Aerolite, for example. Parents tell us the strollers' vaunted one-hand fold/step-up is a pain to use in real life (the stiff release mechanism frustrates users) and design goofs like the wider rear wheelbase cause the stroller to get caught in tight spaces at the mall.

Bottom line: Cosco disappoints. Unless you are picking up one as a steal on Craigslist, we suggest skipping these strollers. *Baby Bargains Resale Rank: Poor.* **Rating: C+**

Cybex *Cybex-online.com* German stroller brand Cybex is best known for their Aton infant car seat, a pricey but well designed entry in that category. Less well known are Cybex's strollers, which have seen much less success. Some of this has been due to design snafus (white frames and wheels?). High retail prices didn't help.

So Cybex is launching an entire new line of strollers for 2015. Here's an overview:

The models. Cybex is mainly known for its souped-up umbrella strollers with precious gem names (the Ruby, Onyx, etc). For 2015, the brand is taking a hard right turn into more expensive multi-function and tri-wheels. Cybex has four model groups: Agis, Eternis, Balios, Priam. They will be released in the first quarter of 2015.

The Agis M-Air 3 is a jazzed Baby Jogger City Mini—that is, a tri-wheel stroller with height adjustable handle, two-step fold and a no rethread harness, which is common on car seats but unusual for strollers. A four-wheel version of this stroller is called the M4.

The Eternis is similar to the Agis, but features larger wheels. Again, there are both three-wheel (Eternis M3) and four-wheel (Eternis M4) versions of this model.

The Balios M stroller is similar to the Eternis but adds a reversible, removable seat. With the seat removed, you can pop in a Cybex Aton infant car seat.

FYI: Pricing has not been set for the Agis, Eternis and Balios as of this writing.

The flagship model for the 2015 Cybex stroller line is the Priam, a multi-function stroller that can be customized with three different wheel and two seat options. The frame features a telescoping handle and self-standing fold. The fully reclining seat will have an adjustable footrest—you can put the seat on the frame forward or rear facing. And yes, you can fold the stroller with the seat attached (take that, Bugaboo). Price: $1200-$1300.

Cybex will carry over two older models into 2015—the Onyx and Callisto.

The Onyx ($260-$360, 16 lbs.) features more padding and full seat recline. A double version of the Onyx is called the Twinyx (for children starting at six months of age; $450). The Callisto is Cybex's top of the line model ($350, 22 lbs.) with plush fabric and wheel suspension.

In the past year, Cybex has rolled out designer versions of its strollers, such as the Jeremy Scott "Food Fight." Don't fall in love with these looks if you don't have a serious bankroll, however—the designer Cybex versions run three *times* the retail price of the non-designer models.

Our view. Reader feedback on the Cybex has been thin, probably due to their poor sales. One mom who bought an Onyx posted to our stroller message board that she loved the stroller's canopy, high handles and decent steering. But the ride was rickety, especially on cracked sidewalks. Overall, she was impressed—but she only paid $65 for the stroller on Overstock.com. "It would absolutely not be worth it at the full $200 retail price point."

Other readers agreed, saying they liked but didn't love their Cybex. While most folks compliment the bright colors and overall features, critics knock the use of flimsy plastic (such as the canopy attachment) and too high prices. If you can find one of these strollers at a steep discount, go for it.

The new 2015 Cybex strollers weren't out as of this writing; we'll update this review as we get feedback on these models. Baby*Bargains Resale Rank: Excellent. **Rating: B**

Eddie Bauer *See Cosco.*

Evenflo evenflo.com Most Evenflo strollers are sold as travel systems, paired with Evenflo's infant car seats. The emphasis is on price—you can typically pick one of these systems up at Walmart for about $160. But are they a good deal? Read on.

The models. Most of Evenflo's strollers are what we'd call first-time parent strollers—when folks think they need a large stroller with every bell and whistle to ferry baby. While these features are nice, they tended to add weight and bulk to Evenflo's strollers. Recognizing the weight issue, Evenflo has apparently sent its stroller line-up to Weight Watchers . . . the newer models have shed some serious poundage compared to the 30 lb. models of the recent past.

Evenflo's current line-up includes two models: the FlexLite and JourneyLite.

The FlexLite is Evenflo's flagship model ($90, 15 lbs.). It features a multi-position reclining seat, one-hand fold and parent console with two cup holders. The JourneyLite ($74, 22 lbs.) is very similar to the FlexLite, but has a deeper basket and weighs about five more pounds than the FlexLite.

The main feature of most Evenflo strollers is their one-hand fold—a twist of the handlebar and the stroller collapses. Yet apparently this isn't fast enough in today's market. Evenflo now has a "SmartFold" stroller: same basic features as their Journey or FlexLite, but now the handlebar fold is replaced by a strap in the seat that folds the stroller (like Baby Jogger). Price: $160 for a travel system, a Walmart exclusive.

Perhaps the best thing about Evenflo strollers is their amazing parent trays complete with two cup holders with "automotive cup grippers" and a storage area with "privacy lid." If only Evenflo had put as much effort into the rest of the stroller as they did the parent tray.

Our view. About the best we can say about Evenflo's strollers is that they get slightly better marks from readers than similarly priced Cosco travel systems. But that is a low bar. We aren't fans of Evenflo's infant car seats, which of course are paired with all these strollers sold as travel systems.

At $90 as stand-alone models, Evenflo strollers compete against Chicco, Summer and Graco's lightweight offerings—and those brands get much better marks from our readers for quality, durability and ease of use. While we like the fact that Evenflo's strollers have shed weight, the company will have to do more to win fans in a competitive market.

One final note: we should commend Evenflo for their customer service, which earns good marks from our readers for promptly taking care of problems. ***Rating: B-***

GB *gbchildusa.com* Chinese baby goods manufacturer and designer Good Baby (or, as the brand is referred to here in North America, GB) has been on a roll in the past couple of years. The company got its start designing and manufacturing car seats and other gear for other major baby goods makers (Dorel/Cosco, etc), but lately it has set its eyes on selling its goods directly to U.S. parents.

To that end, the company has snapped up baby gear companies Cybex and Evenflo. And launched Urbini, a new car seat/stroller brand that is exclusive to Walmart. If that weren't enough, the company is also rolling out strollers under its own brand GB. Here's an overview:

The Models. GB debuts in this category with two lightweight strollers: the Zuzu and Ellum. A third model, the Evoq, is sold as a

strollers

travel system. All GB strollers are exclusive to Babies R Us.

The Zuzu ($180-$200, 15.8 lbs.) has two handles with an umbrella-like standing fold and partially reclining seat. It has build-in adapters for Graco and Chicco car seats.

The Ellum ($220, 15.4 lbs.) is a single handle stroller with adjustable footrest, airflow canopy, compact fold and quick fold with a center strap. The biggest differences between the Ellum and Zuzu? Besides, the handlebar, the seat on the Ellum has a full recline and the canopy is extended.

The Evoq ($430) is a travel system that pairs a multi-function stroller with GB's new infant car seat, the Asana35 AP.

Our View. GB's first strollers have only been on the market for a short time, so we've received little reader feedback yet on the models. But we did have time to evaluate the models at a recent trade show. Our verdict: they're overpriced. At $180-$200, the Zuzu is aimed squarely at the top of the umbrella market, where UPPAbaby's G-Luxe reins. And on paper, both of these strollers are similar (adjustable footrest, standing fold, etc). But look at the canopy—while the Zuzu has an interesting ventilated zippered extension, the G-Luxe's pop out sunshade is more practical and offers better coverage.

And let's talk weight: at 15.8 lbs., the Zuzu is about 20% heavier than the G-Luxe. Yes, we are only talking two pounds, but every ounce counts when hauling a stroller in and out of a trunk.

Finally, we like the removable fabrics (for washing) on the G-Luxe and other premium umbrella strollers, a feature the Zuzu lacks.

The Zuzu wins when it comes to car seat compatibility, with built-in adapters . . . but the Zuzu's fold pushes the stroller's footrest to the ground, which is guaranteed to get the fabric grimy when you fold it in a parking lot. The G-Luxe keeps the fabric off the ground when it is folded down.

Bottom line: the Zuzu is a decent first effort, but overpriced. We'd be more happy with this stroller at $125.

The Ellum has similar pros and cons to the Zuzu—overpriced for what you get. Oddly, the Ellum's storage basket is largely blocked by two large cross bars in back. That is a rookie mistake we wouldn't expect GB to make, given their extensive stroller design background.

The Evoq is a multi function stroller that has a reversible seat and height adjustable handle bar. The shallow basket is an odd oversight here, as GB's other strollers feature better basket designs. As a travel system, the Evoq fits the brand's Asana35 AP infant car seat—but that's about it. There are no other adapters, which limits the appeal of the Evoq. In fact, there are no other accessories for this model, which is major negative (want a cup holder? No cup holder for you!).

The Evoq system is so new as of press time, we've seen little real world feedback on it. Given both the stroller and infant seat are brand new, it would be a major leap of faith to invest $400+ on this package.

The take home message: GB's first efforts as a stand-alone brand in the stroller category show promise but ultimately fall short. Unless pricing comes down, these strollers will have a tough time competing. **Rating: C**

Graco gracobaby.com Graco's main stroller niche is the travel system combining an infant car seat and stroller and aimed at first-time parents who want all the bells and whistles. The secret to their success is their excellent infant car seat, the SnugRide.

Graco is like the Honda of strollers—a mid-priced brand with decent quality, but not a lot of pizzazz. Graco leaves the low-end, opening price-point market to Dorel/Cosco.

Graco's line is huge, so let's get to the highlights:

The models. Graco divides their stroller line into three areas: lightweight, three-wheel and multi-child strollers.

The lightweight models include the Breeze, Modes, UrbanLite, Dynamo Lite, FastAction Fold and LiteRider. New for 2015: the Verb and Comfy Cruiser.

The three-wheel models include the FastAction Fold Jogger/Sport and Trekko, Aire3, Relay.

In the double or multi-child category, Graco offers the FastAction Fold Duo, Ready2Grow, RoomFor2 Duo and DuoGlider.

FYI: some of Graco's strollers are exclusive to certain chains. Example: until recently, only Babies R Us carried the Air3. Strollers often go on exclusive for a year or more, then come off exclusive and are more widely available.

Whew. Deep breath. Let's look at the stand-outs in each Graco stroller category:

◆ **Lightweight.** The Modes and Fast Action strollers are the stars here.

The Graco Modes Click Connect stroller is 23.3 lbs. (which pushes the concept of light weight to the outer limits of reality) and features a reversible seat, one-hand standing fold and removable child tray. You can use Modes just as a stroller frame to transport the infant car seat (by removing the stroller seat). All told the Modes stroller converts into ten different configurations.

As with all Graco strollers, you also get Graco's generous parent tray with cup holders. Feedback on the Modes has been quite positive and we'd recommend it. Price: $250 as a stand-alone model or $370 as part of a travel system with the SnugRide Click Connect 35. Our only reservation about the Modes: at $250, you are getting up into Baby Jogger City Mini price territory. And the City Mini, while lacking the reversible seat, is six pounds lighter with an easier fold.

Speaking of Baby Jogger, Graco is hoping to conjure up some

strollers

of that Baby Jogger Quick Fold magic with its new FastAction Fold LX stroller ($130-$160, 20.9 lbs.). As the name implies, this stroller folds in a single-step and stands when folded. It features a multi-position reclining seat, three or five-point harness and all the standard Graco stroller features you'd expect (large storage basket, parent tray with cup holders, etc). It holds all Graco infant seats. Sold as a stand-alone model or as a travel system ($200).

The Graco Aire3 is very similar to the Baby Jogger City Mini or Britax B-Agile—a tri-wheel stroller with a quick fold, parent console and fully reclining seat. Price: $230.

The Graco Breaze ($170, 17.5 lbs) is a one-hand fold lightweight stroller with full recline, extended canopy and front wheel suspension. It is car seat compatible.

New for 2015, the Verb (18.2 lbs.) features front suspension and a one-hand fold. It will be sold as a stand-alone stroller ($100) or as a travel system ($200) with the infant seat the Graco Dangling Participle (just kidding).

Also new: the Graco Comfy Cruiser (16 lbs.) features a one-hand, standing fold. Price: $190 as a travel system with a Graco SnugRide 30.

◆ **Three-wheel strollers.** Graco's main entry here is the FastAction Fold Sport ($160), a Baby Jogger City Mini knock-off. This tri-wheel stroller features a multi-position reclining seat and large storage basket.

Graco also makes other tri-wheel strollers with air-filled tires under the FastAction moniker (FastAction Fold Joggers). Even though these strollers are billed as joggers, they really are designed for walking on trails, not running. The turnable/lockable front wheels on the FastAction Fold Joggers make the strollers more maneuverable, but less ideal for actual running.

Also in the three-wheel category is Graco's Trekko ($160 stand-alone, $280 travel system). This full-size stroller has a front wheel that can be locked and features a 180 degree rotating canopy, full seat recline, one-hand fold, rubber tires, and a height adjustable handle. And it works with any Graco infant car seat. Our only concern with this stroller: the rear-wheel width at 25.5" may make negotiating tight spaces difficult (most strollers have a 20-24" rear wheel width). Also this stroller clocks in at 26.9 lbs., about 10% heavier than the similar Valco Tri-Mode. FYI: The Trekko has "never flat" rubber tires, not air filled.

The Graco Relay ($290, 27 lbs.) is an all-terrain stroller featuring air-filled tires, suspension and an included car seat adapter. The canopy features reflective fabric and UV50 protection.

◆ **Double strollers.** Most of Graco's offerings here are tandem (front/back) doubles, such as the Ready2Grow. It features 12 seating positions, the ability to hold two infant seats, and a removable rear jump seat with harness that can hold an older toddler. The

Ready2Grow runs $180 to $200 and weighs in at a hefty 32.4 lbs. This stroller seems squarely aimed at the Joovy Big Caboose market.

The DuoGlider ($122, 29 lbs.) is also a front/back tandem. Graco's claim to fame in this niche is "stadium seating," where the rear seat is elevated. Of course, you get all the standard features: huge storage baskets, removable canopies, etc. Cool feature: The DuoGlider holds two Graco infant car seats.

New to the lineup is a model that is similar to the Baby Trend's Sit N Stand: the RoomFor2. This stroller holds a 50 lb. child in both front or rear jump seat and features a large basket, one-hand fold, parent tray and the ability to hold a car seat in front. The child in the rear can sit or stand. Price: $120, 24.7 lbs.

Finally in the double stroller category, Graco offers one side-by-side model: the FastAction Duo ($280), a Babies R Us Exclusive. This stroller is essentially a double version of the FastAction Fold Sport.

◆ *Misc.* Graco has a couple of other strollers that don't quite fit into the above categories.

Graco's entry in the stroller frame category, the Snug Rider, is a winner—this $70 frame holds the (what else?) Graco Snug Ride infant car seat with a secure lock-in feature and has a one-hand fold and basket. New in the past year, Graco rolled out a Snug Rider Elite: this $90 model has integrated cup holders, zippered storage and one-hand fold. It holds both Graco's Classic and Click Connect infant seats.

Travel systems are a major part of the Graco stroller line-up, where a Graco stroller (like the ones reviewed above) is paired with a Graco infant seat in one box. Graco does sell some travel systems that include older model strollers not sold separately.

There are a slew of other Graco travel system models out there (Stylus, etc.)—most of these strollers are "full-feature" models with large storage baskets, parent trays and reclining seats.

Our view. Graco has slowly improved its stroller line over the past several years. The brand used to be known for selling mostly bulky travel systems with hulking strollers that weighed 30 lbs. empty. Today there are more three-wheel options and strollers that have slimmed down, weight wise.

The best options here are the Modes and FastAction Fold Sport strollers. Fans of the Modes like its ability to have baby face you or out—the ten riding configurations are a plus. The fact that the seat removes and you can use the remaining frame to snap in an infant car seat is another major plus. Critics of the Modes point out the stroller is still rather heavy and bulky—23.3 lbs. with seat is light for Graco, but heavy when compared to the competition. The $250 Modes is pricey.

The FastAction Fold Sport is also a winner—a credible alternative to the Baby Jogger Mini at a price that's 40% less. We also like the

Graco Aire3, which is a credible alternative to the Baby Jogger City Mini or Britax B-Agile, even if the canopy coverage isn't as generous.

Of course, despite the generally positive reviews, Graco strollers aren't without their faults. Look at how some Graco strollers fold up . . . when folded, the front tray hits the ground, inevitably damaging or scratching it in a parking lot. Parents also complain about canopies that offer less than full coverage (note that several of Graco's new models include fully enclosing canopies). And the steering on most Graco strollers is only so-so. These strollers were designed for the mall or smooth sidewalks.

Graco strollers are bulky when folded—even the lightweight ones can eat up the entire trunk of an average sized car. Factor this into your decision if your ride is a small compact.

Bottom line: Graco's strollers are designed for the mall or other light duty shopping trips. Don't expect these strollers to do well in urban environs with cracked sidewalks. Stick with Graco's lightest weight models and set your expectations accordingly. *Baby Bargains Resale Rank: Poor.* **Rating: B**

Harmony This brand is reviewed on the free side of our web site at BabyBargains.com/?p=15969

Hauck/i'coo This brand is reviewed on the free side of our web site at BabyBargains.com/?p=1294

Ingenuity *kidsii.com.* Ingenuity is new to the stroller biz, but the company behind the brand (Kids II) is well known as the maker of Bright Starts, Baby Einstein and Taggies toys and gear.

Ingenuity debuted its first stroller in fall 2014 at the same time they also debuted an infant car seat (the InTrust 35 Pro). We were impressed with the car seat, but how does the stroller stack up?

The Ingenuity InVenture Pro Multi-Function stroller (a mouthful for sure) is a $200, 26.7 lb. model that, as you might guess, works with Ingenuity's own car seat. Features include a height adjustable handle, reversible multi-position reclining seat, infant insert and parent tray with covered storage.

Overall, not bad for $200. So what's not to love? Well, even though Ingenuity boasts of a "lightweight aluminum frame," at nearly 27 lbs., the InVenture is pushing the definition of lightweight. Closer to 20 lbs. would be better.

The canopy with sunshield is good, but doesn't fully enclose the stroller. And while we like the parent console with a place for a phone and cord slot, the small, shallow storage basket is disappointing.

As of this writing, the InVenture only works with Ingenuity's own infant car seat—and not with other brands. Also missing: any accessories like a rain cover.

This stroller was too new to get any parent feedback as we went to press. FYI: Even though this stroller is sold on Amazon, it is cheaper on other sites like Babies R Us. ***Rating: Not Yet.***

InStep *See Schwinn.*

i'coo/Traxx *See Hauck.*

Inglesina *Inglesina.com* Given the success of fellow Italian stroller makers Peg Perego and Chicco, you'd think Inglesina would be another slam-dunk here in the U.S. Yet the company has struggled for several reasons. First, it lacks an infant car seat—that means Inglesina is frozen out of the big travel system market. Second, distribution—these strollers aren't sold in many big box stores, so seeing them in person takes quite a bit of effort.

The models. Inglesina has two umbrella-style models: Trip and Swift.

The Trip ($160, 14.9 lbs.) is a lightweight umbrella model with a four-position seat recline, adjustable footrest, cup holder and included rain cover. The Swift ($140, 13 lbs.) is a scaled down version of the Trip, but still has the same seat recline. It omits the cup holder and rain cover and has a less fancy canopy.

FYI: the Trip and Swift are made in China.

Inglesina recently made some small improvements to the Trip: bigger wheels, improved suspension and a larger extended canopy. The Trip also recently added a bumper bar and rain cover with no increase in price; the Trip is also now available in a white frame option.

New for 2015, the Net is a new entry-price point stroller ($150, 11.9 lbs.) with two position seat recline and a standing fold. The Net lacks a storage basket.

Inglesina has two full-size strollers: the Quad and Trilogy.

The Quad ($600) is an all-terrain stroller with front and rear suspension, a full recline, reversible seat and one-hand fold (that only works without the seat in place, unfortunately). The Quad weighs in at a hefty 26.1 lbs. Included in the price is a cup holder, rain cover and boot. A optional bassinet is $250. The Quad is compatible with Combi infant car seats.

The Trilogy ($500) features a reversible seat, rain cover, one-hand, self-standing fold with seat (in either direction). The weight is 22.7 lbs.

Our view. We've always liked this brand, despite its lack of distribution and market success. The Trip and Swift are the most popular models and get good marks for quality. Fans like the tall handles and ease of use, but critics say the seats are too shallow for larger toddlers. Also disappointing: no cup holder and a seat position some folks think is too reclined.

The Quad and Trilogy are tougher sells, given their high price points. The feedback on these models has been very thin, given the limited distribution. From what little we've heard, however, folks like the features and ease of use—especially on the Quad.

One negative for Inglesina: the brand's resale values land at the bottom of our rankings. In the past year, Inglesina has occasionally dumped strollers at deep discounts—this has depressed values for Inglesina strollers on the second-hand market.

Bottom line: Inglesina strollers are well made; we like all the included extras (cup holder, rain cover on some models) that cost extra elsewhere. *Baby Bargains Resale Rank: Poor.* **Rating: A**

Jane *Jane-USA.com* This brand is reviewed on the free side of our web site at BabyBargains.com/?p=17640

JJ Cole *jjcolecollections.com* JJ Cole's stroller is made by The First Years. The JJ Cole Broadway 360 ($365) has a unique selling point: the seat can swivel 360 degrees. It also has larger rear wheels and a seat that makes into a bassinet. Included is a universal car seat adapter.

Parents seem to like the Broadway overall although some complain the basket is hard to access and rather skimpy. However, the Broadway is priced very reasonably for all the features it offers.

FYI: Even though the First Years is giving up on selling strollers sold under its own name, the JJ Cole Broadway will live on. **Rating: A**

Joovy *joovy.com* Joovy was launched in 2002 with a single model—the Caboose Stand-on Tandem ($138, 26 lbs.), which can cart a baby in the stroller seat and toddler on a stand-up board (or seat) in back. Similar to the Baby Trend Sit N Stand, Joovy's Caboose features a higher handle height, foam handle, improved car seat attachment and nicer canopy.

Over the last few years, Joovy has refined the Caboose—now the seat recline doesn't interfere with the space for the toddler. And the infant car seat attachment sits higher than the previous model. FYI: the Joovy works with 13 infant seats, including the Britax B-Safe and Chicco KeyFit.

In recent years, Joovy has rolled out several spin-offs of the Caboose: the Caboose Ultralight, Big Caboose, Ergo Caboose, Big Caboose Stand On Triple, and Caboose VaryLight.

The Caboose Ultralight ($200, 24.3 lbs.) is 20% lighter than the original Caboose and features a larger canopy and neoprene parent organizer. In the past year, this stroller got a fancier canopy and taller seat. A rear seat accessory (Caboose Too seat) is available for an additional $60. Or you can buy it together as a complete package as the Caboose Too Ultralight ($250).

Got three kids? The Big Caboose ($350, 37 lbs.) has two seats plus a toddler jump seat/standing area. This model can also handle two infant car seats—so if you have twins and an older toddler, this would be one of the few models out there to hold all three tykes.

The Ergo Caboose ($300, 28.5 lbs.) looks like a pregnant Bugaboo—it features air-filled rear tires, ergonomic mesh seat with two-position recline, a longer frame with better access to the storage basket and a slew of accessories (rain cover, fleece canopy, etc).

The latest Caboose model is the Caboose VaryLight ($400, 34 lbs.)—this Caboose features a frame that expands, turning the stroller from a single to double strollers. The VaryLight is car seat compatible (Graco Classic Connect 32/35, Chicco KeyFit 30, Perego SIP 30-30) and features a one-hand fold, storage basket and front wheel suspension.

While the Caboose is Joovy's flagship model, the company has several other strollers. The Scooter X2 ($230) is a lightweight side-by-side twin stroller with an elliptical frame. It also features a deep (but not full) seat recline. Like all Joovy strollers, the Scooter X2 features an oversized canopy and large storage basket. There are even two cup holders/storage pockets on the back of each seat. FYI: The single version of the Scooter is quite different than the double, with a ten-position adjustable handle bar and sealed bearing wheels.

For 2015, the Scooter X2 boasts larger wheels (7" front, 9" rear), new graphite frame and improved fold.

The compact, two-handle Groove ($183, 17 lbs.) umbrella stroller has a partial seat recline (150 degrees) and an extended canopy with sun visor plus six-inch wheels with suspension. The Groove Ultralight ($140) has much the same features as the Groove, but has a lighter weight frame (13.9 lbs.) as well as smaller wheels and somewhat less seat padding.

Joovy's Zoom 360 ($250) is billed as a jogger with front swivel wheel, no rear axle (so you can run without kicking the back), full canopy, car seat adaptor (seats click in) and parent tray. New for 2015, this model gets a spin-off: the Zoom 360 Ultralight, which is 10% lighter than the original.

Joovy's stroller frame is the Roo, which comes in both single ($60, 16.2 lbs.) and double versions (TwinRoo, $120, 21.6 lbs.). Both feature a one-hand fold, parent organizer and work with Chicco, Graco and Peg Perego infant seats. Unlike other stroller frames, Joovy's Roo positions the infant car seat sideways. You can click the car seat into the frame and release it with the seat's release lever.

New for 2015, a new Roo spin-off dubbed the TwinRoo+ allows you to mount the infant car seats in the same or opposite directions (the original TwinRoo just allows one configuration). The new TwinRoo+ also works with Graco's newer car seats (the Click Connect 35/40) as well as the Britax B-Safe and UPPAbaby Mesa.

strollers

Joovy's entry in the multi-function stroller category is the Qool, available both in single and double (Too Qool) versions. The Qool ($460, 21.5 lbs.) features a reversible seat, telescoping handlebar, four wheel suspension, large canopy, and an adjustable footrest. The seat offers a 140 degree recline. The Too Qool ($700, 36.5 lbs.). double is an inline double, with the second seat in the back (like Phil & Teds). As with other Joovy strollers, the Too Qool has car seat adapters available as accessories.

For 2015, the Qool gets a new dark grey graphic frame or silver frame option. The latter models are called the Qool Silver. Also new: several car seat adapter accessories for the Qool.

The TooFold by Micralite ($800) has a one-handed quick folding frame and can go from single to double with optional stand-on board or second seat. (Joovy is importing this stroller from UK-based Micralite).

Our view. Of all the Caboose variations, we recommend the Joovy Caboose Ultralight as tops. Reader feedback on this model is mostly positive—the lighter weight makes it a worthy upgrade over the regular Caboose. Fans like the easy fold and compatibility with most infant car seats. Critics note that infant car seats must be strapped down (there is no click-in lock). And even when collapsed, the Caboose takes up a large amount of trunk real estate.

Feedback on Joovy's other strollers has been generally positive. Readers like the Zoom as a great value, but a few parents criticized the weight (27 lbs.), which is hefty compared to the similar strollers in this category. It appears Jovvy is addressing the weight issue with the new Zoom 360 Ultralight.

The Groove has less feedback (but again, mostly positive).

As for Joovy's other offerings, the Scooter X2 also gets good marks for its easy fold, although it takes two hands. This stroller is a good choice for those looking at an affordable option for a side-by-side stroller. (We haven't tested the 2015 Scooter X2 yet, which has been modified to make the fold easier).

The Joovy models that are least popular are probably its largest/heaviest strollers: the Ergo Caboose and Big Caboose. These strollers are large and bulky—and when weighed down with two or three kids, they can require Herculean effort to push and maneuver.

Bottom line: it's unusual for a stroller company to have mostly positive reviews across nearly all its models, especially a line as large as Joovy's. Fans love the overall value and features like oversized canopies. We are raising Joovy's rating this year to reflect this. *Baby Bargains Resale Rank: Good.* **Rating: A-**

Kinderwagon This brand is reviewed on the free side of our web site at BabyBargains.com/?p=12623

Kolcraft *kolcraft.com* Kolcraft is the exception to the rule that you need a successful infant car seat to succeed in the stroller market—despite the lack of any travel systems, Kolcraft has survived, thanks to a focus on under-served market segments (namely double strollers).

The models. Kolcraft sells strollers under two brands: Kolcraft and Contours. Kolcraft is sold as entry-level models at chains stores like Walmart; Contours is the mid-price offering with multi-function strollers. (Kolcraft used to sell strollers under the Jeep brand, but that license ended in 2014).

Kolcraft's entry-level offering is the Cloud umbrella stroller sold at Walmart for $30. The Cloud is your basic umbrella stroller with cup holder, storage basket and extended canopy—not a bad deal for $30. The Cloud Plus (11.8 lbs.) adds a one-hand fold, multi-position seat recline and child snack tray for $60.

New for 2015, Kolcraft is adding all-terrain and jogging strollers to the mix. The Adventure is an all-terrain with large canopy, air-filled wheels, front basket access and one-hand fold. It also is infant car seat-compatible. Price: $170. The Sprint is Kolcraft's first jogger that will come in two versions: the Sprint X features fixed 16″ wheels while the Sprint Pro will have a front swivel wheel that can be locked and height adjustable handle. Both will retail for about $230.

Contours is Kolcraft's premium offering with upgraded features and styling. The flagship model is the Contours Bliss (25.3 lbs.) a 4-in-1, multi-function stroller. The $400 Bliss features a reversible seat that can convert into a bassinet. Yep, this is like a poor man's Uppa Baby Vista. At $400, the Bliss is pricey but includes an infant car seat adapter, a fold with or without the seat attached, cup holder and more. For 2015, Kolcraft tweaks the Bliss with a new extendable canopy, rubber coated back wheels and a bigger foot rest.

The biggest sellers in the Contours line are their double strollers. The Options tandem stroller ($280, 32 lbs.) has seven different configurations with seats that can reverse or mix one (or two) infant car seats and a seat. The Options ships with a universal car seat adapter and features a standing fold, reclining seats, adjustable footrests and decent size canopies.

The Options is a Babies R Us exclusive. There is also an upgraded version of the Options called the Options Elite ($300, 37.4 lbs.), which is a Buy Buy Baby exclusive. The Elite adds rubber coated rear wheels, side storage basket access and seat back storage. The Elite also has an extra, extendable canopy with mesh air vent as well as taller seats.

Contours has both single and double strollers. On the single side, the Contours Options 3 Wheel Stroller ($170, 26 lbs.) has an infant car seat adapter and reversible seat, so you can see baby while pushing. The Contours Lite stroller ($88, 15.5 lbs.) features a large

strollers

storage basket, partial seat recline and a value price.

Our view. Dollar for dollar, these are the best affordable strollers on the market. Compared to other low-end brands (Graco, Cosco), Kolcraft shines.

We like the affordable Cloud strollers—parents tell us they are a good value for the dollar, praising the simple fold and extended canopy (something often missing in the under $100 stroller market).

At $400, the Contours Bliss seems a world away from the affordable Cloud—yet, amazingly Kolcraft pulls off this model as well. Fans like the multi-function feature and memory foam. Critics knock the fact the Bliss is rather bulky when folded; and the plastic wheels seem out of place in this price range (foam or rubber-coated wheels would have been a better choice). While we like the Bliss, the fabric quality and finish is not quite as nice as other $400 strollers, in our opinion.

The Contours Options tandem is an excellent double stroller. The only disadvantage: weight. At 30+ lbs., the Options is bulky when folded (it can easily eat up the entire trunk in a vehicle). While fans loved the multiple configurations and overall ease of use, the lack of a parent console (save one skimpy cup holder) is a bummer. *Baby Bargains Resale Rank: Fair.* **Rating: B+**

Mima *MimaKids.com* This brand is reviewed on the free side of our web site at BabyBargains.com/?p=17573

Maclaren After this company's bankruptcy in 2012, we no longer recommend Maclaren. See our blog for an archive of these events.

Mamas and Papas *mamasandpapas.com* No, not the 1960's folk rock group. Mamas and Papas is the UK-based baby product manufacturer and retailer that landed in the U.S. in 2010. In Britain, the brand is similar to Graco, selling products across several categories. Unlike U.S. competitors, Mamas and Papas not only makes baby gear but also runs their own chain of stores in Britain.

The models. The flagship model here is the oddly named Armadillo, a "big little stroller" as the company bills it. The Armadillo ($280, 20 lbs.) features a wide seat, full recline, adjustable footrest, one hand fold, large basket and wheel suspension. Car seat adapters are available for the Chicco, Maxi Cosi and Cybex car seats.

In case you missed it, the Armadillo is clearly "inspired" by the Bugaboo Bee, down to the animal name and bright yellow canopy. On the plus side, the Armadillo is less than half the Bee's $700+ price tag. The Armadillo has been so successful that Mamas and Papas has rolled out three spin-offs: the Armadillo City, Flip and Flip XT. The Armadillo City ($270, 18.7 lbs.) is a slimmer, more compact version of the regular Armadillo (even the wheels are smaller). At first blush, it doesn't look much different, but Mamas and Papas addressed some complaints about the old model—namely, the buckle that was hard to work. The hood is now detachable and the fabric doesn't get dirty when the stroller is folded. One trade-off: the foot rest that was adjustable on the Armadillo is now non-adjustable on the Armadillo City.

As you might guess from the name, the Armadillo Flip ($500, 21.6 lbs.) has a reversible seat, upgraded padding and a huge canopy that can enclose the stroller. You can fold the stroller with the seat facing either direction.

If that weren't enough, there is also the Armadillo Flip XT ($600, 23.4 lbs.)—an upgraded version of the Flip with height adjustable handle, faux leather trim, larger basket and wheels. The canopy is even larger than on the Flip. The Armadillo Flip XT will be out by the time you read this.

Does Mamas and Papas make strollers that aren't named Armadillo? Yes, they do.

Mamas and Papas other major offering is the Urbo ($380), a 22.3 lb. shiny aluminum model with reversible seat, large canopy and fully reclining seat. Infant car seat adapters are available for Graco and Maxi Cosi infant seats ($30). New in the past year, the company debuted a revised version of the Urbo (called the Urbo 2) that adds front and rear wheel suspension, a reversible fully reclining seat and flip flop friendly brakes. The Urbo 2 ($580, 23.7 lbs.) has an optional bassinet ($220) and an easier fold (with the seat facing forward only, however).

The spider-like Mylo 2 stroller is heavy (32 lbs.) and pricey ($800), but includes a carrycot, foot muff, fully reclining seat that reverses, telescoping handle and adjustable footrest.

The Sola 2 ($400, 26.1 lbs.) is Mamas and Papas' riff on the Bugaboo Cameleon, with smaller front wheels and reversible seat. Like the Urbo, it has an optional infant car seat adapter and features adjustable handle height. The Sola has four wheel suspension, a lay flat seat and included rain cover. FYI: The Sola is Mamas and Papas best-selling model in the UK.

New in the past year, the Sola MTX ($480) features upgraded fabrics and bigger basket/wheels.

Our view. When Mamas and Papas invaded the U.S. a few years ago, they fell victim to one of the classic blunders of European stroller companies. The most famous of which is "never get involved in a land war in Asia." But only slightly less well known is this: never assume the stroller that sells well in the UK will appeal to Americans.

Hence, the first round of Mamas and Papas strollers brought to these shores were met with the sound of one hand clapping. They were too heavy, too expensive, had dinky storage baskets, lacked cup holders and were cumbersome to fold. They might be a hit in

strollers

London, but in Houston, they bombed.

To their credit, Mamas and Papas regrouped and released the Armadillo. Despite being clearly derivative of other animal-named strollers, at least this stroller hits all the right notes—relatively light in weight (although at 20 lbs., they are pushing it), easy to fold and spacious in storage. Parent reviews of this stroller are positive.

Feedback on Mamas and Papas other models have been mixed. While fans like the overall features of the strollers, critics point out little problems are always popping up—a cup holder that doesn't stay in place, wheels that squeak or click after a month of usage.

The fold of many models (like the original Urbo) is probably the biggest criticism here—"user unfriendly" is how one parent described it. Even the Armadillo, while an improvement still requires two steps—you fold over the seat then fold over the handle. While that isn't overly complex, compare it to the one-step, one-hand fold of Baby Jogger. And the Armadillo stroller can't fold when the car seat adapters are attached.

And why no car seat adapter for Graco for the Armadillo? Did they miss the millions of these infant seats being sold?

Bottom line: it is mixed review for Mamas and Papas. Kudos to the Armadillo for hitting the mark. But a miss for the Urbo, Mylo and Sola. The new Armadillo spin-offs were just hitting the market as we wrote this, so no feedback there. But we are raising the grade for this brand a half grade to reflect their continued improvement. *Baby Bargains Resale Rank: Excellent.* **Rating: B-**

Maxi Cosi *maxi-cosi.com* Dorel brought its European subsidiaries Maxi Cosi and Quinny to the U.S. a few of years ago to bolster the brand's efforts in the upper end of the stroller market.

The models. Maxi Cosi's main focus in the U.S. is car seats, but they do offer one stroller: the Kaia ($200-$235, 16 lbs.).

This lightweight umbrella stroller stands when folded and works with Maxi Cosi's Mico infant car seat (adapters are included). It also is sold as a travel system with the Mico ($300).

The basket is smallish, but has decent access. Ditto for the canopy—not the largest on the market, but decent enough. The partial seat recline will work for most toddlers, but not for napping—hence Maxi Cosi suggests using this stroller (without the car seat) for babies six months and older.

One plus: the Kaia has a long distance (12") between the seat and leg rest, a plus for toddlers with longer legs. On the downside, the Kaia only comes in two colors: you better like black or red.

New for 2015, Maxi Cosi is coming out with a stroller frame—the Maxi Taxi ($130, 14.7 lbs.). It features an umbrella-style, standing fold and fits any Maxi Cosi infant seat (or infant seats that are compatible with the Maxi Cosi adapters like the Cybex Aton).

Our view. Maxi Cosi has jettisoned many of their heavier models from past years. The Kaia is probably more in tune with the market—a higher-end umbrella stroller that weighs just 16 lbs.

Feedback on the Kaia has been mostly positive, although the limited canopy coverage and partial seat recline suggest this is aimed more at parents with older toddlers for trips to the mall. *Baby Bargains Resale Rank: Poor.* **Rating: B**

Mountain Buggy *mountainbuggy.com* Mountain Buggy is best known for their all terrain strollers. Founded in New Zealand, Mountain Buggy is now part of Phil & Teds, the fellow Kiwi stroller maker that scooped Mountain Buggy out of bankruptcy in 2009. Like Phil & Teds, Mountain Buggy is made in China.

The models. Mountain Buggy's forte is the tri-wheel stroller with lightweight aluminum frames (21-24 lbs., depending on the model), 12" air-filled tires with polymer rims, fully reclining seats, height adjustable handles and one-step folds. While you could certainly use these stroller in a city with rough sidewalks, the main focus is on all terrain adventures (hiking, beach, etc).

The brand's flagship model is the Urban Jungle ($400 single, 24 lbs.; $600 double—called the Duo, 36 lbs.). It has a front wheel that can swivel or lock into place, plus a raft of available accessories, including a car seat adapter, carry cot, rain cover and more. Unfortunately, the cup holder is an extra expense.

Coming in 2015, a redesigned Urban Jungle will add a one-hand, self-standing fold, new brake on the handlebar and extendable leg rest. The new model is bit more compact but weighs about the same as last year (24.9 lbs). List price: $500, but online sites will probably sell it for less, as is the case for the current model.

The Terrain ($500) used to be a fixed wheel stroller, but the most recent version lets you lock or swivel the front wheel. The big difference between the Terrain and Urban Jungle: 16" wheels (versus 12" for the Urban Jungle). This adds about four pounds of weight (29 lbs.). With the larger wheels, the Terrain is pitched more for joggers and runners.

The Swift ($400, 21 lbs.) is a compact version of the Urban Jungle—it has smaller, 10" tires. In a recent update, Mountain Buggy added a higher canopy with extendable visor and bumper bar to the stroller.

Following the trend of tri-wheel stroller makers adding four wheel models (re: Baby Jogger), Mountain Buggy debuted their first four wheeler in the past year: the Cosmopolitan ($550, 26 lbs.). It features a reversible seat that turns into a lay-flat bassinet for newborns, EVA/rubber tires (12" in rear, 8" in back), two step fold and large canopy.

Obviously, the Cosmopolitan is drifting away from Mountain Buggy's core market (note the lack of air-filled tires). This model is clearly aiming at the multi-function market dominated by Uppa

strollers

Baby and Britax's B-Ready. One note: the Cosmopolitan has accessory car seat adapters for Graco, Maxi Cosi and Cybex ($40 or so).

Along the same lines is the MB Mini stroller ($300)—basically, this is a Swift that substitutes foam filled wheels for the air tires. This helps shave off four pounds in weight—the MB Mini is 17.5 lbs.

You can see Phil & Ted's influence on this line with the new +one Mountain Buggy ($600)—this inline stroller can hold two kids in a front/back position. Sort of like a tandem version of the Urban Jungle.

New in the past year, Mountain Buggy launched what it claims to be the lightest weight stroller on the market—the Nano ($200, 13.1 lbs.). This travel stroller has universal infant car seat straps (to fit any infant car seat) and is clearly aimed at folks who do a lot of airplane travel. The Nano comes with a travel bag and doesn't need to be gate checked, claims Mountain Buggy (try explaining that to the grumpy airline gate attendant, however).

Our view. Mountain Buggy generally gets high marks for quality and useability. Fans love the off road ability, although critics wish the canopies was larger. We've also seen a few complaints from heavy users on the durability of tires—some folks go through one or two replacement sets because the tread wears too quickly. If Mountain Buggy could offer heavy duty tires as an accessory, that might do the trick.

Early feedback on the Cosmopolitan has been positive. The Nano also has won over parents with its compact design, but detractors note, again, the canopy doesn't offer much coverage.

It will be interesting to see if Mountain Buggy picks up more fans as it moves away from its all terrain niche with the Cosmopolitan and MB Mini. *Baby Bargains Resale Rank: Fair.* **Rating: A**

Mutsy *Mutsy.com* This brand is reviewed on the free side of our web site at BabyBargains.com/?p=1282

MÜV *muvbaby.com* MÜV is the new upper-end stroller brand that is part of the Baby Trend empire. The company plans to debut two new strollers in 2015: the Gaan, a three-wheel model for $690 and the Reis, a four-wheel model for $700. Both models are available as stand-alone models or travel systems, paired with MÜV's Kussen infant car seat.

Both strollers feature an extended, height adjustable canopy with six windows, reversible seat, three-position full recline, and large storage basket with access from the front or rear of the stroller. And, yes, you can fold the stroller with the seat on. A winter boot (thermal compartment) and rear-wheel suspension round out the features.

What makes these strollers unique is the relatively high seat position, which MÜV pitches as a high chair replacement (you can wheel one of these strollers up to a table).

The only difference between the models is the Gaan is a three-wheel version and the Reis is four wheels.

As you'd expect with a high-end stroller, MÜV has all the bells and whistles: a three-position footrest and height-adjustable handle. All this tends to add to the weight of the stroller, unfortunately. We weighed the Reis at 27 lbs.; the Gaan at 26.1 lbs. Another negative: there are only two colors (black and red, and two frame colors—silver and black) as of this writing.

Despite the Dutch model names and branding, these strollers are made in China. And if MÜV's strollers look a bit like that other Dutch stroller brand that starts with a B, that's because one of their ex-employees is a founder of the company.

These strollers were not on the market as of this writing; MÜV's web site still has a "coming soon" sign. We'll update this review once these strollers are released. ***Rating: Not Yet.***

Nuna *Nuna.eu* Dutch-based baby gear maker Nuna landed in the U.S. in 2013 and is the latest European stroller company to give it a go here. Apparently, Europe has an endless supply of these companies, all looking to expand in North America.

The problem with European baby gear makers is they simply don't get how Americans use a product like a stroller. Yes, European strollers have four wheels—and American strollers (for the most part) have four wheels. But the lifestyles of European parents are much different than here—their use of mass transit, where they walk . . . and even their need for cup holders. Example: Italian strollers don't have cup holders because when an Italian mom goes for coffee with her baby, she walks to a cafe, sits down and drinks coffee. We, on the other hand, drive to the nearest mall, hit the Starbucks for a coffee . . . and need a cup holder because we are walking and strolling. We're a busy nation and we're off to invent the next tech wonder gadget. Europeans? Not so much.

Hence, most European strollers bomb in the U.S. for several reasons. They are often heavy, cumbersome to fold (because you don't often fold them in Amsterdam) and generally lack features like cup holders.

The models: The Nuna Pepp is a case in point. This $300 stroller aims to be a lightweight, super-maneuverable stroller for shopping the mall. And at 21.8 lbs., it does avoid the trap of other European strollers that are way too heavy to haul in and out of a trunk. But still . . . the Pepp is 20% (four pounds) heavier than the best-sellers in this category like the Baby Jogger City Mini or Britax B-Agile.

And the Pepp's other specs are equally disappointing—there is no full seat recline (only partial). And the seat reclines with two zip-

strollers

pers, which are difficult to re-zip without getting the fabric stuck, etc. That's why most U.S. strollers have simpler reclines. And the fold? That requires two hands and several steps. Again, Europeans must have extra time on their hands because the one-hand, one-step fold is what wins parents' hearts here.

We liked the height adjustable handle and extra sun visor for the canopy; but the canopy's overall coverage pales in comparison to the canopies on a BOB stroller, for example. The Pepp's car seat adapter (an extra accessory) will work with only the Maxi Cosi and Cybex seats. The Pepp has an odd, low-to-the-ground profile—we wonder if taller parents will find it cumbersome to buckle in baby. And of course, there is no standard cup holder.

Nuna's latest stroller is the IVVI ($800). This full feature stroller includes rain cover, carry cot and car seat adapters, full extendible canopy and rotating removable bumper bar. The tires are run flat rubber with lockable front wheels and quick release for a more compact fold. Nuna has included front and rear wheel suspension as well and it has full recline. This stroller is so new (no surprise at this price) we have no feedback on it yet.

Another recent model, the MIXX, is a $500 stroller that includes car seat adapters (Maxi Cosi), reversible seat, full recline, large canopy, rain cover and an easy flat fold. Nuna said they are aiming for a 24 lb. final weight, although the prototype we viewed was 27 lbs.

New in early 2015, Nuna will add its first stroller frame to the line, the Tavo. Similar to the Snap N Go, you'll be able to snap in Nuna's infant car seat into the Tavo for a stroller solution. Price: $320

Our view. We haven't heard much feedback from parents on Nuna, but the little feedback we've heard from readers on the Pepp has been positive. Fans like the smooth ride of the Pepp, flat fold and high style. But the limited distribution (the Pepp is only sold in a handful of pricey stores and web sites like Giggle) makes it hard to get a good reading on it.

The classic mistake of European stroller makers is to take a stroller that sells like hotcakes in Barcelona and try to sell it in Boston with minimal or no changes. Nuna is falling into that trap—the brand needs to do some more homework and better adapt its designs to American parents' needs. ***Rating: C-***

Orbit orbitbaby.com Fans of *The Office* may remember the Orbit fondly, after Dwight Schrute spent an entire episode trying to destroy the pricey travel system, to no avail. While that episode may qualify as the best baby product placement in a TV series ever, it showcased the Orbit's quality to withstand the show's extreme road test.

The model. What set off Dwight? It was Orbit's über expensive price tag ("$1200 is more than I spent on my entire bomb shelter!").

Actually, the Orbit "starter kit" runs $980, including the infant car seat reviewed in the past chapter. And no, the Orbit doesn't come with a toddler stroller seat—that's an extra $380.

In the past year, Orbit rolled out a third generation of its travel system. The G3 model upgrades the stroller's steering, handling and fold (its faster). You can now customize your Orbit with various color packs and accessories, sold a la carte. There are now two cup holders.

Our view. The verdict? Folks who have the Orbit love it—the unique car seat base makes for simple, rock solid installation, as we noted in the last chapter. The engineering on the Orbit is top notch: parents like the stroller frame's simple one-hand fold and ergonomic handles. And the frame lets you shift the car seat in a 360-degree range of motion.

Downsides? Even though the infant car seat works to 30 lbs., most kids will outgrow it by height before they hit that weight limit. Some bigger kids will age out of the Orbit at six months—and that's a lot of money to spend for such brief usage. Yes, you can pony up another $225 for a toddler stroller seat—but that means a total investment of $1000.

As we noted in the Orbit car seat review, the infant car seat carrier is heavy (nearly ten lbs.) and bulky, making it a tight fit in smaller vehicles. Once your baby is near the weight limits of the seat, carrying the Orbit's 30 lb. weight (baby plus car seat) will be a hardy upper-body workout.

Got two babies? Orbit's twin option is the Double Helix stroller. This stroller holds two infant seats, two toddler seats or one of each. The cost: a whopping $1200 (for a model with two toddler seats). You can also buy a Helix kit if you already have an Orbit stroller for $500. The kit allows you to add a second seat to your existing stroller.

New for 2015, Orbit is debuting its first jogging stroller: the O2. It will have two modes: city and performance. City mode has a higher seating position—hit a lever and the seat lowers for the performance mode. This is designed for running, complete with a front wheel that locks. The O2 will feature an adjustable handle, self-standing fold and parent console. It will be available in June 2015 for $620 for the frame or $900 for a complete system (frame plus infant seat).

The take-home message: if you are looking for a travel system that is a conversation starter, then Orbit is your brand. Parents love the Jetsons-like look . . . and having a stroller/car seat that no one on the block has is appealing.

Critics knock the overall bulk and weight of the Orbit. Some folks found the Orbit's handle bars to be uncomfortable. And while most fans like the infant car seat/frame combo, there is noticeably less love for the toddler configuration, when the weight/bulk of the system begins to outweigh the Orbit's advantages.

strollers

We saw a demo of the new O2 jogging stroller and were impressed with the innovative features. Our only concern—this thing is much bigger in person than it looks online. We measured the O2 in performance mode and came up with a whopping 50″ length from the handle bar to the wheel. You might want to see this stroller in person before committing to its $600 price. *Baby Bargains Resale Rank: Fair.* **Rating: B**

Peg Perego *perego.com* Peg Perego is the Italian stroller maker that was among the first European brands to land in North America, way back in the 1980's. The company traces its roots back to 1949 when its founder Giuseppe Perego created a carriage for his infant son.

Unlike most other European brands who long ago abandoned production on the Continent in search of lower labor costs in Asia, Peg Perego still makes all its strollers in Italy

That all-Italian mantra for Peg has been both a blessing and curse. On the upside, the company's fabrics are considered among the most fashionable (although, admittedly, other companies have since closed the fashion gap). Peg's reputation for quality is also excellent. In an era where parents are concerned about Chinese imports and their safety, recalls on Perego strollers are rare.

But . . . the made-in-Europe label has its price—in the last few years, Peg's strollers have jumped in price. Many new Peg models run $500 or more . . . that's a tough sell in any economy.

This brand has had its ups and downs in the past decade. They missed out on the all-terrain craze, as well as the boom in tri-wheel strollers. You'd think Perego would be strong player in the multi-function stroller market, first pioneered by Bugaboo and then perfected by Uppa Baby, Britax and others. But they missed that one too.

Peg also lost a bit of its cache after unloading its overstock strollers in closeout discounters like Marshall's.

So can Peg get its mojo back? Let's look at their current line up.

The models. Perego has a lengthy list of strollers that includes single models, doubles and what they dub "systems," modular models that include an infant car seat. Below is the current model line-up. We'll break this down into single, double and systems.

Single strollers. Peg's line-up includes eight single strollers: the Uno, Switch Four, Pliko Four, Vela Easy Drive, Pliko Mini, Book, Book Plus and Book Pop Up.

The Uno ($300 to $370, 23 lbs.) features a Bugaboo-ish wheel design with smaller wheels up front and larger ones in the back. It includes a reversible handle so you can face baby, as well as a boot and height adjustable handle. The only bummer: when you reverse the handle on the Uno, you have the turnable wheels in back (rear-wheel drive), which is awkward.

The Switch Four ($500, 23.8 lbs.) has a 150 degree reclining seat, reversible seat, foot muff and rain shield.

The Pliko Four ($320, 18.7 lbs.) features all wheel suspension and ball bearings for a smooth ride. This latest generation Pliko features a two-handle design, 150 degree reclining seat, adjustable leg rest, adjustable height handle and removable/washable seat cushions. There is also a one-hand fold. Compared to past versions of the Pliko, this model has a more compact fold.

If you like the Pliko but are turned off by the weight, there is a Pliko spin-off called the Pliko Mini ($250, 14 lbs.), Peg's lightest weight stroller. The Mini features a three-position reclining seat, cup holder, adjustable footrest and height adjustable handle.

The latest addition to the Perego family is the Book ($400, 22.6 lbs.), which gets its name from its fold: yes, it folds up like a book (and stands when folded). The Book features wider front wheels with suspension and a wider seat (it can also hold a car seat). Perego recently tweaked the Book basket to make it larger and more accessible. Other features include a height adjustable handle bar, fully reclining seat, ball bearing wheels for a smooth glide and one-hand fold. The Book is also sold as a travel system, paired with Peg's infant car seat.

The Book Plus ($500, 24.4 lbs.) adds a reversible seat and can be folded with or without the seat. The Book Plus comes with a boot and rain shield. You can snap in a Perego infant car seat right to the chassis, which can be bought separately for $270 (you can later add the stroller seat).

The newest versions of the Book are the Book Pop-Up and Booklet. The Book Pop Up ($800, 25.6 lbs.) is similar to the Book, but adds a seat and bassinet that both pop-up when opened. You can fold the Book Pop Up with the seat facing either direction and it takes a Peg infant seat without an adapter.

The less expensive Booklet ($400, 19 lbs.) features the same Book fold, but the seat doesn't reverse and is three pounds lighter than the base Book model. The Booklet has an extended canopy and full recline—it takes the Peg 4.35 infant car seat with no additional adapter.

For 2015, Perego is trimming back its single stroller offerings. The Book and Book Plus are being discontinued; the Book Pop-Up and Booklet will continue. While the Pliko Mini goes forward, the Uno, Switch Four and Pliko Four are not being manufactured, but Perego is still selling through existing stock.

Double strollers. Peg makes two double strollers: the Aria Twin ($300 to $350, 17 lbs.), a side-by-side model and the Duette SW ($800, 32 lbs.), a tandem model. The Aria has a 60/40 configuration that holds a car seat in the larger space. While the Aria Twin has been discontinued (Perego isn't making any more of them), it is still being sold in stores as Peg sells through existing stock.

Got triplets? Peg even makes a triple stroller, dubbed the Triplette SW for $1000. It weighs a whopping 61 lbs.!

Modular systems. Peg sells two modular models: the Switch Four Modular System and the Skate.

The Switch Four Modular System is like the single version described above, but adds a bassinet and infant car seat plus a raft of accessories (bassinet stand, child tray, rain cover, foot muff, etc). Price: $1100.

The Skate was introduced in 2008 with much fanfare—it featured a Bugaboo-like multifunction frame, a height-adjustable handle, four-wheel suspension, ball-bearing wheels for a smooth glide, three seat heights and (drum roll) a cup holder. But it also cost an outrageous $900 and weighed 33.7 pounds . . . 70% more than the Bugaboo. The Skate was a bust.

Peg has since tweaked the Skate to fix its shortcomings. The current version now weighs 28.8 lbs. and is discounted to $534 online, which includes a bassinet, an improved fold and other refinements. Yes, there's even a storage basket now.

FYI: Peg has discontinued the Switch Four and Skate, but is continuing to sell through existing stock.

Our view. Peg Perego's DNA is making expertly tailored full-size strollers. And bless their hearts, they have made these things no matter how the stroller market has changed over the years. Call them dedicated, crazy or just Italian—Peg Perego is . . . Peg Perego.

The Peg strollers we think are the best are their lightest weight offerings—the Pliko Mini is probably our favorite here, with its compact fold and overall good design. We wish it folded up quicker, with fewer steps, however. The Pliko Four is also a good choice.

Fans of Perego like their overall quality, features like a standing fold (in some models), and made-in-Italy fabrics. Critics bristle at the price (the Pliko Mini is $250—for a lightweight umbrella stroller?). Another negative: the storage baskets on many Peregos are small.

Peg's full-size strollers are a tougher sell, given their weight and price. The Book series strollers are the stars here, with fans liking the reversible seats. They are credible alternatives to the Uppa Baby Vista and Cruz models. The Skate, however, is a bust.

As for the double strollers, we are less enthusiastic about the Aria Twin, which gets low marks from readers—there are better options out there than this. *Baby Bargains Resale Rank: Fair.* **Rating: B+**

Phil & Teds philandteds.com Phil & Ted's brand mojo is a tri-wheel stroller with inflated tires that can morph from a single stroller to a double with a toddler seat accessory. The company calls these "inline" strollers. The pitch is the ability to use the stroller from birth (with optional car seat adapter or bassinet) through toddlerhood, with a second child.

Founded in New Zealand, Phil & Teds exudes a Kiwi vibe: outdoorsy and unpretentious. FYI: Phil & Teds snapped up competitor and fellow New Zealand stroller line Mountain Buggy out of bankruptcy a few years ago and now runs that line as a separate brand.

The models. Phil & Teds flagship stroller is the Navigator ($500, 27.5 lbs.). The stroller features a large canopy, one-hand fold, adjustable handle and is car seat compatible. The Navigator has a large number of accessories, from storm/sun covers, to a travel bag, cold weather boot, cup holder and more. Examples include a Snug Carry Cot ($150) and a face-to-face seat ($50), where the baby faces you. You can also use the doubles kit (the extra toddler seat) and an infant car seat at the same time.

What sets Phil & Ted apart is their second-child seat ($150 extra; for kids six months and up), which can attach to the FRONT or BACK of the stroller (for comparison, Valco's toddler seat only attaches to the front). The rear seat configuration turns off some parents (safety hint: the child in the backseat has to be removed first to prevent tipping). And if you put a larger toddler in the back seat, the access to the stroller's storage basket is limited.

Feedback on the Navigator has been positive—parents tell us the stroller's all-terrain 12" air-filled wheels are perfect for both the mall and hiking trails, plus the wide seat accommodates children for many years.

If the Navigator looks too big for your tastes, Phil & Ted's has a compact stroller—the Dot ($450, 26 lbs.). The Dot and the Navigator share the same basic features and accessories (with one exception: the face-to-face seat is a Navigator exclusive). Even though the Dot is more compact than the Navigator (a little over an inch in width), the seat size is the same. The Dot's width is a slim 23".

If a $400-$500 stroller is out of your budget range, the company sells a stripped down version of the Navigator, dubbed the Classic ($400, 24 lbs.). The Classic omits the height adjustable handle and has less fancy padding. But it still has a large canopy and one-hand fold. Reader reviews on the Classic are not as effusive as the Navigator or Dot, however—the trade-off of fewer features and less fancy padding for a lower price is too much, say critics.

Two other strollers round out the inline category at Phil & Teds: the Verve and Promenade. The Verve ($550, 28 lbs.) drops the front air-filled wheels for foam tires—and adds a fourth wheel up front. You still get the option of adding a second seat, but there are only seven seat configurations for the Verve (versus 26 for the Navigator). Hence, the Verve is more aimed at city dwellers than those who plan off-road adventures. (A three-wheel version of this stroller with air-filled tires is called the Vibe, $600).

The Promenade ($600, 28 lbs.) is also aimed at urban parents, with a reversible seat that converts to a lay flat bed, adjustable han-

strollers

dle, adjustable footrest and foam tires.

If all these presto-chango features are too much for your tastes, Phil & Teds does make a simple lightweight stroller. The Smart ($250, 18 lbs.) has smaller wheels up front and bigger tires in back, and features a compact fold and one-touch brake, but no cup holder. In a recent update, the Smart got a reversible seat with a car seat adapter accessory ($29). New in the past year, Phil & Teds rolled out an upgraded version of the Smart called the Smart Lux ($400). It features air-filled rear tires and a lay-flat reversible seat (like the Promenade), as well as upgraded seat fabric. The upgrades (notably the air-filled rear tires) add quite a bit of weight to this version, however: it is 26.2 lbs.

For serious runners with a serious bank account, Phil & Teds also has a jogging stroller: the Sub 4 ($1117). Billed as the "world's fastest jogger," it features wishbone suspension, disc brakes and quick-release wheels. The seat is made from a variable density foam. And yes, it costs $1117.

FYI: Phil & Teds also makes a Costco exclusive stroller, the S4 ($400). This stroller is a less-fancy Classic, with "aerotech" tires and an included doubles kit. Aerotech tires are not air-filled; instead they are a blend of EVA foam and rubber—the same tires that are on the Verve and Promenade.

Our view. These strollers are perfect for the outdoors—the air-filled tires are great for hikes, gravel paths or rough sidewalks.

Readers give Phil & Teds an enthusiastic thumbs up for a smooth ride and second-seat functionality. The height adjustable handle also wins raves. We like the little touches such as the flip-flop friendly brake pedal and new, bigger canopy. Cons: a few parents complain of tire blowouts (requiring the purchase of extra tubes). And why no included cup holder? For 500 bucks, the least Phil & Teds could do is include a place to hold a water bottle.

Critics wish there was wheel suspension on the Navigator for a smoother ride. And one trade-off of the inline design is the rather long distance from the front to back of this stroller, making it a tight fit in smaller elevators. Some of the complaints about Phil & Teds come from parents who tried to use their inline strollers for jogging— even when you lock the front wheel into place, these strollers make a poor choice for runners. The weight and bulk of loading a Phil & Teds with two kids also makes jogging or running difficult. We suggest a fixed wheel jogger like the BOB Ironman for running.

Phil & Ted's more urban-focused models (Promenade, Verve) receive good marks from readers.

In the stroller wars, Phi & Teds has been somewhat eclipsed in recent years by Baby Jogger and BOB—thanks to the former's quick fold and the latter's more affordable prices. A BOB Revolution Double runs about $100 less than a Phil & Ted's Navigator with second seat accessory, but is wider with its side-by-side seat configuration.

Bottom line: if you need to transport two kids and like the idea of an in-line, all-terrain stroller, then Phil & Teds is a good bet. *Baby Bargains Resale Rank: Excellent.* **Rating: A-**

Quinny *quinny.com* Quinny is Dorel's (Cosco, Safety 1st) Dutch subsidiary known for its stylish multi-function strollers.

The models. The Buzz Xtra (29.4 lbs.) is Quinny's flagship model—this clever tri-wheel stroller has an innovative "automatic unfolding" feature plus a sleek look with a fully reclining seat that can face forward or back toward the parent. Price: $600, which includes the car seat adapters for the Maxi Cosi Mico (sold separately, of course).

In the past year, the Buzz Xtra added a quieter, extendable zippered canopy, height adjustable handle and an easier lay-flat fold.

The Zapp Xtra ($350, 20.1 lbs.) is Quinny's lightweight stroller with compact fold and reversible seat. This model also accommodates a Maxi Cosi car seat (Mico or Prezi). Unlike the Zapp's European counterpart, the U.S. Zapp Xtra has a storage basket. A cup holder, however, is an extra $25.

Quinny's most expensive model is the The Moodd, which is available as a $700 version with a white frame or as an $800 multi-colored "Britto" model. The Moodd features one-touch automatic unfold, reversible seat and funky T-bar front attachment, which makes the stroller look like something out of the Jetsons. A separate car seat adapter accessory works with Maxi Cosi or other brand infant seats.

The final stroller in the Quinny line is the odd ball of the group—the Yezz, which is billed as an ultralight weight urban stroller. At 12.7 lbs., it certainly is among the lightest strollers on the market, but this $280 stroller sacrifices storage to get there: no under seat storage basket, no parent storage, cup holder, etc. The skimpy canopy won't block much sun. The Yezz has a funky frame and small, skateboard like wheels. In the past year, Quinny simplified the fold to avoid ruining your pedicure.

Our view. Quinny's hardcore fans love the sleek design and gee-whiz features like the Buzz's automatic unfolding trick. But Quinny has failed to achieve mainstream success here and a look at parent feedback gives you a clue why.

At 30 lbs. the Buzz Xtra is extra heavy. And while Quinny has improved the stroller in recent years (we like the new canopy and reversible seat), the wide 25.5" rear wheels makes negotiating tight spaces difficult.

The Zapp has similar faults. Yes, it is much lighter in weight than the Buzz, but it lacks the simple quick fold found in competitors like Baby Jogger. Instead—the Zapp requires multiple steps, buttons you have to push, and a bottom latch that must be wrestled with. The skimpy canopy is the final nail in the coffin for the Zapp.

Fans say the pricey Moodd pushes like a dream—and for $700, it darn well should. But the skimpy canopy and shallow seat (larger babies will quickly outgrow it) keep this stroller from achieving greatness.

The Yezz is an expensive, niche offering for those looking for the lightest weight stroller . . . and not much else.

One universal issue for Quinny: the smallish seats may be a tight fit for older toddlers. A clue to this issue comes in the top age recommendation for these strollers: at just three and a half years and 50 lbs., bigger toddlers may outgrow these pricey strollers too soon. And even the 50 lb. weight seems optimistic, considering the small seat dimensions.

In Quinny's defense, we should point out that the company has tried to address their strollers' shortcomings with recent upgrades and improvements. And feedback on the strollers (especially the Buzz) has improved in the past year.

But if Quinny wants to charge a premium for these models, they must address the skimpy canopies on the Zapp and Moodd. When the entire stroller market has moved to the simple, quick fold you see on Baby Jogger models, Quinny looks like a dinosaur. And a pricey one at that. We can understand if folks are attracted to the look here, but be prepared to pay through the nose for a stroller that just doesn't perform as well as its peers. *Baby Bargains Resale Rank: Fair.* **Rating: C**

Recaro recaropromotion.com Best known for their car seats, Recaro has tip toed into the stroller market with two offerings: the Denali and Easylife. Here's an overview.

The models. The Denali ($280, 21.9 lbs.) is a full-size stroller that includes a large canopy, huge storage basket, one-hand quick fold and front and back wheel suspension. A parent cup holder and storage pocket at the back of the seat round out the Denali's features. As you might guess, the Denali works with Recaro's infant car seat, the Performance Coupe.

The Easylife ($220, 13.2 lbs.) is coming in summer 2015 and features an interesting one-handed Z-fold, where the stroller collapses down into a small footprint. The Easylife has a basic canopy and wheels with all-around suspension.

Our view: Recaro's convertible car seats are considered to be among the best in class—excellent design with safety features that rival category leader Britax.

That's why we we're somewhat disappointed with the brand's first stroller efforts. While the Denali is too new as of this writing to get much real world feedback, we had a chance to try out a sample at a trade show. There are two glaring negatives here.

First, the Denali only works with Recaro's infant car seat. That seems incredibly short sighted, considering Recaro's infant seat is still quite new to the market. Furthermore, there are no accessories available for this stroller—no rain cover, no winter boot, etc. At this price level, accessories like this are a common way for parents to customize their ride.

Finally, the seat on the Denali is somewhat small—at 18″ in height, it is about 3-4″ shorter than Baby Jogger's seats. That means larger toddlers will quickly outgrow this stroller.

We do like the wheel suspension and included parent cup holder, but the canopy coverage could be better. And the Denali's chrome accents come in for a mixed reception from parents.

Overall, we expected more innovation from Recaro . . . instead, we got a shiny elliptical stroller with limited utility unless you own a Recaro infant seat.

So it is a lukewarm review for Recaro's first stroller efforts (the Easylife wasn't out yet as we wrote this review). ***Rating: C***

Safety 1st *See Cosco.*

Schwinn / Instep This brand is reviewed on the free side of our web site at BabyBargains.com/?p=9846

Stokke *stokkeusa.com* Stokke (pronounced Stuck-Ah) is a Norwegian based baby gear company that traces its roots back to 1932. As you might guess, Norway's influence on the world baby gear market has been slight, but Stokke has had modest success here in the U.S., especially in the high chair category with the Tripp Trapp.

Stokke's strollers, however, have never quite gained much traction. Why? Exhibit A: The Stokke Xplory.

The futuristic Xplory might look like something George Jetson would have pushed his boy Elroy around in, but it failed to make a splash when it was introduced to the U.S. ten years ago. Here's an overview of the Xplory and Stokke's newer strollers.

The models. Like Bugaboo's Cameleon, the Xplory ($1100) is a modular system that includes a frame with rubber tires and a seat that can attach to the frame either forward or rear facing. The Stokke's key feature is its high-altitude seating. The pitch, according to Stokke, is to keep baby higher off the ground so they are away from exhaust fumes, slobbering Labradors, etc. (the target market is urban parents).

In addition to a generous canopy, adjustable footrest and a raft of accessories, Xplory has optional car seat adapters for Maxi Cosi, Nuna, Peg Perego and Cybex. What's missing? If you answered, "storage basket," you are correct—instead Stokke throws in a shopping bag that is attached to the front of the unit.

New for 2015, Stokke is introducing summer and winter kits for the Xplory—the summer kit ($160) has an umbrella/shade and terry cloth pram liner. The winter kit ($200-$300) has a handmuff and stroller liner.

After not releasing a new model for several years, Stokke rolled out not one but three new strollers in the past year: the Crusi, Scoot and Trailz.

The Crusi (26 lbs., $1250) clearly riffs on Phil & Ted's inline buggy, with the optional second seat riding below the main seat. The Crusi includes a bassinet and stroller seat which can face forward or rear. Unlike the Xplory, however, the Crusi's seat can't change height. (The handle, however, is height adjustable). Very pricey at $1250, but at least you get a rain cover, bug net and cup holder. The second seat runs $300.

The Stokke Scoot is the lighter weight cousin to the Crusi—it weighs 23 lbs. and runs $600. While you get the same reversible seat as the Crusi, this model omits the optional carry cot or sibling seat. The basket is also smaller, as are the wheels. For 2015, Stokke tells us the Scoot will get air-filled tires (the current offering has foam filled wheels).

Finally, Stokke has added an all terrain stroller dubbed the Trailz (30 lbs.). This $1300 model features air filled tires, height adjustable handle, a five-position reversible seat with full recline and a water-proof shopping basket. Car seat adapters are available for Peg Perego, Maxi Cosi, Nuna and Cybex infant seats.

Our view. So why haven't you seen the über rich pushing the Stokke Xplory around Greenwich Village? That's because for the most part, the Xplory has been a bust. For years and for reasons unexplained, Stokke resisted making infant car seat adapters for the Xplory—this was a major strategic blunder that cut the Xplory's appeal in the U.S.

Second, little design issues plagued the stroller. Example: the handle and most of the Xplory's frame is injection-molded plastic . . . not something you'd expect from a $1000+ stroller. The "plastic-y" feel turns off many, while the lack of a basket is another major negative. Instead the Xplory has a "shopping bag" that attaches to the frame . . . right.

And look at the fold for the Xplory—it folds into *four separate pieces*. You first remove the foot rest, bumper bar and seat before you fold the chassis. Really? We're guessing the same person in Norway who thought this was smart also considers boiled cod a delicacy.

Add in the dinky canopy and hotel mini bar prices for accessories ($300 for a winter foot muff?) and you can see why the Stokke Xplory just doesn't make the cut.

Stokke's trio of new models (Crusi, Scoot, Trailz) have garnered very little real world feedback from parents, probably due to the $1000+ price tags and (in the case of the Trailz) the relatively little time on the market.

Bottom line: Stokke is a pass. *Baby Bargains Resale Rank: Good.*
Rating: C-

Stroll Air *stroll-air.com* This brand is reviewed on the free side of our web site at BabyBargains.com/?p=1300

Summer *summerinfant.com* Best known for its video baby monitors, Summer debuted a stroller line in 2010—the focus is on lightweight, umbrella-style models. Here's an overview.

The models. Summer's first effort in this category was the Prodigy travel system that paired a stroller with Summer's first infant car seat in 2010. That stroller would go on to earn Biggest Stroller Bomb Of The Year Award . . . if we had that award to give out.

The Prodigy looked like a Graco stroller circa 1998—bulky, heavy and ugly. And those were its better features.

Summer wisely buried that model like Atari ET video game cartridges and rebooted its stroller line with four lightweight umbrella strollers under the 3D sub-brand: 3D lite, 3Dflip, and 3Dyzre.

The 3D lite ($70, 12 lbs.) is a two-handled umbrella-style stroller that features a full seat recline, pop-out canopy, easy access to the basket and cup holder.

As you might guess from the name, the 3D Flip ($130, 16.3 lbs.) features a seat that flips over so baby can face the parent or out. The canopy also flips around.

The 3Dzyre ($120, 14.6 lbs.) is an upgraded version of the 3D lite—nicer fabric, upgraded wheel bearings, extra seat padding and zippered canopy. The seat has a near full recline on the 3Dzyre.

New for 2015, the 3D-One focuses on one-hand operation—one-hand fold, one-hand recline, etc. Also new: the Go Lite, a super lightweight (11.4 lbs.) stroller with smaller wheels and partially reclining seat. It is very similar to the 3D lite.

Now discontinued but still for sale online is the Fuze ($300, 25.4 lbs.)—it features a reversible seat, full canopy, fully reclining seat, large basket, height adjustable handle, cup holder and drop down fold. An included car seat adapter works with Summer's Prodigy infant seat as well as those from Perego, Chicco and Graco.

The Spectra ($220, 19.8 lbs.) looks similar to the Fuze, but lacks the reversible seat. The Spectra does have a full seat recline, full canopy, adjustable foot rest and self-standing fold.

Our view. Summer 2.0 is definitely an improvement—we like the lower prices and feature mix here. The 3D lite is probably the pick of the litter—we liked the seat recline, although it does require two hands.

Reader feedback on the 3D lite has been mostly positive. Fans love the value and ease of use. Critics say the stroller is great while it lasts—but we see scattered reports that the stroller broke after a few months. Others knock the skimpy canopy, which is unfortunately common in under $100 umbrella strollers. Notably, the newer models (3Dzyre, 3Dflip) have better canopies . . . but of course, they

strollers

cost more than the 3D lite.

We're less enthusiastic about Summer's pricey, full size models (Fuze and Spectra). The lower priced umbrella strollers are better bets, as long as you keep your expectations in check. All in all, we'll raise Summer's rating this time out to reflect the improved parent feedback. *Rating: B+*

Thule Chariot *ChariotCarriers.com* Outdoor gear brand Thule Chariot (formerly the Canadian brand, Chariot bought by Swedish brand Thule) takes a different approach to the jogger market—they make bicycle trailers that covert into jogging strollers, plus they've introduced their first sport strollers

The models. If you are an avid bicyclist who also wants to occasionally jog with baby, Thule Chariot offers four models of bike trailers (and corresponding double trailers) with optional kits that turn the trailers into jogging strollers. Example: the Cougar ($650, includes strolling kit), which features plush harness straps, padded seats and adjustable suspension. A plus: the Cougar has expanded legroom for the kiddies. A double version (Cougar 2) is $800.

Other convertible bike trailers include the CX 1 ($1050), the Cheetah ($450) and the Chinook ($1150). Double versions these trailers range from $550 to $1250.

New this year are a couple sports strollers: the Thule Glide ($330), and the Urban Glide ($380 to $400). The Glide is a fixed wheel dedicated jogging stroller with 16" front wheel and 18" rear wheels. It comes with height adjustable handle, hand brake, and adjustable canopy. The fold is one handed although to get it compact you need to remove the wheels. The stroller weighs 22 lbs. and the price is $350. Accessories include a parent console and infant car seat adapter.

The Urban Glide (23 lbs.) is similar to the Glide but includes a full recline, a 12.5" front wheel that swivels or locks in 2 positions and 16" rear wheels. Price: $400. A double version (the Urban Glide 2, $650) will be out in Spring 2015 and will weigh 31 lbs.

Our view. While this brand is pricey (some models run well over $1000), we've been impressed with Thule Chariot's quality—no, they aren't cheap . . . but you'll be amazed by the ease of use and adjustments. (Yes, there is even a cross-country ski kit). The downside: these trailers/joggers are too wide to take into most stores, so this isn't a good solution for shopping. Obviously, unless you are a serious biker or runner, a Thule Chariot is probably overkill. But if you want a quality bike trailer that can morph into a stroller, this brand should be on the top of your shopping list.

If you're looking at their jogging stroller or all-terrain option, both the Glide and the Urban Glide are sturdy, well made options. The fold isn't as compact as competitors (unless you remove the wheels) but the quality is impressive. *Rating: A*

Trends For Kids *trendsforkids.com* This brand is reviewed on the free side of our web site at BabyBargains.com/?p=1304

UPPAbaby *UppaBaby.com* UPPAbaby was launched in 2006 by Bostonians Bob and Lauren Monahan. Bob worked for First Years and Safety 1st in product development before launching UPPA; Lauren provides the PR and design mojo. Obviously, the Monahans have kids, as you can tell from the well thought-out designs of their strollers.

The models. UPPAbaby has a hit with their flagship model, the multi-function Vista (27.5 lbs.). Made with an aircraft alloy frame, the Vista stroller system includes a bassinet and stroller seat, telescoping handle and easy fold. We liked all the included extras, such as a rain shield, mesh sunshade and bug cover. Plus the Vista uses rubber-like foam wheels that give a smooth ride, but don't go flat. Unlike the Bugaboo, you can fold the Vista with the seat attached.

For 2015, UPPAbaby is giving the Vista a complete make-over. The biggest changes include a simpler one-step fold (like the Cruz, described below). And the Vista will be able to hold two seats—two UPPAbaby Mesa infant seats, two toddler seats, two bassinets, etc. With eight configurations, this is similar to the Baby Jogger Select.

Other improvements include bassinet fabrics that easily zip off for washing, removable wheels, and a new lighter frame (although we weighed the 2015 Vista at 29.8 lbs., which is more than the 26.3 lbs. for the 2014 Vista).

The 2015 Vista will retail for $820-$860 (which includes a bassinet and toddler seat); extra seats run $200. While the Vista is the flagship, UPPA's most popular strollers are their lightweight G umbrella models. These are anchored by the G-Lite ($160 to $180, 8.3 lbs.), a super lightweight umbrella stroller with a standing fold and mesh seat and seat pad. The G-lite doesn't recline, so it is best for babies six months and up. For 2015, the G-lite is losing its seat pad, which will now be available as an accessory.

There is also an upgraded version of the G-Lite, dubbed the G-Luxe ($260 to $280, 13.4 lbs.). It features a standing fold, bigger wheels, and partial seat recline. In a recent update, the G-Luxe got a removable, washable seat pad and an improved canopy.

In a recent refresh, the G-Lite and G-Luxe got new wheels, a new, easier closing mechanism, reinforced frame and removable washable seat pads. The G-Luxe also has a three-position seat recline.

New for 2015, UPPA is adding a double version of their G-Luxe stroller, called the G-Link (22.2 lbs.). It features adjustable footrests and a quick fold from a center strap. The G-Link is listed as coming in summer 2015, with a price not set as of press time.

The final stroller in the UPPA line is the Cruz ($460, 22 lbs.), positioned between the G-Lite and the Vista. It features a reversible seat

strollers

(but no bassinet) and adjustable height handle. Car seat adapters for the Maxi-Cosi, Graco, Chicco and Peg Perego infant seats are available for $30 to $40. Accessories include a bumper bar ($30), snack tray ($40) and travel bag ($90). Interesting note: the travel bag guarantees against damage by the gorillas at the airlines. Just register the bag with Uppa Baby's TravelSafe Program before you leave on your vacation.

Our view. We like UPPAbaby—parent feedback on their strollers has been quite positive.

Readers who like the Vista praise its quality, huge basket and high-riding seat and bassinet. The no-flat foam tires also win raves. The negatives include a basket that is a bit hard to reach with the bassinet attached—and the rear wheelbase (25") on the Vista is rather wide, making the stroller harder to maneuver in tight aisles or doorways. Another bummer: the seat doesn't have a full recline, which irks some users. But . . . the footrest is adjustable (something the Bugaboo lacks) and the fold is much easier and more compact compared to Bugaboo. Another parent told us she loved the stroller as a single, less so as a double (the attached toddler seat made the steering difficult). We blogged about that issue back in 2011.

The new 2015 Vista wasn't on the market as of this writing, so no parent feedback yet. The comments above are on the previous model Vista.

Those criticisms aside, folks who have the Vista give it high marks for quality and durability. The company's customer service is also excellent. If you live in the city and need a durable, multi-function stroller (and can live with the weight/bulk), the Vista is a good choice.

The G-Lite wins similar kudos, with fans citing its super light weight and included cushions. The lack of seat recline in the G-lite is one major negative, but folks with older toddlers say it is fine for them. We picked the G-Lite as our "better" picks on our umbrella stroller website.

So, we will recommend UPPAbaby—for urban parents, the Vista or Cruz is a good bet. For those in the suburbs, the G-Lite or G-Luxe are top contenders for best lightweight strollers. *Baby Bargains Resale Rank: Good.* **Rating: A**

Urbini *urbinibaby.com* Urbini is the Walmart exclusive stroller brand owned by Goodbaby.

Chinese baby goods behemoth Goodbaby has stayed largely below the radar in North America, despite rapid sales growth (2012 sales: $587 million). Their claim to fame is as a past manufacturer for Dorel (Cosco, Safety 1st, Quinny, Maxi Cosi), the world's largest baby goods maker.

Not content to merely design and manufacture baby gear for other companies, GoodBaby has gone on an acquisition spree in recent years. First, they snapped up Cybex and then, in 2014, Evenflo.

At the same time, Goodbaby has decided to sell direct, under the both the GB and Urbini brands. Urbini is exclusive to Walmart, while GB is sold in other stores.

The models. The company has three main stroller offerings:

Omni Travel System: 3-in-1 travel system ($200, 22 lbs. features an infant car seat (the Petal) and a multi-function stroller with reversible seat. The infant car seat works from 4-35 lbs. and features a two-position base recline and infant body support pillow. The Petal also has side impact protection (deep side walls lined with EPS foam). The Omni is also available solo for $149.

The Touri Travel System features same infant car seat (Petal) paired with an umbrella-style stroller for $150. The Touri stroller includes a large canopy with sun visor, multi-position reclining seat and cup holder.

The Hummingbird is a $99 super lightweight stroller with one-hand, self-standing fold. Goodbaby claims the Hummingbird is the "world's lightest stroller," weighing in at under 7 lbs.

The Avi all terrain stroller is a $200 model featuring air-filled wheels, one-hand quick self-standing fold and two-position canopy. It is sold as a stand-alone stroller or as part of a travel system ($300).

Our view. The Omni is clearly the best-selling stroller in the Urbini line. Most impressive: it is one of the lowest-price models we've seen with a reversible seat. The Urbini Omni seems to be aiming to be a poor man's Britax B-Ready ($350) or Uppa Baby Vista ($730, with bassinet). Most parent feedback on this model has been positive, with fans citing its overall ease of use (opening, closing). Detractors point out there is no separate base for the infant seat and the fabric on the stroller doesn't remove for cleaning.

The Urbini Tour's lightweight umbrella stroller is also unique—similar to the Chicco C6, but with a better canopy and single wheels that are popular in Europe. Feedback on this model is also quite positive.

Meanwhile the Urbini Hummingbird looks much like a Combi stroller, although the square canopy doesn't look very effective at blocking sun. The weight at 6.6 lbs. is impressive—but the feedback on this model is nowhere near as positive as the Touri or Omni. Critics knock the wheels as "horrible" . . . this model is clearly designed for the mall. The minimal seat recline makes the Hummingbird only appropriate for older babies.

The Avi all terrain stroller was too new as of this writing to get a read on parent feedback yet, but initial reports are positive.

Bottom line: Urbini offers impressive value, with the Omni and Touri the best bets. **Rating: B+**

Valco valcobaby.com Australia-based Valco's mojo are all terrain and double strollers. Their flagship model is the Tri-Mode EX, a tri-wheel stroller whose key selling point is expandability.

The models. The basic Tri-Mode EX comes in both a single

($500, 23 lbs.; pictured) and double ($715, 33 lbs.) version and features a five-position, fully reclining seat, large storage basket, aluminum frame, newborn insert and swivel front wheel that can be locked in a fixed position. The Tri-Mode has 12" air-filled tires.

That's nice, but what separates Valco from other stroller makers are the plethora of add-ons: a bassinet ($200) and toddler seat ($80 to $100) that extend the use of this stroller. The bassinet is fine, but the toddler seat is really cool, turning the Valco into a double stroller. Valco's other accessories include a car seat adapter ($30 to $40) and foot muff ($65 to $120).

The twin version of the Tri-Mode (the Tri-Mode EX Twin) is Valco's top selling model.

In the past year, Valco revamped the Valco frame, adding wheel suspension and an easier fold with self lock. The newest Tri-Mode is somewhat lighter, landing at 21.3 lbs. Also new: a four-wheel version of the Tri-Mode with air tires at 25.1 lbs.

New for 2015, Valco is rolling out a smaller Tri-Mode, dubbed the Tri-Mode X. It features adjustable foot rests, a cell phone pocket and air filled tires. This model will be available in three and four wheel (Quad X) versions—pricing was not set as of this writing.

How does the Valco stack up versus its main competitors in the swivel wheel, all terrain category? Well the Valco is a touch heavier than the Mountain Buggy Urban Jungle, although Valco has reduced its weight in recent years to be more comparable. And folks seem to like the Valco's toddler seat configuration better than Phil & Ted, although there is a split opinion here. Fashion wise, Valco is a bit dull, with only four choices.

Besides the Tri-Mode, Valco has three other models: the Snap, Zee and Spark.

At a mere 13 lbs. for the single version, the Snap ($260 to $280) is a feature-packed three-wheel stroller. Included are a padded napper bar, extendable canopy, full recline, adjustable foot rest, extra compact fold, "flip flop friendly" brake and large basket. There is also a four-wheel version of the Snap (dubbed the Snap4, $280, 15.3 lbs.). Air filled tires are an option on the Snap4.

New for 2015, Valco has rolled out two spin-offs of the Snap: the Snap Ultra and Snap Duo. The upgraded Snap Ultra ($390, 18.3 lbs.) features a full recline seat that reverses, foam tires and zippered canopy with UV protection. The Snap Duo ($500, 24 lbs.) has adjustable footrests, the ability to hold one or two bassinets as well as to mix and match canopies in different colors.

The Zee ($300 to $330, 17 lbs.) is a bit of a departure for Valco: this four-wheel in-line stroller features a compact fold, adjustable footrest, compact/standing fold and one-touch seat recline. The Zee also has a companion double stroller, called the Zee Two

($550). This side-by-side double also has swivel double front wheels like the single version as well as two independent canopies. In the past year, the Zee gained a height adjustable handle and a canopy with two-position height adjustment.

The Spark ($500, 24 lbs.) is Valco's offering in the multi-function category now dominated by the UPPAbaby Vista. The Spark's seat morphs from bassinet mode (full recline) to a full seat that is reversible. Other features include air-filled 10″ tires, an extended canopy and a storage basket with both rear and side access. A double version of the Snap (Snap Dual) runs $400 and weighs 21.7 lbs. The Spark looks like it will be discontinued sometime in 2015.

Valco's Matrix ($375, a tri-wheel model with air-filled tires) is discontinued, although you may see a few still available online.

Our view. Parent feedback on the Tri-Mode has been positive, with folks lauding the stroller's quality, maneuverability and sturdy ride. We've been impressed with how Valco has trimmed the weight on the Tri-Mode, as that was previously a major drawback. Readers love all the storage and air-filled tires, which make the Tri-Mode a better bet for folks who want to use it on trails or rough sidewalks.

Valco's other models also earn high marks on quality, ease of use and overall design. Perhaps the only complaint here is the lack of included cup holders or parent consoles—that's an extra $20-$40 accessory. The storage baskets on Valco strollers also come in for criticism—they are smallish compared to other strollers in this price range.

Finally, we should note that Valco's retail distribution is somewhat thin, concentrated in independent baby stores (not chains). That makes seeing one in person a challenge—example: Texas has just one retail dealer, as of this writing. Oregon? Zero.

Despite these drawbacks, we like Valco. The company's niche of all-terrain strollers (with an emphasis on doubles) fills a void in the market. *Baby Bargains Resale Rank: Good.* **Rating: A**

Our Picks: The Best Strollers

Lifestyle #1: Mall Crawl

You live in the suburbs and drive just about everywhere you go. Besides the mall, you take quick strolls around the block, which has paved sidewalks in good condition.

The ideal mall crawler stroller has small wheels that enable tight cornering in narrow aisles—it can't be too wide or bulky. As for weight, you'll be hauling this stroller in and out of a trunk several times a day . . . so anything over 20 lbs. is asking for trouble. Other nice features for a mall stroller include a decent cup holder and good-sized basket. The canopy and accessories like a rain cover are a bit less important, since this stroller is used more indoors than out.

strollers

Common first-time parent mistake: buying a giant travel system, with matching infant car seat and stroller. These are common shower gifts and many folks fall for that coordinated look . . . and think their stroller should be built like a M1 tank to protect a newborn from thermonuclear attack. But many travel system strollers are behemoths—and that huge weight and bulk make them impossible to use as baby gets older, not to mention wrestling it in and out of trunk.

Good. Ok, you have two choices here: get a stroller that is infant-car seat compatible or go for a stroller frame.

Good news: more strollers now have adapters that fit infant car seats. Some brands like Baby Jogger have car seat adapter accessories that work with several major infant car seats.

Another option: buy a simple stroller frame, like the **Graco Snug Elite Rider** ($100) or **Chicco KeyFit Caddy** ($100). If you can't decide what main stroller you want just yet, this could be a placeholder. When your baby outgrows the infant car seat, you'll end up buying a good lightweight stroller like the ones recommended below.

Finally, a caveat about over-use of the infant car seat for newborns in strollers. Pediatricians generally recommend limiting the amount of time newborns spend in an infant car seat—this is especially true for preemies or infants with certain medical conditions (ask your doctor for advice if there is a concern). While there is no hard and fast rule, it makes sense to take your baby out of the seat fre-

STROLLER ROUND-UP

Here's our round-up of popular lightweight models by the major stroller manufacturers.

Maker	Model	Weight	Price	Recline
Baby Jogger	City Mini	17.1	$250	Full
Chicco	C6 / Capri	11.0	$80	Partial
Combi	Cosmo	13.0	$115	Full
GB	Ellum	15.4	$220	Full
Graco	Breaze	17.5	$170	Full
Inglesina	Swift	13.0	$140	Partial
Joovy	Groove Ultralight	13.9	$140	Partial
Kolcraft	Cloud Plus	11.8	$60	Partial
Peg Perego	Pliko Mini	14.0	$250	Partial
Uppa Baby	G-Lite	8.3	$160	None
	G-Luxe	13.4	$260	Partial
Valco	Snap	13.0	$260	Full

quently so there is a change in position.

Better. Your baby has now outgrown the infant car seat and you are looking for a lightweight stroller. Among the better bets would be the **Chicco C6** (aka the Capri; $70 to $80, 11 lbs.) which features a two-position seat recline, five-point harness and basic canopy . . . it is a best bet for the mall.

We also like the **Summer Infant 3D lite** stroller ($70, 12 lbs.)—it is a two-handled umbrella style stroller with a full seat recline, pop-out canopy, cup holder and easy access to the basket.

A bit more money but still excellent would be **UPPAbaby's G-Lite** ($160, 8.3 lbs.). Compared to the other two mall strollers, the G-Lite has upgrades like a removable washable seat pad.

FYI: The Chicco C6 and UPPAbaby G-Lite have partial seat reclines and hence are best for babies six months and older. The maximum weight capacity for G-Lite is 50 lbs.; the C6 is 37 lbs.

Best. Here's our top pick for the mall crawl: the **Baby Jogger City Mini** ($250, 17.1 lbs.). The Baby Jogger City Mini is an excellent tri-wheel stroller with oversized canopy and fully reclining seat. Baby Jogger's quick fold technology is amazing—you lift a strap in the middle of the stroller and zip! It's folded. An optional car seat adapter can turn a City Mini into a travel system if you wish.

strollers

COMMENTS

Quick-fold technology, extended sun canopy, tri-wheel.

Compact umbrella fold, decent-size basket. aka the Capri.

Affordable, compact fold, can be paired with Combi infant seat.

Quick, compact fold, air-flow extended canopy. Pricey

Full recline, extended canopy, front wheel suspension.

Skimpy canopy, no cup holder, two handle design.

Two handle design, extended canopy.

One hand, standing fold, child snack tray.

Height adjustable handle, lightest weight Pliko model.

Lightest weight. Standing fold, mesh seat, seat pad is extra.

Bigger wheels, improved canopy, washable seat pad.

Extendable canopy, adjustable footrest, compact fold.

Airline travel. Experienced parent rule #429: *never* gate-check an expensive stroller. Instead, if you plan to do much airline travel, go for a super cheap, lightweight model. Our suggestion: The *Kolcraft Cloud Plus* ($60) has a good size canopy and removable snack tray. At $60, this stroller is easily replaced if an airline destroys it.

Lifestyle #2: Urban Jungle

When you live in a city like New York, Boston or Washington D.C., your stroller is more than just baby transportation—it's your primary vehicle. You stroll to the market, on outings to a park or longer trips on weekend getaways.

Weight is crucial for these parents as well. While you are not lugging a stroller in or out of a trunk like a suburbanite, you may find

BUGABOO SMACKDOWN!

The Bugaboo Cameleon ($890, 20 lbs.) is the reir ing champ of ultra expensive, three componer strollers (combining a bassinet, stroller frame an seat). Whether you think it is a cleverly designe

CONTENDER		PRICE	WEIGHT	BUGABOO-ISH?
BABY JOGGER CITY SELECT		$500	28.1 LBS.	
BRITAX B-READY		$400	28.1 LBS.	
CHICCO URBAN		$400	24.1 LBS.	
MAMAS PAPAS SOLA		$400	26.1 LBS.	
NUNA IVVI		$800	29.8 LBS.	
QUINNY BUZZ XTRA		$600	29.4 LBS.	
PHIL & TEDS SMART LUX		$400	26.2 LBS.	
UPPA BABY VISTA		$820	27.5 LBS.	

yourself climbing up subway stairs or trudging up to a fourth-floor walk-up apartment. It's a major trade-off here: full-featured strollers that are outfitted for the weather (full boot, rain cover) can weigh more than lightweight models designed for the mall. Basically, you want a rugged stroller that can take all the abuse a big city can dish out—giant potholes, uneven sidewalks, the winter from Hell . . . without the weight of a bulldozer.

In the past, carriage strollers or prams were the primary "urban jungle" stroller, but these have fallen out of favor for their bulk, weight and other disadvantages (prams typically have front wheels that don't turn).

Multi-function strollers are now the rage for urbanites—these combine a chassis with stroller seat for older babies and a bassinet

---

stroller that embodies urban chic . . . or a sign of wretched excess, Bugaboo sure has been one thing: a design leader. Now competitors are nipping at Bugaboo's wooden shoes. We rate the contenders on a scale of one to three klompen! (Google it.)

COMMENTS/VERDICT

Swiss Army knife of strollers with 16 configurations. 2nd seat runs $160, bassinet is $90. **But it weighs 40% more than Bugaboo.**

Reversible seat, 14 different seat configurations. 2nd seat is $150. Wheel suspension, large storage basket. Fashion is a bit dull.

Telescoping handle, aluminum frame, standing fold, large basket, quick release EVA tires. **Reversible seat that converts to carry cot.**

Reversible seat, height adjustable handle bar, lay flat seat. **Includes rain cover.** Affordable. But tiny basket won't hold much.

Includes car seat adapter, **full canopy extends to cover entire stroller**, run flat rubber wheels. But weight is nearly 30 lbs.

Price includes stroller, carry cot and infant car seat. **Extendable zipper canopy, air-filled front tire.** Full recline. Reversible seat. Tri-wheel.

Modular seat has 21 configurations,; air filled wheels. Affordable, but car seat adapters and bassinet are separate purchases.

Pricey, but includes bassinet, height adj. handle, rain shield, mesh sun shade, rubber-like foam wheels. Bonus: $130 rumble seat for toddlers.

strollers

for newborns. Some models include the bassinet, others offer it as an optional accessory.

While multi-function strollers are nice, they do have one disadvantage. They're heavy (many are 20+ lbs.) and most don't fold compactly. When you are trying to ascend subway stairs with baby in one arm and a stroller in another, the last thing you need is a bulky stroller.

So we recommend a lightweight second stroller—but unlike a stroller for the mall, this one needs more weatherproofing for the city. Of course, if you live in a tiny apartment, all you may have room for is the lightweight stroller.

Hence, we will break down our picks for the urban jungle into two categories: multi-function and lightweight, but weather proof:

Best (multi-function). The winner here is the *UPPAbaby Vista* ($820, 27.5 lbs.., pictured), which includes a bassinet and stroller seat, plus many extras (rain shield, mesh sun shade, bug cover, etc). Readers love how functional this stroller is (you can fold it with

the stroller seat attached, for example), plus its smooth ride on no-flat foam tires is a must for urban dwellers. FYI: the Vista got a complete make-over for 2015; see review earlier in this chapter for details.

If you plan to have two kids close in age, we'd suggest the *Baby Jogger City Select* ($500, 28.1 lbs.). It can be configured 16 ways with an optional second seat ($170). An excellent stroller with a quick fold.

Finally, a close runner-up in the multi-function stroller race is the *Britax B-Ready* ($400, 28.1 lbs.). It also has the second seat option, but lacks the cool quick-fold of the Baby Jogger. The B-Ready works out of the box with the Britax infant car seat, which is a nice plus.

You'll note we didn't mention Bugaboo in the above picks—sorry, their $1000+ Cameleon just doesn't offer the same value and features as the others we mentioned. See the "Bugaboo Smackdown" box nearby for a look at how the Bugaboo stacks up to the competition.

Best (light weight). Our top pick is the *Baby Jogger City Mini* ($250, 17.1 lbs.; pictured).

There are two key reasons to go with the City Mini over an umbrella-type stroller: fold and canopy. Baby Jogger's "quick fold" is amazing— grab it by a strap on the seat and zip! It's folded in one simple step. That's a key advantage over many umbrella-type strollers, most of which require a parent to hit a couple of levers and then fold the stroller to the ground . . . not easy to do with a baby in your arms. Seconds count in the big city—and the Baby Jogger's quick fold is, well, quicker.

Ditto for the canopy. The City Mini has an awesome, giant canopy that completely shields baby from sun, wind and all the urban weather you can think of.

The **Britax B-Agile** ($215, 16.5 lbs.) is also a top choice here—its curved back axle might be a better bet for taller parents. And the included car seat adapter for Britax seats is a great value (versus the extra $60 you'd shell out for a Baby Jogger adapter). We also like how easy it is to adjust the harness on the B-Agile, which can be done without the re-clipping that the City Mini requires. On the downside, the B-Agile has a foam handle versus rubber for the Baby Jogger—the rubber is probably more durable than the foam. There are also little differences that tip the scales to Baby Jogger—the hidden brake cables on the City Mini versus the exposed one on the B-Agile. The City Mini also has a deeper, more enclosed storage basket than the B-Agile.

Lifestyle #3: Green Acres

If you live on a dirt or gravel road or in a neighborhood with no sidewalks, you need a stroller to do double duty. First, it must handle rough surfaces without bouncing baby all over the place. Second, it must be able to "go to town," folding easily to fit into a trunk for a trip to a mall or other store. And what about snow? Most mall strollers simply don't work in snow.

The answer: an all-terrain stroller with air-filled tires.

Good. *Phil & Ted's Navigator* ($500, 27.5 lbs.) is a tri-wheel stroller with swivel front wheel and air-filled tires. It features a large canopy and one-hand fold. What's unique about the Phil & Ted's: a toddler seat accessory ($90-$100) that attaches to the front or back of the seat, giving you added flexibility  if you have multiple kids. That's what makes Phil & Ted special: the flexibility to use the same stroller for newborn, toddler, BOTH toddler and newborn at the same time and two toddlers. Hence, this is a good bet if you are planning on having more than one kid. If not, consider one of the next two picks.

Better. Similar to the Phil & Ted's Explorer (in fact, they are owned by the same company), the *Mountain Buggy Urban Jungle* ($400, 24 lbs.) is our better pick in this category. The polymer spoke wheels won't earn fashion

strollers

points, but at least they don't rust (helpful for folks who live near an ocean). Fans of Mountain Buggy love the way these strollers push and handle the most extreme weather (Snow? Sleet? Bring it on). We also like the stroller's overall weight (24 lbs.). One drawback: there is no second seat option like the Phil & Ted's Navigator.

Best. The crown for best all-terrain stroller goes to the *BOB Revolution* stroller ($330-$390, 24.9 lbs.). It comes in two versions: polymer wheels (SE or Sport Experience) or aluminum alloy rims (CE or City Experience). The polymer wheels are a pound heav- ier (24.9 lbs.) than the aluminum option (23.9 lbs.); the aluminum version is about $60 more expensive. We love the new infant car seat adapter accessory ($60) that can be removed from the stroller without tools. FYI: if you need a height adjustable handlebar, the new *Bob Revolution Flex* ($390) adds that feature. Fans of BOB love the stroller's quality and durability.

See the chart below for a comparison of all-terrain models.

Lifestyle #4: Exercise (Jogging & Sport Strollers)

If you want to exercise with a stroller, you have two choices: tri-wheel strollers with fixed front wheels, or a model with a front wheel that swivels.

Fixed-wheel jogging strollers with air-filled tires are best for folks who want to actually jog or run with a stroller—you can push them in a straight line. The disadvantage to these strollers: to turn them, you have to pick up the front wheel and move it. Hence, fixed wheel joggers aren't good for walking or shopping trips.

ALL-TERRAIN STROLLERS

How top all-terrain strollers compare—each of these

MODEL	WEIGHT	PRICE	BRAND RATING
BABY JOGGER CITY ELITE	31.3 LBS.	$400	A
BOB REVOLUTION SE	24.9	$330	A
BRITAX B-READY	21.8	$400	A-
BUMBLERIDE INDIE	20.0	$500	B+
MOUNTAIN BUGGY URBAN	24.9	$500	A
PHIL & TED NAVIGATOR	27.5	$500	A-
VALCO TRI-MODE	23.0	$500	A

Strollers with turnable front wheels are NOT recommended for folks who want to run—even if the stroller has the option to lock the front wheel. That said, strollers with a swivel front wheel are great for folks who just want to walk the neighborhood or trails. So you need to ask yourself, exactly how do you plan to exercise with the stroller?

Another issue to consider: how young can your baby be and ride in a jogger? First, determine whether the seat reclines (not all models do). If it doesn't, wait until baby is at least six months old and can hold his or her head up. If you want to jog or run with the stroller, it might be best to wait until baby is at least a year old since all the jostling can be dangerous for a younger infant (their neck muscles can't handle the bumps). Ask your pediatrician for advice if you are unsure.

Another decision area: the frame. The cheapest strollers (under $200) have steel frames—they're strong but also heavy (and that could be a drawback for serious runners). The most expensive models ($300 to $400) have aluminum frames, which are the lightest in weight. Once again, if you plan casual walks, a steel frame is fine. Runners should go for aluminum.

Finally, remember the Trunk Rule. Any jogger is a lousy choice if you can't get it easily in your trunk. Check the DEPTH of the jogger when it is folded—compared this to your vehicle's trunk. Many joggers are rather bulky even when folded. One tip: quick release wheels help reduce the bulk, so check for that option.

So, which jogging stroller do we recommend? Let's break that down into two categories: power walking and serious runners. Note that our pick for serious runners has a fixed front wheel; if you want a stroller with a turnable front wheel (more suited to the mall or light duty outdoor activities), go for the power walking pick or see the Green Acres section above.

models are tri-wheels with air-filled tires and front wheels that swivel.

COMMENT

12" AIR-FILLED TIRES, PARENT CONSOLE, QUICKEST FOLD ON MARKET.

POLYMER RIMS (OR ALUMINUM $20 EXTRA). CAR SEAT ADAPTER $50 EXTRA.

14 CONFIGURATIONS; OPTIONAL BASSINET AND 2ND SEAT.

ADJUSTABLE HANDLE, FULL RECLINE, BOOT AND BIG STORAGE BASKET.

2015 REDESIGN ADDS ONE-HAND STANDING FOLD, EXTENDED LEG REST

WIDE SEAT, HEIGHT ADJUSTABLE HANDLE. OPTIONAL SECOND CHILD SEAT.

FULLY RECLINING SEAT, LARGE BASKET, TODDLER SEAT ACCESSORY.

Best (power walking). *Graco FastAction Fold Jogger Click Connect* ($151, 27 lbs.) has a swivel front wheel that can be locked, plus a quick fold feature that earns kudos from readers. Add in a generous storage basket, parent console with cup holders plus an affordable price and you've got a great stroller for extended walking.

Best (serious running). *BOB Ironman* ($335, 21 lbs.) is a fixed wheel jogger with smooth 16" tires with steel wheel spokes and

---

Three mistakes to avoid when buying a jogging stroller

With jogging strollers available everywhere from Target to high-end bike stores, it is easy to get confused by all the options. Keep in mind these traps when shopping for a jogger:

◆ *Rust.* Warning: cheaper jogging strollers are made of steel—rust can turn your jogging stroller into junk in short order. This is especially a problem on the coasts, but can happen anywhere. Hint: the best joggers have ALUMINUM frames. And make sure the wheel rims are alloy, not steel. All-terrain strollers like Mountain Buggy use polymer wheels (in most models) to get around the rust problem.

◆ *Suspended animation.* The latest rage with joggers is cushiony suspensions, which smooth out bumps but can add to the price. But do you really need it? Most jogging strollers give a smooth ride by design, so no added suspension is necessary. And some kids actually LIKE small bumps or jostling—it helps them fall asleep in the stroller.

◆ *Too narrow seats.* Unlike other baby products, a good jogging stroller could last you until your child is five years old—that is, if you pick one with a wide enough seat to accommodate an older child. The problem: some joggers rather narrow seats. Great for infants, not good for older kids. We noticed this issue after our neighbors stopped using their jogging stroller when their child hit age three, but our son kept riding in his until five and beyond. Brands with bigger seats (like BOB) offer more long-term value. (As always, confirm seat dimensions before committing to a specific stroller; seats can vary from model to model).

adjustable tracking. Thanks to an aluminum frame, this jogger weighs just 21 lbs.

Need a double jogger? Our advice would be the same: BOB makes a double version of the Ironman for $455.

Plan to take your jogger out in the cold weather? Instead of bundling up baby, consider a stroller blanket. One of our favorites is the *JJ Cole Bundle Me* (bundleme.com), which comes in several versions for $30. And what can you use to keep a blanket on your stroller? Try the *BlankyClip*, a $20 tension clip (blankyclip.com) cleverly disguised as a stuffed bear or duck.

Of course, you could have the opposite problem: you live somewhere where the summer weather is brutal. If your stroller seat fabric doesn't breathe, consider a *Cool Mee Seat Liner* from Meeno Babies (MeenoBabies.com). Their machine washable seat liner ($25) is made of three-ply mesh material that promotes airflow to cool baby.

Double The Fun: Strollers for two

There are two types of strollers that can transport two tikes: tandem models and side-by-side styles. A tandem stroller has a "front-back" configuration, where the younger child rides in back while the older child gets the view. These strollers are best for parents with a toddler and a new baby.

Side-by-side strollers, on the other hand, are best for parents of twins or babies close in age. In this case, there's never any competition for the view seat. The only downside: some of these strollers are so wide, they can't fit through narrow doorways or store aisles. (Hint: make sure the stroller is not wider than 30" to insure door compatibility). Another bummer: few have napper bars or fully reclining seats, making them impractical for infants.

So, what to buy—a tandem or side by side? Our reader feedback shows parents are much happier with their side-by-side models than tandems. Why? The tandems can get darn near impossible to push when weighted down with two kids, due to their length-wise design. Yes, side by sides may not be able to fit through some narrow shopping aisles, but they seem to work better overall.

Double strollers can be frustrating—your basic choices are low-price duos from Graco or Kolcraft or high-price doubles like those from Baby Jogger. There doesn't seem to be much in between the low-price ($200 range) and the high-end ($400 and up).

Best tandem strollers (front/back double). *Kolcraft Contours Options Tandem* ($280, 32 lbs.) has seven different configurations with seats that can reverse to face each other—or use one (or two) infant car seats. The Options ships with a universal car seat adapter and features a standing hold, reclining seats, adjustable footrests and decent size canopies.

On the downside, there is no parent tray (just one small cup holder) and no child snack trays or cup holders (you can add an aftermarket cup holder if need be). And, yes, this stroller is heavy and quite bulky when folded—but so are most tandem strollers.

The Options is a Babies R Us exclusive. There is also an upgraded version of the Options called the Options Elite ($300, 37.4 lbs.), which is a Buy Buy Baby exclusive. The Elite adds rubber coated rear wheels, side storage basket access and seat back storage. The Elite also has an extra, extendable canopy with mesh air vent as well as taller seats.

Runner up: Chicco has a winner with the **Chicco Cortina Together** ($300, 30 lbs.). This front/back tandem stroller holds two car seats and features an aluminum frame, a storage basket with trap door access, three-position handle and flat fold. Readers love the steering and overall quality of this stroller.

E-MAIL FROM THE REAL WORLD
Biting the bullet on a pricey twin stroller

Cheapo twin strollers sound like a good deal for parents of twins, but listen to this mother of multiples:

"Twins tend to ride in their strollers more often and longer, and having an unreliable, bulky or inconvenient stroller is a big mistake. As you suggest, it's a false economy to buy an inexpensive Graco or other model, as these most likely will break down before you're done with the stroller. My husband and I couldn't believe that we'd have to spend $400 on a stroller, but after talking to parents of multiples, we understand why it's best to just bite the bullet on this one. We've heard universally positive feedback about side-by-side strollers for their maneuverability, durability and practicality. We've heard much less positive things about front-back tandems for twins. These often are less versatile, as only one seat reclines, so you can't use them when both babies are small (or tired). And when the babies get bigger, they're more likely to get into mischief by pulling each others' hair and stuff."

Another runner up in this category: the **Joovy Caboose Stand-on Tandem** ($138, 26 lbs.). It really isn't a tandem, but a pushcart—the younger child sits in front while the older child *stands* in back (there is also a jump seat for the older child to sit on). This is a better solution when you have an older toddler who doesn't want to ride all the time in a stroller . . . but still gets tired and needs a place to sit on long outings.

Best side by side strollers. For parents of two little ones on a tight budget, we like the **Chicco Echo Twin** ($190, 30.5 lbs.), which is a Target exclusive. We like the one-hand seat recline (each seat can be reclined individually), as well as the zip-off rear canopy to allow for air flow.

If your budget allows, we'd suggest the **Graco FastAction Fold Duo** ($280, 33 lbs.). Yes, it is three lbs. heavier than the Chicco, but you get a bigger storage basket, better canopies with sun visors as well as quick fold. A similar good bet here is the **Joovy Scooter X2** ($265, 28 lbs.).

Is Grandma offering to buy your twin stroller? If so and the budget allows, we recommend the **Baby Jogger City Mini Double** ($450, 26.6 lbs., pictured), with its excellent extended canopies and quick fold.

Need a double that can handle rough sidewalks? The **Baby Jogger City Mini GT** ($580) adds larger foam tires for a cushy ride.

Finally, for outdoor treks with two kids, we'd suggest looking at our top-rated all-terrain stroller brands (Phil & Ted, Mountain Buggy and BOB). They each make swivel wheel doubles that, while pricey, feature great quality and comfort.

Bike Trailers, Seats & Helmets

Bike Trailers. Yes, lots of companies make bike trailers, but the gold standard is **Burley** (burley.com; pictured left). Their trailers (sold in bicycle stores) are considered the best in the industry. A good example is the **Burley D'Lite**. It features a multi-point safety harness, built-in rear storage, 100 lb. carrying capacity and compact fold (to store in a trunk). Okay, it's expensive at $630 but check around for second-hand bargains. And there is a $160 jogger conversion kit that turns a Burley into a jogging

bike trailers

stroller (we've heard mixed reviews on this for its wobbly steering).

If the D'Lite is too expensive, consider Burley's newer Honey Bee at just $300 to $400. It comes out of the box with everything to attach it to a bike or convert it to a stroller. It's basically like their D'Lite, with seating for up to 2 kids and all of Burley's safety features.

A close runner-up to Burley in the bike trailer race is **Thule Chariot** (thule.com). "These are the best engineered bike trailers I've ever seen," opined a reader and we agree. The Thule Chariot Cheetah is $450.

Baby Jogger, the stroller company reviewed earlier, has an entry in the bike trailer race as well—the POD. This model is sold as a chassis for $350—you can add a stroller kit for $50, jogger for $60 and bike trailer adapter for $40. The POD is 30" wide so it can fit through most standard doorways, yet still accommodate up to two kids. FYI: the POD has been discontinued, but we still see it for sale online.

What about the "discount" bike trailers you see for about $100? **InStep** makes a few of these models:, including the Quick N EZ ($134). InStep also makes four Schwinn bike trailers, which are upgraded versions of their regular line. Cost: $120 to $300.

What do you give up for the price? In general, lower priced bike trailers have steel frames and are heavier than the Burleys (which are made of aluminum). And the cheaper bike trailers don't fold as easily or compactly as the Burleys, nor do they attach as easily to a bike.

The key feature to look for with any bike trailer is the ease (or lack thereof) of attaching the trailer to a bike. Quick, compact fold is important as well. Look for the total carrying capacity and the quality of the nylon fabric.

So, should you spring for an expensive bike trailer or one of the $150 ones? Like jogging strollers, consider how much you'll use it. For an occasional (once a week?) bike trip, we'd recommend the cheaper models. Plan to do more serious cycling, say two or three times a week? Then go for a Burley or Thule Chariot. Yes, they are expensive but worth it if you really plan to use the trailer extensively. Hint: this might be a great item to buy second-hand on eBay or Craigslist.

Safety information: you should wait on using a bike trailer until your child is OVER one year of age. Why? Infants under age one don't have neck muscles to withstand the jolts and bumps they'll encounter with bike trailers, which don't have shock absorbers. Remember you might hit a pothole at 15+ mph—that's not something that is safe for an infant to ride out. Be sure your child is able to hold his head up while wearing a helmet as well. Your child should always wear a helmet while riding in a bike trailer—no exceptions. And, no, there is no bike trailer on the market that safely holds an infant car seat, which might cushion the bumps. Most trailers will accommodate children up to about age six.

Bike seats & helmets. When considering whether to buy a bike seat or a bike trailer, the low price of many bike seats (which start at $100) may be tempting. However, for safety reasons, we recommend a bike trailer.

Why? Bike seats are inherently less safe for baby than a trailer. That's because if you crash on a bike with a bike seat, both you and baby hit the ground. Even if your baby is wearing a helmet, that can still be ugly. Meanwhile, a trailer doesn't hit the ground the same way in a crash—and it is closer to the ground to begin with. Also: bike seats can make even the best of bikes unstable. That's because the additional weight of a child plus the bike seat can make a bike hard to handle even for experienced riders. Of course, bike trailers have their own issues—since they sit lower to the ground, they can be hard for motorists to see (always use an orange flag on the trailer). And they can be tippy, especially on tight turns. Since a trailer is wider than a bike, you have to be careful when negotiating tight spaces. That said, we still think bike trailers are a better (and safer bet) than a bike seat. As a result, we will no longer recommend bike seats in this edition.

One final tip: don't forget the helmet. If your child is strapped in securely to a bike trailer, she still needs a helmet that is properly fitted and adjusted. *Consumer Reports* does a good job rating and reviewing kid bike helmets: we agree that their most recent top pick (the Schwinn Thrasher Youth helmet) is a good option. Price: $22.

A few tips on helmets: sometimes it is hard to fit a helmet on a toddler. The best advice is to go to a bike store for help. One tip: add in thick pads (sold with some bike helmets) to give a better fit. Don't glue pads on top of pads, however—and adding a thick hat isn't a safety solution either. If your child cannot wear a bike helmet safely, put off those bike adventures until they are older. Be sure your child wears the helmet well forward on his head. If a helmet is pushed back and your child hits the ground face first, there is no protection for the forehead.

Diaper Bags

We consider ourselves experts at diaper bags—we got five of them as gifts. While you don't need five, this important piece of luggage may feel like an extra appendage after your baby's first year. And diaper bags are for more than just holding diapers—many include compartments for baby bottles, clothes, and changing pads. With that in mind, let's take a look at what separates great diaper bags from the rest of the pack. In addition, we'll give you our list of nine items for a well-stocked diaper bag.

Best Online Sources

Just because you have a new baby doesn't mean you have to lose all sense of style. And there is good news: an entire cottage industry of stylish diaper-bag makers has sprung up to help fill the style gap. One good place to start: our message boards. Go to BabyBargains.com, click on the message boards and then to Places to Go (All Other Gear, Diaper Bags, etc). There you'll find dozens of moms swapping tips on the best and most fashionable diaper bags. Here's a round up of our readers' favorite custom diaper bag makers (most sell direct off their sites, but a few also sell on other sites):

Amy Michelle	amymichellebags.com
California Innovations	californiainnovations.com
Fleurville	fleurville.com
Haiku Diaper Bags	haikubags.com
Holly Aiken	hollyaiken.com
I'm Still Me	imstillme.com
Ju Ju Be	ju-ju-be.com
Kate Spade	katespade.com.
Kipling	kipling.com
Lexie Barnes	lexiebarnes.com
Oi Oi	oioi.com.au
One Cool Chick	onecoolchick.com
Reese Li	reeseli.com
Skip Hop	skiphop.com
Timbuk2	timbuk2.com
Vera Bradley	verabradley.com

No doubt there are dozens more, but that's a great starting point. You can expect prices to be commensurate with style. Kate Spade can cost over $300 a diaper bag. But there are some great looking options for under a $100 too. One caveat: many of these manufacturers are small boutique companies. Often it may be the owner who's taking the order. . . and also sewing the bag! While we admire the entrepreneurship of these companies, many are so small that a minor event can put them off kilter. All it takes is one hurricane or a deluge of orders to turn a reputable company into a customer service nightmare. Check the feedback on these companies on our message boards before ordering.

Smart Shopper Tips

Smart Shopper Tip #1
Diaper Bag Science
"I was in a store the other day, and they had about one zillion different diaper bags. Some had cute prints and others were plain. Should I buy the cheapest one or invest a little more money?"

The best diaper bags are made of tear-resistant fabric and have all sorts of useful pockets, features and gizmos. Contrast that with low-quality brands that lack many pockets and are made of cheap, thin vinyl—after a couple of uses, they start to split and crack. Yes, high-quality diaper bags will cost more ($50 to $150 versus $30 to $45), but you'll be much happier in the long run. High-end diaper bags (like those made by Kate Spade and other designers) can reach the $300 mark or more. Of course, many of our readers have found deals on these bags, so check out our message boards for shopping tips.

Here's our best piece of advice: buy a diaper bag that doesn't *look* like a diaper bag. Sure those bags with dinosaurs and pastel animal prints look cute now, but what are you going to do with it when your baby gets older? A well-made diaper bag that doesn't look like a diaper bag will make a great piece of carry-on luggage later in life.

Smart Shopper Tip #2
Make your own
"Who needs a fancy diaper bag? I just put all the necessary changing items into my favorite backpack."

That's a good point. Most folks have a favorite bag or backpack that can double as a diaper bag. Besides the obvious (wipes and diapers), put in a large zip-lock bag as a holder for dirty/wet items. Add a couple of receiving blankets (as changing pads) plus the key items listed below, and you have a complete diaper bag.

You can buy many items found in a diaper bag (such as a changing pad) a la carte at most baby stores.

Top 9 Items for a Well-Stocked Diaper Bag

After much scientific experimentation, we believe we have perfected the exact mix of ingredients for the best-equipped diaper bag. Here's our recipe:

1 **GET TWO DIAPER BAGS**—one that is a full-size, all-option big hummer for longer trips (or overnight stays) and the other that is a mini-bag for a short hop to dinner or the shopping mall. Here's what each should have:

The full-size bag: This needs a waterproof changing pad that folds up, waterproof pouch or pocket for wet clothes, a couple compartments for diapers, blankets/clothes, etc. Super-deluxe brands have bottle compartments with Thinsulate to keep bottles warm or cold. Another plus: outside pockets for books and small toys. A zippered outside pocket is good for change or your wallet. A cell phone pocket is also a plus.

The small bag: This has enough room for a couple diapers, travel wipe package, keys, wallet and/or cell phone. Some models have a bottle pocket and room for one change of clothes. If money is tight, just go for the small bag. To be honest, the full-size bag is often just a security blanket for first-time parents—some think they need to lug around every possible item in case of a diaper catastrophe. But, in the real world, you'll quickly discover schlepping that big full-size bag everywhere isn't practical. While a big bag is nice for overnight or long trips, we'll bet you will be using the small bag much more often.

2 **EXTRA DIAPERS.** Put a dozen in the big bag, two or three in the small one. Why so many? Babies can go through quite a few in a very short time. Of course, when baby gets older (say over a year), you can cut back on the number of diapers you need for a trip. Another wise tip: put whole packages of diapers and wipes in your car(s). We did this after we forgot our diaper bag one too many times and needed an emergency diaper. (The only bummer: here in Colorado, the wipes we keep in the car sometimes freeze in the winter! As they say, you don't know cold . . .)

3 **A TRAVEL-SIZE WIPE PACKAGE.** A good idea: a plastic Tupperware container that holds a small stack of wipes. Some wipe makers sell travel packs that are allegedly "re-sealable" to retain moisture; we found that they aren't. And they are expensive. For example, a Huggies travel pack of 16 wipes is $6. That works out to 38¢ per wipe compared to 2¢ per wipe if you buy a Huggies refill box of 384 from Kmart.

4 **BLANKET AND CHANGE OF CLOTHES.** Despite the reams of scientists who work on diapers, they still aren't leak-proof—plan for it. A change of clothes is most useful for babies under six months of age, when leaks are more common. After that point, this becomes less necessary.

5 **A HAT OR CAP.** We like the foreign legion-type hats that have flaps to cover your baby's neck and ears (about $10 to $20). Warmer caps are helpful to chase away a chill, since the head is where babies lose the most heat.

6 **BABY TOILETRIES.** Babies can't take much direct exposure to sunlight—sunscreen is a good bet for all infants. Besides sunscreen, other optional accessories include bottles of lotion and diaper rash cream. The best bet: buy these in small travel or trial sizes. Don't forget insect repellent as well. This can be applied to infants two months of age and older.

7 **DON'T FORGET THE TOYS.** We like compact rattles, board books, teethers, etc.

8 **SNACKS.** When baby starts to eat solid foods, having a few snacks in the diaper bag (a bottle of water or milk, crackers, a small box of cereal) is a smart move. But don't bring them in plastic bags. Instead bring reusable plastic containers. Plastic bags are a suffocation hazard and should be kept far away from babies and toddlers.

9 **YOUR OWN PERSONAL STUFF.** Be careful putting your wallet or checkbook into the diaper bag—we advise against it. We left our diaper bag behind one too many times before we learned this lesson. Put your name and phone number in the bag in case it is lost.

Our Picks: Brand Recommendations

Here we go with our top picks for best diaper bag. We realize a diaper bag is a fashion choice and our tastes may not always agree with yours, but if one style by the following manufacturers doesn't appeal to you, check out the other options by that brand. You may find something else you like and you'll be getting commensurate quality.

Good. It's impossible to find a good diaper bag for $25, you say? True, many of these cheaper diaper bags are basically a bag with few or no accessories. The *SoHo diaper bag* ($25 on Amazon) is an exception to the rule—it has seven pieces: the large main bag, zippered mini purse, insulated bottle bag, Grips stroller attachments, two accessory cases and changing pad. The diaper bag itself has a several outside pockets and zip closure on top.

diaper bags

Better. The *Ju-Ju-Be* line of diaper bags gets raves from readers. Most of their designs are over $100, but the *Hobo Be* is a great option at only $86 (sold on Amazon.com). This messenger style bag comes with five zippered pockets, five outside pockets, anti-microbial treated inner fabric, Teflon-treated outer fabric, a changing pad, and memory foam padded strap. A wide variety of colors and styles are available.

Best. Okay, you need more than a basic bag—but you don't want to spend the equivalent of a used car price on a diaper bag? Our readers love the Skip Hop line of bags (skiphop.com). The company offers nine different designs, but our favorite is the *Skip Hop Duo* ($40-$60). The Duo is their largest bag with eleven pockets including a cell phone pocket, magnetic closures instead of zippers and their cool Shuttle Clips, which allow you to clip it to a stroller. Yes, it has a shoulder strap too and changing pad, as you'd expect. Some parents say the bag holds less than they expected and the magnetic closures don't work as well if you stuff the bag really full. Those complaints aside, Skip Hop is a great option if you are looking for a full-size diaper bag with a bit more style. The Duo also comes in a Deluxe, Special Edition and Signature option (fabric changes mainly).

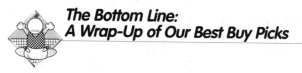

The Bottom Line:
A Wrap-Up of Our Best Buy Picks

Wow . . . and you thought car seats were complex!

Here's the take-home message on strollers: match a stroller to your lifestyle. That means thinking about HOW you'll use the stroller. Mall? Park? Hikes? Read our lifestyle recommendations to match the right stroller to your needs.

Overall, the best strollers brands are UPPAbaby, Britax, Phil & Ted's and BOB. But even brands that get a lukewarm rating can have an occasional winner—witness Graco and Kolcraft's twin strollers.

No matter which stroller you get, it is always smart to go for the lightest weight model you can find. Another key factor: rear wheel width, especially for urban parents. Some new strollers have wide rear wheel widths . . . making negotiating a narrow doorway or tight elevator darn near impossible.

For diaper bags, we like Soho, Ju-Ju-Be and Skip Hop's offerings. Designer diaper bags are nice to get as gifts . . . but go for practical here and you'll be happier.

Next up: baby carriers—which are best for you, baby . . . and your back!

CHAPTER 10 CARRIERS

Baby Carriers

Inside this chapter

Ever wonder what a mai tai is? Here's your 411 on baby carriers, from mai tais to slings to frame carriers. We'll show you which style is best for what you need and give you the inside scoop on our best picks in each category. We'll also explore safety tips to wearing your baby as well as advice on how to be comfortable in any type of carrier.

Advocates of baby wearing from pediatricians to your next-door neighbor tout the benefits of closeness with your child. But even if you don't subscribe to attachment parenting, you have to admit carriers are darn convenient. When you have a baby who just won't take a nap and you've got dinner to get on the table, a carrier that gives you two hands free is a godsend. In this chapter, we'll look at the different types of carriers and they're uses,

Just to make it more confusing, though, it seems like there are 437 different carrier makes and models on the market, from simple slings to fancy backpacks. And we've noticed over the years that every single one of those models has a parent who's a big fan. Of course, the key is to find the right carrier for you. One idea: we like an instructional DVD on baby wearing called **Tummy 2 Tummy**. It covers different types of carriers and how to wear them—a good introduction to the world of carriers. Another tip: we recommend buying a carrier that either has a DVD with instructions or provides an instructional video on their web site.

Getting Started:
When do you need this stuff?

Many parents recognize the benefit of baby wearing and want to begin as soon as they bring their baby home from the hospital. Hence, most folks are shopping for this item in the last trimester of your pregnancy. Unfortunately, there is no knowing if your baby will like the type of carrier you buy, so we recommend parents keep the original packaging and receipts in case you need to return it. Another note of caution: if you have a c-section, you may not be able to use your carrier immediately. And most carriers have a minimum weight requirement of about seven to eight lbs. (backpack carriers minimums are around 16 lbs.). So if you have a smaller baby, you won't want to use your carrier until your baby gains some weight.

Best Online Sources

The Baby Wearer

thebabywearer.com The Baby Wearer is a message board that focuses on carriers. We liked their forum on choosing and comparing carriers; there are also specific forums on different types of carriers (ring slings, wraps, etc).

What Are You Buying?

Carriers come in several flavors: slings, hip carriers, front carriers, mei tais, wrap arounds and frame carriers. Here's a look at each:

◆ **Slings and Pouches.** Slings allow you to hold your baby horizontally or upright. Made of soft fabric with an adjustable strap, slings drape your baby across your body and use rings to connect the strap (see picture). The first slings were made by NoJo, but many other manufacturers have jumped into the sling market.  Whichever brand you choose, devoted sling user Darien Wilson from Austin, Texas has a great tip for new moms: "The trick for avoiding backache when using a sling is to have the bulk of the baby's weight at the parent's waist or above."

Some parents complain that there isn't much between your baby's head and a collision with a wall, furniture, etc. It's true you have to watch where you're going and what you're doing, but sling aficionados say once you get the hang of it, slings are simple to use.

Slings come in padded and unpadded versions in a variety of fabrics. They may also be called Rebozos (they tie together instead of using rings).

Pouches (pocket slings) work in a similar way to slings across mom's body, but they are really just one continuous piece of fabric with an area of fabric that forms a pouch or pocket. No tying or looping fabric through rings; instead buckles or velcro are used.

◆ *Mei Tai or Asian Carriers.* This type of carrier is made up of a fabric rectangle with straps at each corner. The bottom straps tie around your waste while the top straps go over your shoulders and attach to the carrier or are tied together.

◆ *Wrap Around Carrier.* These are like those Guatemalan carriers we mentioned earlier. They are basically made by wrapping a long (three to six meter) piece of fabric around and around your body forming a pouch around baby. Wrap arounds can be positioned to go around the shoulders and waist for better support. But there is a learning curve—wrap around carriers require some practice for correct use.

◆ *Hip Carriers.* Hip carriers are a minimalist version of the sling. With less fabric to cradle baby, they generally work better for older babies (over five or six months). Baby is in a more upright position all the time, rather than lying horizontally. And like a sling, the hip carrier fits across your body with baby resting on your hip.

◆ *Front (Soft) Carriers.* Front carriers are basically a fabric bag worn on your chest. Your baby sort of dangles there in an upright position either looking in at you (when they're very young) or out at the world (when they gain more head control). Some front carriers will convert to a back carrier. Structured soft carriers have more rigid padding so they maintain their shape even when not in use.

◆ **Frame (or backpack) Carriers.** Need to get some fresh air? Just because you have a baby doesn't mean you can never go hiking again. Backpack manufacturers have responded to parents' wish to find a way to take their small children with them on hikes and long walks. The good news is that most of these frame carriers are made with lightweight aluminum, high quality fabrics and well-positioned straps. Accessories abound with some models including sunshades, diaper packs that Velcro on, and adjustable seating so Junior gets a good view.

More Money Buys You . . .

When you spend more money on a carrier, you generally get more luxurious fabrics like from organic cottons to washable silk. Some manufacturers also add embroidery or ruffle accents. Patterns can also cost more than basic solids.

Safe & Sound

Back in 2010, the Consumer Product Safety Commission issued a warning to parents about sling use for infants under four months of age. At least 14 deaths have been associated with the use of slings in the last 20 years. Here are the CPSC's tips for using a sling:

◆ *Premature infants and those with low birth weight (including twins or infants with breathing issues such as a cold) should not be placed in a sling.*

◆ *Make sure the infant's face is not covered* and can be seen at all times regardless what type of carrier you're using.

◆ *Frequently check on your baby to make sure he is breathing.*

◆ *Check the graphic below.* This shows both the correct way (chin up, face visible, nose and mouth free) and the improper way to wear your baby.

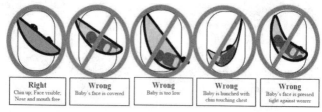

| Right
Chin up; Face visible;
Nose and mouth free | Wrong
Baby's face is covered | Wrong
Baby is too low | Wrong
Baby is hunched with
chin touching chest | Wrong
Baby's face is pressed
tight against wearer |

Smart Shopper Tips

Smart Shopper Tip #1
Try More than One

"My friends are all experienced moms and they have very different opinions on what carrier I should by for my baby. Why can't I get any consensus from them?"

The best carrier works for you *and* your baby. That's why we suggest you buy one or two styles that interest you and keep the packaging/receipts. That way, if your baby loves the Ergobaby soft carrier, but hates the Maya Wrap sling, you're covered. Or you may find that certain carriers are more comfortable—like wrap-arounds, which can be infinitely adjusted for the right fit. Finally, some of our readers own more than one type of carrier. Certain carriers work better with infants but not so great with toddlers. Some carriers are too hot to wear in the summer.

Smart Shopper Tip #2
How Does It Work?

"My new carrier came in today. I was so excited until I tried to get it to work. What am I doing wrong?"

Great question. Here's how you find out. Before you even buy a carrier, check the manufacturer's web site for instructions. We prefer sites that have videos you can watch. Some even send a DVD with the product. And as a last resort, check YouTube to see if any moms posted helpful videos on how to use your carrier. If you notice the manufacturer only has written instructions, beware! It can be as bad as an IKEA shelving unit.

Waste of Money

"All these carriers look the same; a sling is a sling, a front carrier is a front carrier. Can't I just buy the cheapest one I find in the store or on the 'net?"

You could, but you might also be wasting your money. Cheap carriers are typically made with scratchy fabrics, little or no padding, no waist belts for parents, and so on. The key is to find a carrier that is comfortable for both you and your baby. A carrier that lacks support will be quickly discarded.

The Name Game: Carrier Reviews

Here are our reviews of baby carriers. We've divided them into different categories (slings/pouches, front carriers, mai tais, wrap arounds, hip carriers and frame carriers). You'll find that manufacturers often make more than one type of carrier so they'll appear in different categories. While we've attempted to include weight ranges, some manufacturers only list their maximum weights. Most manufacturers also have online videos as well as written instructions included with their products. If they don't have videos, customers often post videos to YouTube to help other parents. Finally, we can't stress enough that you should always practice putting on your carrier and taking it off before you put your baby into it. Some carriers are complex and need practice to use.

Slings and Pouches

THE BABASLING

Joovy.com
Price: $80 to $130
Weight Range: 7.7 to to 33 lbs.
Comments: Around since 1999 (but recently introduced in the U.S.), the BabaSling allows you to carry your baby in five different positions (three carrying positions, two breastfeeding positions). They use heavy duty "ski buckles" to secure and adjust the sling. The shoulder straps are padded as well as the sides of the sling. Fabrics include solid colors, plus one pattern. They have organic options as well as lighter weight, warm weather styles (the BabaSling Lite). Overall, parents are happy with the BabaSling. Some have complained that it's too tight or too complicated to figure out. If you need more adjustability, a ring sling gives you that. Joovy's web site does have videos to help parents use it correctly.

As a side note, there is a similar Australian sling called Baba Sling (without the "The"). We have not reviewed this sling. The Joovy version has a Joovy logo on the front. ***Rating: B-***

BABY K'TAN

babyktan.com
Price: $50 to $60.
Weight Range: 8 to 35 lbs.
Comments: The best thing about a Baby K'Tan carrier: it rests on both shoulders. That's right, unlike the usual slings, which lay across your body and put the weight on one shoulder, the K'Tan distributes the weight evenly.

Another plus: it works like a mei tai, but you don't have to do any wrapping or knotting and you don't have all that excess fabric.

However, when baby is placed in certain positions, a sash must be tied around baby and your waist for additional support (comes with your purchase). Great videos on the web site tell you how to choose the correct size, how to use the carrier and how to remove it as well. Fabrics are all cotton except for the Breeze version which is a mesh fabric for hot weather.

New this year is the Baby K'Tan Active which is made of a hi-tech polyester fabric. It blocks UVA and UVB rays and wicks away moisture. All the carriers now have a personalization option—you can get your baby's name embroidered on the sling for $15.

One complaint we hear: the Baby K'Tan works best for young or small babies. Once you get beyond 20 lbs., they tell us it's too small. Others are frustrated by the sizing: either it's too tight or too loose, or the fabric stretches out too much. But those issues are the exceptions. Most parents love their Baby K'Tan sling carrier. ***Rating: A-***

BALBOA BABY SLING BY DR. SEARS

BalboaBaby.com

Price: $60.

Maximum weight: 8 to 35 lbs.

Comments: Dr. Sears was the original advocate for "baby wearing." He worked for years with NoJo (owned by Crown Crafts) who manufactured his version of a sling. Now he's moved on to a new manufacturer, Balboa Baby, which is making his approved slings. It's basically a pouch with a contoured and padded strap that slips through an adjustable ring system. There is elastic and padding around the edges that help create the pouch and a small front pocket for minimal storage. Parent feedback is mixed on this sling: fans liked the comfortable padded strap while others complain that if they don't position baby just right, the sling becomes quite uncomfortable. Check YouTube for videos to help you position your baby correctly. Parents also noted it works best for small infants. Once they hit 15 lbs. it's difficult to wear for long periods. ***Rating: B***

HOTSLINGS ADJUSTABLE POUCH

HotSlings.com

Price: $38 to $52

Weight Range: 8 lbs. to 35 lbs.

Comments: They were here; they were gone; they're baaack! Yep, HotSlings has been revived. So how have the new owners changed HotSlings? Their new adjustable slings (called AP or adjustable pouches) come in two sizes which can adjust to fit nine size ranges based on a measurement across your body from shoulder to hip. The fabric now has higher thread counts and they're using more durable buckles (no rings here) than in the past.

HotSlings AP comes in 14 fabrics for as little as $40 online. Readers like the price and the sling for the most part. Some moms complained that the sling was too small and others recommended waiting until baby can hold her head up. While all carriers have information on how to use their product safely, we like HotSlings safety motto: Visible & Kissable. Easy way to remember how your baby should be seated in the sling. Rating: **B+**

MAMMA'S MILK BABY SLING

mammasmilk.com

Price: $50 to $95 depending on fabric.

Maximum weight: 35 lbs.

Comments: Made of stretch cotton, the Mamma's Milk slings are probably the simplest style of sling available. They are infinitely adjustable and use Aplix (a stronger version of Velcro) to keep the sling in the correct position for the parent. Comfortable foam padding is included in the area where toddlers' legs rest. Most of the designs are made of cotton stretch fabric, although they also offer one solar veil option, three organic fabrics and two beautiful silk fabrics (dry clean only). Videos are available online as well as photos to help you use and adjust your sling. Feedback is positive. **Rating: A**

MAYA WRAP

mayawrap.com

Price: $60 to $80

Weight Range: 8 to 35 lbs.

Comments: Maya Wrap has consistently been recommended to us by readers who love its flexibility and comfort. Helpful instructional videos are available on their web site and a DVD is included with your purchase. The rings are made of 1/4" anodized aluminum, the fabrics are 100% cotton hand-loomed and are only made of one layer of fabric (there is padding at the shoulder area for comfort). As a result, the Maya Wrap is quite lightweight. It comes in four sizes with nearly ten fabric options. Reader feedback on the Maya Wrap is positive, although some parents complain about the long piece of fabric that hangs from the rings when the sling is being used. If you want to avoid a lot of extra fabric, you can size down your wrap so the hanging fabric is shorter. Another complaint: it can be painful to use with older babies or for long periods of time. **Rating: A**

NEW NATIVE BABY CARRIER

newnativebaby.com

Price: $50.

Maximum weight: 35 lbs.

Comments: New Native's focus is eco-friendly slings made from mostly organic cotton. This sling is styled as a one-piece pouch with no adjustments. Check the size chart carefully since you can make the sling smaller, but not larger. That lack of adjustment is a negative here and parents complain that the sizes run small. An infant support pillow can be purchased separately to improve fit for both preemies and newborns. Online instructional videos are available as are written instructions on the web site. Recently, we noticed New Native has a factory seconds option with carriers priced as low as $20. ***Rating: B-***

THE PEANUT SHELL

thepeanutshell.com

Price: $30 to $50.

Maximum weight: Adjustable: 8 to 26 lbs.; Classic: 8 to 36 lbs.

Comments: Peanut Shell was one of our readers' favorite slings a few years back, but the owners were ready to give up the company so they could focus on family and other projects. They were bought out and the new owners completely re-launched the line. They now offer two sling options: Adjustable and Classic.

The Adjustable is a one size fits all sling with a cool safety strap and catch plus padded rails in a stretch cotton fabric. The Classic comes in two sizes (S/M and L/XL), includes a pocket for storage and has only light leg padding.

Parents definitely had mixed feelings about the Peanut Shell Adjustable. For some it worked great, but others complained that it was difficult to use, couldn't safely accommodate a newborn and was hard to adjust. Parents like the Classic version better as long as you get the correct size. So it's a mixed bag for the Peanut Shell. ***Rating: B***

WALKING ROCK FARM SLING

abaybe.com

Price: $58.

Maximum weight: 35 lbs.

Comments: Readers love the Sling Baby Sling because it's so easy to use—no rings, no knots or ties, no tails of fabric hanging down. The strap works like a duffle bag strap—just slide it one way or the other to lengthen or shorten. It's so easy to adjust, maker Walking Rock claims you can hand baby off from one parent to the other without waking your baby. The Sling Baby is available in three fabrics: micro fleece for cold climates, pique air flow fabric for warm climates and "all-climate" Ponte Roma knit. Unfortunately, this sling appears to only be available directly from the abaybe.com web site. ***Rating: A-***

ZoloWear Adjustable Pouch
zolowear.com
Price: $39
Weight Range: 8 to 40 lbs.
Comments: Unlike the ring-design of Zolo Wear's sling, the company's adjustable pouches are a single loop of fabric with a shaped pocket for baby. True to the name, the pouches can be adjusted by using four button holes. The advantage to this: no long tail of fabric. A free instructional DVD is included with the pouch. Reader feedback on the adjustable pouches has been sparse, but given the company's overall reputation, we will recommend them. ***Rating: B***

ZoloWear Sling
zolowear.com
Price: $50 to $125 depending on fabric.
Weight Range: 8 to 35 lbs.
Comments: Zolo Wear's mojo are cool fabrics: cotton (including organic), silk brocade and breathable mesh. Yep, it's the gorgeous silk material (machine washable) that catches your eye. Designed with a front ring, these slings include a front pouch and come in four sizes and two styles (pleated or classic). The Zolo Wear sling can be used with baby in six different positions. Check their web site for sales, plus there is a factory outlet. Reader feedback on Zolo Wear is positive, although a few moms told us it takes a bit of practice to use the sling. An instructional video is included plus you'll find videos and illustrations on their site. If you're trying to choose between a pouch or a traditional sling, the web site offers a comparison of their pros and cons under their FAQ section. ***Rating: A***

Front Carriers

Baby Bjorn Miracle
BabyBjorn.com
Price: $100 to $130, depending on the fabric. See price trend.
Weight: 8 to 26 lbs.
Comments: The Miracle builds on some of the features of Bjorn's other discontinued carriers (the Comfort, mainly). The Miracle has an adjustable waist belt for starters, and includes a

unique measuring tape adjustment inside the carrier so you can make sure the seat is a best fit for your child. For parents, the adjustable weight belt combines with infinite adjust shoulder straps allowing parents to evenly distribute the weight on shoulders and waist, or take weight off either the waist or the shoulders. This makes the fit even more customized. Also, the waist belt flexes as it pivots meaning it stays flat on the stomach and doesn't dig in.

The Miracle was a lot more expensive when it first came out, almost $200! We're pleased to see they've lowered the price significantly. That good news plus the mostly positive reviews from parents make the Miracle a great carrier for infants up to 26 lbs. **Rating A-**

BABY BJORN ONE

BabyBjorn.com

Price: $180

Weight: 8 to 26 lbs. forward facing; up to 33 lbs. inward facing and as a back carrier (over one year of age).

Comments: The Baby Bjorn One is pitched as the Ginsu Knife of baby carriers—it works for infants. And toddlers. As a front carrier—facing in or out. And as a back carrier.

So does it live up to all the hype? Yes, it actually does.

The clever design feature of the Bjorn One is its ability to morph from a carrier that works for the smallest infants to a carrier for larger toddlers. Like the Bjorn Comfort, the One has a waist belt for lumbar support and to distribute the baby's weight on your hips. The carrier has a newborn height position that utilizes a simple zipper to position the baby high up in the carrier and facing inward. No need for a separate infant insert.

Then at about four months—and here's the One's secret sauce—you can unzip the seat and your baby drops down lower in the carrier. This makes the carrier more comfortable for parents as baby gets bigger. An audible click on the buckles let's you know when the carrier is attached properly.

Once your baby hits five months, you can position your baby to look outward and then at 12 months you can convert the One to a back carrier. To use as a backpack carrier, you'll need to adjust it into the wide leg position. Just open the zipper on each side to change from normal to wide leg. You'll want to load your child into the carrier in the front position, then slide the carrier around to your back.

Even though the price tag seems steep, we've seen it online for as little as $135. And let's look at what it would cost to buy a carrier that morphs into all these uses: a basic front carrier (that works for infants) runs about $75 to $125. To get a carrier that also works for toddlers and as a back carrier, you'd have to shell out another $100

carriers

or more. So that makes the One seem reasonable, especially if you are an attachment parenting fan and want to carry your baby beyond the newborn stage.

So what are parents telling us about the One? Most are enthusiastic about it. They love the flexibility and find the waist belt quite comfortable. While some complain it took a while to figure out how to get the carrier on in all positions, others noted that it is easy to adjust and transfer between different size parents. Baby Bjorn has hit a home run with the One. *Rating: A*

BABY BJORN ORIGINAL

BabyBjorn.com
Price: $60, depending on the fabric.
Weight: 8 to 25 lbs.
Comments: Baby Bjorn is the 800-pound gorilla in the carrier category. The Original is the carrier that made the company famous. As one of the first easy to use, adjustable options, it set the bar for other front carriers. Baby can ride facing in or out and, best of all, you can snap off the front of the Bjorn to put a sleeping baby down in a crib.

The Active ($190), based on the Original design but with added lumbar support and wider straps for longer walks, is being discontinued although some web sites are still selling through their inventory.

Baby Bjorn consistently gets high ratings from parents who purchase front carriers—they like the ease of use and the fact that baby can face outward eventually. But detractors point to the high price and limited use (babies outgrow it fast). Plus size moms, as well as moms with larger breasts, complain the Original is uncomfortable because babies sit so high. Back/neck strain is a common complaint of Bjorn users. Some babies also don't like the Bjorn for whatever reason. We recommend keeping the receipt just in case you have a picky baby. *Rating: B*

BABYHAWK OH SNAP!

BabyHawk.com
Price: $113 to $150
Weight Range: 15 to 45 lbs.
Comments: It's a bit difficult when you visit BabyHawk's web site to find the information about the Oh SNAP! carrier—click on "in-stock carriers" to locate them (they're also available on Amazon.com now). A soft structure carrier similar to the Ergobaby, the Oh SNAP! has triple padded top straps and a foam core bottom strap with adjustable webbing and buckles. BabyHawk also offers customizing options on their website. Choose a main fabric and a strap color or you can use your own fabric. And the site does have some ready-made Oh SNAPs! for $115 to $130. All their

carriers are made in the U.S.

The only complaints we heard about this carrier were from petite or small framed women who couldn't get a comfortable fit because the waist belt was too wide across their backs. For average size women, this carrier should work just great. **Rating: A-**

BABY TREKKER

babytrekker.com

Price: $150

Weight Range: 8 to 50 lbs.

Comments: Baby Trekker was first recommended to us by our Canadian readers who raved about this made-in-Canada, multi-use carrier. Yes, it works as your typical front carrier with baby facing in when young and out when older. But the carrier also has a cool nursing option and a backpack position allows baby to either face your back or out to see the world (though not until your baby is at least three months old or 15 lbs.). Special safety straps in the carrier are recommended when baby is under 16 lbs. to keep her from slipping out of the leg holes. And Baby Trekker also offers accessory stirrups for toddlers 18 and older for additional support ($14).

The Trekker stores in its own attached pocket making it easy to pack in your diaper bag. All six colors are organic cotton. We liked the extra padding under every buckle for baby's comfort. FYI: As we were going to press, we noticed that Baby Trekker has ceased prodution, unfortunatley. As a result, you may have to search eBay or other second-hand sources to find this carrier. **Rating: A**

BECO GEMINI

BecoBabyCarrier.com

Price: $130 to $180 (depending on fabric).

Weight Range: 7 to 35 lbs.

Comments: Unlike Beco's Butterfly 2 carrier, the Gemini allows baby to face forward. It comes with head support, waist belt, adjustable chest strap and adjustable base. This base alternates to allow for small infants facing mom, then, when baby gets bigger, facing out. You don't need a separate infant insert. And you can also adjust the carrier so baby rides on your back or hip. Reader feedback on the Gemini is overwhelmingly positive. Yes, it is pricey, but a bit less than the Butterfly 2. **Rating: A**

BELLE BABY CARRIER

BelleBabyCarriers.com

Price: $40 to $60 directly from Belle Baby; $84 to $130 online.

Weight Range: 8 to 35 lbs.

Comments: Looking for a lightweight, easy to pack

carrier? Belle Baby carriers forgo all the extra padding to make a lighter, cooler carrier that allows baby to face both in and out. Based in California, they are made of microsuede and mesh with cotton/spandex lining. They offer two collections: the Cruz (more padding at waist belt, shoulder straps and leg openings) and the Fit (no padding). A removable head support comes with the carrier for sleeping babies.

We liked the ergonomic design and how the densely padded straps on the Cruz cross in the back like the Baby Trekker. Buckles are similar to what you see in quality backpacks. An independent waist belt puts the weight on your hips, not your back. *Rating: A-*

BOBA 4G

Boba.com
Price: $125
Weight Range: 7 to 45 lbs.
Comments: For parents who want to begin baby wearing immediately with their newborn, our readers recommend the Boba 4G. The beauty of this carrier: you can use it for newborns with a special integrated insert. And it works with children seven to 45 lbs. as a front or back carrier. No, you can't face baby out (and that's really the only negative here) but it has pretty cool accessory foot straps that attach to the adult waist belt for toddlers being carried on the back. Additional features include a lowered shoulder strap connection, slightly wider seat and stronger buckles. The sleep hood is also lighter and longer. Compared to similar carriers like the Ergobaby, parents liked the longer body and less bulky straps on the Boba. *Rating: A*

BRITAX BABY CARRIER

BritaxUSA.com
Price: $80
Weight Range: 8 to 32 lbs.
Comments: Britax has slowly been adding categories to its product lines over the years. Originally, car seats was their mojo, then strollers. And now they've added a front carrier with the exciting name of (drumroll) the Britax Baby Carrier.

The carrier's key feature: Britax's CarryLong System, a padded waist belt and shoulder straps that claim to "distribute weight across shoulders, back and hips for maximum extended wear comfort." The carrier includes a multitude of features: padded leg openings; easy on/off design with one hand buckles and snaps; easy adjust front harness straps; "easy-adjust waist belt" (22" to 56"); bib; adjustable head support; leg loops sized for small infants. Whew! Clearly, Britax did their homework.

The Baby Carrier used to carry a price tag of $130, making it comparable to a Bjorn. But we notice that online prices hover around $80, making it a more reasonably priced option.

Whatever the price, is it worth it? Feedback is mixed. Parents really seem to like the high weight limit—the Britax Baby Carrier can be used up to 32 lbs., versus the Bjorn carriers which only go up to between 22 and 26 lbs. The carrier's light weight (3 lbs.) also comes in for praise. But some parents complain the carrier doesn't fit well or adjust easily. This negative feedback leads us to lower Britax's rating a bit. ***Rating: B***

CATBIRD BABY PIKKOLO
CatBirdBaby.com
Price: $130.
Weight Range: 8 to 40 lbs.
Comments: Maker Catbird Baby started off with a mei tai carrier, but recently expanded into a soft carrier with buckles. The straps are shorter than a mei tai, addressing a common complaint with those carriers. The Pikkolo can be used front and rear facing, on the back and on the hip like a mei tai. They offer it in only one size and recommend their original mei tai if you are very petite or large. The Pikkolo comes with an attached hood, memory foam straps, chest strap to use in the piggyback position and instruction booklet. Fabric options are limited (one solid, two patterns), made of brushed cotton canvas. Reader feedback on the Pikkolo has been very positive—the hybrid style of a soft carrier with mei tai like options makes it a favorite. Our only complaint: we wish they had videos on their site to show parents how to use the Pikkolo. ***Rating: A***

ERGOBABY 360°
ErgoBaby.com
Price: $160
Weight Range: 8 to 35 lbs.
Comments: One concern for forward-facing carriers is the risk for hip dysplasia. Some carriers unintentionally position baby's legs in an unhealthy position where the legs are dangling; this can be a risk for hip dysplasia if the carrier is used for an extended period of time. The Ergobaby 360° attempts to address this issue with an innovative design—the carrier can be worn front or back, with baby facing front or back. (Ergobaby's original carrier only allowed for baby to face in).

Why the switch to a carrier that allows for forward facing? Ergobaby notes that they've had many requests for just such an option over the years. And they claim they've found a way to allow baby to face out without worry of hip issues. The new 360° is made with a structured bucket seat that effectively avoids the dangling legs problem. It comes with a wide waist belt which can be worn high when baby is little and adjusted down to carry the weight of older babies and toddlers. The forward facing carry is recommended for babies six months old and older.

The Ergobaby 360° allows you to wear your child in four positions like the Baby Bjorn One ($250) but at $160, it's considerably less than the One. Feedback from parents has been mostly positive. They like the fact the 360° doesn't require a special infant insert for little ones plus it's super easy to use. And they're happy to be able to face baby out, a position unavailable with the original Ergo. Some did complain they didn't like the hood (too small; doesn't store away), and the back latch is uncomfortable/hard to buckle. But these are minor quibbles—overall, parents are very pleased with this carrier **Rating: A**

ERGOBABY ORIGINAL BABY CARRIER
ErgoBabyCarrier.com
Price: $115 to $140 depending on fabric.
Weight Range: 7 to 45 lbs. (7 to 12 lbs. with optional newborn insert, priced separately)
Comments: Made by Hawaii-based Ergobaby, the Ergobaby Original carrier has won kudos on our boards for its ease of use (you can wear it in front or back or on the hip) and less strain on the back. While most front carriers put the strain on your shoulders and back, the Ergobaby comes with a padded hip belt that takes the strain off your upper back.

Best of all, you can use it from birth (with a newborn insert, $22 to $38) up to an amazing 45 lbs. (toddlers)—most front carriers can only be used for a short time (the Bjorn limit is 25 lbs.). And the Ergobaby can be used as a hip carrier. One important caveat: you cannot face your baby out when wearing it in the front position; baby always rides facing you. On the plus side, Ergobaby offers four versions: Original, Performance (special light-weight fabric), Organic, and Designer (exclusive prints).

Feedback on the Ergobaby is mostly positive. In fact, the only negatives parents note are a bit of a learning curve and the fact that you have to buy the infant insert or wait till baby is 12 lbs. Another issue: the carrier can be quite hot for babies in the summer months with its cocooning fabric. Otherwise, they praise lack of back pain and the comfortable straps and belt. **Rating: A-**

KINDERCARRY KINDERPACK
KinderCarry.com
Price: $180
Weight Range: Infant version is 8 to 50 lbs.; Standard is 18 to 50 lbs.; Toddler is 25 to 50 lbs.; Preschool is 35 to 50 lbs.
Comments: Kindercarry offers yet another version of the Soft Structured Carrier (SSC): the Kinderpack. This carrier is sort of an

amalgamation of other styles with a structured body but straps that work a little like a mei tai. Except they don't tie, they buckle. Anyway, the real selling point is that they are very wide so they support legs rather than leave them dangling and they can accommodate large kids. They come in four sizes. The newborn size has an adjustable base that changes the crotch width to accommodate infants. The standard version works for babies starting at 20 lbs., the toddler is for 25 lbs. and up and the preschool model works starting at 35 lbs. (if you can carry your child at that point!).

All the carriers are rated up to 50 lbs. although its doubtful you could carry a child that size. Kinderpacks come with buckles on the contoured straps and waistband, a hood, and contoured body panel made of canvas and twill. Handy videos help explain how to use your Kinderpack. Parents comment that they like Kinderpacks but would mainly recommend them for older children and they are expensive compared to other soft structured carriers. However, feedback is very positive so we'll give them our recommendation. ***Rating: A***

LILLEBABY COMPLETE

lillebaby.com

Price: $115 to $150

Weight Range: 7 to 45 lbs.

Comments: Lillebaby boasts their carrier, the Complete, "offers more carrying positions, lasts longer and includes more features than any other carrier." Them's fightin' words, you might say, if you were in the carrier business.

So are their claims true? Yes, in our opinion. The Complete can be used in a fetal position (inward facing with legs inside the carrier), inward facing with legs out, forward facing, hip carry, and back carry (facing in or out). The Complete also includes a hood and neck support. And the company offers a host of fabrics including organic cotton, airflow breathable mesh and new "All Seasons" fabric (warm in winter, cool in summer).

Fans of the Complete love the flexibility of Lillebaby's carriers. The lumbar support, light weight and extra long shoulder straps—no extensions needed—are also plusses. The only complaints from readers: Lillebaby no longer includes a front pocket on the newest versions, the carriers can be bulky and they may work better with older/bigger babies. Despite these drawbacks, we think the Lillebaby Complete is a winner. So we'll give this carrier our top rating. ***Rating: A***

MAMAS & PAPAS MORPH

MamasandPapas.com

Price: $75 to $139

Weight: 8 lbs. to 27 lbs.

Comments: Mamas and Papas front carrier, the Morph, is the product of lots of parent research—and that's a good thing. First they discovered that most parents are flummoxed when they take their carrier out of the box. So the Morph is meant to be intuitive out of the box. The straps go on just like a jacket, not over your head, and it snaps and zips together. Another plus: the Morph allows parents to adjust the shoulder straps and waist strap easily for a great fit. The carrier comes in two sizes (sm/med and med/lg) and additional harnesses are available ($22 to $65 each). One hand adjustable straps and waist belt are wide and well padded with lumbar support built in.

Putting baby in the harness is simple too. The "pod" (structured pouch for baby) has adjustable sides and slides into the front belt then snaps to the harness straps. The pod also includes a head rest and dribble cloth. Baby can be positioned facing in or out. Cost for the complete set of harness and pod runs $139 and comes in five colors.

So what do we think of the Morph? We're impressed. It has features similar to Baby Bjorn's $200 Miracle at a much better price. Most parents like it although a few noted it's more complicated than the company claims. Their favorite feature is how easy it is to transfer baby from one person to another (if you buy another harness). *Rating: A*

MOBY WRAP MOBY GO
MobyWrap.com
Price: $63
Weight Range: 15 to 45 lbs.
Comments: The Moby GO is a structured soft carrier manufactured by the folks who gave us the Moby Wrap. Intended for older babies from 15 to 45 lbs., the GO has straps that cross at the shoulders to distribute baby's weight similar to the Pikkolo carrier. The carrier includes a padded waist belt and uses buckles to secure baby. You can loosen the straps to remove baby without having to unbuckle it. One complaint: this carrier does not allow for back carrying like other soft carriers. Older babies might prefer a back carry position to the front carry, especially since baby can't face out either.

Parental feedback is mostly positive. It's much easier to put on, take off and adjust than the Moby Wrap plus it's very affordable. Only complaint: newborns can't use this carrier and they don't offer an infant insert. But overall, we'll recommended the Moby GO. *Rating: A-*

STOKKE MYCARRIER
Stokke.com
Price: $210
Maximum weight: 7.7 to 33 lbs.
Comments: After seeing the $200+ price tag mentioned above, we're betting we lost quite a few dear readers before we even got to the comments section. For those of you still

with us, yes, that is quite a hefty investment—the pitch is the MyCarrier by Stokke also works for kids as a backpack carrier up to 33 pounds (about three years of age).

The carrier comes with one harness and two pouches. The first pouch works facing in from birth then facing out at about four months. The second pouch is for kids that can sit up on their own and are at least 28 inches tall.

The harness includes a support belt for parents as well as two pockets for keys, etc., a chest clip and an integrated sunshade/sleep support. Carabiners are used to attach the pouches to the harness as well as quite a few buttons and zippers. In fact, you might be a bit overwhelmed when you first try to put together your MyCarrier. To help, Stokke has posted detailed how-to videos on its site for the MyCarrier. After watching these, however, we can guess some folks will still be flummoxed by the carrier's ease of use, or lack thereof.

The back carrying position seems to be the MyCarrier's secret weapon. Stokke includes an aluminum support bar with the carrier (this is installed down the back of the carrier for extra support). Again, the online video is helpful. This added feature is a real must have when you want to use this carrier with older children. Now that Baby Bjorn has come out with the One which has similar features, the Stokke faces some tough competition

As you might expect from eco-focused Stokke, the carrier uses only organic fabrics. Yet, for this amount of money, we kept looking for gold leaf accents on the MyCarrier. They also make a MyCarrier Cool with breathable fabric ($200-$220). Parent feedback has been mixed. Some parents complain about a lack of padding in the shoulder straps, and it can be difficult to put on. Others, however, liked that the carrier doesn't require an infant insert and grows with the child. Overall we think the Stokke has enough negatives to assign them only an average rating. ***Rating: C***

TULA ERGONOMIC BABY

TulaBabyCarriers.com
Price: $150 (baby version); $170 (toddler version)
Weight Range: 15 lbs. to 45 lbs.; 8 lbs. to 15 lbs. with infant insert
Comments: Tula's founders, Ula and Mike, were inspired by their travels all over the world to use carriers when their children were born. But they were never really satisfied with existing carriers on the market. So they designed their own: the Tula Ergonomic Baby Carrier. The design allows parents to use it as both a front and back carrier. FYI: baby cannot face out when in the front carry position (similar to the Ergobaby Original).

The Tula features organic cotton fabrics, a hood for support and sun protection, hip belt for parent support with a pocket for storage, padded adjustable shoulder straps and leg openings. To use a Tula with infants, there is a separate insert (included).

One unique feature: Tula offers a $30 two week rental of their carriers in case you want to try them out first. If you decide to purchase, you get a $15 off coupon, so you recoup half your rental fee. Of course, there is an easier alternative: you could just order a carrier from Amazon, try it out and return it if it's not right for you. But we salute Tula for giving parents a try before you buy option.

So what do readers think of Tula? Most thought it was easy to use and very comfortable. Fans like how easy it is to adjust between different size parents. The only negative, as we mentioned above: baby can only face toward the parent when in the forward-facing position. And Tula is a bit pricey—a similar Ergobaby is about 20% less. But Tula includes an infant insert, which is an extra $20-$40 accessory for Ergobaby. So in the end, it is a wash.

With all the positive feedback, we'll give the Tula Ergonomic Baby Carrier a top rating. FYI, the company also has a carrier for older babies: Tula Toddler Carrier ($170) works for kids 18 months to 4 years of age. It's made of the same fabric with similar features to the baby carrier. ***Rating: A***

Mei Tai/Asian Carriers

BABYHAWK
babyhawk.com
Price: $89 to $99.
Weight Range: Two sizes: newborn to 40 lbs. and 15 to 40 lbs.

Comments: BabyHawk offers quite a few options to custom design your own mei tai. Start with a strap color (6 options) and main body color (over 40), and then decide whether you want extra long straps ($5), toy rings ($5 each) or reversible fabric ($10). Without all the extras, a basic BabyHawk is $85. Unfortunately, BabyHawk has changed their web site, removing the prices for each feature, meaning you'll have to choose features then see the final price. If you just want to buy an in-stock mei tai, we saw 13 options available when we last visited.

BabyHawk makes two types of mei tais: one for smaller babies up to 40 lbs. and the other for older babies to 15 to 40 lbs. (called the ToddlerHawk). This allows for a more customized fit.

We like all the unique fabrics including Amy Butler designs as well as florals, Asian prints, and geometrics. Like other mei tais, BabyHawk can be used in front, back or on the hip. Readers most like the customization options (but be forewarned: customized BabyHawks are non-returnable) and the comfortable fabrics. On the other hand, some readers complained that the straps were too long . . . and it takes a while to figure out how to use these carriers. **Rating: A**

CATBIRD BABY MEI TAI

CatBirdBaby.com

Price: $85 to $99

Weight: 8 to 40 lbs.

Comments: Catbird Baby makes one of our favorite front carriers, the Pikkolo, so we were excited to see they also make a mei tai. Priced at around $100 and available in 12 fabric options, this is a great choice for parents who want carrier flexibility. You can use the Catbird mei tai in four positions including front carry, forward facing. For parents with older, heavier babies Catbird sells a support belt ($25) to make it more comfortable. In fact, this is our only complaint about the brand: it would be nice if the support belt came with the mei tai. Regardless, fans give the Catbird Baby excellent reviews and the reasonable price leads us to rate them highly. **Rating A-**

KOZY CARRIER

kozycarrier.com

Price: $90

Weight Range: 8 to 40 lbs.

Comments: Kozy Carrier's mei tai-inspired carrier has no buckles or rings—just tie it on. You'll notice it has wide shoulder straps with light padding, a lightly padded curved head support and is reversible. Extra long straps are available as an option ($5 additional) . All Kozy Carriers are made to order so you can customize them to your taste: pick a base fabric (natural, black or canvas) and a solid or print accent fabric plus a pocket can be added for $10. Like other mei tai carriers, baby can be worn in front (facing in or out), on the side or on your back and used for infants up to toddlers. You'll need to check the web site for instructions on how to use the carrier. Reader feedback has been quite positive on the Kozy Carrier.

FYI: Kozy Carrier was recently bought by a New Zealand couple (owners of a baby store and long time supporters of the Kozy Carrier). They continue to sell the carrier in the U.S. in nearly 80 stores. **Rating: A**

Wrap Around Carriers

BOBA WRAP

BobaFamily.com

Price: $38 to $50

Weight Range: 7 to 35 lbs.

Comments: Boba Wrap gets universally positive

feedback from readers. And it's priced very affordably. Made of cotton with a bit of spandex for stretch, this wrap is relatively easy for newbies to get the hang of. The key is make sure you get a very snug fit to yourself before you put baby in. That spandex makes it really work, but if it's too loose when you put baby in, it will begin to sag and hurt your back. The online videos and graphic instructions are helpful since you tie this wrap rather differently from similar products. We especially love the "helpful tips" section of the instructions plus the numerous safety reminders. Parents note that the fabric holds its shape well even after long term use although it can be a pain for beginners to use. ***Rating: A***

ERGOBABY WRAP

ErgoBaby.com
Price: $80
Weight Range: 7-45 lbs.
Comments: Wrap carriers have long had a disadvantage for a lot of moms: you can get it tight enough to support baby for awhile, but eventually it stretches out with use. Ergobaby thinks they've solved the problem. They call their Wrap a "hybrid": strong like a woven but with added stretch equally in all directions. They claim this will cause the wrap to rebound back to its original shape after every use. And you can remove and put your child back in the carrier multiple times without re-wrapping. Baby can be wrapped into six different positions and folds into it's own pocket. Parent feedback is mostly positive with most complaints centered around frustration around a steep learning curve with all the fabric. ***Rating: B+***

GYPSY MAMA WRAPSODY

gypsymama.com
Price: $70 to $90.
Maximum weight: 35 lbs.
Comments: Gypsy Mama makes three Wrapsody wraps in different fabrics: the Wrap DuO (can be used in water $70), The Breeze Wraps (cotton gauze, $80), and the Stretch-Hybrid (like t-shirt material, $86, pictured).

The Breeze wraps are the lightest weight but not stretchy and are made of fabric hand dyed and batiked in Bali. It folds down into a built-in storage pocket, making it easy to toss in the diaper bag. Gypsy Mama recommends the Stretch-Hybrid wraps ($84) for beginners as they are "more forgiving of sloppy wrap jobs." The fabric is similar to a t-shirt and is very soft for both newborns and older kids.

The Wrap DuO is made to use in the water and on land for babies until they reach about 35 lbs. in the water or 25 lbs. on land.

Made of high tech sports knit, it's intended to keep mom and baby cool on those hot summer days.

Online instructions (both videos and printed) were clear and easy to follow. We recommend the Breeze for parents in hot climates or for summer wearing. ***Rating: A***

MOBY WRAP

mobywrap.com

Price: $42 to $60.

Weight Range: 8 to 35 lbs.

Comments: Moby Wraps are one-size-fits-all carriers designed to allow moms to adjust the fit by how tight they wrap the baby. The wrap uses three sections of fabric for extra security. The lack of padding means its not bulky to wear or store. They use cotton stretch fabric to get a close fit to the body. The Original version sells for $42 to $45 and comes in solid colors. Fabrics get fancier with cute patterns ($50) and organics ($63). But the most expensive options are the Dolcino styles made with organic yarn from Germany for up to $160.

You can expect some shrinkage when you wash the Moby Wrap, although they add extra fabric to account for that. A downside: it takes a bit of time to learn to use it, and even once you have it figured out, the Moby Wrap takes some time to put on. Although they include an instruction book with each wrap, you'll want to check YouTube for video help as well. The Moby Wrap can be used for both front and back wearing. Parent reviews are mostly positive, with the exception of the learning curve. Plus size moms will love the Moby Wrap as it can be adjusted to any parent's body type. ***Rating: B+***

VATANAI

vatanai.cz

Price: $145.

Weight Range: 8 to 35 lbs.

Comments: Manufactured in the Czech Republic, Vatanai wraps have a world wide following. In the U.S., they are sold on GranolaBabys.com. Vatanai wraps are made of lightweight cotton and are recommended for warm climates. They can be tied in eight different ways from cradle carries to hip to backpack style. They claim to have a unique "cross-wise stretch" that makes them easier to tie plus a three year guarantee. While instructions are included, check YouTube for videos to help you the first few times. These wraps are available in four sizes from 4 to 5.5 meters of fabric. ***Rating: A***

Hip Carriers

CUDDLE KARRIER
cuddlekarrier.com
Price: $60
Maximum weight: up to six years of age; we recommend three years

Comments: Cuddle Karrier won't win any design awards for their web site, but their hip carrier is the Swiss Army knife of carriers. It converts from carrier to shopping cart restraint, high chair cover . . . and four more uses. The Cuddle Karrier adjusts and repositions with just one hand (the online video is helpful to see this). One caveat: you may need a waist belt to make the Cuddle Karrier work most comfortably. Oddly, the site doesn't sell this accessory, but you can use a regular belt threaded through the crotch strap. ***Rating: B-***

ORIGINAL HIP HAMMOCK
hiphammock.com
Price: $54
Weight Range: 15 lbs. to three years of age
Comments: The Original Hip Hammock was designed to make the usual baby-on-the-hip carry easier on moms' backs. Attach the waist belt, slide your baby into the seat, then wrap the shoulder strap around your back and snap to the front of the carrier. In a nutshell, it is similar to a messenger bag. The Hip Hammock only works with children who are at least 15 pounds, so it's not for newborns. FYI: avoid the Playtex version of the Hip Hammock—readers didn't like it much and it was involved in a recall, both in 2005 and again in 2013. ***Rating: A-***

SCOOTABABY HIP CARRIER
scootababy.com
Price: $120.
Weight Range: 12 to 37 lbs.
Comments: Scootababy makes just one product: a hip carrier that's a bit like a mei tai and a bit like a sling. It positions baby to sit on your hip (although you can use it as a back pack or front carrier too) by using a wide, padded strap that goes around your back and over the shoulder. The wide, padded waist belt provides added support and the body of the carrier is shaped to fit your baby. Videos on the site are helpful. Overall, parents rave about their Scootababy hip carrier. The only downside: price. At $120, Scootababy is pretty expensive. ***Rating: A-***

WALKING ROCK FARM HIP BABY

abaybe.com

Price: $78 to $98

Maximum weight: 44 lbs.

Comments: We mentioned Walking Rock Farm's sling in another section, but their hip carrier is the company's biggest seller. The Hip Baby comes in three types of fabric: Inprints, which is a lycra knit with heat reducing lining; Cooler II, a waterproof fabric with breathable lining; and Air Flow, a special water proof athletic fabric. Walking Rock touts their strap for its length and no-slip padding. A few readers complain the strap digs into their necks, despite the padding. The Hip Baby adjusts pretty much the same way all-hip carriers work with a backslide adjustment. All in all, this is a good choice among hip carriers. ***Rating: B+***

Frame Carriers

DEUTER KID COMFORT II

Deuter.com

Price: $250

Maximum weight: 48.5 lbs.

Comments: Deuter is a German company with a long history in this category—Deuter rucksacks debuted in 1934 and were used on expeditions to the Himalayas in 1953. The company branched out into child carriers in 1991 and now offers four models. The most popular version is the Kid Comfort II (pictured), which features a contoured hip belt, zipped compartment under the seat, 35-point harness, side entry, large mesh storage pockets, and breathable seat cushions. Parents love the multiple adjustments for parent and child, as well as the storage. Others rave about how comfortable it is. The only complaint: more than one reader told us they hate the Kid Comfort's numerous zippers. ***Rating: A-***

KELTY TRANSIT 3.0 CHILD CARRIER

Web: *kelty.com*

Price: $200 retail

Weight Range: 16 lbs. to 30 lbs.

Comments: While the Kelty Transit 3.0 requires a lot of adjustment at first to get baby strapped in, readers tell us this backpack carrier is one of the best options on the market. The adjustable lumbar support gets kudos, parents find it easy to get on and off, and it is comfortable for long hikes. Kelty includes features like a sun hood, changing pad, toy loops, organizer pocket, and hip-belt water bottle pocket. Kelty offers four other frame carrier options—readers like the Transit 3.0 best. ***Rating: A***

TOUGH TRAVELER KID CARRIER

This carrier is reviewed on the free side of our web site at BabyBargains.com/?p=5112

Our picks: Brand recommendations

Here are our top carrier recommendations:

In the sling category, we have a tie: the **Mama's Milk** baby sling ($50-$75) and the **Maya Wrap** ($80). Parents love the simplicity of the Mama's Milk and the flexibility and comfort of the Maya Wrap.

In the front carrier category, our top pick for front carriers this year is the **Ergobaby 360°**. As one reader put it: "finally a front facing Ergo!" The new structured bucket seat makes forward facing more comfortable for baby and avoids those dangling legs. You can wear baby in four different positions like the Baby Bjorn One, but at $160, it's a lot less expensive. And parents love it!

Our runner up is last year's top pick, the **Cat Bird Baby Pikkolo** ($130). It's really a mash-up of a front carrier and a mei tai with buckles instead of long ties. It's also more flexible than most other front carriers—it can be used in front facing both in and out, on the back and as a hip carrier.

What about a recommendation for the soft structured carrier sub category? We do have a top pick for those of you who don't mind that baby can't face out: the **Boba 4G Carrier** ($125). This one can be used as a front carrier comfortably by babies without a special insert (it's already integrated into the design) and it goes up to 45 lbs. as a back carrier.

Let's talk hip carriers. If you have an older child and want to try hip carrying, the best option is the **Original Hip Hammock** for $54. It's easy to use and easy on your wallet. Just make sure you avoid the Playtex Hip Hammock.

Mei tais or Asian carriers have really made inroads in the carrier market. Our top pick for this category is the **BabyHawk** ($80-$100). The customization options, great fabrics and ease of use made this mei tai a favorite. The **Kozy Carrier** ($90) mei tai is a runner-up.

Wrap carriers have front and back carrying flexibility. Our favorite is the **Wrapsody Baby Breeze** gauze carrier ($85). If you get hot when wearing your baby, this is the coolest, lightest fabric on the market.

Finally, frame carriers. For those up for long hikes with baby, a frame carrier is a great option. Our favorite is the **Kelty Transit 3.0** ($200). It's comfortable for parents and baby, easy to use and reasonably priced. A runner-up is the **Deuter Kid Comfort II** ($250) It's got everything you could ever need: adjustability, storage and great safety features.

CHAPTER 11

CONCLUSION

What Does it All Mean?

ow much money can you save if you follow all the
tips and suggestions in this book? Let's take a look
at the average cost of having a baby from the introduction and compare it with our Baby Bargains budget.

Your Baby's First Year

ITEM	AVERAGE	BABY BARGAINS BUDGET
Crib, mattress, dresser, rocker	$1570	$1433
Bedding / Decor	$350	$222
Baby Clothes	$615	$301
Disposable Diapers	$865	$400
Maternity/Nursing Clothes	$1300	$550
Nursery items, high chair, toys	$515	$225
Baby Food/Formula	$1015	$350
Stroller, Car Seats, Carrier	$730	$490
Miscellaneous	$490	$500
TOTAL	$7450	$4323
TOTAL SAVINGS:		**$3127**

WOW! You just saved over $3100! We hope the sav-
ings makes it worth the price of this book. We'd love to hear from
you on how much you saved with our book—feel free to email, write
or call us. See the "How to Reach Us" page at the back of this book.

What does it all mean?

At this point, we usually have something pithy to say as we end
the book. But, as parents of two boys, we're just too tired. We're
going to bed, so feel free to make up your own ending.

And thanks for reading *Baby Bargains*.

conclusion

APPENDIX A

Registry Cheat Sheets

Time is tight—we know. So to help juice your baby registry, here are the Baby Bargains Registry Cheat Sheets.

These sample registries follow our Good, Better, Best recommendations earlier in the book. If you need more detail about a particular recommendation, see the index to find a full review. Enjoy!

Good

Item	Baby Bargains recommends	Price
Crib	IKEA Sniglar	$70
Mattress	Lullaby Earth Super Lightweight	$170
Dresser	Ikea Hemnes 3-Drawer Chest	$149
Changing pad	Summer Infant Contoured Changing Pad	$20
Glider Rocker	Dutailier Ultramotion Glider	$390
Bedding	American Baby Co. sheets (4)	$52
Wearable blanket	Halo SleepSack	$16
Breast pump	Medela Swing mini-electric	$150
Bottles	The First Years Breastflow Starter Set	$16
High Chair	Fisher-Price Space Saver	$42
Bathtub	First Year's Infant to Toddler Tub with Sling	$29
Potty seat	Fisher Price Precious Planet Potty	$13
Audio monitor*	VTech Safe & Sound Digital Audio Monitor	$40
Video Monitor	Infant Optics DXR-5	$99
Play Yard/Bassinet	Joovy Room2 Portable Play Yard	$104
Bouncer	Fisher Price Comfy Time Bouncer	$32
Humidifier	Honeywell HCM-350	$70
Swing	Kids II's InGenuity Power Adapt Swing	$90
Safety gate	KidCo Safeway Gates (2)	$86
Thermometer	Safety 1st Gentle Read Rectal Thermometer	$9
Infant Car Seat	Graco SnugRide Click Connect 40	$170
Convertible Seat	Cosco Scenera Next	$46
Stroller	Chicco C6 Capri	$70
Diaper Bag	SoHo diaper bag	$35
Carrier	Mama's Milk baby sling	$50
Clothing	Wait until after showers; see page 201.	
TOTAL		**$2018**

Better

Item	*Baby Bargains recommends*	Price
Crib	DaVinci Kalani	$220
Mattress	Moonlight Slumber Little Dreamer	$190
Dresser	Imagio Baby Summit Park 3-Drawer	$300
Changing pad	Summer Infant Contoured Changing Pad	$20
Glider Rocker	Little Castle Cottage Glider	$825
Bedding	Land of Nod sheets (4)	$96
Wearable blanket	zzZipMeSack	$36
Breast pump	Philips Avent Double Electric Comfort	$200
Bottles	Mam bottle starter set	$20
High Chair	Fisher-Price Healthy Care	$100
Bathtub	EuroBath by Primo	$25
Potty seat	Fisher Price Precious Planet Potty	$13
Audio monitor*	VTech Safe & Sound Digital Audio Monitor	$40
Video Monitor	Samsung's BabyVIEW (SEW-3036WN)	$169
Play Yard/Bassinet	Chicco's Lullaby LX Play Yard	$190
Bouncer	Fisher Price Infant to Toddler Rocker	$40
Humidifier	Honeywell HCM-350	$70
Swing	Graco Glider LX Gliding Swing	$107
Safety gate	KidCo Safeway Gates (2)	$86
Thermometer	Safety 1st Gentle Read Rectal Thermometer	$9
Infant Car Seat	Chicco KeyFit 30	$190
Convertible Seat	Chicco NextFit	$280
Stroller	UPPAbaby G-Lite	$160
Diaper Bag	Ju-Ju-Be Hobo Be	$86
Carrier	Ergobaby 360 baby carrier	$160
Clothing	Wait until after showers; see page 201.	
TOTAL		**$3632**

*Audio monitor is optional—you can get either audio or video. You most likely will NOT need both!

See the next page for the best picks.

registry cheat sheets

SAMPLE REGISTRY

Best

Item	*Baby Bargains recommends*	Price
Crib	Pali Imperia	$400
Mattress	Naturepedic Organic Cotton Lightweight	$260
Dresser	Pali Designs Bolzano Double Dresser	$750
Changing pad	Summer Infant Contoured Changing Pad	$16
Glider Rocker	Dutailier upholstered glider	$1200
Bedding	Carousel crib sheets (4)	$120
Wearable blanket	zzZipMeSack	$36
Breast pump	Medela Pump In Style Advanced	$225
Bottles	Avent Classic Infant Starter Set	$25
High Chair	Graco Blossom	$145
Bathtub	Puj Tub	$45
Potty seat	Fisher Price Precious Planet Potty	$13
Audio monitor*	VTech Safe & Sound Digital Audio Monitor	$40
Video Monitor	Samsung's SafeVIEW (SEW-3037WN)	$179
Play Yard/Bassinet	Graco Pack N Play On the Go	$65
Bouncer	4Moms MamaRoo	$200
Humidifier	Sunpentown SPT SU-4010 Ultrasonic	$65
Swing	Fisher Price Snugabunny Cradle 'n Swing	$150
Safety gate	KidCo Safeway Gates (2)	$86
Thermometer	Safety 1st Gentle Read Rectal Thermometer	$9
Infant Car Seat	Britax B-Safe 35 Elite	$200
Convertible Seat	Britax Boulevard ClickTight	$280
Stroller	Baby Jogger City Mini	$250
Diaper Bag	Skip Hop Duo	$55
Carrier	Boba Carrier 4G	$125
Clothing	Wait until after showers; see page 201.	
	TOTAL	**$4939**

Grandparents

Item	*Baby Bargains recommends*	Price
Crib	Dream on Me portable crib	$120
Mattress	Sealy Soybean Foam-Core	$133
Bedding	American Baby Co. sheets (4)	$52
High Chair	Cosco Flat Fold	$34
Thermometer	Safety 1st Gentle Read Rectal Thermometer	$9
Safety gate	KidCo's Safeway Gates (2)	$86
Convertible Seat	Cosco Scenera Next	$46
	TOTAL	**$480**

Audio monitor is optional—you can get either audio or video.

APPENDIX B TWINS
Advice for multiples

Yes, this year, one in 32 births in the US will be twins. Here's our round-up of our picks for the best gear for parents of multiples.

◆ **Cribs.** Since twins tend to be smaller than most infants at birth, parents of multiples can use bassinets or cradles for an extended period of time. For those on a tight budget, we like a portable playpen with a bassinet feature as an alternative (**Graco Pack N Play** is one popular choice for under $100). We also like the **Halo Bassinest Swivel Premiere Sleeper** ($250).

Here's a neat idea for parents of multiples—how about a crib that converts to two twin beds? HGTV Home Baby (made by Bassett and sold at Buy Buy Baby) makes the Hayden collection, a crib that converts to two twin beds. Yes, most twins sleep in separate cribs; so one could sleep in the Hayden and the other in a simpler IKEA model.

◆ **Nursing help.** Yes, nursing one baby can be a challenge, but two? You might need some help. To the rescue comes **Mothering Multiples: Breastfeeding & Caring for Twins and More** by Karen Kerkoff Gromada ($18.95). This book was recommend to us by more than one mother of twins for its clear and concise advice.

Looking for a nursing pillow for twins? Check out **My Brest Friend's Twins Plus Deluxe** pillow for $55 to $80. Moms note this pillow helps keep their babies in the correct position so they can nurse in tandem.

FYI: Skip buying a glider-rocker if you plan to nurse your twins. The large nursing pillows won't fit! Instead, go for a loveseat.

◆ **Car seats.** Most multiples are born before their due date. The smallest infants may have to ride in special "car beds" that enable them to lie flat (instead of car seats that require an infant to be at least five or six pounds and ride in a sitting position). The car beds then rotate to become regular infant car seats so older infants can ride in a sitting position.

Some hospitals sell infant car beds—they can be used for premature infants up to nine pounds. The key feature: a wrap-around harness to protect a preemie in an accident. FYI: ALL premature infants should be given a car seat test at the hospital to check for breathing problems— ask your pediatrician for details.

As you might guess, some car seats fit smaller babies than others. We like the **Maxi Cosi Pria 70 with TinyFit** ($232), which starts at just 4 lbs. This version of the Pria has an insert specifically designed for preemies; it is an excellent car seat.

multiples

Another idea: check with your hospital to see if you can RENT a car bed until your baby is large enough to fit in a regular infant car seat.

◆ **Strollers.** Our complete wrap-up of recommendations for double strollers is in Chapter 8 (see Double the Fun in the lifestyle recommendations).

Our top pick for tandem strollers: the **Kolcraft Contours Options Tandem** ($280, 32 lbs.). Cool feature: the seats reverse to face the parents or each other. The runner up: the **Chicco Cortina Together,** which accepts two infant seats ($300).

For side-by-side strollers, we suggest the **Chicco Echo Twin** ($190, 30.5 lbs.; Target exclusive). It comes with a one-hand recline and sip off rear canopy. We also liked the **Graco Fast Action fold Duo** ($280, 33 lbs.) with big storage basket and canopies with sunvisors. Finally, if grandma is buying, we like the **Baby Jogger City Mini Double** ($450, 26.6 lbs.), with its excellent extended canopies and quick fold.

◆ **Deals/Freebies.** Chain stores like Babies R Us and Baby Depot offer a 10% discount if you buy multiples of identical items like cribs. Buy Buy Baby has a similar program—and they even allow you to use one of their 20% coupons in addition to a 10% twin discount (for the second item only).

The National Mothers of Twins Clubs (nomotc.org) has fantastic yard/garage sales. Check their web page for a club near you.

Another good source: *Twins Magazine* is a bi-monthly, full-color magazine published by The Business Word (twinsmagazine.com).

◆ **Clothes and Diaper Bags.** For clothes, make sure you get "preemie" sizes instead of the suggestions in our layette chapter—twins are smaller at birth than singleton babies.

One of our readers with multiples sent us an extensive list of tips from her experience with twins. Go to BabyBargains.com/twins to download this free PDF.

With twins, you'll need a bigger diaper bag. We recommend **Skip Hop's Forma Pack and Go Diaper Tote Bag** for $60. It comes with two smaller zippered backs, a changing pad, exterior zippered compartments, one mesh packing cube, one insulated packing cube, changing pad and more. It's also water resistant. A good value at $60!

◆ **Our message boards.** On the free side of our message boards, you'll find all sorts of help as a parent of multiples. Our Bargain Alert forum features discount codes and other sales info for baby-related sites. There is a freebie list that is updated frequently: babybargains.com/freebies. And if you just need another mom or dad to chat with, go to the Baby Bargains Lounge.

index

index

index

index

index

index

index

index

INDEX

Washcloths, 166, 173, 174, 201
Water, formula and, 251-252
Water heaters, turning down, 299
Waverly, bedding from, 128
Waverly Baby, 142
Wels, Kelly, 197
Wendy Bellissimo, 45, 97
Wes and Willy, 181, 182
Westwood, 30, 36, 49, 99, 126
  rating of, 100-101
Westwood Design, 45
  review of, 98-99
Wheels, stroller, 479-480, 480-481
Whistle & Wink, 146
  rating of, 148-149
White noise, 301
White River Concepts, 234
Whole Foods, 192, 250
Whozit Activity Spiral, 311
Wilson, Darien, 564
Wipe warmers, avoiding, 302, 354
Wipes, 198, 200
  packages/travel-size, 560
Withings
  features of, 346-347
  review of, 344-345
Woodcraft Industries, 45
Wooden Soldier, 182
  review of, 160
Woombie, 134
Workout videos, 226-229
Wrap around carriers, 565, 567
  review of, 583-585
Wrapsody Baby Breeze, 588

Yard sales, 156-157
Yelp, 177
Yoga Journal, 227
Yoga Zone, 227
Young America, 99
  rating of, 100-101

Yummy Spoonfuls, review of, 267

Zenoff Products, 244
Zippers, 171-172
ZoloWear Adjustable Pouch, review of, 572
ZoloWear Sling, review of, 572
Zoolikins.com, review of, 187
Zulily, 35
  review of, 160
Zutano, 45, 99, 118
zzZipMe Sack, 134, 147

Notes

BabyBargains.com

What's on our web page?

◆ *Updated blog with news and safety recalls.*

◆ *Learn about our ebooks for your Kindle, iPad or Nook.*

◆ *Message boards with in-depth reader feedback.*

◆ *The latest coupon codes and freebies!*

◆ *Corrections and clarifications.*

◆ *Links to our Facebook page and Twitter feed.*

◆ *Subscribe to read reviews online!*

BabyBargains.com
Email: authors@babybargains.com
Phone: (303) 442-8792